Mastering AutoCAD

Mastering Autocad®

Second Edition

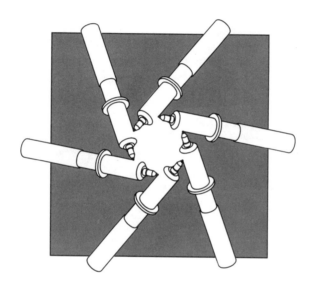

GEORGE OMURA

San Francisco • Paris • Düsseldorf • London

Cover art by Thomas Ingalls + Associates, Casey Cartwright, and Omura
Illustration.
Book design by Jeffrey James Giese
Illustrations by Omura Illustration

To my wife and dearest friend, Cynthia
my son, Arthur
my mother, Shizuko Omura
and the memory of my father, Shomatsu Omura

Acknowledgments

My thanks to the many people at SYBEX who were instrumental in creating this second edition of *Mastering AutoCAD*: Fran Grimble for her great editorial work and her many helpful suggestions; Linda Ackerman for copyediting; Harold Price for technical review and advice; John Kadyk, Jocelyn Reynolds, and Scott Campbell for word processing; Aidan Wylde for typesetting; Winnie Kelly for proofreading; Bob Thomas for indexing; Eleanor Ramos for graphics; and Michelle Hoffman for graphics production.

I would also like to thank Paul Richardson and Christine Meredith of Technical Publications and Edwin Rutsch for their advice on desktop publishing, and Pierrette Montroy at Autodesk.

And finally, thanks to Tarthang Tulku Rinpoche for the inspiration to do the impossible, and to Cynthia for her support and understanding.

The people at SYBEX who worked on the first edition of *Mastering AutoCAD* were Fran Grimble, editor; Chuck Ackerman, acquisitions editor; Barbara Gordon, initial developmental editor; Greg Hooten, technical reviewer; Olivia Shinomoto, Paul Erickson, and Scott Campbell, word processors; Charles Cowens, typesetter; Eileen Walsh and Aidan Wylde, proofreaders; Paula Alston, indexer; Jeff Giese, graphic artist; and Michelle Hoffman, graphics assistant.

Larry Knot, Mark Otavka, Allan Terry, and Fred Willsea provided many comments and insights. At Autodesk, David Kalish, Greg Kerrigan, Laura London, Paul Panish, Raymond Roy, Kevin Seavar, Joyce Williams, and the people in technical support provided help and information.

Contents

Introduction

THIS BOOK SHOWS YOU HOW TO USE AUTOCAD, the popular computer-aided design and drafting program, quickly and effectively. It is a guide for those who are beginning to use computer-aided design and drafting (CAD) in their work, whether as users or managers. You don't have to have any computer background to use *Mastering AutoCAD*. We do assume some knowledge of basic mechanical drafting principles and terms.

This book assumes you are using AutoCAD on an IBM PC, XT, AT, or compatible. In an effort to be comprehensive, we describe the most recent version of AutoCAD, version 9, with the full complement of drafting extensions (the ADE3 package). The most noticeable feature of version 9 is the advanced user interface (AUI), which allows you to select commands from pull-down and icon menus. Also new with version 9 are spline curves, which allow you to generate smooth, natural-looking curves, 20 different text typefaces, and other features that allow greater flexibility in customizing AutoCAD. These updates are available on computers equipped with IBM or compatible displays like CGA, EGA, and Hercules. You can, however, complete most of the exercises in this book even without one of these display systems or with versions 2.6 or 2.5 of AutoCAD.

Even if you don't have a computer and the AutoCAD software, reading this book is a way to look over the shoulder of someone using AutoCAD. The numerous illustrations (all created with Auto-CAD) show the results of each step in the exercises. You may want to just read the book if you must deal with AutoCAD as a manager rather than a user, though some time spent using the program will further your understanding of it.

The bulk of this book consists of a tutorial, designing an apartment building. We chose an architectural exercise because most people have some interest in and understanding of architecture, even if they are not architects. You don't have to be an architect to understand and complete the exercises. They can be followed easily by anyone who is a designer, illustrator, drafter, or engineer, or who is studying one of these professions.

HOW TO USE THIS BOOK

Rather than just showing you how each command works, the tutorial shows you AutoCAD in the context of a meaningful activity and how to use commands together to reach a goal. It provides a foundation from which you can build your own methods for using AutoCAD. For this reason, we don't cover every single command and every permutation of a command response. The help system and the *AutoCAD Reference Manual* are quite adequate for this purpose. You should think of this book as a supplement to the reference manual and as a way to get a detailed look at AutoCAD as it is used in a real project. As you follow the exercises, we encourage you to also explore AutoCAD on your own, applying the techniques you learn to your own work.

Mastering AutoCAD is intended to be read from front to back, since later chapters rely on the skills and information you learned in earlier ones. The first five chapters introduce you to the program, and in them you will create and print a simple drawing. Chapter 1, "Before You Start," explains some basic CAD and microcomputing concepts and describes the equipment you will need. In Chapter 2, "Getting Familiar with AutoCAD," you will learn how to start and exit the program and give input. Chapter 3, "Creating a Drawing," tells you how to set up a work area, edit objects, and lay out a drawing. In Chapter 4, "Getting Organized," you will explore some tools unique to CAD: symbols, blocks, and layers. And in Chapter 5, "Getting Your Drawing on Hard Copy," you will print and plot the drawing you worked on in Chapters 2–4.

In the next 11 chapters, you will gain hands-on experience in more advanced drawing and editing techniques. Chapter 6, "Using Existing Information," tells you how to reuse drawing setup information and parts of an existing drawing. In Chapter 7, "Managing a Large Drawing," you will learn how to assemble and edit a large drawing. Chapter 8, "Using Text," tells you how to annotate your drawing and edit the notes. Chapter 9, "Using Dimensions," gives you practice in using automatic dimensioning, another unique CAD capability. Chapter 10, "Using Attributes," tells you how to attach information to drawing objects. In Chapter 11, "Entering a Hand-Drafted Drawing," you will learn three techniques for transferring such a drawing to AutoCAD. Chapter 12, "Drawing Curves and Solid Areas," teaches you about such special drawing objects as polylines. In Chapter 13, "Getting and Exchanging Information," you will practice getting information about a drawing and interacting with other programs, such as spreadsheets and desktop-publishing programs. Chapter 14, "Using 3D," covers AutoCAD's features for creating three-dimensional drawings. Chapter 15, "Expanding AutoCAD's 3D Capabilities with AutoShade," shows how you can use AutoShade to render AutoCAD 3D models. And in Chapter 16, "Managing the Drawing Process," you will complete the apartment building tutorial, and in the process learn techniques for working with a set of project drawings.

The last three chapters tell you how to optimize your AutoCAD use and management. Chapter 17, "Increasing Input and Processing Speed," discusses creating keyboard macros and enhancing your hardware. Chapter 18, "Customizing AutoCAD," teaches you such customization techniques as creating lines and patterns, and introduces the basics of AutoLISP. And Chapter 19, "Incorporating Auto-CAD into Your Projects," discusses using AutoCAD in an office environment, including CAD management techniques.

Finally, this book has five appendices. Appendix A, "Hardware Options," should give you a start on selecting hardware appropriate for AutoCAD. Appendix B, "Installing AutoCAD and AutoShade," contains a tutorial that you should follow before starting Chapter 2, if AutoCAD is not already on your system. If you're a DOS beginner, you may want to read Appendix C, "Using Some Common DOS Commands," in conjunction with the earlier chapters. You should read Appendix D, "AutoLISP Programs," around the time you read Chapter 18. And Appendix E, "Setvar Options," will illuminate references to the Setvar command scattered throughout the book.

HOW TO OBTAIN THE AUTOLISP PROGRAMS

If you would like to use the AutoLISP programs in Appendix D but do not want to enter them into your computer, you can obtain them on disk using the order form at the end of this book. The disk also includes an AutoCAD AEC overlay, a library of architectural symbols, and a utility for converting AutoCAD and AutoShade plot files into Encapsulated PostScript files.

Chapter 1

Before You Start

COMPUTER-AIDED DRAFTING AND DESIGN, otherwise known as CAD, has been around since 1964. However, it wasn't widely used until around 1982, when CAD systems such as AutoCAD became available on microcomputers, as opposed to mainframes and minicomputers. Since then, the number of CAD users has grown steadily. Before we take a look at AutoCAD and its development over the past few years, we should provide some background on CAD and its features.

WHAT CAD IS AND WHAT IT CAN DO

CAD's features include ease of use, accuracy, intelligence, and customization. Each will be discussed in this section.

Ease of Use

One of CAD's nicest features is its ease of use. Compared to traditional methods, it is a clean and comfortable approach to drafting. Anyone who has spent hours over a drawing erasing and redrafting can appreciate a method that allows you to sit up straight, make changes without leaving a trace of an erased line, and make those changes more quickly. CAD enables you to create drawings as fast as hand-drafting methods, or even faster—with the added features of easy duplication and editing, accuracy, and "intelligence." If for no other reason, CAD is a valuable tool because it makes the tedious and inevitable task of revising drawings more pleasant.

CAD is often compared to word processing because both make editing a much simpler task than traditional methods. When you edit a drawing, you can "cut and paste" objects to other parts of the drawing or to an entirely different drawing. You can store parts of drawings for future use or simply discard them. There is even a way to do a type of "search and replace." In word processing, the "search and replace" feature looks for all occurrences of a word or phrase in a document and replaces them with a different word or phrase that you specify. When you use CAD for a drawing containing the same object in several places, you can draw the object once, then insert it wherever it is needed. If you later want to redraw the object, you can do so once and it will be updated automatically wherever it occurs. Or you can modify one occurrence of the object without affecting the others.

But unlike word processing, CAD can be used to create a visual model of an imagined object. You can quickly see whether an idea will work by using CAD to construct a graphic model, then checking in detail the design's critical elements. For example, if you are a mechanical designer you can use CAD to draw the gears and cams in a piece of machinery with great accuracy at full scale. You can then check tolerances in the drawing, thus eliminating some of the guesswork you may be faced with using traditional methods. If you are an architectural designer, you can experiment with design elements while controlling their dimensions. Elements can be mixed and matched, stored and redisplayed at will.

CAD may not completely replace sketching on tracing paper for initial design concepts, but it can be an enormous aid when you're trying to make your ideas work. It may even enable you to see your design in ways you never considered before.

Accuracy

CAD allows greater accuracy than traditional hand-drafting methods. Rather than depending on a graphic scale and the clarity of your sight to determine dimensions, you can use CAD's built-in measuring capabilities to check the dimensions of the drawings you create. Checking long strings of dimensions by conventional methods can be a tedious, error-ridden task, but a CAD system makes it much simpler. Many CAD systems even offer an automatic dimen-sioning feature that draws in dimension arrows and distances.

Zooming and *panning* features enable you to magnify the smallest detail of a drawing and work as though you were looking through a microscope (see Figure 1.1). Zooming with a CAD system is similar to zooming in with a camera; you pick a small area in the drawing and expand it to fill the screen. Panning is a way to get around once you've zoomed in on an area. You can work on a drawing represent-ing a square mile while maintaining a one-inch accuracy. Imagine doing this using traditional drawing methods!

Intelligence

Another CAD feature not found in manual drafting is the ability to attach textual information to an object or an entire drawing. Such a piece of information is called an *attribute*, and the ability to attach attributes to a drawing is often referred to as "intelligence." An attrib-ute can be visible or invisible. It can be a part number attached to a gear, the number of a phone line attached to a desk, or even the work history of an employee in an organizational chart. These attributes can be extracted and manipulated in a database-management or spreadsheet program. This added "intelligence" helps you generate parts lists from a mechanical drawing or keep track of the number and types of desks in an interior design proj-ect. Attributes can also be used to automate certain aspects of drafting, such as inserting notes or part symbols. For example, you can set up a drawing so that whenever a note is inserted, the pro-gram "reads" the attribute of the associated part and displays that information as part of the note.

Customization

Many CAD programs have customization features that enable you to automate repetitive tasks. For example, while creating an archi-tectural design, you may find that you have to draw the symbols for doors, windows, sinks, and other fixtures repeatedly. CAD enables you to store such frequently used symbols and later insert them into any drawing. Another example is the numbering of park-ing stalls in a parking lot plan. You could customize the program to automatically insert a sequence of numbers from 1 to 100, leaving you the task of indicating where the sequence begins and ends.

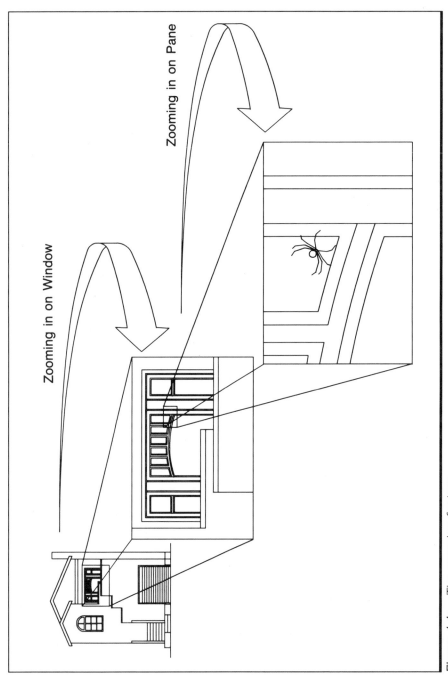

Zooming in on Pane

Zooming in on Window

Figure 1.1: The zooming feature

Micro vs. Mini or Mainframe

It is said that microcomputer-based CAD systems offer 80 percent of the functions of mainframe CAD systems at 10 percent of the cost. This is often referred to as the 80/10 rule for micro-CAD. So what do you give up in a micro-CAD system? Larger computers offer features that make operating the CAD system much easier. They are capable of greater speed, so complex drawings are more easily edited. Because of their greater power, mainframe and mini systems can handle three-dimensional modeling with greater ease.

Larger CAD systems also support multiple workstations and *multi-tasking*. Having multiple workstations connected to one computer simplifies project management on large jobs. Multitasking allows you to edit two files simultaneously on one computer, or to have more than one program operating at the same time. And, multitasking allows you to view different parts of the same drawing at one time, thus taking some of the guesswork out of your editing sessions.

Recent technical advances in computer hardware are blurring the distinction between mini- and microcomputers. Soon we will see very inexpensive desktop computers with the same power as mainframes and minis. These advances will make the more powerful micro-CAD systems, such as AutoCAD, easier to use.

AUTOCAD AS AN IMPLEMENTATION OF CAD

There are many microcomputer CAD systems available with all the features we've been discussing, but AutoCAD is by far the most popular. Let's take a look at this program and see what makes it special.

Speed and Accuracy

AutoCAD drawings are actually mathematical databases. The position of each object in a drawing is stored as a coordinate in a database. The database is then translated into an image on the screen. Whenever a drawing file is opened or a display is substantially changed, the display must be *regenerated* by recalculating the values in the database.

AutoCAD uses two methods of calculation: *floating-point calculation* and *integer-based calculation*. To establish the sizes and positions of objects in its database, AutoCAD uses floating-point calculation. This is the most accurate method, because it can manipulate real numbers (numbers that include decimals). Integer-based calculation is faster but less accurate. Because it can deal only with whole numbers, the range of values is much more limited. AutoCAD uses integer calculation to control what is displayed on the screen. This combination gives you the speed of an integer system and the accuracy of floating-point calculation, enabling you to efficiently create very complex drawings on your PC.

Hardware Customization

AutoCAD enables you to use a wide variety of display systems and input devices that can be added to the PC (more on these later). CAD/camera, another software product from Autodesk, enables you to use an optical scanner, which can convert a hand-drafted drawing into an AutoCAD file. These hardware customization options allow you to create a system suited to your needs and budget. You can start with a small system and expand it as your needs grow; there are few limits on your system's ultimate capability. And if you do eventually find that AutoCAD on the PC doesn't completely suit your needs, there are versions available for the IBM/RT, the DEC MicroVAX, and the Apollo Domain Series 3000 CAD workstation.

With version 9, files are interchangeable between dissimilar computer systems. This means that if you have AutoCAD on both a PC and a DEC MicroVAX, and these systems are connected together by a network or modem, both computers can open and edit the same files with no modifications. If you find you need to transfer AutoCAD files to other CAD software, AutoCAD supports the IGES standard for computer graphics. This standard allows file transfer between different programs. AutoCAD's DXF file format has also become a standard, and many micro-CAD software systems support it.

Software Customization

As we mentioned earlier, most CAD systems allow you to customize their software. Two kinds of customization are available to you in AutoCAD. The first is the ability to develop *macros*. Macros are strings of commands and responses you set up to reduce the amount of command input (and therefore time) required to accomplish a task. For example, suppose you need to insert a symbol for a door into several places in an architectural drawing. Normally you would have to select or type in the insertion command, then the name of the symbol to be inserted, its scale, orientation, and insertion point. AutoCAD lets you write a macro to invoke the insertion command and supply all the other variables automatically, leaving you the single task of giving the insertion point. Each time you need to insert that door symbol, you can just start the macro and point to the position for the door.

The second kind of customization is the ability to create new commands. For example, you can create a command to automatically insert a door opening in a wall after the door has been inserted. You can even create a command that creates other macros. Even if you find that AutoCAD lacks a command or feature you need, and if you haven't found a suitable AutoCAD or third-party add-on, you may be able to create the feature yourself.

When you create an AutoCAD command, you use Autodesk's version of Common LISP, called AutoLISP. Chapter 17 gives a brief introduction to AutoLISP. If you already know some LISP, you should be able to create AutoCAD commands after examining the sample programs in Appendix D of this book. If you're a programmer or an experienced AutoCAD user who would like to try your hand at programming, you will find the *AutoLISP Programmer's Reference* extremely useful. It contains a chapter showing you step-by-step how to create a program. If you are a beginner, read this book and practice using AutoCAD. With a good understanding of AutoCAD, you can learn to program in AutoLISP more easily and quickly. AutoCAD's programmability is a key advantage of the program, so if you intend to use AutoCAD extensively, I strongly suggest that you give programming a try. It's not as difficult as you might think and it can boost productivity significantly. You don't need any formal computer programming training—just consider it part of learning AutoCAD.

Several Kinds of Support

Because AutoCAD has a fairly large user community, you can take advantage of several user publications, a CompuServe user forum, and numerous third-party software add-ons. Two independent publications, *CADalyst* and *CADENCE*, are devoted to AutoCAD users. Autodesk publishes a third, *Final Draft*. The CompuServe user forum allows an active interchange of ideas and problems between users and the people at Autodesk. AutoCAD's third-party software add-ons are listed in Autodesk's guide to third-party software. There are also a growing number of consultants who specialize in customizing AutoCAD.

YOUR COMPUTER IN A NUTSHELL

Next we will examine AutoCAD's hardware requirements. Before we do, however, we should look into some of the basic concepts of your computer's operations. If you're already familiar with these, you may want to skip ahead to "AutoCAD and Your Computer."

A computer is not very intelligent. It requires very complex and detailed instructions before it can do anything. These instructions compose the computer *program*. The program works with the computer's main processor to perform certain tasks on information you supply. These tasks can be anything from word processing to running Space Invaders, and the information may be in the form of a file on a disk or directly provided by you through the keyboard or other input device.

Input and Output

The process of giving your computer instructions and information is known as *input*. A computer receives input from various devices. The most common devices are the keyboard, the *hard disk*, and the *floppy disk* (see Figure 1.2). The keyboard allows you to give the computer instructions interactively, while a disk gives the computer access to programs and files you have previously saved.

When you tell the computer to start a program, it reads the program from the disk and places a copy in an electronic work space referred to as random-access memory, or *RAM*, located on the computer's main circuit board. RAM gives the computer's main processor instant access to the program's instructions. It is also the space where your computer keeps a file while you are working on it. When you're using AutoCAD, that file will be a drawing.

Both while you're working on a file and after you're through, you'll want the computer to show you the results of your work. Results are shown as *output*, and the devices used to display output are the *monitor* and the *printer* (or *plotter*). The disk is also an output device since the computer stores files there, but the files are not displayed in a form understandable to you until they are brought up on screen or printed.

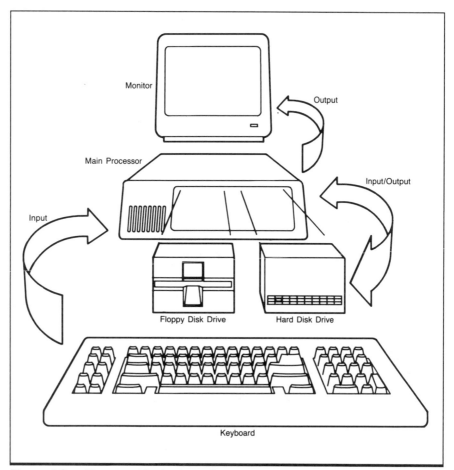

Figure 1.2:   *How input/output works*

Memory

When you finish working on a file, and at intervals during your task, you should save the file, moving it from RAM to a more permanent location on your disk. Because RAM depends on electrical power to maintain information stored there, as soon as you turn your computer off any information in RAM will vanish. Information on your disk is stored magnetically, in a more permanent way. As well as providing more permanent storage, a hard disk provides a much larger amount of storage than RAM.

Then why can't you just use the disk for working memory as well as storage? The answer to that question is "speed." RAM can transfer information instantaneously because it is an electronic medium, but the disk, being a mechanical device, is limited in speed by its own mechanics. Both types of memory have a useful role: the RAM's speed makes it ideal for a working space where information is constantly manipulated, while the disk's greater capacity and lack of volatility make it ideal for storage.

The Operating System

Your computer needs a program to help you direct all these input and output activities. This program is called the *disk-operating system;* on your PC, it is PC-DOS or MS-DOS. You could look at the operating system as the conductor of an orchestra directing the very complex interactions among you, the computer, and the computer's many activities (see Figure 1.3). It provides a standard environment in which your application programs, such as Lotus 1-2-3, dBASE III PLUS, or AutoCAD, can work. Since DOS handles many of the computer's basic functions, other programs don't have to include instructions on managing these. This standard allows you to use the same programs and files on different computers, as long as they share the same operating system.

Sometimes a program calls for input and output devices that are not normally connected to a microcomputer and which the operating system does not know how to manage. In this case, the program must provide its own instructions for managing the devices. AutoCAD provides a number of these *drivers*, enabling you to use such devices as a plotter for printing out large drawings.

This book assumes a working knowledge of PC-DOS or MS-DOS. You should understand how to create and use directories, copy files, and do general file maintenance. If you are not familiar with DOS, take some time now to read Appendix C, which covers some of the basics. If you need more information, you might want to read *Mastering DOS*, by Judd Robbins (SYBEX, 1987).

With these things in mind, let's look at some of the options Auto-CAD gives you.

AUTOCAD AND YOUR COMPUTER

Microcomputer hardware can be set up, or *configured*, in any number of ways. The computer most commonly used for AutoCAD is an IBM PC/AT or AT compatible, though an IBM PC/XT can also be used. Your computer should have at least one floppy disk drive and

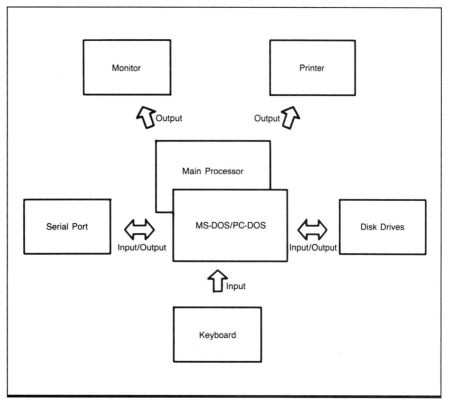

Figure 1.3: *The operating system and your computer's activities*

one hard disk drive, a *serial port*, a *printer port*, a *math coprocessor*, and at least 512K of RAM. It should also be equipped with a high-resolution color *display card* and *monitor*, an input device such as a *mouse* or a *digitizing tablet*, and a plotter for printing out drawings. And, it is helpful to have a *dot-matrix printer* to print out information about your drawings. The printer can double as a plotter if you don't need high-quality or large-format output.

Here's some more detail on the available hardware options.

Disk Drives and Disks

The two most common types of drives are the floppy disk drive and the hard disk drive. The floppy disk drive uses a removable floppy disk, and the hard disk drive uses a nonremovable or "fixed" disk. The floppy disk has the advantage of transportability, but it does not store much information and slows down the performance of tasks requiring the disk to be read frequently. The hard disk, on the other hand, is not transportable but has much greater storage capacity and can transfer information many times faster than a floppy disk. You can view the floppy disk drive as the "loading dock" where files and programs from outside are brought in and out, and the hard disk drive as the "warehouse" where the computer has quick access to files and programs. The ideal setup is to have both types of disk drives in your computer system (see Figure 1.4).

The Graphics Display

A high-resolution display card is a device that allows your computer to display graphic images in greater detail, or *resolution*, than a standard graphics display. Its higher resolution often requires a monitor capable of displaying the output from such a card. Because of this, the card and monitor combination is often considered a unit.

Resolution is measured by the number of *pixels* the device can display. A pixel can be loosely described as the smallest unit of light the screen can produce. In the case of a color system, a pixel is the smallest unit of light containing the red, green, and blue color elements. The more pixels a display card and monitor can display, the higher the resolution. The very popular Enhanced Graphics Adapter, or EGA, has a resolution of 640 x 350 pixels. A system with this resolution is adequate for most AutoCAD applications, but resolutions of 640 x 400 and greater are preferred. Monitor and display cards with resolutions of 1024 x 1024 are available, but very costly. However, as interest in high-resolution graphics rises, prices of these display systems will drop.

Other factors affect the quality of the image from your computer. The ratio between the number of vertical pixels to horizontal pixels, for example, can affect an image's smoothness. The closer this ratio is to one-to-one, the less jagged the image will appear. Lack of flickering and uniform sharpness of the screen image are also important qualities. Nothing can give you a headache faster than a dull, flickering screen, no matter what its resolution.

Color is very useful because it can convey considerably more information at a glance. For example, you can use color to separate electrical information from architectural information in a floor plan. Color allows you to assign line thicknesses to objects and to organize your drawing. If you don't use color, you will miss some of the key advantages of AutoCAD.

Although this description simplifies the factors affecting a display's clarity, it does give you a general idea of them. If you are

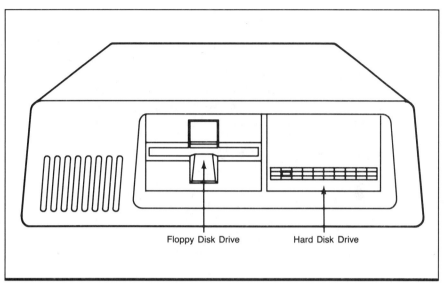

Figure 1.4:   *A floppy disk drive and a hard disk drive*

using version 9, you will need a display that is not only clear but supports the advanced user interface's pull-down menus, icon menus, and dialog boxes. Because AutoCAD has at least 44 different display options, we won't cover them all here. AutoCAD's *Installation and Performance Guide* describes them thoroughly, and Appendix A of this book gives some guidelines for installing your hardware and choosing a display that supports the AUI.

The Keyboard

The keyboard is the most important input device you have. You use it to start programs, initiate commands, and provide names and other responses to commands. When you're working feverishly with AutoCAD to meet a deadline, you may find yourself using the keyboard more frequently; a subtle indication that it is the quickest means for certain types of input. It helps if you're a touch-typist, because ultimately your input speed depends on your typing speed.

If you are new to the PC, take some time to familiarize yourself with its keyboard, which is shown in Figure 1.5. You will use some of the same keys you use on a typewriter, but others may be new to you.

The two rows of keys labeled F1 through F10 at the left of the keyboard are called *function keys*. These keys are often used by a

MASTERING AUTOCAD

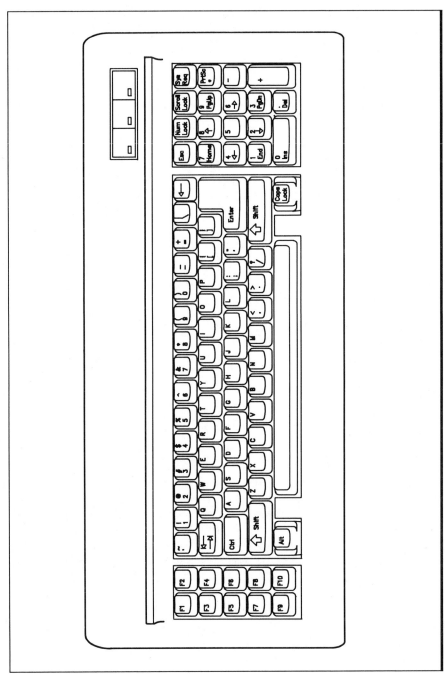

Figure 1.5: A PC/AT keyboard

program to perform tasks specific to that program. Different programs can assign different tasks to the same function key. For
example, a word-processing program might use F1 to cancel a command, while a database-management program might use it to add a
record to a database. AutoCAD uses six function keys to control
certain options. We'll tell you how to use these keys when we discuss the options.

At the right of the keyboard is a set of keys used for controlling
the cursor and for entering numbers (see Figure 1.5 again). These
two tasks are usually shared by the same set of keys; you switch
between them using the Num Lock key. Some keyboards have separate cursor and numeric keys. The cursor keys are essential if
you don't have a mouse, digitizing tablet, or other pointing device.
We'll cover how to use them when you start creating AutoCAD
drawings.

Drawing Devices

The *cursor* is a visual device that shows your position on the
screen. In DOS or in most word processors it is a small, blinking rectangle. In AutoCAD, the cursor is a cross formed by intersecting
horizontal and vertical lines. To draw with a computer, you need a
device to convert your hand movement into cursor movement on
your computer screen.

The Digitizing Tablet

The digitizing tablet shown in Figure 1.6 is such a device. It is usually a rectangular object with a penlike *stylus*, or a device called a
puck that resembles a mouse. It has a smooth surface on which to
draw. The most popular size is 11 x 11 inches, but digitizing tablets
are available in sizes up to 60 x 70 inches. The tablet gives a natural feel to drawing with the computer because the movement of
the stylus or puck is directly translated into cursor movement.

A digitizing tablet's puck often has *function buttons*. These buttons can be programmed to start your most frequently used commands, which is much faster than searching through an on-screen
menu. You can also select commands from the tablet's surface if
you install the *menu template* supplied with AutoCAD. A menu template is a flat sheet of plastic with the AutoCAD commands printed
on it. You can select commands simply by pointing at them on the
template. If you have a digitizing tablet, refer to Appendix B, which
tells you how to install a template.

MASTERING AUTOCAD

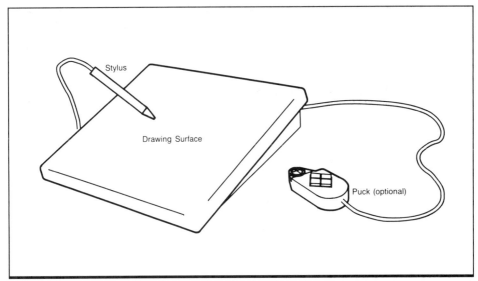

Figure 1.6:   *A digitizing tablet*

The Mouse

If you don't plan to use an AutoCAD tablet template or if you don't intend to trace drawings, the mouse is a reasonable substitute for a tablet. Its drawbacks are a less natural feel and the inability to trace drawings. You also can't use the mouse to select items from some of the available tablet menus, which can provide very useful features. However, some of the third-party software products designed for AutoCAD offer on-screen menus containing some of the same features available on the tablet menus.

On the plus side, the mouse allows a much faster cursor movement than the keyboard. Most mice have three buttons, two of which can be programmed like a tablet's puck (see Figure 1.7). And the mouse can be used with many other programs, particularly some of the graphic operating environments such as GEM, Microsoft Windows, and IBM's Topview. Since they are more common than digitizing tablets, mice are relatively inexpensive.

The Trackball

An alternative, though less commonly used, option is the *trackball*. This consists of a ball about two inches in diameter mounted in a small, flat box with part of the ball exposed (see Figure 1.8). The ball's movement moves the cursor on the screen. The trackball's housing usually has buttons that enable you to add programmable

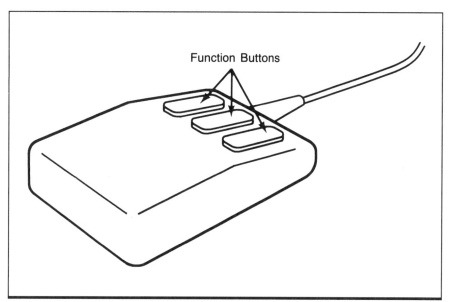

Figure 1.7: *A mouse*

functions. The trackball's main advantage over the mouse and the digitizing tablet is that it requires little arm movement, and shifting between it and the keyboard is easier (you will have to go to the keyboard often). Another advantage is that the trackball takes up considerably less desk space than a tablet or even a mouse. Like the mouse, the trackball can be used with programs other than AutoCAD. Usually it can be used with any program that requires cursor movement through the keyboard. There are even keyboards for the IBM PC that include a trackball.

The Joystick

Finally, there is the *joystick*, shown in Figure 1.9. You may be familiar with the joystick from playing computer games, but it is also often used for creating computer graphics. The joystick shares many of the trackball's characteristics; it is usually connected to a game port on your computer (make sure your computer has one before you buy the joystick).

AutoCAD supports at least 30 drawing devices, ranging from the cheapest mouse to the largest, most expensive digitizing tablet. Be sure AutoCAD supports the particular make you have chosen. See Appendix A for installation guidelines.

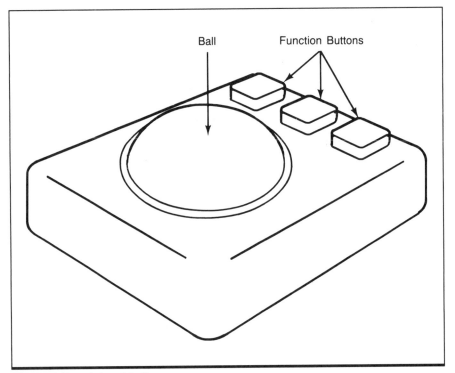

Ball   Function Buttons

Figure 1.8:   *A trackball*

Printing Devices

Printing devices include the plotter, the dot-matrix printer, and the laser printer.

The Plotter

A plotter is a mechanical drafting device used to draw a computer image on sheets of paper, vellum, or polyester film (see Figure 1.10). Unlike a dot-matrix printer, which is also capable of printing out graphic images, a plotter uses pens. Its drawings are composed of continuous lines rather than dots, and are clearer and sharper than those produced by the dot-matrix printer. Some plotters can use multiple pens, enabling you to vary color and line thickness without manually changing pens. Plotter drawing sizes range from 11 inches × 17 inches to 30 inches × 42 inches and up. Most drafting applications require at least a 24-inch × 36-inch sheet. If you're drawing technical illustrations or business graphics, you can get by with an 11-inch × 17-inch format.

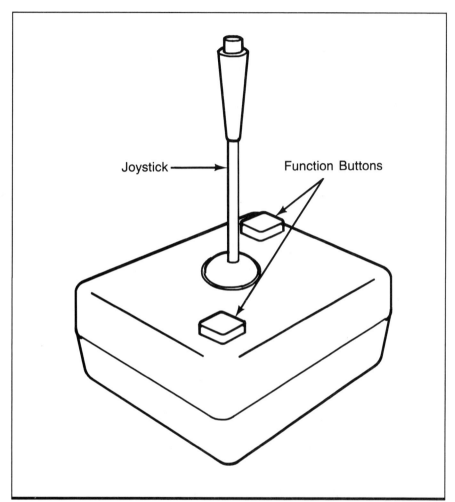

Figure 1.9:   *A joystick*

It is in this size that you will find the most variety in features, quality, and cost. AutoCAD gives you at least 19 plotter options, ranging from an 8½-inch × 11-inch format to a 48-inch-wide continuous-sheet format.

If you need large plots but feel you can't afford a large plotter, many blueprint companies are beginning to offer plotting as a service. This can be a very good alternative to purchasing your own plotter. Check with your local blueprinter.

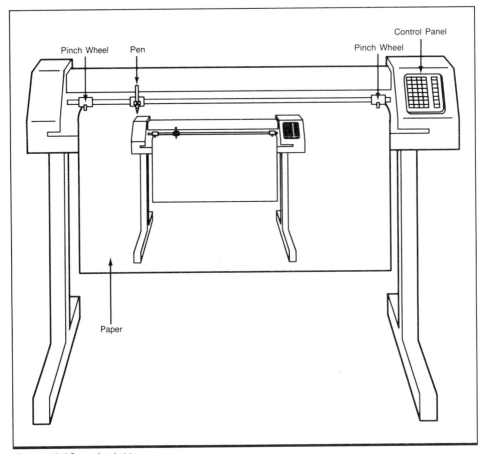

Figure 1.10: A plotter

The Dot-Matrix Printer

You'll want to use a plotter to produce high-quality, finished draw-ings. But in the course of your work, you may also want to print quick preliminary drawings. In this case, you may not care much about a drawing's appearance, as long as you can read it. This is where a dot-matrix printer can be of great use. What you give up in quality, you get back in sheer speed. If you plan to use a printer for this purpose, check Appendix A to make sure the printer you choose is supported by AutoCAD. Also note whether you need a serial or parallel port for connecting it.

A printer is also useful for getting nongraphic information from AutoCAD; for example, a list of symbols used in a drawing. You might also print the status of a drawing to record what settings are active during a particular editing session. As your drawings get more complex, the printer will be more and more valuable to you.

The Laser Printer

Another type of output device AutoCAD supports is the *laser printer*. This device can produce the best-quality output of all the devices we mentioned (see Figure 1.11). Just make sure your laser printer will give you a full 8½ x 11-inch plot at a resolution of 300 dots per inch. With many laser printers, you must reduce the drawing size to get a resolution this high. Another advantage of the laser printer is that it can produce multiple copies of your drawings.

If you are involved in producing technical manuals, some of the desktop-publishing software packages will accept AutoCAD drawings as line art. This may be a way of getting high-quality plots of your artwork and combining them with your text. However, you will have to learn to use more software.

The Serial Port

Virtually all plotters and most input devices are connected to the computer's serial port (see Figure 1.12). This is a type of connector that allows your computer to communicate with other hardware, even other computers. It shouldn't be confused with the parallel port, which is generally used only with printers. Both ports use the same type of 25-pin connector; the only visual difference between them is that *usually* the computer's serial port is a male connector, while the printer port is female. However, the ports are not interchangeable because they use entirely different communications standards. Since you will be using more than one device requiring a serial port, for example a digitizing tablet and a plotter, you may want to have two serial ports. Another option is to purchase a switch box that will allow you to switch between two devices on the same port.

The Math Coprocessor

The math coprocessor is a microprocessor specifically designed to do floating-point calculations (see Figure 1.13). It is required to run version 9. In earlier versions, a math coprocessor reduces the time AutoCAD takes to open large files and regenerate drawings by as much as 80 percent. If you are using other programs designed to use a math coprocessor, such as Framework or Symphony, you will

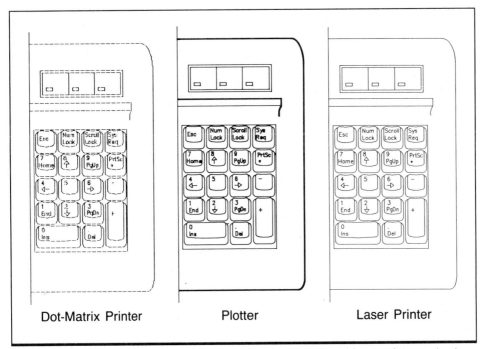

Dot-Matrix Printer   Plotter   Laser Printer

Figure 1.11:   *A comparison of dot-matrix printer, plotter, and laser printer output*

notice speed gains in those programs as well. All IBM PC and PC compatibles provide a space for a math coprocessor on the main system board. If you are using an IBM/AT, the speed increase will be less noticeable than with an IBM/XT, due to the AT's faster overall processing power.

You have to be careful when you install the math coprocessor, because its connector pins are easily bent and it may be difficult for you to determine the coprocessor's proper orientation in the main board of the computer. It is also very sensitive to static charges. If you don't already have a math coprocessor and you are not comfortable with handling electronic devices, you should have your dealer install this item.

The Minimum System Requirements

This book assumes you have an IBM PC/XT or AT, or an XT or AT compatible that will run AutoCAD and supports a mouse. If you intend to create a lot of very complex drawings, it's best to use an

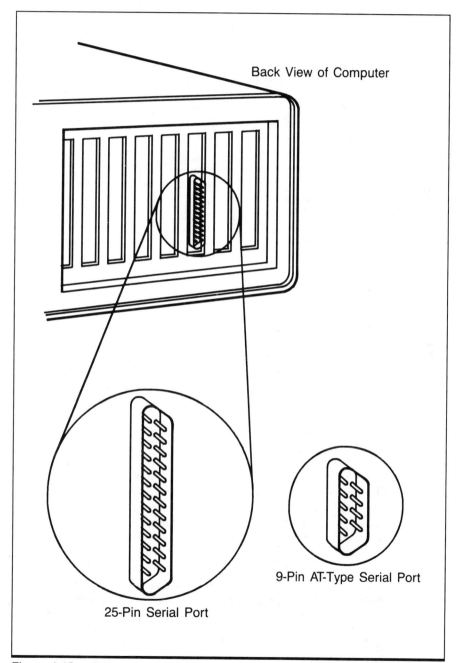

Back View of Computer

25-Pin Serial Port

9-Pin AT-Type Serial Port

Figure 1.12:   The serial port

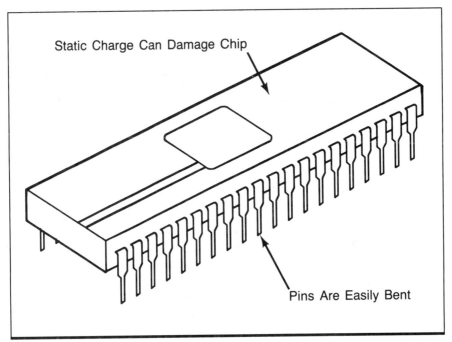

Figure 1.13: *The math coprocessor*

AT or AT compatible. Creating a complex drawing slows down Auto-CAD's performance when opening files and regenerating drawings, and the AT or compatible handles large files faster than the XT. The ATT 6300 and the Compaq Deskpro are very good alternatives to the IBM PC/AT, but make sure you purchase the software specifically designed for these machines.

Your computer should have at least one disk drive capable of reading 360K disks, and a hard disk with 5MB or more free (about 1.9MB for the AutoCAD program, another 3MB available for drawing files). AutoCAD needs a minimum of 512K of RAM.

The computer should also have a high-resolution monitor and a color display card such as the Enhanced Graphics Adapter, or any card with a higher resolution. (A standard IBM Color Graphics Adapter can be used in a monochrome mode, but this is not recommended because the resolution is so low.) It should have at least one serial port. You should consider having a second serial port installed, or at least getting a switch box.

We also assume you are using a mouse and possess a dot-matrix printer, a plotter, and a math coprocessor.

THE AUTOCAD PACKAGE

This book assumes you are using AutoCAD version 9, 2.6, or 2.5 with the ADE-3 drafting extension. The drafting extensions are software enhancements to the basic AutoCAD package. Each extension adds more functions to AutoCAD. ADE-3 is the complete package with all the drafting extensions.

AutoCAD comes in a large box containing a tutorial, the *Reference Manual*, the *Installation and Performance Guide*, the *AutoLISP Programmer's Reference* (if you have ADE-3), and nine program disks. You may also get sample issues of magazines devoted to the AutoCAD user and information on other Autodesk products.

The Manuals

You receive four manuals with AutoCAD: a brief tutorial, the *Installation and Performance Guide*, the hardbound *Reference Manual*, and the *AutoLISP Programmer's Reference*. They are all pretty intimidating, especially if you feel uncomfortable with user manuals in the first place. But take some time to browse through them and get to know their contents. You'll probably want to read the installation guide first. Then you might want to work through the tutorial, which will give you some hands-on experience from which you can gain a better feel for the program. After the tutorial, you'll probably want to look at the *Reference Manual*. The *AutoLISP Programmer's Reference* is useful when you start customizing AutoCAD.

The Disks

Before you do anything else, make copies of your disks and put the originals in a safe place. To do this, follow the instructions outlined in Appendix C.

The ten disks you receive can be broken into three categories. Disks one through six are your program disks. Disk seven contains sample drawing files and menus that you can look at and experiment with. Disk eight contains sample AutoLISP programs and additional sample drawings. The ninth and tenth disks contain the drivers for the numerous hardware options available with AutoCAD. These drivers are used only when you are setting up AutoCAD to run with your equipment.

If you look at the contents of your disks, you will notice that each file has a name followed by a period and three letters (as in *Filename*.DWG). The part of the file name that follows the period is called the file *extension*, and indicates what kind of file it is. Some of the extensions are explained below; others are explained when the related type of AutoCAD file is introduced.

When you send off your registration card, you will receive a template for use with an 11-inch x 11-inch digitizing tablet (see Figure 1.14). If you have a tablet, this template will aid you in command selection.

The Program Files

Disks one, two, and three contain *overlay files*, which are like subprograms AutoCAD uses during its operation. Sometimes a program is too large to fit into RAM. When this happens the program is often broken into smaller pieces. When such a program is initialized, the main part of the program is loaded into RAM and the other parts reside on the disk. When the part of the program on disk is needed, another part already in memory is discarded. The part on the disk is then loaded into RAM. As the program is used, these overlays are continually swapped in and out of RAM. You can recognize them by their extension, .OVL.

Disk four contains the main AutoCAD program along with more overlays. You can recognize the main program by its extension, .EXE.

Disks five and six contain support files that include the menu, help file, and files that tell AutoCAD how to set up a typical drawing. There are also files for fonts, line types, and special shapes. You can modify these files if you wish to create your own fonts, line types, or drawing shapes; set up a different default drawing; or customize the on-screen menu. We'll examine those possibilities later on in the book.

Disks nine and ten contain files used by AutoCAD to set up, or configure, the program to work with your particular hardware. These files do not have to be on your hard disk for AutoCAD to run, but it would be a good idea to load them whenever you configure AutoCAD. If you copy them to their own directory you will have all of them in one place and AutoCAD can access them considerably faster. Once you have finished configuration, you can remove the files from the hard disk and free up some disk space. See Appendix B for more details on configuration.

The Sample Drawing and AutoLISP Files

You are also given several sample drawings on disk seven. You may want to look at these files to see how they are organized. These files and any files you create will have the extension .DWG.

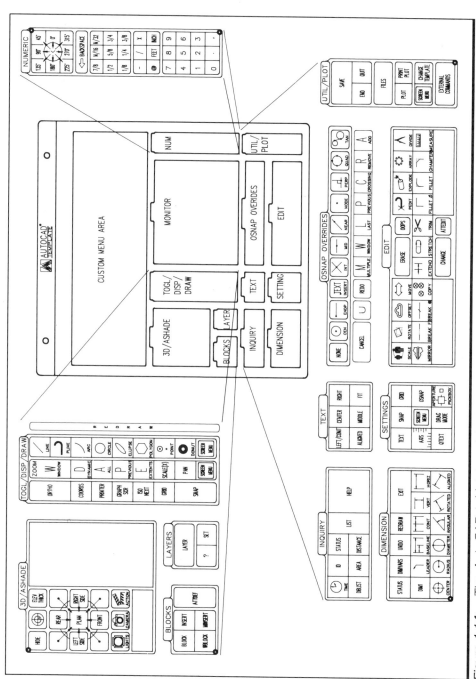

Figure 1.14: The AutoCAD tablet template

AutoCAD will also make a backup file whenever you edit an existing drawing. This backup file will have the extension .BAK. If for some reason you edit a drawing and decide you want the unedited version back, use the DOS renaming command to change the .BAK extension of your drawing to .DWG. Check Appendix C for more details on the renaming command.

Disk eight contains several AutoLISP files that you can experiment with or use as they are. AutoLISP files have the extension .LSP. We discuss AutoLISP in Chapter 18.

AUTOCAD INSTALLATION

Installing AutoCAD is straightforward and is explained clearly in the *Installation and Performance Guide*. If you are buying a complete system for AutoCAD, your vendor will usually install the program for you. If you are putting together your own system and want to get started quickly, go to Appendix B and follow the installation instructions there.

CONCLUSION

We've covered some of the background on AutoCAD so you could get a feel for what it has to offer. We've also looked at the many AutoCAD options and what you get with the AutoCAD package. Next we'll make ourselves more comfortable with the program's operations.

Chapter 2

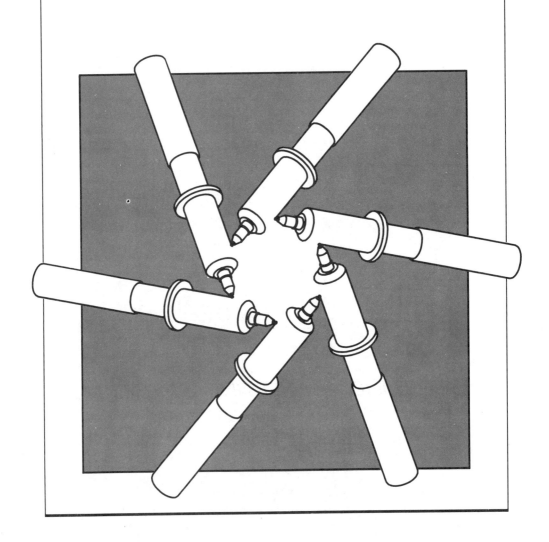

Getting
Familiar with AutoCAD

IN THIS CHAPTER we'll look at some of AutoCAD's basic functions and practice using the drawing editor by building a simple drawing to use in later exercises. We'll cover entering and exiting AutoCAD; the screen and menus for versions 9, 2.6, and 2.5; giving input; interpreting prompts; and getting help when you need it. We'll also cover using coordinate systems to give AutoCAD exact measurements for objects, selecting objects you've drawn, and specifying *base points* for moving or copying.

If you're not a beginning AutoCAD user, you might want to complete the drawing quickly and move on to the more complex material in Chapter 3.

STARTING AN EDITING SESSION

Turn on your computer and go to the directory that contains AutoCAD. To do this, type

cd *directory name*

and press the Return key. If you followed the installation guide in Appendix B, type

cd \\ACAD

and again, press Return. Start AutoCAD by typing

acad

and press Return.

The first thing you see is the introductory message. Press Return twice, and the Main menu appears (see Figure 2.1). It shows a number of options available to you.

Select option 1, Begin a new drawing, by typing

1

and press Return. At the prompt

Enter NAME of drawing,

type

door

and press Return. The drawing editor will appear.

We won't keep reminding you to press Return, since you should do so each time you enter an AutoCAD command or response to a command through the keyboard.

USING THE AUTOCAD DRAWING EDITOR

You'll see that the screen is divided into four parts, as shown in Figure 2.2. To the right is the *side menu area*; at the bottom is the *prompt area*; and along the top is the *status line*. The rest of the screen is occupied by the *drawing area*.

The *side menu* displays options available to you; it always appears on your screen and is the only type of menu available in versions previous to version 9. The prompt area displays AutoCAD's responses to your input. It is important to pay special attention to this area because this is how AutoCAD communicates with you. The status line displays current information about your drawing. If you have the version 9 advanced user interface, the status line doubles as the *pull-down menu area*. It gives you access to *pull-down menus*, *icon menus*, and *dialog boxes*. A pull-down menu is displayed only when you move your mouse cursor onto the status line. An icon menu provides graphic, rather than textual, representations of such options as typefaces and symbols. A dialog box displays a number of command options and allows you to set these options all at once, so that you can control program settings more easily. The drawing area is where you will create your drawings.

```
          A U T O C A D
Copyright (C) 1982,83,84,85,86,87 Autodesk, Inc.
Release 9.0 (9/17/87) IBM PC
Advanced Drafting Extensions 3
Serial Number:  10-113610

Main Menu

    0.   Exit AutoCAD
    1.   Begin a NEW drawing
    2.   Edit an EXISTING drawing
    3.   Plot a drawing
    4.   Printer Plot a drawing

    5.   Configure AutoCAD
    6.   File Utilities
    7.   Compile shape/font description file
    8.   Convert old drawing file

Enter selection:  _
```

Figure 2.1:   The Main menu

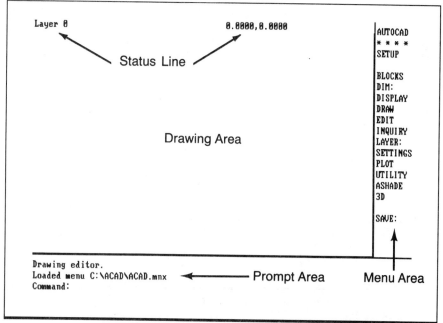

Figure 2.2:   The AutoCAD screen, showing the menu area, the prompt
               area, the status line, and the drawing area

Using the Cursor

If you move your mouse around you will see two crossed lines move across the screen. This is the drawing editor *cursor*, and you use it to select positions on the screen when you create objects (see Figure 2.3). When you select objects to be edited, the cursor will change in shape to a small square.

Take a moment to look at the keyboard cursor keys. There are four keys with arrows on them. Each key moves the cursor in the direction indicated by the arrow. Press the key with the arrow pointing right a few times and watch the response of the cursor (if there is none, press the Numeric Lock key). Now hold the key down. Notice that the cursor continues to move as long as you hold down the key. The key labeled Home will make the cursor appear on the screen if it is not already there. The key labeled End will delete the cursor from the screen. Press these two keys alternately and see what happens to the cursor.

The Page Up and Page Down keys allow you to control the speed of cursor movement. Press Page Up once, then move the cursor using the arrow keys. Notice how the cursor takes larger steps as you press the keys. Press Page Up again and try the arrow keys

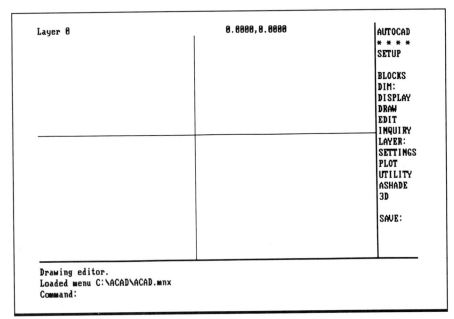

Figure 2.3:   The screen cursor

again. Each time you press Page Up the step distance of the cursor increases. There are two step increments, after which pressing Page Up won't do anything. To reduce the step distance press Page Down.

If you are using a mouse, you won't often use these keys, but it is useful to know how in case you find yourself working on a system without a pointing device. Using your mouse, move the cursor over to the far right. A bar will highlight an item on the menu.

Selecting Items from the Side Menus

The first menu you see when you open a drawing file is the Root menu. As you look at the menu you will notice that three of the items listed, Dim, Layer, and Save, are followed by colons. A colon tells you that this item starts an AutoCAD command. All other items on the Root menu display other menus (submenus) containing the commands related to that particular activity. For example, if you pick Edit, another menu will appear that contains the commands for editing objects.

Highlight the item Edit, then press the *pick button* (usually the left mouse button). Figure 2.4 shows the editing menu that appears. Note that nothing changes on the prompt area at the bottom of the screen. You will now see a new menu with several items followed by colons. Each of these items invokes a command.

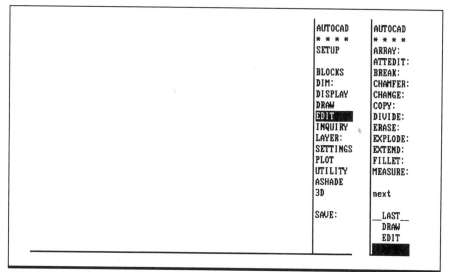

Figure 2.4: The Root menu and the Edit menu

To pick a menu option without a mouse, type the first one, two, or three letters of the option. Type

A

Notice that the option Autocad at the top of the menu is now highlighted. If two or more options have the same first letter, just keep typing the name of the option you want until it is highlighted. Now type

R

The option Array is highlighted. Press the backspace key and Autocad will again be highlighted. Now press the Ins key (see Figure 2.5). The menu changes back to the Root menu. The Ins key picks the option you highlight. From the Root menu, type

E

to highlight the Edit option, then press the Ins key to go back to where you were.

The AutoCAD menu system is set up like a tree (see Figure 2.6). The Root menu is the trunk that branches to other menus specific to particular types of activity. From the branches, like leaves, spring the various commands related to the activity you have chosen.

Near the bottom of the menu you will see Next. Pick Next and note that another set of editing commands appears. To get back to the original editing menu you can pick Previous (see Figure 2.7).

You will also see Last, Draw, and Edit at the bottom of the menu. These items allow you to go directly to the last menu or the Edit or Draw menu from wherever you may be in the menu tree. At the top, the item Autocad can be selected to bring you back to the Root menu. Just below the item Autocad is a row of asterisks. If you pick this item the Osnap (object snap) overrides will appear. The Osnap overrides menu is shown in Figure 2.8. These subcommands allow you to pick specific locations in a drawing, such as the midpoint of a line or the intersection of two lines. You will see how these work later.

The items Autocad; the row of asterisks; and Last, Draw, and Edit appear on nearly every menu. No matter where you are, you can get to the most commonly used menus.

Selecting Items from the Pull-Down Menus

If you use the advanced user interface, you can also use pull-down menus to select commands. You should be aware, however, that

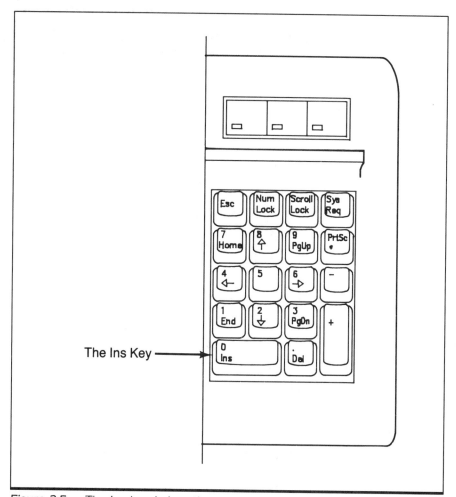

Figure 2.5: *The Ins key below the cursor keys*

these menus are not accessible through the keyboard, only through a mouse or other pointing device.

Move the cursor to the top of the screen so it touches the status line. A bar will appear overlaying the status line (see Figure 2.9). This bar contains seven options, some of which are the same as the options on the Root menu on the right side of the screen. As you move your mouse horizontally, the options are highlighted. Highlight the Edit option and press the pick button on your mouse. A menu drops down below the Edit option displaying some of the editing commands available on the side menu (see Figure 2.10).

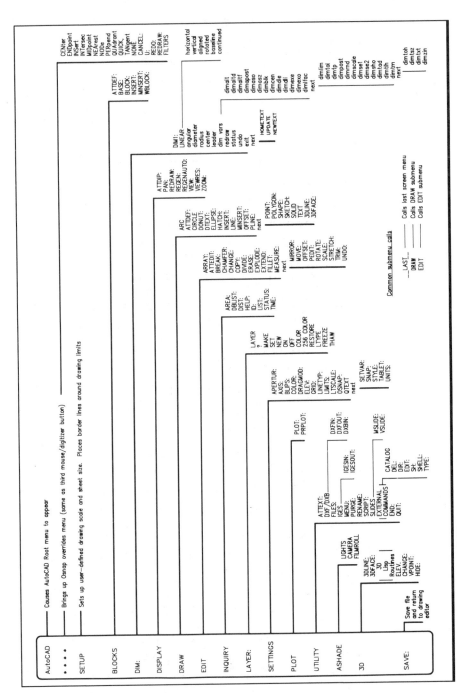

Figure 2.6: The AutoCAD menu system

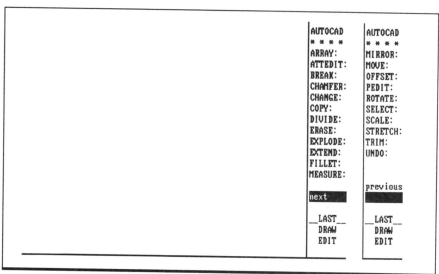

Figure 2.7: The Edit menu and the Next menu

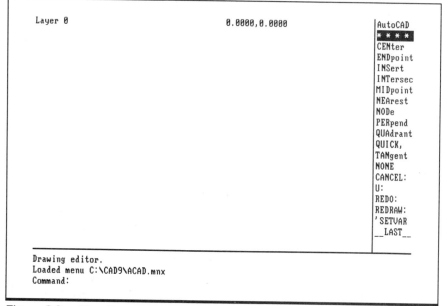

Figure 2.8: The Osnap overrides menu

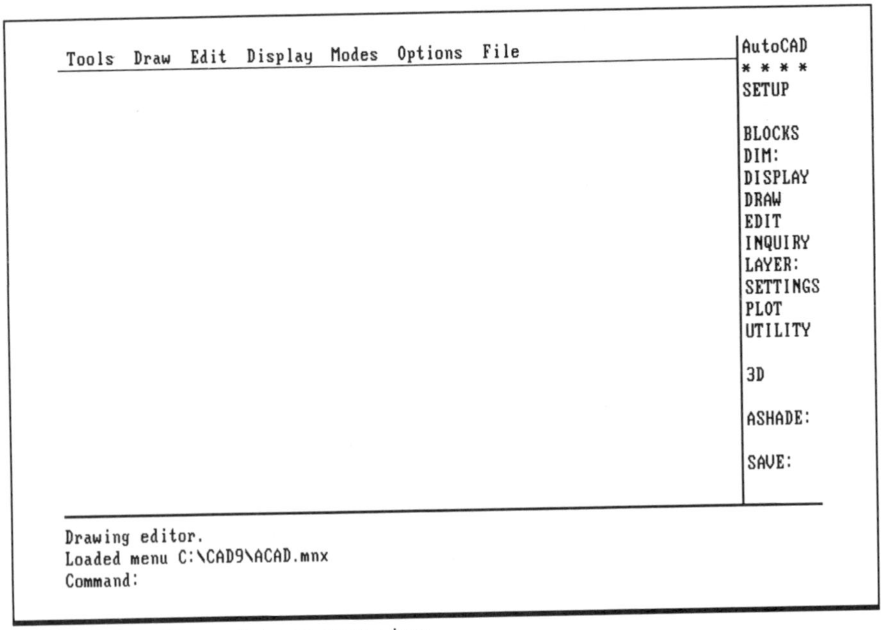

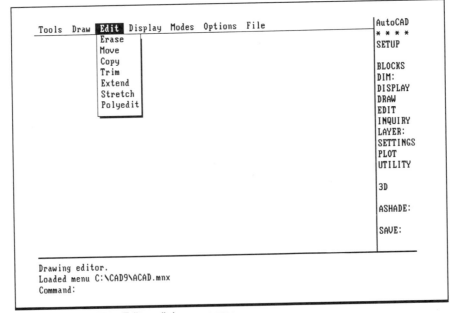

Figure 2.9: The pull-down menu bar

Figure 2.10: The Edit pull-down menu

As you move the cursor down, these options are highlighted. You can now pick commands from the menu that has been pulled down, or you can select another option from the top menu bar. If you select Tools from the menu bar, a menu appears below the Tools option that is nearly identical to the Osnap overrides menu (see Figure 2.11). The Edit menu disappears. To leave the pull-down menu, pick a point in the drawing area. The pull-down menu disappears and the status line is restored.

Figure 2.12 shows all the options available from the pull-down menus. The range of commands is limited compared with the side menus, but access to them is easier. Throughout this book, we will tell you to select commands from side menus and pull-down menus. Both kinds of menus offer new users an easy-to-remember method for accessing commands. As you have seen, you can also enter commands and subcommands through the keyboard. In fact, as you become more familiar with AutoCAD, you may prefer the keyboard over the menus. Keyboard entry of commands can actually speed up drawing input since it eliminates paging through the many layers of menus. Also, knowing the basic AutoCAD commands will allow

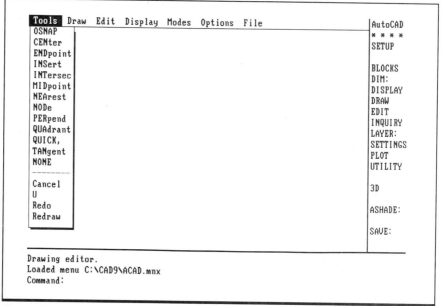

Figure 2.11: The Tools pull-down menu

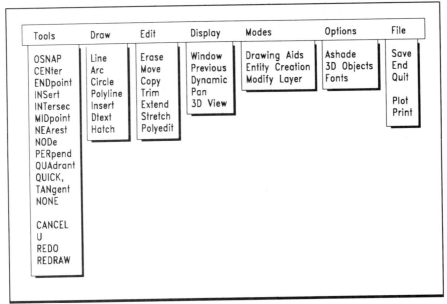

Figure 2.12: Options available on the pull-down menus

you to work on any AutoCAD system no matter what kinds of custom menus and program overlays the system may have. Keep this in mind as you proceed through the tutorials in this book.

Interpreting Prompts

Now you will draw a door symbol to use in later exercises. Go back to the Root menu by picking the item Autocad at the top of the menu area. Then select Draw from the Root menu (see Figure 2.13). Next pick Line. AUI users should pick the Draw option from the pull-down menu bar and select Line from that Draw menu.

When you select an item that invokes a command, you will see the prompt area at the bottom of the screen change to display a new prompt. The prompt is a way of telling you that AutoCAD is waiting for instructions. When you see the command prompt, you can enter any legal AutoCAD command either from the keyboard or from the on-screen menu. As you enter a command, other messages appear in the prompt area, asking you for additional information. The menu will also change to show subcommands available for the command. In this case you selected Line from the screen menu. AutoCAD responds with the new prompt

Command: LINE From point:

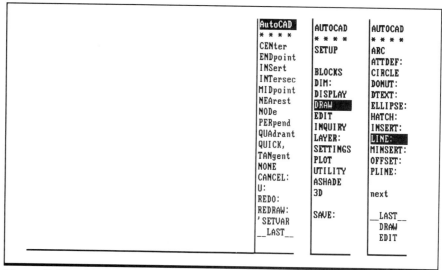

Figure 2.13:   *The Osnap menu, the Root menu, and the Draw menu*

asking you to select a point to begin your line.

Using the Drawing Area

The drawing area occupies most of the screen and is your work space. Everything you draw appears in this area. At the top of the screen are the *status lines* (see Figure 2.14). You can get information about the drawing from these lines. For example, the *layer* you are presently working on is displayed in the upper-left corner. A layer is like an overlay that allows you to separate different types of information. AutoCAD allows an unlimited number of layers. On new drawings the default layer is 0. The upper-right corner displays the coordinates of the cursor's position on the screen. We will cover these status lines in more detail a little later.

Move your mouse around. You will see the cursor follow your movements within the drawing area. Using the pick button, select a point on the screen near the center. As you select a point the prompt becomes

To point:

Now as you move the mouse around, you will notice a line with one end fixed on the point you just selected and the other end following the cursor as you move the mouse (see Figure 2.14). This is called *rubber banding*. You will also see a tiny cross marking the first

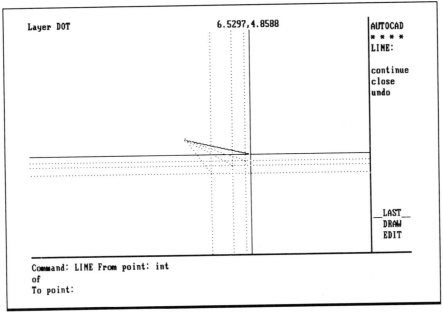

Figure 2.14:   *A rubber-banding line*

endpoint of the line. This cross is called a *blip,* and it appears every time you select a point during a command. Though it shows up on the screen, it is not part of the drawing. It is just a visual aid to you while you draw.

Move the cursor to a point to the right of the first point you selected and press the pick button again. The rubber-banding line is now fixed between the two points you selected, and a second rubber-banding line appears (see Figure 2.15).

If the line you drew isn't the exact length you want, you can back up during the Line command and change it. Pick Undo from the Line menu shown in Figure 2.16 or enter U. The line you drew previously will rubber band as if you hadn't selected the second point to fix its length.

SPECIFYING DISTANCES

For this exercise, you will draw a plan view (an overhead view) of a door to no particular scale. Later you will resize the drawing to use in future exercises. You will make this door 3.0 units long and 0.15 units thick. To specify exact distances in AutoCAD, you can use relative polar or Cartesian coordinates.

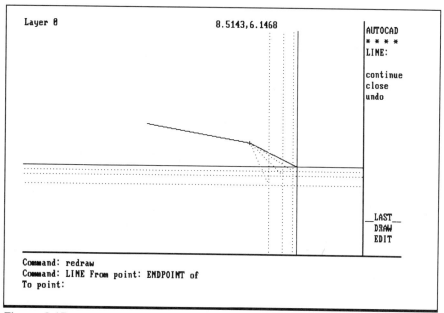

Figure 2.15: *A line fixed between two endpoints and a rubber-banding line*

Figure 2.16: *The Undo option*

Giving Polar Coordinates

To enter the distance of three units to the right of the last point you selected, type

@3<0

A line appears starting from the first point you picked and ending three units to the right of it (see Figure 2.17).

The at sign tells AutoCAD that the distance you specify is from the last point you selected. The 3 is the distance. The less-than symbol tells AutoCAD that you are giving it the angle at which the line is to be drawn. The last figure is the value for the angle, which in this case is 0. This is how to use polar coordinates to tell AutoCAD distances and direction.

Angles are given based on the system shown in Figure 2.18. 0 degrees is a horizontal direction from left to right. 90 degrees is straight up. 180 degrees is horizontal from right to left, and so on. You can specify degrees, minutes, and seconds of arc if you want to be that exact. We'll discuss angles in more detail later.

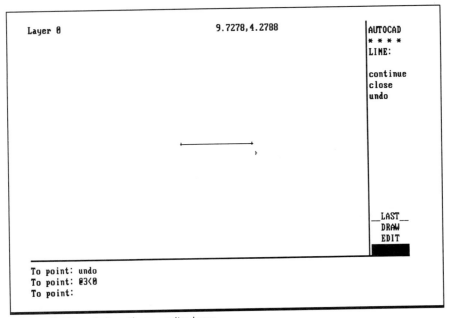

Figure 2.17:   A line three units long

Giving Cartesian Coordinates

For the next line let's try another method of specifying exact distances. Enter

@0,.15

A short line appears above the endpoint of the last line. Once again the at sign tells AutoCAD that the distance you specify is from the last point picked. But in this example, you give the distance in x and y values. The x distance, 0, is given first, followed by a comma, and then by the y distance, .15. This is how to specify distances in relative Cartesian coordinates.

Now let's continue with the door. Type

@-3,0

The result is a drawing that looks like Figure 2.19.

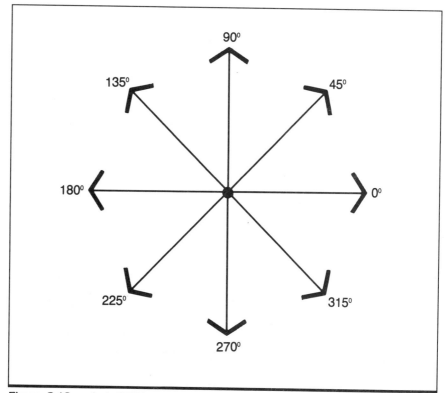

Figure 2.18: AutoCAD's system for specifying angles

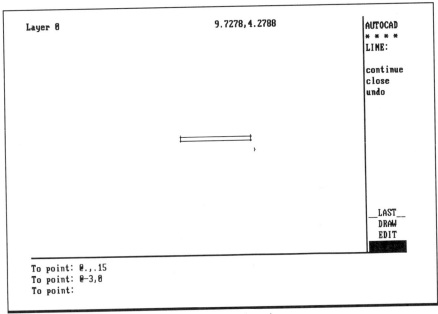

Figure 2.19:   Three sides of the door in the plan

The last distance you entered was in x,y values. But you used a negative value to specify the x distance. Positive values in the Cartesian coordinate system are from left to right and from bottom to top (see Figure 2.20). If you want to draw a line from right to left, you must give it a negative value.

Now pick Close from the menu, as shown in Figure 2.21, or enter C. You can close any sequence of lines by picking Close from the menu during the Line command. A line connecting the first and last points of a sequence of lines will be drawn, and the Line command will terminate (see Figure 2.22).

GIVING INPUT

In this section you will become familiar with some of the ways AutoCAD prompts you for input. Understanding the format of the prompts will help you to learn the program more easily.

The simple rectangle you just drew represents a plan view of a door. Usually, in a drawing of a floor plan, an arc is drawn to indicate how the door swings.

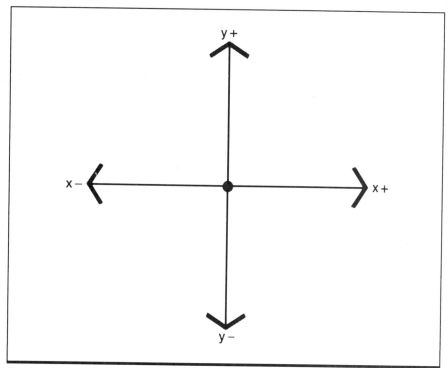

Figure 2.20:   Positive and negative Cartesian coordinate directions

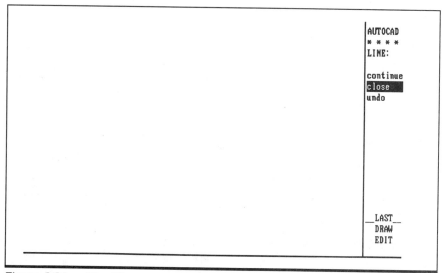

Figure 2.21:   The Close command

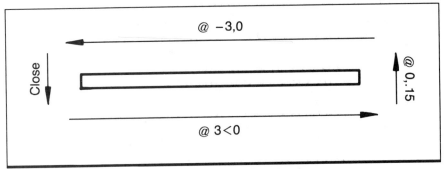

Figure 2.22:   *Distance and direction input for the door*

Responding to Prompts

Virtually every command in AutoCAD has more than one option. The Arc command illustrates this point quite well. First, initiate the command by typing

arc

The following prompt appears:

Center/<Start point>:

This prompt tells you that you have two options. The *default* option always appears between angle brackets, and all options are separated by a slash. The default is the option AutoCAD assumes if you don't tell it otherwise. If you choose to take the default, you can simply input a point by picking a location on the screen with the mouse or entering a coordinate.

Try selecting the Center option. Type

C

The following prompt appears:

Center:

Now pick a point representing the center of the arc near the upper-left corner of the door (see Figure 2.23). The following prompt appears:

Start point:

Notice that you only had to type in the C and not the whole word "Center." When you see other options in the prompt, note the capitalization. The capitalized letters are the only ones you need to

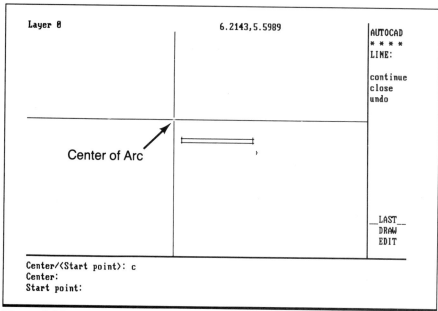

Figure 2.23:   *The center point for the arc*

enter to select that option. In some cases the first two letters are capitalized to differentiate between two options that begin with the same letter, such as LAyer/LType. Now type

@3<0

The following prompt appears:

Angle/Length of chord/<End point>:

Move the mouse and you will see an arc originating from a point three units to the right of the center point you selected, and rotating about that center, as in Figure 2.24.

As the prompt indicates, you have three options. You can enter an angle, length of chord, or endpoint of the arc. The default is endpoint. To select this option, you need only pick a point on the screen indicating where you want the endpoint. Pick a point directly vertical from the center of the arc. The arc is now fixed in place, as in Figure 2.25.

You could have selected the C,S,E: (center, start, end) option from the Arc menu and gotten the same results. The exercise you just completed, however, has given you some practice using the prompt and entering keyboard commands.

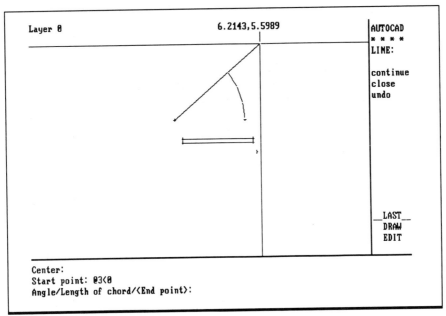

Figure 2.24:   The arc

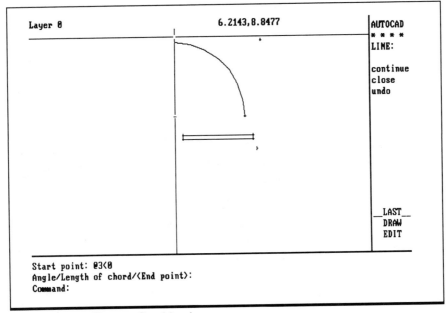

Figure 2.25:   The arc fixed in place

Selecting Objects

AutoCAD provides many options for selecting drawing objects. Because the AUI offers a few options new to version 9, we have split this section into two main parts. The first part deals with object selection for those who do not have the AUI; the second part deals specifically with object-selection options using the pull-down menus. We suggest you read both parts even though you may not have both options.

Selecting Objects without the AUI

Some AutoCAD commands prompt you to

Select objects:

Whenever you see this prompt, you have several options while making your selection. Often, as you select objects on the screen, you may change your mind about a selection or accidentally pick an object you do not want. In this section, you will try out most of the available selection options and learn what to do when you make the wrong selection.

Pick the Edit option, then select Next (see Figure 2.26). Pick the Move command near the top of the menu. Now pick, one at a time, the four lines that compose the door. Do this by moving the cursor to a line, then pressing the pick button. Notice that the cursor has changed into a small square. This tells you that you are in *object-selection mode*. As you pick an object, the object *ghosts*; that is, it changes from a solid image to one composed of dots (see Figure 2.27). Ghosting visually tells you that you have chosen that object to be acted upon by whatever command is active.

After making your selections you may decide to unselect some items. Pick the Undo subcommand from the Move menu or enter U (see Figure 2.28). Notice that a line unghosts. The Undo subcommand unselects objects, one at a time, in reverse order of selection.

There is also another way to unselect objects. Pick the Remove subcommand from the Move menu.

Now you can proceed to unselect objects just as you selected them. Pick two of the lines you selected to move, and they will unghost to show that they are no longer among the selected objects.

By now you have probably unselected nearly everything. If you decide to reselect an object, pick Add from the Move menu. Another option for selecting objects is to *window* them. Pick Window from the menu.

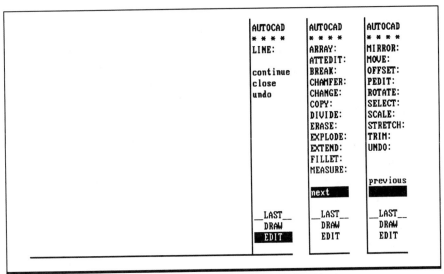

Figure 2.26:   The Line menu, the Edit menu, and the Next menu

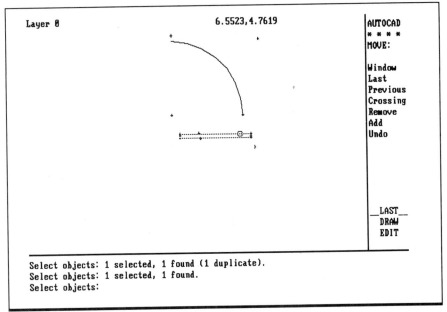

Figure 2.27:   The ghosted door

Now pick a point to the lower left of the rectangle representing the door. As you move your cursor across the screen, a box, or window, appears to stretch across the drawing area. When the window completely encloses the door, but not the arc, press the pick button and all of the door will ghost. The Window subcommand selects only objects that are completely enclosed by the window, as in Figure 2.29.

There are three other subcommands you haven't tried: Crossing, Last, and Previous. The Crossing subcommand is similar to Window, but will select anything that *crosses* *through* the window you define. You can select the last item you input by picking Last from the menu. The Previous subcommand picks the last object that was edited or changed. We won't try these options yet, but keep a mental note of how they can be used.

When you have selected the entire door but not the arc, press Return and a new prompt will appear:

Base point of displacement:

It is important to remember that you must press Return as soon as you have finished selecting the objects you want to edit. The space bar also acts like the Return key. Or, if you have a three-button mouse, you can use its center button like the Return key.

Figure 2.28:   The Move menu

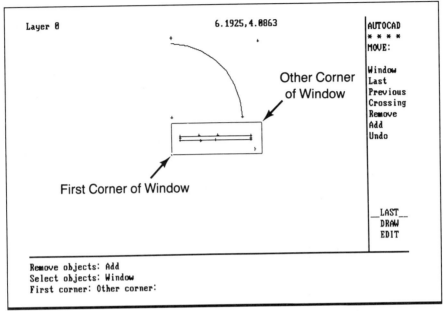

Figure 2.29: *The selected door*

The point is that you must tell AutoCAD when you have finished selecting objects.

Providing Base Points

One difficult concept to grasp is that of a base point. When you move or copy objects, AutoCAD must be told specifically *from* where and *to* where the move occurs. The base point is the exact location from which you determine the distance and direction of the move. Once the base point is determined, you can tell AutoCAD where to move the object in relation to that point.

To select a base point, pick the row of asterisks near the top of the menu. Then pick the Intersec command from the Osnap menu that appears (see Figure 2.30).

Notice that a square appears on the cursor. Now pick the upper-right corner of the door. When you see the square in the cursor you don't have to point exactly at the intersection. Just get the inter-section within the square, and AutoCAD will find the exact point where the two lines meet (see Figure 2.31).

The following prompt appears:

Second point of displacement:

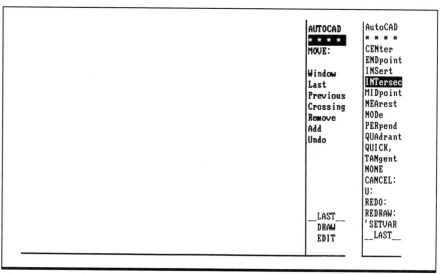

Figure 2.30: *The Move menu and the Osnap menu*

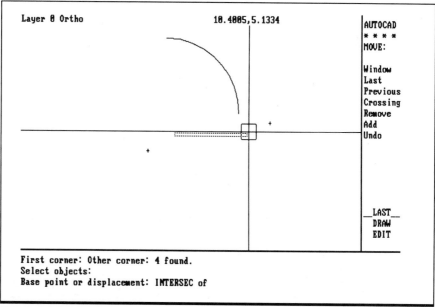

Figure 2.31: *The Osnap cursor*

Pick the asterisks again and pick Endpoint from the Osnap menu. Now pick the lower-right end of the arc you drew earlier. Remember, you need place only the end of the arc within the square. The door moves so that the intersection of the door you picked connects exactly with the endpoint of the arc (see Figure 2.32).

The Osnap overrides allow you to select specific points on an object. You used Endpoint and Intersec in this exercise, but other options are available. We will look at some of those later.

If you want to specify an exact distance and direction for moving or copying objects, you can select any point on the screen as a base point. Or you can just type an at sign at the base point prompt, then enter the second point's location in relative coordinates. Remember that the at sign means "the last point selected."

Try moving the entire door an exact distance of 1 unit in a 45-degree angle. Pick the Edit menu, then Next, then Move, then Window, as in Figure 2.33. Pick a point to the lower left of the door. Now drag the window across to the upper right of the door until the window completely encloses the door. Press the pick button. The entire door, including the arc, will ghost as shown in Figure 2.34.

Now press Return to tell AutoCAD you have finished your selection. The prompt

Base point of displacement:

will appear. Pick a base point on the screen between the door and the left of the screen (see Figure 2.30). Move the cursor around

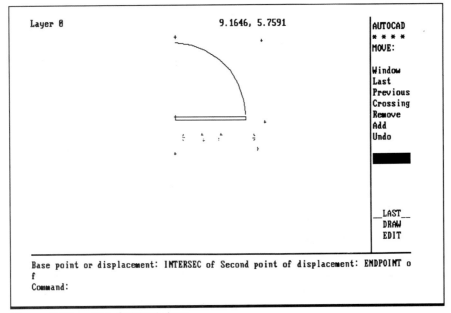

Figure 2.32: *The finished door*

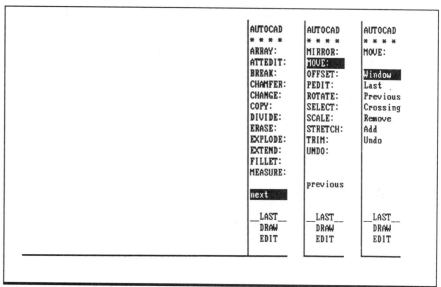

Figure 2.33: *The Edit menu, the Next menu, and the Move menu*

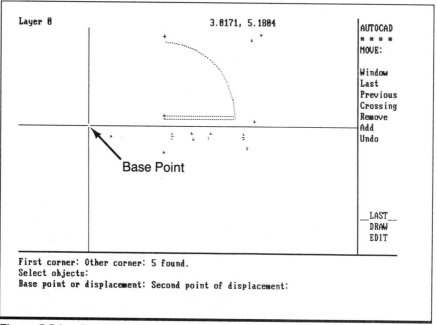

Figure 2.34: *The ghosted door and the base point just left of the door*

slowly and notice that the door moves as if the base point you selected were attached to the door. The door moves with the cursor at a fixed distance from it. This visually shows you how the base point relates to the objects you select.

Now type

@1<45

The door will move to a new location on the screen at a distance of one unit from its previous location and at an angle of 45 degrees. This shows that the base point does not have to be on the object you are manipulating if you provide specific distances. It can be virtually anywhere on your drawing, so long as you can control it.

Selecting Objects Using the AUI

When you select Erase, Move, Copy, Trim, or Extend from the Edit pull-down menu, you get the object-selection prompt. You now have several options for selecting objects. You can select a single object by pointing to it and picking it, or you can select a group of objects by using a window or a crossing window. Once you pick the object, you are prompted for a base point. This means you cannot select and unselect objects the way you can when you select these commands from the side menu or enter them through the keyboard.

Pick the Edit option from the pull-down menu bar, and then pick the Move command from the Edit menu. The object-selection prompt and the object-selection cursor (or pick box) appear. Pick the arc representing the door swing. The arc ghosts, and the base point prompt appears immediately, telling you that you have finished selecting objects and must now select the base point for the move.

Object selection works differently when you use the pull-down Edit menu because the pull-down menu implements two selection options that are new to version 9. These new options are Si (for single) and Auto (for automatic). In fact, if you watch the prompt line when you pick any of the editing commands mentioned above from the pull-down menu, you will see the name of the command first followed by Si, then by Auto. The Si option forces AutoCAD to allow only one selection rather than several. This is why you are limited to only one pick when using the Move command from the pull-down menu. The Auto option tells AutoCAD automatically to use a standard window or crossing window if no object is selected using the pick box. You can achieve the same result manually by entering the Si Auto and options through the keyboard at the object-selection prompt, but this may seem redundant because Si and Auto are intended for use in a custom menu where the single and automatic selection modes make more sense than the standard object-selection process.

Si and Auto offer an alternative means of editing objects. Pick any point on the screen and enter

@1<0

The arc will move to a new location one unit to the right. Notice that the object-selection prompt appears again at the prompt line. The Move command automatically restarts and you can select another object to move. Unlike a command selected from the side menu or entered through the keyboard, a command selected from a pull-down menu continues to be active until a new command is selected, or until you cancel it by pressing Control-C or by selecting Cancel from the Tools pull-down menu.

Next you will move the rest of the door in the same direction by using a window. Since you are still in the Move command, your cursor is in object-selection mode. Pick a point just above and to the left of the rectangle representing the door. Be sure not to pick the door itself. Now a window appears to drag across the screen as you move the cursor. If you move the cursor to the left of the last point selected, the window appears dotted (see Figure 2.35). If you move the cursor to the right of that point, it appears solid (see Figure 2.36).

These two different windows, the dotted and the solid, respectively represent a crossing window and a standard window. If you use a crossing window, anything that crosses through the window will be selected. If you use a standard window, anything that is completely contained within the window will be selected. These window options start automatically if no object is picked while you are in object-selection mode.

Now pick a point below and to the right of the door, so that the door is completely enclosed by the window (see Figure 2.36). The door ghosts and the base-point selection prompt appears. Pick any point on the screen, then enter

@1<0

The door will join with the arc.

Now try using the crossing window. As before, you are still in the Move command. Pick a point below and to the right of the door. As you move the cursor to the left, the window appears dotted. Select the next point so that the window encloses the door and part of the

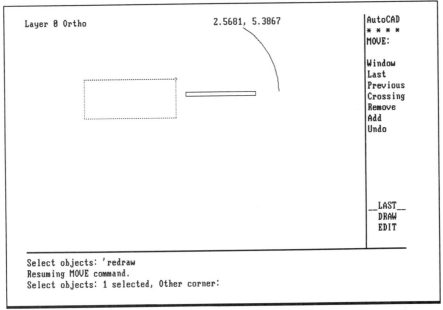

Figure 2.35: *The dotted window*

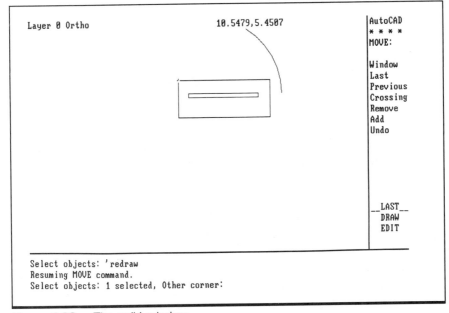

Figure 2.36: *The solid window*

arc (see Figure 2.37). The entire door, including the arc, ghosts. Pick any point on the screen, then enter

   @1<180

The door will move back to its original location.

GRASPING SOME BASIC DRAWING TOOLS

As you begin with AutoCAD there are a few commands you will use often. The following are some of the more important commands you should know about.

Updating the Display

By now the screen looks a bit messy with all the blips. To clean up a screen image, use the Redraw command. Go to the Root menu and pick Display to bring up the menu shown in Figure 2.38. Pick Redraw and the screen will quickly redraw the objects, clearing them of the blips.

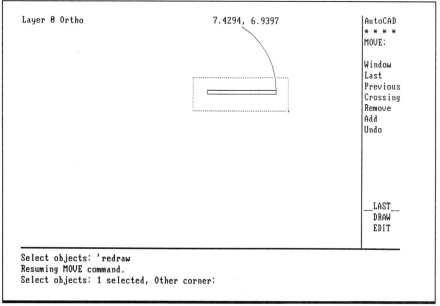

Layer 0 Ortho   7.4294, 6.9397   AutoCAD
                                                          * * * *
                                                          MOVE:

                                                          Window
                                                          Last
                                                          Previous
                                                          Crossing
                                                          Remove
                                                          Add
                                                          Undo

                                                          __LAST__
                                                           DRAW
                                                           EDIT

Select objects: 'redraw
Resuming MOVE command.
Select objects: 1 selected, Other corner:

Figure 2.37:   The door enclosed by a crossing window

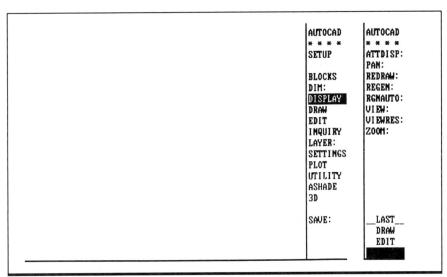

Figure 2.38:   *The Root menu and the Display menu*

Redraw can also be found on the Osnap overrides menu. Another command, Regen, does the same thing, but also updates the drawing database—which means it takes a lot longer to restore the drawing. In general you will want to avoid the Regen command. You will see how to use it in Chapter 7.

Correcting Errors

If you make a typing error before you press Return, you must use the backspace key to back up to your error, then retype your command or response. If you start a command and then decide not to use that command after all, you must hold down the Control key and simultaneously press C to cancel your last entry. Finally, if you accidentally change something in the drawing and want to reverse that change, you can use the U command. It will undo everything you have done, in reverse order; that is, the most recent command performed will be undone first, then the next to last, etc., each time you type U. To use it, type

U

The prompt will display the last command used, and the drawing will revert to its condition prior to the last command.

Getting Help

You can get help from AutoCAD by typing a question mark at the command prompt. Type

?

You will see the following prompt:

Command name (RETURN for list):

Press Return and you will see a list of commands like those shown in the top half of Figure 2.39. Press Return again, and another list of commands like those shown in the bottom half of Figure 2.39 appears. These help screens are a list of commands available to you. They also indicate which commands are available with each drafting extension.

```
         AutoCAD Command List  (+n = ADE-n feature, ' = transparent command)

  APERTURE +2    BREAK +1      DIM/DIM1 +1    END            HIDE +3
  ARC            CHAMFER +1    DIST           ERASE          ID
  AREA           CHANGE        DIVIDE +3      EXPLODE +3     IGESIN +3
  ARRAY          CIRCLE        DONUT +3       EXTEND +3      IGESOUT +3
  ATTDEF +2      COLOR         DOUGHNUT +3    FILES          INSERT
  ATTDISP +2     COPY          DRAGMODE +2    FILL           ISOPLANE +2
  ATTEDIT +2     DBLIST        DTEXT +3       FILLET +1      LAYER
  ATTEXT +2      DDATTE +3     DXBIN +3       FILMROLL +3    LIMITS
  AXIS +1        'DDEMODES +3  DXFIN          'GRAPHSCR      LINE
  BASE           'DDLMODES +3  DXFOUT         GRID           LINETYPE
  BLIPMODE       'DDRMODES +3  ELEV +3        HATCH +1       LIST
  BLOCK          DELAY         ELLIPSE +3     'HELP / '?     LOAD

  Press RETURN for further help. _

         AutoCAD Command List  (+n = ADE-n feature, ' = transparent command)

  LTSCALE        PEDIT +3      REGENAUTO      SNAP           UNDO
  MEASURE +3     PLINE +3      RENAME         SOLID          UNITS +1
  MENU           PLOT          'RESUME        STATUS         'VIEW +2
  MINSERT        POINT         ROTATE +3      STRETCH +3     VIEWRES
  MIRROR +2      POLYGON +3    RSCRIPT        STYLE          VPOINT +3
  MOVE           PRPLOT        SAVE           TABLET         VSLIDE
  MSLIDE +2      PURGE         SCALE +3       TEXT           WBLOCK
  MULTIPLE       QTEXT         SCRIPT         'TEXTSCR       'ZOOM
  OFFSET +3      QUIT          SELECT         TIME           3DFACE +3
  OOPS           REDEFINE +3   'SETVAR        TRACE          3DLINE +3
  ORTHO          REDO          SHAPE          TRIM +3
  OSNAP +2       'REDRAW       SHELL/SH +3    U
  'PAN           REGEN         SKETCH +1      UNDEFINE +3

  At the "Command:" prompt, you can enter RETURN to repeat the last command.

  Press RETURN for further help. _
```

Figure 2.39:   *Two help screens showing a list of commands*

Press Return again, and another screen will appear (see Figure 2.40). The top screen gives you a brief description of AutoCAD's coordinate format; the bottom screen shows a list of selection options, the same information we covered in this chapter.

If you type ? Return, then the name of a command, you will get a brief description of that command and how to use it. Type

?

move

```
You can enter points, or coordinates, in any of the following ways:

    Absolute:   x,y
    Relative:   @deltax,deltay
    Polar:      @dist<angle

For the commands that accept 3D points, you can include a Z coordinate
in the absolute and relative formats:

    Absolute:   x,y,z
    Relative:   @deltax,deltay,deltaz

If you omit the Z coordinate, the current elevation is used.

X/Y/Z filters can be used to compose a full point from the X, Y, and
Z components of intermediate points.  For instance, the filter ".X"
will instruct AutoCAD to use just the X coordinate of the following
point.  The Y (and possibly Z) values will then be requested.

See also:   Section 2.9 of the Reference Manual, and
            the Release 9 supplement.

Press RETURN for further help. _

Object selection:  ("Select objects:")

    (point)  =  One object
    Multiple =  Multiple objects selected by pointing
    Last     =  Last object
    Previous =  All objects in the Previous selection-set
    Window   =  Objects within Window
    Crossing =  Objects within or Crossing window
    BOX      =  Automatic Crossing (to the left) or Window (to the right)
    AUto     =  Automatic BOX (if pick in empty area) or single object pick
    SIngle   =  One selection (any type)
    Add      =  Add mode: add following objects to selection-set
    Remove   =  Remove mode: remove following objects from selection-set
    Undo     =  Undo/remove last

When you are satisfied with the selection-set as it stands, enter RETURN
(except for "Single" mode, which does not require an extra RETURN).

See also:   Section 2.10 of the Reference Manual.

Command: _
```

Figure 2.40:   Two help screens describing AutoCAD's coordinate options

You will get a screen like the one in Figure 2.41. This help screen displays a brief description of the Move command, how to use it, and where to look in the *AutoCAD Reference Manual* to get more detailed information.

You can also get information about a command while you are in the middle of using it. For example, if you start the Move command and forget what to do next, you can enter

'?

and you will get the same help screen you see in Figure 2.41.

Flipping Between Text and Graphics Screens

You may be wondering how to get back to the drawing editor screen. Some commands, like Help, will flip the display from the drawing editor into a text mode. This happens when you are trying to get information about the drawing. To shift between text and graphics, press the F1 function key (the flip-screen key). Try it a few times and see what happens.

```
The MOVE  command is used to move one or more existing drawing
entities from one location in the drawing to another.

Format:     MOVE  Select objects: (select)
            Base point or displacement:
            Second point of displacement:  (if base selected above)

If you have the ADE-2 package, you can "drag" the object into position
on the screen.  To do this, designate a reference point on the object in
response to the "Base point..." prompt, and then reply "DRAG" to the
"Second point:" prompt.  The selected objects will follow the movements
of the screen crosshairs.  Move the objects into position and then press
the pointer's "pick" button.

See also:   Section 5.2 of the Reference Manual.

Command: _
```

Figure 2.41:   A help screen describing the Move command

SAVING, QUITTING, AND ENDING FILES

After you have had enough, you can either *save* your drawing file, *quit* it, or *end* it. The Save command will save the drawing in its most recent form without exiting the program. Enter

save

You will get the prompt

File name <Door>:

Press Return, and the drawing you have been working on will be saved. By pressing Return you accept the default file name you see within the brackets, "Door." AutoCAD will create a new file on the disk with the name "Door" and add the file extension .DWG. If this were a drawing you had saved previously, AutoCAD would update it. You can now take a break or continue to edit knowing that if you have a power failure now you won't lose all the work you've done. When you are spending a lot of time on a drawing, it is a good idea to use the Save command every 20 minutes or so as a precaution against power problems that may occur.

Both Quit and End will exit the drawing editor. If you quit an unsaved file, the file will no longer exist once you've exited the program. If you quit a file that was previously saved, you will exit the program without saving the changes you made in this editing session—so be sure that when you use Quit, you really mean it. If you end a file, it will be saved along with any changes you have made up to now. Type

end

This brings you to the Main menu. Type

0

You are now back in DOS.

CONCLUSION

You now have the basic knowledge to start doing some serious drawing. At this point you could try using some of the commands just to see how far your understanding can take you. You should be able to open a new file, input distances, and select commands from a menu with some confidence. In the next chapter you will start a project that shows you some of AutoCAD's basic drawing commands.

Chapter 3

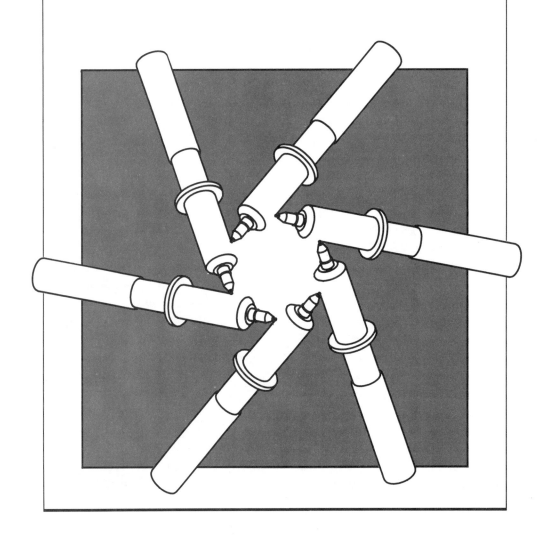

Creating a Drawing

SO FAR WE HAVE COVERED the most basic information you need to understand the workings of AutoCAD. Now you will put your knowledge to work by drawing a studio apartment building. This architectural tutorial illustrates how to use AutoCAD commands and will give you a solid understanding of the basic AutoCAD package. With that understanding, you can use AutoCAD to its fullest potential regardless of the kinds of drawings you intend to create or the enhancement products you may use in the future. In this chapter you will start drawing an apartment's bathroom fixtures. In the process, you will learn how to use AutoCAD's basic tools.

As you go through the exercises, we will frequently ask you to enter a command by picking it from a side or pull-down menu. Often, picking a command from a screen menu brings up a side menu of subcommands to select from. If you enter the commands through the keyboard, however, these subcommands will not appear on the menu, so you must also enter them through the keyboard as described in Chapter 2. Keep this in mind as you progress through the exercises.

SETTING UP A WORK AREA

Before beginning most drawings, you will want to set up your work area. By doing this you will determine the *measurement system*, the *drawing sheet size*, and the *scale* you want to use. The default work area is 9 x 12 inches at full scale, using a decimal measurement system where one unit equals one inch. If these are appropriate settings for your drawing, then you don't have to do any setting up. It is more likely that you will be doing drawings of various sizes and scales. For example, you may want to do a drawing in a measurement system where you can specify feet, inches, and fractions of inches at 1" = 1' scale, and print it on an 8½ x 11-inch sheet of paper. Once you have set up a drawing, you can use the setup for future drawings; we explain how later in the book. In this section, you will learn how to set up a drawing the way you want.

Choosing a Measurement System, Drawing Sheet Size, and Scale

Open a new file called Bath the same way you opened the Door file in Chapter 2. Pick the menu option Setup. You will see a menu listing the different unit formats available (see Figure 3.1).

In the last chapter, you input distances in units using the default measurement system, decimal. The *decimal system* allows you to enter distances in inches and decimals of inches. The Unit Type menu allows you to select another measurement system. For

Figure 3.1:   *The Unit Type menu*

example, if you choose the *metric system*, all units will be in millimeters and decimals of millimeters. If you choose the *architectural system*, the unit will be inches, and you will be able to enter values in feet, inches, and fractions of inches. Table 3.1 shows the options available to you and a sample of how measurements are entered.

Pick Archtect from the Unit Type menu to select the architectural system. The Archtect submenu appears, showing your options for selecting the scale for the drawing. These options are typical scales used in architectural drawings. For our example, you will want a scale of one inch to one foot. Pick 1" = 1' (see Figure 3.2).

Choosing 1" = 1' brings up a menu of sheet sizes to choose from (see Figure 3.3). These options are standard sheet sizes for technical drawings. This is where you select the size you want your drawing to be when you finally plot or print it out. Pick 8.5 x 11 for an 8½ x 11-inch sheet.

A rectangle appears, filling the screen, and the Root menu comes up. The rectangle represents the edge of your 8½ x 11-inch sheet. Now as you draw you will input distances in the actual dimensions of the objects you are drawing, and they will appear at the proper scale within the sheet area defined by that rectangle (see Figure 3.4).

Using the Drawing Sheet

To get a clearer understanding of what Setup does, let's check the size of this rectangle. Pick the Inquiry option from the Root

Measurement System	AutoCAD's Display of Measurement	
Scientific	1.55E + 01	(inches)
Decimal	15.5000	(inches)
Engineering	1'-3.5"	(input as 1'3.5")
Architectural	1"-3 1/2"	(input as 1'3-1/2")
Metric	15.5000	(converted to metric at plot)
Fractional	15 1/2"	(input as 15-1/2")

Table 3.1:   Measurement systems available in AutoCAD

Figure 3.2:   *The Archtect menu of scale options*

Figure 3.3:   *The Horizontl Sheet Size menu*

menu, then the Dist command (see Figure 3.5). Bring up the Osnap overrides by picking the asterisks on the menu, then pick Intersec.

Now point to the lower-left corner of the rectangle. Bring up the Osnap overrides menu again, and pick Intersec. Pick the upper-right

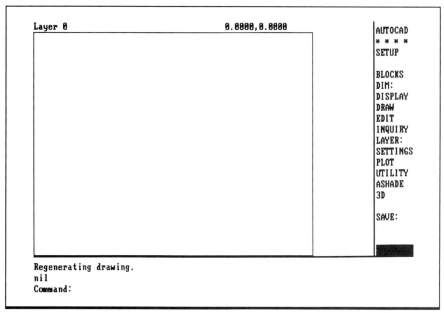

Figure 3.4: *The rectangle in the drawing area representing the edge of the 8¹/₂ × 11-inch drawing sheet*

Figure 3.5: *The Inquiry menu*

corner. You will see the prompt line display the message

Distance = 13'-10 13/16" Angle = 38
Delta X = 11'-0" Delta Y = 8'-6" Delta Z = 0'-0"

As you can see, the rectangle defining your sheet in the drawing editor is 8'-6" x 11', which allows you to draw at full scale. The Setup program converted the 11-inch side of the sheet to 11 feet and the 8½-inch side to 8 feet 6 inches. It is as if you were drawing full size on a sheet of paper or film 11 feet wide by 8 feet 6 inches high. Later when you plot the drawing you will tell AutoCAD the scale of the drawing, 1" = 1', and it will reduce everything to fit on an 8½ x 11-inch sheet of paper. Table 3.2 shows how AutoCAD determines drawing sheet size in the drawing editor according to the scale of the drawing and final plotted sheet size.

Understanding the Setup Option

If you display the list of AutoCAD commands by entering a question mark, you won't see Setup on the list. This is because Setup is actually an external AutoLISP program intended to simplify the drawing setup process. Setup prompts you for the information it needs, then runs two AutoCAD commands, Units and Limits. While running these commands, Setup passes the setup information to them to save you the work of figuring out how to convert an 8½ x 11-inch sheet into the proper size for a 1" = 1' scale drawing. It also draws a rectangle around your work area. The following is a brief description of the Units and Limits commands.

Specifying Units

The Units command allows you to select any measurement system available on the Unit Type menu (except for metric). This command also allows you to set the level of accuracy or the smallest fraction or number of decimal places you can use while specifying distances. You can also determine how angles are input and displayed. If you want to enter values smaller than those allowed by the Setup option, or if you want to use a different method for entering angles, you should use the Units command independently of Setup.

You should note that fractions of a unit can only be used in the architectural and fractional systems and that hyphens are only used to distinguish those fractions from whole inches. You cannot use spaces while giving a dimension. For example, you can specify eight feet four and one-half inches as 8'4-1/2" or 8'4.5, but not as 8'-4 1/2".

Plotted Sheet Size in Inches

Scale	8 1/2×11	11×17	17×22	18×24	22×34	24×36	30×42	36×48
1"=10'	85×110	110×170	170×220	180×240	220×340	240×360	300×420	360×480
1"=20'	170×220	220×340	340×440	360×480	440×680	480×720	600×840	720×960
1"=30'	255×330	330×510	510×660	540×720	660×1020	720×1080	900×1260	1080×1440
1"=40'	340×440	440×680	680×880	720×960	880×1360	960×1440	1200×1680	1440×1920
1"=50'	425×550	558×850	850×1100	900×1200	1100×1700	1200×1800	1500×2100	1800×2400
1"=60'	510×660	660×1020	1020×1320	1080×1440	1320×2040	1440×2160	1800×2520	2160×2880
3"=1'-0"	2.83×3.67	3.67×5.67	5.67×7.34	6×8	7.33×11.34	8×12	10×14	12×16
1 1/2"=1'-0"	5.67×7.34	7.34×11.34	11.34×14.67	12×16	14.67×22.67	16×24	20×28	24×32
1"=1'-0"	8.5×11	11×17	17×22	18×24	22×34	24×36	30×42	36×48
3/4"=1'-0"	11.33×14.66	14.67×22.67	22.67×29.34	24×32	29.34×45.34	32×48	40×56	48×64
1/2"=1'-0"	17×22	22×34	34×44	36×48	44×68	48×72	60×84	72×96
1/4"=1'-0"	34×44	44×68	68×88	72×96	88×136	96×144	120×168	144×192
1/8"=1'-0"	68×88	88×136	136×176	144×192	176×272	192×288	190×336	288×384
1/16"=1'-0"	136×176	176×272	272×352	288×384	352×544	384×576	480×672	576×768

Table 3.2: Sheet size in the drawing editor according to the drawing scale and final plotted sheet size

This is a source of confusion to many architects and engineers new to AutoCAD, since AutoCAD displays architectural dimensions in the standard architectural format but does not allow you to *enter* dimensions that way.

Specifying Limits

The Limits command helps determine the size of the area you are working on. It defines the view area displayed when you use the Zoom All command and it also allows you to force your drawing to stay within the view area boundary. If you are using an unusual scale, you will want to run the Limits command independently of the Setup option.

The limits are defined by two points using absolute Cartesian coordinates. These points locate two diagonal corners of a rectangular area, which are the limits of a drawing. In general, the Cartesian coordinate 0,0 is used for the lower-left corner, and the upper-right corner varies depending on the scale and sheet size of your drawing. If for example you want to do a drawing that is 1" = 1' scale on an 8½ x 11-inch sheet, multiply the width and height of the sheet by a factor of 12 to get the coordinate of the sheet's upper-right corner, 11',8'6".

The 12 comes from the fact that it takes 12 one-inch units to make one foot. For other scales, you must find out how many units are needed to make one foot. The 1/16" = 1' scale requires 192 units, while the 1/8" = 1' scale requires 96 units (see Table 3.3).

In later chapters you will use this scale conversion to determine the size of text and dimensions.

USING THE AUTOCAD MODES AS DRAFTING TOOLS

After you have set up your drawing sheet, you can begin the plan of a typical bathroom in your studio. We will use this example to show you some of AutoCAD's tools. These tools might be compared to a background grid, scale, T square, and triangle.

Using the Grid Mode as a Background Grid

Using the *grid mode* is like having a grid under your drawing to help you with layout. The F7 function key toggles the grid mode on and off. Press F7. An array of dots appears. These dots are the

Scale	Scale Factor
1″ = 10′	120
1″ = 20′	240
1″ = 30′	360
1″ = 40′	480
1″ = 50′	600
1″ = 60′	720
1/16″ = 1′-0″	192
1/8″ = 1′-0″	96
1/4″ = 1′-0″	48
1/2″ = 1′-0″	24
3/4″ = 1′-0″	16
1″ = 1′-0″	12
1 1/2″ = 1′-0″	8
3″ = 1′-0″	4

Table 3.3:   *Scale conversion factor*

grid points. They will not print or plot with your drawing. If the grid seems a bit too dense, you can alter the grid spacing by using the Grid command. Pick Settings from the Root menu, then pick Grid from the Settings menu (see Figure 3.6).

Note that the prompt displays options for the grid mode. Enter 10 to select the default option, grid spacing(X), and press Return. The grid spacing is now ten inches.

Pull-down menu users can select Drawing Aids from the Modes pull-down menu. This brings up a dialog box that allows you to select and adjust drawing modes. You can see all of your current mode settings at a glance and modify one or all of them at once.

Pick Modes, then Drawing Aids from the Modes pull-down menu. A dialog box displaying all the mode settings appears (see Figure 3.7). An arrow appears that follows the motion of your mouse. As you move the arrow into one of the boxes inside the dialog box, the setting is highlighted. Highlight the X Spacing setting that contains the number 10.0000, just below the Grid heading (see Figure 3.7). This type of box is called an *input button*.

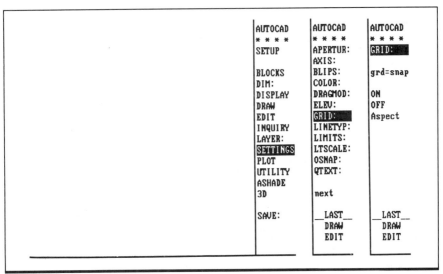

Figure 3.6: The Root menu, the Settings menu, and the Grid menu

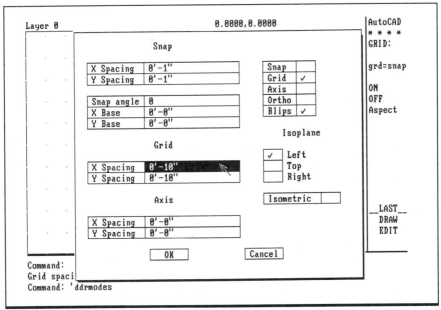

Figure 3.7: The Drawing Aids dialog box with the X Spacing input button highlighted

With the X Spacing input button highlighted, enter the number 20 through the keyboard. As you enter the number, two other *action buttons* appear to the right of the one you are modifying. These buttons contain the words Cancel and OK. Move the arrow to highlight the OK, and press the pick button to confirm your entry of 20. Both the number you edited and the number directly below it, the Y Spacing, change to 20.0000. If you select the Cancel button, the grid settings revert back to their original settings.

You may notice a set of *check buttons* to the right of the input buttons. These buttons allow you to turn modes on and off. A check beside the button means that mode is turned on. Notice that there is a check by the word Grid, indicating that the grid mode is on. These settings can be changed by simply highlighting the button and picking it.

Now highlight and pick the Cancel input button at the bottom of the dialog box. This tells AutoCAD to ignore the changes you have made to the settings. If you had picked the OK input button, any changes you had made in the dialog box would become the new settings. Since you don't really want to change anything, pick Cancel.

You may notice the word Ddrmodes appear on the prompt line when you pick Drawing Aids from the Modes pull-down menu. This is the actual AutoCAD command that brings up this dialog box. You can enter this command through the keyboard to access this dialog box if you wish.

Using the Snap Mode

The *snap mode* has no equivalent in hand drafting. This mode forces the cursor to step a specific distance. It is useful if you want to maintain accuracy while entering distances with the cursor. The F9 function key toggles the snap mode on and off. Press F9, then move the cursor slowly around the drawing area. Notice how the cursor seems to step rather than move in a smooth motion. Also note that the word Snap appears in the status line. This tells you that the snap mode is on.

The default snap distance is one inch. You can adjust this distance using the Snap command. Pick Last from the Grid menu, then Next, then Snap (see Figure 3.8). Note that the prompt displays options for the snap mode.

Snap spacing or ON/OFF/Aspect/Rotate/Style<X>:

Enter 4 to set the snap setting to four inches. Now move the cursor around. Notice how it steps at a greater distance than before.

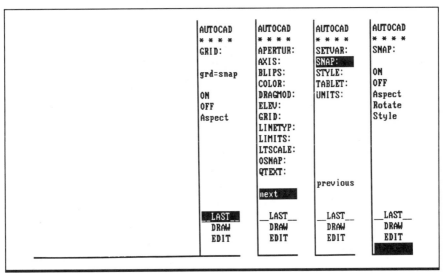

Figure 3.8: The Grid menu, the Settings menu, a Settings submenu, and the Snap menu

Other options allow you to set the snap origin point (Rotate option), rotate the cursor to an angle other than its current 0-90 degrees (Rotate option), and set the horizontal snap spacing to a value different from the vertical spacing (Aspect option). You can also change the cursor shape to allow isometric-style drawings (Style option). Because these useful options are buried in a command you may not associate with them, we are calling attention to them now. We will look at these features in Chapters 6 and 14.

If your display system supports pull-down menus, you can use the dialog box that appears when you select Drawing Aids from the Modes pull-down menu. The snap modes are set like the grid modes—you pick the appropriate button to either toggle the setting on or off or to adjust the snap spacing.

Using Cursor Keys with the Snap Mode On

In the last chapter, you saw how to use the cursor keys to move the cursor. At that point, however, you weren't able to control the distance the cursor moved very well. With the snap mode, you can control the distance the cursor moves each time a cursor key is pressed. If the snap distance is 4, the cursor will move four inches. If you press the Page Up key, this distance will increase by a factor of 10 to 40 inches. Press Page Up again, and the distance increases again by a factor of 10 to 400 inches. As before, pressing Page Down will reduce the cursor step distance.

Using Grid and Snap Together

You can set the grid spacing to reflect the snap setting, allowing you to see every snap point. Pick Last from the current menu, then Previous, then Grid, then enter 0. The grid now equals the snap setting. As you move the cursor, it snaps to the grid points. Pick Snap from the current menu and enter 1 to change the snap setting to one inch. The grid now changes to reflect the new snap setting. At this density, the grid is overwhelming. Pick Grid from the Settings menu and enter 10 to change the grid spacing back to ten inches. Whenever the grid setting is greater than zero, it will no longer reflect the snap points.

Using the Coordinate Readout as Your Scale

Now you will draw the first item in the bathroom, the toilet. The toilet will be composed of a rectangle representing the tank and a truncated ellipse representing the seat. Press the F6 key and watch the coordinate readout in the upper right of the screen. As you move the cursor, the coordinate readout dynamically displays its position in absolute Cartesian coordinates. This allows you to find a position on your drawing by locating it in reference to the drawing origin, 0,0, which is in the lower-left corner of the sheet. Throughout these exercises, coordinates will be provided to enable you to select points using the dynamic coordinate readout.

Pick Draw from the Grid menu and select Line from the Draw menu. Pull-down menu users can pick Line from the Draw pull-down menu. Start your line at the coordinate 5'-7", 6'-3". As you move the cursor you will see the coordinate readout change to polar coordinates. AutoCAD switches to polar coordinates to allow you to see your current location in reference to the last point selected. This is helpful when you are using a command that requires distance and direction input. Move the cursor until the coordinate readout lists

1'-10" < 0

Pick this point. By using the snap mode in conjunction with the coordinate readout, you can measure distances as you draw lines. This is similar to the way you would draw using a scale. You could have entered the distances through the keyboard or, if you have a digitizing tablet, through the menu template. Although this method works well for short distances, it doesn't work when you are dealing with distances of 20 feet or more, because of the combined limitations of your monitor and pointing device.

Using the Ortho Mode as Your T Square and Triangle

As you move the cursor around, the rubber-banding line follows it at any angle. You can also force the line to be orthogonal. Press F8 to toggle on the *ortho mode,* and move the cursor around. If your display system supports pull-down menus, you can use the Drawing Aids dialog box to toggle the ortho mode on or off. Now the rubber-banding line will only move vertically or horizontally. The ortho mode is analogous to the T square and triangle. Note that the word Ortho appears on the status line to tell you that the ortho mode is on. Move the cursor down until the coordinate readout lists

0'-9″< 270

Continue drawing the other two sides of the rectangle by using the coordinate readout. You should have a drawing that looks like Figure 3.9.

The drawing modes can be indispensable tools when used prop-erly. If you have the advanced user interface, the Drawing Aids dia-log box helps you visualize the modes in an organized manner and simplifies their management.

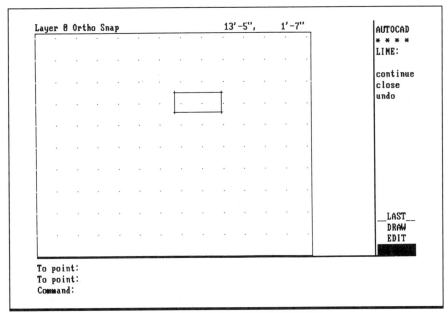

Figure 3.9: Plan view of the toilet tank

EXPLORING THE DRAWING PROCESS

In this section, you will look at some of the more common commands and use them to complete this simple drawing. As you draw, watch the prompts and notice how your responses affect them. Also note how you use existing drawing elements as reference points.

While drawing with AutoCAD, you create gross geometric forms to determine the basic shapes of objects, then modify the shapes to fill in detail. This is where the differences between drawing with AutoCAD and manual drafting become more apparent.

AutoCAD provides nine basic drawing object types: lines, arcs, circles, traces, polylines, points, 3D lines, 3D faces, and solids. All drawings are built on these objects. You are familiar with lines and arcs, and these, along with circles, are the most commonly used objects. As you progress through the book, we will introduce you to the other objects and how they are used.

Locating an Object in Reference to Others

To define the toilet seat you will use an ellipse. AutoCAD's ellipse is actually a type of object called a *polyline* that we will discuss in detail in Chapter 12. Go to the Draw menu and pick the Ellipse option. The following prompt appears:

<Axis endpoint 1>/Center:

For the first axis endpoint, pick the midpoint of the bottom horizontal line of the rectangle. Do this by bringing up the Osnap overrides and selecting Midpoint, then pick the bottom line. The prompt

Axis endpoint 2:

appears. Next move the cursor down until the coordinate readout lists

1'-10"< 270

Pick this as the second axis endpoint. The prompt

<Other axis distance>/Rotation:

appears. Next move the cursor horizontally from the center of the ellipse until the coordinate readout lists

0'-8"< 180

Pick this as the axis distance defining the width of the ellipse. Your drawing should look like Figure 3.10.

Getting a Closer Look

During the drawing process, you will want to enlarge areas of a drawing to more easily edit the objects you have drawn. The Zoom command is used for this purpose. Pick Autocad from the top of the menu to return to the Root menu. Pick Display, then pick Zoom from the Display menu (see Figure 3.11), or just pull down the Display menu from the Status line.

The following prompt appears:

All/Center/Dynamic/Extents/Left/Previous/Window/ < Scale(x) >:

Pick Window, then pick a point below and to the left of your drawing at coordinate 5'-0", 6'-3". Next pick a point above and to the right of the drawing at coordinate 8'-3", 6'-8" so that the toilet is completely enclosed by the view window. The toilet enlarges to fill more of the screen (see Figure 3.12).

Note that the Window subcommand works in the same way it did in Chapter 2 when you learned about selecting objects. The only difference between the two is that here you are defining a view, while in Chapter 2 you were selecting a group of objects.

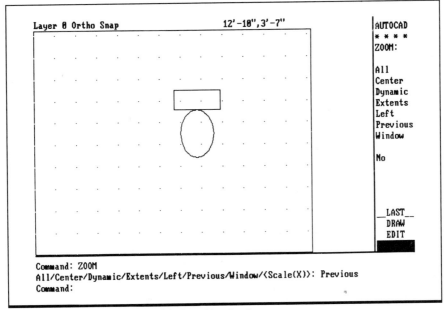

Figure 3.10: The ellipse added to the tank

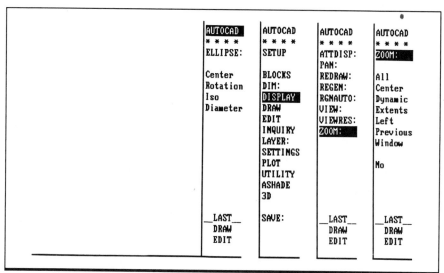

Figure 3.11:   The Ellipse menu, the Setup menu, the Display menu, and the
Zoom menu

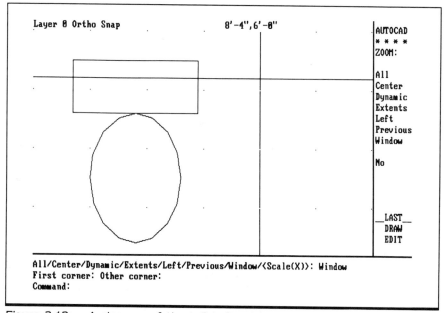

Figure 3.12:   A close-up of the toilet drawing

Modifying an Object

To define the back edge of the seat, copy the line defining the front of the toilet tank three inches toward the center of the ellipse. Pick the Edit option at the bottom of the Zoom menu, then pick Copy from the Edit side or pull-down menu. The object-selection prompt appears. Pick the horizontal line that touches the top of the ellipse; once the line ghosts, press Return to confirm your selection. (If you used the Edit pull-down menu, you don't have to press Return). The

Base point:

prompt appears. Pick a base point near the line, then move the cursor down until the coordinate readout lists

0'-3" < 270

Pick this point. Your drawing should look like Figure 3.13.

You will notice that the Copy command acts exactly like the Move command you used in Chapter 2, except that Copy does not alter the position of the object(s) you select.

Now you must delete the part of the ellipse that is not needed. You will use the Break command to break it off, then you will erase

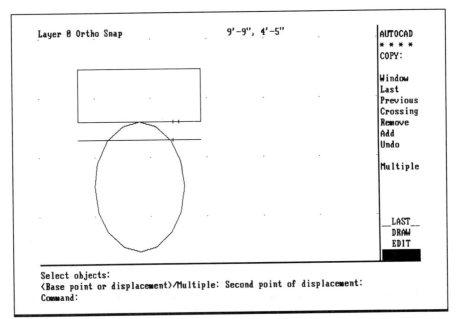

Figure 3.13:   The line copied down

the broken-off section. Breaking an ellipse is a bit tricky. The best thing to do is to make two small breaks, rather than one large break. If you don't do this, you can break the ellipse in the wrong direction.

First, turn the snap mode off by pressing the F9 function key. Snap may be a hindrance at this point in your editing session because it may keep you from picking the points you want. The snap mode forces the cursor to move to points at a given interval, so you will have difficulty selecting a point that doesn't fall exactly on one of those intervals.

To break the ellipse, go to the Edit menu, then pick Break (see Figure 3.14). The object-selection prompt appears. Select a point on the ellipse above the left intersection of the line and the ellipse near coordinate 6'-3", 5'-5". Next bring up the Osnap overrides and select Intersec, then pick the left intersection of the ellipse and the line. The ellipse breaks between the two points you selected. Pick Break again, and this time pick a point on the ellipse toward the right of the first break near coordinate 6'-9", 5'-5". Now pick the Intersec Osnap override, then the rightmost intersection of the ellipse and line. Your drawing should look like Figure 3.15.

Break can be used to break any object except *blocks*, solids, 3D lines, and 3D faces. We will discuss blocks in the next chapter.

Now that you've broken the ellipse, erase the part you don't need. Go to the Edit side or pull-down menu and pick Erase. The

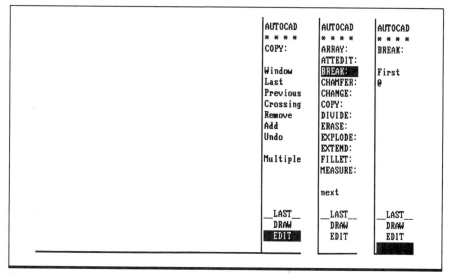

Figure 3.14:   *The Copy menu, the Edit menu, and the Break menu*

object-selection prompt appears in the prompt area and the Erase menu of selection options appears. Pick the remaining fragment of the ellipse just below the toilet tank. When the object ghosts, press Return to confirm your selection and complete the Erase command (unless you are using the pull-down menu, in which case the fragment will be automatically erased as soon as you pick it).

Now you need to trim the line defining the back of the seat. Go to the Edit menu, then pick Change. The object-selection prompt and options appear as before. Pick the horizontal line touching the ellipse. When the line ghosts, press Return to confirm your selection. The prompt changes to

Properties/<Change point>:

Now use the Osnap overrides to pick the left endpoint of the ellipse touching the line. Go through the same process to shorten the right side of the line.

Change can be used to alter an object in several ways. In this example we took the default option, to change the length of a line. However, Change can also be used to alter such properties of an object as its layer, color, or line type. We will cover these options in Chapter 4. If you are creating a 3D model, Change can be used to

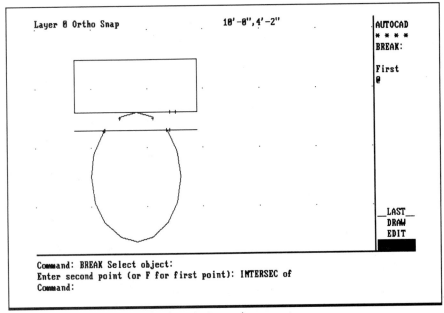

Figure 3.15: *The ellipse broken in two places*

modify shapes and volumes in the z axis; this feature is explained in Chapter 14.

Now you want to restore your view to its original size. Go to the Root Menu, then pick Display, then Zoom, then Previous. Or pick Previous from the Display pull-down menu. Your view will return to the one you had before the last Zoom or Pan command (AutoCAD can remember up to four previous views). Your drawing should look like Figure 3.16.

PLANNING AND LAYING OUT A DRAWING

For the next object, the bathtub, you will use some new commands to lay out parts of the drawing. This will help you get a feel for the kind of planning you must do to use AutoCAD effectively.

Using the Line command, draw a rectangle 2'-8" x 5'-0" on the left side of the drawing area. Start your drawing so that the lower-left corner of the rectangle is at the coordinate location 0'-9", 0'-10", and orient the rectangle so that the long side is vertical. This will be the outline of the tub. Remember, if you are entering dimensions through

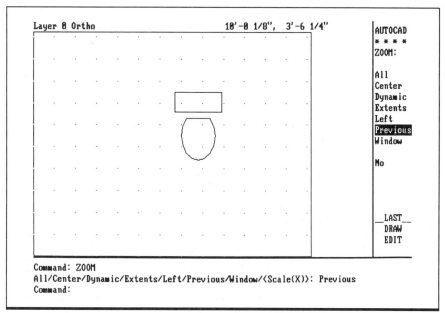

Figure 3.16:   *The finished toilet*

the keyboard, enter feet and inches without hyphens or spaces. 2 feet 8 inches is typed as 2'8".

Making a Preliminary Sketch

The following exercise will show you how planning ahead can make your use of AutoCAD more efficient. When drawing a complex object, you will often have to do some layout before you do the actual drawing. This is similar to drawing an accurate pencil sketch that you later trace over to produce a finished drawing. The advantage of doing this in AutoCAD is that your drawing doesn't lose any accuracy between the sketch and the final product. Also, AutoCAD allows you to use the geometry of your sketch to aid you in drawing. While planning your drawing, think about what it is you want to draw, then think what drawing elements will help you create that object.

You will use the Offset command to establish reference lines to help you draw the inside of the tub. This is where the Osnap overrides are quite useful.

Setting Up a Layout

The Offset command allows you to copy an object, such as the rectangle forming the outside of your tub, a specified distance. It differs from the Copy command in that it allows only one object to be copied at a time, but it can remember the distance you specify. Go to the Edit menu, then Next, and pick Offset. At the prompt

Offset distance or Through <Through>:

type 3. This enters the distance of three inches as the offset distance. The following prompt appears:

Select object to offset:

Pick the bottom line of the rectangle you just drew. The following prompt appears:

Side to offset?

Pick the point 2'-0", 3'-6" inside the rectangle. You will again be prompted to select an object to offset. Repeat this process for the other three sides of the rectangle (using 2'-0", 3'-6" for the side to offset) until you have a drawing that looks like Figure 3.17.

Continue to offset the four lines inside the rectangle toward the center. You will have a drawing that looks like Figure 3.18. End the Offset command by pressing Return.

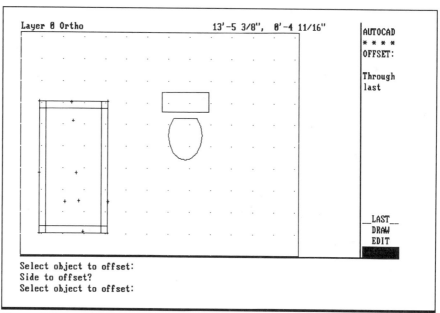

Figure 3.17: The first set of layout lines

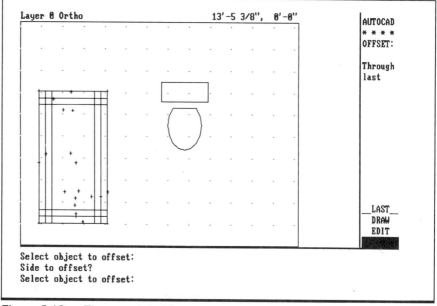

Figure 3.18: The completed layout

Using the Layout

Now you will begin to draw the inside of the tub, starting with the narrow end. You will use your offset lines as references to construct the arcs that make up the tub. Go to the Draw side menu and select Arc to bring up the Arc menu shown in Figure 3.19. Or, you can pick Arc from the Draw pull-down menu, and the Arc menu will appear at the right of the screen. Pick 3-point from the menu, then pick the intersection of the two lines located at coordinate 2'-11", 5'-4" (see Figure 3.20 for an explanation of 3-point and the other options on the Arc menu). Next pick the midpoint of the second horizontal line near the top. Finally, pick the intersection of the two lines at coordinate 1'-3", 5'-4". Figure 3.21 shows the sequence we've just described. An arc appears.

Next you will draw the left side of the tub. Pick S,E,D (start, end, direction) from the Arc menu and enter an at sign. This selects the last point you picked as the start of the arc. In the lower-left corner of the tub, pick the intersection of the two lines at coordinate 1'-0",1'-4" to select the end of the arc. See Figure 3.21 for the location of this point. You will see the arc drag as you move the cursor along with a rubber-banding line from the starting point of the arc. (Be sure the ortho mode is off, as this will force the arc in a direction you don't want.) This rubber-banding line indicates the direction of the arc. Move the cursor to the left of the dragging arc until it

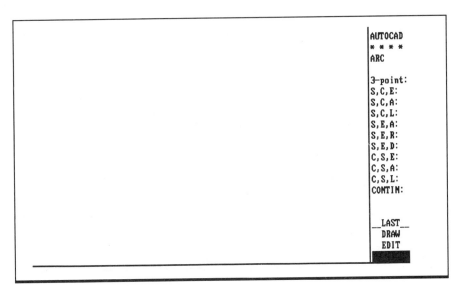

Figure 3.19: The Arc menu

touches the middle line on the left side of the tub. Then pick that point (see Figure 3.22).

Now you will draw the bottom of the tub. Pick 3-point from the Arc menu, and pick the endpoint of the bottom of the arc just drawn. Pick the midpoint of the middle horizontal line at the bottom of the tub. Finally, pick the intersection of the two lines at coordinate 3'-2", 1'-4" (see Figure 3.23).

Now you will create the right side of the tub by mirroring the left side. Go to the Edit menu, then Next, then pick Mirror. Pick the long arc on the left side of the tub and when it is ghosted, press Return. The prompt will display the message

First point of mirror line:

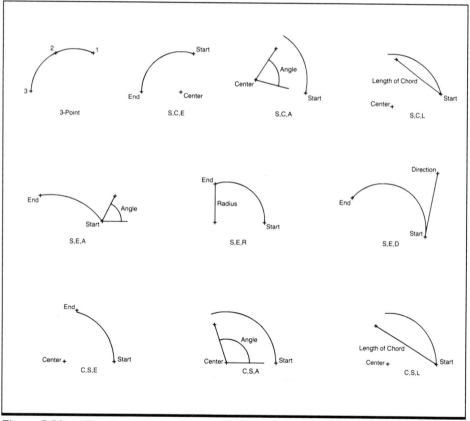

Figure 3.20:   The Arc options and what they mean

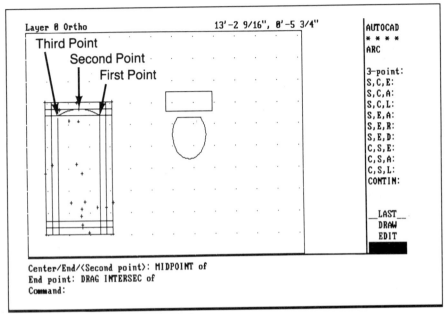

Figure 3.21: The top of the tub

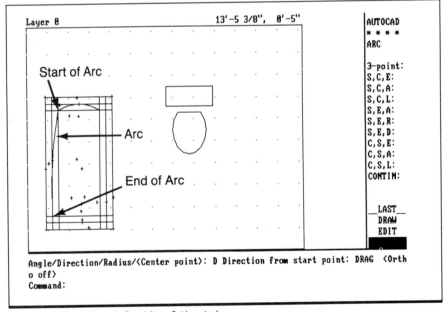

Figure 3.22: The left side of the tub

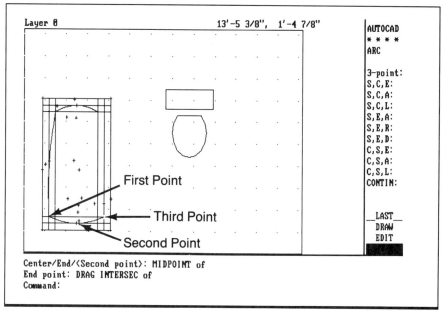

Figure 3.23: *The bottom of the tub*

Pick the midpoint of the top horizontal line. The next prompt appears:

Second point:

Turn on the ortho mode and pick a point directly below the last point selected. The prompt will display the message

Delete old objects?<N>

The default is no, so you can press Return to accept the default. A mirror image of the arc you picked appears on the right side of the tub. Your drawing should look like Figure 3.24.

Now erase all the layout lines. Because the arcs and lines are so close together, avoiding the arcs may be difficult. If you have problems selecting just the lines, try using the Window selection option to select single lines. Remember that a window selects only objects that are completely within the window. If you enter the Erase command from the keyboard or from the side menu, you can use the Remove subcommand to unselect objects from your current selection set. In general, entering commands from the keyboard or the side menu will offer more flexibility in your selection of objects. If you foresee the need to select a group of objects that are difficult to pick with only a single pick or a window, use the side menu or enter the command through the keyboard.

Notice how parts of the arcs you drew are missing. Don't be alarmed; they are still there. When an object that overlaps another object is changed or moved in any way, the overlapped object seems to disappear. This frequently occurs while you are using Change, Fillet, Move, Mirror, and Erase. Use the Redraw command on the Osnap overrides menu or the Display menu to refresh the drawing. After you've done that your drawing should look like Figure 3.25.

Putting on the Finishing Touches

The inside of the tub still has some sharp corners. To round out these corners, you can use the Fillet command. Fillet allows you to join lines and arcs end to end, and it can add a radius where they join so there is a smooth transition from arc to arc or line to line. The Fillet command can join two lines that do not intersect, or it can trim two crossing lines back to their point of intersection. This is one of the more frequently used commands because of its versatility.

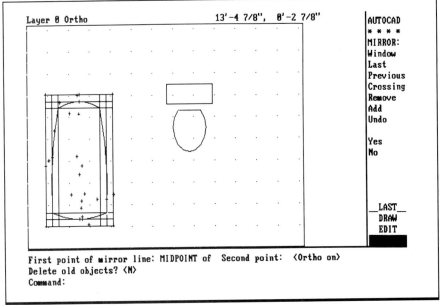

Figure 3.24:   The inside of the tub completed

Go to the Edit menu and pick Fillet (see Figure 3.26). The prompt will display the message

Polyline/Radius/<Select two objects>:

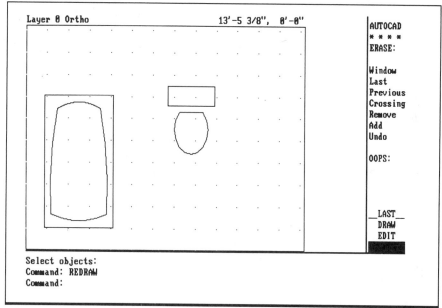

Figure 3.25: *The redisplayed drawing*

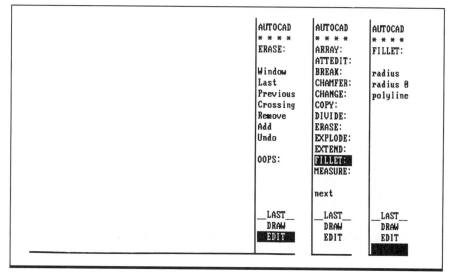

Figure 3.26: *The Erase menu, the Edit menu, and the Fillet menu*

You will notice that the menu also contains the two nondefault options indicated by the prompt. Pick Radius from the menu and enter 4 from the keyboard to indicate that you want a four-inch radius for your fillet. Now pick two adjacent arcs and watch the fillet appear. Press Return to invoke the Fillet command again, and this time just pick two adjacent arcs. Fillet each corner of each arc in this manner. Your drawing should look like Figure 3.27.

Now use End to exit the Bath file.

CONCLUSION

As you went through these commands, you probably noticed that many of them used the object-selection prompt introduced in Chapter 2. Change, Copy, Mirror, and Erase all allow you to select multiple objects, though in these examples you only had to choose one

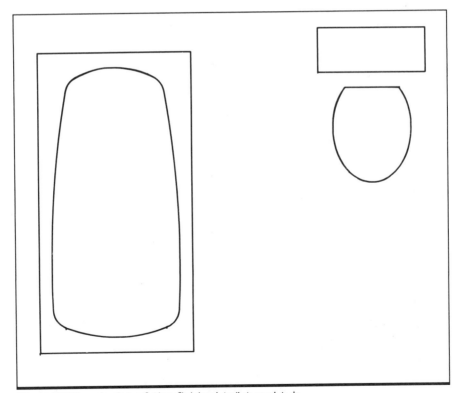

Figure 3.27: A plot of the finished toilet and tub

object. You also used the Osnap overrides to select exact points on the objects you were editing.

As you draw you will notice that you are alternately creating objects and editing them. This is where the differences between hand drafting and CAD really begin to show up. Planning the way you draw becomes an important aspect of your work. To plan, you need to know the tools you are working with. You got a glimpse of the planning process in this chapter. We will explore this theme further as you progress through the book.

Try drawing an object or two that reflects the kind of drawing you intend to do: IC sockets, wide flange sections, widgets, or whatever.

Chapter 4

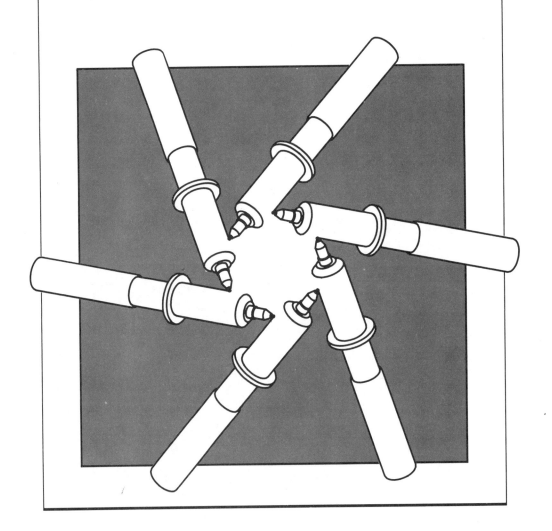

Getting Organized

You may think it took you an inordinate amount of time to draw the tub and toilet. As you continue to use AutoCAD, however, you will be able to draw objects faster. You will also need to draw fewer of them because you can save drawings as *symbols* to be used like rubber stamps, duplicating them instantaneously wherever they are needed. Reusing such symbols can save you a lot of time when composing drawings.

To make effective use of AutoCAD, you should have a *symbol library* of drawings you use frequently. A mechanical designer might have a library of symbols for fasteners, cams, valves, or any number of parts for his or her application. An electrical engineer might have a symbol library of capacitors, resistors, switches, and the like, while a circuit designer may have another set of frequently used symbols.

In Chapter 3 you drew two objects, a bathtub and a toilet, that architects often use. In this chapter you will learn how to create symbols from those drawings. You will also learn about layers and how you can use them to organize information.

CREATING A SYMBOL

To save a drawing as a symbol, you use the Block command. If you use a word processor, you are probably familiar with the idea of a block. In word processing a block is used to group words or sentences to be copied elsewhere within the same file, other files, or saved separately on disk for future use. AutoCAD uses blocks in a similar fashion. Within a file, you can turn parts of your drawing into blocks that can be saved and recalled at any time. You can also use entire existing files as blocks.

Start AutoCAD and open the existing Bath file. The drawing appears just as you left it in the last session. Select Blocks from the Main menu, then select Block from the submenu to bring up the Block menu (see Figure 4.1). The prompt area will display

BLOCK Block name (or ?):

asking you to supply a name for the block you are about to define.

Type

Toilet

and the next prompt

Insertion base point:

asks you to select a base point for the block. The insertion base point of a block is similar to the base point you used as a handle on

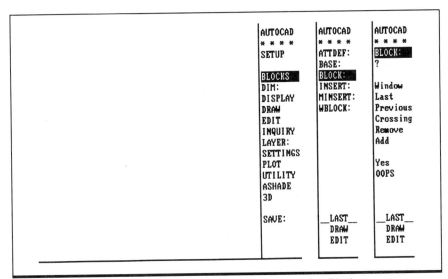

Figure 4.1: The Main menu, the Blocks menu, and the Block menu

an object in Chapter 2. Use the Osnap overrides and pick the mid-point of the back of the toilet. You will now see the familiar object-selection prompt. Notice that the Block menu contains the selection options discussed in Chapter 2. Pick Window from the menu and window the entire toilet. The toilet will ghost. Press Return to confirm your selection, and the toilet will disappear. It is now a block with the name Toilet.

Go through the same process for the tub, but this time use the upper-left corner of the tub as the insertion base point and give the block the name Tub.

When you turn an object into a block, it is stored within the drawing file, ready to be recalled at any time. The block remains part of the drawing file even when you end the editing session. When you open the file again, it will be available for your use. A block acts like a single object even though it is really made up of several objects. It can only be modified by unblocking it using the Explode command, editing it, then turning it back into a block. We will look at the block-editing process later in this chapter.

If for some reason you want to restore the object you just turned into a block, you can use the Oops command. Pick Oops from the Block menu. The tub reappears in its former condition, not as a block. This technique can be useful when you want to create several blocks that are only slightly different. For example, suppose you want several versions of the tub. You can save the tub as a block, then use the Oops command to restore it, then modify it to a different shape, then save this new tub as a different block. The Oops command can also be used in any situation where you want to restore an object you erased by accident.

Since you don't need this restored tub, enter U to undo the Oops command. Be careful you don't press Return more than once.

INSERTING A SYMBOL

Although the tub and toilet blocks disappeared, they can be recalled at any time, as many times as you want. Before you recall them, draw the interior walls of the bathroom. Do this by drawing a rectangle 5 feet × 7 feet 6 inches. Orient the rectangle so the long sides go from left to right and the lower-left corner is at coordinate 1'-10", 1'-10". Your drawing will look like Figure 4.2.

Now you can place the tub and toilet in the bathroom. Go to the Blocks menu, then pick Insert from the side menu or from the Draw pull-down menu (see Figure 4.3). The following prompt appears:

INSERT block name (or ?):

Enter Tub. The next prompt appears:

Insertion point:

Move the cursor across the screen slowly. Notice that the tub now appears and follows the cursor. The upper-left corner you picked for the tub's base point is now on the cursor intersection. Pick the upper-left intersection of the room as your insertion point. The next prompt appears:

X scale factor <1> / Corner / XYZ:

You can specify a scale different from 1 if you choose to stretch the tub in the x direction by whatever value you enter. You can even specify a negative value to insert a mirrored block. Since you don't want to change the size of the tub, press Return to accept the default, 1, and bring up the next prompt:

Y scale factor (default = X):

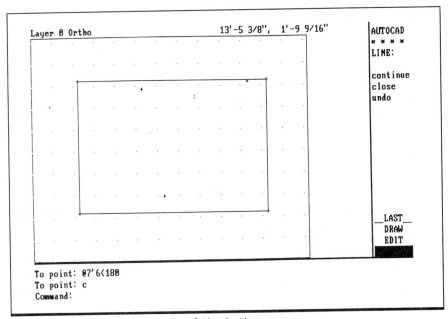

Figure 4.2:   The interior walls of the bathroom

You can also specify a y value different from the x value in the previous prompt. This allows you to reshape the object by changing its x and y proportions. Since you don't want to distort the tub, press Return to accept

(default = X)

The next prompt appears:

Rotation angle <0>:

Move the cursor around. Be sure the ortho mode is off. Notice that the tub rotates around its insertion point as you move the cursor. You could visually select a point to determine the angle or enter a value through the keyboard. Since you want the default angle, 0, press Return. You should have a drawing that looks like Figure 4.4.

Repeat the same procedure with the toilet. Place it along the top of the rectangle representing the room and just to the right of the tub, at coordinate 5'-8", 6-10", as shown in Figure 4.5.

If you prefer, you can select Insert from the Draw side or pull-down menu or enter it through the keyboard.

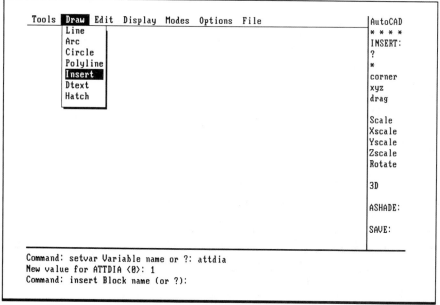

Figure 4.3: *The Insert command on the Draw pull-down menu and the Blocks side menu*

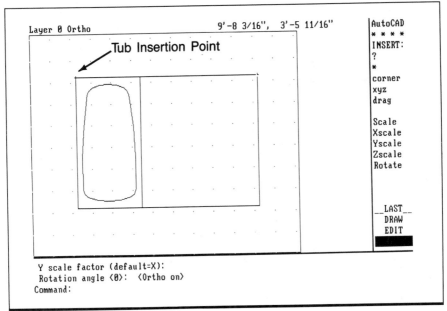

Figure 4.4: The bathroom with the tub inserted

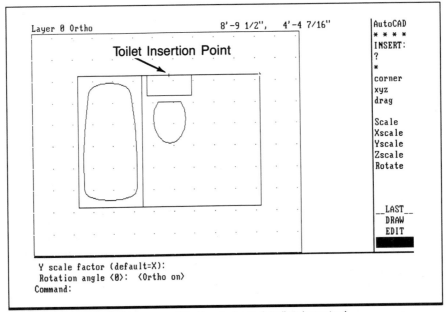

Figure 4.5: The bathroom with the tub and toilet inserted

Using an Existing Drawing as a Symbol

You need a door into the bathroom. Since you already drew a door and saved it as a file, you can bring the door into this drawing file and use it as a block. If, during the insertion command, AutoCAD does not find a block within the current drawing file, it looks on the hard disk for a drawing file with that name. If it finds a file with the name you entered as a block name, it uses that file just as it uses blocks within the current file.

Pick Insert from the Block menu again. Enter Door for the block name. The light on your computer indicating hard disk activity comes on for a moment as AutoCAD looks for the Door file. As you move the cursor around, you will notice the door appear above and to the right of the cursor intersection as in Figure 4.6.

The door looks too small for this bathroom. This is because you drew it 3 units long, which translates to three inches. Pick a point near coordinate 7'-2",2'-4", so that the door is placed in the lower-right corner of the room. If you take the default setting for the x scale of the inserted block, the door will remain three inches long. But, as we explained earlier, you can specify a smaller or larger size for the inserted object. In this case, you want a three-foot door. To get that

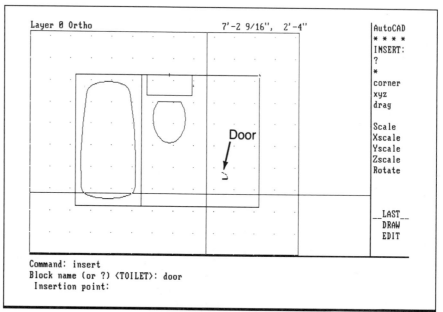

Figure 4.6: The door drawing being inserted

from a three-inch door you must enter an x scale factor of 12 (see Table 3.3). Enter 12 at the

x scale factor

prompt. Press Return twice to accept the default y = x and the rotation angle of 0.

The command prompt appears, but nothing seems to happen to the drawing. The reason is that when you enlarged the door, you also enlarged the distance between the base point and the object. This brings up another issue to be aware of when considering drawings as symbols. All drawings have base points. The default base point is the absolute coordinate 0,0, otherwise known as the *origin*, which is located in the lower-left corner of any new drawing. When you drew the door in Chapter 2, you didn't specify the base point. So, when you try to bring the door into this drawing, AutoCAD uses the origin of the door drawing as its base point (see Figure 4.7).

Use the Zoom command and pick the All option. The view of the room will shrink away and the door will be revealed. Notice that it is now the proper size for your drawing (see Figure 4.8).

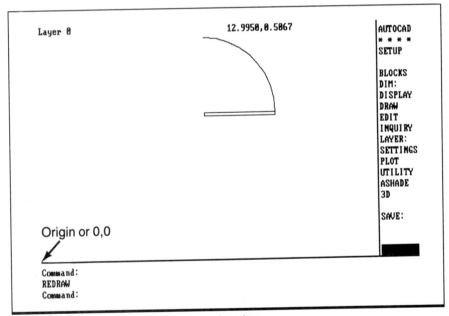

Figure 4.7:   The origin of the door drawing

Since the door appears outside the bathroom, you must use the
Move command to move it to the right side wall of the bathroom.
When you are prompted to select objects pick a point anywhere on
the door. Notice that now the entire door ghosts. This is because a
block is treated like a single object even though it may be made up
of several lines, arcs, etc. After you move the door, your drawing
should look like Figure 4.9.

Because the door is an object you will use often, it should be a
common size so you don't have to specify an odd value every time
you insert it. It would also be helpful if the door's insertion base
point were in a more convenient location. Next, you will modify the
Door block to better suit your needs.

Unblocking a Block

You can modify a block by breaking it down into its components,
editing them, and then turning them back into a block. To break a
block into its components you use the Explode command.
(However, Explode will not work if the block you want to edit is mirrored or if its x scale factor differs from its y scale factor.) Go to
the Edit menu and pick Explode (see Figure 4.10).

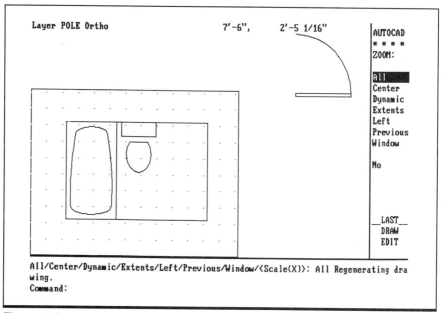

Figure 4.8: *The enlarged door*

Pick the door. You can now edit the individual objects that make up the door if you so desire. In this case, you only want to change the door's insertion point because you already made it a more

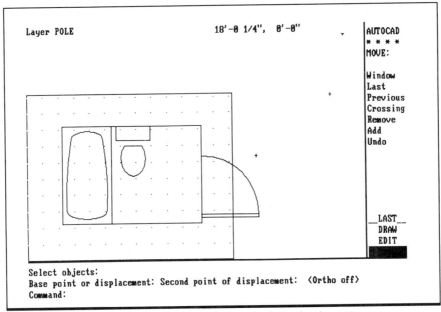

Figure 4.9: The door on the right side wall of the bathroom

Figure 4.10: The Explode menu

convenient size. Now turn the door back into a block, this time using the door's lower-left corner for its insertion base point. When you enter Door for the name of the block, the prompt

Block DOOR already exists.
Redefine it? <N>

appears. AutoCAD provides this prompt so you won't inadvertently change a block you want to leave alone. Enter Y for yes. At the base-point insertion prompt, pick the lower-left corner of the door, then proceed with the rest of the command. Once you are done the drawing will regenerate.

Now insert the door again, but this time use the Nearest Osnap override and pick a point on the right side wall of the bathroom near coordinate 9'-4", 2'-1". After you complete this, mirror the door using the wall as the mirror axis so that the door is inside the room. Your drawing will look like Figure 4.11.

You've seen that, with very little effort, you can create a symbol that can be placed anywhere in a file. Suppose you want to use this symbol in other files.

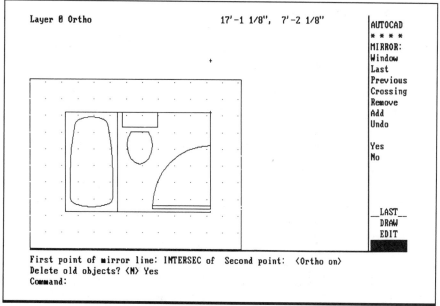

Figure 4.11: The bathroom floor plan thus far

Saving a Block as a Drawing File

When you create a block using the Block command, the block exists only within the current file until you save it as a drawing file on disk. For an existing drawing that has been brought in and modified, like the door, the drawing file on disk associated with that door may have to be updated. You do this using the Wblock command. To turn the tub and toilet blocks into individual files on disk, go to the Blocks menu and select Wblock. The prompt

File name:

appears. Enter the name Tub. The next prompt appears:

Block name:

Enter the name of the block you wish to save on disk as the tub file—in this case also Tub. The light on your computer indicating hard disk activity will come on for a second. The tub block is now saved as a file.

AutoCAD gives you the option to save the file of a block under either the same name as the original block, or a different one. Usually you will want to use the same name, which you can do by entering an equal sign after the block name prompt or picking it from the Wblock menu. Save the toilet block to disk in this manner:

File name: toilet
Block name: =

Use the Wblock command again to save the door block you modified. This time after you enter the file name you get the prompt

A drawing with this name already exists.
Do you want to replace it? <N>

This prompt tells you that the door exists already as a drawing file. It keeps you from inadvertently writing over the existing file. In this case, you want to update the door you drew in Chapter 2, so enter Y. When you are prompted for a block name, pick the equal sign on the Wblock menu, or enter the equal sign through the keyboard. The new door will replace the old one.

So far, you have used Block to create symbols and Wblock to save those symbols to disk. As you can see, symbols can be created and saved any time while you are drawing. The tub and toilet symbols are now drawing files you can see when you check the contents of your current directory. However, creating symbols is not the only use for the Insert, Block, and Wblock commands. You can use them in any situation that requires grouping objects. Wblock also allows you to save to disk a part of a drawing that is not a block without making it into a block in the current drawing. These other uses of Block and Wblock are explained in Chapters 7 and 16.

Block and Wblock are both very useful, and if used judiciously can boost your productivity and make your work easier. If you are not careful, however, you can also get carried away and create more blocks than you can keep track of. Planning your drawings helps you determine what elements work best as blocks and where other methods of organization are more suitable.

An Alternative to Blocks

Another way to create symbols is by creating *shapes*. Shapes are special objects made up of lines, arcs, and circles. They can regenerate faster than blocks and they take up less file space. Unfortunately shapes are considerably more difficult to create and less flexible to use than blocks. You create shapes by using a coding system developed by Autodesk. The codes define the sizes and orientations of lines, arcs, and circles. You first sketch your shape, then convert it into the code, then copy that code into a DOS text file. We won't get into detail on this subject, so if you want to know more about shapes look in Appendix B of your *AutoCAD Reference Manual*.

One way to get around the difficulty of creating shapes is to purchase one of the third-party software products available for this purpose, such as the CAD Systems Unlimited AutoShapes program. These are add-on programs capable of converting AutoCAD drawings into shape libraries. They usually require that you draw your shape within a predefined area in a special drawing file supplied with the software. If you intend to do drawings that will be composed mostly of very simple symbols, you may want to look into this alternative. Since AutoCAD fonts are created the same way shapes are, these programs also allow you to create your own fonts.

ORGANIZING INFORMATION WITH LAYERS

Another tool for organization is the layer. A layer is like an overlay on which you keep various types of information (see Figure 4.12). In a floor plan of a building, for example, you want to keep the walls, ceiling, plumbing fixtures, wiring, and furniture separated, so you can display or plot them separately or combine them in different ways. You also want to keep notes and reference symbols on their own layers, as well as dimensions. As your drawing becomes more complex, these different layers can be turned on and off to allow easier display and modification.

For example, one of your consultants may need a plot of just the dimensions and walls without all the other information, while another consultant may need only a furniture layout. Using manual drafting, you would have to redraw your plan for each consultant. Using AutoCAD, you can turn off the layers you don't need and plot a drawing containing only the required information. A carefully

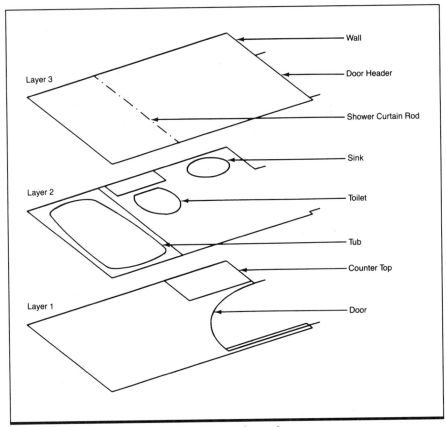

Figure 4.12:   *A comparison of layers and overlays*

planned layering scheme helps you produce a document that combines the different types of information you and different consultants need.

Using layers also enables you to modify your drawings more easily. For example, suppose you have an architectural drawing with separate layers for the walls, the ceiling plan, and the floor plan. If any change occurs in the wall locations, you can turn on the ceiling plan layer to see where the new wall locations affect the ceiling and make the proper adjustments.

AutoCAD allows an unlimited number of layers, and you can name each layer anything you want.

Creating and Assigning Layers

To continue with your bathroom, you will create some new layers. Pick Layer from the Root menu, and pick New from the Layer menu (see Figure 4.13). Enter the word Wall at the prompt

New layer name(s):

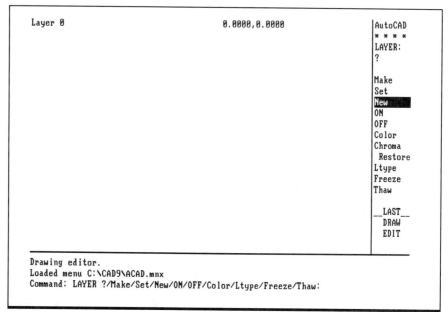

Figure 4.13: The Layer menu

MASTERING AUTOCAD

Pick Color from the Layer menu. Then pick Yellow from the Color menu (see Figure 4.14). The prompt

Layer name(s) for color 2 (yellow) <0>:

appears. At this prompt you can enter the name of the layer you wish to assign yellow to. The default will always be the current layer. In this case, you want the layer Wall to be yellow, so type Wall and press Return. Press Return again to exit the Layer command.

Using the Modify Layer Dialog Box

Pull-down menu users can pick the Modify Layer option from the Modes pull-down menu. The Modify Layer dialog box will appear (see Figure 4.15). Highlight the New Layer input button toward the bottom of the dialog box, then enter the word Wall. Next, pick the OK action button that appears to the right of the text you just entered or simply press the Return key. The Wall layer is added to the list of layers in the dialog box.

Set the color of the Wall layer by picking the button under the column labeled Color next to the Wall input button. The Select Color dialog box appears, listing the available colors (see Figure 4.16). If you have a color display, bars in the actual colors available appear to the right of the color list. Pick Yellow, then pick the OK action button at the bottom of the dialog box. The Select Color dialog box disappears

Figure 4.14: The Color menu

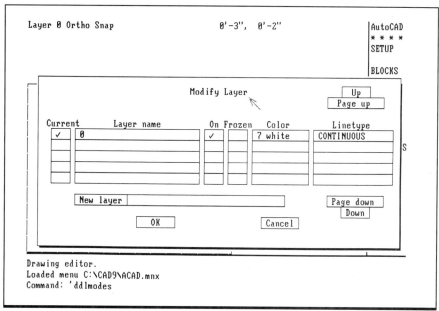

Figure 4.15:   *The Modify Layer dialog box*

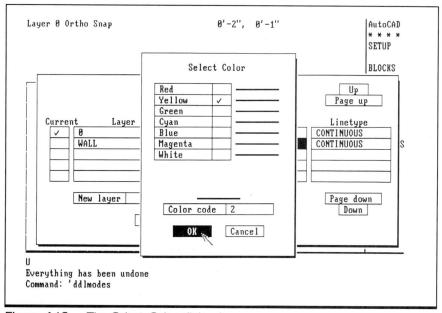

Figure 4.16:   *The Select Color dialog box*

and the word Yellow appears in the color column next to the Wall input button. When you have finished and are satisfied with the settings, pick the OK action button.

Understanding Colors

If you entered the layer settings using the keyboard, the color prompt displayed a 2 for color with the word yellow in parentheses. When you use the dialog box, the 2 is displayed next to the color name.

AutoCAD assigns a number to each color, and you can use this number to select it. Number assignments vary among the numerous display options available with AutoCAD, so 2 may not always correspond to the color yellow. AutoCAD provides a quick way to find the number that corresponds to a color. On the Layer menu you will see the item Chroma (see Figure 4.13). By picking this item, you will get a display of the colors available on your monitor, along with the numbers they correspond to. The topmost row of colors shows the first nine. The first column to the left shows the next ten colors, with even-numbered colors in the upper half and odd-numbered colors in the lower half. As you move from left to right, the color numbers increase by ten.

The Chroma image is an AutoCAD slide file. We will discuss slides in Chapter 16. To restore your previous view, you can pick Restore from the Layer menu or enter redraw.

Assigning Layers to Objects

Go to the Edit menu and pick Change. Pick the four lines representing the bathroom walls. If you have problems singling out the wall to the left, use a window. Press Return to confirm your selection. At the

Properties/<Change point>:

prompt enter P to select the Properties option. A new prompt appears.

Change what property (Color/Elev/LAyer/LType/Thickness) ?

You were probably unaware of some of these options; they are explained later in the book. Notice that the Change menu also displays some of these options. Pick Layer. The prompt

New layer <0>:

appears. Enter the name Wall. You will be prompted for another property to change. Press Return to exit the Change command instead.

The bathroom walls are now on the new layer, Wall. If you have a color monitor, you will see the walls change to yellow. Layers are more easily distinguished from each other when colors are used to set them apart.

Create a new layer called Fixture. Give it the color blue, then use the Change command to change the tub and toilet to that layer. Now create a new layer for the door. Call the layer Door and make it red. Change the door to that layer. Create three more layers for the ceiling, door jambs, and floor, and assign magenta to Ceiling, yellow to Jamb, and white to Floor.

We should mention that you are able to change the layer assignment of a block only when the objects within the block are on layer 0. Layer 0 is a special layer designed to allow objects used in a block to take on the characteristics of the layer the block is inserted on. If those objects are on a layer other than 0, they will maintain their original layer assignment no matter what layer the block is inserted on or changed to. For example, suppose you draw the tub on the Door layer, turn it into a block, then insert it on the Fixture layer. The objects the door is composed of will maintain their assignment to the Door layer although the Door block is assigned to the Fixture layer.

AutoCAD allows you to have more than one color or line type on a layer. You can use the Properties option on the Change menu to alter the color or line type of an object on layer 0, for example. That object then maintains its line type and color assignment when used in a block, just as if it were drawn on a layer other than 0. This feature can help you if you want to draw an entire block on layer 0 but still have parts of the block maintain line types or colors other than continuous and white.

Working on Layers

So far you have created layers then moved objects to those layers. You are still on layer 0, the default layer, and everything you draw will be on layer 0. To change the current layer, you use the Layer command with the Set subcommand. Start the Layer command, then pick Set from the Layer subcommands. Enter Jamb at the

New current layer <0>:

prompt. Press Return to exit the Layer command. Notice that the status line displays the word jamb to indicate that you are now on that layer.

You can also set the current layer by simply bringing up the Modify Layer dialog box and picking the check button next to the layer you wish to set as current. The Current check button is located to the far left of the Layer Name input button (see Figure 4.17).

As you open the dialog box, you don't see the Jamb layer listed. The dialog box displays only five available layers at one time. If your drawing contains more than five layers, you can scroll through additional layers with the Page Up, Up, Page Down, and Down buttons. Page Up and Page Down advance or reverse the list five layers at a time, while Up and Down move it one layer at a time. Pick the Down button (see Figure 4.17). The Jamb layer appears at the bottom of the list (see Figure 4.18).

Zoom into the door and draw a line four-and-a-half inches long toward the right from the lower-right corner of the door. Draw a similar line from the top right end of the arc. Your drawing should look like Figure 4.19. The two lines you just drew to represent the door jambs are yellow.

Now you will use the part of the wall between the jambs as a line representing the door header (the part of the wall above the door).

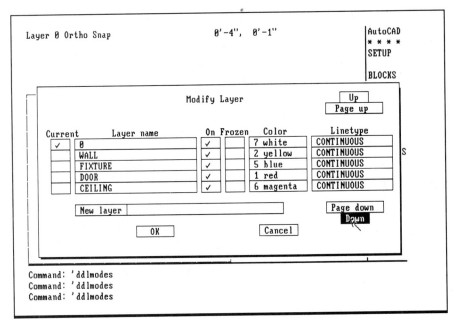

Figure 4.17:   *The Current check button and the Down button*

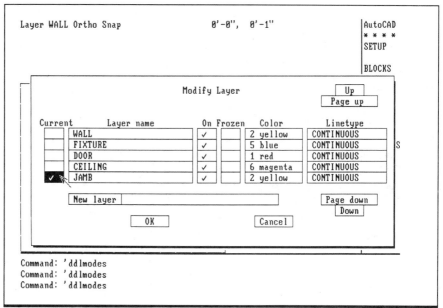

Command: 'ddlmodes
Command: 'ddlmodes
Command: 'ddlmodes

Figure 4.18:   How to scroll through the list of layers and select the Current check button

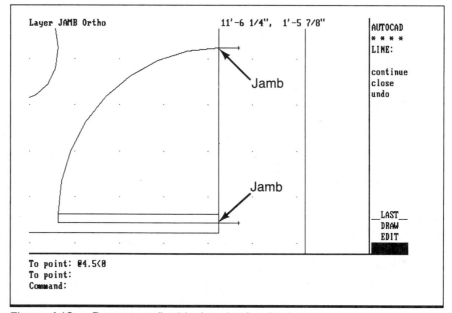

Figure 4.19:   Door at wall with door jamb added

Pick the Break command from the Edit menu, then pick the wall between the two jambs. Pick the First subcommand from the Break menu and pick the endpoint of the arc touching the wall. At the

Enter second point:

prompt, pick the at sign on the Break menu. This breaks the wall line into two lines at the intersection of the wall, the jamb, and the arc. Repeat this procedure at the jamb near the door hinge location. Now change the line between the two jambs to the Ceiling layer. Be sure that when you select the object to be changed, the line ghosts only between the two jambs. When you complete the change, the line will turn to magenta, telling you it is now on the Ceiling layer. Use the Zoom command to return to the previous view.

We've shown you the New and Set options on the Layer menu. The Make option combines New and Set to allow you to create a layer and specify it as the current layer at the same time. Start the Layer command and pick the Make option. Enter the name Casework at the

New current layer <JAMB>:

prompt. (Casework is a term used for cabinets, counter tops, and the like.) Assign the color blue to this layer. Notice that the default is the new layer, Casework. When you exit the Layer command the status line indicates that the current layer is Casework. If you are using the pull-down menus, you can create the Casework layer, set its color to blue, then make Casework the current layer—all with the dialog box. You don't need to use the Make command.

Finish the bathroom by adding a sink. Use the Zoom command and pick the All subcommand. Draw a rectangle 28 inches x 18 inches representing a sink counter top. Orient the counter top so it fits into the upper-right corner of the room as in Figure 4.20. Use coordinate 7'-0", 5'-4" for the lower-left corner of the counter. Draw an ellipse 17 inches x 14 inches in the center of the counter top. Change the ellipse to the Fixture layer. Your drawing will look like Figure 4.20.

Controlling Layers

We mentioned earlier that at times you want to be selective about what layers you are working with on a drawing. In this bathroom, a door header is shown that normally only appears in the ceiling plan. To turn off a layer so that it becomes invisible, use the Off

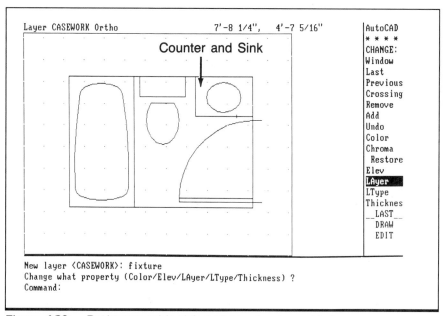

Figure 4.20: Bathroom with sink and counter top added

command on the Layer menu. Enter the Layer command and pick Off. The prompt

Layer name(s) to turn off:

appears.

As the prompt implies, you can turn off multiple layers. You can enter each layer name separated by a comma or, just as in DOS, you can use an asterisk or question mark to designate wild-card layer names. For example, if you have several layers whose names begin with C-, like C-lights, C-header, and C-pattern, you can enter C-* at this prompt to turn off all the layers beginning with those two letters. You can use the question mark to be more selective about names. For example, you may have layers with names like redfloor-tile, redwallstile, and whtwanestile. You can select all the layers with the tile ending by entering ????????tile, or you can select all the lay-ers with red tile by entering red?????tile. Keep the wild-card fea-ture in mind as you name layers; you can use it to group layers and later select those groups to turn on and off. Pull-down menu users can use the Modify Layer dialog box to turn layers on and off by picking the check buttons next to the layers (see Figure 4.15).

Since you now want to turn off only one layer, enter the layer name Ceiling and press Return (see Figure 4.21). The header over the door is no longer visible (though it is still there).

You can turn off all the layers except Wall and Ceiling and be left with a simple yellow rectangle (see Figure 4.22). Try turning off all the layers by entering an asterisk at the prompt for layer names to turn off (see Figure 4.22). The following prompt appears:

Really want layer CASEWORK (the CURRENT layer) off? <N>

Press Return to accept the default, No, then press Return again to exit the Layer command. All that is displayed is the current layer.

This is a quick way to isolate a layer for editing. For example, if you want to delete the contents of an entire layer you can set the current layer to the one you want to edit, then turn off all the others. You can then erase the entire contents of that layer by choosing the Erase command, then the Window option, from the Erase menu to select everything visible in the drawing.

You may have noticed the Layer subcommands Freeze and Thaw. These commands are similar to On and Off. However, the Freeze command not only makes layers invisible, it also tells AutoCAD to

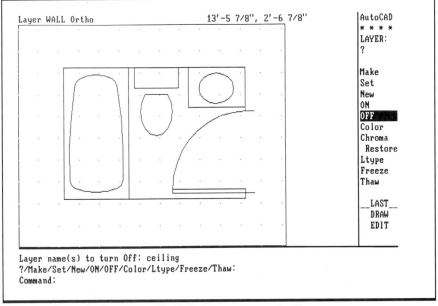

Figure 4.21: Bathroom with Ceiling layer turned off

ignore the contents of those layers when AutoCAD has to recalculate vectors during regenerations. Freezing layers can save a lot of time when you regenerate a complex drawing because it reduces the number of components AutoCAD has to recalculate. You will get first-hand experience with the Freeze and Thaw commands in Chapter 7.

Before you continue, turn on all the layers. You can use the wild card again by entering it at the prompt

Layer name(s) to turn on:

ASSIGNING LINE TYPES TO LAYERS

You will often want to use different line types to show hidden lines, or center lines, or other noncontinuous lines. You can set a layer to have not only a color assignment, but a line type assignment. In the bathroom plan, you will show a shower curtain rod as a dash-dot line type. Start the Layer command again and pick the Make subcommand. Enter the name Pole and give it the color cyan. Before you exit the Layer command, pick the Ltype option. You will

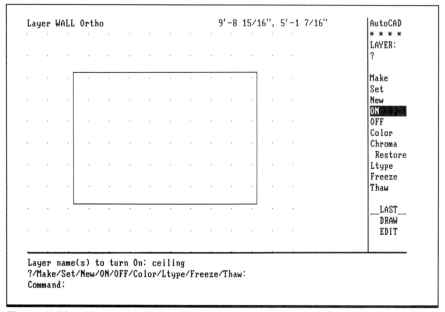

```
Layer WALL Ortho                        9'-8 15/16", 5'-1 7/16"      AutoCAD
                                                                     * * * *
                                                                     LAYER:
                                                                     ?

                                                                     Make
                                                                     Set
                                                                     New
                                                                     ON
                                                                     OFF
                                                                     Color
                                                                     Chroma
                                                                       Restore
                                                                     Ltype
                                                                     Freeze
                                                                     Thaw

                                                                     __LAST__
                                                                       DRAW
                                                                       EDIT

Layer name(s) to turn On: ceiling
?/Make/Set/New/ON/OFF/Color/Ltype/Freeze/Thaw:
Command:
```

Figure 4.22: Bathroom with all layers except Wall and Ceiling turned off

see a list of line types appear on the resulting Linetype menu (see Figure 4.23).

Pick dashdot at the

Linetype (or ?) <CONTINUOUS>:

prompt. The prompt

Layer name(s) for linetype DASHDOT <POLE>:

appears. At this prompt you can enter the name of the layer you wish to assign the dash-dot line type to. The default is always the current layer. Since you just used Make to create and set the Pole layer, you can take the default, POLE. Exit the Layer command. You can use the Modify Layer dialog box to set a layer to a line type by picking the Linetype button for the layer you wish to change. When you do this, a Select Linetype dialog box appears (see Figure 4.24). However, the line type must already be loaded before it can be selected through the dialog box. If you instead set the line type with the side menu or the keyboard, AutoCAD will automatically load the line type from an external file and assign the chosen layer to the new line type. We give a more detailed description of the way line types are created and loaded in Chapter 18.

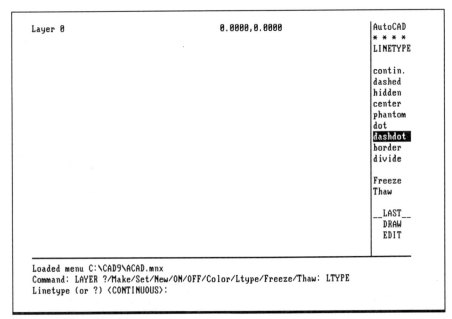

Figure 4.23:   The Linetype menu

Now draw a line across the opening of the tub area from coordinate 4'-4", 1'-10" to coordinate 4'-4", 6'-10". Although this line should have been a dash-dot line, it appears to be solid. If you zoom into a small part of the line, you will see that the line is indeed a dash-dot line. Since you are working at a scale that is not one to one, you must adjust the line-type scale. You do this by using the Ltscale menu. Go to the Root menu and pick Settings, then pick Ltscale (see Figure 4.25).

The prompt

LTSCALE New scale factor <1.0000>:

appears. The default setting for Ltscale is 1.0000, which works fine if you are drawing at a scale of one to one. Since this drawing is at a 1" = 1' scale, enter 12, the scale conversion factor (see Table 3.3). The drawing regenerates, and the rod is shown as the line type you want. Your drawing will look like Figure 4.26.

AutoCAD comes with eight line types and also allows you to create your own very easily. Remember that if you assign a line type to a layer, everything you draw on that layer will be that line type. This includes arcs, polylines, circles, and traces. As we mentioned earlier, you can also have several different colors and line types on the

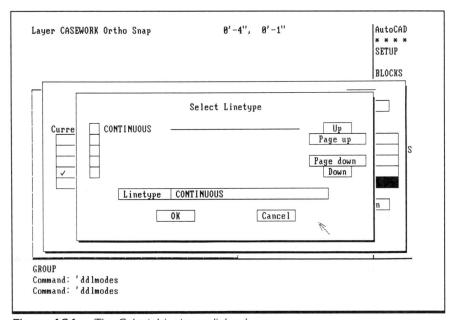

Figure 4.24:   *The Select Linetype dialog box*

Figure 4.25: The Ltscale menu

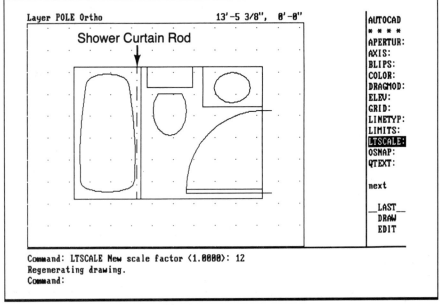

Figure 4.26: The completed bathroom

same layer. However, this can create confusion as your drawing becomes more complex. You should avoid using multiple colors and line types on a layer until you have some experience with AutoCAD and a good grasp of your drawing's organization.

KEEPING TRACK OF BLOCKS AND LAYERS

You may have noticed the question mark option on the Layer, Block, and Line Type menus. This option enables you to view information on layers, blocks, and line types. (The advanced user interface enables you to view all the layers in the drawing using the Modify Layer dialog box, but does not provide any special way to view information on blocks and line types.) For example, as you continue a drawing, you may forget the names of some blocks you've created and want a list of them all. To get one, start the Insert command and enter a question mark at the

Block name (or ?):

prompt. You will see a list of blocks in the order of creation. You can also get a list of layers and their status by selecting the question mark from the Layer menu during the Layer command. You can get a list of available line types in the same way, by entering a question mark during the Linetype command.

You may also forget what layer an object resides on. The List command on the Inquiry menu enables you to get information about individual objects. Pick List, then pick the tub at the object-selection prompt. The text screen will appear, and you will see not only the layer that the tub is on but its insertion point, name, color, line type, rotation angle, and scale. List is a useful command when a drawing becomes complex or when you are working on a drawing unfamiliar to you.

You may want a permanent record of these listings. Hold down the Control key and press Q (be sure your printer is on and connected to your computer). Now enter the Layer command and a question mark. Your printer will print the same information that appears on the screen. This Control-Q feature acts like the Control-Print Screen feature in PC-DOS. To stop printing listings, press Control-Q again.

CONCLUSION

Such AutoCAD features as blocks and layers can help you organize your drawing task in ways not possible in manual drafting. In this chapter, you learned some of the ways to use these features effectively. If your application is not architecture, you may want to experiment with creating some symbols more in line with your work. You might also start thinking about a layering system that suits your particular needs. If you did another drawing after Chapter 3, think of ways you might best utilize the Block and Layer commands in that drawing.

Figure 4.27 is a plot of the finished bathroom. In the next chapter you will learn how to use the Plot command to control your final output to paper.

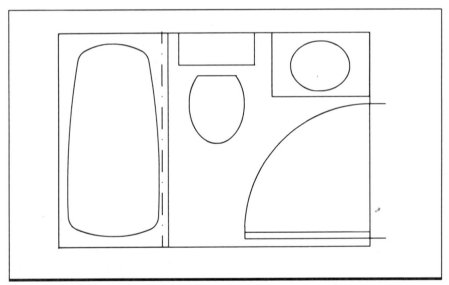

Figure 4.27: Plot of bathroom floor plan

Chapter 5

Getting Your Drawing on Hard Copy

BECAUSE IT IS DIFFICULT to spot errors on a computer monitor, you will periodically want to print your unfinished drawing to check for errors and omissions. When you finish it, you will want to get high-quality output you can reproduce for your clients. In this chapter, you will generate both kinds of output for your bathroom drawing, using a dot-matrix printer and a plotter. In the process, you will learn how to control the size of your drawing and its location and orientation on the sheet you print or plot on. You will also learn how to control line weight in a plotted drawing and how to use different pens and plotter media.

CHOOSING BETWEEN YOUR PRINTER AND PLOTTER

The dot-matrix printer is your best choice for producing a quick check plot as long as your drawing isn't larger than 17 x 22 inches. It will do a reasonable job of printing your drawing, though it won't produce the best-quality line work and drawing size is limited to the carriage width of the printer (anywhere from 8½ inches to 20 inches, depending on the printer). The printer's chief advantage is speed. A dot-matrix printer can print any drawing in under ten minutes, regardless of complexity. In contrast, a plotter can take an hour or more, particularly if your drawing contains a lot of text. Some dot-matrix printers also offer color printing.

The laser printer falls into the category of dot-matrix printers as far as AutoCAD is concerned. Laser printers have the same limitations as dot-matrix printers, but they are capable of better line quality and higher speeds. They are usually limited to 8 1/2 x 11-inch paper.

Plotters can produce much larger drawings than dot-matrix printers, ranging from 8 1/2 x 11 inches to 36 x 48 inches and up. For this reason, you may want to use a plotter to do check plots of large drawings. If your drawing is fairly simple, your plotter can give you results in minutes (most of the plotted illustrations in this book were done in less than ten minutes). However, many applications require fairly complex drawings, which in turn take much longer to plot. A typical architectural drawing, for example, takes 45 minutes on a good-quality, large-format plotter using wet-ink pens on polyester film. By using pens capable of faster speeds, you can reduce the time it takes to plot a drawing by 40 percent and still get an accurate reproduction. Although you won't get dot-matrix printer speeds from a plotter, you are not limited in the size of your plot.

The plotter also produces better line quality than a dot-matrix printer, enables you to vary line weights and colors in a drawing, and can plot drawings onto polyester film and vellum as well as paper. When you want large plots, sharp, clear lines, or reproduction quality, the plotter is the way to go.

USING THE DOT-MATRIX PRINTER

This section describes the process you go through to print your drawing. Plotting uses the same process with a few additional steps. Keep this in mind as you work through this section.

Determining What to Print

Start AutoCAD and open the Bath file. Pick Plot from the Root menu to bring up the Plot menu. The Plot menu shows the options Plotter and Printer. Pick Printer, or enter Prplot from the keyboard. Or you can pick Print from the File pull-down menu (see Figure 5.1). The first prompt you see is

What to plot – Display, Extents, Limits, View, or Window <D>:

These options allow you to specify what to print. If you pick Display, your printout will be of what is currently displayed on the screen. An important point to remember is that the lower-left corner of the current display is the origin point of the printout (see Figure 5.2). The origin of the printout is in the lower-left corner of the sheet as you face the printer. If your printer is limited to 8½ x 11-inch sheets, the print appears near the top of the sheet with the short dimension of the sheet being horizontal.

Extents draws the entire drawing and forces the lower-left corner of the entire drawing, rather than the display, to become the origin of the plot (see Figure 5.3).

Limits uses the limits of the drawing to determine what to print (see Figure 5.4). In general, this makes the origin of the drawing equal to the origin of the printout because, as we mentioned in Chapter 3, the Setup option uses 0,0 as one corner of the AutoCAD drawing sheet.

View uses a previously saved view to determine what to print (see Figure 5.5). As you zoom and pan over your drawing, you may want to save a particular display so you can return to it without having to display the entire drawing first. You can accomplish this

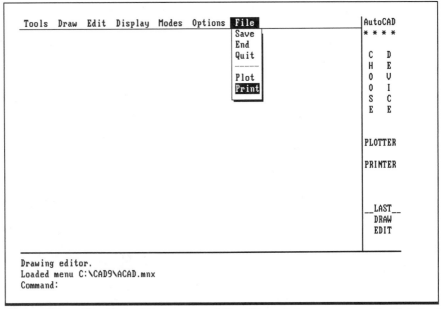

Figure 5.1: *The Plot side menu and the File pull-down menu with Plot and Print options*

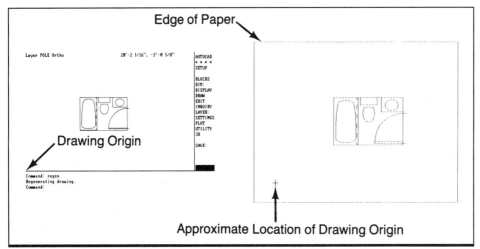

Figure 5.2: *The screen display and the printed output when Display is chosen and no scale is used (drawing is scaled to fit sheet)*

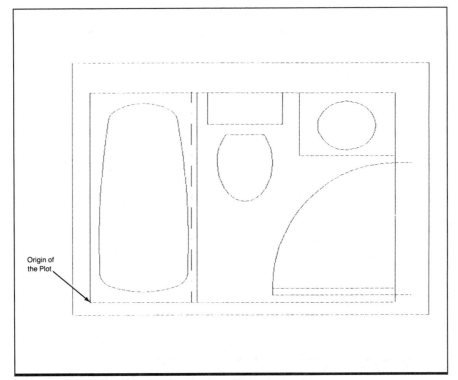

Figure 5.3: *The printed output when Extents is chosen*

by using the View command. You can select a view by either using a window or saving a current display as a view.

Window allows you to pick a window on the screen that the Printer command uses to determine what to print (see Figure 5.6). Nothing outside the window will print, and the lower-left corner of the window becomes the origin of the printout.

Choosing a Drawing's Orientation, Sheet Size, and Scale

Press Return to accept the default, Display. The screen changes to text mode and the message

Plot will NOT be written to a selected file
Sizes are in Inches
Plot origin is at (0.00,0.00)
Plotting area is 10.50 wide by 8.00 high (A size)
Plot is NOT rotated 90 degrees
Hidden lines will NOT be removed
Plot will be scaled to fit available area
Do you want to change anything? <N>

appears. Although you can accept the default settings, for this example enter Yes. The next prompt appears:

Write the plot to a file ? <N>

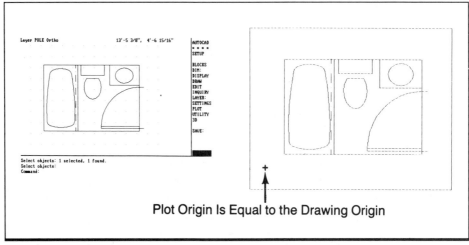

Plot Origin Is Equal to the Drawing Origin

Figure 5.4:   *The screen display and the printed output when Limits is chosen*

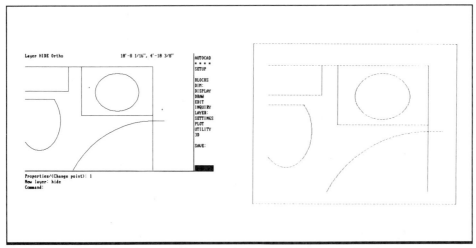

Figure 5.5: A comparison of the saved view and the printed output

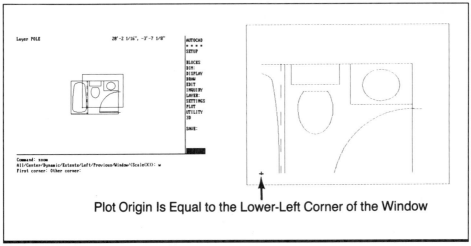

Figure 5.6: A selected window and the resulting printout

This option enables you to divert your printout to a file on disk and print it later. It is discussed in more detail in the section on plotting. Press Return to accept the default, No. The next prompt appears:

Size units (Inches or Millimeters) <I>:

Press Return to accept the default, Inches. If you did your drawing in millimeters, you would have had to pick Millimeters. You cannot do a drawing in inches, then pick Millimeters at this prompt and expect to get a scale drawing. The next prompt appears:

Plot origin in inches <0.00,0.00>:

This prompt allows you to change the position of your drawing on the paper. Normally, the origin point of the printed drawing is slightly above and to the right of the lower-left corner of your sheet (to avoid printing beyond the edge). This position varies a little from printer to printer. Figure 5.7 gives you an idea of the location of the origin.

To change the location of that origin and thus change the location of the drawing on the sheet, you can give a coordinate in inches or millimeters at this prompt. You should use the same measurement system you chose at the previous prompt. The printer adjusts the origin to your specification. Figure 5.8 shows how your input here affects your plot.

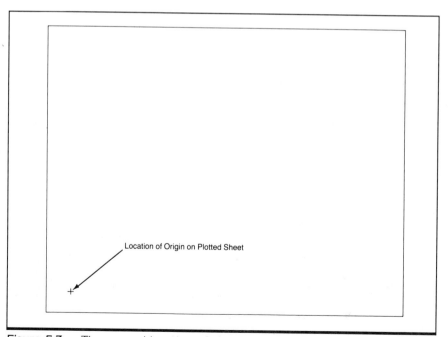

Figure 5.7:   *The general location of the drawing origin on the paper*

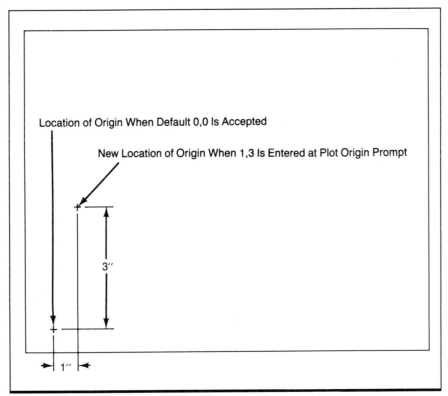

Figure 5.8: *The locations of the default and new origins*

Press Return to accept the default origin, 0.00,0.00. The next prompt appears:

Standard values for plotting size

Size	Width	Height
A	10.50	8.00
MAX	13.50	11.00

Enter the size or Width,Height (in inches) <A>:

In most cases, you will have more than one choice here for the size, but some printers allow only an A size (8½ x 11-inch) sheet. You can specify a width and height by entering a numeric value at this prompt. If you enter a sheet size that is too large for the printer, the warning message

Warning plotting area exceeds plotter maximum
Plotting area truncated to maximum

appears just before the last prompt in this sequence. If you proceed to print the drawing, AutoCAD fits as much of the drawing on the sheet as possible and cuts off anything that does not fit within the maximum area allowed.

Notice that the default Width and Height values for the A size sheet are half an inch smaller than the standard A size. The printer will not print an image beyond a quarter-inch margin around the edge of the medium.

Be sure you have an A size sheet of paper in your printer, then press Return to accept the default, A. The next prompt appears:

Rotate 2D plots 90 degrees clockwise ? <N>

As this prompt indicates, you can rotate the drawing so that it is oriented on the sheet 90 degrees from its normal position. You may want to use this option if your printer can only handle 8½-inch-wide paper. This option places the origin in the upper-left corner of your sheet (see Figure 5.9). Notice that the prompt singles out 2D drawings. This is because 3D drawings cannot be rotated. They are always printed in the same orientation. We will discuss printing 3D drawings in Chapter 14.

Enter Y to rotate the plot 90 degrees so it can fit on the 8½ x 11-inch paper. The next prompt appears:

Remove hidden lines ? <N>

This option affects only 3D drawings. We will discuss it in Chapter 14. Press Return to select the default, No. The next prompt appears:

Specify scale by entering:
Plotted Inches = Drawing Units or Fit or ? <F>

This is an important printing option, because this is where you must tell AutoCAD what scale you used in your drawing. If you set up your drawing to accept fractions or feet and inches, you can enter values here in fractions or feet and inches. For example, if your drawing is 1/8" = 1' scale, you can enter

1/8" = 1'

Otherwise you would have to enter

.125 = 12

Notice that in both cases no spaces were entered between values.

You can also enter the scale conversion factor in Table 3.2, 1 = 96. Using the scale conversion factor may help you keep things straight in your mind since you have to convert sizes to scale from time to

Origin of the Plot

Figure 5.9: *The drawing rotated 90 degrees on an 8¹/₂-inch-wide sheet*

time. You can specify a different scale from the one you chose while setting up your drawing, and AutoCAD will plot your drawing to that scale. Entering the right scale is important, because if it is too large, AutoCAD will think your drawing is too large to fit on the sheet. If your printer doesn't seem to be working and you're sure everything else is set up properly, check your scale setting.

The other option, Fit, allows you to avoid giving a scale altogether and forces the drawing to fit on the sheet. This works fine if you are doing illustrations that are not to scale. Press Return to select the Fit option. The next prompt appears:

Effective plotting area: 5.06 wide by 8.00 high
Position paper in printer.
Press return to continue:

This prompt tells you the size of your plotting area and reminds you to put paper in your printer. Prepare your printer, then press Return. You see the message

Processing Vector

in the prompt area. This message is equivalent to seeing the drawing regenerate. Since the display is in text mode, the drawing regeneration can't be displayed, so AutoCAD tells you how many vectors are being processed as it plots your drawing.

In a few seconds your printer starts to print. The drawing should look like Figure 5.9. When it is done you will see the prompt

Press return to continue:

Press Return and you will return to the drawing editor. The next time you print a drawing using the dot-matrix printer, the settings you selected in this session will be the default settings and will remain so until you change them again.

Printing an AutoCAD drawing with a dot-matrix printer takes from one to five minutes, depending on the area the drawing takes up on the paper. (The drawing's complexity has little effect on the printing time.) You can speed up the process using a *printer buffer*, or gain more flexibility in your printing schedule by saving the plot to a file on disk and printing it later using a *print utility program*. Because these options are also available for plotting, which is a much more time-consuming process than printing, they are discussed in detail in the section on plotting.

Printing from the Main Menu

If you prefer, you can print AutoCAD drawings from the Main menu instead of the Plot menu. Quit this file and then enter 4 from the Main menu to select Printer Plot a Drawing. You will be asked the name of the file to print. After that, the rest of the process is identical to what we have just described. You will not enter the drawing editor, so you won't be able to change your drawing. Printing from the Main menu is useful if you have several drawings already set up to be printed, because you can print them without having to open and close the files.

USING THE PLOTTER

Plotting a drawing can be a frustrating process, for two reasons. First, it can use up a lot of computer time. You must plan your work so you can do noncomputer tasks while you plot drawings. You have some options, however, that can help you manage plotting time. You can speed up the process using a *plotter buffer,* or gain more flexibility in your plotting schedule by saving the plots to disk as *plot files* and printing them later using a *plot utility program.* These options are also available for printing drawings with a dot-matrix printer, but generally you must obtain separate buffers and utility programs for your plotter and your printer.

A plotter buffer electronically stores the information sent to the plotter, then meters out that information as the plotter needs it. This way AutoCAD can send the plotter information without having to worry about how fast it is actually plotted. The buffer can be either a hardware or a software product. Hardware buffers usually contain the memory required to store the plotter information and can be quite expensive. Software buffers (or *spoolers*) are less expensive, but they will use some memory from your system— memory you might prefer to use for AutoCAD.

Using a plot utility program doesn't actually save plotting time, but it can give you a lot more flexibility in your plotting schedule. First you save the drawing and its specified settings as a plot file on disk, which takes less computer time than actually plotting. You later use the plot utility program to plot the saved drawings at another time, or on another computer. Or you can have someone unfamiliar with AutoCAD plot them. Autodesk does not provide a plot utility program, but you can probably get one from an Auto-CAD users' group or from CompuServe—or even write one if you're a programmer.

The second reason plotting can be frustrating is that there are many different plotter pens and media, which must be carefully chosen for each drawing. This section gives you the basic information you need on pens and plotter media.

Setting Up the Plotting Parameters

The plotter settings are almost identical to those for the dot-matrix printer, with the exception of the plotter pen assignments and options allowing the plotter to adjust for pen widths. Start AutoCAD and open the Bath file. To initialize a plot you can pick the Plot option from the Root menu, then pick Plotter. Or you can enter

plot

through the keyboard. Pick Plotter from the Plot side menu or Plot from the File pull-down menu (see Figure 5.1). At the prompt

What to plot – Display, Extents, Limits, View, or Window <D>:

press Return to accept the default, Display. The screen switches to text mode and you see the following list of settings:

Plot will NOT be written to a selected file
Sizes are in Inches
Plot origin is at (0.00,0.00)
Plotting area is 10.50 wide by 8.00 high (A)
Plot is NOT rotated 90 degrees
Pen width is 0.010
Area fill will NOT be adjusted for pen width
Hidden lines will NOT be removed
Plot will be scaled to fit available area
Do you want to change anything? <N>

This list is similar to the one you saw when you started the Printer command, with the addition of the lines concerning pen width and area fill. Enter Y. You will get the following list:

Entity Color	Pen No.	Line Type	Pen Speed	Entity Color	Pen No.	Line Type	Pen Speed
1 (red)	1	0	60	9	1	0	60
2 (yellow)	1	0	60	10	1	0	60
3 (green)	1	0	60	11	1	0	60
4 (cyan)	1	0	60	12	1	0	60
5 (blue)	1	0	60	13	1	0	60
6 (magenta)	1	0	60	14	1	0	60
7 (white)	1	0	60	15	1	0	60
8	1	0	60				

Line types   0 = continuous line
1 = ...
2 = – – – – – – – –
3 = – –· – –· – –· – –·
4 = – – –· – – –· – – –· – – –·
5 = – – · – – · – – · – – ·
6 = –· · · –· · · –· · · –· · ·

Do you want to change any of the above parameters? <N>

The *entity color* in the first column of this list is the color you have assigned to an object in your drawing. Usually an object is automatically assigned the color of the layer it is on, but you can also give an object a color assignment independent of its layer assignment. You can plot the object in either the same color you used in the drawing file or in a different color. Generally, it is easier to keep track of your colors and pens if you use the same color.

Although this list does not explicitly enable you to assign different line weights to colors, you can do so by varying the line weights of your pens. You might assign the color red to pen 1 on your plotter, a pen with a fine line weight. The color yellow might be assigned to pen 2, a pen with a medium line weight. Finally, the color green might be assigned to pen 3, a pen with a heavy line weight. Keep your plotter pen assignments in mind when you assign colors to objects and layers during the drawing process.

If you have a single-pen plotter and you want to do a multiple-pen plot, AutoCAD stops the plotter and prompts you to change pens whenever a different pen is called for.

This prompt also enables you to control the pen speed. This is important because different pens have different speed requirements. Refillable technical pens that use india ink generally require the slowest settings, while roller pens are capable of very high speeds. Selecting pens and media for your plotter can be a trial-and-error proposition. Later in this chapter we will examine this issue more closely.

If your plotter can generate its own line types, you can also assign line types to colors. This feature is very seldom used because it is simpler to assign line types to layers directly in the drawing.

If you want to change pen assignments, enter Y at the prompt

Do you want to change any of these parameters? <N>

The following prompt appears:

Enter values, blank = Next value, Cn = Color n, S = Show current values, X = Exit

Entity Color	Pen No.	Line Type	Pen Speed	
1 (red)	1	0	60	Pen number <1>:

Enter values, blank = Next value, Cn = Color n, S = Show current values, X = Exit

Entity Color	Pen No.	Line Type	Pen Speed	
1 (red)	1	0	60	Pen number <1>:

Notice how this prompt duplicates the information on the first color listed in the previous prompt. To the right is a line prompting you to enter a pen number for the color. The default is 1. You can select a pen number corresponding to the color red, or accept the default pen number, 1. Enter 2 to indicate that you want pen 2 to be assigned the color red. The bottom line of the prompt changes to show the following:

1 (red)	2	0	60	Line type <0>:

The prompt reflects the change in pen assignments you just made and asks you what line type you wish to use. If you look back to the list of pen assignments, you will see a list of line types from 0 to 6. The default, 0, is a continuous line and as we mentioned earlier, is nearly always used. Press Return to select the default. The prompt will change again to:

1 (red)	2	0	60	Pen speed <60>:

Now AutoCAD prompts you for pen speed (unless your plotter does not offer the pen speed option). Every plotter has its own maximum speed, corresponding to the number provided here by Auto-CAD. The 60 in this example is the fastest setting available for the Hewlett-Packard 7585 plotter. Generally, the fastest setting should be used only with felt-tip or roller pens. For wet-ink or technical pens on polyester film, use the slower settings. You may have to do some experimenting here to see just what speeds give you the best results.

Table 5.1 gives you a sample of settings used successfully with a Hewlett-Packard 7585 plotter. If you have another make of plotter, find out what AutoCAD pen speed settings correspond to the plotter speeds in this table and use those values. Generally, the plotter speed corresponds to the AutoCAD pen speed. We will look at the available types of plotter pens and the pros and cons of each later in this chapter.

Now press Return to accept the default pen speed, 60 (your default pen speed may be different). The prompt now displays the settings for color number 2, yellow. You can now select pen number, pen speed, and line type for yellow the same way you did for red. You can then continue through all 15 colors, or you can review your new settings by entering S.

You may be wondering why only the first 8 colors are listed in the pen assignment list, although there are 15 numbers. The first eight colors are assigned the same numbers no matter what display adapter you use. This means that color number 3 is green whether you have an Enhanced Graphics Adapter, a Tecmar Graphics Adapter, or a BNW Graphics Adapter. After 8, AutoCAD does not assign specific colors to the numbers. Color number 9 on an Enhanced Graphics Adapter might be magenta, while on a Tecmar Graphics Adapter it might be cyan. Some display adapters even allow you to assign your own numbers to the colors during their configuration.

Pen Type	Plotter Speed	AutoCAD Setting	Media Use
Refillable wet-ink	15 cm	18	Polyester film, vellum
Disposable wet-ink	30 cm	36	Polyester film, vellum
Felt-tip	30–60 cm	36–56	Vellum, bond
Roller-ball	60 cm	56	Vellum, bond

Table 5.1:   Pen speeds and pen types for the HP 7585 plotter

Enter S now to review the settings. The screen displays all the current pen settings as before, but this time it reflects any changes you have made. If you decide you want to change a pen assignment, type C followed by the number of the color you wish to reassign. Enter C1 and the following prompt appears:

1 (red) 2   0   60   Pen number <2>:

Now you can change the pen assignments for red again.

Once you are satisfied with your pen assignments, enter X. The following prompt appears:

Write the plot to a file? <N>

At this prompt you can tell AutoCAD to send the plot information to a plot file instead of to the plotter, as we discussed in the introduction to the plotting section. Press Return to accept the default, N. The next prompt appears:

Size units (Inches or Millimeters) <Inches>:

This is where you select your base unit of measurement. Press Return to accept the default, Inches. The next prompt appears:

Plot origin in Inches <0.00,0.00>:

Just as in the printer settings, this option allows you to specify a plot origin other than the lower-left corner of the sheet. Some plotters orient the sheet sideways, so check your plotter manual to see exactly where the plot origin is located. If you've forgotten what this prompt means, refer to the section on printing your drawing.

Press Return to accept the default, 0.00,0.00. A prompt similar to the following one appears:

Standard Values for plotting size

Size	Width	Height
A	10.50	8.00
B	16.00	10.00
C	21.00	16.00
D	33.00	21.00
E	43.00	33.00
MAX	44.72	35.31

Enter the Size or Width,Height (in Inches) <A>:

The sizes listed depend on your plotter. This prompt is typical for an E size plotter. If you have a small plotter, you may only have sizes up to B, which would be designated as the MAX size. You can select a listed size by entering either its ANSI designation, A, B, C, etc., or any size (6,6 for example, for a sheet six inches square). If you enter a size that is too large, you will get the error message

Warning plotter area exceeds plotter maximum

before the last prompt in this sequence. If you continue to plot any-way, AutoCAD will truncate the drawing to fit on the sheet.

Enter A if the default is not already A. The following prompt appears:

Rotate 2D plots 90 degrees clockwise? <N>

At this point you can tell AutoCAD to do the plot rotated 90 degrees on the sheet. This is useful when you have drawn an object that is taller than it is wide and will not fit on the sheet. Press Return to accept the default, N. The next prompt appears:

Pen width <.010>:

AutoCAD provides four drawing commands, Trace, Pline, Solid, and Donut, to create solid-fill areas (we will cover their use in Chapter 12). Whenever these commands are used, the pen plotter must draw a series of lines close together to duplicate the solid fill (much as you would do by hand). To do this efficiently, AutoCAD must know the thickness of the pen being used. By giving a value here, you tell Auto-CAD how far over to move the pen each time it draws a line in a solid area. Figure 5.10 gives a graphic example of what this option does.

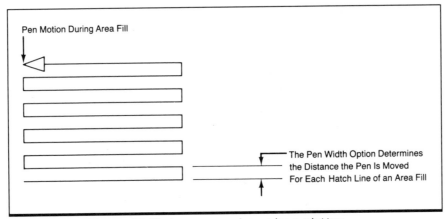

Figure 5.10: *How solid filled areas are drawn by a plotter*

If the value you give here is too high, the solid area will come out as a vertical or horizontal hatch pattern. If it is too low, the plotter will waste time drawing over areas it has already covered. The default pen width, .010 (ten thousandths of an inch) is equivalent to a .30-millimeter wet-ink pen nib. This thickness is adequate for felt-tip pens. If you use a smaller pen, you will get a hatch pattern instead of a solid fill.

Accept the default by pressing Return. The next prompt appears:

Adjust area fill boundaries for pen width? <N>

This option tells AutoCAD to compensate for pen width around the edges of a solid area. If a solid filled area is to be .090 inches wide and you have drawn it at .090 inches, the plotter normally makes the solid area .090 inches wide plus the pen width, .010 inch, because it draws the border of the solid area using the border's center line to determine where to place the pen. If you enter Y to this prompt, AutoCAD pulls in the border of the solid area half the pen width you specified. Figure 5.11 shows you what area fill adjustment does. Generally, compensation for pen width is critical only when you are producing drawings as a basis for photo etchings or similar artwork where close tolerances must be adhered to.

Press Return to accept the default, N. The next prompt appears:

Remove hidden lines? <N>

This option affects only 3D drawings; it will be discussed in Chapter 14.

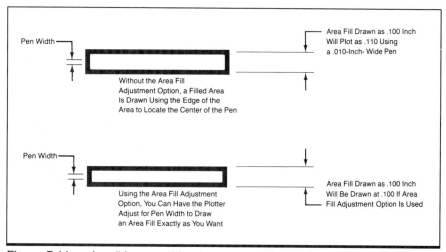

Figure 5.11: A solid area without compensation and with compensation

Press Return to select the default, No. The next prompt appears:

> **Specify scale by entering:**
> **Plotted Inches = Drawing Units or Fit or ? <F>**

This is the same scaling option found in the Printer command, and it works in the same way. Press Return to select the option Fit.

AutoCAD now saves the settings you just selected. The next time you plot, AutoCAD will use these settings as the defaults, so you don't have to enter the same values every time you plot. The next prompt appears:

> **Effective plotting area: 5.06 wide by 8.00 high**
> **Position paper in plotter.**
> **Press return to continue or S to Stop for hardware setup.**

At this point you can press Return to start the plot. Or, if you have a plotter with controllable options such as pen force and acceleration, you can enter S, then set up your own options on your plotter. Generally, these options are controlled automatically by the plotter, as it can sense the type of pen it is using. If you want to experiment with pens and media you can override the plotter. Enter S and the following prompt appears:

> **Do hardware setup now.**
> **Press RETURN to continue:**

If you try setting up your plotter without using the S option, AutoCAD overrides your settings when it starts to send its information to the plotter.

If you have only one serial port and your plotter is not connected to it, connect it now. If you have a switch box connecting your plotter to your serial port, switch to the plotter. Although this is a simple operation, it is often forgotten and the computer can lock up, causing you to lose your drawing or any changes made since the last time you saved. The only thing you can do if this occurs is to restart your computer.

Once you have the plotter connected and set up, press Return. The vector-processing message appears at the bottom of the screen. In a moment the plotter begins to draw. If you have a single-pen plotter and you have assigned different pens to each color, AutoCAD stops the plot when it has completed plotting one color and a prompt similar to the following appears:

> **Install pen number 1, color 1 (red)**
> **Press RETURN to continue:**

You can now change the pen in the plotter to the next pen size or color. Once the plot is done, the last prompt in the plot command appears:

Plot complete.
Press RETURN to continue:

Press Return and you will return to the drawing editor. Your plot should look like Figure 5.12.

Plotting from the Main Menu

Just as you can print from the Main menu, you can plot from it. Start AutoCAD in the normal way, then at the Main menu enter 3, Plot a Drawing. You will be asked for the name of the file you want to plot. The rest of the process is identical to what you've just practiced.

USING PLOTTERS, PENS, AND MEDIA

The most difficult part of plotting is the use and selection of pens. Although your overall drawing quality depends a great deal on the quality of the plotter, you can control the line quality to some

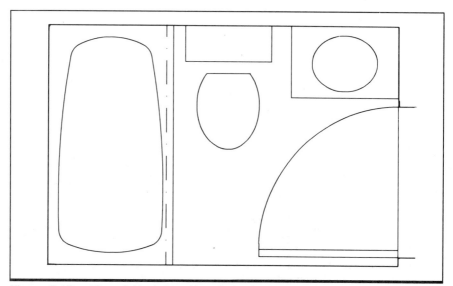

Figure 5.12:   The plotted drawing of the bathroom

degree by selecting the right pen and medium for the job. In this section, we discuss the use of these pens and media and what the alternatives are.

Using Wet-Ink Pens

The best line quality can be obtained using wet-ink refillable pens on polyester film, but this is also the most difficult combination to use. (Figure 5.13 shows a wet-ink pen.) If you have never used wet-ink pens before, be prepared for a mess. They require a good deal of attention and cleaning and you will have to replace them frequently. When these pens wear out, they cause skips in the ink flow; you can end up wasting time and materials trying to use a worn-out pen.

If your plotter allows you to control the pen force, the best type of wet-ink pen nib to use is a tungsten V-groove nib. The ability to control pen force is important when using this type of nib, since heavy pressure can cause the pen to gouge the film and plug the nib. The nib is the actual point of the pen and it is replaceable. We have found that this type of nib used with the proper ink (KOH-I-NOOR Rapidograph #3074-F, for example) yields the most trouble-free results when plotting on polyester film at slow speeds.

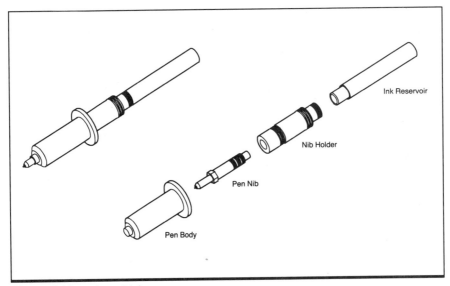

Figure 5.13: A wet-ink pen

If you want to use a nib size smaller than 0, you may run into difficulty no matter what you try. If you must use these smaller nibs, use the slowest speed possible and be sure to keep your media and work area clean and free of dust and static. In fact, keeping the media, the plotter, and its surroundings clean is a good idea no matter what type of pen you use.

An alternative to the refillable wet-ink pen is the disposable wet-ink pen (see Figure 5.14). Hewlett-Packard and KOH-I-NOOR have introduced a line of disposable wet-ink pens specifically designed for use on polyester film. The pen sizes are limited, but if they are adequate for your drawings and you have a plotter that will accept disposable pens, they may well be worth a try. They may seem expensive, but not when you compare them to the cost of frequently replacing refillable pen nibs. These disposable pens are relatively trouble-free, which adds to their economy, since you can spend hours trying to get a refillable wet-ink pen to work properly.

Some plotters, particularly small-format plotters, do not work well with the tungsten V-groove nibs because pen force cannot be controlled. The regular tungsten nibs combined with a latex-based india ink are a better choice for this type of plotter, but you must keep the pen nibs clean. If you intend not to use the pens for a long

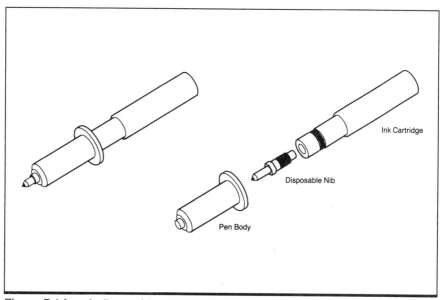

Figure 5.14: *A disposable wet-ink pen*

time—say a week—it is a good idea to empty and clean them. Otherwise, the ink can ruin the delicate internal parts of the nib.

Because of the growing interest in computer-aided design and drafting, the number of plotter inks available is increasing. You may want to experiment with different inks to see what works best in your plotter.

Vellum is next in quality to polyester film. Both refillable and disposable wet-ink pens are available for this medium. The best pens are the disposable wet-ink pens. If you must use a refillable wet-ink pen, the jewel-tip nibs work best.

Choosing Media

The choice of media is often determined by what you are used to using and what you are willing to spend. As we mentioned, the combination of polyester film and wet ink yields the best-quality line work. It also reproduces the best and is the most durable. Correcting ink drawings is easier on polyester film than on vellum. If you are doing overlay drafting, it is the only medium to use because of its dimensional stability.

However, most people use vellum rather than polyester film because it is cheaper and they are used to drawing on it. If you don't need the longevity and stability of polyester film, vellum is a good alternative. Its biggest drawback is that it handles ink erasures and corrections poorly.

Finally, there is bond paper. This medium isn't often used in hand drafting, but is good for checking CAD drawings because it can take the faster ball- and felt-tip pens. Bond is reproducible using blueprint techniques, but the quality is poor. The reproductions are good enough, however, for check plots.

If you want to use preprinted title blocks on polyester film, be sure your printer or supplier is aware that you intend to use the film in a plotter. Normally, the process used to print on polyester film requires talc to help dry the ink. Due to the talc's tendency to clog plotter pens, a different drying process is used when the film is intended for a plotter. If you already have preprinted title blocks, check to see if there is a residue of powder on the film. If there is, be sure to clean it off before you use it in your plotter.

The thickness of polyester film affects the quality of the plot, particularly in plotters that use pinch rollers to hold the film. In general you should follow the plotter manufacturer's recommendations on mil thickness of polyester film, but you should not exceed four-mil polyester. When the film is too thick, plot registration becomes a problem. As the plotter runs, it crosses the polyester film several times. The film gradually slips in the plotter and throws off the alignment of drawing objects. Plotter quality also determines the thickness of film allowed. A high-quality plotter will do beautiful plots on six-mil polyester film, while a low-quality plotter won't even do a decent plot on three-mil film.

Vellum thickness is less crucial. Vellum's biggest drawback is its tendency to expand and contract depending on environmental humidity. This isn't a problem unless you intend to do overlays where registration between two different plots is critical.

Bond paper is probably the most commonly used plotter medium because it provides an inexpensive and fast way to get check plots. You should use a plotter to do check plots of drawings that are larger than your printer permits, usually 17 x 22 inches and up. Using bond paper with a pen capable of high speeds can take half the time of a wet-ink plot.

Keeping Your Pens Flowing

If you do not cap your pens while they are not in use, you run the risk of having a pen that won't write at a crucial moment. This is especially important with multipen plotters. Many plotters offer a pen holder that will cap the pens, but other plotters rely on frequent pen switches to keep all the pens flowing. If you have the latter type, AutoCAD allows you to set the pen-selection sequence so that the plotter alternates between pens more frequently. Because you can determine the pen-selection sequence only during plotter configuration, we have included details on it in Appendix B.

Sometimes dried pens are inevitable. It's a good idea to have an ultrasonic pen cleaner to loosen dried ink. This device can help get a clogged pen running if it isn't too dried or dirty. If you still have problems getting a pen to work, as a last resort you can take it apart and soak the nib in a pen-cleaning solution. This is a last resort because cleaning pens is a messy job and you risk breaking the delicate inner workings of the pen nib.

Using Ceramic, Ball-Tip, and Felt-Tip Pens

As we mentioned earlier, bond paper is often used for quick check plots. Ball-tip pens are capable of the highest speed and are often used in conjunction with bond paper for this purpose (see Figure 5.15). They are usually available only on high-quality plotters. Felt-tip pens are available on virtually every plotter made, and they can also be

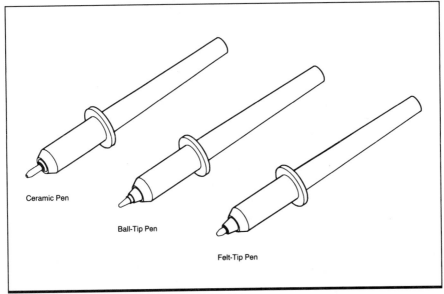

Figure 5.15:   *Ceramic, ball-tip, and felt-tip pens*

used at high speeds. They tend to dry out faster than the ball-tip pens, however.

If you are producing a color rendering on a plotter, felt-tip pens can provide a good solid color. You could combine the use of wet-ink and felt-tip pens to produce a very clean color rendering. New colors are being offered in the felt-tip pens, some of which can be over-lapped to create even more colors. The possibilities are limited only by your creativity in using AutoCAD and your plotter.

Ceramic-tip pens can be used at the same speeds as the ball- and felt-tip pens. Because they are capable of finer lines, you might want to use them where a fine line is required in a finished plot. You can get good-quality reproducible plots by using ceramic-tip pens with certain types of uncoated vellums. Ceramic-tip pens also come in a limited range of colors.

All these pens can also be used on polyester and vellum with mixed results. You may want to experiment to see how to use them on these media. One idea is to use ball- or ceramic-tip pens on polyester film or vellum to draw hatch patterns that should appear very light in the final drawing. They might be used in place of a very small pen nib, a 000 nib size, for example.

PostScript Printer Output

To use a PostScript output device for printing, you need to configure the AutoCAD plotter option for it (see Appendix B). AutoCAD treats PostScript devices as plotters. Once the configuration is done, you get hard copy through the same process described earlier in this chapter—with a couple of differences.

First, you can set the default overall line width of your output by entering the line width value at the prompt

Pen width <.010>:

when setting up the plot. All the lines drawn by the PostScript device will be the width you specify unless you have drawn polylines of varying thicknesses. Polylines will plot at their drawn thickness. In fact, using polylines of varying thicknesses is the only way to vary line weight on PostScript output.

Second, you can have AutoCAD create a file that stores the plot information on your hard disk for plotting at a later time. You can then take this file to an MS-DOS compatible computer connected to a PostScript device and have that computer send the file to the printer for output. To create a plot file, you enter Y at the prompt

Write the plot to a file <N>

during the plot setup. At the end of the plot setup, you will get the prompt

Enter file name for plot *default:*

where the default name is the name of the file you are plotting. If you press Return without entering a name, the plot file will have the same name as the original drawing file but with the extension .PLT instead of .DWG.

Once the plot is complete, you will find the plot file on the default directory. You can then load that file onto another computer connected to a PostScript device and print it out by entering

copy *file name*.plt com1:

where *file name* is the name of the plot file. Com1: in the example above is the serial port address the printer is connected to.

By plotting to a file, you can use another output device to get hard copy. Many photocopy services now rent time on computers connected to output devices. Even if a service does not have AutoCAD, you can still get high-resolution output on its hardware.

SENDING YOUR DRAWINGS TO A SERVICE

Using a plotting service can be a good alternative to purchasing your own plotter. Or you might consider using a low-cost plotter for check plots, then sending the files to a service for your final plots.

There are *service bureaus* that will take your AutoCAD files and plot them on a pen or *electrostatic* plotter. An electrostatic plotter is like a very large laser printer capable of producing color plots. Because it is costly and often requires a minicomputer or powerful microcomputer to run it, you probably won't want to purchase one yourself. However, the electrostatic plotter is excellent for situations where high volume and fast turnaround are required, as in a service bureau. It produces high-quality plots, often better than a laser printer, and it is fast. A 30 × 42-inch plot can take as little as eight minutes.

The one drawback to using a service bureau is it usually requires your drawings to conform to certain guidelines. The service assigns a standard line thickness to each layer color, so if you want your line thicknesses to be correct, you must assign the colors to your layers according to these guidelines. Another drawback is the electrostatic plotter's inability to accept preprinted media. It often requires specially treated media that preclude the use of your standard title block sheets.

These are minor problems since layer colors can be easily changed and you can have your title block as a drawing file that you add to all your drawings. Services usually have the hardware and software to do any file conversion necessary to use their output devices, so all you have to do is give them your AutoCAD drawing file on a floppy disk.

Blueprinters are also beginning to offer plotting in conjunction with their usual services. They usually offer the same services as service bureaus, complete with high-quality plotters.

CONCLUSION

At this point, when you aren't rushing to meet a deadline, you may want to experiment with some of the plotter and printer variables and see firsthand what each one does. There are many plotters available and each has its own features and drawbacks. It's up to you to find the optimum method for using your particular plotter.

And it's worth the time to become thoroughly familiar with the plotting process, since it can be a major bottleneck in your drawing schedule.

In the next chapter, you will see how to make the best use of existing work. You will learn how to use existing files as the basis for new ones and how to make multiple copies of objects. We will also discuss using lines to aid you in drawing.

Chapter 6

Using Existing Information

ONE AUTOCAD CAPABILITY is duplicating existing information. You have already seen how the Copy command can quickly and easily copy any object or group of objects. In this chapter, while you finish drawing the studio apartment unit, you will explore some of the ways to exploit existing files and objects while constructing your drawing. For example, you will use existing files as *templates* for new files, eliminating the need to set up layers, scales, and sheet sizes. With AutoCAD you can also duplicate objects in multiple *arrays*. You have already seen how to use the Osnap commands on objects to locate points to draw complex forms. We will look at other ways of using lines to aid your drawing.

And, because you will begin to use Zoom more, you will review this command as you go along. We'll also introduce you to the Pan command, another tool to help you get around in your drawing.

USING AN EXISTING DRAWING AS A TEMPLATE

Because you're already familiar with many of the commands you will use to draw the apartment unit, we won't take you through every step of the drawing process. Instead, we will sometimes ask you to copy the drawing from a figure, using the notes and

MASTERING AUTOCAD

dimensions as guides and putting objects on the indicated layers. If you have trouble remembering a command you've already learned, review the appropriate section of this book.

AutoCAD allows you to use an existing drawing as the starting point or template for a new drawing. A template is a file that contains necessary settings and/or objects to do a drawing. For example, you may want to create a drawing with the same scale and sheet size as an existing drawing. You may even want to use some of the objects, layers, and blocks in that drawing. By using the existing drawing to begin your new one, you can save a lot of time.

This is exactly what AutoCAD does when you open a new file. The ACAD.DWG file that comes with AutoCAD contains the default settings for modes, text, limits, etc. AutoCAD copies the ACAD.DWG file, then gives the copy the name you enter for your drawing. When you save your drawing file or exit it using the End command, the ACAD.DWG file is left untouched. If you find most of the default settings unsatisfactory for your application, you can actually open ACAD.DWG and reset them however you want. Then each time you open a new file, your most common default settings will already be established.

But you may have several sets of default settings you would like to use. In this case, you can create several empty drawing files, each with its own default settings. One may have layers already set up, while another may have predefined blocks ready to use. Then when you want to use one of these files as a template, proceed as if you were opening a new file and enter the new file name followed by an equal sign and the template file name. The following exercise guides you through creating and using a template for your studio's kitchenette.

Because the kitchenette will use the same layers, settings, scale, and sheet size as the bathroom drawing, you can use the Bath file as a template. First start AutoCAD in the usual way. At the Main menu enter 1 to start a new drawing. At the next prompt enter

kitchen = bath

The bathroom drawing now appears in the drawing editor. This does not mean that you have opened the Bath file, however. Because the Kitchen file used the Bath file as a template, it contains everything in the Bath file, including objects. You don't need these objects, so erase them. Your template still contains the layers and settings used in the Bath file, and is set up for a 1" = 1' drawing on an 8½ x 11-inch drawing area.

COPYING AN OBJECT MULTIPLE TIMES

First you will draw the gas range. In the process you will learn how to use the Array command to create arrays, or multiple copies of an object, and to control the number and orientation of the copies. An array can be in either a circular pattern called a *polar array*, or a matrix of columns and rows called a *rectangular array*.

Making Circular Copies

Set the current layer to Fixture and toggle the snap mode on. Draw a circle with a three-inch radius, with its center at coordinate 4'-0", 4'-0". This represents the outside edge of the first gas burner. Pick Circle from the Draw menu, then pick Cen,Rad (Center, Radius) from the Circle menu (see Figure 6.1). At the prompt

Diameter/<Radius>: Drag

enter 3. The circle appears.

Next, you will draw the burner grill. Draw a line four inches long starting from the coordinate 4'-1", 4'-0" and ending to the right of that point. Now zoom into the circle and line to get a better view. Your drawing should look like Figure 6.2.

Figure 6.1: The Circle menu

MASTERING AUTOCAD

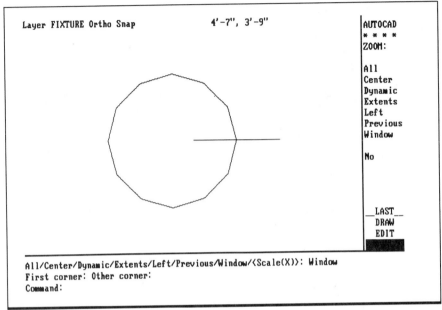

Figure 6.2:   Close-up of circle and line

Go to the Edit menu and pick Array. Pick Last from the Array menu to select the last object drawn (see Figure 6.3). The line you just drew will ghost. Press Return to confirm your selection and pick Polar from the Array menu at the

Rectangular or Polar array (R/P):

prompt to begin creating a polar array.

A polar array is a series of copies that rotates about a center point. You just drew one line of the gas burner grill; now you will use the polar array option to copy that line around to complete the grill. Pick the center of the circle at the next prompt

Center point of array:

At the next prompt

Number of items:

enter 8. This tells AutoCAD you want seven copies of the original line, leaving you with eight lines altogether. At the next prompt

Angle to fill (+ = ccw,- = cw) <360>:

press Return to accept the default, 360 degrees. By doing so, you

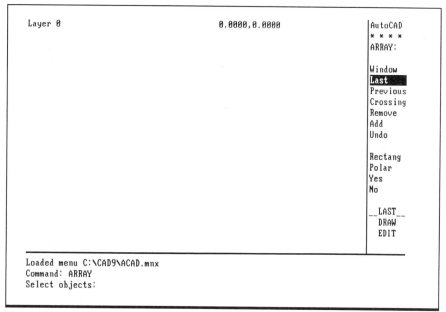

Figure 6.3:   The Array menu

are telling AutoCAD to copy the objects so that they are spaced evenly over a 360-degree arc. (If you had instead entered 180 degrees, the lines would be evenly spaced over a 180-degree arc and fill only half the circle.) The lines will be copied in a counterclockwise direction. If you want to copy in a clockwise direction, you must enter a minus sign before the number of degrees.

The next prompt is

Rotate objects as they are copied? <Y>:

Here you can have the line maintain its horizontal orientation as it is copied around. Since you want it to rotate about the array center, accept the default, Y.

The line copies around the center of the circle, rotating as it copies. Your drawing will look like Figure 6.4.

Now you will draw the other three burners of the gas range by creating a rectangular array from the burner you just drew. First zoom back a bit to get a view of a larger area. You can control the amount of magnification by entering a value at the Zoom command prompt. Start the Zoom command and enter .5x at the first prompt. Your drawing will look like Figure 6.5.

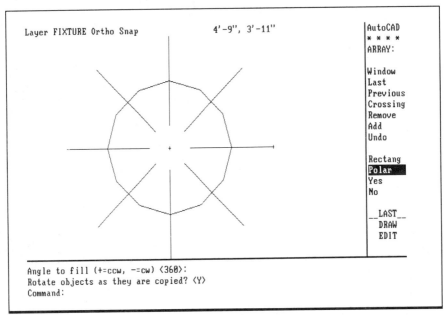

Figure 6.4: The completed gas burner

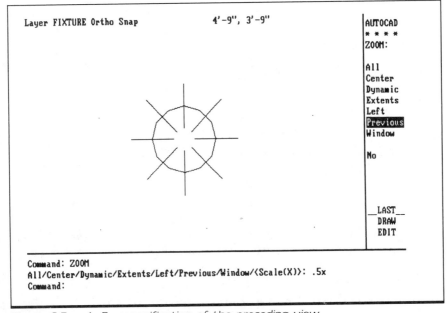

Figure 6.5: A .5x magnification of the preceding view

By entering .5x, you told AutoCAD you want a view that reduces the width of the current view to fill half the display area, allowing you to see more of the work area. If you specify a value greater than 1, 5 for example, you will magnify your current view five times. If you leave off the x, your new view will be in relation to the drawing limits rather than the current view.

Making Row and Column Copies

Now start the Array command again. Select the entire burner using the Window option at the object-selection prompt. Then at the

Rectangular or Polar array (R/P):

prompt pick the Rectangular option from the Array menu. As we mentioned earlier, a rectangular array is a matrix of columns and rows. Since the range has four burners, you want two rows and two columns. Enter 2 at the

Number of rows (----) <1>:

prompt. Then enter 2 again at the

Number of columns (||||) <1>:

prompt. Enter 14 at the

Unit cell or distance between rows (----):

prompt. This tells AutoCAD that the distance between the rows of burners is 14 inches. Then enter 16 at the prompt

Distance between columns (||||):

to tell AutoCAD the distance between the columns of burners, 16 inches. Your screen will look like Figure 6.6.

AutoCAD usually draws a rectangular array from bottom to top, left to right.

You can also use the cursor to graphically indicate an *array cell* (see Figure 6.7). An array cell is a rectangle defining the distance between rows and columns. You may want to use this option when an object is available to use as a reference from which to determine column and row distances. For example, you may have drawn a crosshatch pattern like a calendar within which you want to array an object. You could use the intersections of the hatch lines as references to define the array cell, which would be one square in the hatch pattern.

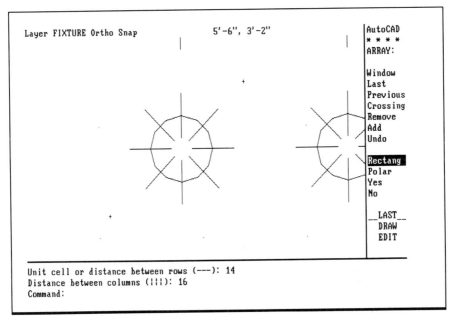

Figure 6.6:   *The burners arrayed*

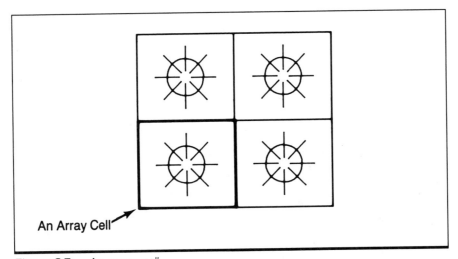

Figure 6.7:   *An array cell*

At times you may want to do a rectangular array at an angle. To accomplish this you must first use the Rotate option on the Snap menu to rotate the grid and cursor to the desired angle. Then proceed with the Array command.

You'll notice that most of your burners do not appear on the display shown in Figure 6.6. You can use the Pan command to move the view over so you can see all the burners. Pan is similar to Zoom in that it changes your view of the drawing. However, Pan does not alter the magnification of the view the way Zoom does. Instead it maintains the current magnification while moving your view across the drawing, just as you would pan a camera across a landscape. This is especially helpful when you have magnified an area to do some editing and you need to get to part of the drawing near your current view. Go to the Display menu, then pick Pan to bring up the Pan menu, or pick Pan from the Display pull-down menu (see Figure 6.8).

The prompt

PAN Displacement:

appears to ask you the distance and direction of your pan. Pick coordinate 3'-7", 3'-7". The prompt

Second point:

appears. Turn the ortho mode off if it is still on, then move the cursor to the lower-left corner of the screen as in Figure 6.9. The rubber-banding line you see indicates the pan displacement. Pick this

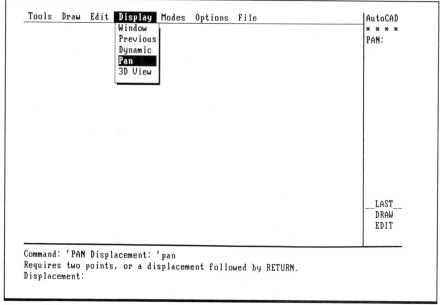

Figure 6.8: The Pan side menu and the Pan command on the Display pull-down menu

point. Your drawing will be panned to the view shown in Figure 6.10.

The burners are still not entirely visible. This is because the current zoom magnification is too great to allow you to view the entire range. Use the Zoom command and enter 1 at the zoom prompt. This gives you a view with the magnification value of one to one, enabling you to view an area equivalent to the limits of your drawing using your current view as the center of the next view. Whenever you enter a value for the zoom magnification, you get a magnification relative to this one-to-one view. If you add an x after the zoom value, as you did when you entered .5x, you will get a magnification relative to the current view.

Now complete the kitchenette as indicated in Figure 6.11. Make sure you change all the objects to the Fixture layer. If you have problems, refer to the sections on layers in Chapter 4.

When you are done, use the Base command to establish an insertion point for this drawing. Go to the Blocks menu and pick Base. At the

Base point <0'-0'',0'-0''>:

prompt, pick the upper-left corner of the kitchenette as indicated in Figure 6.11.

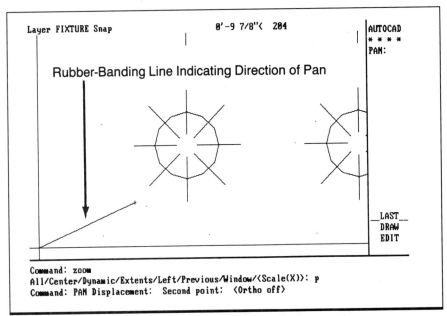

Figure 6.9:   *Rubber-banding line indicating pan displacement*

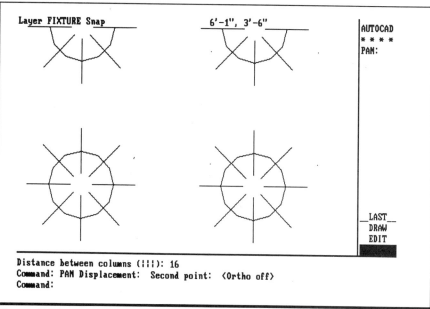

Figure 6.10: *The panned view of the gas range*

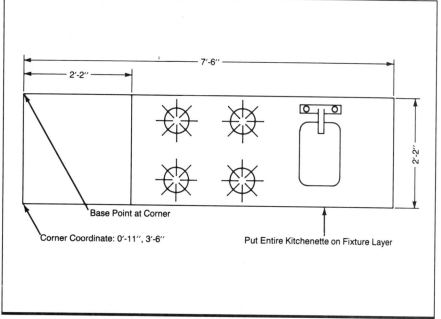

Figure 6.11: *Drawing the kitchenette*

The kitchenette drawing is complete. Exit this file using the End command.

Making Multiple Copies Using the Copy Command

You can also use the Copy command to make multiple copies of an object. Copy has an option that allows you to make several copies placed randomly over a drawing, rather than in a regular pattern as with the Array command. To use this option, you start the Copy command in the usual way. At the object-selection prompt you pick the objects you want to copy, then press Return to confirm your selections. Then when you see the prompt

<Base point of displacement>/Multiple:

you enter M for multiple. You then get the base point prompt and select a base point as usual. The prompt for a second point appears next, enabling you to select a point for the position of the copy. But instead of ending the Copy command after making a copy, AutoCAD prompts you again for a second point, allowing you to make yet another copy of your object. You can continue to copy the object this way until you press Return.

DEVELOPING YOUR DRAWING

We mentioned briefly in Chapter 3 that when using AutoCAD, you first create the most gross forms of your drawing, then refine them. In this section you will create two drawings, the studio apartment unit and the lobby, that demonstrate this process in more detail. As you go through the exercise, observe how the drawings evolve from simple forms to complex, assembled forms.

First you will construct the typical studio apartment unit using the drawings you have created thus far. In the process, you will explore the use of lines as reference points that are a relative distance from an object but not necessarily on the object.

You will also further explore how to use existing files as blocks. In Chapter 4, you inserted a file into another file. There is no limit to the size or number of the files you can insert. As you may have already guessed, you can also nest files and blocks. Nesting can help reduce your drawing time by allowing you to build one block out of smaller blocks. For example, the door drawing you created can be inserted into the bathroom plan. The bathroom plan in turn can be inserted into the studio unit plan, which also contains doors. Finally the unit plan can be inserted into the overall floor plan for the studio apartment building.

In the next exercise, you will use the Bath file as a template for the studio unit plan. However, you must make a few changes to it. First, open the Bath file. Since you will use this file in another file, erase the rectangle representing the sheet edge. Then use the Base command and select the upper-left corner of the bathroom as the new base point for this drawing, so you can locate the Bath file more easily.

Importing Settings

Open a new file called Unit. Use the Setup option to set up a 1/4" = 1'-0" scale drawing on an 8½ x 11-inch sheet. Turn the snap mode on and set the grid spacing to 12 inches. Begin the unit by drawing two rectangles, one 14 feet wide by 24 feet long, the other 14 feet wide by 4 feet long. Place them as shown in Figure 6.12.

The large rectangle represents the interior of the apartment unit, while the small rectangle represents the balcony. Insert the bathroom drawing using the upper-left corner of the unit's interior as the insertion point (see Figure 6.13).

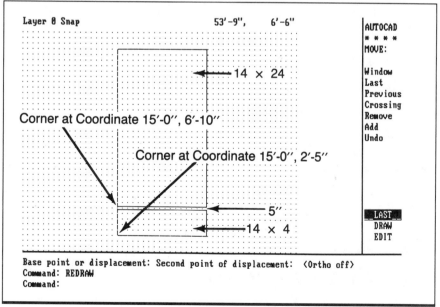

Figure 6.12:   The apartment unit interior and balcony

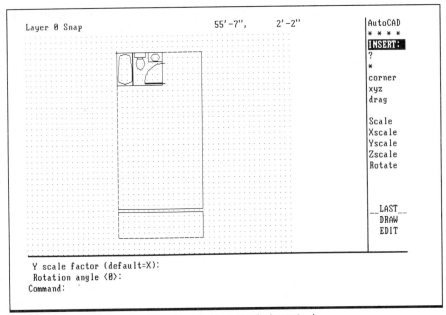

Figure 6.13:   The unit after the bathroom is inserted

By inserting the bathroom, you imported the layers and blocks contained in the Bath file. You could set up several drawings containing different layering schemes, then insert them into new drawings as a quick way of setting up layers. This method is similar to using an existing drawing as a template, but allows you to start and work on a drawing without having to decide which template to use right away.

Now change all the lines you drew to the Wall layer.

Using and Editing Lines

The majority of your work involves drawing lines, so it is important to know how to manipulate them to your best advantage. In this section, you will look at some of the more common ways to use and edit this primary drawing object.

The bathroom you inserted in the last section has only one side of its interior walls drawn (walls are usually shown by double lines). Next you will draw the other side. Zoom into the bathroom so that the entire bathroom and part of the area around it is displayed on the screen, as in Figure 6.14.

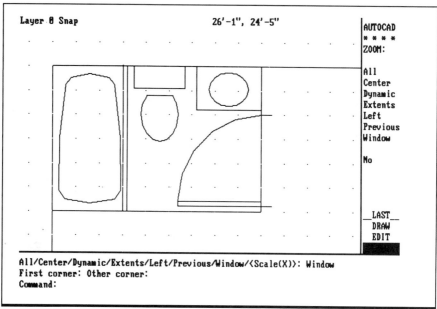

Figure 6.14:   *The enlarged view of the bathroom*

When you create your zoom window, you may notice that the
arcs are not smooth. Don't be alarmed; this is due to the way Auto-
CAD displays enlarged views that are not regenerated. The arcs will
be smooth when they are plotted, or, if you want to see them as
they actually are, you can regenerate the drawing using the Regen
command on the Display menu. We will look more closely at regeneration in the next chapter.

Make Wall your current layer and draw a line from the lower-right
corner of the bathroom down a distance of 5". This is only a reference line establishing the thickness of the wall; it will be erased. Continue the line horizontally to the left to slightly cross the left wall of
the apartment unit, as in Figure 6.15.

Erase the first short line you drew from the corner of the bathroom. Draw another line from the endpoint of the top door jamb at
coordinate 22'-11", 29'-2" upward to meet the top wall of the unit. Use
the ortho mode and the Perpend Osnap override to pick the top wall
of the unit. This will cause the line to end precisely on the wall line in
perpendicular position, as in Figure 6.16.

Draw a line connecting the two door jambs. Then change that line
to the Ceiling layer (see Figure 6.16). Next draw a line six inches

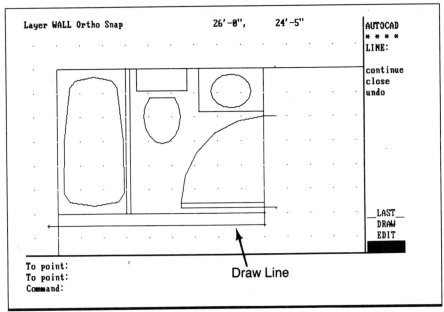

Figure 6.15: The first wall line

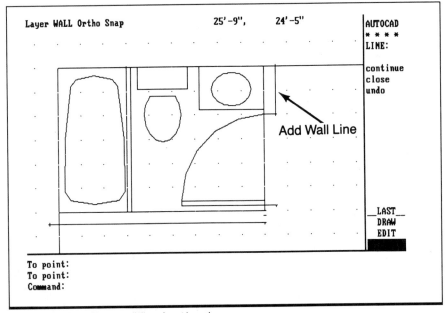

Figure 6.16: The wall line by the door

downward from the endpoint of the jamb nearest the corner at coordinate 22'-11", 26'-0", as in Figure 6.17.

Now use the Fillet command to join the line you just drew with the bottom horizontal wall line. First, make sure the fillet radius is zero by using the radius 0 option on the Fillet menu. Then proceed to fillet the two lines by picking the vertical line at coordinate 22'-11", 25'-7" and the horizontal line at coordinate 22'-0", 25'-5". Your drawing will look like Figure 6.18.

Fillet the bottom wall of the bathroom with the left wall of the unit. Next use the Trim command to join the top wall of the unit with the right side wall of the bathroom. Go to the Edit menu, then pick Trim on the Next menu to bring up the Trim menu (see Figure 6.19).

At the prompt

> **Select cutting edge(s) ...**
> **Select objects:**

pick the vertical wall line at coordinate 22'-11", 30'-0". Then press Return. By doing this, you are selecting a reference line to which you will trim your line. You can pick several objects, lines, arcs, and circles, as long as they are not blocks. The prompt

> **Select object to trim:**

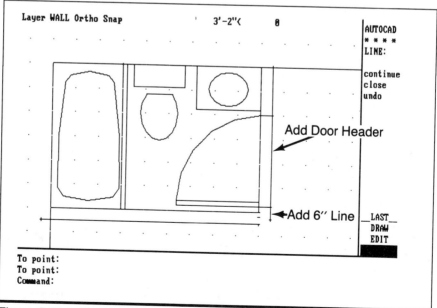

Figure 6.17: *The corner of the bathroom wall*

appears. At this prompt you must pick the objects you want to trim on the side of the cutting edge you wish to delete. If you have several objects to trim, you can pick them one by one. They must cross the object you selected as the cutting edge, however.

Pick the top wall line of the unit just left of the ghosted line at coordinate 22'-8", 30'-10". The line you just picked will trim back to the vertical wall line. Press Return to end the Trim command. Use the Redraw command to refresh the drawing. Your drawing should now look like Figure 6.20.

Both Trim and Fillet accomplished the same thing in the previous examples. The reason you used Trim instead of Fillet in the last corner is because Fillet connects the two closest endpoints of a line or an arc. In this case it would have filleted the right-hand end of the unit wall to the vertical wall line, to give you the drawing shown in Figure 6.21. Since you wanted the left end to connect to the vertical wall, you had to use Trim. Trim allows you to shorten a line back to another reference line regardless of which end is closest to the reference line. Trim also can be used to trim multiple lines.

Chamfer is another command that accomplishes the same thing as Fillet, but unlike Fillet, it allows you to join two lines with an intermediate beveled line as opposed to an arc. Chamfer can be set to join two

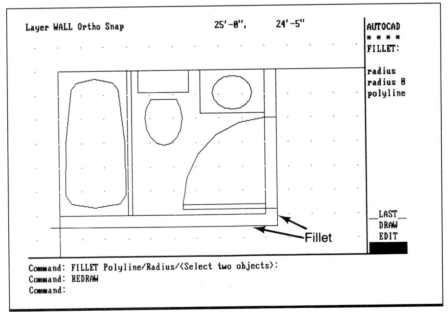

Figure 6.18: The filleted wall around the bathroom

Figure 6.19:   *The Trim menu*

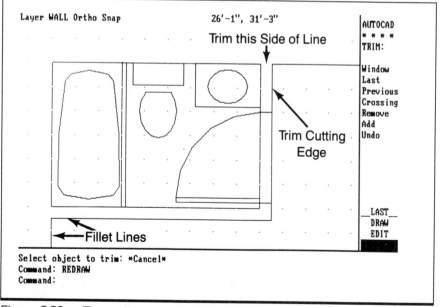

Figure 6.20:   *The wall intersections cleaned up*

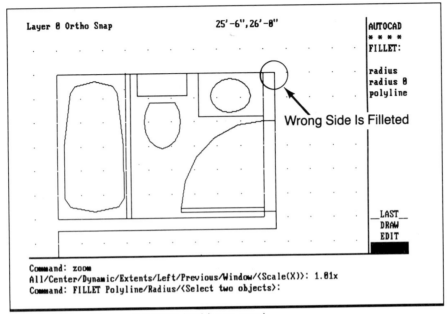

Figure 6.21:   The wall if Fillet had been used

lines at a corner in exactly the same manner as Fillet. Insert the kitchen drawing at the wall intersection at coordinate 15'-0", 25'-5". Pan your view so that the upper-right corner of the bathroom is in the center of the drawing area. Your view will look like Figure 6.22.

Insert a door on the unit wall at coordinate 23'-4", 30'-10". When you are prompted for a rotation angle, enter 270 or use the cursor (make sure ortho mode is on) to orient the door so that it is swinging into the unit. Make sure the door is on the Door layer. Add five-inch door jambs and break the header over the door the same way you did in Chapter 3 for the bathroom door (see Figure 6.23). Be sure the door jambs are on the Jamb layer.

To finish this end of the unit, draw the door header on the Ceiling layer. Then copy the top wall lines of the unit and the door header up five inches so they connect with the top end of the door jamb, as shown in Figure 6.24. Don't forget to include the short wall line from the door to the bathroom wall.

Now you need to extend the upper wall line five inches beyond the right side interior wall of the unit. To accomplish this, draw a reference line at a 45-degree angle from the upper-right corner of the unit at coordinate 29'-0", 30'-10" (see Figure 6.25). The length of this line is not important.

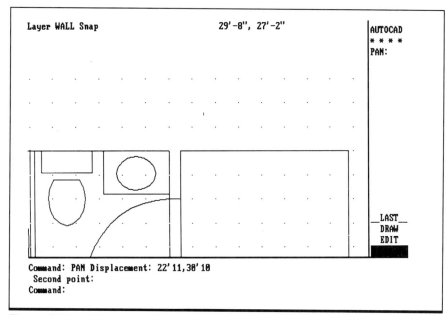

Figure 6.22: The view after using Pan

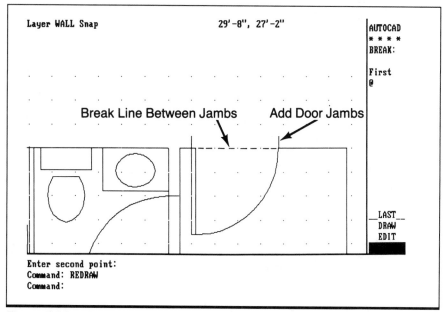

Figure 6.23: The door inserted and the jamb and header added

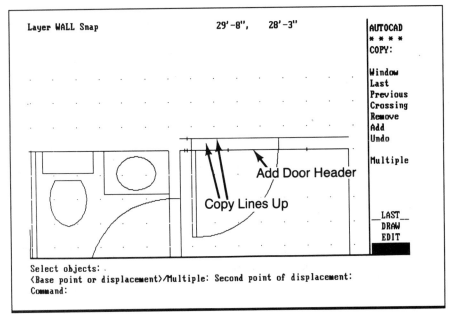

Figure 6.24: The other side of the wall

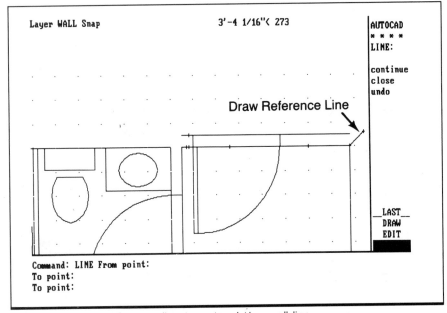

Figure 6.25: A reference line to extend the wall line

Now fillet this diagonal line with the wall line you wish to extend, then erase the diagonal line when you are done. Your drawing should look like Figure 6.26.

Repeat the process to extend the short wall line to the left of the door five inches beyond the left side of the unit. Use the Previous option on the Zoom menu to view the left side of the unit. This time draw your reference line at 135 degrees (see Figure 6.27).

Use the All option on the Zoom menu to view the entire drawing. Your drawing will look like Figure 6.28.

Now you will finish the balcony by adding a sliding glass door and rail. First, you will add the door jamb by drawing a short line, then moving and copying it into position to locate the door.

Zoom into the balcony area. Draw a line connecting the lower-right corner of the unit's interior to the upper-right corner of the balcony from coordinate 29'-0", 6'-5" to 29'-0", 6'-10". Move that line to the left 3'-6", then copy the line 7'-0" to the left. Change these lines to the Jamb layer. Break the wall lines between the two jambs using the First option in the Break menu. Do this by picking Break from the Edit menu, then pick the line you wish to break. Next pick First from the Break menu and proceed to pick the points on the

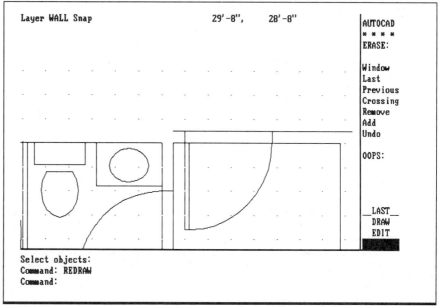

Figure 6.26: The wall line extended

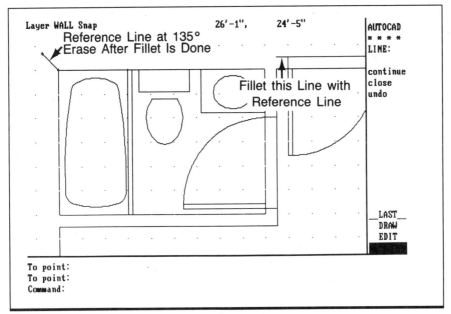

Figure 6.27: The left side wall line extended

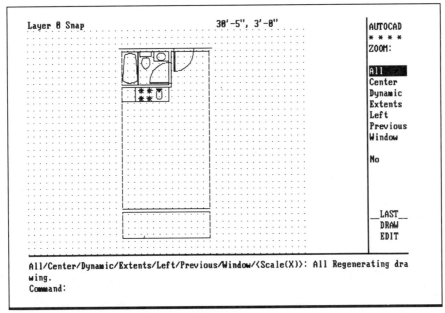

Figure 6.28: The unit plan thus far

ghosted line that intersect with the door jambs. Your drawing will look like Figure 6.29.

Add lines on the Ceiling layer to replace the broken lines. Now draw lines between the two jambs to indicate a sliding glass door (see Figure 6.30).

Copy the bottom line of the balcony vertically a distance of three inches to represent the rail. Create a new layer called F-rail and change this line to it. Add a five-inch horizontal line to the lower corners of the balcony as shown in Figure 6.30. Now use the Base command to set the base point at the lower-left corner of the balcony. Change the lines indicating walls to the Wall layer and the sliding glass door to the Door layer (see Figure 6.30). Zoom back to the previous view. Your drawing should look like Figure 6.31.

Your studio apartment unit plan is now complete. End out of the Unit file.

Now you will draw the apartment house's lobby. Create a new file called Lobby using the Unit file as a template. Erase the entire unit. Draw the lobby as shown in Figure 6.32.

As is usual in floor plans, the box with the cross through it indicates an elevator and the box with the row of vertical lines

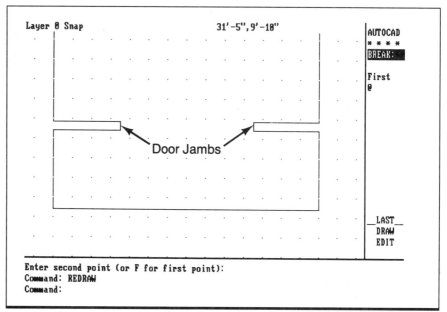

Figure 6.29: The door opening

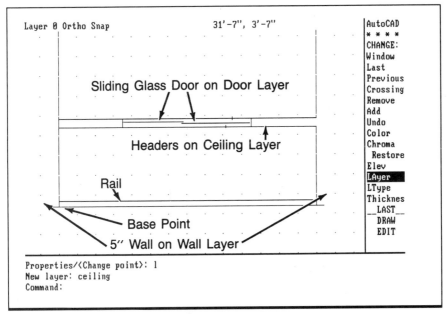

Figure 6.30: The sliding glass door

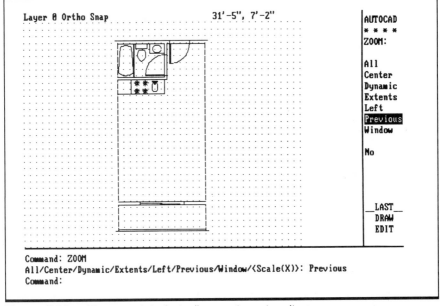

Figure 6.31: The completed studio apartment unit

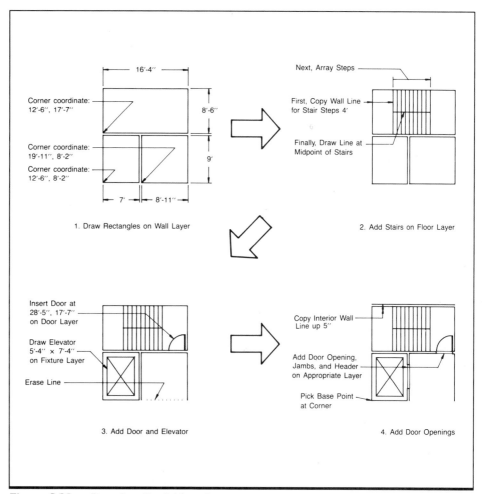

Figure 6.32: Drawing the lobby plan

indicates the stair shaft. Draw the three main rectangles representing the outlines of the stair shaft, the elevator shaft, and the lobby first. Then fill in the detail of the stairs, elevators, and door. To draw the stairs, copy the left wall of the stair shaft to the right a distance of four feet to create the first line representing the steps. Array this line in one row of seven columns using a ten-inch column spacing. Draw the center line dividing the two flights of stairs. Draw the elevator, insert the door, draw in the door jambs, and edit the door openings to add the door headers as you did in Chapter 4 for the bathroom.

Creating a Drawing Using Parts of the Current Drawing

You can create a separate stair drawing using the stair you've already drawn, and later use the drawing for a fire escape. Use the Wblock command and create a new file called Stair. Although you haven't turned the stair into a block, you can still use Wblock to turn it into a file. Start the Wblock command. At the prompt

File name:

enter Stair. At the next prompt

Block name:

press Return. By doing this, you are telling AutoCAD that you want to create a file from part of the drawing, rather than a block. A new prompt appears:

Insertion base point:

Pick the lower-right corner of the stair shaft at coordinate 28'-10", 17'-7". This tells AutoCAD the base point for the new drawing. At the object-selection prompt use a window to pick the stair shaft as shown in Figure 6.33.

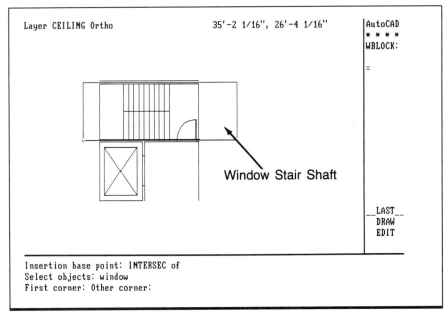

Figure 6.33: Window enclosing the stair shaft

When the stair shaft, including the door, has ghosted, press Return to confirm your selection. The stair disappears. Since you want the stair to remain in the lobby drawing, use the Oops command to bring it back. Once you are finished, end out of the Lobby file.

GETTING RID OF BLOCKS, LAYERS, LINE TYPES, SHAPES, AND STYLES

A template may contain blocks and layers you don't need in your new file. For example, the lobby you just completed contains the bathroom block because you used the Unit file as a template. Even though you erased this block, it remains in the drawing file's database. It is considered "unused" because it doesn't appear as part of the drawing. Such extra blocks can slow you down by increasing the amount of time needed to open the file. They can also unnecessarily increase the size of your file. There are two commands for getting rid of unused elements: Purge and Wblock.

Selectively Removing Unused Elements

The Purge command is used to remove unused individual blocks, layers, line types, shapes, and text styles from a drawing file. It must be the first command you enter after opening the file. For example, if you open a file from which you wish to purge some blocks, start adding lines, then issue the Purge command, AutoCAD gives you the message

The PURGE command cannot be used now.
★Invalid★

Open the Lobby file and pick Utility from the Root menu to bring up the Utility menu (see Figure 6.34). Then pick Purge. The following prompt appears:

Purge unused Blocks/LAyers/LTypes/SHapes/Styles/All:

You can now choose the category of elements you want to purge. Pick Blocks.

Purge block Border? <N>

appears. Border is a block that AutoCAD inserts automatically when you use the Setup option. It is the rectangle representing the sheet

Figure 6.34: *The Utility menu*

edge. Press Return to accept the default, N. The prompt

Purge block BATH? <N>

appears, giving you the opportunity to keep or purge the Bath block. Enter Y. This process continues until most of the blocks have been listed. Continue to enter Y to all the prompts until the Purge command is completed.

Now end out of this file. The Lobby file is now purged of most, but not all, of the unused blocks. In the next section, you will learn how to delete all the unused elements at once.

Removing All Unused Elements

The Purge command has its limitations. We already mentioned that it can be used only as the first command upon opening a file. Purge also does not remove nested blocks. For example, although you purged the Bath block from the Lobby file, it still contains the Tub and Toilet blocks that were nested in the Bath block. And last, using Purge is a time-consuming way to delete large numbers of elements.

The Wblock command enables you to remove *all* unused elements, including blocks, nested blocks, layers, line types, shapes, and styles, at any time in the editing session. You cannot select specific elements or types of elements to remove. Because a block you want to keep may be unused, you may want to keep a copy of the unpurged file.

Open the Lobby file again. Start Wblock and at the prompt

File name:

enter Lobby1. This tells AutoCAD to create a new file called Lobby1, which will be the Lobby file with the unused elements removed. If you pick the name of an existing file, you will get the following prompt:

A drawing with this name already exists.
Do you want to replace it? <N>

This keeps you from inadvertently writing over an existing file you want to keep. The next prompt

Block name:

appears. Enter an asterisk. This tells AutoCAD that you want to create a new file containing all the drawing elements of the current file, including settings. AutoCAD now saves the current file to the disk less all the unused blocks, layers, etc.

Now quit the Lobby file. Open the Lobby1 file and get a list of blocks by using the question mark option on the Insert menu. You get the following message:

Defined Blocks.
  DOOR
1 user blocks, 0 unnamed blocks.
All the unused blocks have been purged, leaving the Door block.

CONCLUSION

You have seen how you can use existing drawings to help you create new ones in many different ways. By understanding these capabilities, you can save yourself a good deal of time. Creative use of lines for reference points can also help you speed up drawing time. Try using the techniques you learned in this chapter to create new files from ones you have created on your own. Perhaps you have several symbols that are similar, but vary enough to warrant separate drawings for each one. Or you may need two separate drawings that use the same elements. You could draw one, then use it as a template for the other.

As your drawings become more complex, you will have to use different strategies to edit them. In the next chapter, you will assemble the components you have created into a larger file. You will then look at ways to edit and view a file more easily once it becomes very large.

Chapter 7

Managing a Large Drawing

NOW THAT YOU HAVE CREATED drawings of a typical apartment unit and the apartment house's lobby and stairs, you can assemble them to complete the first floor of the apartment house. As your drawing becomes larger, you will have to take a different approach to moving around in it and to editing it. You will find yourself using the Zoom and Pan commands more often, and along with that comes more frequent regeneration. Also, as the drawing becomes more dense, regeneration takes longer. In this chapter you will see how regeneration affects the time you spend on a drawing and how it can be controlled. You will also learn how to edit a large drawing and how to update a block once it has been changed.

ASSEMBLING THE PARTS

Open a new file, called Plan, to contain the drawing of the apartment house's first floor. Set up the drawing for a 1/8" = 1'-0" scale on an 18 x 24-inch drawing area. Use the Make option on the Layer menu to create a layer called Plan1. Turn the snap mode on, set the grid to five feet, and erase the border. Insert the unit drawing at coordinate 31'-5", 43'-8". Accept the default values at all the prompts since you want to insert this drawing just as you drew it.

If you have problems using your mouse to pick the exact point we specify, enter the values through the keyboard. Or you can move the cursor close to the specified point using your cursor, then switch to the cursor keys with the snap mode on and close in on the point.

Zoom into the apartment unit plan. Draw a line from the upper-right corner of the unit's interior at coordinate 45'-5", 72'-1" to the right three inches. Use the endpoint of that line to mirror the unit plan to the right. By mirroring the unit at the endpoint of the three-inch line, you will get a wall thickness of six inches between studio units. Keep the original unit plan in place. Your drawing should look like Figure 7.1.

Now erase the short line you used as a mirror reference and draw another line vertically from the same corner a distance of 24 inches. Use the endpoint of that line to mirror the two unit plans on a horizontal axis. Use the Extents option on the Zoom menu to get a view of the four plans. Your drawing will look like Figure 7.2.

The Extents option forces the entire drawing to fill the screen and leftmost side of the display area. Erase the reference line and copy the four units horizontally a distance of 28'-11", the width of two units. Insert the lobby at coordinate 89'-3", 76'-1". Copy all the

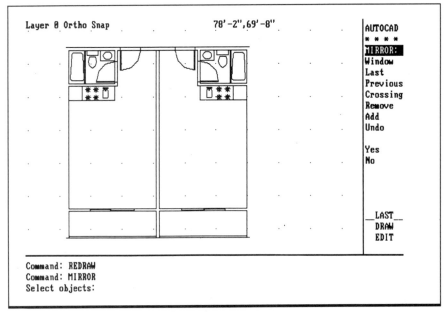

Figure 7.1:   The unit plan mirrored

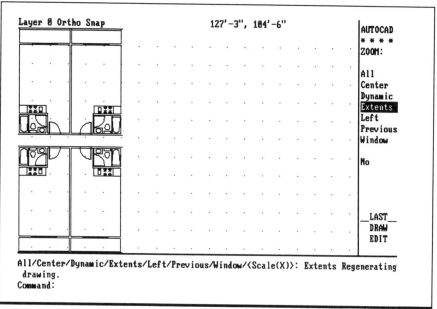

Figure 7.2: The unit plan duplicated four times

unit plans to the right 74'-7", the width of four units plus the width of the lobby. Now use the All option on the Zoom menu to view the entire drawing. Your display will look like Figure 7.3.

Now use the Save command to save this file to disk.

CONTROLLING REGENERATION

You may have noticed that the drawing takes considerably longer to regenerate than it did before. This is because AutoCAD must recalculate more information during Zoom, Pan, and other commands that regenerate the drawing. In this section, you will discover how to minimize the number of regenerations during an editing session, thus making it easier to create a large and complex drawing. You can control regeneration in three ways: by using the *virtual screen* to speed up zooming and panning, by saving views to return to without zooming, and by freezing layers that do not need to be viewed or edited.

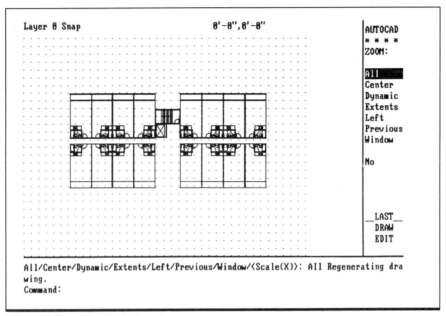

Figure 7.3: The Plan drawing

Using the Virtual Screen

As we mentioned in Chapter 1, AutoCAD uses two types of information to control the screen display and update the drawing database: floating-point calculation and integer-based calculation. When AutoCAD does a regeneration, it recalculates vector coordinates in the floating-point drawing database. Since this database is made up of real numbers, the recalculation time can be lengthy. AutoCAD then converts the drawing coordinates to screen pixel integer coordinates: the virtual screen. AutoCAD can recalculate these integer coordinates much faster than the floating-point coordinates when you do zooms and pans. As long as you select view windows within the virtual screen area, your zooming speed will be as fast as a redraw.

Redrawing is used to refresh the screen drawing area by clearing blips and restoring any lines that appear to get lost during editing. This can take as little as one-tenth the time of a regeneration. A typical architectural drawing can take three minutes and more to regenerate using a PC/AT or similar computer. At that rate, you can find yourself spending more time waiting for a drawing to regenerate than you spend on actual editing. With this in mind, you can appreciate the speed of redrawing while moving around in your drawing.

Figure 7.4 shows the relationship between the drawing database, the virtual screen, and the display area of the drawing editor.

The virtual screen is on by default. You can turn it off or on using the Viewres command on the Display menu. This command also controls the smoothness of line types, arcs, and circles when they appear in an enlarged view. With the virtual screen active, line types sometimes appear as continuous even though they are supposed to be dotted or dashed. Also, you may have noticed in previous chapters how arcs appeared to be segmented lines on the screen, though they always plotted as smooth curves. You can use Viewres to control the number of segments an arc appears to have. The fewer the segments, the faster the redraw and regeneration.

The size of the virtual screen is roughly determined by the most recent regeneration of the drawing. For example, if a Zoom All command causes the entire drawing to regenerate, the virtual screen is roughly the area defined by the drawing's limits. You can set the virtual screen area by setting the Limits check button to on, then issuing a Zoom All command. The virtual screen is then forced to the same area as the drawing limits. You can see the virtual screen dynamically by using the Dynamic option on the Zoom menu,or picking Dynamic from the Display pull-down menu.

Pick Zoom from the Display menu, then pick Dynamic. You will get a display that looks like Figure 7.5. You see several boxes and the drawing redrawing on the screen. The solid white box represents the drawing limits. The dotted box represents the current display area. The corner marks show the virtual screen area. The box that

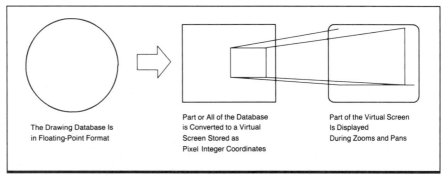

The Drawing Database Is
in Floating-Point Format

Part or All of the Database
is Converted to a Virtual
Screen Stored as
Pixel Integer Coordinates

Part of the Virtual Screen
Is Displayed
During Zooms and Pans

Figure 7.4:   *The relationship between the drawing database, the virtual screen, and the display area*

MASTERING AUTOCAD

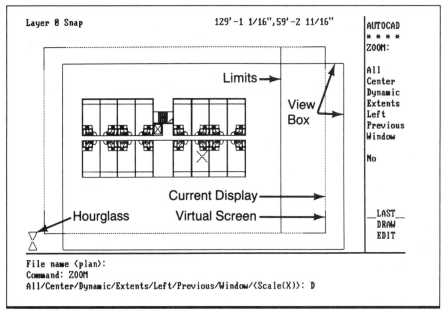

Figure 7.5: *The Dynamic Zoom display*

moves with your cursor input is your *view box*, which determines the next view you will select.

Press the pick button on your mouse. As you move the mouse from left to right, the lower-left corner of the view box remains stationary, while the opposite corner changes as you move your mouse. As you move the mouse up and down, the view box also moves up and down. This allows you to determine the window size of your zoom. If you make the view box too small, an hourglass appears in the lower-left corner of the screen to tell you that if you pick that view box, AutoCAD must regenerate the drawing to display it.

Notice how the view box maintains its proportion of width to height when you select a zoom window. AutoCAD forces the box to maintain the same proportions as the drawing area. If you were allowed to select a window in the manner you normally do, you would risk inadvertently picking a window outside the virtual screen, causing the drawing to regenerate. By forcing the view box to maintain the same proportions as the display, AutoCAD ensures that the window you pick is what will be displayed.

Adjust the size of the box to about a quarter of the display area, then press the pick button again. The view box is now smaller and it moves freely as it did before.

Now you can pick a view framed by the view box. Move it to a position outside the virtual screen. You will notice that the hourglass appears again. As you move the view box completely within the virtual screen, the hourglass disappears, telling you that view will not be regenerated. When you finally decide on a view, press Return to select it. The new view will be displayed.

Using Dynamic Zoom is another way to move from one part of the drawing to another without having to do a Zoom All to see the entire drawing. The Dynamic Zoom window does not display the entire drawing very quickly unless the view box is held still. If your drawing is dense and you are in a hurry, you can approximate a view position with the view box, and then, once the view is on the screen, pan to the exact position. An alternative is to stop the view box movement by lifting your mouse off the desktop until the entire drawing finishes redrawing, then select your view.

Another way to control regeneration is by turning off the Regenauto command on the Display menu. If you then use Pan, Zoom, or another command that automatically performs regeneration, AutoCAD tells you it is about to regenerate the drawing and asks if you are sure you want to proceed. Some commands that normally regenerate a drawing won't give you a regeneration prompt. When you globally edit attributes, redefine blocks, freeze and thaw layers, change the Ltscale setting, or change a text style, you must use the Regen command to display the effects of these commands. If you don't care whether you see the changes, then you won't have to regenerate the drawing. The drawing database is still updated when you save or end the file.

Saving Views

A few walls in the Plan drawing are not complete. You have to zoom into the areas that need work to add the lines, but these areas are spread out over the drawing. You could use the Dynamic option on the Zoom menu or the Display pull-down menu to view each area. Another way to edit widely separated areas is to first save views of the areas you want to work on, then jump from view to view. This technique is especially helpful when you know you will often want to return to a specific area of your drawing.

Pick the View command from the Display menu. At the prompt

VIEW ?/Delete/Restore/Save/Window:

pick Window. At the next prompt

View name to save:

enter 1. Pick a window enclosing the leftmost wall of the Plan draw-ing. Use coordinate 26'-3", 40'-1" for the first point and 91'-2", 82'-8" for the second. Repeat this procedure using Figure 7.6 as a guide to where to define your windows.

Now start the View command again, but this time pick the Restore option from the View menu and enter 1. Your screen dis-plays the first view you selected. Set your current layer to Wall and proceed to add the stairs and exterior walls of the building as shown in Figure 7.7.

Use the View command again to restore view 2. Then add the wall indicated in Figure 7.8. Continue to the other views and add the rest of the exterior walls as you have done in these examples. Use Fig-ure 7.9 as a guide to completing the views.

Now use the All option on the Zoom menu to view the entire drawing again. You may want to save the view to plot since the Plot command allows you to specify saved views. You can also save the overall view of the drawing to get a quick look at it from time to time.

Now save the Plan file to disk.

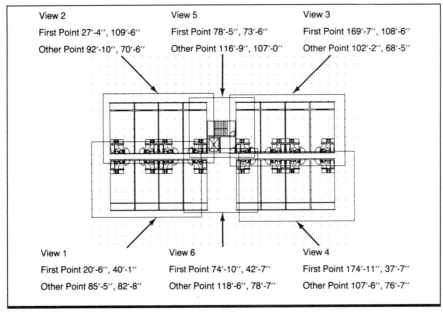

Figure 7.6: *Where to select view windows*

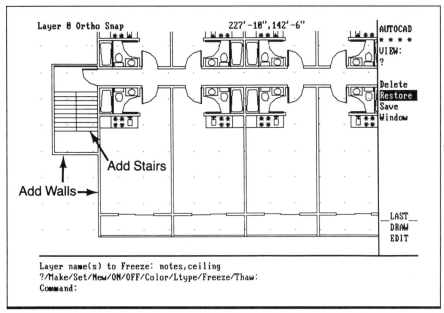

Figure 7.7: The stairs added to the restored view 1

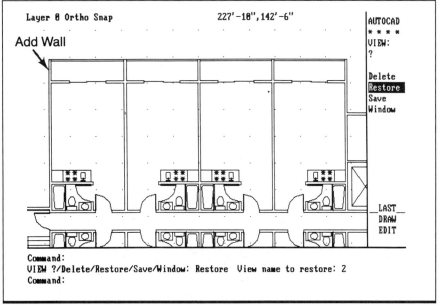

Figure 7.8: A wall added to the restored view 2

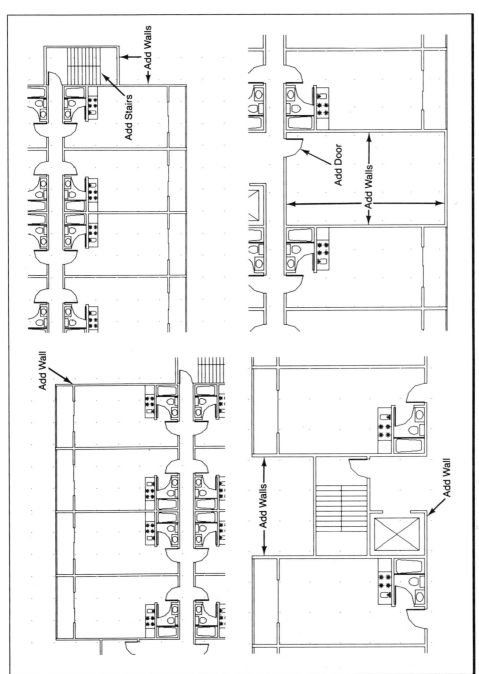

Figure 7.9: The rest of the walls added to views 3-6

Zooming and Panning During Other Commands

At times you may want to do something that requires you to pan beyond the current view while in the middle of another command. You can do this by using the Zoom, Pan, and View commands. For example, suppose you have view 1 on the screen and you want to draw a line from the lower-left corner of the building to the upper-right corner. You can start the Line command, pick the starting point of the line, then pick Pan from the Display side menu or pull-down menu and pan your view so that the upper-right corner of the building appears on the screen. Once the view appears, the Line command automatically continues and you can pick the other corner.

This only works within the virtual screen area, however, and you cannot use the Zoom subcommands All or Extents. If you save a view of the overall drawing, you can recall that view using the View command in place of Zoom All. If you are entering these commands through the keyboard, precede them with an apostrophe as in

'zoom

Commands that can be used in the middle of other commands are called *transparent commands*. Setvar, the command that allows you to access system variables, and the help question mark are also transparent commands. We will discuss Setvar in Chapters 12 and 14.

Freezing Layers to Control Regeneration Time

We mentioned earlier that you may wish to use the Off option to plot a drawing containing only selected layers. We also mentioned that the Freeze option on the Layer menu acts like the Off option, except that Freeze causes AutoCAD to ignore frozen layers when regenerating a drawing. By freezing layers that are not needed for reference or editing, you can speed up operations that automatically regenerate the drawing, such as redefining blocks and line type scales.

Freeze also affects blocks in a way that Off does not. Turn on all the layers, then turn off the Plan1 layer. Nothing happens because none of the objects were drawn on that layer. Now use the Freeze option to freeze the Plan1 layer. Every block you inserted disappears. Even though none of the objects within those blocks were drawn on layer Plan1, when Plan1 is frozen, so are the blocks assigned to that layer. Table 7.1 shows the relationships between blocks and layers.

	Freeze		Off	
	Layer A	**Layer B**	**Layer A**	**Layer B**
Objects on layer A	Off*	On	Off	On
Objects on layer B	On	Off	On	Off
Block containing objects on layer 0 inserted on layer B	On	Off	On	Off
Block containing objects on layer A inserted on layer B	Off	Off	Off	On

* An off in the matrix indicates that the screen does not display objects indicated in the left-hand column.

Table 7.1: *How freezing a layer containing blocks differs from turning off that layer*

You should consider the Freeze option when creating blocks and layers in your drawings. For example, you can insert several drawings as blocks on different layers. When you want to view a particular drawing, you can freeze all the layers except the one containing that drawing. You can also put parts of the drawing you may want to plot separately on different layers. For example, three floors in your apartment house plan may contain the same information with some variation from floor to floor. In this case, you can have one layer contain blocks of the objects common to all the floors. Another layer contains the blocks and objects specific to the first floor, and yet other layers contain information specific to the second and third floors. When you want to view or plot one floor, you can freeze the layers associated with the others. You will practice this technique in Chapter 15.

Using layers and blocks this way requires careful planning and record keeping. It also makes your files quite large, slowing down overall regeneration time and making it difficult to transfer files from your hard disk to floppy disks. If used successfully, however, it can save a great amount of time with drawings that use repetitive objects or that require similar information that can be overlayed.

Now thaw all the layers you froze and turn off the Ceiling layer.

ALTERING A PART

As you progress through a design project, you make countless revisions. If you are using traditional drafting methods, revising a drawing like the studio apartment floor plan takes a good deal of time. If the bathroom layout is changed, for example, you have to erase every occurrence of the bathroom and redraw it 16 times. If you are using AutoCAD, however, revising this drawing can be a very quick operation. The studio unit in your example can be updated throughout the drawing by editing the original Unit file, then replacing the current Unit block with the edited version. AutoCAD automatically updates all occurrences of the Unit block.

In the following example, we show you how this is accomplished. First you will edit the Unit file by adding a floor pattern. By doing this, you will also be introduced to the Hatch command. Next, you will update the Unit block in the Plan file to reflect the changes in the Unit file.

Open the Unit file and zoom into the bathroom and kitchenette area. Use the New option on the Layer menu to create a floor pattern layer called Flr-pat. Use the Make option on the Layer menu to create a layer called Layout. Pull-down menu users can use the Modify Layer dialog box to create these two layers with the New Layer input button, then set the current layer to Layout by picking the Current check box next to the Layer Name input button.

Now draw a line outlining the area you want to hatch (see Figure 7.10). You can use the Osnap overrides to select the intersections or endpoints of lines you are using to define the hatch area. When you get to the toilet seat, you will have to draw short line segments to follow the curve of the arc. Be sure the outlines are closed. Once you finish, turn off all the layers except the current one by using the asterisk wild card in place of the names of layers to be turned off. Press Return when AutoCAD asks if you are sure you want the current layer turned off.

Now start the Hatch command by picking Hatch from the Draw menu to bring up the Hatch menu, or pick Hatch from the Draw pull-down menu (see Figure 7.11). If you use the keyboard or the side menu to start this command, the prompt

Pattern (? or name/U,style):

appears. You can now select from the 41 patterns AutoCAD provides, or define a simple hatch pattern of your own. If your system does not display pull-down menus, pick U from the menu to tell AutoCAD you want to define your own hatch pattern.

Using Icons to Select Hatch Patterns

If you use the pull-down menu to select the Hatch command, an icon menu appears showing several hatch patterns (see Figure 7.12).

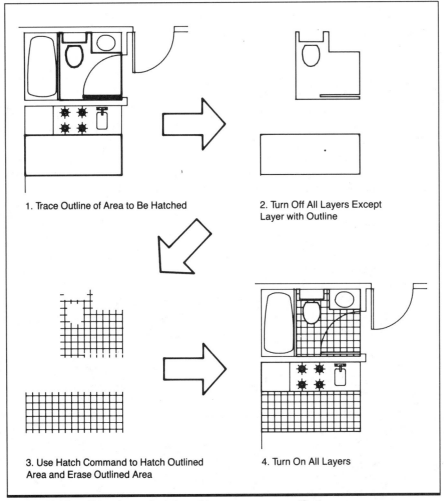

1. Trace Outline of Area to Be Hatched

2. Turn Off All Layers Except Layer with Outline

3. Use Hatch Command to Hatch Outlined Area and Erase Outlined Area

4. Turn On All Layers

Figure 7.10: Drawing a hatch pattern over a specified area

Each icon in the menu has a small box to the lower left. When you move the arrow to that box, it is highlighted. You will also notice two blank boxes labeled Next and Exit to the lower right of the icon menu. Highlight the box labeled Next and press the pick button. Another group of hatch patterns appears. Pick the box labeled Next again and a third group of icons appears (see Figure 7.12).

Now pick the box labeled Beginning. As you can see, you can scroll through three groups of icon menus to select any of 41 patterns available. Pick the box labeled Previous/User in the upper-left corner of the first icon menu.

Completing the Hatch Pattern

Once you have selected a hatch pattern, the prompt

Angle for crosshatch lines <0>:

appears. You get this prompt no matter which method you use to start the Hatch command. You now have the option to set an angle for the hatch pattern. Press Return to accept the default, 0 degrees. At the

Spacing between lines <1.0000>:

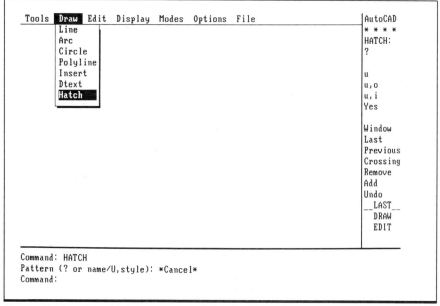

Figure 7.11: The Hatch menu and the Draw pull-down menu

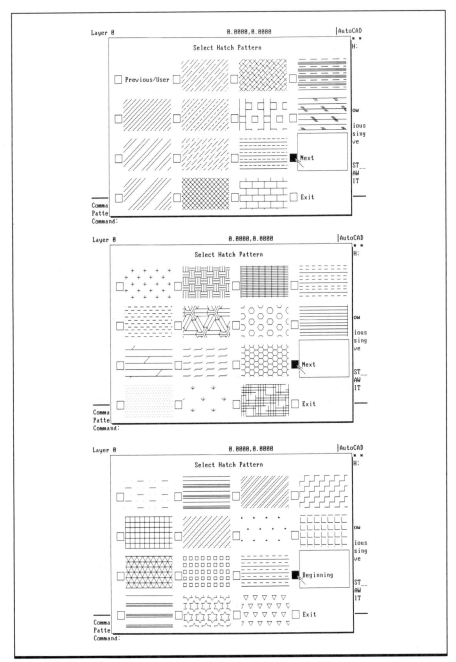

Figure 7.12: The three hatch pattern icon menus

prompt, enter 6" for six-inch tiles. At the

Double hatch area? <N>

prompt, pick Yes. This tells AutoCAD you want the hatch pattern to run both vertically and horizontally. At the object-selection prompt, pick Window and window the entire area you've drawn. The hatch pattern appears.

If you want to use a different hatch pattern and you do not have access to the icon menu, you can get a list of AutoCAD's predefined patterns by entering a question mark at the pattern name prompt. If you are adventurous, you can even create your own predefined hatch patterns—but don't attempt it unless you feel you are quite familiar with AutoCAD. If you are interested, read Chapter 18 or the appendix on customization in the *AutoCAD Reference Manual.*

Now change the hatch pattern to the Flr-pat layer. The pattern disappears because it is now on a layer that is turned off. Erase all the lines on the current layer. Turn the other layers back on. Your drawing will look like Figure 7.13.

The hatch pattern acts like a block in that the entire pattern is one object. If you find you need to edit it, you can use the Explode command to unblock the pattern just like a block.

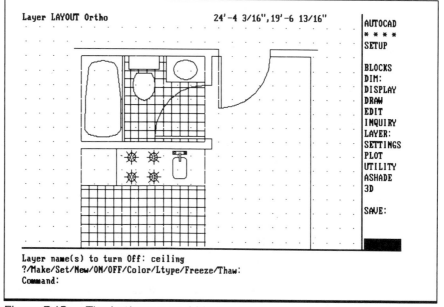

Figure 7.13: *The bathroom and kitchenette with floor pattern added*

In some situations, you may have to locate the hatch pattern precisely. The pattern uses the same origin as the snap point and the drawing, 0,0. You can change the snap origin and thus the hatch pattern origin by using the Rotate option on the Snap menu. To do this, you pick Snap from the Settings menu, then pick Rotate from the Snap menu. The prompt

ROTATE Base point (0.0000,0.0000):

appears. You can select a point on the drawing either by using the screen cursor or by specifying a point through the keyboard. Once you have done this, your snap points are aligned with this new origin. The next time you draw a hatch pattern, it will originate from this point.

After you pick a point, the prompt

Rotation angle (0):

appears. At this prompt, you can specify a new rotation angle for the screen cursor, grid, and snap points. Its current setting, 0, allows you to draw vertical and horizontal lines. If you enter a new angle, your cursor, snap points, and grid will rotate to that new angle. If you use the ortho mode, your lines will be forced to the new angle or 90 degrees to that angle. If you enter 45, for example, the grid and cursor will change to a 45-degree angle. This is similar to having an adjustable triangle where you can specify a different angle from horizontal.

If you like, try redrawing the hatch pattern after specifying a new snap base point to see how you can control the position of the pattern. Now end out of the Unit file.

Updating Blocks

Since you changed the apartment unit plan, you need to update it in your Plan drawing. Start by opening the Plan file. When the drawing editor appears, press Control-C to cancel the initial regeneration. You don't have to wait for the drawing to regenerate to edit it, and canceling this regeneration can save some time when you update blocks. Start the Insert command. When you are prompted for the name of the block to insert, enter

unit =

Your prompt displays a series of messages telling you that Auto-CAD is ignoring duplicate blocks. Then, unless you have Regenauto turned off, the drawing regenerates. At the insertion point prompt, cancel the Insert command by pressing Control-C, because the Unit block is now updated. If Regenauto is turned off, you must use the Regen command to force a regeneration of the drawing before the updated Unit block will appear on the display, even though the drawing database has been updated.

Now zoom into one of the units. You will see that the floor tile appears in the unit as you drew it in the Unit file (see Figure 7.14).

You must be careful about updating nested blocks. For example, if you had modified the Toilet block while editing the Unit file, then updated the Unit drawing in the Plan file, the old Toilet block would not be updated. This is because even though the toilet is part of the Unit file, it is still an individual block in the Plan file and AutoCAD will not modify it unless specifically instructed to do so. In this situation, you must edit the original Toilet file, then update it in the Plan file just as you did with the Unit plan.

Substituting Blocks

In this example, you updated a block in your Plan file by using the equal sign with the Insert command. You can also replace a block with another block or file. The operation is the same, except that when you enter the name of the block to be replaced, you add an equal sign and the name of the block to replace it with, as in

Block name (or ?) <*default*>: unit = *altrnate*

You can use this method of replacing blocks if you would like to see how changing one element of your project can change your design. For example, you could draw three different apartment unit plans, each with a different name. One might be a low-cost alternative, the next a medium-priced alternative, and the last a very expensive alternative. You could then create and plot three different apartment house drawings in a fraction of the time it would take you to do it by hand.

You can also use block substitution to reduce a drawing's complexity and speed up regeneration, instead of using the virtual screen. To do this, you temporarily replace large, complex blocks with schematic versions of those blocks. For example, you could replace the Unit block in the Plan drawing with another drawing that contains just a line representation of the walls. You still have the wall lines for reference when inserting other symbols or adding mechanical or electrical information, but the drawing regenerates much faster.

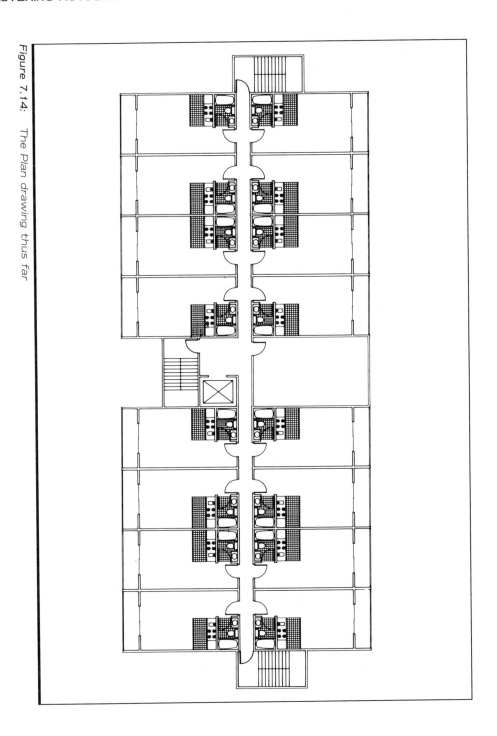

Figure 7.14: The Plan drawing thus far

When it comes time to do the final plot, you reinsert the original Unit block showing every detail.

CONCLUSION

Speed is always important when you are doing computer-aided drafting. With some intelligent use of AutoCAD commands, you can save a lot of time.

You may want to experiment with some of the options we discussed but didn't use in the exercises, such as turning off Regenauto, using different snap rotation settings, or substituting blocks. You may want to try to fill in some of the details in the Plan drawing, such as closet space in the units. If you do, save a copy of the files you created in this chapter to use in future exercises.

In the next chapter, you will learn how to enter and edit text in AutoCAD drawings.

Chapter 8

Using Text

ONE OF THE MORE TEDIOUS DRAFTING TASKS is applying notes to your drawing. Anyone who has had to draft a large drawing containing lots of notes knows the full effects of writer's cramp. AutoCAD not only makes this job go faster by allowing you to type your notes, it enables you to create more professional-looking notes by using a variety of fonts, type sizes, and type styles.

In this chapter you will add notes to your apartment house plan. In the process, you will explore some of AutoCAD's text creation and editing features. You will learn how to control the size, slant, type style, and orientation of text, and how to *import* external text files.

USING TEXT AS LABELS

In this first section you will add simple labels to your Unit drawing to identify the general design elements: the bathroom, kitchenette, and living room. Start AutoCAD and open the Unit file. Then turn off the Flr-pat layer. Otherwise, the floor pattern you added previously will obscure the text you will enter in this chapter.

Entering Text

It is a good idea to keep your notes on a separate layer so you can plot drawings containing only the graphic information or freeze the notes layer to save regeneration time. Start the Layer command and use the Make option on the Layer menu to create a layer called Notes. You can also use the Modify Layer command on the Modes pull-down menu. Notes is the layer on which you will keep all your text information. Go to the Draw menu and pick Next. Then pick Text to bring up the Text menu (see Figure 8.1).

At the prompt

TEXT Start point or Align/Center/Fit/Middle/Right/Style:

pick the starting point for the text you are about to enter, just below the kitchenette at coordinate 16'-2", 21'-8". By picking a point, you are accepting the default justification, left justification.

You also have five other options for justifying your text: Right, Center, Middle, Fit, and Align. If you choose the Right option, your text is justified on the right instead of the left. Center and Middle cause the first line of text to be centered on the starting point. The difference between these subcommands is that Center uses the starting point as a baseline for the text, while Middle centers the text on the starting point both vertically and horizontally. If you are entering a column of

Figure 8.1: The Text menu

text, each line is centered. Figure 8.2 shows you the differences between the Center and Middle options.

The subcommands Fit and Align allow you to specify a dimension within which the text must fit. For example, you may want the word Refrigerator to fit within the 26-inch-wide box representing the refrigerator. To do this, you could use either the Fit or the Align option. Fit asks you for a text height, then stretches or compresses the letters to fit within the width and text height you specify. You use this option when the text must be a consistent height throughout the drawing and you don't care about distorting the font. Align automatically adjusts the text height to fit within the specified width without distorting the font. You use this option where it is important to maintain the font's shape and proportion. Figure 8.3 shows you how these options work.

At the next prompt

Height <0'-0 3/16">:

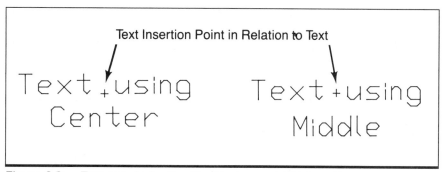

Figure 8.2: *Text inserted using the Center and Middle options*

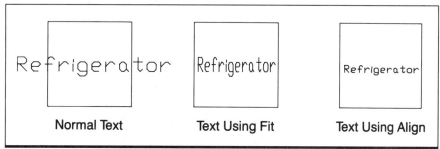

Figure 8.3: *The word Refrigerator as it appears normally, using the Fit option, and using the Align option*

enter 6" to indicate the text height. You may wonder why you would want the text to be so high. Remember that you are drawing at full scale and anything you draw will be reduced in the plotted drawing. We will discuss text height in more detail later in this chapter.

At the next prompt

Insertion angle <0>:

press Return to accept the default, 0 degrees. You can specify any angle other than horizontal if you wish; for example, if you want your text to be aligned with a rotated object. At the next prompt

Text:

enter the word Kitchenette. If you make a typing error, you must back up to the error with the Backspace key, then retype the rest of the word. Press Return and the word appears, beginning at the point you selected.

Now press Return again to restart the Text command. Notice how the word Kitchenette ghosts. This tells you that if you don't enter a point to determine the beginning of the next line of text, AutoCAD will place the text below the ghosted line. This feature allows you to stop while you are entering a column of text, do something else, then return to the last line to continue your note.

This time you want to label the bathroom. Pick a point to the right of the door swing at coordinate 19'-11", 26'-5". The next prompt

Height <0'-6">:

displays six inches as the new default text height. Press Return to accept the default. Press Return again to accept the default insertion angle. At the text prompt, enter Bath. Figure 8.4 shows how your drawing should look. The text is in the default font, Txt; we discuss fonts later in this chapter.

Understanding Text and Scale

Text scale conversion is a concept many people have difficulty grasping. As you discovered in previous chapters, AutoCAD allows you to draw at full scale, that is, to represent distances as values equivalent to the actual size of the object. When you later plot the drawing you tell AutoCAD what scale you wish to plot it to and the program reduces the drawing accordingly. This allows you the freedom to input

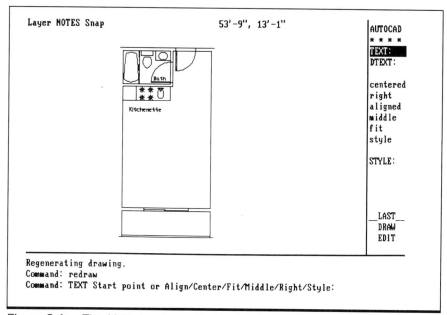

```
Layer NOTES Snap                53'-9", 13'-1"          AUTOCAD
                                                        * * * *
                                                        TEXT:
                                                        DTEXT:

                                                        centered
                                                        right
                                                        aligned
                                                        middle
                                                        fit
                                                        style

                                                        STYLE:



                                                        _LAST_
                                                         DRAW
                                                         EDIT

Regenerating drawing.
Command: redraw
Command: TEXT Start point or Align/Center/Fit/Middle/Right/Style:
```

Figure 8.4:   *The Unit drawing with the kitchenette and bath labeled*

measurements at full scale and not worry about converting them to various scales every time you enter a distance. Unfortunately, this feature also creates problems when you enter text and dimensions. Just as the Setup option converts the plotted sheet size to an enlarged size equivalent to full scale in the drawing editor, you have to convert your text size to its equivalent at full scale.

Imagine you are drawing the Unit plan at full size on a very large sheet of paper. When you are done with this drawing, it will be reduced to a scale that will allow it to fit on an 8½ x 11-inch sheet of paper. So, you have to make your text quite large to keep it legible once it is reduced. This means that if you want text to appear 1/8" high when the drawing is plotted, you must convert it to a considerably larger size when you draw it. To do this, you multiply the desired height of the final plotted text by a scale conversion factor. If your drawing is at 1/8" = 1' scale, you multiply the desired text height, 1/8", by the scale conversion factor of 96 found in Table 3.3 to get a height of 12". This is the height you must make your text to get 1/8"-high text in the final plot. Table 8.1 shows you some other examples of text height to scale.

Drawing Scale	Scale Factor	AutoCAD Drawing Height for 1/8"-High Text
1/16" = 1'-0"	192	24.0"
1/8" = 1'-0"	96	12.0"
1/4" = 1'-0"	48	6.0"
1/2" = 1'-0"	24	3.0"
3/4" = 1'-0"	16	2.0"
1" = 1'-0"	12	1.5"
1/2" = 1'-0"	8	1.0"
3" = 1'-0"	4	0.5"

Table 8.1:   1/8-inch-high text converted to size for various drawing scales

ENTERING A COLUMN OF TEXT

You will often want to enter a note or description of an object that requires more than one line of text. You have two options at your disposal for this purpose: the Text and Dtext commands. This section discusses them.

Continuing Text from Where You Left Off

We mentioned that you can end the Text command, do something else, then return to the Text command and continue to add text in a column below the last line you entered. This exercise shows you the process.

Using the Text command, place the word Entry by the entrance door at coordinate 24'-0", 26'-5". Now zoom into that area. Start the Text command again and press Return at the text starting point prompt. The text prompt appears (skipping the height and insertion angle prompts). Enter the dimensions 6'-0" x 7'-0". Then press Return three times until the text prompt appears again. Enter the words "to the kitchenette," to indicate that the previous dimension entered is the dimension of the studio entry from the door to the

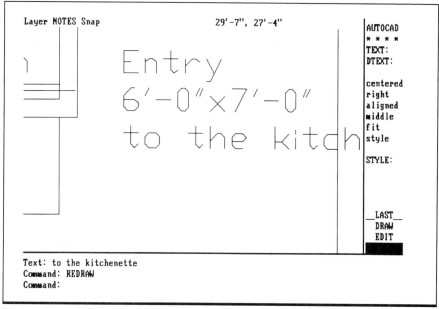

```
Layer NOTES Snap          29'-7", 27'-4"              AUTOCAD
                                                      * * * *
  )                                                   TEXT:
                                                      DTEXT:
         Entry
                                                      centered
         6'-0"x7'-0"                                  right
                                                      aligned
                                                      middle
         to the kitch                                 fit
                                                      style

                                                      STYLE:



                                                      _LAST_
                                                       DRAW
                                                       EDIT

Text: to the kitchenette
Command: REDRAW
Command:
```

Figure 8.5:   *The column of text you just entered*

kitchenette. You should have something that looks like Figure 8.5.

As you can see, you can continue adding text to your last entered line by pressing Return at the text starting point prompt.

Using Dtext to Enter Notes

Another way of entering text is to use the Dtext command. Dtext allows you to see your text as you type, just as it will appear on your drawing.

Zoom back to your previous view, then go to the Text menu again and pick Dtext. You can also pick Dtext from the Draw pull-down menu. Notice that the same starting point prompt appears as when you use the Text command. Pick a point on the balcony at coordinate 19'-8", 4'-4". Press Return twice to accept the default height and angle. When the text prompt appears, you will notice a box where you selected the point to start your text. This box shows you the height of your text. Enter the word Balcony. As you type, the letters appear on the drawing. When you press Return, the box moves down one line ready for you to type the next line (see Figure 8.6). You can enter another line of text, or you can press Return again to end the Dtext command. Press Return to end Dtext.

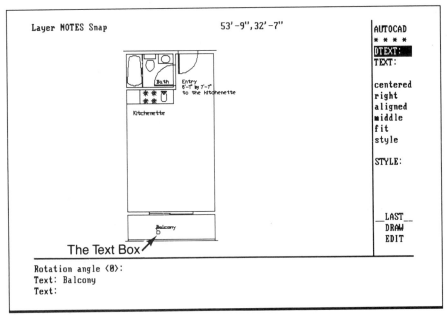

Figure 8.6:   *The word Balcony added*

The Dtext command affords a more natural way to enter text than the Text command, and it allows you to see where the text will end up when you need to make sure your text will fit. Dtext is easier to use than the Text command because you can back up all the way to the beginning of your text column to make corrections.

CHOOSING FONTS AND SPECIAL CHARACTERS

AutoCAD offers 20 fonts that can be set up to display in a number of different ways. These include two foreign fonts, Greek and Cyrillic. Symbols for astronomy, mapping, math, meteorology, and music are also provided. You can compress or expand these fonts and symbols, or you can modify them to create different *type styles.* Figure 8.7 shows you the fonts available with AutoCAD.

We should mention that the more complex the font, the longer it takes AutoCAD to regenerate your drawing. Before you choose a font for a particular job, consider how much text the drawing will contain. Use the Txt font if you like its looks; it regenerates the fastest. Monotxt is a fixed-width font (like a typewriter font) that is

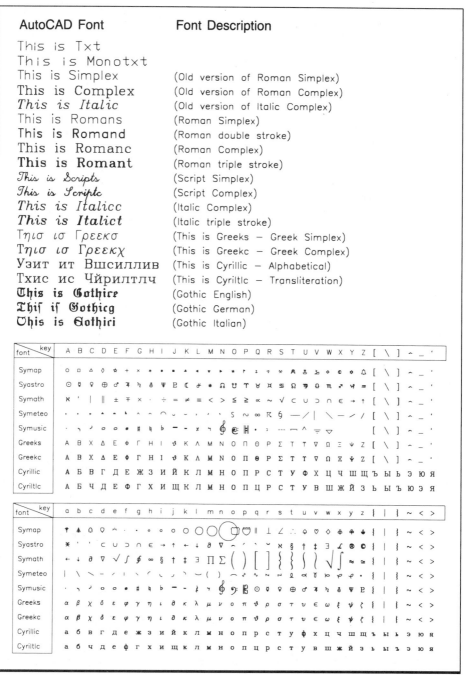

Figure 8.7: The AutoCAD script and symbol fonts

MASTERING AUTOCAD

useful for aligned columns of numbers or notes (see Figure 8.8). If you want something less boxy looking, you can use the Romans font. Use the Romanc, Italicc, and other more complex fonts sparingly as they will slow down the drawing regeneration considerably. Use the more complex fonts where you want a fancier type style, such as in drawing titles, or labels in an exploded parts diagram (see Figure 8.9). You could use the Greeks font in conjunction with the Symath symbols for mathematical text (see Figure 8.10).

AutoCAD's fonts are contained in the files with the .SHX extension in your AutoCAD directory. Although these are the only fonts you get with AutoCAD, you can get others from third-party software companies. Some third-party vendors offer a wide range of

Txt Font

Room #	Door #	Thick	Rate	Matrl	Const
116	116	1 3/4'	20 MIN	WOOD	SOLID CORE
114	114	1 3/4'	20 MIN	WOOD	SOLID CORE
112	112	1 3/4'	20 MIN	WOOD	SOLID CORE
110	---	1 3/4'	45 MIN	METAL	MINERAL CORE
108	108	1 3/4'	20 MIN	WOOD	SOLID CORE
106	106	1 1/2'	NO RATE	WOOD	HOLLOW
102	102	1 1/2'	NO RATE	WOOD	HOLLOW
104	104	1 3/4'	20 MIN	WOOD	SOLID CORE
107	107	1 3/4'	45 MIN	METAL	MINERAL CORE
105	105	1 3/4'	20 MIN	WOOD	SOLID CORE
101	101	1 3/4'	20 MIN	WOOD	SOLID CORE

Monotxt Font

Room #	Door #	Thick	Rate	Matrl	Const
116	116	1 3/4'	20 MIN	WOOD	SOLID CORE
114	114	1 3/4'	20 MIN	WOOD	SOLID CORE
112	112	1 3/4'	20 MIN	WOOD	SOLID CORE
110	---	1 3/4'	45 MIN	METAL	MINERAL CORE
108	108	1 3/4'	20 MIN	WOOD	SOLID CORE
106	106	1 1/2'	NO RATE	WOOD	HOLLOW
102	102	1 1/2'	NO RATE	WOOD	HOLLOW
104	104	1 3/4'	20 MIN	WOOD	SOLID CORE
107	107	1 3/4'	45 MIN	METAL	MINERAL CORE
105	105	1 3/4'	20 MIN	WOOD	SOLID CORE
10 1	10 1	1 3/4'	20 MIN	WOOD	SOLID CORE

Figure 8.8:   *Columns in the Txt and Monotxt fonts*

fonts, including Helvetica, Times Roman, and monospaced versions of Roman fonts. One notable product, CAD Lettering Systems Lettercase, offers accurate renditions of popular fonts in both outline and solid forms, which provide the near-typeset-quality text you need for applications where the text appearance is important, such as desktop-publishing line art. Both the accuracy of the letter forms and the solid fills required by large text make it nearly impossible to create high-quality fonts using the AutoCAD .SHX file format. CAD Lettering Systems solves the problem by making each letter a drawn object and using it as a drawing file. Text is entered and

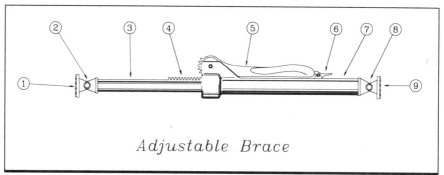

Figure 8.9:   *Italic font used as title of parts diagram*

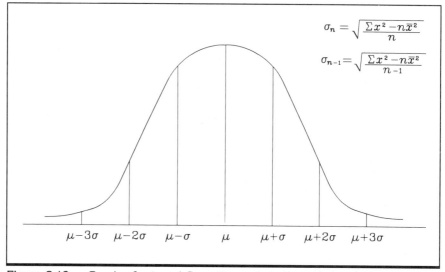

Figure 8.10:   *Greeks font and Symath symbols in mathematical text*

edited using an AutoLISP program provided with the fonts (see Figure 8.11).

You can also obtain high-quality text by entering it with a desktop-publishing program, such as PageMaker or Ventura. However, drawing size is limited by the output size used by the desktop-publishing program. See Chapter 13 for more information on using PageMaker and Ventura with AutoCAD.

If you are willing to spend the time, you can create your own fonts. *Advanced Techniques in AutoCAD*, by Robert M. Thomas (SYBEX, 1987) gives instructions for creating fonts, but keep in mind that it can be a very time-consuming process.

Adding Special Characters

AutoCAD offers the ability to add special characters to your text. For example, you can add the degrees symbol to a number or underscore text. To accomplish this, you need to use a double percent sign in conjunction with a special code (see Table 8.2). For example, to underline text, you enclose it with the underline code. To get the following text

This is <u>underscored</u> text.

you would enter:

This is %%uunderscored%%u text.

Figure 8.11: A comparison of AutoCAD, CAD Lettering Systems, and typeset fonts

Overscore operates in the same manner. You just place the other codes in the correct positions for the symbols they represent. For example, to enter

100.5°

you would type

100.5%%d

Creating and Selecting a Type Style

To use a font, you must create a type style using the Style command. Style enables you to create a type style based on any font you choose. It allows you to specify a height, slant the font as in an italic style, and condense or expand the font. It also asks you to name the style since you can have many variations of one font in a drawing. The name can be anything you want; type style names have no relation to font names.

Now you will create a new type style using the Style command. Pick Style from the Text side menu. The prompt

Text style name (or ?) <STANDARD>:

Code	Description
%%o	Toggles overscore on and off
%%u	Toggles underscore on and off
%%d	Places a degrees sign where the code occurs
%%p	Places a plus-minus sign where the code occurs
%%%	Forces a single percent sign. This is useful where a double percent sign must be entered or when a percent sign must be entered in conjunction with another code
%%nnn	Allows the use of extended ASCII characters when these characters are used in a text definition file. The nnn is the three-digit value representing the character

Table 8.2: Codes for adding special characters to AutoCAD text

appears. Enter the name Note. The next prompt

Font file <txt>:

appears. Enter Romans to select the Romans font. If you are using version 2.6 or earlier, enter Simplex. The next prompt appears.

Height <0'-0">:

If you accept the 0 value here, you will be prompted for a height every time you use the Text and Dtext commands. If you need to use several different text heights in a drawing, you may want to keep the text height at 0. However, if you are using only two or three heights, you would be better off creating two or three different type styles having different heights. Once you enter a value at this prompt, it becomes the new default height for this style.

Enter a height of 12". The next prompt appears.

Width factor <1.00>:

At this prompt, you can compress or expand the Romans font. You may find that you need a compressed font to fit into tight spaces. Or you may want to expand a font because of some graphic design consideration (see Figure 8.12).

Enter .8. The next prompt

Obliquing angle <0>:

allows you to slant the font backwards or forwards (see Figure 8.13). This allows you to give an italic look to any font but it doesn't slow down regeneration the way the Italic font does.

Press Return to accept the default, 0. The next prompt

Backwards? <N>

allows you to have the text appear backwards as if in a mirror (see Figure 8.14). You may want to do this when using both hand drafting and computer drafting on the same sheet. You plot the drawing

---

This is the Complex font expanded by 1.4

This is the Complex font using a width factor of 1

This is the Complex font compressed by .6

Figure 8.12: *Examples of compressed and expanded fonts*

backwards on the back of the sheet, then add other parts of the drawing by hand on the front. By doing this, you can hand draft on one side without having to worry about accidentally erasing or smudging the plotted side. This means, however, that the graphics of your AutoCAD drawing must also be backwards.

Press Return to accept the default. The next prompt

Upside-down? <N>

allows you to set the style to appear upside down, rather than entering the text, then rotating it (see Figure 8.15).

Press Return to accept the default, N. The last prompt

Vertical? <N>

allows you to arrange lines of text vertically (see Figure 8.16).

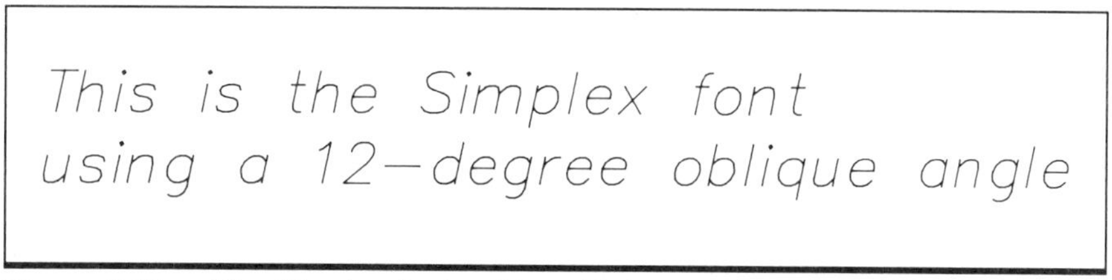

This is the Simplex font using a 12-degree oblique angle

Figure 8.13:   The Simplex font with a 12-degree oblique angle

Figure 8.14:   A text style using the backwards option

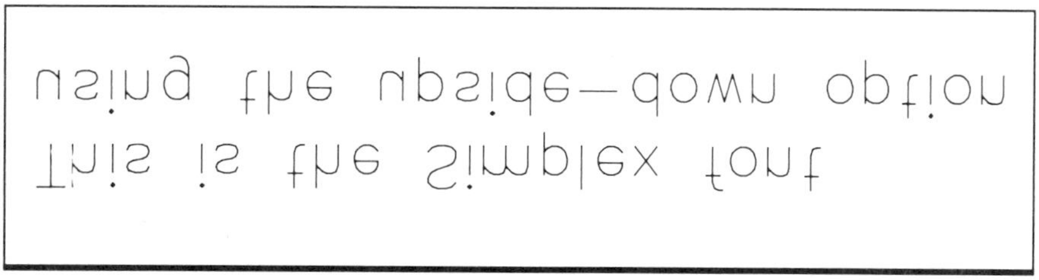

Figure 8.15:   A text style using the upside-down option

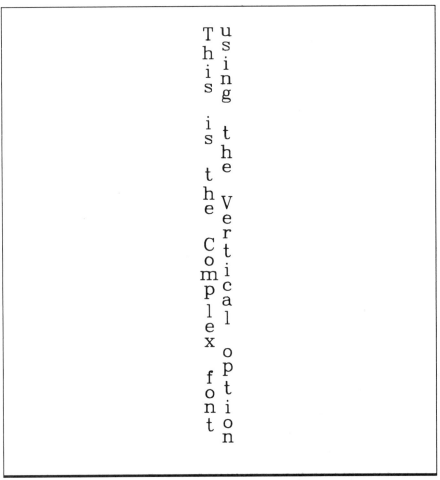

Figure 8.16: A text style using the vertical option

The last prompt

NOTE is now the current text style.

tells you that now when you enter text, it will be in the style you just created, Note.

Selecting a Type Style from the Icon Menus

If your system supports the advanced user interface, an icon menu is available that allows you to visually select the font you

want to use. Pick Fonts from the Options pull-down menu (see Figure 8.17). An icon menu appears displaying seven fonts and two buttons labeled Next and Exit. This menu works the same way the
hatch pattern icon menu works. You can select a font by highlighting the pick button to the lower left of the font you want, or you
can use the Next button to display more fonts. The Exit button cancels the font-selection operation. Pick Next to view the next group
of fonts. Pick Next again to view the last group of fonts and symbols. Note that a button labeled Beginning appears in place of the
Next button. This button brings you back to the first group of icons
(see Figure 8.18).

Pick the Beginning button, then pick the Roman Simplex button.
The icon menu disappears and the following prompt appears:

Font file <txt>: romans Height <0'-0">:

Select style options as desired. The rest of the command operates
exactly as if you had entered the Style command from the side
menu or through the keyboard.

Renaming a Type Style

If you used the icon menu to select a font, the prompt will read

ROMANS is now the current text style.

Romans is the default name AutoCAD gives to any style that uses
this font when you select it from the icon menu. However, you
want to call this font Note. To do this, pick Rename from the Utility
side menu. The following prompt appears:

RENAME Block/LAyer/LType/Style/View:

The Rename side menu appears (see Figure 8.19). Pick Style from
the side menu. The prompt then asks

Old text style name:

Enter Romans. At the next prompt

New text style name:

enter the word Note. You have just renamed the text style you created using the icon menu.

As you can see, the Rename command allows you to rename
blocks, layers, line types, and views as well as text styles.

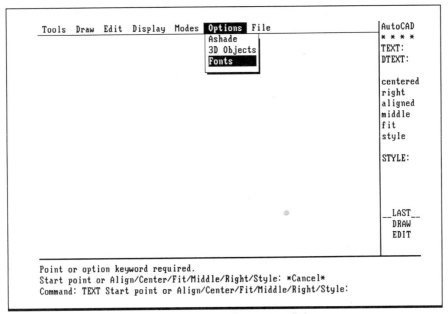

Figure 8.17:   *The Fonts option on the Options pull-down menu*

Selecting a Type Style

Now start the Dtext command and pick the Centered option. Pick a point near the center of the living room at coordinate 21'-11", 15'-2". You will get the insertion angle prompt, but not the text size prompt. For the text, enter Living room. Then press Return again to exit the Dtext command. Notice how the text centered on the point you selected.

When you use the Style command, your default style becomes the one you most recently edited or created. You can use the Style option from the Text and Dtext menus to select a style you create by name. Start the Text command and pick Style from the Text menu. The prompt

Style name (or ?) <NOTE>:

appears. You can now enter a question mark to get a list of available styles, enter the name of an available style, or press Return to accept Note, the current style.

Enter Standard. The starting point prompt appears again, allowing you to pick a point to locate your text. Pick the Center option from the Text menu, then pick the point at coordinate 21'-11", 14'-4". This

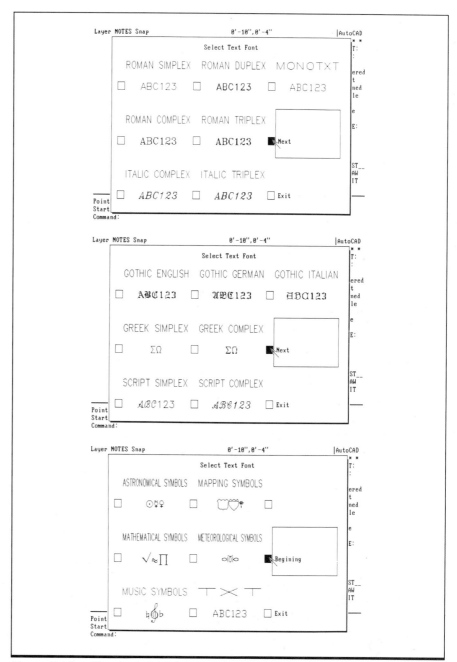

Figure 8.18: The text font icon menus

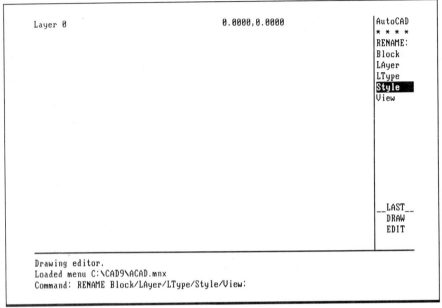

Figure 8.19: *The Rename side menu*

time the height prompt appears because you are now using a font whose height is set to 0. Notice how the default height is still at the last size you selected. Press Return to accept the default height. Press Return again to accept the default angle, then enter 14'-0" by 16'-5".

Zoom into this group of text. Now you can see the different styles you entered (see Figure 8.20). The words Living room use a smoother letter form than the dimensions 14'-0" by 16'-5".

Start the Dtext command and at the starting point prompt press Return. The box indicating the text location appears just below the last text entry, and the angle prompt does not appear. Enter 230 square feet. Notice how the text you just entered is centered below the previously entered text (see Figure 8.21). AutoCAD remembers not only the location of the last text you entered, but the starting point you selected for it. If you had moved the last line of text, the new text would still appear below it. Now zoom to your previous view.

EDITING TEXT

You can edit not only the contents of entered text, but the style, insertion point, angle, and, in cases where the style height is 0, the

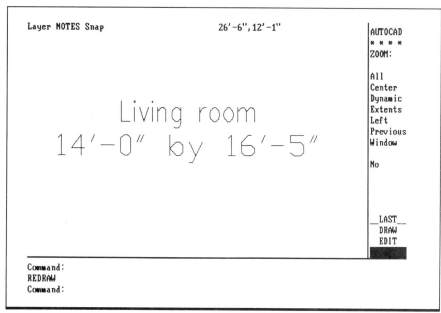

Figure 8.20: *A close-up showing the Note and Standard styles*

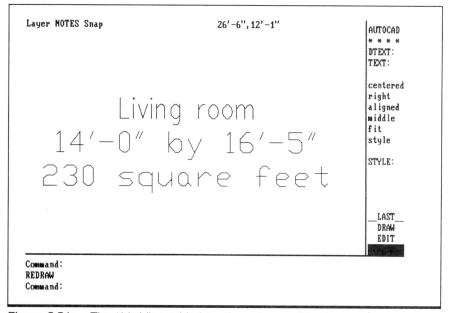

Figure 8.21: *The third line added to the column of text*

text size. To do this you use the Change command.

Modifying Text

Zoom into the entry area again. Start the Change command and pick the bottom two lines of the currently displayed text. At the prompt

Properties/<Change point>:

press Return. The next prompt

Enter text insertion point:

appears. At this prompt, you can pick a new point for the text. Press Return again. The next prompt

Text style: Standard
New style or RETURN for no change:

appears. At this point you can change the text to a different style. Enter Note at this prompt. The text changes into the Note style (see Figure 8.22).

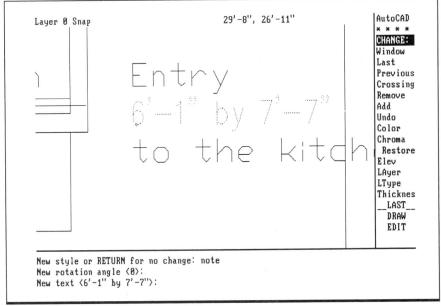

Figure 8.22: The style changed to Note

We should mention that if you modified the Standard style and wanted to update your existing labels, you would still have to enter the word Standard at this prompt even though Standard is the default. Styles are not automatically updated in your drawing.

At the next prompt

New rotation angle <0>:

you can alter the text angle. If you move the cursor around, you will see the text rotate about its insertion point. Press Return to accept the default. At the final prompt

New text <6'-0'' by 7'-0''>:

you can enter new text for this line. Enter 6'-1'' by 5'-5''. The next line ghosts, and you can repeat the process. Cancel the command by pressing Control-C, then erase the last line of text.

You can also change the layer assignment of the text using the Change command, just as you assigned objects to layers in Chapter 4. Unfortunately, you cannot globally change the size of a text style.

Controlling Mirrored Text

At times you may want to mirror a group of objects that contain some text. Normally, if you do this, the mirrored text appears backward. You can change a setting in AutoCAD to make the text read the regular way. Pick Next from the Settings menu, then pick Setvar from the Next menu. You get the prompt:

Variable name or ?:

Setvar provides an alternate way to access certain settings in your drawing; others, such as the one you will change below, are accessible only through Setvar. As we mentioned in Chapter 7, Setvar is a transparent command. Appendix E of this book lists variables accessible by Setvar. For more information, read the appendix on system libraries and variables in the *AutoCAD Reference Manual*.

Enter Mirrtext at this prompt. The next prompt appears:

New value for MIRRTEXT (1):

Enter 0 to keep the Mirror command from causing the mirrored text to read backward. Once you have done this, any mirrored text that is not in a block will read normally. The text position, however, will still be mirrored as shown in Figure 8.23.

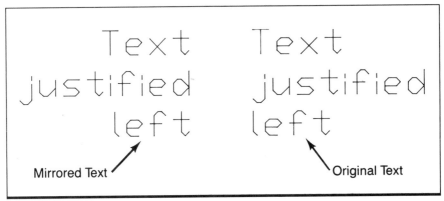

Figure 8.23:   Mirrored text with Mirrtext set to 0

Editing Text Using an AutoLISP Program

When you send in your registration form for the AutoCAD software package, you receive a disk containing some AutoLISP programs. One of these programs, Chgtext.LSP, allows you to edit part of the text in a line without reentering the entire line, unlike the Change command. To use it, make sure that the program is on your current directory. You can get a listing of your current directory by entering

   dir

just as you would in DOS. Do this now. At the prompt

   File specification:

enter Chgtext.LSP. If the file is there, you will get the following prompt:

   Volume in drive c has no label
   Directory of C:\acad

   CHGTEXT   LSP   1576   3-05-83   11:32a

If the file is not found, copy the Chgtext.LSP file from your bonus disk onto your AutoCAD directory. Then enter

   (load "chgtext")

at the command prompt. The message

   C:CHGTEXT

appears and the command prompt returns. You have now loaded

the Chgtext program and you can access it any time while you are editing the current drawing. If you leave this drawing file and enter another one, you must reload Chgtext.

There are a number of other AutoLISP routines on the bonus disk; you will recognize them by their extension, .LSP. You can load any of them using the procedure described above. Just substitute the name of the desired program for Chgtext.

Now enter Chgtext and at the object-selection prompt pick the line of text that reads 6'-1" by 5'-5". Then press Return. At the next prompt

Old string:

enter 5'-5". At the next prompt

New string:

enter 7'-7". The new text appears.

Chgtext can also be used to change a repeated word or phrase to a different word or phrase, much like a search-and-replace function. Unfortunately, you can't use Chgtext very many times during an editing session because it fills up part of the memory AutoCAD reserves for AutoLISP variables. If you do reach the limit, you exit the drawing file, then reopen it and reload the Chgtext program. You can also use a simple AutoLISP utility program to clear the memory, which we will discuss in Chapter 18.

Now end out of this file and exit AutoCAD.

SAVING TIME WITH QTEXT

If you need to edit a drawing that contains lots of notes, but you are not going to edit the notes, you can use the Qtext command to help speed up regenerations. Qtext turns lines of text into rectangular boxes, saving AutoCAD from having to form every letter. If you freeze the layer your notes are on to speed up regeneration, you won't be able to see the locations of your notes. Qtext allows you to see the note locations so you don't accidentally draw over them.

You can enter Qtext by picking it from the Settings menu or entering qtext through the keyboard. Figure 8.24 shows the Qtext menu.

When Qtext is off, text is generated normally, as in Figure 8.25. When Qtext is on, a rectangle appears showing the approximate size and length of text as shown in Figure 8.26.

Figure 8.24:   *The Qtext menu*

IMPORTING TEXT FROM OUTSIDE AUTOCAD

If you have a good deal of text in a drawing, or a sheet of general notes for a set of drawings, you may want to create it in a word processor with advanced features for moving around in, editing, and copying text. You may also want a drawing to contain text already generated with a spreadsheet or database program. AutoCAD's Script command enables you to import such text into an AutoCAD drawing, after preparing it as described below.

The text file you create must be in the DOS, or ASCII, format. ASCII stands for American Standard Code for Information Interchange. As the name implies, the ASCII format was created to allow different computing systems to communicate with each other. Most word processors allow you to generate files in this format. WordStar, for example, uses what it calls a nondocument mode to read and write ASCII text files. In WordPerfect, you use special options to open or save a file in ASCII format. Some word processors, like PC Write, automatically generate ASCII files.

In Chapters 17 and 18, you will use a word processor to customize the AutoCAD menu and to create an AutoLISP program. If you

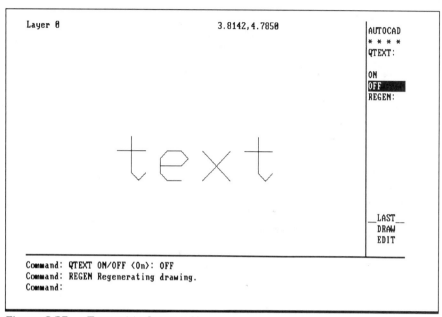

Figure 8.25: Text with Qtext off

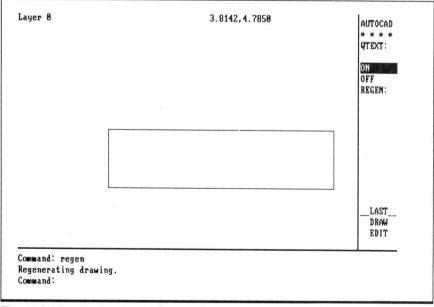

Figure 8.26: Text with Qtext on

would like to do these things, we strongly suggest you obtain a word processor if you don't already have one.

If your notes are not too long, and you are careful while you enter them, you can use the COPY CON command to create a DOS text file directly from DOS. The problem with COPY CON is that if you make a typing error and press Return, you must start all over again. You will use it, however, in the following exercise to create a file that you will later import into a drawing. If you have problems or questions about COPY CON, refer to your DOS manual.

At the C: prompt, enter

copy con note.scr

After you press Return, the cursor moves down one line. Now enter the following text. Like any file you wish to import, it starts with the word text followed by a Return, an at sign, then two Returns. Then the body of the text starts, using three Returns between each line, one to end the line of text and two to triple-space the rest of the file. Each line must be a fixed length. This means you must enter a Return at the end of each line when you use a word processor, rather than using its word-wrap feature. However, if your word processor allows you to adjust the line spacing globally within a file, you can modify your text files for importation without inserting Returns.

The text on your screen will look like this:

text
@

2 x 4 studs

@ 16 inches

on center

Press Return for the last time, then press the F6 function key. A Control-Z appears. This tells DOS that you are finished writing the file. Press Return to save the file to disk. If you list the disk directory, you will find the file you just created, Note.SCR, among the AutoCAD files.

Start AutoCAD and open the Unit file. Be sure your current text style is Standard with a height of 0. If the height is not 0, change it now using the Style command. The Script file is set up to accept the default text height by entering a Return after the at sign near its beginning. If the current style has a nondefault height, the script file will contain one too many Returns, causing AutoCAD to read the file out of order and not import the text.

Use the Point command on the Draw menu and select a point just below the word Kitchenette at coordinate 16'-2", 19'-8". Now pick the Utility command from the Root menu to bring up the Utility menu (see Figure 8.27). Then pick Script.

At the prompt

Script file <unit>:

enter Note. This tells the Script command to use the file Note.SCR. The note you just created while in DOS appears in the drawing starting from the point you entered. Your drawing should look like Figure 8.28.

When you use the Script command, the text is entered in the current style. In this example, you used the Standard text style, which uses the Txt font.

Entering external text into a drawing is only one of many uses for the Script command. Script is actually a means of saving keyboard entries that can be played back all at once. This is similar to batch files in DOS. If you analyze the text file you created in DOS, you will see that the entire file is actually the keyboard entry sequence of the notes you entered. Once you understand this, you can set up the import file to automatically select the style and

Figure 8.27:   *The Utility menu*

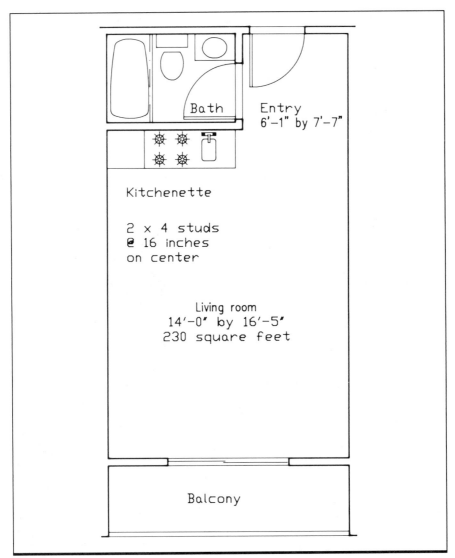

Figure 8.28:   *The Unit plan with notes*

height it is to be in the drawing file. We will explore other uses for the Script command in Chapter 16.

Programs such as AutoWord by Technical Software, Inc. and AutoEDITOR by Ai/Systems, which convert a text file to an Auto-CAD drawing without your having to specially format your ASCII file for importation, are available from third-party software companies.

These can be real timesavers when you want to include large text files in your drawings, as well as giving you more control over how the text will appear. You could also use the AutoLISP programming language to import external files. A sample of an AutoLISP program that imports text files without modification is in Appendix D.

CONCLUSION

In this chapter we have introduced you to AutoCAD's features for entering, editing, and importing text. You may end up using only a few of the available options, but it is useful to be aware of them all. You never know when you will have to enter a large text file into an AutoCAD drawing, or when you will have to replace every occurrence of the word "widget" with the word "dodad" in a drawing full of text.

At this point you may want to try adding notes to drawings you have experimented with outside this tutorial. You might try importing a schedule using the Monotxt font to see how that works. You could even create a logo and letterhead.

Along with notes, dimensions help convey information about a design. In the next chapter, you will add dimensions to the studio unit plan.

Chapter 9

Using Dimensions

BEFORE YOU DETERMINE the dimensions of a project, your design is in flux and many questions may be unanswered. Once you begin dimensioning, you see if things fit or work together. Dimensioning can be crucial to how well a design works and how quickly it develops. Communicating even tentative dimensions to others can speed up design development.

With AutoCAD, you can easily add tentative or final dimensions to any drawing. AutoCAD gives you an accurate dimension without your having to take measurements. You simply pick the two points to be dimensioned and the dimension line location, and AutoCAD does the rest. AutoCAD's *associative dimensioning* capability automatically updates dimensions wherever the size or shape of the dimensioned object is changed. These dimensioning features can save you valuable time and reduce the number of dimensional errors in your drawings.

This chapter shows you the basics of AutoCAD dimensioning.

GETTING STARTED WITH DIMENSIONS

The dimension command Dim is like a self-contained program. Once you enter it, you get the prompt Dim: instead of the familiar Command: prompt. You also cannot use any other AutoCAD commands (with the exception of transparent commands); only the commands that relate to dimensioning are allowed. You should use the Dim command when you are adding strings of dimensions to a drawing or when you want to add several dimensions at once.

AutoCAD also provides the Dim1 command, which allows you to enter a single dimension then automatically returns you to the standard command prompt to enter other AutoCAD commands. This is useful for dimensioning parts of an object quickly, when you don't have to enter lots of dimensions. Because Dim1 uses the same settings as Dim, we won't discuss it explicitly in this chapter.

Using the Default Dimension Settings

Like most other AutoCAD commands, Dim has default settings. But unlike those of other commands, its set of defaults is quite extensive. In this section you will enter some dimensions to see what happens when you use the default settings.

Start AutoCAD and open the Unit file. Be sure your current layer is Notes. Pick Dim from the Root menu. By doing this, you automatically start the Dim command. Pick Linear from the Dim menu, then Vrtical from the Linear Dimension menu (see Figure 9.1).

The prompt

Dim: VERT
First extension line origin or Return to select:

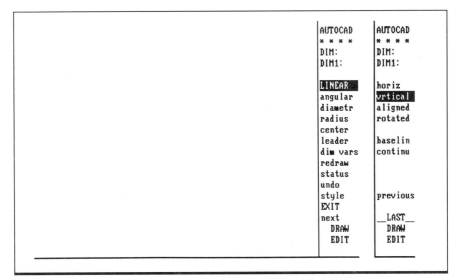

Figure 9.1:   The Dim menu and the Linear Dimension menu

appears. This prompt is asking you for the first point of the distance to be dimensioned. The *extension line* connects the points being dimensioned to the dimension line. For example, if you dimension one side of a square, the lines drawn from the two ends of the side to be dimensioned are the extension lines.

Notice the word VERT. Although you pick the word Vrtical from the menu, the actual subcommand name is Vert and it must be entered that way through the keyboard. As we go through these exercises, note the subcommand on the prompt line as you select each menu item. You can also refer to Figure 9.2, which shows the dimensioning menu hierarchy and the keyboard entries equivalent to the menu items. Or you can just use the menus for your input.

Now notice the option to press Return to select. If you press Return at this prompt, you are prompted to pick the object you wish to dimension. It can be a line, arc, or circle. We'll look at this option later.

Pick the upper-right corner of the entry at the coordinate 29'-0", 30'-10" (you can use the Intersec Osnap override). The prompt

Second extension line origin:

appears. This prompt is asking you for the second point of the distance to be dimensioned. Pick the lower-right corner of the living room at coordinate 29'-0", 6'-10". The prompt

Dimension line location:

appears. The *dimension line* is the line indicating the direction of the dimension and contains the arrows or tick marks. You could pick a point using your cursor, but you may want to place the dimension line more accurately. Enter @4'<0 to tell AutoCAD you want the dimension line four feet to the right of the last point you selected. The prompt

Dimension text <24'>:

appears. The value shown as the default is the distance between the two extension line origins you selected. This is what will appear as the dimension if you press Return to accept the default.

You could append text to the default value by entering

< >*appended text*

By using the less than and greater than signs, you can add text either before or after the default dimension. Just place the two

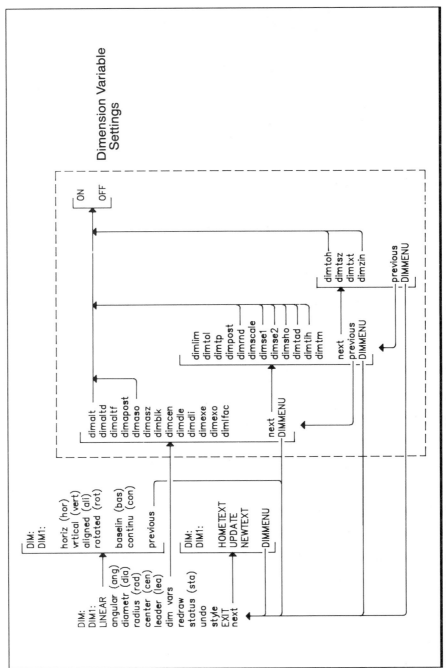

Figure 9.2: The dimensioning menus and keyboard commands

signs within the text wherever you want the default to appear. For example, if your prompt reads

Dimension Text <8″>:

and you enter

Add <> to the length

you get

Add 8″ to the length

for the dimension text. You can also add a *dimension suffix* to all, rather than selected, dimension text using the Dimpost and Dima-post options described below.

Press Return to accept the default, 24′. The dimension lines appear but there are no dimensions or arrows (see Figure 9.3). To see what happened, use the transparent Zoom command and the Center subcommand. You will get the prompt

Center point:

Pick a point midway between the two dimension extension lines as

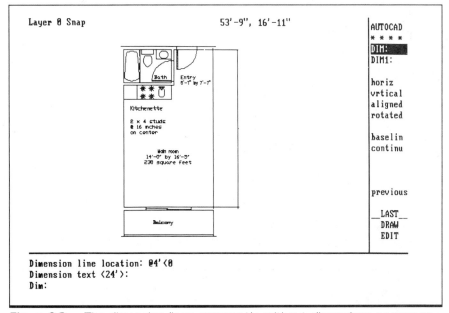

Figure 9.3: *The dimension lines, apparently without dimensions or arrows*

shown in Figure 9.4. You get the prompt

Magnification or Height (34'-0") :

The value in the brackets indicates the current view height. Enter 8 for an eight-inch height. Your view will look like Figure 9.5. The dimension is there after all, but it is so small that it cannot be read in a normal view.

Setting a Dimension Scale

A new user will often try the Dimension command only to find that many things seem not to work. Most of these problems come from not understanding that dimensions require a scale adjustment, just as sheet sizes and text do.

Zoom back to the overall view of the unit plan by starting the Zoom command, then using the All option on the Zoom menu. The default dimension arrows were also inserted, but because they are so small and so close to the extension lines, they don't appear. Next you will set the dimension scale so the dimension will appear at the right scale for this drawing.

To set the proper scale for the dimension, you must adjust the Dimscale setting. Go to the Dim menu and pick Dim Vars, then pick

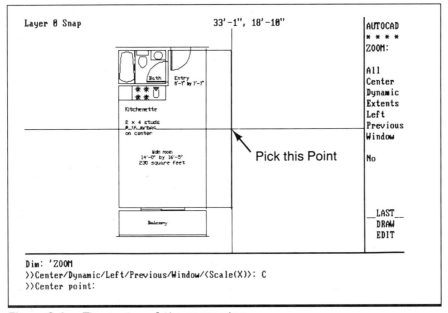

Figure 9.4:   *The center of the zoom view*

the Next option on the Dim Vars menu (see Figure 9.6). Pick Dimscale from the Next menu. The prompt

Dim: DIMSCALE Current value <1.0000> New value:

appears. As you can see from the default value, the current setting is for a one-to-one scale. Your current scale, however, is 1/4" = 1'-0". You know from previous chapters that the scale conversion factor for 1/4" scale is 48. A simple way to figure out scale factors is to divide 12 by the decimal equivalent of the inch scale. For 1/4" you divide 12 by .25 to get 48. For 1/8" you divide 12 by .125 to get 96. For 1 1/2" you divide 12 by 1.5, and so on.

Enter 48 at this prompt. Now pick Next from the Dim menu, then pick Update from the Next menu to bring up the Update menu (see Figure 9.7). You will get the object-selection prompt. Pick the dimension line you just entered or pick Last from the Update menu, then press Return. The dimension will appear at the proper scale as in Figure 9.8.

A dimension acts as a single entity even though it is composed of lines, arrows, and text. You can edit an entire dimension using the Update, Hometext, and Newtext commands. You have just used Update to update a dimension to the current settings. Hometext

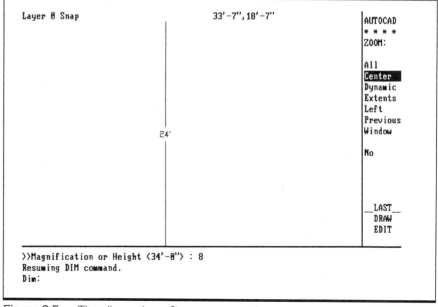

Figure 9.5: *The dimension after you zoom in*

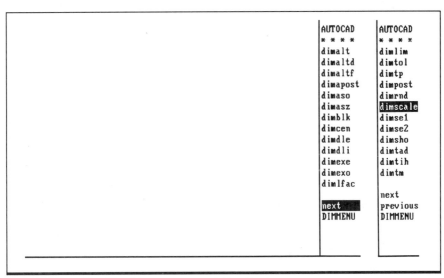

Figure 9.6:   *The Dim Vars menu and the Next menu*

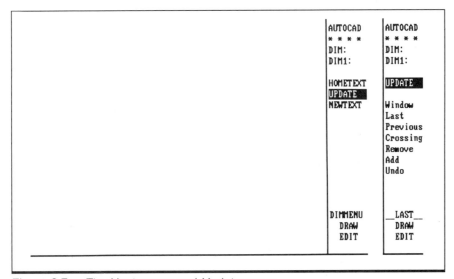

Figure 9.7:   *The Next menu and Update menu*

moves the dimension text to its default position, and Newtext allows you to edit it. If you have to edit the dimension lines individually, you can use the Explode command to break a dimension down into its components. Once you explode a dimension, however, you cannot use AutoCAD's associative dimensioning features.

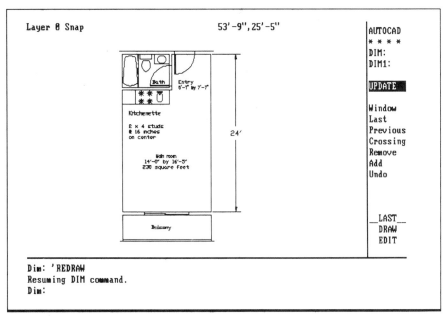

Figure 9.8: The dimension updated

Continuing a Dimension String

You will often want to input a group of dimensions strung together in a line. For example, you may want to dimension the balcony and have it aligned with the dimension you just entered. To do this, you use the Continu option. Pick Continu from the Dim menu. You get the prompt

Second extension line origin:

Pick the lower-right corner of the balcony above the rail at coordinate 29'-0", 2'-8". The prompt

Dimension text <4'-2">:

appears. Press Return to accept the default. See Figure 9.9 for the results.

You should be aware that to enter this option through the keyboard, you need only enter the word Cont at the Dim: prompt.

Entering Horizontal Dimensions

Next, you will use the Horiz option to dimension the bathroom. Go to the Dim menu and pick Linear. This time pick Horiz from the

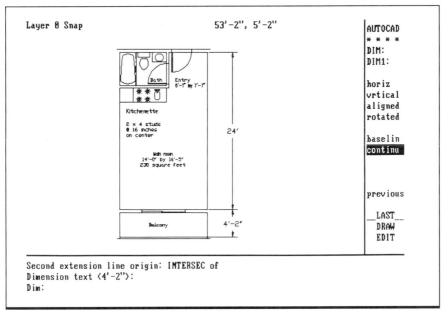

Figure 9.9: *The dimension string continued*

Linear Dimension menu. Pick the upper-left corner of the bathroom near coordinate 15'-0", 30'-10" at the first extension line prompt. Next pick the upper-right corner of the bathroom near coordinate 22'-6", 30'-10". Pick a point near coordinate 22'-5", 33'-5" to set the dimension line location. Then press Return at the dimension text prompt (see Figure 9.10).

Entering a Set of Dimensions from a Common Extension Line

At times you will want several dimensions to originate from the same extension line. To accommodate this, AutoCAD provides the Baselin option. Pick this option from the Linear Dimension menu, then pick the upper-right corner of the entry at the prompt

Second extension line origin:

Press Return at the dimension text prompt. Although you cannot see it, the overall width dimension appears above the 7'-6" dimension. Exit the Dim command by picking Exit from the Dim menu. Then use the All option on the Zoom menu to see the entire drawing, as shown in Figure 9.11.

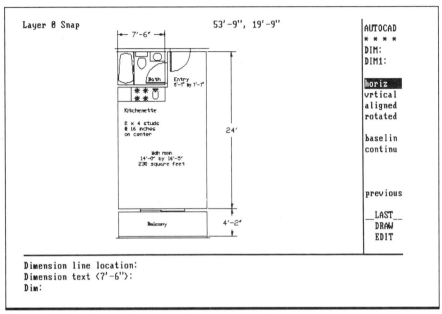

Figure 9.10: The bathroom with horizontal dimensions

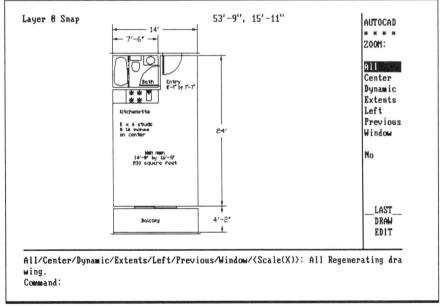

Figure 9.11: The overall width dimension

In this example, you see that the Baselin option is similar to the
Continu option, except that it allows you to use the first extension
line as the base for a second dimension. You should note that you
must enter the option as Base through the keyboard.

Updating Dimensions Automatically

AutoCAD provides the associative dimensioning capability to automatically update dimension text when a drawing is edited, as long as
you include the dimension or *definition points*. The definition points
are located at the points you pick when you determine the dimension location, plus another definition point at the center of the
dimension text. For example, the definition points for linear dimensions are located at the extension line origin and the intersection of
the extension line and the dimension line. The definition points for a
circle diameter are the point used to pick the circle and the opposite
side of the circle. The definition points for a radius are the points
used to pick the circle, plus the center of the circle. As long as you
include these points when you select objects to be processed, and
you see the dimension lines ghost, you know you have selected the
definition points. The points are located on a layer called Defpoints.
Definition points are displayed regardless of whether Defpoints is
on, but you must turn Defpoints on to plot them. The following
exercise demonstrates associative dimensioning.

Suppose you want to enlarge the balcony by moving the wall
between the balcony and the living room closer to the bathroom
wall. You can move a group of lines and vertices using the Stretch
command and the Crossing option. Go to the Edit menu and pick
Next. Then pick Stretch from the Next menu. The Stretch menu
shown in Figure 9.12 will appear. You will get the prompt

Select object to stretch by window...
Select object: C
First corner:

You must always use a crossing window with the Stretch command to select all the objects associated with the vertices being
edited. Because you selected Stretch from a menu, the Crossing
option has been automatically entered. When you enter this command through the keyboard or repeat it by pressing Return, you
must enter a C at the object-selection prompt, then pick your window. Pick a crossing window as indicated in Figure 9.13.

Figure 9.12: The Stretch menu

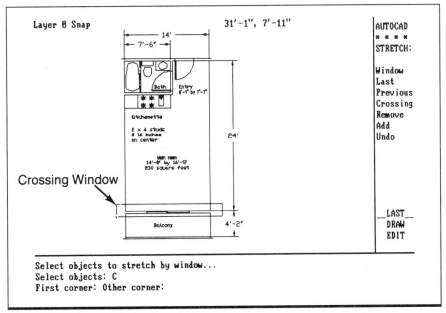

Figure 9.13: The Stretch crossing window

Once you have picked the window, press Return to confirm your selection. At the base point prompt pick any point on the screen. Then at the new point prompt enter

@2′ <90

to move the wall two feet in a 90-degree direction. The wall will move and the dimension text will change to reflect the new dimension as shown in Figure 9.14.

You can use the Mirror, Rotate, Scale, and Stretch commands with dimensions. The Array command will also work using polar arrays, and Extend and Trim can be used with linear dimensions. When editing objects using these commands, be sure you select the dimension line associated with any point that is being edited. Using the Crossing option when selecting objects to be edited will help you include the dimensions.

If you don't want to use the associative dimensioning feature, for example when you want to edit dimension lines easily, you can turn it off. Go to the Dim menu, then the Dim Vars menu. Then set the Dimaso setting to off by picking Off from the Dimaso menu or entering off. Also, you can control whether the dimension value is

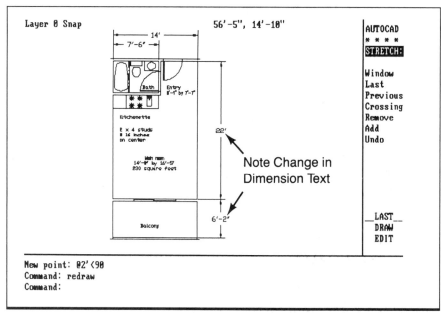

Figure 9.14:   The wall moved and the dimensions updated

dynamically updated while a dimension line is being dragged using the Dimsho setting, which is also on the Dim Vars menu.

Since associative dimensioning is rather complex, you may want to refer to the *AutoCAD Reference Manual* for more detailed information.

Now use the U command to return the apartment unit to its previous dimensions.

Using Osnap to Select Dimension Points

You may find that when you pick intersections and endpoints frequently, as during dimensioning, it is a bit inconvenient to use the Osnap overrides menu. Fortunately, you can set a default active Osnap mode or combination of modes. To do this, go to the Settings menu and pick Osnap to bring up the Osnap Settings menu (see Figure 9.15).

The prompt

Object snap modes:

appears. You can now select the desired default mode. You can even pick more than one mode, say Intersect, Endpoint, and Midpoint, so that whichever geometry you happen to be nearest will be the point selected. You use the comma between Osnap overrides when more than one is to be active at the same time. Pick Endpoint, then the comma near the bottom of the menu. Then pick Intersec to select both endpoints and intersections. Press Return.

Figure 9.15:   The Osnap Settings menu

Now whenever you are asked to select a point, you will see the Osnap box appear on the cursor. You can still use the Osnap overrides as you did before to override the current setting. The only drawback to setting a constant Osnap mode is that when your drawing gets crowded, you may end up picking the wrong point by accident. When you want to pick a point at random, use the None option on the Osnap menu.

Now end out of the Unit file.

CHOOSING A DIMENSION STYLE

Because different professions use different styles of dimensioning, AutoCAD allows you to modify the way its dimensions appear. In your apartment unit plan, you used the default dimension settings, which are more frequently used in engineering and mechanical drawings than in architectural ones. Other available options include tick marks, which are usually used instead of arrows in architectural drawings. You can align the dimension numbers along a vertical dimension line, and you can place them above the dimension line rather than breaking them. You can even have the dimension automatically display a plus or minus value, which is useful if you are doing mechanical drawings of machined parts. In this section we will look at how you can alter some of the dimension settings to suit your type of drawing.

Table 9.1 shows you a list of the settings that can be modified, their current status, and a brief description of what they do. You can get a similar listing by picking the Status option from the Dim menu while the Dim command is active. The name of a setting may help you remember its purpose. For example, Dimasz adjusts the Arrow SiZe.

If you want to change a setting, pick the Dim Vars option from the Dimension menu. You can also enter a setting through the keyboard so long as you see the Dim: prompt. Then pick the setting you want to change. You will be prompted for a new setting value. You can enter a new value from the keyboard, or, if the setting is a toggle, you can pick On or Off from the menu that appears when you select that setting.

Controlling Associative Dimensioning

As we said earlier, you can turn off associative dimensioning using the Dimaso setting. The default for Dimaso is on. The Dimsho setting controls whether the dimension value is dynamically updated while a dimension line is being dragged. The default for this setting is off because it can slow down the display on less powerful computers.

Specifying Scales of Dimension Elements

In the previous exercise, you used the Dimscale setting to set the dimension scale. Dimscale controls the overall *scale factor*. The other dimension settings are multiplied by this factor. For example, the default arrow size is 3/16". With Dimscale set to 1, the dimension arrows are drawn at 3/16". If Dimscale is set to 48, the arrows are drawn at 48 times 3/16", or 9 inches. The use of an overall scale factor allows quick adjustment of all these settings. Otherwise, you would have to convert every setting individually for every different scale you use.

The Dimtxt setting controls text size. Remember that the setting height is multiplied by the Dimscale setting. In the exercise, you set Dimscale to 48. With a Dimtxt value of 3/16", that made your dimension text 9 inches high. If the current text style has a fixed height, that height overrides this setting. For example, if you had used the Note text style in your dimension example the text height would be six inches.

The Dimasz setting controls the arrow size. The size indicated is the actual size of the arrows in the plotted drawing, provided the Dimscale option is set to the drawing scale.

Setting Name	Default Setting	Description
Associative Dimensioning		
Dimaso	On	Turns associative dimensions on and off
Dimsho	Off	Updates dimensions dynamically while dragging
Scale		
Dimscale	1.0000	Overall scale factor of dimensions

Table 9.1:   The default settings for the Dim command

Dimtxt	3/16″	Text height
Dimasz	3/16″	Arrow size
Dimtsz	0″	Tick size
Dimcen	1/16″	Center mark size
Dimlfac	1.0000	Linear unit scale factor
Offsets		
Dimexo	1/16″	Extension line origin offset
Dimexe	3/16″	Amount extension line extends beyond dimension line
Dimdli	3/8″	Dimension line offset for continuation or base
Dimdle	0″	Amount dimension line extends beyond extension line
Tolerances		
Dimtp	0″	Plus tolerance
Dimtm	0″	Minus tolerance
Dimtol	Off	Shows dimension tolerances when on
Dimlim	Off	Shows dimension limits when on
Rounding		
Dimrnd	0″	Rounding value
Dimzin	0	Controls display of 0 dimensions. Has four settings: 0, 1, 2, and 3. 0 leaves out zero feet and inches. 1 includes zero feet and inches. 2 includes zero feet, and 3 includes zero inches.

Table 9.1: The default settings for the Dim command (cont.)

Dimension Text Orientation

Dimtih	On	Text inside extensions is horizontal when on
Dimtoh	On	Text outside extensions is horizontal when on
Dimtad	Off	Places text above the dimension line when on

Extension Line Suppression

Dimse1	Off	Suppresses the first extension line when on
Dimse2	Off	Suppresses the second extension line when on

Alternate Dimension Options

Dimalt	Off	Alternate units selected are shown when on
Dimaltf	25.4000	Alternate unit scale factor
Dimaltd	2	Alternate unit decimal places
Dimpost	*Suffix*	Adds suffix to dimension text
Dimapost	*Suffix*	Adds suffix to alternate dimension text
Dimblk	*Block name*	Alternate arrow block name

Table 9.1:   *The default settings for the Dim command (cont.)*

The Dimtsz setting controls dimension tick mark size. If this setting is a value greater than 0, the dimensions produce a tick mark. (The arrow still appears when you dimension radii or use leaders for notes.) The value you enter here determines the orthogonal distance from the midpoint of the tick mark to one end (see Figure 9.16).

Dimcen controls the size of the center mark AutoCAD uses when dimensioning arcs and circles. The center mark is a small cross placed at the center of the circle or arc.

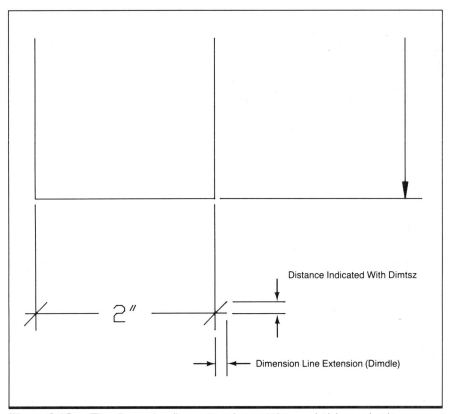

Figure 9.16:   *The dimension line extension setting and tick mark size*

The Dimlfac setting affects the numeric value of the dimension. The default setting, 1.0000, multiplies the distance to be dimensioned by 1 and enters this value as the actual dimension measured. If you want to show the distance converted to millimeters, for example, you make the Dimlfac value 25.4. This multiplies a one-unit distance by 25.4 and displays a dimension of 25.4000.

Setting Dimension Line Offsets

Dimexo controls the distance between the point you pick and the beginning of the extension line. Dimexe controls the distance the extension line passes beyond the dimension line (see Figure 9.17).

At times it is necessary for AutoCAD to offset dimensions when the Continu or the Base option is used. The Dimdli setting controls the distance of that offset (see Figure 9.18).

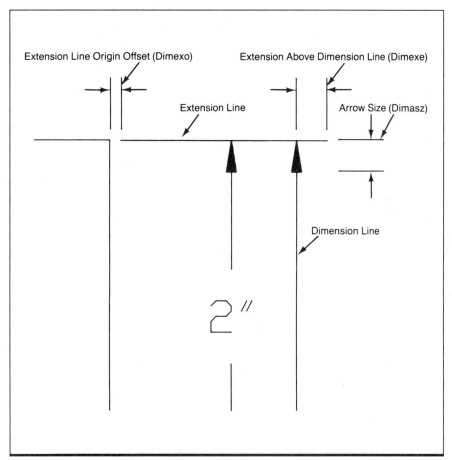

Figure 9.17:   *The extension line offset*

The Dimdle setting is effective only if you use tick marks. It controls the distance the dimension extends beyond the extension lines (see Figure 9.16). This is one setting that is not affected by Dimscale. For example, if you set Dimdle to 1/8", no matter what the Dimscale value is the dimension line will extend only 1/8" beyond the extension line.

Dimensioning with Tolerances

You may want to indicate a plus tolerance in your dimensions. The Dimtp setting determines what that value will be. A 0" setting shows a 0" plus tolerance, for example. The Dimtm setting works

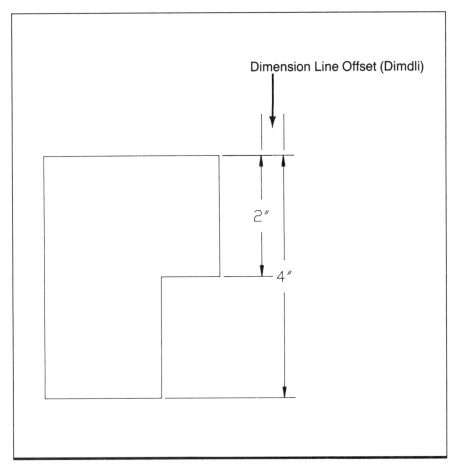

Figure 9.18: *How Dimdli controls offset distances*

the same as the Dimtp setting, but for minus tolerances. Plus and minus tolerances do not appear unless Dimtol or Dimlim is set on (see Figure 9.19).

Dimtol controls whether the dimension tolerance values set with Dimtp and Dimtm are added to the dimension text. With Dimtol on, you get a dimension followed by the plus and minus values you specified using Dimtp and Dimtm (see Figure 9.20).

Dimlim is similar to Dimtol. However, rather than giving the plus and minus values, it gives two values reflecting the range deter-mined by the dimension and tolerance values (see Figure 9.19). Since Dimlim and Dimtol do similar things, if one is turned on the other is automatically turned off.

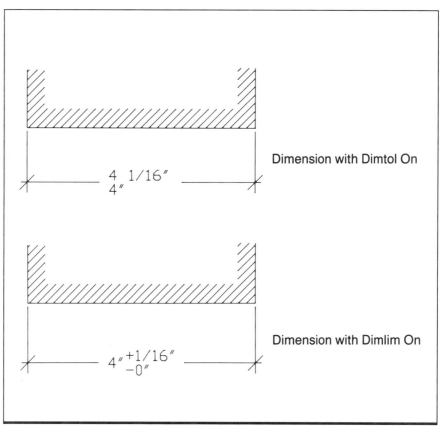

Figure 9.19:   The effect of Dimlim on dimension text

Controlling Dimension Rounding

To round the dimension values, use the Dimrnd command. A .125 value here will round your dimensions to the nearest 1/8".

If your measurement system uses feet and inches, the Dimzin setting determines how a zero-inch value is displayed. It can be set to one of four integer values: 0, 1, 2, or 3. 0 leaves out zero feet and inches; for example, 1'0" is displayed as 1', and 0'6" is displayed as 6". 1 includes zero feet and inches. 2 includes zero feet only, and 3 includes zero inches only.

Positioning Dimension Text

Dimtih controls whether the dimension text is inserted horizontally or aligned with the dimension line. When Dimtih is on, text is always

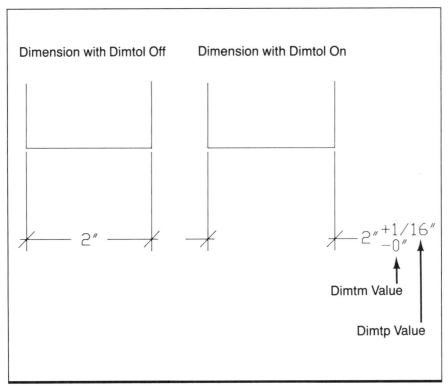

Figure 9.20: *The effect of Dimtol on dimension text*

inserted horizontally. If off, the text is aligned with the dimension line except when it does not fit between the extension lines (see Figure 9.21).

Dimtoh controls the orientation of dimension text that does not fit between the extension lines. As with Dimtih, when on, it forces the text to be horizontal (see Figure 9.22).

When the Dimtad setting is on, the dimension text is placed above the dimension line and aligned with it. If you are doing architectural drawings, you will probably want to set Dimtad on (see Figure 9.23).

Suppressing Dimension Line Extensions

At times you may not want the first extension line to be drawn as in Figure 9.24. You can control the insertion of extension lines by setting Dimse1 and Dimse2 on or off. Setting Dimse1 on suppresses the insertion of the first extension line, while setting Dimse2 on suppresses the second extension line.

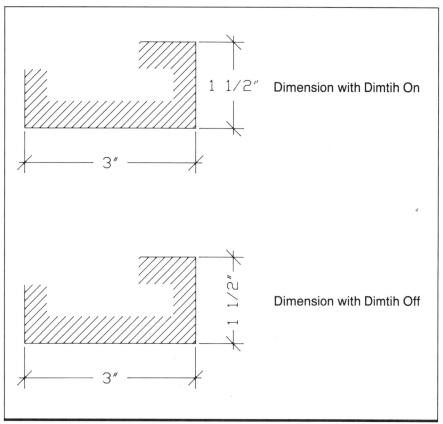

Figure 9.21: Text inserted with Dimtih on and off

Using Alternate Dimensions and Arrows

Dimalt controls whether the Dimaltf and Dimaltd settings are operative. The Dimaltf setting determines a conversion factor for the AutoCAD drawing unit and displays that alternate dimension in brackets. For example, the current setting, 25.4000, converts the unit measure, inches, to millimeters. If the Dimalt setting is on, a one-inch measurement is displayed along with the alternate millimeter equivalent, 25.4000, in brackets (see Figure 9.25). This is useful if you must show dimensions in both English and metric measurements. The Dimaltd setting controls the number of decimal places shown when you use Dimaltf.

If you want a dimension suffix added to your dimensions, you can use the Dimpost option. For example, if you want the word units to

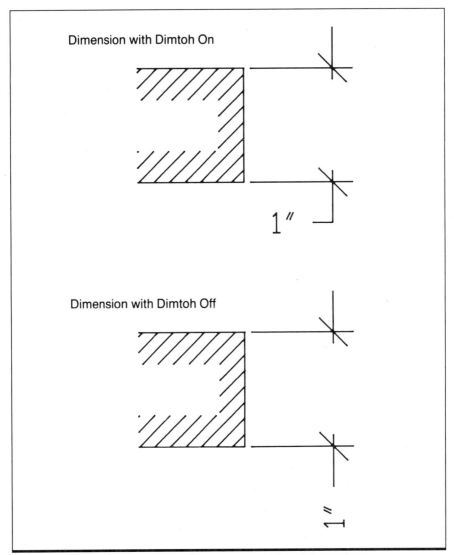

Figure 9.22: Text inserted with Dimtoh on and off

always appear after a dimension value you can set Dimpost to "units". A four-unit dimension would read

4 units

instead of just 4. Dimapost has the same effect, except it applies only to alternate dimensions as in

1″ [25.4 *units*]

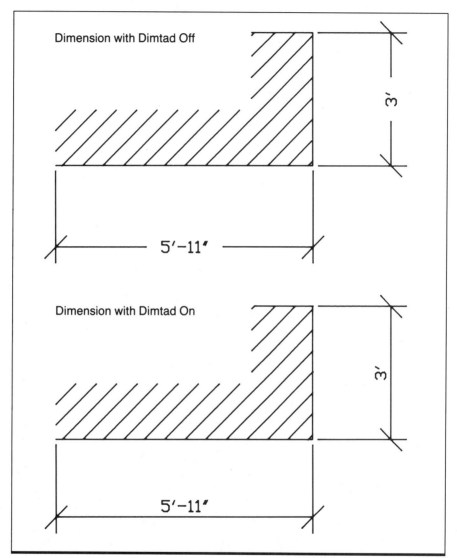

Figure 9.23: *Dimensions inserted with Dimtad on and off*

If you don't want the default arrow or tick mark for your dimension lines, you can create a block of the desired arrow or tick and enter the block name for the Dimblk setting. For example, you may want to have a tick mark that is thicker than the dimension lines and extensions. You could create a block of a tick mark on a layer you assign to a thick pen weight, then assign that block to the Dimblk setting.

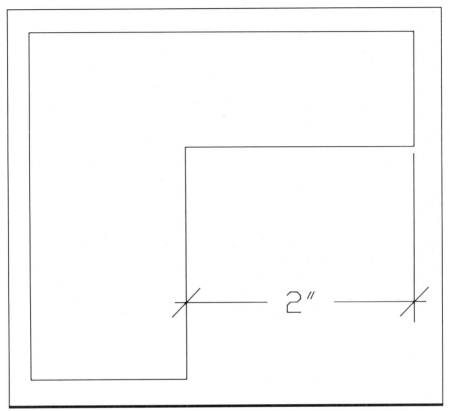

Figure 9.24:   *When you want to suppress an extension line*

The original block should be drawn one unit long. The block's insertion point will be the endpoint of the dimension line, so be sure the
insertion point is at the point of your arrow. The block will be
rotated 180 degrees for the left side of the dimension line. Because
the right side's arrow will be inserted using a zero rotation value,
orient the arrow so that it is pointing to the right (see Figure 9.26).

If you set a block for a different arrow, then decide to use the
standard AutoCAD arrow, enter a period as a response to the
Dimblk option.

If you know you will use certain dimension settings all the time,
you may want to change the default settings in the ACAD.DWG file,
as we discussed in Chapter 6, or set up a template file.

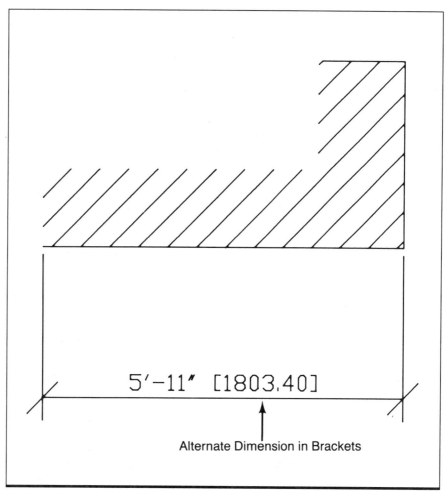

5'-11" [1803.40]

Alternate Dimension in Brackets

Figure 9.25: *A dimension with Dimalt on and Dimaltf set to 25.4000*

DIMENSIONING NONORTHOGONAL OBJECTS AND ADDING LEADERS

Some options on the Dim and Linear Dimension menus allow you to dimension nonorthogonal objects, such as circles, arcs, triangles, and trapezoids (see Figure 9.1). If you want to dimension an object that has no vertical or horizontal sides, you will have to use the

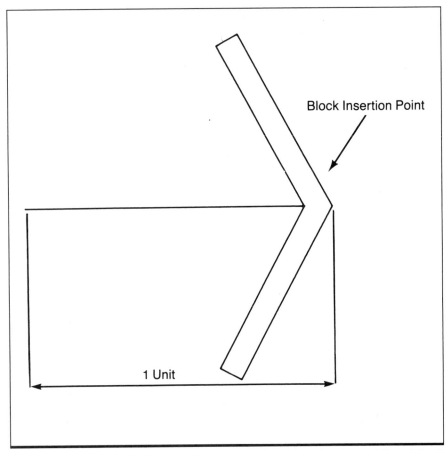

Block Insertion Point

1 Unit

Figure 9.26:   The orientation and size of a block used in place of the default arrow

Aligned or Rotated options on the Linear Dimension menu. If you want to dimension a circular object, the Angular, Diametr, Radius, or Center options on the Dim menu must be used. In this section you will practice dimensioning nonorthogonal objects by drawing an elevation of a window that might appear as part of the set of plans for your studio apartment building.

Open a new file called Window. Set the file up as an architectural drawing at a scale of 3" = 1'-0" on an 8½ x 11-inch sheet. Go to the Draw menu, then Next. Then pick Polygon to bring up the Polygon menu (see Figure 9.27).

Figure 9.27: The Polygon menu

At the prompt

Number of sides:

enter 6. At the next prompt

Edge/<center of polygon>:

pick the center of the polygon at coordinate 1'-10", 1'-6". At the next prompt

Inscribed in circle/Circumscribed about circle (I/C):

pick C-Scribe from the Polygon menu. Now as you move the cursor, you can see the hexagon drag along with it. You could pick a point with your mouse to determine its size. But instead, enter 8 through the keyboard to get an exact size for the hexagon. Draw a circle with a radius of seven inches using coordinate 1'-10", 1'-6" as its center. Your drawing will look like Figure 9.28.

Dimensioning Nonorthogonal Distances

Now you will dimension the window. The unusual shape of the window prevents you from using the Horiz or Vrtical options on the Dim menu. However, the Aligned option on the Linear Dimension menu allows you to enter a dimension across a line that is not horizontal or vertical. Start the Dim command by picking Dim from the Root menu.

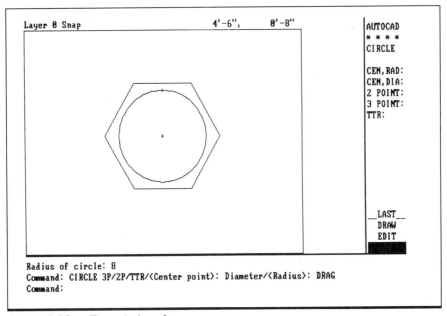

Layer 8 Snap   4'-6'',   8'-8''   AUTOCAD
                                                                 * * * *
                                                                 CIRCLE

                                                                 CEN,RAD:
                                                                 CEN,DIA:
                                                                 2 POINT:
                                                                 3 POINT:
                                                                 TTR:

                                                                 _LAST__
                                                                 DRAW
                                                                 EDIT

Radius of circle: 8
Command: CIRCLE 3P/2P/TTR/<Center point>: Diameter/<Radius>: DRAG
Command:

Figure 9.28: The window frame

Then set the Dimscale option to 4. Pick Linear from the Dim menu, then pick Aligned from the Linear Dimension menu. At the prompt

First extension line origin or RETURN to select:

press Return. You could have picked extension line origins as you did in earlier examples, but using the Return to select option will show you firsthand how it works. At the prompt

Select line, arc, or circle:

pick the upper-right face of the hexagon near coordinate 2'-5'', 1'-10''. As the prompt indicates, you can also pick an arc or circle for this type of dimension. At the next prompt

Dimension line location:

pick a point near coordinate 2'-10'', 2'-2''. Press Return at the prompt

Dimension text <9 1/4''>:

to accept the default dimension. The dimension appears parallel to the line you picked, as in Figure 9.29.

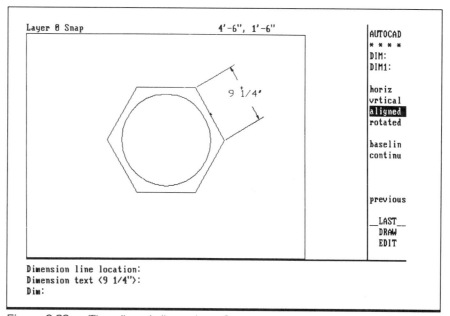

Figure 9.29: The aligned dimension of a nonorthogonal line

Next you will dimension a face of the hexagon. But instead of its actual length, you will dimension a distance at a specified angle. In this example, you will dimension a face of the hexagon to show the distance from the center of the face. To do this, pick the Rotate option on the Linear Dimension menu. At the prompt

Dimension line angle <0>:

enter 30. Press Return at the next prompt

First extension line origin or RETURN to select:

then at the prompt

Select line, arc, or circle:

pick the lower-right face of the hexagon near coordinate 2'-6", 1'-4". At the prompt

Dimension line location:

pick a point near coordinate 2'-11", 0'-8". Press Return at the prompt

Dimension text <8">:

and the dimension of the line at 30 degrees appears. Your drawing will look like Figure 9.30.

Dimensioning Radii, Diameters, and Arcs

The four options Angular, Diameter, Radius, and Center on the Dim menu allow you to generate nonlinear dimensions. While still in the Dim command, pick Angular from the Dim menu. This option allows you to dimension the angle between two lines. At the prompt

Select first line:

pick the upper-left face of the hexagon near coordinate 1'-3", 1'-10". At the next prompt

Second line:

pick the top face at coordinate 1'-9", 2'-2". At the next prompt

Enter dimension line arc location:

pick a point near coordinate 1'-8", 1'-11". Press Return at the prompt

Dimension text <120>:

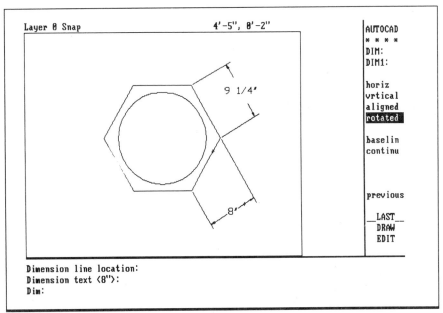

Figure 9.30:   *A linear dimension using the Rotate option*

and at the last prompt

Enter text location:

pick a point near coordinate 1'-8", 1'-9". The angle between the two lines you picked appears with an arrow indicating the angle (see Figure 9.31).

Now try the Diametr option, which shows the diameter of a circle. While still in the Dim command, pick Diametr from the Dim menu. At the prompt

Select arc or circle:

pick the circle near coordinate 2'-5", 1'-6". Then press Return at the prompt

Dimension text <1'-2">:

Your drawing should look like Figure 9.32.

The diameter dimension line starts at the point on the circle you selected. If the dimension text can't fit within the circle, AutoCAD gives you the message

Text does not fit.
Enter leader length for text:

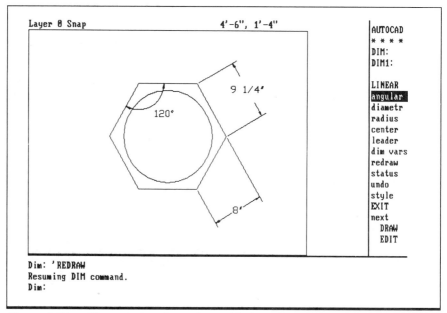

Figure 9.31:   *The angular dimension added to the window frame*

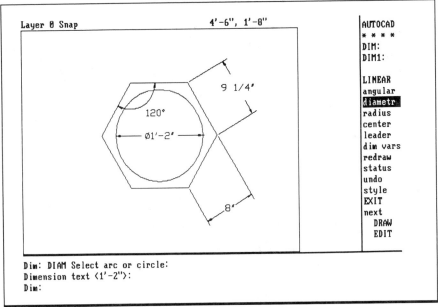

Figure 9.32: *Dimensions showing the diameter of a circle*

You can then pick a distance using your mouse or enter a distance value from the keyboard. The value you enter determines the length of the leader. The dimension appears outside the circle with an arrow pointing to the circle.

The Radius option works the same way as the Diametr option, except that it gives you a radius dimension (see Figure 9.33). The Center option just places a center mark in the shape of a cross at the center of the selected arc or circle.

Finally, there is the Leader option. This option allows you to add a note with an arrow pointing to the object the note describes. While still in the Dim command, pick Leader from the Dim menu. At the prompt

Leader start:

pick a point near coordinate 1'-4", 2'-0". At the prompt

To point:

enter @6'<110. The leader appears and the prompt for a to point reappears. You could continue to pick points just as you would draw lines. Press Return instead. A short horizontal line appears at the end of the leader line, and you see the prompt

Dimension text <1'-2">:

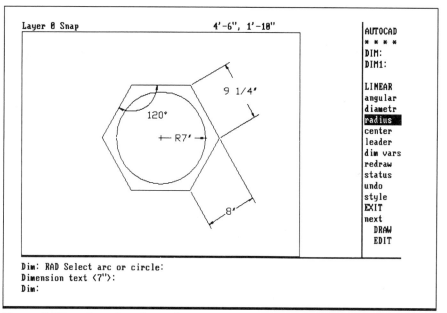

Figure 9.33:   A radius dimension

The default value for this prompt is the last dimension you entered. If this is the first option used in the Dim command, it will be a blank. You can enter a different value or press Return to accept this default. Enter the note Window frame. Your drawing will look like Figure 9.34.

The problem with the Leader option is that it does not allow you to enter more than one line of text. If you have a lot of text you would like to use with the leader, you will have to enter the text using the Text command, then use the Leader option on the Dim menu to add the leader. When you do this, enter a blank at the dimension text prompt.

Now end out of the Window file.

CONCLUSION

AutoCAD's dimensioning capabilities are extensive and take some practice. This chapter has given you the necessary background on the dimension menu hierarchy and the command settings, and some practice in issuing dimension commands. At this point, you might want to experiment with the settings to identify the ones that are most useful for your work. You can then set these up as defaults in

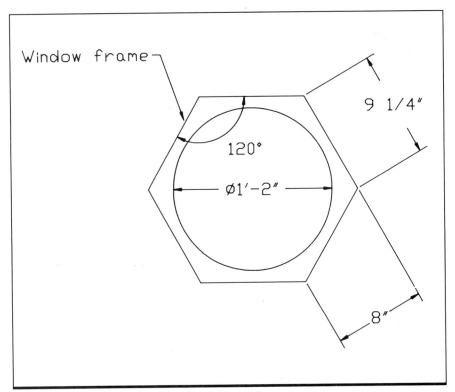

Figure 9.34: *The leader with a note added*

a template file or the ACAD.DWG file. Because you will still have to alter them from time to time, it's also a good idea to experiment with the settings you don't think you will need often.

In the next chapter, you will learn about attributes and how they are used.

Chapter 10

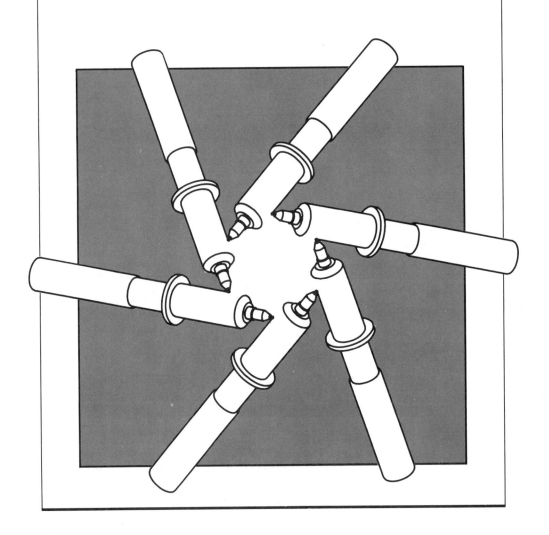

Using Attributes

ATTRIBUTES ARE UNIQUE to computer-aided design and drafting; nothing quite like them exists in traditional drafting. Because of this, they are often poorly understood. Attributes enable you to store information as text you can later extract to use in database managers, spreadsheet programs, and word processors. By doing this, you can keep track of virtually any object in a drawing.

But keeping track of objects is just one way of using attributes. You can also use them in place of the Text command where you must enter the same text, with minor modifications, in many places in your drawing. For example, if you are drawing a schedule that contains several columns of information, you can use attributes to help simplify your data entry. Attributes can also be used where you anticipate global editing of text. For example, suppose a note that refers to a part number occurs in several places. If you think you will want to change that part number in every note, you can make the number a block with an attribute. Later when you know the new part number, you can use the global editing capability of the attribute feature to change the old part number in one step.

In this chapter you will use attributes for one of their more common functions—maintaining lists of parts. In this case, the parts are doors. We will also describe how to import these attributes into a database-management program. As you go through these exercises, think about the ways attributes can help you in your particular application.

For the exercises in this chapter, you will need to know how to create and manipulate ASCII files, and you should be familiar with DOS. If you need more information on DOS, look at Appendix C of this book or your DOS manual. It is helpful, but not essential, if you also know how to use a database-management program.

CREATING ATTRIBUTES

In this exercise, you will create a door type symbol, which is commonly used to describe the size, thickness, and other characteristics of any given door in an architectural drawing. The symbol is usually a circle or diamond with a number in it. The number can be cross-referenced to a schedule that lists all the door types and their characteristics.

Adding Attributes to Blocks

Attributes depend on blocks. You might think of an attribute as a tag attached to a block that contains information about that block. For example, if you add an attribute to the door drawing you created in Chapter 2, every time you subsequently insert the door, you will be prompted for a value associated with that block. The value can be a number, height and width value, a name, or any type of text information you like. When you insert the block, you get the usual prompts, then a prompt for an attribute value. Once you enter a value, it is stored as part of the block within the drawing database. This value can be displayed as text, or it can be made invisible. You can set up the attribute so it prompts you for specific information, such as the door name or door number. You can even set up a default value for the attribute, such as hollow core or hc. That way you only have to enter a value when it deviates from the default.

But suppose you don't have the attribute information when you design the door. You want to avoid adding an attribute to a block that will not have a specific value early in the design process. Instead, you add the attribute to a symbol that is later placed by the door when you know enough about the design to specify what type of door goes where. The standard door type symbol suits this purpose nicely because it is an object that can be set up and used as a block.

In the following exercises, you will create a door type symbol with attributes for the different values normally assigned to doors, namely size, thickness, fire rating, material, and construction. To create the door type symbol with these attributes attached, open a new file and call it S-door (for symbol-door). Draw a circle .25 units in diameter with its center at coordinate 7,5. Next zoom into the circle. Pick Attdef from the Blocks menu. You will see the prompt

**Attribute modes – Invisible:N Constant:N Verify:N Preset:N
Enter (ICVP?) to change, RETURN when done:**

and the Attdef menu appears (see Figure 10.1).

At this point you can tell AutoCAD whether you want the attribute to be *invisible, constant,* or *verifiable* after the attribute is entered. The Invis option allows you to control whether the attribute is shown as part of the drawing. The Constant option allows you to create an attribute that does not prompt you to enter a value. Instead the attribute simply has a fixed value you give it during creation. Constant is used in situations where you know you will assign a fixed value to an object. When you use the Verify option, AutoCAD shows you the attribute value you entered and asks you if it is correct. The Preset option is used if you want an attribute to be automatically assigned its default value when its block is inserted. This saves time since a preset attribute will not prompt

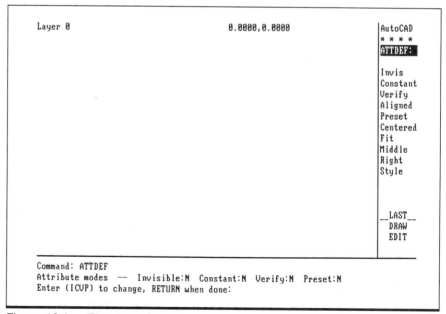

Figure 10.1:   The Attdef menu

you for a value. Unlike the Constant option, you can edit an attrib-ute that has the Preset option on.

The N after each option in the prompt above means that mode is currently off. You can enter I, C, V, or P to toggle any of the modes on or off until you have the settings you want. You can have all four modes on, all four off, or any combination of modes. Once a mode has been selected, however, you cannot change it, with the exception of the invisible mode. Later in this chapter we will discuss how to make an invisible attribute visible.

Pick Verify from the menu or enter V through the keyboard. The attribute modes prompt appears again, only this time the Verify option has a Y following it to indicate that the verify mode is on. Press Return to continue. The next prompt

Attribute tag:

appears. At this prompt, you must enter the attribute name. It is important to keep track of this name because later when you edit your attributes, you will want to know what attribute relates to what information. For this reason, attributes need simple, easy-to-remember names. Enter Type for door type. The next prompt

Attribute prompt:

appears. Here you enter the text for the prompt that appears when you insert the block containing this attribute. Often the prompt is the same as the tag, but it can be anything you like. Enter Door type. The next prompt

Default Attribute value:

appears. This is where you enter a default value for the door type prompt. Even if you haven't yet determined a default value you should enter something, since entering a blank now will make it diffi-cult to edit this attribute later.

However, you may sometimes want the default value to begin with a blank space. This enables you to specify text strings to be modified when you edit the attribute. For example, you may have an attribute value that reads "3334333". If you want to change the first 3 in this string of numbers, you have to specify "3334" when prompted for the string to change. If you start with a space as in " 3334333" you isolate the first 3 from the rest by specifying " 3" as the string to change. You must enter a backslash character before the space in the default value to tell AutoCAD to interpret the space literally, rather than as a press of the space bar (which is equivalent to pressing Return).

Enter a hyphen for the door type default value (a hyphen is often used in architectural drawings to indicate that a symbol is not assigned a value). The next prompt

Start point or Align/Center/Fit/Middle/Right/Style:

will look familiar. The rest of the prompts are the same as those for the Text command. You can choose a text style, whether the attribute is centered, left-justified, right-justified, etc. Pick Middle from the menu, then pick the center point of the circle. Enter a height of .125 and an insertion angle of 0. Your drawing will look like Figure 10.2.

Press Return to start the Attdef command again. This time pick Invis for the attribute mode. Enter D-size for the tag, Door size for the prompt, and a hyphen for the default value. When you see the starting point prompt, press Return. Your drawing will look like Figure 10.3.

Just as you can add more lines of text to the most recent line entered, you can continue to add attributes. Add the attributes listed in Figure 10.4, and make them invisible. After you have entered all the attributes, make the base point of this drawing the center of the circle.

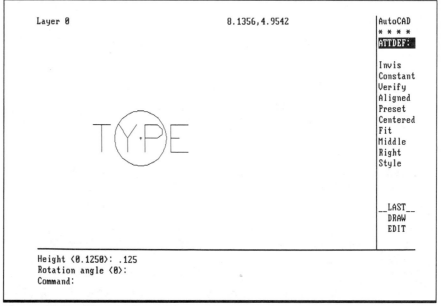

Figure 10.2:   *The attribute inserted in the circle*

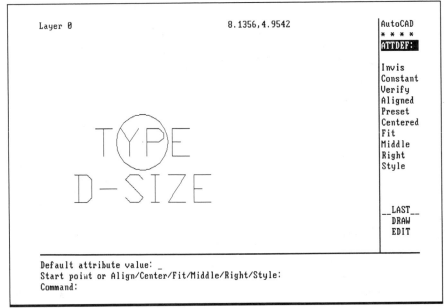

```
     Layer 0                          8.1356,4.9542        AutoCAD
                                                           * * * *
                                                           ATTDEF:

                                                           Invis
                                                           Constant
                                                           Verify
                                                           Aligned
                                                           Preset
          TYPE                                             Centered
                                                           Fit
          D-SIZE                                           Middle
                                                           Right
                                                           Style


                                                           __LAST__
                                                           DRAW
                                                           EDIT

     Default attribute value: _
     Start point or Align/Center/Fit/Middle/Right/Style:
     Command:
```

Figure 10.3:   *The second attribute added*

Tag	Prompt	Default
D-number	Door number	-
D-thick	Door thickness	-
D-rate	Fire rating	-
D-matrl	Door material	-
D-const	Door construction	-

Figure 10.4:   *Attributes for the door type symbol*

Changing Attribute Specifications

In all the attributes except the first, you added the prefix D- to the tag. This helps you separate the door type symbol attribute tags from other symbols that might contain similar tags. You will want the first tag, type, also to have the D- prefix. To change an attribute tag, you can use the Change command. Pick Change from the Edit menu and pick the Type attribute. Press Return to confirm your selection and continue to press Return until you get to the prompt

Properties/<Change point>:
Enter text insertion point:
New style or RETURN for no change:
New height <0.1250>:
New rotation angle <0>:
New tag <TYPE>:

Enter D-type. The next two prompts

New prompt <Door type>:

and

New default value <->:

allow you to change the prompt and default value. Press Return twice to keep the old ones. The Type tag will change to D-type.

Now you have finished creating your door type symbol with attributes. End out of the S-door file and open the Plan file.

Inserting Blocks Containing Attributes

In the last section, you created a door type symbol at the size desired for the actual symbol. This means that whenever you insert that symbol you have to specify the x scale factor of the drawing you are inserting the symbol into. This technique allows you to use the same symbol in any drawing, regardless of its scale. You could have several door type symbols, one for each scale you anticipate using, but this would be inefficient.

Use the View command to restore view 1 (refer to Chapter 7 if you need to refresh your memory about views). Be sure the Ceiling layer is off. Normally in a floor plan the door headers are not visible, and they will interfere with the placement of the door symbol. Start the Insert command from the Draw side or pull-down menu and enter S-door at the block name prompt. Insert the symbol at coordinate 41'-3", 72'-4". Then at the x scale factor prompt enter 96. Press Return at the y scale factor prompt and the rotation angle prompt. Unless your system uses the advanced user interface, you get a new prompt

Door type <->:

This is the prompt you created along with the default value you specified in the previous section. Now you can enter the door type value you want to assign to this particular block. Enter A. The next prompt

Door size <-> :

is the prompt you created for the door size attribute. Enter 7'-0". This represents the door height. The next prompt will be the door number, 116. This represents the apartment the door is associated with. Continue to enter the values for each prompt as shown in Figure 10.5.

When you are done entering the values, the prompts repeat themselves to verify your entry (because you set the verify mode to N). You can now either change an entry, or just press Return to accept the original entry. When you are done and the symbol appears, the only attribute you can see is the one you selected to be visible, the door type.

If you select Insert from the pull-down menu, you get a dialog box after entering the S-door scale and rotation angle (see Figure 10.6). This dialog box allows you to enter the values for each attribute using the input buttons next to the attribute name. Since it lets you change your mind about a value before confirming your entry, the dialog box allows greater flexibility in entering attributes. You can also see all the attributes associated with a block at once, making it easier to understand what information is required for the block.

You should note that attributes set with the Preset mode on will also appear in the dialog box and are treated no differently from other

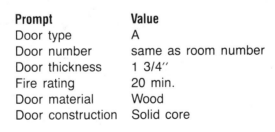

Prompt	Value
Door type	A
Door number	same as room number
Door thickness	1 3/4"
Fire rating	20 min.
Door material	Wood
Door construction	Solid core

Figure 10.5:   *Attribute values for the typical studio entry door*

editable attributes. If you picked the Insert command from the Draw pull-down menu, fill in the dialog box as shown in Figure 10.5.

Add the rest of the door type symbols for the apartment entry doors. You can use the previously saved views to help you get around the drawing quickly. Use Figure 10.7 as a guide to the apartment numbers.

Next, end out of the Plan file and create the apartment number symbol shown in Figure 10.8. Give its attribute the tag name A-number, the prompt Apartment number, the hyphen default, and a text height of .125 inches. Name this symbol file S-apart for Symbol-apartment. Open the Plan file again and insert the apartment number symbol into each studio. Figure 10.9 shows you what view 4 should look like once you have entered the door symbols and apartment numbers.

EDITING ATTRIBUTES

Because drawings are usually in flux even after actual construction or manufacturing begins, you sometimes have to edit previously entered attributes. In the example of the apartment building, many things can change before the final set of drawings is completed.

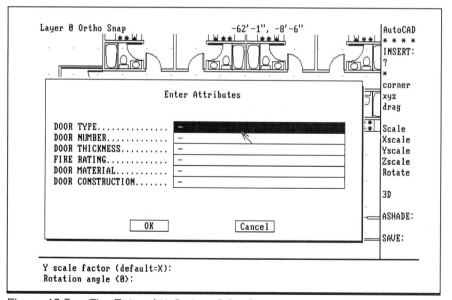

Figure 10.6: *The Enter Attributes dialog box*

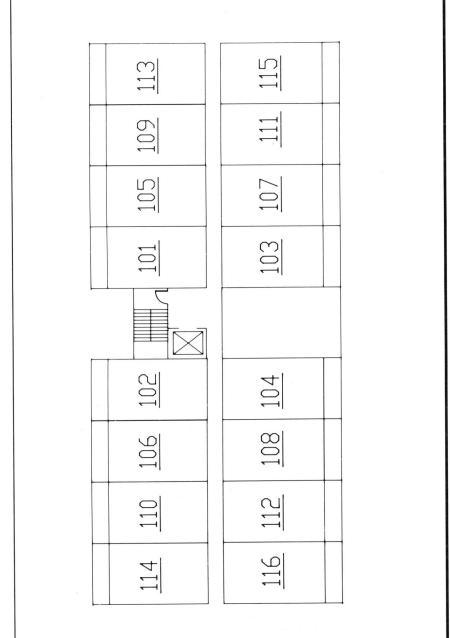

Figure 10.7: Apartment numbers for one floor of the studio apartment building

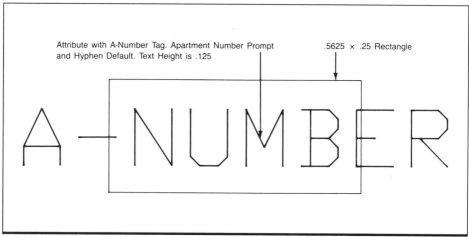

Attribute with A-Number Tag. Apartment Number Prompt and Hyphen Default. Text Height is .125

.5625 × .25 Rectangle

Figure 10.8: The apartment number symbol

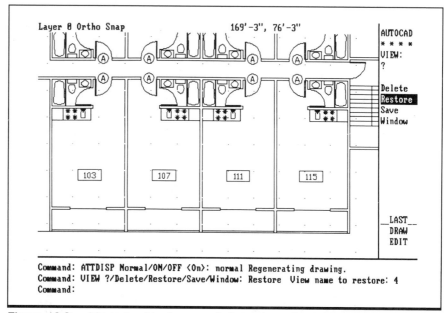

Figure 10.9: View 4 with door symbols and apartment numbers added

Attributes can be edited globally, meaning you can edit several occurrences of a particular attribute tag at once, or individually. However, if your system does not support the advanced user interface, you cannot edit invisible attributes individually unless you make them visible. In this section you will make changes to the attributes you have entered so far using both individual and global editing, and you will practice editing invisible attributes.

Editing Individual Attributes

The Attedit command allows you to alter not only the value of the attribute, but its position, height, angle, style, layer, and color. You will use this option to edit one of the door type symbol attribute values. Use the View command to restore view 1. Pick Attedit from the Edit menu to bring up the Attedit menu (see Figure 10.10). The prompt

Edit attributes one at a time? <Y>

appears. The default is yes, so press Return. The next prompt

Block name specification < * >:

appears. Note that the default is an asterisk, which can be used like a wild card as for layers and other prompts that display the asterisk as a default value. If you accept the default, all blocks containing attributes will be considered for editing. Or you can enter instead the name of the block containing the attribute you want to edit.

Figure 10.10:   The Attedit menu

Since you have two blocks with attributes, enter S-apart to edit the apartment number symbol. The next prompt

Attribute tag specification < * >:

appears. You can now enter the name(s) of the attribute tag or tags you want to edit. Only the tags you enter here will be considered for editing. Enter S-apart. The next prompt

Attribute value specification < * >:

appears. Now you can even narrow your selection to specific values. For example, if you want to change only those attributes with the value 116, you could enter 116 at this prompt. If you later pick an attribute with a different value, AutoCAD will ignore it. If you wish to add a value to an attribute that has none, you can enter a backslash here.

Press Return to accept the default. The next prompt

Select Attributes:

asks you to pick the attributes you wish to edit. You can pick them one by one, or use a window to select a group, then press Return. Each selected attribute that conforms to the specifications you just entered ghosts, and an X appears at its base point.

Pick the apartment number attribute at unit 116. The next prompt

Value/Position/Height/Angle/Style/Layer/Color/Next <N>:

appears, and an X appears at one of the attributes you selected (see Figure 10.11).

As you can see from the prompt, you have many options to choose from. With the exception of Value, these are accessible only through the individual editing option. Because most of these options should be familiar by now, you'll practice only the most commonly used option, Value. Pick Value from the Attedit menu. The next prompt

Value Change or Replace? <R>:

appears. You can enter R to replace the current value, or you can enter a C to change part of the existing text. The Change option is useful if you have a long sentence where only two or three words need to be replaced.

Enter C for change. The prompt

String to change:

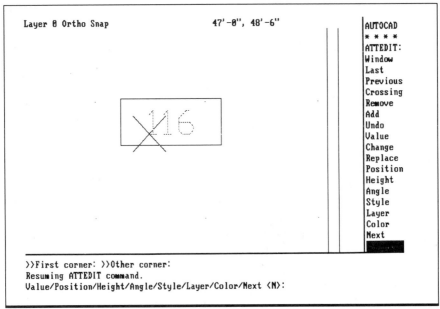

```
Layer 0 Ortho Snap                    47'-0", 48'-6"              AUTOCAD
                                                                 * * * *
                                                                 ATTEDIT:
                                                                 Window
                                                                 Last
                                                                 Previous
                                                                 Crossing
                                                                 Remove
                                                                 Add
                                                                 Undo
                                                                 Value
                                                                 Change
                                                                 Replace
                                                                 Position
                                                                 Height
                                                                 Angle
                                                                 Style
                                                                 Layer
                                                                 Color
                                                                 Next


 >>First corner: >>Other corner:
 Resuming ATTEDIT command.
 Value/Position/Height/Angle/Style/Layer/Color/Next <N>:
```

Figure 10.11:   *Close-up of attribute with X*

appears. Now you can modify any part of the attribute text you wish. First you enter the group of letters or string you want to change, then you enter the new string. Enter 16 at this prompt. At the next prompt

New string:

enter 00 and watch the apartment number become 100.

Using a Dialog Box to Edit Attributes

Pull-down menu users can edit attributes with a dialog box by entering the command Ddatte. The following prompt appears:

Select block:

Pick the apartment number block. A dialog box similar to the one that appeared when you inserted the block appears. You can now change the value button. For now, leave the value as it is and pick the OK action button at the bottom of the dialog box (see Figure 10.12).

The Ddatte command is useful for reviewing attributes as well as editing them because both visible and invisible attributes are displayed in the dialog box. If you wish to review several attributes, you can use the multiple command modifier to force AutoCAD to

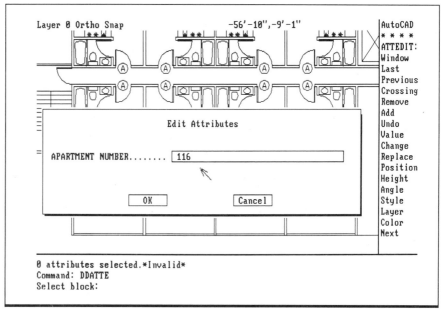

Figure 10.12:   The Edit Attributes dialog box

repeat the Ddatte command. First, enter multiple at the command prompt, then enter ddatte. Now, as you pick blocks containing attributes, a dialog box appears as before. Once you exit the dialog box, however, AutoCAD automatically restarts the Ddatte command. This enables you to pick the next block without reentering the Ddatte command, and makes it possible to view several attributes easily. To exit the Ddatte command, press Control-C or pick Cancel from the Tools pull-down menu or from the Osnap side menu. The multiple command modifier affects all other commands in the same way by automatically repeating them until a cancellation is issued.

Editing Multiple Attributes

Global editing allows you to change a group of attributes all at once. Unlike individual editing, global editing allows you to edit only the attribute values. In the following exercise, you will make a global change of attribute values.

Suppose you decide you want to change all the entry doors to a type designated as B, rather than A. Perhaps door type A was an input error, or type B happens to be better suited for an entry door.

Use the View command to restore view 4. Start the Attedit command again, but this time at the prompt

Edit attributes one at a time? <Y>

enter N for no. A different prompt appears.

Global edit of attribute values.
Edit only attributes visible on screen? <Y>

Now you must tell AutoCAD if you want to edit only the visible attributes. The default is yes, so press Return. The next three prompts are the same as before. You can filter out the block name, attribute tag, and value to be edited. Enter S-door for the block name, D-type for the attribute tag, and press Return for the value. The attribute-selection prompt appears. Window the door type symbols for units 101 to 107. The prompt for a string to change appears. Enter A. The prompt for a new string appears. Enter B. The door type symbols all change to the new value.

Try the same procedure again, but this time enter N at the prompt to edit only visible attributes. Another message appears.

Drawing must be regenerated afterwards.
Block name specification < * >:

The display will flip to text mode. Once again, you are prompted for the block name, the tag, and the value. Respond to these prompts as you did before. Once you have done that, you get a new message.

16 attributes selected.
String to change:

This tells you the number of attributes that fit the specifications you just entered. Enter A at this prompt to indicate you want to change the rest of the A attribute values, then B at the prompt for a new string. A series of Bs appears, indicating the number of strings that were replaced (unless Regenauto is off, in which case you must regenerate the drawing to see the change).

Making Invisible Attributes Visible

You just used the global editing option to change a visible attribute, but you can use it to change invisible ones as well. Or, as we mentioned earlier, you can make the invisible attributes visible, then edit them individually. To do this, pick Attdisp from the Display menu to bring up the Attdisp menu (see Figure 10.13).

Figure 10.13: *The Attdisp menu*

The Attdisp menu shows three options: Normal, On, and Off. Normal is the current option and this displays the attributes just as you specified when you selected the attribute modes; that is, visible attributes are visible and invisible attributes are not. Off causes all the attributes to become invisible, and On makes them all visible. Pick On. If Regenauto is off, regenerate the drawing. It will look like Figure 10.14. Since the door type symbols are so close together, the attributes overlap. At this point you could edit the invisible attributes individually, as in the first attribute-editing exercise. For now, however, just set Attdisp to Normal.

EXTRACTING ATTRIBUTE INFORMATION

Once you have entered the attributes into your drawing, you can extract the information contained in them and use it in other programs. You may, for example, want to keep track of the door information in a database manager. This is especially true if you have a project that contains thousands of doors, such as a large hotel.

The first step in extracting attribute information is to create a template file using a word processor or the DOS COPY CON command. This shouldn't be confused with the drawing file you use to set up various default settings. The template file used with attributes is a DOS text file containing a list of the attributes you wish

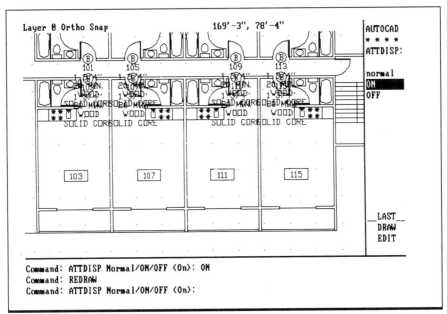

Figure 10.14: *The drawing with all the attributes visible*

to extract and their characteristics. You can also extract information about the block an attribute is associated with. The block name, its x and y coordinates, its layer, orientation, and scale are all available for extraction.

Creating a Template File

In the template file, for every attribute you wish to extract, you must give its tag name followed by a code that determines whether the attribute value is numeric or text, how many spaces to allow for the value, and, if it is a numeric value, how many decimal places to give the number. If you are familiar with database-management programs, you know these are typical variables you determine when you set up a database, even though this template file format is used for all the types of programs into which information can be imported.

To get a list of rooms containing the B door type, you create a DOS text file that looks like the one below.

```
D-ROOM N005000
D-TYPE C001000
```

The first item on the line is the tag of the attribute you want to list, D-ROOM or D-TYPE. It is followed by a code that describes the attribute. The first character of the code is always a C or an N to denote a character or numeric value. The next three digits are where you enter the number of spaces the value will take up. You can enter any number from 1 to 999, but you must enter zeros for null values. This example shows the value of 5 for five spaces. The last three digits are for the number of decimal places to allow if the value is numeric. For character values, these must always be zeros. You cannot have a blank line anywhere in the template file, or Auto-CAD will reject it. Also, the last line in the file must be ended with a Return.

Now you will use the Shell command to temporarily exit AutoCAD to create your template using COPY CON. In Chapter 8 you used COPY CON while you were in DOS to create an ASCII file. In the following exercise, you will use AutoCAD's Shell command to enter DOS temporarily and use the COPY CON command again.

Pick External Commands from the Utility menu, then pick Shell to bring up the External Commands menu (see Figure 10.15). You will get the prompt

DOS Command:

You can now enter any DOS command or even start another program if it is small enough. Some word processors, such as PC Write, will run in AutoCAD's Shell command because they require very little memory to operate. You will explore these uses of the Shell command in Chapter 13.

Now enter COPY CON Door.TXT. Template files must have the extension TXT in order to work. Enter the following text as it is shown. Enter one line then press Return, then the next line until you are done.

```
D-NUMBER C005000
D-THICK C007000
D-RATE C010000
D-MATRL C015000
D-CONST C015000
  ^Z
```

Remember to use the F6 function key to get the ^Z character. Once you are done, the message

1 File(s) copied

appears at the bottom of the list.

Figure 10.15:   *The External Commands menu*

We mentioned that you can extract information regarding blocks, as well as attributes. To do this you must use the following format.

```
BL:LEVEL     N000000
BL:NAME      C000000
BL:X         N000000
BL:Y         N000000
BL:LAYER     C000000
BL:ORIENT    N000000
BL:XSCALE    N000000
BL:YSCALE    N000000
```

If the line BL:LEVEL is included in the attribute template file, the attribute block's nesting level will be extracted. If the line BL:NAME is included, the attribute block's name will be extracted. If the BL:X and BL:Y lines are included, the attribute block's coordinates will be extracted. BL:LAYER, BL:ORIENT, BL:XSCALE, and BL:YSCALE extract the attribute block's layer, orientation in degrees, x scale, and y scale, respectively. A template file containing these codes must also contain at least one attribute tag because AutoCAD must know which attribute it is extracting before it can tell what block the attribute is associated with. The code information for blocks works the same as for attributes. The zeros in the example would normally be filled in with numbers to reflect the size of the block value you want to extract.

You are now ready to extract the attribute information from your drawing.

Extracting Information from Your Drawing

The Attext command allows you to extract attribute information from your drawing as a list in one of three different formats. These are the CDF (comma delimited format), SDF (system data format), and DXF (data exchange format). Each format is discussed below.

Using the CDF Format

The CDF format can be read by many popular database-management programs, as well as programs written in BASIC. To select it, pick Attext from the Utility menu, then pick CDF from the Attext menu (see Figure 10.16). The prompt

Template file:

appears, asking you for the name of the template file to use for your data extraction. Enter Door. The next prompt

Extract file name <plan>:

asks you what to name the file containing the list. The default file name, Plan, comes from the current file name. Press Return to accept the default. The computer will pause for several seconds and when it is done, the message

16 records in extract file.

appears. AutoCAD has created a file called Plan.TXT that contains the extracted list. The program automatically adds the extension TXT to files created using the CDF or the SDF option.

To display the contents of the DOS text file, pick External Commands from the Utility menu, then pick Type from the External Commands menu. At the prompt

File to list:

enter Plan.TXT. You will get the following list:

```
'116','1 3/4''','20 MIN','WOOD','SOLID CORE'
'114','1 3/4''','20 MIN','WOOD','SOLID CORE'
'112','1 3/4''','20 MIN','WOOD','SOLID CORE'
'110','1 3/4''','20 MIN','WOOD','SOLID CORE'
'108','1 3/4''','20 MIN','WOOD','SOLID CORE'
'106','1 3/4''','20 MIN','WOOD','SOLID CORE'
```

Figure 10.16:   The Attext menu

'102','1 3/4''','20 MIN','WOOD','SOLID CORE'
'104','1 3/4''','20 MIN','WOOD','SOLID CORE'
'107','1 3/4''','20 MIN','WOOD','SOLID CORE'
'105','1 3/4''','20 MIN','WOOD','SOLID CORE'
'101','1 3/4''','20 MIN','WOOD','SOLID CORE'
'103','1 3/4''','20 MIN','WOOD','SOLID CORE'
'111','1 3/4''','20 MIN','WOOD','SOLID CORE'
'109','1 3/4''','20 MIN','WOOD','SOLID CORE'
'113','1 3/4''','20 MIN','WOOD','SOLID CORE'
'115','1 3/4''','20 MIN','WOOD','SOLID CORE'

The AutoCAD Type command, like the DOS TYPE command, displays the contents of any DOS text file. Since you picked the comma delimited format option, AutoCAD placed commas between each extracted attribute value (or *field* in database terminology). The commas are used by some database-management programs to indicate the separation of fields in ASCII files. Notice that the individual values are enclosed in single quotes. These quotes delimit character values. If you had specified numeric values, the quotes would not appear. Also note that the fields are in the order they appear in the template file. This example shows everything in uppercase letters because you used them to enter the attribute information. The extracted file maintains the case of whatever you enter for the attribute values.

Some database managers require the use of other symbols, such as double quotes and slashes, to indicate character values and field separation. AutoCAD allows you to use a different symbol in place of the single quote or comma. If the database manager you use requires double-quote delimiters, for example, in the file to be imported, you can add the statement

c:quote "

to the template file to replace the single quote with a double quote. You can also add the statement

c:delim /

to replace the comma delimiter with the slash symbol.

Using the SDF Format

The SDF format, as well as the CDF format, can be read by most database-management programs. You can also use this format if you intend to enter information into a word-processed document. You can even import it into an AutoCAD drawing using the method described in Chapter 8 to import text.

Now try using the SDF option to extract the same list. Pick Attext, then SDF. Use the same template file, but for the Extract file name use Plan-SDF to distinguish this file from the last one you created. After you have extracted the list, use the Type command to view the contents of the file. You should get the following list:

```
116 1 3/4" 20 MIN WOOD SOLID CORE
114 1 3/4" 20 MIN WOOD SOLID CORE
112 1 3/4" 20 MIN WOOD SOLID CORE
110 1 3/4" 20 MIN WOOD SOLID CORE
108 1 3/4" 20 MIN WOOD SOLID CORE
106 1 3/4" 20 MIN WOOD SOLID CORE
102 1 3/4" 20 MIN WOOD SOLID CORE
104 1 3/4" 20 MIN WOOD SOLID CORE
107 1 3/4" 20 MIN WOOD SOLID CORE
105 1 3/4" 20 MIN WOOD SOLID CORE
101 1 3/4" 20 MIN WOOD SOLID CORE
103 1 3/4" 20 MIN WOOD SOLID CORE
111 1 3/4" 20 MIN WOOD SOLID CORE
109 1 3/4" 20 MIN WOOD SOLID CORE
113 1 3/4" 20 MIN WOOD SOLID CORE
115 1 3/4" 20 MIN WOOD SOLID CORE
```

Using the DXF Format

The third file format is the DXF format. There are actually two DXF commands. The one on the Attext menu extracts only the data on blocks containing attributes. The Dxfout command on the Utility menu converts an entire drawing file into a special format for data exchange between AutoCAD and other programs (for example, other PC CAD programs). Dxfout creates a text file containing all the information in the drawing. We will discuss the DXF format in more detail in Chapter 13.

Finally, you may have noticed the Entities option in parentheses on the Attext prompt or the Attext menu. By entering E at this prompt, you can single out attributes to extract by picking their associated blocks from the display.

USING EXTRACTED ATTRIBUTES WITH OTHER PROGRAMS

Suppose you want to import the list you just created into dBASE III PLUS using the CDF option. First you create a database file with the same field characteristics you entered for the template file. Then enter:

Append from *AutoCAD directory*\plan.txt Delimited

where *AutoCAD directory* is the directory where the Plan.TXT file can be found. To use the file created by the SDF option, replace Delimited in the line above with SDF and use Plan-SDF.TXT instead of Plan.TXT.

You can import any of these lists into any word-processing program that accepts ASCII files. They will appear as shown in our examples. You may want to use the SDF format for word processing because it leaves out the commas and quotes.

You can also use the SDF format for importing files to Lotus 1-2-3. However, you must change the SDF file extension from .TXT to .PRN. Once you have done this, you can use Lotus's File Import command to create a spreadsheet from this file. Use the Numbers option on the Lotus Import submenu to ensure that the numeric values are entered as discrete spreadsheet cells. Any items containing text are grouped together in one cell. For example, the last three items in the Plan-SDF.TXT file are combined into one cell because each item contains text.

As we mentioned earlier, the extracted file can be made to conform to other data formats. If you are using a database manager other than dBASE III PLUS, find out what its format requirements are for imported files and use the Quote and Delim options described earlier to make adjustments.

CONCLUSION

AutoCAD's attribute feature offers flexibility and power to those who take the time to master its use. It may seem a bit cumbersome at first, but with some standardization of procedures and names for attributes and template files, you can simplify the process of extracting information.

If you have the advanced user interface, you can easily access attributes, which gives you more freedom to create an intelligent drawing. Also, with the Ddatte command, you can display or modify attribute information instantaneously. This is like having a graphic database—easily accessed graphic symbols that can store written information.

In this chapter, you used attributes in your door type symbols. In an actual apartment-design project, you would also add window and wall types as well as elevation targets, section lines, and perhaps even equipment symbols. An electrical engineer might add light fixtures, outlets, fans, switches, and electrical equipment symbols. A mechanical engineer might add valve and register locations. All these things can be made into symbols with attributes that can be extracted and used in other programs or turned into schedules in other drawing files. You may want to go through these exercises again using symbols suited to your application.

At times you will want to enter hand-drafted drawings to be used as templates or backgrounds for other drawings. In the next chapter, you will look at alternate methods of input, such as tracing, that enable you to quickly enter existing drawings. You will also learn what to do with a drawing once it has been traced.

Chapter 11

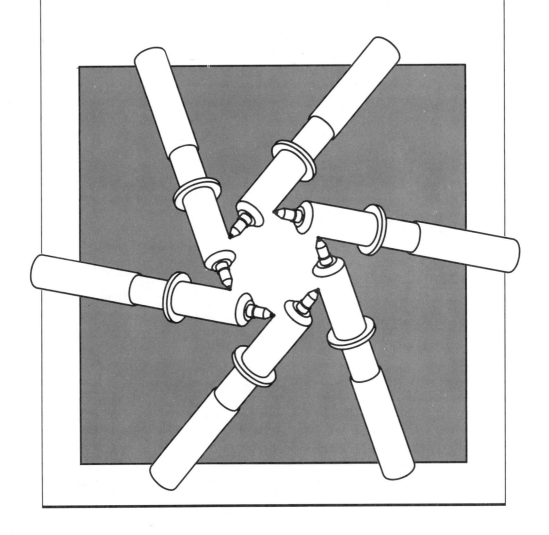

Entering a Hand-Drafted Drawing

AT TIMES YOU WILL WANT to turn a hand-drafted drawing into an Auto-CAD drawing file. It may be because you are modifying a design you created before you started using AutoCAD, or because you are converting your entire library of drawings for future AutoCAD use. This chapter discusses three ways to enter a hand-drafted drawing: *tracing*, *scaling*, and *scanning*.

Each method of drawing input has its advantages and disadvantages. Tracing with a digitizing tablet is the easiest method, but a traced drawing usually requires some cleaning up and reorganization. If dimensional accuracy is not too important, tracing is the best method for entering existing drawings. It is especially useful for entering irregular curves, such as the contour lines of a topographical map.

Scaling a drawing is the most flexible method since you don't need a tablet to do it and you usually have less cleaning up to do afterwards. It also affords the most accurate input of orthogonal lines since you can read dimensions directly from the drawing and enter those same dimensions into AutoCAD. Its main drawback is that if the drawing does not contain complete dimensional information, you must constantly look at the hand-drafted drawing and measure distances with a scale. Also, irregular curves are difficult to scale accurately.

Scanning produces a file that requires the most cleaning up of all these input methods. In fact, you often spend more time cleaning up a scanned drawing than you would have spent tracing or scaling it. It is also difficult to scan text in a drawing (even though some scanners can read straight text files). Unfortunately, there is no easy way to transfer text from a hand-drafted drawing to an AutoCAD file. Scanning is best used for drawings that are difficult to trace or scale, such as complex topographical maps containing more contours than are practical to trace, or nontechnical line art.

If you don't have a digitizing tablet, you can use scaling to enter the utility room drawing used in the tracing exercise (you will insert it into your apartment house plan in Chapter 16). Be sure to read the tracing information anyway, because some of it will help you with your editing. For example, because traced lines are often not accurately placed, you will learn how to fix such lines in the course of cleaning up a traced drawing.

TRACING A DRAWING

The most common and direct method for entering a hand-drafted drawing is tracing. If it is a large drawing, and you have a small tablet, you may have to cut the drawing into pieces your tablet can manage, trace each piece, then assemble the completed pieces into the large drawing. The best solution is to have a large tablet to begin with, but many of us can't afford the eight or ten thousand dollars these large-format tablets usually cost.

In the following exercises, we assume you have an 11 x 11-inch or larger tablet. The sample drawings are small enough to fit completely on this size tablet. You can use either a stylus or a puck to trace them, but the stylus offers the most natural feel since it is shaped like a pen. A puck has cross hairs that you have to center on the line you want to trace. This requires a bit more dexterity, but it can be done.

Reconfiguring the Tablet for Tracing

When you first installed AutoCAD, you configured the tablet to use most of its active drawing area for AutoCAD's menu template. Since you will need the tablet's entire drawing area to trace this drawing, you now have to reconfigure the tablet to get rid of the menu. Otherwise you won't be able to pick points on the drawing outside the 4 x 3-inch screen pointing area AutoCAD normally uses (see Figure 11.1).

Start AutoCAD and open a new file called Utility. Set up the file as a 1/4" = 1' scale architectural drawing on an 8½ x 11-inch sheet. Pick Settings from the Root menu, then pick Next. Then pick Tablet from the Settings menu to bring up the Tablet menu (see Figure 11.2).

You will get the prompt

TABLET Option (ON/OFF/CAL/CFG):

Enter CFG. This tells AutoCAD you want to configure your tablet. (We will discuss the other options later in this section.) At the next prompt

Enter number of tablet menus desired (0-4) <4>:

enter 0. At the next prompt

Do you want to respecify the screen pointing area? <N>

enter Y. Then, at the prompt

Digitize lower left corner of screen pointing area:

pick the lower-left corner of the tablet's active drawing area. On some tablets, a light appears to show you the active area; other tablets use a permanent mark, such as a corner mark. AutoCAD won't do anything until you have picked a point, so you don't have to worry about picking a point outside this area. At the next prompt

Digitize upper right corner of screen pointing area:

pick the upper-right corner. Now as you move your stylus or puck you will notice that the relationship between your hand movement and your screen cursor is different. The cursor moves more slowly and it is active over more of the tablet surface.

Calibrating the Tablet for Your Drawing

Now photocopy Figure 11.3, which represents a hand-drafted drawing of a utility room for your apartment building. Place the photocopied drawing on your tablet so that it is aligned with the tablet and completely within the tablet's active drawing area (see Figure 11.4).

Before you can trace anything into your computer, you must *calibrate* your tablet. This means that you must give some points of

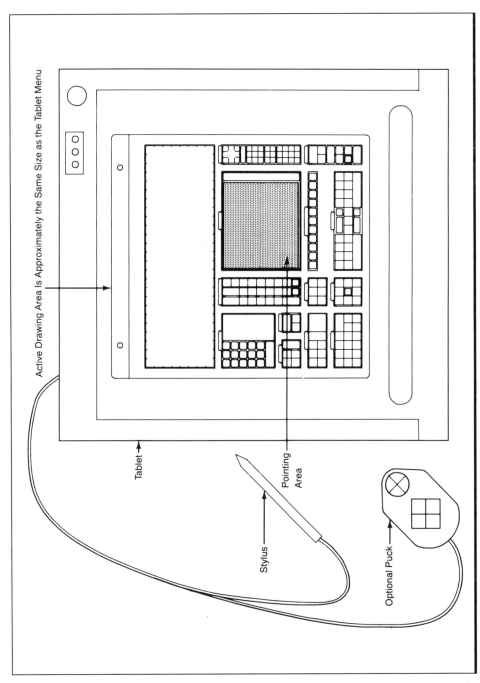

Active Drawing Area Is Approximately the Same Size as the Tablet Menu

Tablet

Pointing Area

Stylus

Optional Puck

Figure 11.1: The template's active drawing area

Figure 11.2: The Tablet menu

reference so AutoCAD can tell how distances on the tablet relate to distances in the drawing editor. For example, you may want to trace a drawing that was drawn at a scale of 1/8″ = 1′-0″. You will have to show AutoCAD two specific points on this drawing, then where those two points should appear in the drawing editor. This is accomplished by using the Tablet command.

On Figure 11.3, we have already determined the coordinates for two points on a reference line. To calibrate your tablet, pick Tablet from the on-screen Tablet menu. The prompt

TABLET Option (ON/OFF/CAL/CFG):

appears. Pick Cal from the on-screen menu. The message

Calibrate tablet for use...
Digitize first known point:

appears, asking you to pick the first point that you know the absolute coordinates for. Pick the X on the left end of the reference line. At the next prompt

Enter coordinates for first point:

enter 0,0. This tells AutoCAD that the point you just picked is equivalent to the coordinate 0,0 in your drawing editor. The next prompt

Digitize second known point:

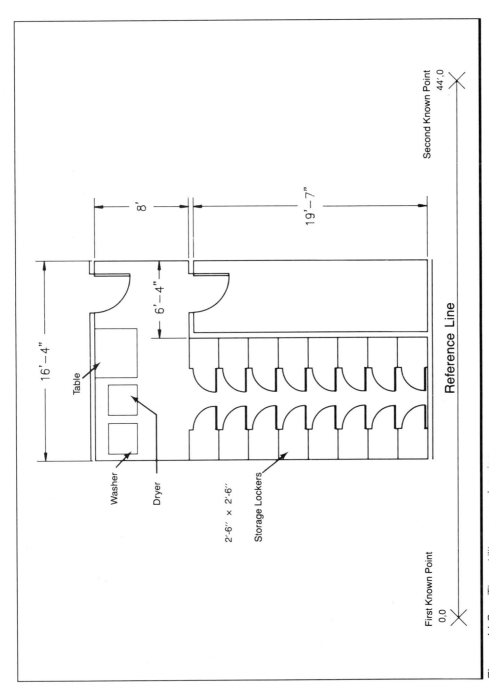

Figure 11.3: The utility room drawing

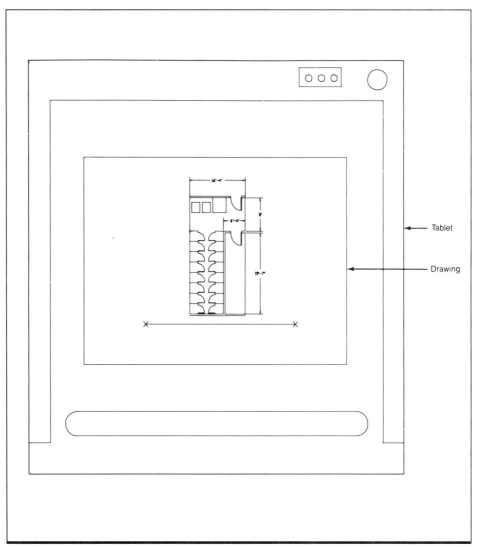

Figure 11.4: The drawing placed on the tablet

is asking you to pick another point that you know the coordinates for. Pick the X on the right end of the reference line. At the prompt

Enter coordinates for second point:

enter 44',0. The tablet is now calibrated.

The word Tablet appears on the status line to tell you that you are in *tablet mode*. While in tablet mode, you can trace the drawing, but you can not access the menus. If you want to pick a menu item, you must toggle the tablet mode off using the F10 function key. Or you can enter commands through the keyboard. If you have forgotten a keyboard command, enter help, then press Return to get a list.

Entering Lines from a Drawing

Now you are ready to trace the utility room. Start the Line command by entering the word line. Press F10 to turn the tablet mode on and trace the outline of all the walls except the storage lockers. Add the doors by inserting them at the appropriate points, then mirroring them. Trace the washer and copy it over to the position of the dryer. Since the washer and dryer are the same size, you can use the same object for both of them.

Your drawing should look something like Figure 11.5. It is a close facsimile of the original drawing, but not as exact as you might like. Zoom into one of the doors. Now you can see the inaccuracies of tracing. Some of the lines are crooked, and others don't meet at the right points. (The raggedness of the door arc, however, is due to the way AutoCAD displays arcs when you use the Zoom command; see Chapter 7 for details.) These inaccuracies are caused by the limited resolution of your tablet, coupled with the lack of steadiness in

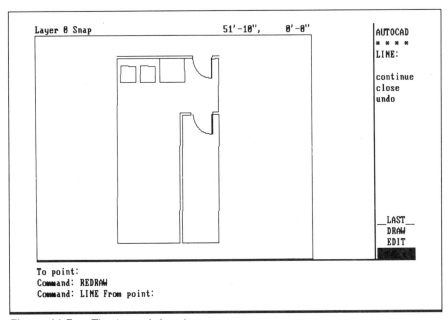

Figure 11.5: The traced drawing

the human hand. The best digitizing tablets have an accuracy of .001 inch, which is actually not very good when you are dealing with distances of 1/8 inch and smaller. In the following section you will clean up your drawing.

Cleaning Up a Traced Drawing

In Figure 11.5, one of the door jambs is not in the right position (see the close-up in Figure 11.6). You can move a group of objects keeping their vertices intact by using the Stretch command, which was introduced in Chapter 9. Go to the Edit menu, then pick Next. Then pick Stretch to bring up the Stretch menu.

Next, pick a crossing window enclosing the corners you wish to move (see Figure 11.7). Press Return to confirm your selection. You are then asked for a base point. Pick the corner of the jamb that is to meet the endpoint of the arc. The jamb and the wall stretch as you move the cursor (see Figure 11.8).

Next, pick the new position for that corner, which is the endpoint of the arc. The jamb repositions itself and all the lines follow (see Figure 11.9).

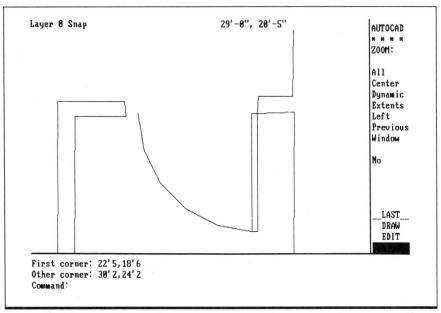

Figure 11.6: A close-up of the door

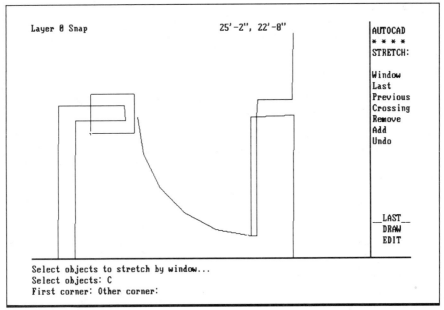

Figure 11.7:   A window crossing the door jamb

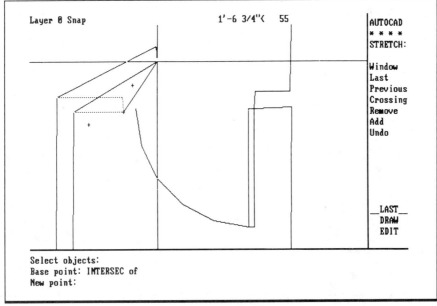

Figure 11.8:   The door jamb being stretched

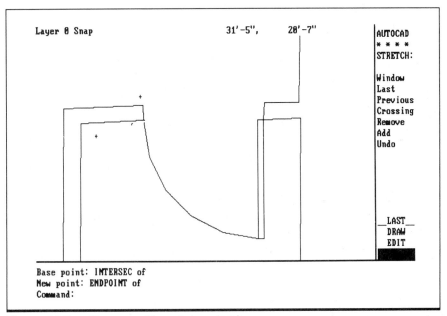

Figure 11.9: The repositioned door jamb

Another problem in this drawing is that some of the lines are not orthogonal. The Change command together with the ortho mode can be used to straighten them. Toggle the ortho mode on and start the Change command. At the object-selection prompt, pick the two lines representing the wall just left of the door. Press Return to confirm your selection. Then use the Perpendicular Osnap override and pick the wall to the left of the lines you just selected. The two lines will straighten out and their endpoints will align with the wall left of the two lines (see Figure 11.10).

As you have just seen, you can use Change not only to straighten lines, but to make them meet another line at a perpendicular angle. This only works with the ortho mode on, however. To extend several lines to be perpendicular to a nonorthogonal line, you have to rotate the cursor to that line's angle, using the Rotate command on the Snap menu, then use the process just described to extend or shorten the others (see Figure 11.11).

When changing several lines to be perpendicular to another line, you must be careful not to select too many. If the width of the group of lines is greater than the distance between the ends of the lines and the line they are to be perpendicular to, some of the lines will not change properly (see Figure 11.12). Once the lines have been straightened out, you can use the Fillet command to make the corners meet.

The overall interior dimension of the original utility room drawing is 16'-4" x 28'-0". Chances are the dimensions of the drawing you traced vary somewhat from these. Use the Dist command on the Inquiry menu to find your drawing's dimensions. Use the Stretch command to adjust the walls to their proper positions (see Figure 11.13). Use the Base command to make the base point the upper-left corner of the utility room near coordinate 13',30'.

To add the storage lockers, draw them in using the dimensions provided on the traced drawing. Draw one locker accurately, then use the Mirror and Array commands. This is actually a faster and more accurate method than tracing for entering repetitive objects. If you tried to trace each locker, you would also have to clean up each one.

Now create a layer called Notes and add the dimensions and labels shown in Figure 11.3. Remember to set the Dim Var dimension setting to 48 before you start dimensioning, and set the text height to 6". When you are done, end out of the Utility file.

Since the previous example had mostly orthogonal lines, you could have set the snap and ortho modes on while you traced. This would

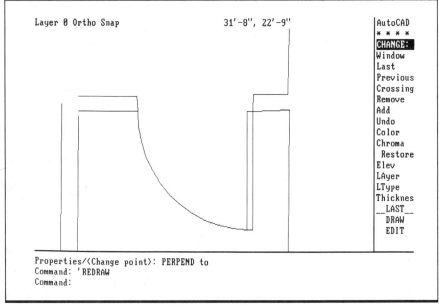

Figure 11.10: *The lines after Change is used*

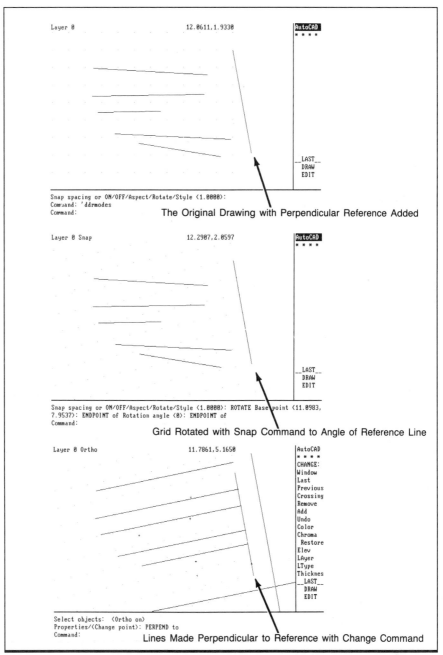

Figure 11.11: How to change lines at an angle other than 0 or 90 degrees

have kept the lines orthogonal and saved you the time of straight-ening them out. By leaving these modes off, however, you practiced some new editing options.

SCALING A DRAWING

If a hand-drafted drawing is to scale, you can use the dimensions on it or measure distances using an architect's or engineer's scale, then enter the drawing as you would a new drawing using these dimensions. Entering distances through the keyboard is much slower than tracing, but you don't have to do as much cleaning up since you are entering the drawing accurately.

If a drawing contains lots of curves, you have to resort to a dif-ferent scaling method, which is actually an old drafting technique for enlarging or reducing a drawing. First draw a grid in AutoCAD to the same proportions as your hand-drafted drawing. Plot this grid on translucent media and place it over the drawing. Then place

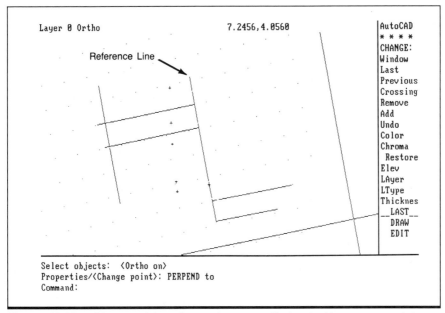

Figure 11.12: *Lines accidentally made perpendicular to the wrong point*

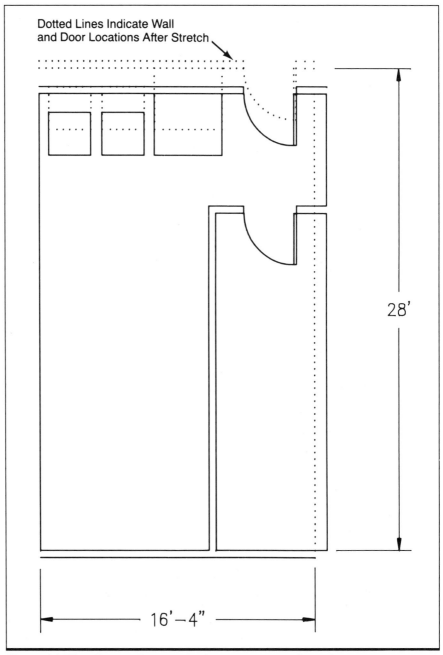

Figure 11.13: The walls stretched to the proper dimensions

points in the AutoCAD grid file relating to points on the grid overlay that intersect with the hand-drafted drawing (see Figure 11.14).

Once you have located these points in your AutoCAD file, you can connect them to form the drawing using polylines. Because this method can be time consuming and is not very accurate, it is best to purchase a tablet if you must enter a lot of drawings containing curves.

If you don't have a tablet, enter the utility room drawing in Figure 11.3 using the dimensions provided (ignore the reference line).

SCANNING A DRAWING

No discussion of drawing input can be complete without mentioning the scanner. The optical scanner has become a subject of interest lately because of its ability to read text from a typewritten page (called *character recognition*), thereby saving the time and effort of typing the text into a word processor. Some scanners can read drawings (though not in conjunction with character recognition). Imagine how easy it would be to convert an existing library of drawings into AutoCAD drawing files by simply running them through one of these devices.

Unfortunately, it is not that simple. Scanners are generally limited to an 8½ x 11-inch sheet size. Larger-format scanners are available but very expensive; they can cost 70 thousand dollars or more. Once the drawing is scanned and saved as a file, it must be converted into a file AutoCAD can use. This conversion process is time consuming and it requires special software (available from Autodesk). Finally, the drawing usually requires some cleaning up, which can be much more involved than cleaning up a traced drawing. The net result is a very expensive alternative to tracing which may or may not save you time.

Whether a scanner can help you depends on your application. If you have drawings that would be very difficult to trace—large, complex topographical maps for example—the scanner may well be worth a look. You don't necessarily have to buy one; there are scanning services. And if you can accept the quality of a scanned drawing before it is cleaned up, you can save a lot of time. On the other hand, drawings composed mostly of orthogonal lines and notes may be more easily traced by hand with a large tablet.

333

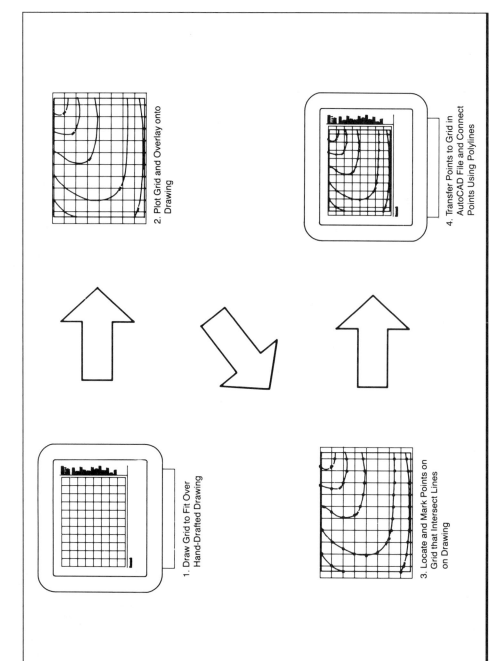

Figure 11.14: Using a grid to transfer a hand-drafted drawing

CONCLUSION

This chapter has shown you the three basic methods of entering a hand-drafted drawing. The method you choose depends on your equipment and the complexity of the drawing to be entered. You may decide you need a digitizing tablet, or you may want to go to a scanning service. Perhaps your input requirements are not very demanding and you can get by with scaling. A careful evaluation of your particular needs will save you time in the long run.

In the next chapter you will practice drawing and editing smooth curves, and creating filled-in areas.

Chapter 12

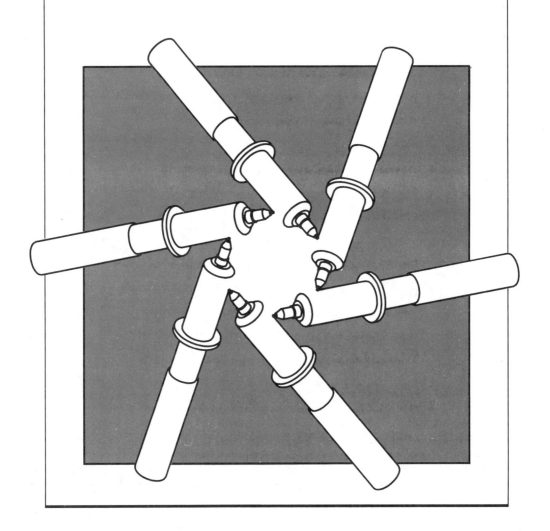

Drawing Curves and Solid Areas

IN CHAPTER 11, you traced a drawing using the normal lines and arcs. In this chapter, you will use polylines to trace curves. Polylines offer many options for creating forms, including solid fills. We will look at these options and a few other object types that allow you to draw solid fills.

DRAWING SMOOTH CURVES

From time to time you will have to trace curved, rather than rectilinear, objects. The Sketch command, in conjunction with the polyline commands, allows you to draw smooth curves. Sketch allows you to draw in a freehand style by drawing a series of short line segments that give the appearance of a continuous, smooth line; that is, a polyline. A polyline is composed of several lines linked together that act like a single object. If you draw a square using polylines, instead of the regular lines, the entire box acts like one object rather than four discrete objects. You can use polylines to design fonts, draw concentric boxes, or draw thick lines such as traces on a circuit board. You can even vary the thickness of a polyline, making it taper and expand as you like.

You draw a polyline using the Pline command on the Draw menu or the Skpoly option on the Sketch menu. The only difference between the two is that Skpoly uses the Sketch command to generate the polyline, while Pline allows you to draw it as you would a normal line.

Figure 12.1 is the site plan for your apartment house. The contour lines (similar to those on geological or relief maps) represent elevation, and the numbers on them represent their height in feet. Tracing or drawing this site plan will give you a good feel for the Sketch and polyline commands.

Open a file called Site and set up the drawing for 1/16" = 1'-0" on an 8½ x 11-inch sheet. Photocopy Figure 12.1 and calibrate the tablet as you did in Chapter 11. For a reference line, use the bottom two corners of the rectangle enclosing the site contours. Use 0,0 for the lower-left corner and 88,0 for the lower-right corner.

If you don't have a tablet, use a grid to scale the site plan as described in Chapter 11. Once you have marked reference points on your grid that correspond to points on the contour line, connect the reference points using the Pline command (see the section on drawing polylines below). Once you have done this, refer to the section on smoothing polylines to change the straight line segments into smooth curves.

If you have a digitizing tablet, proceed with the following exercise. Go to the Draw menu and pick Next, then pick Sketch. Remember, you must toggle the tablet mode off to get to the screen menu. The Sketch menu appears (see Figure 12.2). Pick Skpoly from the Sketch menu and the message

> Command: SKETCH Record increment <0'-0 1/8">: 'SETVAR
> >>Variable name or ?: SKPOLY
> >>New value for SKPOLY <0>: 1
> Resuming SKETCH command.
> Record increment <0'-0 1/8">:

appears. This message shows a series of predefined command entries set up in the AutoCAD menu. The Skpoly menu option is actually a command macro, that is, a means of entering several commands by combining them into one.

The first item in the Skpoly macro starts the Sketch command. Next, the Setvar command is issued, setting a system variable called Skpoly to 1. System variables are settings like grid, snap, and ltscale (see Appendix E for a list). Many of these variables can be changed using Setvar during another command, while others can only be

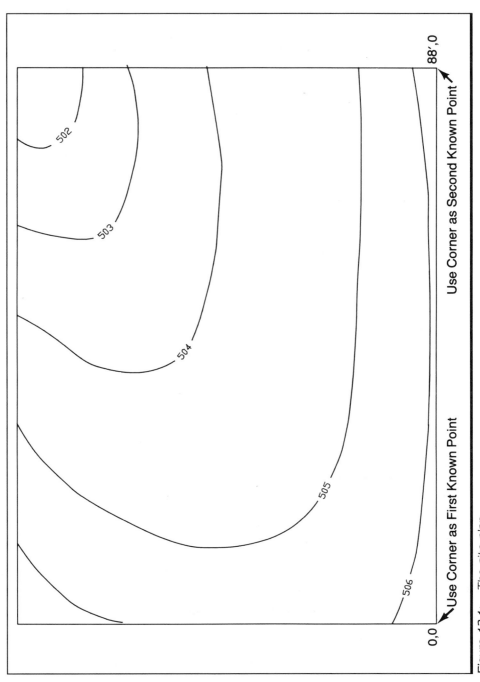

Figure 12.1:   The site plan

Figure 12.2: The Sketch menu

read. Setting Skpoly to 1 causes the Sketch command to draw using polylines rather than the standard ones.

Finally, the Record increment prompt appears, asking you to enter a value for the line segment length. As we said above, the Sketch command draws a series of short lines to simulate a continuous sketched line. The smaller the record increment, the shorter the line segments and the smoother the appearance of the sketch line. If the number you enter here is too small for your drawing scale, however, the Sketch line will use up too much memory and will slow down drawing.

AutoCAD offers a default value of 1/8″, which is fine for drawings at full scale on the default work area of 9 x 12 inches. Since you are drawing at a different scale, you must adjust this value. Generally, it is best to pick a value that allows at least four line segments for the smallest half circle you will draw (see Figure 12.3). We estimate that length to be five feet for this exercise. Enter 5′ to specify your sketch line segment length (see Figure 12.4).

Now the following prompt appears:

Sketch. Pen eXit Quit Record Erase Connect.

Be sure the tablet mode is on and ortho mode is off. Now start to trace the contour lines on the site plan. Do this by placing your stylus or puck at the beginning of a contour line, then pressing the pick

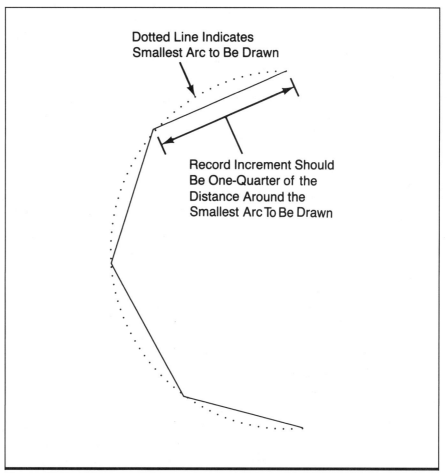

Figure 12.3: *How to estimate the sketch record increment*

button or the P key. The pick button or P key acts as a toggle to "raise" and "lower" the stylus. It tells the AutoCAD cursor when and when not to draw, but doesn't physically move the stylus. If you get the message

Please raise pen!

accompanied by a beep, press the P key (you may have to press it twice). This message appears when your drawing file becomes very complex or if your computer has limited memory. AutoCAD will begin to use disk space as temporary storage, but before it does it asks you to raise the stylus while it prepares to write to the disk.

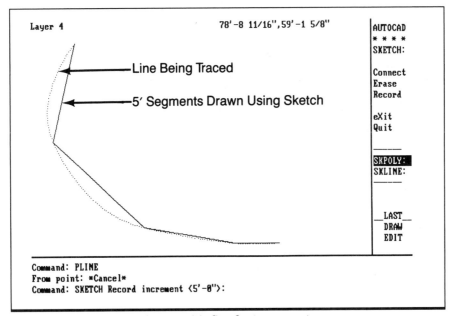

Figure 12.4: A curve drawn with five-foot segments

Then the following message appears:

Thank you. Lower the pen and continue.

Now you can continue.

As you trace the contour line, you will notice a rubber-banding line appear at five-foot intervals. As the line reaches a five-foot length, it becomes fixed, then another rubber-banding line continues. When you reach the end of the contour line, press the pick button again. Your line is temporarily drawn. To permanently save it as a line, pick Record from the Sketch menu or press R. A line drawn with Sketch is temporary until you use Record to save it.

Trace the rest of the contour lines. When you are done, choose Exit or press Return to exit the Sketch command. Your drawing will look like Figure 12.5.

Now use the Text command to enter the elevations shown on the original site plan. When you are prompted for a text angle, use the cursor to visually set an angle tangent to the contour line.

Refer back to the options shown on the Sketch menu and in the prompt above. The Connect and period options offer different ways to draw lines. Connect allows you to continue a line from the

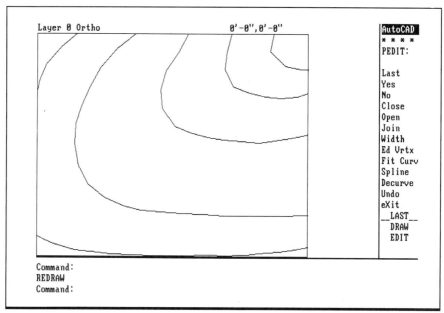

Figure 12.5:   The traced contour lines

end of the last line drawn. You pick Connect or press C, then move the cursor to the endpoint of the line. AutoCAD automatically starts the line and you just continue to draw.

The period option, which is not available on the menu, allows you to draw by moving the cursor to the desired position, then pressing the period key to draw a line segment. First you start a sketch line, then you set the pen up. Then move the cursor to the position for the next endpoint and press the period key. A line segment will be drawn from the endpoint of the last line segment to the current cursor position. This is quite similar to the way you normally draw lines, only without the rubber-banding line. The period option is useful when you are sketching along, then suddenly find you must draw a long, straight line segment.

The Record, Erase, Quit, and Exit commands control recording lines and exiting Sketch. As we said above, the Record command is used to save a sketched line. Once a line has been recorded, you must edit it as you would any other line. Erase allows you to erase lines *before* you record them. Quit ends the Sketch command without saving unrecorded lines. Exit, on the other hand, automatically saves *all* lines you have drawn, then exits the Sketch command.

Smoothing Polylines

Next you will convert the contour line segments into smooth curves. Go to the Edit menu, then pick Next, then pick Pedit to bring up the Pedit menu (see Figure 12.6). Pull-down menu users can pick Polyedit from the Edit pull-down menu. The following prompt appears:

PEDIT Select polyline:

Pick a contour line. The next prompt is

Close/Join/Width/Edit vertex/Fit curve/Spline/Decurve/Undo/eXit
<X>:

Pick Fit Curv from the Pedit menu or enter F. The contour line will change from a series of straight lines to a smooth curve. Press Return to end the Pedit command. Then press Return to start it again and repeat the process for the next contour line. Keep doing this until all the lines are smoothed.

Now reconfigure your tablet to its previous condition, using the Reconfig option on the Tablet menu, so you can use the digitizing

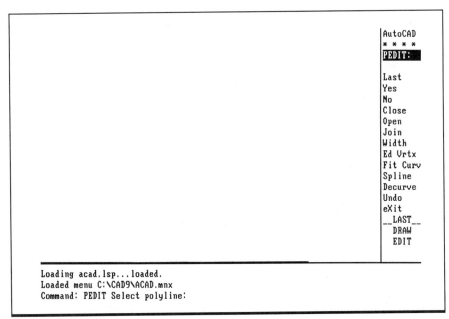

Figure 12.6:   The Pedit menu

tablet menu if you wish. If you need help, refer to Appendix B. Once you have done this, end out of the Site file.

Drawing Polylines

As we mentioned above, you can use the Pline command to draw polylines, and it offers a few more options than the Sketch command. You can, for example, adjust the width of your polyline while you draw, or enter a polyline arc. Pick Pline from the Draw menu. You are prompted for a from point, and the Pline menu appears (see Figure 12.7).

Enter a point to start your polyline. You will get the prompt

Arc/Close/Halfwidth/Length/Undo/Width/<Endpoint of line>:

You can now draw lines just as you would with the Line command. Or you can use the other options on the Pline menu to enter a polyline arc, specify polyline thickness, or add a polyline segment in the same direction as the previously drawn line.

The Arc option allows you to draw an arc that starts from the last point you selected. You are prompted to pick the endpoint of the arc.

The Close option draws a line segment from the last endpoint of a sequence of lines to the first point picked in that sequence. This

Figure 12.7: The Pline menu

works exactly like the Close subcommand on the Line menu. The Length option enables you to specify the length of a line, which will be drawn at the same angle as the last line entered.

Halfwidth allows you to create a tapered line segment or arc by specifying its beginning and ending widths (see Figure 12.8). The Width option generates a polyline of uniform width.

The Undo option deletes the last line segment drawn. The Fill On and Fill Off options are explained in the section on solid fills, below.

To end the Pline command, you press Return without picking a point.

Editing Polylines

You can use any editing command except the Change Point option on the Change menu to edit a polyline. When you use the Offset

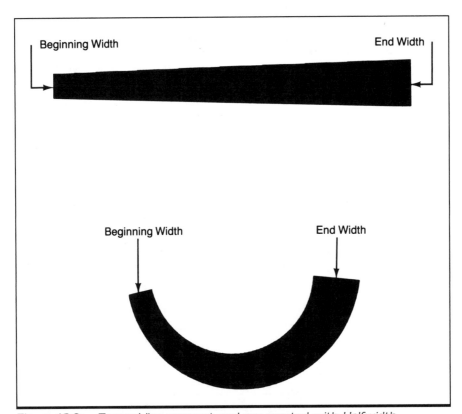

Figure 12.8: Tapered line segment and arc created with Halfwidth

command on a polyline, the entire polyline is offset, allowing you to create concentric boxes or parallel curves as shown in Figure 12.9.

Other editing commands affect polylines as they affect any other object. In addition, there are many editing capabilities offered only for polylines. In this section, we will look at these special options.

In the exercise above, you used the Fit Curv option on the Pedit menu to convert polylines into smooth curves. Other Pedit options enable you to change the thickness of a polyline, alter its shape when used as a curve, straighten it, or convert simple lines and arcs into polylines. For example, you may want to group a series of lines, as in a circuit board trace, so you can see where they all connect. To convert a line or arc simply pick the object at the polyline-selection prompt. You will get the message

Entity selected is not a polyline
Do you want to turn it into one? <Y>

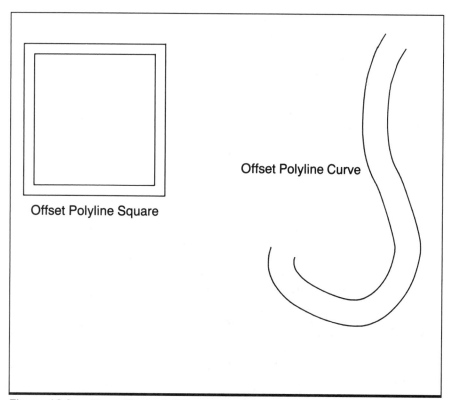

Offset Polyline Curve

Offset Polyline Square

Figure 12.9:   The effect of Offset on polylines

When you press Return, the object is converted into a polyline.

The Join option allows you to join other objects to a polyline. Join uses the object-selection prompt to allow the selection of several objects. However, the objects to be joined must touch the existing polyline exactly endpoint to endpoint. You can use Join together with polyline conversion to convert a series of connected lines into a polyline.

Using the Width option on the Pedit menu, you can change the thickness of a polyline (unlike the Width option on the Pline menu, which determines the width of a line segment as you draw it). This option gives you the prompt

Enter new width for all segments:

The value you enter will be the new thickness.

The Close option connects the two endpoints of a polyline with a line segment. If the polyline you selected to be edited is already closed, this option changes to Open. Open removes the last segment added to a closed polyline. If you want to turn a polyline into a group of simple lines, you can use the Explode command just as you would with blocks.

Editing Vertices

The Edit Vertex option is more complex than the others. You must be careful about selecting the vertex to be edited, because there are six editing options and you often have to use Fit Curv to see the effect of an option on a curved polyline. When you select Edit Vertex you get the prompt

Next/Previous/Break/Insert/Move/Regen/Straighten/Tangent/Width/eXit <N>:

and the Edit Vertex menu appears (see Figure 12.10).

The Next and Previous options, or N and P keyboard commands, enable you to select a vertex. An X on the selected polyline shows the beginning of the polyline; as you select Next and Previous, the X moves from vertex to vertex to show which one is being edited. When you press Return to enter the default Next, the X moves to the next vertex. If you enter P for Previous, the X moves in the opposite direction and the default becomes P.

The other options (except Regen and Exit) offer various ways to edit a vertex. The Break option breaks the polyline between two vertices. To use this option, you must first position the X on one

```
                                                    AUTOCAD
                                                    * * * *
                                                    ED VRTX

                                                    next
                                                    previous
                                                    break
                                                    insert
                                                    move
                                                    straight
                                                    width
                                                    tangent
                                                    go
                                                    regen
                                                    Undo
                                                    eXit

                                                    _LAST_
                                                    DRAW
                                                    EDIT
```

Figure 12.10:   *The Edit Vertex menu*

end of the segment you want to break. Then pick Break from the Edit Vertex menu or enter B. You will get the prompt

Next/Previous/Go/eXit <N>:

Use Next or Previous to move the X to the other end of the segment. When the X is in the right position, pick Go from the Edit Vertex menu or enter G, and the polyline will be broken (see Figure 12.11). You can also use the Break command on the Edit menu to break a polyline anywhere, as you did when you drew the toilet seat in Chapter 3.

The Insert option inserts a new vertex. First position the X *before* the new vertex. You must know which end of the polyline is the beginning and which is the end to use this option properly. To determine which direction is forward in relation to the X, and therefore where the new vertex will be placed, you can use the Next option to move the X. Now pick Insert from the Edit Vertex menu or enter I. The prompt

Enter location of new vertex:

appears and a rubber-banding line appears originating from the current X position (see Figure 12.12).

You then pick a point indicating the new vertex location, and the polyline is redrawn with the new vertex. If the polyline is curved,

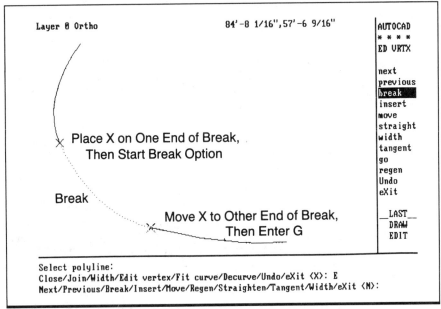

Figure 12.11: How the Break option works

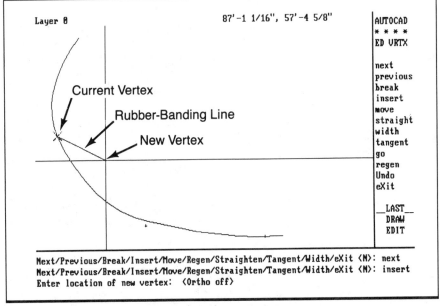

Figure 12.12: The new vertex location

the new vertex will not be shown curved (see Figure 12.13). You must smooth it out by exiting the Edit Vertex option and then using the Fit Curv option as you did to edit the site plan (see Figure 12.14).

The Move option allows you to move a vertex. To use this option, place the X on the vertex you wish to move, then pick Move from the Edit Vertex menu or enter M. The prompt

Enter new location:

appears and a rubber-banding line appears originating from the X (see Figure 12.15). Next, you pick the new vertex position and the polyline is redrawn (see Figure 12.16). Again, if the line is curved, the new vertex appears as a sharp angle until you use the Fit Curv option (see Figure 12.17).

The Straighten option straightens all the vertices between two selected vertices. First select the starting vertex for the straight line, then pick Straight from the menu or enter S. The prompt

Next/Previous/Go/eXit <N>:

appears, allowing you to move the X to the other end of the straight line. Once the X is in the proper position, pick Go from the Edit Vertex

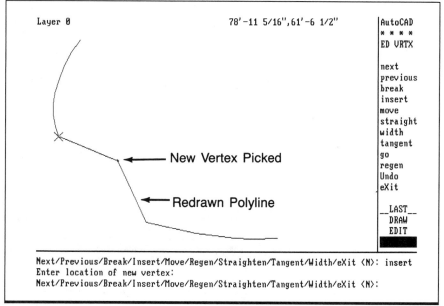

Figure 12.13: *The polyline before the curve is fitted*

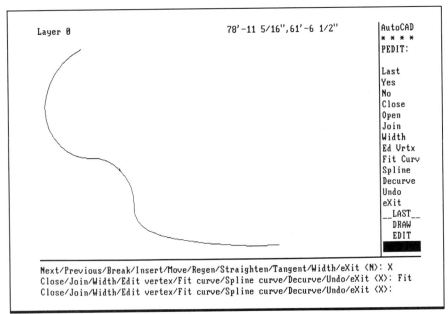

Figure 12.14:   The polyline after the curve is fitted

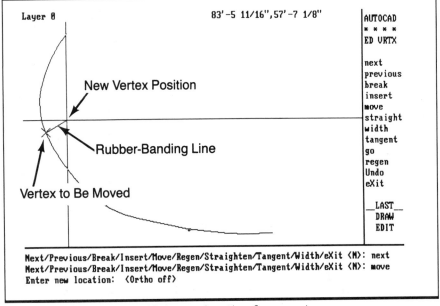

Figure 12.15:   How to pick a new location for a vertex

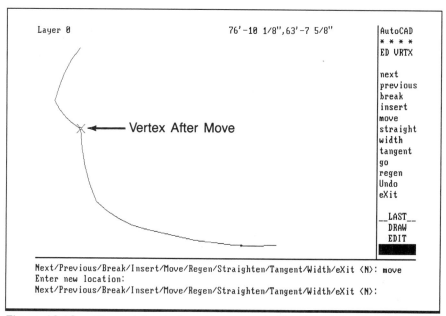

Figure 12.16: *The polyline before the curve is fitted*

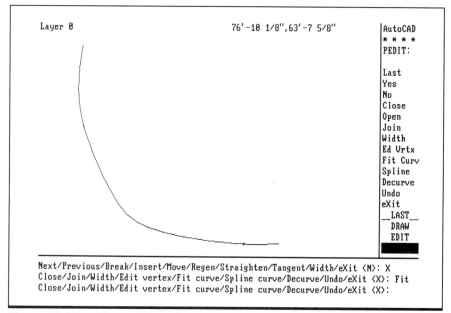

Figure 12.17: *The polyline after the curve is fitted*

menu or enter G. The polyline straightens between the two selected vertices (see Figure 12.18).

The Tangent option alters the direction of a curve on a curve-fitted polyline. First you position the X on the vertex you wish to alter. Then pick Tangent from the Edit Vertex menu or enter T. A rubber-banding line appears (see Figure 12.19). Point the rubber-banding line in the direction for the new tangent, then press the pick button. An arrow appears indicating the new tangent direction (see Figure 12.20). Don't worry if the polyline shape does not change. You must use Fit Curv to see the effect of the Tangent option (see Figure 12.21).

Finally, there is the Width option. Unlike the Width option on the Pedit menu, this option enables you to alter the width of the polyline at any vertex. By doing this you can taper or otherwise vary polyline thickness. This technique is useful when you want to create an area in your drawing that is to be filled in solid. First place the X at the beginning vertex of a polyline segment (this is another option that is sensitive to the polyline direction). Then pick Width from the Edit Vertex menu or enter W. The prompt

Enter starting width <0.0000>:

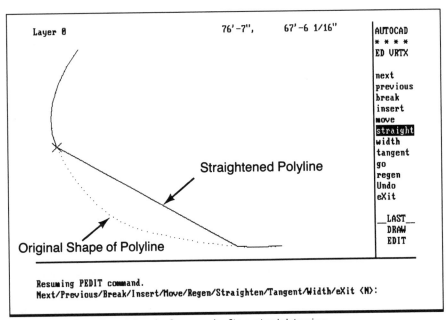

Figure 12.18: A polyline before and after straightening

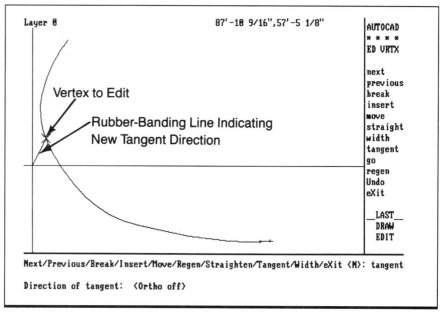

Figure 12.19: How to pick a new tangent direction

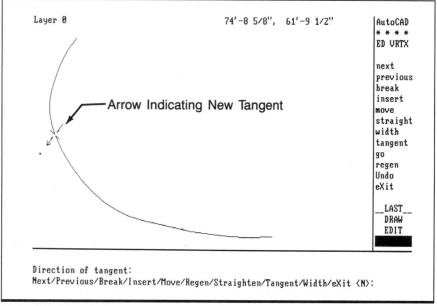

Figure 12.20: The new tangent direction indicated by an arrow

appears. You enter a value indicating the polyline width desired at this vertex. Then the next prompt

Enter ending width <0.0000>:

appears. Here you enter the width for the next vertex. Again, don't be alarmed if nothing happens after you enter this value. To see the result of the Width option, you must use the Regen option on the Edit Vertex menu (see Figure 12.22).

The Undo option undoes the last Edit Vertex option used. You can exit the Vertex option any time by picking Exit from the Edit Vertex menu or entering an X. This brings you back to the polyline-editing prompt.

Using Spline Curves

The Spline command on the Pedit menu (named after the spline manual drafting tool) offers a way to draw smoother and more controllable curves than those produced by the Fit command. (However, too frequent use of splines enlarges your drawing files and causes them to take much longer to redraw and regenerate.) A polyline curved by using the Spline command does not pass through the ver-

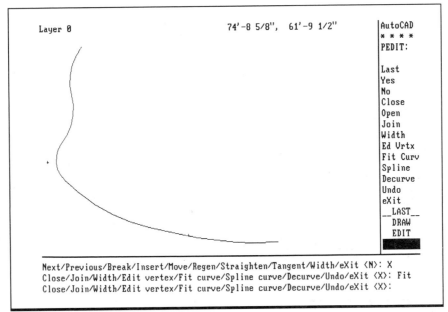

Figure 12.21: The polyline after the Fit Curv option is used

tex points like a fitted curve. Instead, the vertex points act like weights pulling the curve in their direction. The spline polyline only touches its beginning and end vertices. Figure 12.23 illustrates this point.

Start the Pedit command, then pick the curve. At the Pedit prompt, pick Spline from the Pedit menu or enter spline. Your curve will change to look like Figure 12.24.

You can edit a spline curve the same way you would edit a fitted curve, though the results will be different because the vertices pull the curve, rather than the curve passing through the vertices. To see what happens when you move a vertex, pick Edit Vertex from the Pedit menu. Move the X to the next vertex from the top as in Figure 12.25. Notice how the X is located not on the curve but to the left of it. Pick Move from the Edit Vertex menu and reposition this vertex as shown in Figure 12.26. The curve regenerates, reflecting the new position of the vertex. Again, notice that the curve does not pass through the vertex but is just pulled toward it (see Figure 12.27).

AutoCAD offers a Setvar option that allows you to see the locations of all the vertices that control a spline curve. Since the Setvar

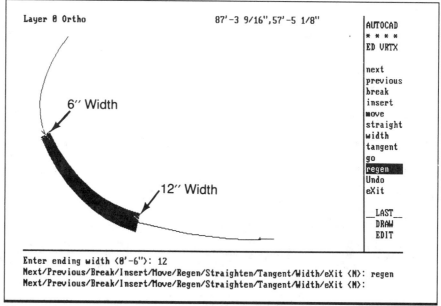

Figure 12.22:   *A polyline with the width of one segment increased*

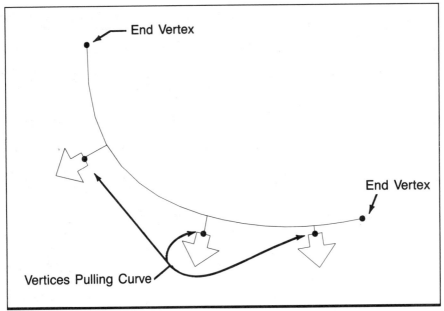

Figure 12.23: The spline curve pulled toward its vertices

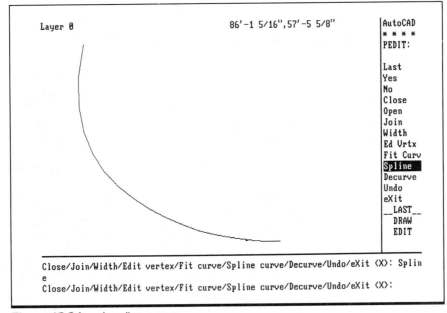

Figure 12.24: A spline curve

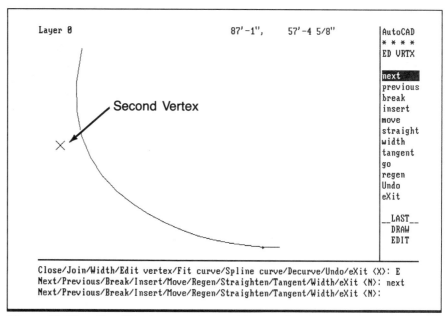

The fitted curve changed to a spline curve

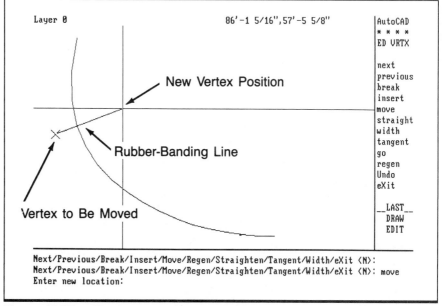

Figure 12.26: *The location of the second vertex*

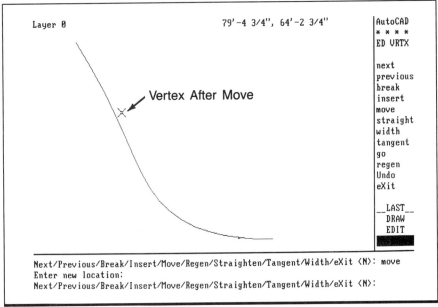

Figure 12.27: *The new location of the second vertex with the new curve*

command can be used transparently, you can view the control vertices while editing a polyline. Bring up the Osnap menu by picking the
row of asterisks at the top of the Edit Vertex menu, then pick Setvar from the Osnap menu, or enter 'setvar at the Pedit prompt.
Enter splframe at the prompt

Variable name or ?:

You will get the prompt

New value for SPLFRAME <0>:

Enter a 1 at this prompt. The statement

Resuming Pedit command.

appears and the Pedit prompt reappears. Now pick the Regen command from the Edit Vertex menu. A line will appear showing the
positions of the vertices (see Figure 12.28). This line does not plot or
print. It is there to help you find spline vertices. If you move the X
to the next vertex, you will see it follow this line. As you can see,
changes in the spline are displayed automatically, allowing you to
edit these types of curves more easily.

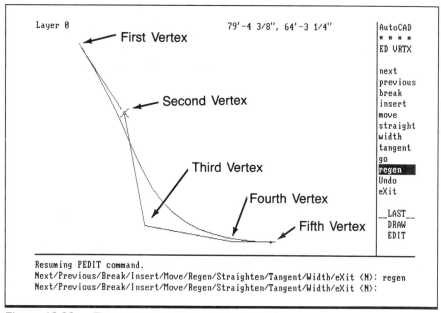

Figure 12.28:   *The spline vertices made visible*

FILLING IN SOLID AREAS

You saw above how you can create a solid area by increasing the width of a polyline segment. But suppose you want instead to create a solid simple shape or a very thick line. AutoCAD provides the Solid, Trace, and Donut commands to help you draw simple filled areas.

Drawing Large Solid Areas

To fill in a large area, you should use the Solid command on the Draw menu. If you pick Solid, you get the prompt

First point:

The Solid command draws a four-sided solid area, so the first point you pick will be one of the area's corners. Once you pick a point, the next prompt appears.

Second point:

At this prompt, you pick the next corner of your solid area. The next prompt is

Third point:

This is where things get a little tricky. If you are drawing a square, your third point represents the corner diagonal to the last corner you picked (see Figure 12.29).

Once you have picked the third point the prompt

Fourth point:

appears. Now you pick the final corner of your fill, and a solid area appears between the four points you selected.

Now the prompt for a third point appears again, allowing you to continue your fill pattern. You select a sequence of points in a Z pattern. If you were to pick points in a circular pattern, you would end up with a filled area shaped like an hourglass (see Figure 12.30).

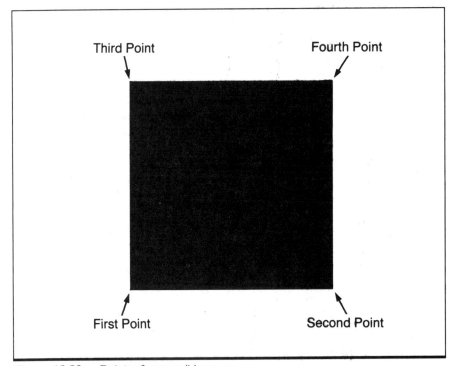

Figure 12.29: *Points for a solid square*

You can create solid filled areas with more than four sides by entering more points in a Z pattern (see Figure 12.31). There is no limit to the number of points you can select. To end the Solid command, press Return without picking a point.

Drawing Thick Lines and Circles

Another way to get a solid fill is to use the Trace command, which can be entered only through the keyboard. The name Trace is derived from the term used for the lines on a printed circuit board. Trace is primarily used to draw very thick lines. It acts like the Line command, except that the first prompt you get is

Trace width <0.0500>:

You enter the desired thickness of the trace, then the prompt for a from point appears just as for the Line command. Once you enter a value, that value becomes the new default.

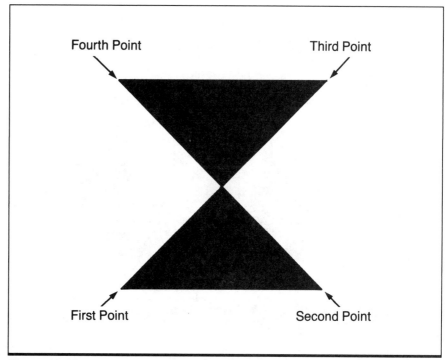

Figure 12.30: An area filled by picking points in a clockwise pattern

It should be noted that you cannot use Change or Fillet on a trace.

If you need to draw a thick circle like an inner tube or a donut, you can select the Donut command on the Draw menu. Or enter donut or doughnut (both spellings are recognized by AutoCAD). When you start this command, you get the prompt

Inside diameter <0.5000>:

This prompt determines the opening at the center of your circle. You can accept the default or enter a different value, which becomes the new default. The next prompt

Outside diameter <1.0000>:

determines the outside diameter of your circle. Finally, you get the prompt

Center of Donut:

and the outline of the thick circle appears on the cursor. You then pick the point locating the circle and it appears as part of your

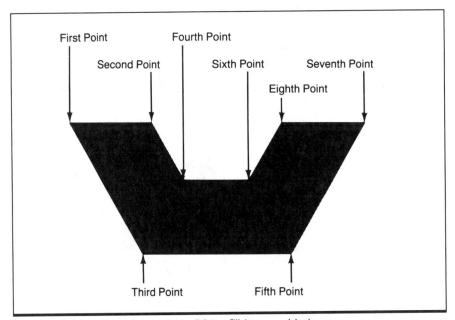

Figure 12.31:   *How to use a solid to fill in an odd shape*

drawing. You can continue to add donuts to your drawing until you press Return (see Figure 12.32). You edit a finished donut like a polyline, with the Pedit or regular object-editing options.

Toggling Solid Fills On and Off

Once you have drawn a solid area with the Pline, Solid, Trace, or Donut command, you can control whether the solid area actually appears as filled in. At times it is useful to not fill in solid areas. For example, you can shorten regeneration time if solids are not filled in. When Fill is turned off, thick polylines, solids, traces, and donuts appear as outlines of the solid areas (see Figure 12.33).

To turn the solid areas on and off, enter fill through the keyboard or choose Fill On or Fill Off from the Solid or Pline menu. You get the prompt

ON/OFF <ON>:

You simply enter on or off depending on whether you want areas to be filled in.

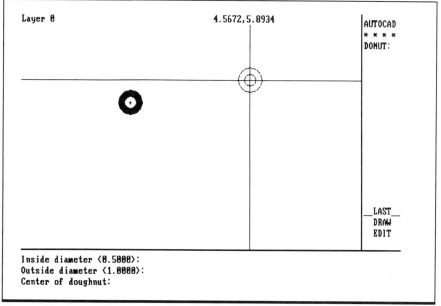

Figure 12.32:   *Filled and unfilled donuts*

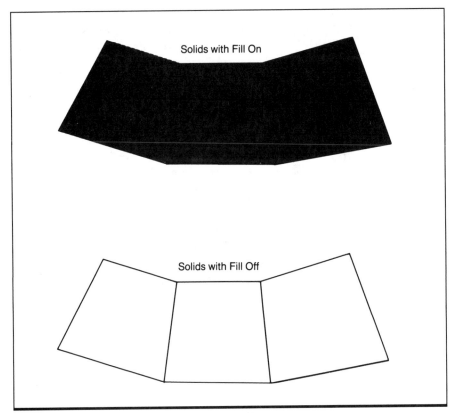

Figure 12.33: Solid fills turned on and off

CONCLUSION

Polylines are not the easiest objects to use but, as you have seen, they are helpful where regular lines and arcs won't work. We have seen polylines used in traffic engineering for roadway striping, and in PCB layout for traces on a circuit board. Think of ways you can use polylines in your own applications.

You have already learned how to use the Dist command to find exact distances. You may want to be able to find areas or other properties of your drawing, or to find out how much disk space you have left or where a file is located. In the next chapter, we will look at ways to get information about your drawing.

Chapter 13

Getting and Exchanging Information

IN THE COURSE OF YOUR WORK with AutoCAD, you will want to get precise information about a drawing and the objects it contains. You have already used the Distance command to find distances between objects, and the question mark option to get information about blocks and layers. In this chapter you will explore how to get other information about objects, plus information about the entire drawing and about AutoCAD files. In addition, you will learn how to use other software, such as DOS, word processors, and spreadsheet programs, without closing your drawing file and exiting AutoCAD. You will practice exporting, editing, and importing data-exchange format files. Finally, you will learn how to use AutoCAD drawings with desktop-publishing programs such as Ventura and PageMaker.

GETTING INFORMATION ABOUT A DRAWING

AutoCAD can instantly give you precise information about your drawing, such as the area, perimeter, and location of an object; the base point, current mode settings, and space used in a drawing; and the time at which a drawing was created and last edited. In this section you will practice getting information about a drawing.

Finding the Area or Location of an Object

If you are an architect, engineer, or facilities planner you might want to know the square foot area of a room or a section of a building. A structural engineer might want to find the cross-sectional area of a beam. In this section you will practice finding the areas of both regular and irregular objects.

Finding Area and Perimeter

First you will get the square foot area of the living room and entry of your studio unit plan. Start AutoCAD and open the Unit file. Next, zoom into the living room and entry area. Pick Inquiry from the Root menu, then pick Area from the Inquiry menu. You get the Area menu shown in Figure 13.1.
The prompt

> <First point>/Entity/Subtract:

appears. Now you can start picking the points defining the area to be measured, as shown in Figure 13.2.

First, pick the lower-left corner of the living room near coordinate 15'-0",6'-10". The prompt

> (Add mode) Next point:

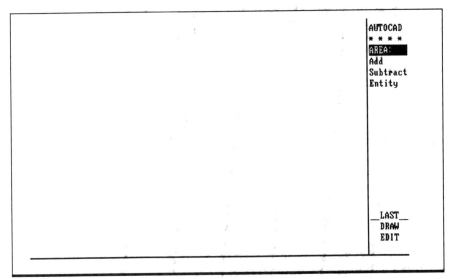

Figure 13.1:   The Area menu

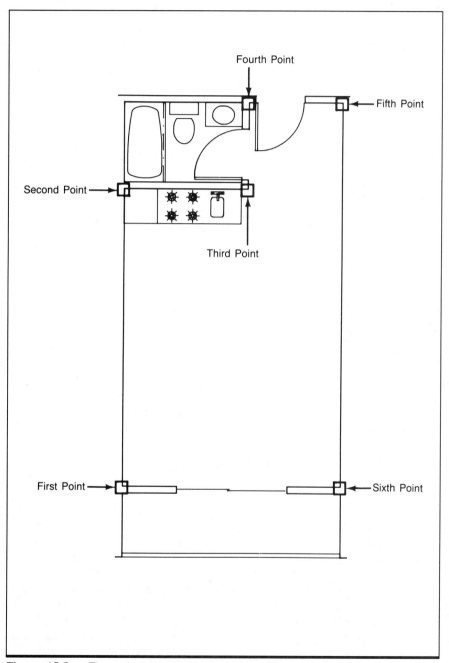

Figure 13.2: The points to select to find the living room and entry area

appears. As you select points determining the area being calculated, AutoCAD keeps a running count of the area. You are currently in *add mode*, that is, adding area values. There is also a *subtract mode* that enables you to subtract area values from the running count. You will learn how to use these options a little later.

Pick the upper-left corner of the kitchenette near coordinate 15'-0", 25'-5". Continue to pick the corners outlining the living room and entry area until you have come full circle to the first point (you don't need to select it a second time).

When you complete the circuit, press Return. You will get the message

> Area = 42209.00 sq in (293.1181 sq ft), Perimeter = 76'-0"
> Total area = 42209.00 sq in (293.1181 sq ft)
> <First point>/Entity/Subtract:

This prompt offers three options: to select a first point, to select an entity, or to subtract an area. Since you have just taken the area of a simple rectangular object, you don't need any of them, so press Return again to exit the Area command.

There is no limit to the number of points you can pick to define an area. This means you can obtain the areas of very complex shapes. Using the Entity option, you can also select circles and poly-lines for area calculations. Using the Subtract option, you can subtract areas from the area being calculated. In your next exercise, you will practice using the Entity and Subtract options.

Exit the Unit file, then open a new file named Flange. First draw the object shown in Figure 13.3 (use the dimensions for reference only). Now you want to find the area of the flange you just drew. You must first turn the arcs into polyline arcs (using the Pedit command as described in Chapter 12) before you start the Area command. Area does not calculate areas for arcs, but it does for polylines.

Next, study the shape to see what rectangular areas can be selected first. Figure 13.4 shows the areas that can be determined by selecting points. Then you must determine the areas to be subtracted from the area calculation. When AutoCAD calculates a poly-line area, it automatically connects the endpoints. The entire area of the large arc in the flange will be calculated, including the area covered by the smaller concentric arc defining the inside of the flange (see Figure 13.5). This means that the area of the smaller arc will have to be subtracted from the overall area calculation.

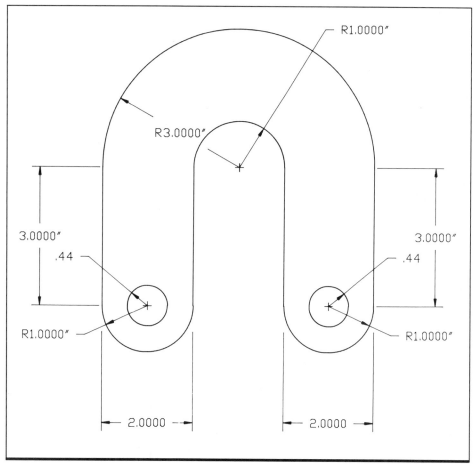

Figure 13.3: A flange to a fictitious mechanical device

Once you have made these determinations, you can proceed to use the Area command. First take the areas of the rectangular shapes. Pick the four corners of one rectangle, then press Return. This causes AutoCAD to calculate the area of that rectangle. You get the prompt

```
Area = 6.0000, Perimeter = 10.0000
Total area = 6.0000
<First point>/Entity/Subtract:
```

Next pick the corners of the other rectangle and press Return again. Another area value appears in the prompt

Area = 6.0000, Perimeter = 10.0000
Total area = 12.0000
<First point>/Entity/Subtract:

The new area is twice the first area calculated because AutoCAD adds the previously calculated area to the current area, and both rectangular areas measured are the same (see Figure 13.6).

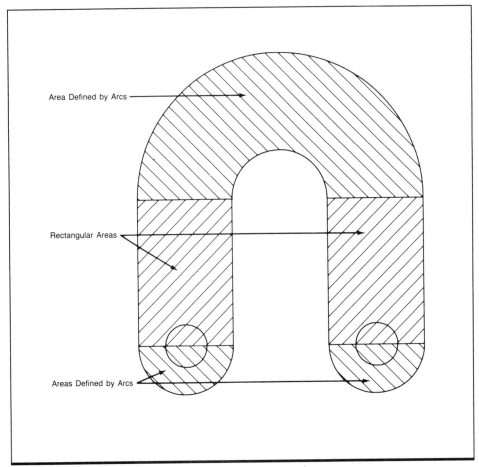

Figure 13.4:   *The flange broken down into types of areas*

Next you add the area defined by the polyline arcs. Pick Entity from the Area menu or enter E through the keyboard. A new prompt will appear.

<ADD mode> Select circle or polyline:

As you can see from this prompt, you are asked to select a circle or polyline. Pick the outer polyline arcs (see Figure 13.7). As you pick the arcs, the running total area is displayed above the prompt, along with the area and perimeter of the object selected. When you

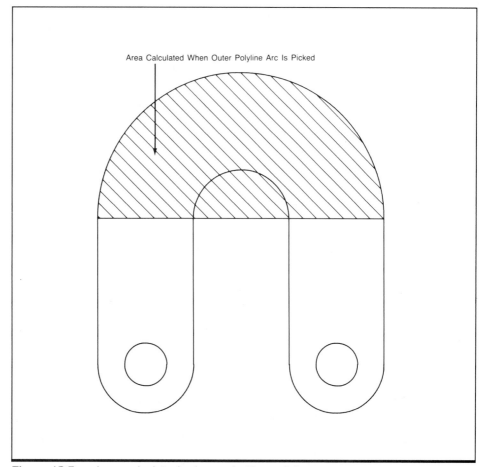

Figure 13.5:   *Area calculated when selecting polyline arcs*

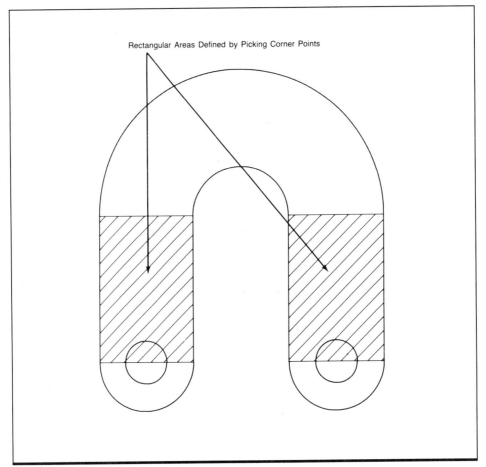

Figure 13.6:   The two rectangular areas

are done selecting the arcs, press Return. This brings you back into the point-selection mode, and the First point/Entity/Subtract prompt returns.

Next pick Subtract from the Area menu or enter S through the keyboard. The prompt then changes to

<First point>/Entity/Add:

Note that now that you are in subtract mode, Add is the current area-selection option.

Pick the Entity subcommand again since you are going to subtract the area defined by polylines and arcs. The following prompt appears.

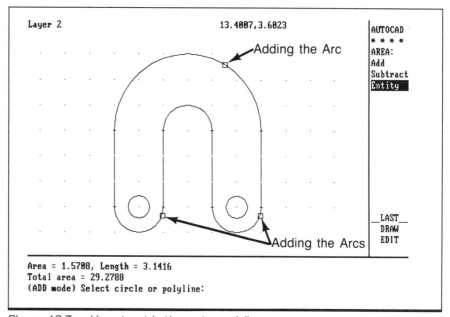

Area = 1.5788, Length = 3.1416
Total area = 29.2788
(ADD mode) Select circle or polyline:

Figure 13.7:   *How to pick the outer polyline arcs*

<SUBTRACT mode> Select circle or polyline:

Pick the two circles and the arc defining the inside of the flange as shown in Figure 13.8. As you pick the objects, the running total is displayed again above the prompt. Once you are done, you see the final total area above the prompt line.

Total area = 26.4940
<SUBTRACT mode> Select circle or polyline:

To exit the Area command, press Return twice.

You must remember that whenever you press Return during an area calculation, AutoCAD automatically connects the first and last points and returns the area calculated. You can then continue to select points or objects defining areas, but the additional areas will be calculated from the next point you pick.

In this example, you obtained the area of a mechanical object. However, the same process works for any type of area you want to calculate. It can be the area of a piece of property on a topographical map, or the area of a floor plan.

You can use the Entity option to find an irregular area like the one shown in Figure 13.9, as long as it is a polyline. If the polyline is not closed, the Area command assumes the first and last points

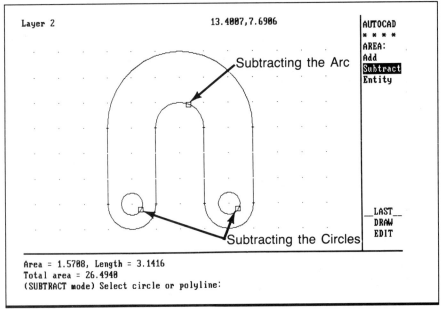

Figure 13.8:   How to pick the subtractive objects

picked are connected and calculates the area accordingly. If you wish to find the area of an irregular object that is not a polyline, you first either have to convert it to a polyline or trace over it on the screen using a polyline. You can then save the traced polyline for future reference or erase it.

Determining Absolute Coordinates

At times it is helpful to know the absolute coordinates of a point on an object. You may need to know for purposes of documentation, or to locate a block for insertion. To find absolute coordinates, first pick the Id command from the Inquiry menu. You will get the prompt

ID Point:

You can then use the Osnap overrides to pick a point. Its x, y, and z coordinates will be displayed on the prompt line.

Finding Out about the Drawing Status

The Status command enables you to obtain some general information about the drawing you are working on, such as the base point,

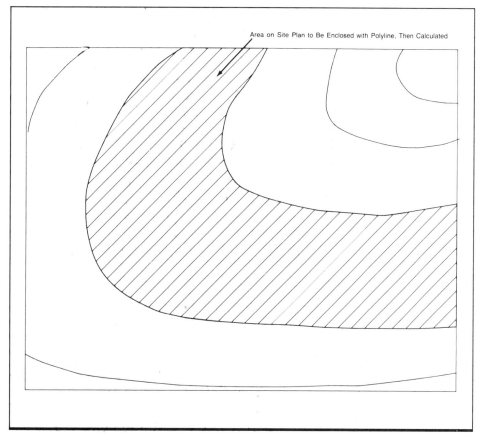

Area on Site Plan to Be Enclosed with Polyline, Then Calculated

Figure 13.9: *The site plan with an area to be calculated*

current mode settings, and work space. Status can be especially helpful when you edit a drawing someone else has worked on because you may want to identify and change settings for your own work. When you pick Status from the Inquiry menu, you get a list like the following:

```
status
74 entities in unit
Limits are        X:  0'-0"        44'-0"       (Off)
                  Y:  0'-0"        34'-0"
Drawing uses      X: 14'-7"        33'-9 3/8"
                  Y:  0'-10 3/8"   34'-7 7/8"  **Over
Display shows     X:  3'-0"        40'-10"
                  Y:  6'-0"        32'-0"
```

Insertion base is	X: 15'-0"	Y: 2'-5"	Z: 0'-0"
Snap resolution is	X: 0'-1"	Y: 0'-1"	
Grid spacing is	X: 0'-10"	Y: 0'-10"	

Current layer: 0

Current color: BYLAYER — 7 (white)

Current linetype: BYLAYER — CONTINUOUS

Current elevation: 0'-0"   thickness: 0'-0"

Axis off Fill on Grid off Ortho off Qtext off Snap on Table off

Object snap modes: None

Free RAM: 12084 bytes Free disk: 4087808 bytes

I/O page space: 47K bytes   Extended I/O page space: 480K bytes

First the number of entities, or objects, is listed. The next few lines give the values of the drawing's settings. The top line tells you the coordinates of the drawing limits. In case you have forgotten, the limits are points describing the drawing area (see Chapter 3 for more details on limits). (Off) means that the limits are off, allowing you to draw outside the limit boundary. The coordinates shown by the heading Drawing uses indicate the area the drawing occupies; **Over means that part of it is outside the limit boundary. The coordinates shown by the heading Display shows indicate the area covered by the current view.

The insertion base, snap resolution, and grid spacing lines tell you what the current default values are for those commands.

The following lines tell you the status of the settings. The current layer is 0 in this example. The current color indicates the default color objects will have as they are drawn. In the example above, Bylayer is the current color. Following Bylayer is the color of the current layer. Bylayer means that an object takes on the color of the layer it is on. You could use the Color command to set the current color to red, for example, instead of Bylayer. Then everything you drew would be red regardless of the current layer color.

Another possible color assignment is Byblock, which you also set with the Color Command. Byblock makes everything you draw white until you turn your drawing into a block, then insert the block on a layer with an assigned color. The objects then take on the color of that layer. This is similar to the way objects drawn on the layer 0 act.

There can be only one current color, and we recommend that you use Bylayer until you feel comfortable with AutoCAD. As we mentioned in Chapter 4, keeping the color setting to Bylayer prevents confusion about color and layer assignments.

The current line type works the same way as the current color. Bylayer can be changed to a specific line type that applies to all the lines you draw regardless of their layers. You set a line type by picking the Set command from the Linetype menu and specifying the desired line type.

The current elevation and thickness settings pertain to 3D drawings and can be changed using the Elev command (see Chapter 14 for details).

The last group of lines gives you information about memory usage. The free RAM and I/O page space lines give you an idea of how much system memory is available as work space for AutoCAD. Free RAM is the memory AutoCAD uses for performing calculations. The size of this area is critical, especially when you are removing hidden lines from a 3D drawing (see Chapter 14). If this value is too small, AutoCAD can dump you out to DOS. I/O page space is RAM that is used to temporarily store the drawing database information. If this space gets filled up, AutoCAD will begin to use your hard disk for temporary storage, or it will use expanded or extended memory if you have it. AutoCAD automatically sets the I/O page space and free RAM values, but these can be adjusted by altering the DOS environment. We will discuss this technique in detail in Chapter 18.

The free disk line tells you how much space you have left on your hard disk for files. The extended I/O page space line is present only if your computer is equipped with an extended or expanded memory board. We'll explain how to use extended memory in Chapter 17.

When you run out of I/O page space or free RAM, AutoCAD tells you by dumping you out of the program. Fortunately, AutoCAD saves your work for you, but being dumped is still an annoyance. You can avoid it by checking the memory information from time to time and making sure you have enough room on your disk drive to accommodate I/O paging to disk. Knowing how much memory is enough takes a little experimentation and experience. Chapter 18 will cover steps for optimizing your memory usage.

Keeping Track of Time

The Time command allows you to keep track of the time spent on a drawing for billing purposes or to analyze time spent on a project. You can also use Time to check the current time and find out when the drawing was created and most recently edited. Because the AutoCAD timer uses the time set on your computer, you must be sure the time is set correctly in DOS.

When you pick Time from the Inquiry menu or enter time, you get a message like the following:

TIME
Current time: 27 Jan 1987 at 06:30:23.850
Drawing created: 12 Jan 1987 at 01:29:40.880
Drawing last updated: 12 Jan 1987 at 01:55:06.600
Time in drawing editor: 6 days 08:13:20.780
Elapsed timer: 6 days 08:13:20.780
Timer on.
Display/ON/OFF/Reset:

The first three lines tell you the current date and time, the date and time the drawing was created, and the last time the drawing was saved or ended. The fourth line shows the total time spent on a drawing from its creation. The elapsed timer allows you to time an activity, such as changing the width of all the walls in a floor plan or redesigning a piece of machinery. You can turn the elapsed timer on or off, or reset it, by entering on, off, or reset at the prompt shown as the last line of the message. The timer will not show any time spent on a drawing between the last time it is saved and the time a Quit command is issued.

Getting Information During Another Command

You may want to know or change the setting of a system variable while you are in the middle of another command. For example, you may want to change the points determining the limits of your drawing, or the snap or grid distance, while you are drawing a line. AutoCAD offers the transparent Setvar command to facilitate this. To use it you enter 'setvar at the AutoCAD command prompt, whether or not another command is active. You will get the prompt

>>Variable name or ?:

You can then enter the name of the desired system variable, or a question mark to get a listing of all the variables and their settings. Appendix E also gives a list of the system variables accessible through Setvar. Once you enter a variable name, you are shown its setting and can change it if you like (except for variables that are *read only*). Then you are returned to the currently active command (if any).

MANAGING FILES WHILE IN AUTOCAD

You may want to list, copy, rename, and delete files while you are working on an AutoCAD drawing. There are several ways of going about file management while in AutoCAD. You can use the Files command, use AutoCAD's external commands, or use the Shell command to enter a single DOS command or to temporarily exit Auto-CAD and perform several DOS commands.

Using the Files Command

The Files command on the Utility menu, and the File Utilities command on the Main menu, switch the screen editor to text mode, then display the File Utility Menu. While in the Flange drawing file, go to the Utilities menu and pick Files to bring up the File Utility menu (see Figure 13.10). To select an option from this menu, enter its number at the prompt

Enter selection (0 to 5) (0):

This works just like the Main menu.

```
          A U T O C A D
Copyright (C) 1982,83,84,85,86,87 Autodesk, Inc.
Release 9.0 (9/17/87) IBM PC
Advanced Drafting Extensions 3
Serial Number:  10-113610

File Utility Menu

   0.  Exit File Utility Menu
   1.  List Drawing files
   2.  List user specified files
   3.  Delete files
   4.  Rename files
   5.  Copy file

Enter selection (0 to 5) <0>:
```

Figure 13.10:   *The File Utility menu*

The List Drawing Files option prompts you for the drive and directory you wish to look at, then lists the drawing files contained there. If you don't supply a drive and directory specification, you get a list of the current directory.

The List User-Specified Files option allows you to specify the files to list. It prompts you for a file search specification, which you can respond to by entering a drive and directory specification followed by the name or names of the files. You can use wild cards to filter certain files to be listed.

The last three options are self-explanatory. To get back to the drawing editor, choose the first option or enter 0.

Using Dir and Catalog

The Dir and Catalog options on the External Commands menu both give you a list of files; Dir gives status information about the files as well. When you pick Dir from the External Commands menu or enter it through the keyboard, you get the prompt

File Specification:

You can enter file specifications here just as you would in DOS. If you press Return without entering anything, you will get a list of the entire current directory. Just as in DOS, if you enter a /P, the program pauses once the list fills the screen so you can view it before some items scroll off. The following list is a sample of what you might get using the Dir command.

Volume in drive C has no label
Directory of C:\acad

.		\<DIR>	9-21-86	10:31a
..		\<DIR>	9-21-86	10:31a
ACAD	OVL	307578	12-28-86	1:21p
ACAD1	MID	125	11-24-86	9:18p
ACAD0	OVL	61130	11-21-86	5:11p
ACA	OVL	111770	11-21-86	5:11p
ACAD3	OVL	189610	12-08-86	2:27p
ACAD2	MID	150	12-08-86	5:41p
ACAD	EXE	232192	12-08-86	2:15p
ACADL	OVL	71088	7-05-86	5:16p
ACAD3	MID	142	12-08-86	5:39p
ACAD	DWG	1349	5-28-86	11:27a

ACAD	HDX	1636	5-30-86	10:16a
ACAD	HLP	83652	5-30-86	10:15a
ACAD	LIN	600	4-21-86	3:12p
ACAD	MNX	46318	11-08-86	5:47a

14 File(s)   4087808 bytes free

This is similar to the list you would get using DIR while in DOS. The first column is the file name, the second is the file extension, the third tells you the size of the file in bytes, and the last two columns tell you the date and time the file was last saved (these depend on the date and time set in DOS).

The Catalog option lists files the same way DOS lists files using the /W option. When you select Catalog or enter catalog through the keyboard, you get a list of file names like the following:

Volume in drive C has no label
Directory of C:\cad25

.		..		ACAD	OVL	ACAD1	MID
ACAD2	OVL	ACAD3	OVL	ACAD2	MID	ACAD	EXE
ACAD3	MID	ACAD	DWG	ACAD	HDX	ACAD	HLP
ACAD	MNX						

14 File(s)   4087808 bytes free

This list shows the same files listed above, but it is abbreviated to show only the file name and extension.

You can also use AutoCAD's Shell command to execute any of the DOS file-management commands. See the section on Shell below.

INTERACTING WITH OTHER PROGRAMS

AutoCAD offers many ways to interact with other programs. The AutoCAD Shell command, which you used in Chapter 10, enables you to use any DOS command and some programs while you are in AutoCAD. The DXF file format, which you were also introduced to in Chapter 10, enables you to create drawings by entering information about them in a DXF file, and to edit drawings outside AutoCAD.

This section assumes some familiarity with DOS commands. If you need help with DOS, refer to Appendix C of this book or your DOS manual.

Using Shell to Access DOS Commands and Other Programs

In Chapter 10, you used the Shell command from the External Commands menu to access the DOS COPY CON command and create an attribute template file, then return to the AutoCAD command prompt. You can use Shell or the Sh command on the same menu to access any other DOS command as well. You can also use these commands to temporarily exit AutoCAD and run other commands or programs that are small enough to fit into the memory left over from AutoCAD. You may, for example, want to write a note using a word processor, then use a spreadsheet to quickly evaluate some attribute information you extracted, before returning to AutoCAD. Your choice of which command to use depends on the amount of memory needed to run the program; Sh allocates about 20K to the program, Shell about 120K. Since the operation of and procedures for using these commands are the same, this section discusses only Shell.

To use Shell to exit AutoCAD temporarily, pick it from the External Commands menu, then press Return. You can also enter shell through the keyboard and press Return twice. You will get the message

Type EXIT to return to AutoCAD

and the C prompt appears with an extra greater-than sign after it. Now you can use your computer as you normally would while in DOS. You can use DOS commands to change directories; type, copy, rename, or delete files; or you can run other programs. Once you are done, you can return to AutoCAD by entering the word exit at the DOS prompt.

The Shell command does not perform *multitasking,* where more than one program runs at the same time. Instead, it suspends AutoCAD while you use DOS. Shell frees up a small amount of memory, then starts the DOS *command handler.* The command handler is a program containing *internal DOS commands;* it also is loaded when you start your computer.

The Shell's 120K of memory is enough for any DOS command and some programs. Some word processors, PC Write and older versions of WordStar, for example, will work in this amount of memory (though you may be limited in the size of the document you can open). If you use a modem, most communications programs will work also. Lotus 1-2-3, SuperCalc, and early versions of Multiplan will also work in Shell, though the size of your spreadsheet may be limited. If you want to use a program with Shell, check to see if less than 120K of memory is required to run it.

There are a few other restrictions on the commands and programs you can use with Shell. One is that you cannot load any *terminate and stay resident* command or program from Shell. A terminate and stay resident program remains in RAM after you close it. These include some external DOS commands like Mode and Print (which is useful for printing text files while you are in Auto-CAD) and programs like Sidekick. You must load such commands and programs *before* you start AutoCAD.

Once a resident program is loaded and AutoCAD is running, you can use it as usual except when you display a graphics screen (unless you have a dual-screen system). Then you must use the F1 key to flip the screen to text mode before bringing up your resident program. Conflicts between your display resolution and the type of display your resident program expects can scramble the image on the monitor. In most cases, if this occurs, you can close the resident program, then use the F1 key to restore your view. Before you use a resident program, test it in AutoCAD to make sure it will work properly.

We must also caution you against using the CHKDSK DOS command with the /F option. AutoCAD often stores unused parts of the drawing on disk temporarily while you work on a file. The /F option can delete these temporary bits of your drawing.

Finally, some programs affect the part of memory used for the screen and can create conflicts with AutoCAD. If you return to the drawing editor and you see the screen full of garbage, try the Redraw command. This will often clear up the screen. If Redraw doesn't work, find out which program causes this problem and stop using it in Shell.

Adding Commands That Start External Programs

You may find yourself using Shell frequently to access another program. You can simplify this by setting up AutoCAD to automatically start your favorite program by entering its name at the Auto-CAD command prompt. To do this, you must edit the AutoCAD program file called Acad.PGP, which can be found in the Auto-CAD directory. Acad.PGP is a small ASCII file that contains information AutoCAD uses for accessing DOS commands. While still in

Shell, enter

> type /acad/acad.pgp

You will get the following list:

> CATALOG,DIR /W,24000,*Files: ,0
> DEL,DEL,24000,File to delete: ,0
> DIR,DIR,24000,File specification: ,0
> EDIT,EDLIN,40000,File to edit: ,0
> SH,,24000,*DOS Command: ,0
> SHELL,,125000,*DOS Command: ,0
> TYPE,TYPE,24000,File to list: ,0

There are several items on each line, separated by commas. Notice that the first item is an option from the External Commands menu. This is the word you enter at the AutoCAD command prompt to start the external command. The second item is the actual command as it is entered in DOS. The third item is the number of bytes to allow for the command. The maximum number of bytes allowable for a program is 125,000, the same as for Shell. The fourth item is the message to display before starting the command. This message is optional, but the comma that follows it must still be present. An asterisk before the message tells AutoCAD that the response may have a space. The 0 at the end is a special AutoCAD code that tells AutoCAD to return to AutoCAD text mode upon completion of the command or program. Other codes are available, but they are reserved for specialized options that you probably won't use. If you are interested in these codes, however, look at the appendix on customization in the *AutoCAD Reference Manual*.

You can add commands or programs to this list by using your word processor or the DOS COPY CON or EDLIN editor. You can access EDLIN with the Edit option on the External Commands menu; note the fourth line of the Acad.PGP file.

Say you want to be able to start Lotus 1-2-3 from the AutoCAD command prompt. First open Acad.PGP using your word-processing program in DOS text file mode. Then add the following line to the bottom of the list:

> Lotus,123,125000,,0

You can add more lines for other programs if you like. When you finish adding lines, be sure to save the file as an ASCII file. The next time you start AutoCAD and open a drawing file, Lotus 1-2-3 will execute by entering Lotus at the AutoCAD command prompt. You must have the Lotus 1-2-3 program on the current default directory or set a path to the directory containing it. See Appendix C for information on setting a path.

To add a line to Acad.PGP with COPY CON, enter

```
copy con addline.txt
Lotus,123,125000,,0
^Z
```

while in the AutoCAD Shell or DOS. This creates a DOS text file called Addline.TXT. Again, the second line can add a program other than Lotus 1-2-3, and you can add more lines for additional programs. Enter the last line by pressing the F6 function key, then press Return.

Next enter

```
type addline.txt >> acad.pgp
```

This line appends the file Addline.TXT to the file Acad.PGP. The double greater-than sign tells DOS to redirect the output from the TYPE command to the file name that follows, which in this case is Acad.PGP. The file must be in the current directory.

Now delete the Addline.TXT file and enter the word exit to return to AutoCAD.

Using the DXF File Format

A DXF file is a DOS text file containing all the information in a drawing. It is often used to exchange drawings created with different programs. Many micro-CAD programs, including some 3D perspective programs, can generate files in DXF format. If you understand the codes used in a DXF file, you can also use it to manipulate a drawing in ways not possible in AutoCAD. For example, you can use a DXF file for *parametric processing*.

Creating Drawings with DXF Files

Parametric processing is a way of drawing an object by entering information regarding that object rather than actually drawing it with the drawing editor. The computer draws the object based on the information provided. Parametric processing allows the creation of fairly detailed drawings that would take many times longer to enter by hand.

For example, a program could be written to draw a stairway. Stairs are fairly complicated because they must follow certain design rules. They must have a certain height-to-tread width ratio, and they cannot be over a certain width without having an intermediate handrail. They must also have a landing before a certain length of stairway is reached. A parametric-processing program would allow you to enter such variables as floor-to-floor distance, stairway shape, and stairway location. Then the program could draw a stair automatically by first incorporating these variables with the typical requirements for stairs, then designing a stair to fit all the requirements. Doing this by hand would require sitting down with a calculator, figuring out the stairway length and exactly how many treads are required, then drawing the stair.

Parametric processing can be accomplished within AutoCAD using AutoLISP, or outside AutoCAD using third-party software. There is currently a program called Synthesis that uses DXF files for parametric processing of AutoCAD drawings. If you are a programmer, you may want to examine the DXF format and try writing your own parametric-processing program.

Importing and Exporting DXF Files

You can also use DXF files to exchange drawings between AutoCAD and other programs. You may want to use a 3D program to view your drawing in a perspective view, or you may just have a consultant who uses a different CAD program that accepts DXF files.

Exporting DXF files is very simple. Pick Dxf/dxb from the Utility menu, then pick Dxfout from the Dxf/dxb menu (see Figure 13.11). You see the Dxfin and Dxfout commands listed on the menu along with the object-selection options and other options that we will discuss shortly. (We will discuss the Dxbin command in Chapter 14.)

You will get the prompt

DXFOUT File name <flange>:

You can enter the name for the DXF file; AutoCAD will automatically add the extension .DXF. The default is the name of the current drawing. Press Return to accept the default.

The next prompt

Enter decimal places of accuracy (0 to 16) (or Entities) <6>:

allows you to specify the degree of accuracy the exported file will have. The exported file will contain information on the location and properties of objects in the drawing in the form of real numbers. The number you enter here determines the number of decimal

```
AUTOCAD
* * * *
DXFIN:

DXFOUT:
16
ENTITIES

Window
Last
Previous
Crossing
Remove
Add
Undo

DXBIN:
_LAST_
 DRAW
 EDIT
```

Figure 13.11: *The Dxf/dxb menu*

places those numbers will be carried to. You can select the 16 option from the Dxf/dxb menu to indicate that you would like the maximum 16-decimal-place accuracy.

You can also pick Entities or enter E to select specific entities to be exported. Perhaps you want to export only a block or a section of a drawing. Rather than exporting the entire drawing, then sorting through the unneeded information, you can isolate the objects you need and not export the rest. If you pick Entities, you will get the object-selection prompt. You can then select objects using the object-selection options on the Dxf/dxb menu.

Once you finish selecting objects, you will be returned to the decimal accuracy prompt. Press Return to accept the default, 6. Auto-CAD will now create the Unit.DXF file. If your drawing is large, this may take several minutes.

Next you will practice importing a DXF file. Close the Flange file and open a new file called Flange1. Go to the Dxf/dxb menu and pick Dxfin. The prompt

File name <flange1>:

asks for the name of the DXF file to import. Enter Flange. AutoCAD will pause about a minute while it reads the file from the hard disk, then the flange appears as a drawing as you exported it, complete with the same settings.

Looking at DXF Files

The DXF file format is quite easy to understand once you become familiar with AutoCAD. To look at the DXF file you created, exit the Flange1 file, then exit AutoCAD. At the DOS prompt, enter

type unit.dxf ¦ more

You will get a listing of the Unit.DXF file; the first part is similar to the one shown below.

```
            SECTION
               2
            HEADER
               9
           $ACADVER
               1
            AC1002
               9
           $INSBASE
              10
            180.0
              20
             29.0
               9
           $EXTMIN
              10
             0.0
              20
             0.0
               9
           $EXTMAX
              10
           – More –
```

Press Return to continue scrolling the file. Press Control-C when you have seen enough.

This shows you that the DXF file is a long list of text, integers, and real numbers. In general, the list contains the drawing settings; the names of line types, text styles, layers, blocks, and views; and finally, the list of objects complete with codes describing what the objects are and their coordinate locations. These values can be manipulated to make changes in the drawing, then imported back into AutoCAD.

To see how this works open a file called Circle. Draw a circle with a radius of two units using the coordinate 6,5 as its center (see Figure 13.12).

Now use the Dxfout command to create a file called Circle.DXF. End out of this file and exit AutoCAD. Start a word processor and open the Circle.DXF file. Remember to open it as an ASCII file. Go to the end of the file. You will see the following text:

BLOCKS
0
ENDSEC
0
SECTION
2
ENTITIES
0
CIRCLE
8
0
10

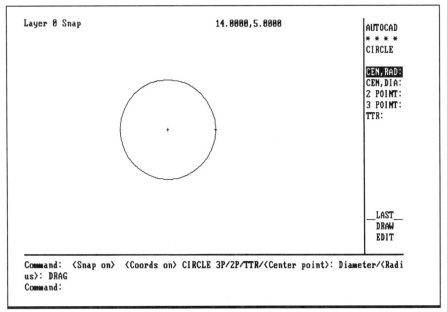

Figure 13.12: The circle

```
                6.000000
                20
                5.000000
                40
                2.0
                0
                ENDSEC
                0
                EOF
```

The items that precede the word entities are the codes defining the drawing's variables, line types, text styles, blocks, layers, and saved views. Everything that follows the word entities represents the actual drawn objects. In this case, the only object is a circle. After the word circle, there is a series of numbers. Each number is a code determining what the following number represents. For example, the number 8 is followed by a 0. The 8 tells you that the 0 is the layer the circle is on. The next number, 10, tells you that the number following it, 6.000000, is the x coordinate for the center of the circle. The number following the 20 is the y coordinate. Finally, the number following the 40 is the radius of the circle, 2. Change the 2 to 4, then save this file as an ASCII file with the same name, Circle.DXF.

Now you will see how editing this DXF file affected the drawing. Start AutoCAD and open a file called Newcirc. Go to the DXF menu and pick Dxfin. You get the prompt

File name <newcirc>:

Enter the name of the DXF file you just edited, Circle. The circle will appear in the drawing area with a radius of 4 instead of 2, as shown in Figure 13.13.

Now quit the Newcirc file.

This may seem like a roundabout way to edit a drawing, but in a large, complicated drawing, some processes may actually go faster using a DXF file and a program written to search for specific items to be processed. For a detailed description of the DXF coding system, refer to the appendix on drawing interchange files in the *AutoCAD Reference Manual*.

Using AutoCAD in Desktop Publishing

The growing popularity of desktop-publishing software is creating a new interest in drawing and paint programs that can be used in

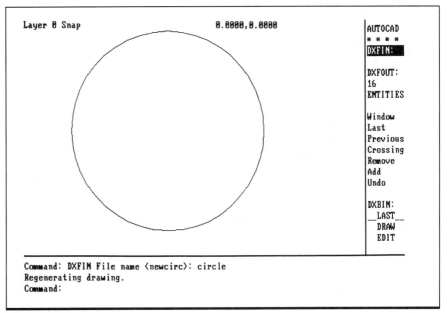

Figure 13.13: The imported circle

conjunction with it. AutoCAD is a natural for creating line art and because of its popularity, most desktop-publishing programs are designed to import AutoCAD drawings in one form or another. Those who employ desktop-publishing software to generate user manuals or other technical documents will probably want to be able to use AutoCAD drawings in their work. In this section, we will discuss ways to output AutoCAD drawings for use by the two most popular desktop-publishing programs available for the IBM PC: Page-Maker (version 1.0a) and Ventura (version 1.1).

Transferring AutoCAD Drawings to PageMaker

There are two methods for transferring AutoCAD drawings to PageMaker. The first is to configure the AutoCAD plotter option as an ADI plotter using the ASCII output format (see Appendix B for details). After configuring the plotter, you must use the Plot command to plot the drawing. Instead of sending the plot information directly to a plotter, AutoCAD creates a file on your default directory. During the plot setup, you will get the prompt

Enter file name for plot <*default*>:

where the default name is the name of the file you are plotting to. If you press Return without entering a name, the plot file will have the same name as the original drawing file but with the extension .PLT instead of .DWG.

Once the plot is complete, you will find the plot file on the default directory. You can then import this file to PageMaker by selecting the Place command from PageMaker's File pull-down menu.

If your drawing is very complex and your plot file exceeds 50K in size, PageMaker may not be able to import the file. If this happens, you will need to break your drawing up into pieces, plot each piece, then import the pieces separately to PageMaker. If your drawing contains text, you may want to transfer the drawing without the text, then add the text while you are in PageMaker. Text can substantially increase the size of a file, so by eliminating it, you improve the chances of PageMaker accepting your file. Also, PageMaker offers higher-quality typefaces than AutoCAD.

The laser printer yields the best-quality output of any desktop printer. You can use a dot-matrix printer with PageMaker, but output quality will be poor. At the other end of the spectrum, you can have your PageMaker output sent to a typesetting device which can give you as much as 2,500 dots per inch resolution.

Figure 13.14 shows an AutoCAD ADI plot that has been imported to PageMaker, then printed on a laser printer. It contains the three variations of polylines that are most troublesome to translate to desktop-publishing software. The object in the upper left is a curve-fitted polyline of varying width. The three objects in the upper right are dots created using the Donut command in AutoCAD. These dots are drawn as completely filled solids. The three lines at the bottom of the figure show how various widths of straight polylines are translated into PageMaker. All three elements of the figure translated accurately, with little distortion. The text in the figure is an AutoCAD Txt font, which appears slightly distorted.

Another method for file transfer is to use the Encapsulated PostScript format. Chapter 5 describes a method for creating a PostScript file from AutoCAD that can be sent directly to a PostScript printer. With some modification, you can also import such a file into PageMaker the same way you import an ADI file. Follow the procedure given in Chapter 5 to create a PostScript plot file. With a word processor capable of editing DOS text files or ASCII files, open the PostScript file. At the beginning of the file, you will see

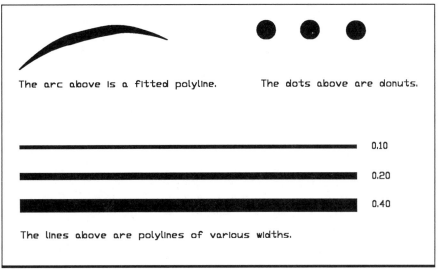

Figure 13.14: *An AutoCAD drawing transferred to PageMaker using the ADI plot file*

comments like

```
%!PS-Adobe-1.0
% File produced by AutoCAD
/m {moveto} def
/l {lineto} def
/s {stroke} def
/n {newpath} def
2 setlinejoin
20 20 translate
0.240000 0.240000 scale
3.000000 setlinewidth
n
1571 1425 m
1577 1421 l
...
```

A few things need to be added to this file to make it conform to the Encapsulated PostScript format. First, you must change the top line to read

```
%!PS-Adobe-1.0 EPSF
```

Next, go to the end of the file and locate the line that begins

```
%%BoundingBox:
```

This is followed by four sets of numbers. These numbers represent the lower-left and upper-right coordinates of the drawing image area in picas. A pica is equivalent to 1/72 of an inch. An example of this line would be

%%BoundingBox: 0 0 500 300

Here the image area is defined by a rectangle whose diagonal corner coordinates are 0,0 for the lower left and 500,300 for the upper right.

If you are using version 2.6 or earlier, this BoundingBox statement is not present in the file. If your file doesn't have the BoundingBox statement, determine the coordinate location of the lower-left and the upper-right corners of your drawing in inches. Convert those coordinates into picas, multiply the converted coordinate values by the scale value at the beginning of the PostScript file, and add 20 to each value. The scale value in the example above appears in the line

0.240000 0.240000 scale

Then add those coordinates to the BoundingBox statement. Once you have located or created this BoundingBox information, move it to just below the top line in the file. Add an extra percent sign to the beginning of the file creation line so that it reads

%%File produced by AutoCAD

Finally, add the following line below the last line that starts with the double percent sign:

%%EndComments

Save the file as a DOS text file or ASCII file. Now you can import the file into PageMaker.

PageMaker will try to load the file, then ask you what type of file it is supposed to be. A list of options will appear. At the bottom of the list will be Encapsulated PostScript. Pick this file type. When you place the file, you will see only a gray area with three lines that read

Title:
Creator:
Cr Date:

as shown in Figure 13.15.

Though the imported AutoCAD drawing appears as a gray rectangle on the screen, the original drawing will appear when the file is

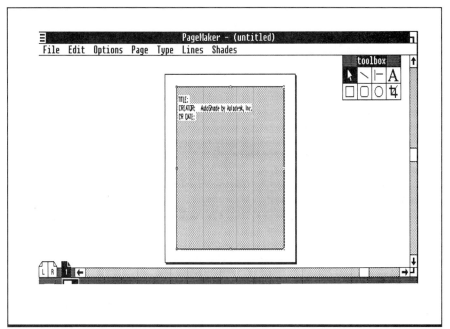

Figure 13.15: Screen view of AutoCAD drawing imported to PageMaker

printed on a PostScript device such as an Apple LaserWriter (see Figure 13.16). As in Figure 13.14, all the drawing elements are reproduced accurately. In fact, Figure 13.16 is slightly better in quality, which is most noticeable in the AutoCAD text. If you look carefully, you will also notice that the dots and the arc are smoother around the edges in Figure 13.16.

A major drawback to using the Encapsulated PostScript format is that it can be used only with a PostScript printer. Another drawback is that you can't see how the drawing is going to look on the page until you actually print it. However, since this method can transfer more complex drawings than the ADI file format, it may be the only way you can bring some AutoCAD drawings into PageMaker.

Whichever file transfer method you choose, PageMaker will produce high-quality line art that accurately maintains the appearance of the original AutoCAD drawing.

Transferring AutoCAD Drawings to Ventura

With Ventura, there are four options for transferring files from AutoCAD. Each has its advantages and disadvantages. The simplest

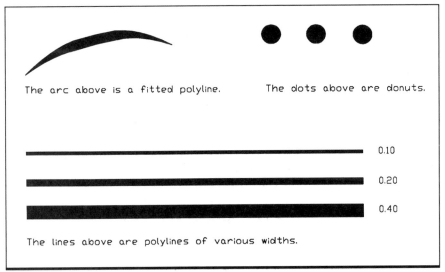

The arc above is a fitted polyline.   The dots above are donuts.

The lines above are polylines of various widths.

Figure 13.16:   *AutoCAD drawing printed from PageMaker using a Post-*
Script laser printer

and quickest way to transfer files from AutoCAD versions 2.6 and earlier is to make an AutoCAD slide file (see Chapter 16 for instructions). Creating slides is simple and quick, and Ventura accepts Auto-CAD slide files directly. The drawback to using this method is its poor image quality. The resolution of the slide depends on the resolution of your display. If you want to fill half a page with your drawing, the slide file will appear rough and clumsy, and small text will be barely readable. Also, if your display has a horizontal-to-vertical pixel ratio of 3 to 4 (as in the Hercules display and IBM EGA), slide images will tend to be flattened when imported into Ventura (see Figure 13.17). Notice in Figure 13.17 how rough the dots and arc appear, and how the text is distorted.

Because of these distortions, AutoCAD slides are best used for artwork that will occupy only a small part of the page. Version 9 users cannot use slides to transfer drawings to Ventura because the slide file format has been changed in that version.

The second method for file transfer is to make a DXF file as described earlier in this chapter. This method requires an intermediate step. Once the DXF file is created, you must convert the file into a format readable by Ventura. Ventura provides the Dxftogem program necessary for this conversion on its utility disk. The quick conversion gives you a file with the extension .GEM, which can then be read by Ventura.

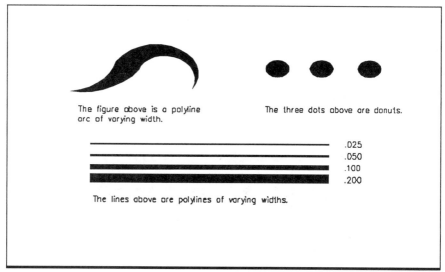

Figure 13.17:   *Slide image printed from Ventura*

This DXF-to-GEM conversion affects the drawing in several ways. First, all text is converted into a Helvetica typeface. Actually, this may be preferable to the sticklike AutoCAD fonts, but the converted text does not fit into the drawing in the same way as the original text. For this reason, you must take care in placing and sizing text in AutoCAD when you intend to transfer files to Ventura. We suggest using the Txt AutoCAD font with a width-scale factor of .65. This will approximate the line length of Ventura's Helvetica typeface.

The second effect of a DXF-to-GEM conversion on AutoCAD drawings is more significant. Polylines that vary in width do not translate. They appear as lines of single widths with rounded ends (see Figure 13.18). Polyline arcs appear as line segments. Donuts are distorted into elongated circles. For this reason, you should avoid using polylines and donuts in drawings you intend to import to Ventura using this method.

Despite these problems, the DXF-to-GEM translation offers a far superior image to the slide file. Lines are straight and clear, and arcs and circles are smooth. And since text is converted to Helvetica, it is very readable so long as it is large enough to be read. If your drawing will occupy a large part of the page, this file transfer method is preferable to the slide file method.

The third method for transferring files from AutoCAD to Ventura is to create an HPGL (Hewlett-Packard Graphics Language) plot file.

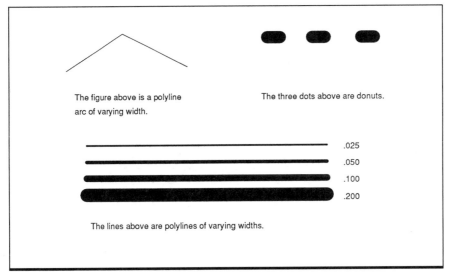

The figure above is a polyline arc of varying width.

The three dots above are donuts.

.025
.050
.100
.200

The lines above are polylines of varying widths.

Figure 13.18: DXF file printed from Ventura

This requires setting up the AutoCAD plotter as a Hewlett-Packard 7470 plotter (see Appendix B for details on configuring the plotter). Once the configuration is done, you plot the file to disk in a way similar to importing to PageMaker, with one difference: You must tell AutoCAD to plot to a file at the beginning of the plot setup.

To create a plot file, enter Y at the prompt

Write the plot to a file <N>

At the end of the plot setup, you will get the prompt

Enter file name for plot <*default*>:

where the default name is the name of the file you are plotting to. If you press Return without entering a name, the plot file will have the same name as the original drawing file, but with the extension .PLT instead of .DWG.

Once the plot is complete, you will find the plot file on the default directory. You can then import this file into Ventura by selecting HPGL as the file format to be imported. The file can be printed on any output device supported by Ventura.

This method of file transfer is one of the two most accurate. Line work is sharp and clear, arcs and circles are smooth, and polylines and text keep their appearance (see Figure 13.19). Notice, however, that the dots in Figure 13.19, which were drawn as solids, have acquired holes during translation.

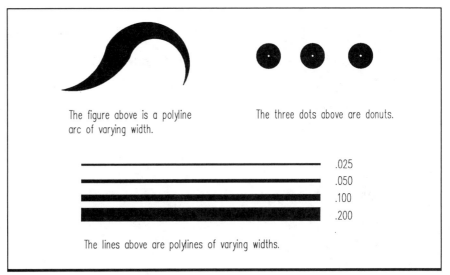

The figure above is a polyline arc of varying width.

The three dots above are donuts.

.025
.050
.100
.200

The lines above are polylines of varying widths.

Figure 13.19: *HPGL plot file printed from Ventura*

The principal drawback of transferring a drawing this way is the time it takes for translation. Plotting to a file can take several minutes. Once the file is imported to Ventura, it is slow to regenerate and print. Also, some files can become too big (over above 200K) for Ventura to import, and you can't import them in pieces because it is difficult to align images in Ventura. With most files, however, size should not be a problem.

With the fourth method, you can import Encapsulated PostScript files, as you did with PageMaker. Follow the instructions in the preceding PageMaker discussion for changing an AutoCAD PostScript plot file into an Encapsulated PostScript file. Ventura displays an Encapsulated PostScript file as a rectangle with an X drawn through it, so you won't be able to see the image until you print the file on a PostScript printer (see Figure 13.20). AutoCAD drawings imported this way load quickly and maintain their appearance accurately, a little more accurately than the HPGL format (see Figure 13.21).

In general, you can save file space by leaving out text in the Auto-CAD drawing and adding it later in Ventura, which allows you to use the high-quality Ventura typefaces. If you don't mind using Helvetica and are careful with the use of polylines, the most expedient way to transfer files is through the DXF-to-GEM conversion. HPGL and Encapsulated Postscript formats give the most accurate results, but they also have their drawbacks. It is worth experimenting with

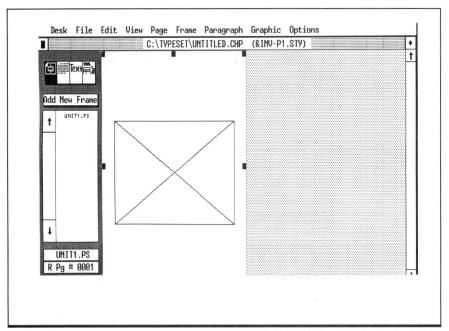

Figure 13.20: A screen of an Encapsulated PostScript file imported into Ventura

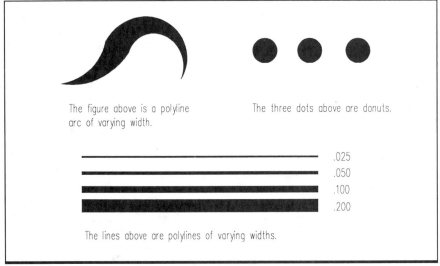

Figure 13.21: The PostScript file printed on a PostScript laser printer

all these methods so you can decide for yourself which is best for your application.

CONCLUSION

In this chapter, you have seen how AutoCAD allows you to access information ranging from areas of objects to information from other programs. You may never use some of these features, but knowing they are there may help you when you are trying to solve a production problem. Try finding the area of a drawing you have done on your own. You might also experiment with entering other programs using the Shell command.

If you use a desktop-publishing program in your work, you may want to experiment with different ways of exporting AutoCAD files to it. If you don't want to open and modify your AutoCAD PostScript plot files every time you use an AutoCAD drawing for desktop publishing, you can obtain a program that does the modification for you by sending for the disk offered in the coupon at the end of this book.

In the next chapter you will learn how to create three-dimensional drawings.

Chapter 14

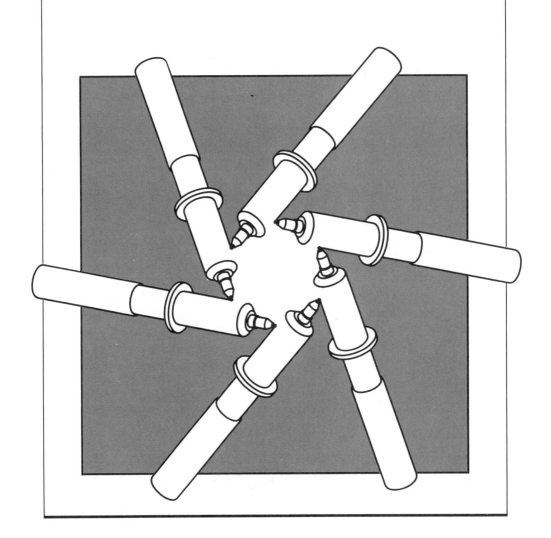

Using 3D

VIEWING AN OBJECT IN THREE DIMENSIONS helps you get a sense of its true shape and form. It also helps you conceptualize the design, which in turn allows you to make better design decisions. Finally, it helps you communicate your ideas to those who may not be familiar with plans, sections, and side views of your design.

AutoCAD allows you to turn any drawing you create into a 3D model by changing the properties of the objects that make it up. AutoCAD does this through a combination of three types of objects: *extruded 2D objects*, *3D lines*, and *3D faces*. It is, however, limited by its inability to give you true perspective views.

In this chapter, you will use AutoCAD's 3D capabilities to see what your studio apartment looks like from various angles.

CREATING A 3D DRAWING

AutoCAD creates three-dimensional forms by *extruding* two-dimensional objects. This means that to draw a cube, you first draw a square, then extrude the square by giving the lines that make it up a *thickness* (see Figure 14.1). This thickness is a value given as a z coordinate. Imagine that the screen's drawing area is the drawing surface. A 0 z coordinate is on that surface. A z coordinate greater

MASTERING AUTOCAD

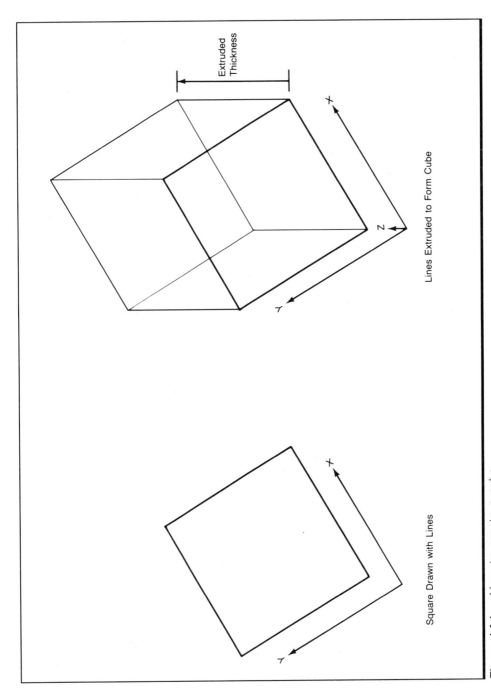

Extruded
Thickness

X

Z

Y

Lines Extruded to Form Cube

X

Y

Square Drawn with Lines

Figure 14.1:   *How to create a cube*

than 0 is a position closer to you and "above" that surface. Figure 14.2 illustrates this point.

When you draw an object with thickness, you don't see the thickness until you view the drawing from a different angle. This is because normally your view is perpendicular to the imagined drawing surface. At that angle, you cannot see the thickness of an object because it projects toward you, just as a sheet of paper looks like a line when viewed from one end. To view an object's thickness, you must change the angle at which you view your drawing.

You can also set AutoCAD so that everything you draw has an *elevation*. Normally, you draw on the imagined surface, but you can set the z coordinate for your drawing elevation so that whatever you draw is above that surface. An object with an elevation value other than 0 rests not on the imagined drawing surface but above it (or below if the z coordinate is a negative value). See Figure 14.3.

We should mention that text and dimensions appear only on the plane defined by the x and y axes. Any text you add to the Unit plan, for example, will appear to be on the floor of the plan. If you turn on the Notes layer while in 3D view, you will see the labels and dimensions you added appear on the floor of the unit.

Changing a 2D Drawing into a 3D Drawing

In this exercise, you will turn the 2D studio unit drawing into a 3D drawing by changing the properties of the wall lines. You will also learn how to view the 3D image.

Start AutoCAD and open the Unit file. Set the current layer to Wall and turn off all the other layers except Jamb. Turn on the grid if it isn't on already. Your screen should look like Figure 14.4.

To view an object in 3D, you must use the Vpoint command on the 3D menu. Pick 3D from the Root menu, then pick Vpoint from the 3D menu (see Figure 14.5). The prompt

Enter view point<0'-0",0'-0",0'-1">:

appears. The default value is a list of the x, y, and z coordinates of your last viewing location relative to your object. We will explain more about this prompt later in this chapter. Enter -1,-1,1. Your view looks as if you are standing below and to the left of your drawing rather than directly above it (see Figure 14.6). The grid shows you the angle of the drawing surface.

The Change command on the 3D menu is used to change the 3D properties of objects. Start Change by picking it from the 3D menu

MASTERING AUTOCAD

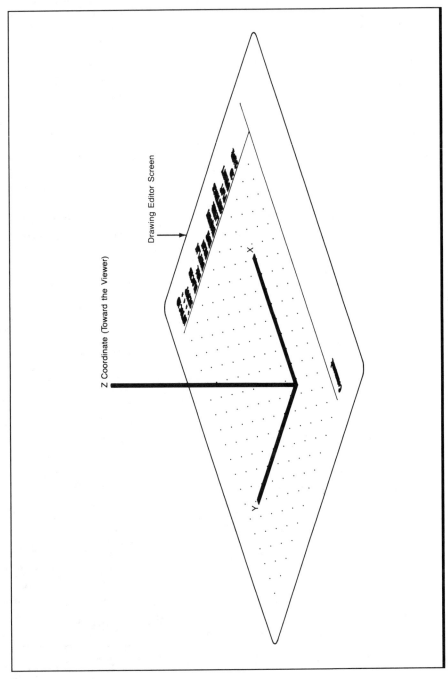

Figure 14.2: The z coordinate in relation to the x and y coordinates

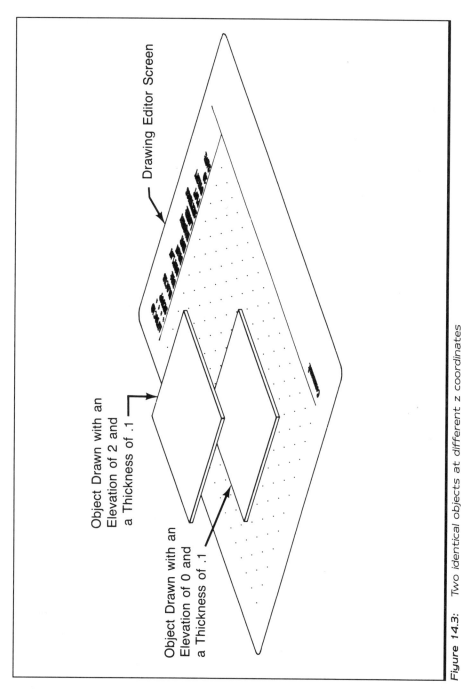

Drawing Editor Screen

Object Drawn with an
Elevation of 2 and
a Thickness of .1

Object Drawn with an
Elevation of 0 and
a Thickness of .1

Figure 14.3:   Two identical objects at different z coordinates

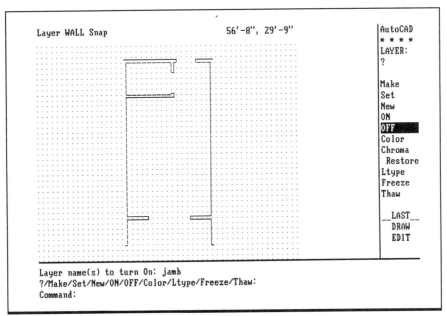

Figure 14.4:   The plan view of the walls and door jambs

Figure 14.5:   The 3D menu

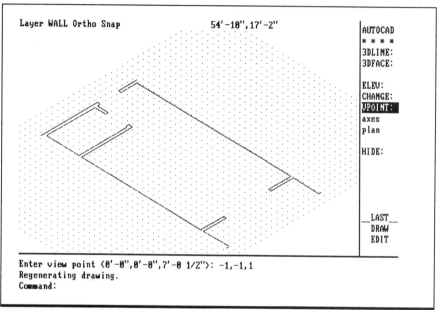

Figure 14.6:   3D view of the floor plan

or entering change through the keyboard. A simplified version of the usual Change menu appears (see Figure 14.7). It contains the Change options, the selection options, and the Elev command. At the object-selection prompt, use a window to pick the entire draw-ing. Press Return. At the properties prompt, pick Thickness from the Change menu or enter P, then T. The following prompt appears.

New thickness<0'-0">:

Enter 8', then press Return to complete the command.

Your drawing will look like Figure 14.8. The walls and jambs now appear to be eight feet high. You are able to see through the walls because this is a *wire frame view*. A wire frame view shows the vol-umes of a 3D object by showing the lines representing the intersec-tions of surfaces. Later we will discuss how to view an object as if the surfaces were opaque.

Next you will use the Change command to change the elevation of the door headers. Turn on the Ceiling layer. You see the door headers appear as lines on the floor of your 3D view. Start the Change command again and pick the two lines representing the header

Figure 14.7: The 3D Change menu

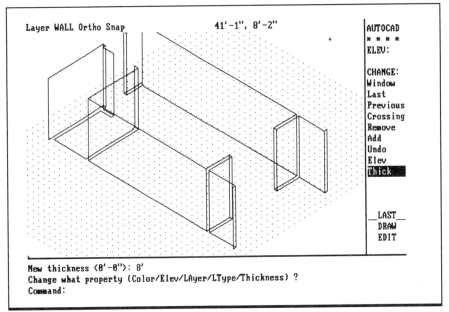

Figure 14.8: The wall lines extruded

over the door to the balcony. Press Return when you have finished your selection. At the properties prompt, pick Elev from the Change menu. You will get the prompt

New elevation<0′-0″>:

Enter 7′ and press Return to complete the command. The header will move from the floor to a position seven feet above the floor (see Figure 14.9).

Change the thickness of the header to 1′ using the procedure you just used to change the thickness of the wall lines. Do the same thing for the door header over the entry. Your drawing will look like Figure 14.10.

Creating a 3D Object

Though you may visualize a design in 3D, you will often start sketching it in 2D and later generate 3D views. If you know from the start what the thickness and height of an object are to be, you can set these values so that you don't have to extrude the object

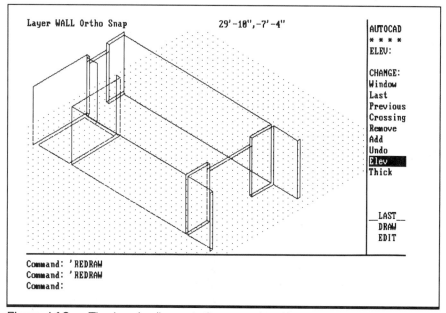

Figure 14.9:   *The header lines at the new elevation*

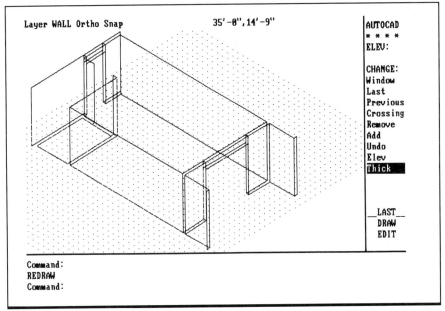

Figure 14.10: *The headers with the new thickness*

later. If you use the same thickness and elevation often, you can even create a template file with these settings so they are readily available when you start your drawing.

The command for setting thickness and elevation is Elev. Pick Elev from the 3D menu. You will get the prompt

New current elevation<0'-0">:

Enter 3". The next prompt appears.

New current thickness<0'-0">:

Enter 12". Pull-down menu users can select Entity Creation from the Modes pull-down menu. The Entity Creation Modes dialog box appears. Enter 3" in the Elevation input button and 12" in the Thickness input button, then pick the OK action button (see Figure 14.11).

The grid changes to the new elevation. Now as you draw objects, they appear 12" thick at an elevation of 3". Draw a circle representing a planter at one side of the balcony (see Figure 14.12). Make it 18" in diameter. The planter appears as a 3D object with the current thickness and elevation settings.

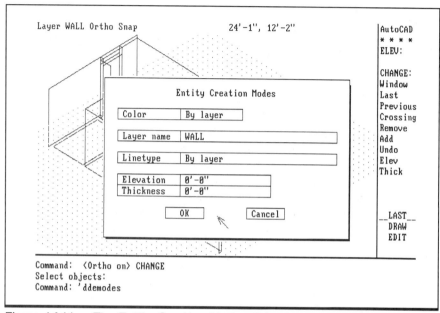

Figure 14.11:   The Entity Creation Modes dialog box

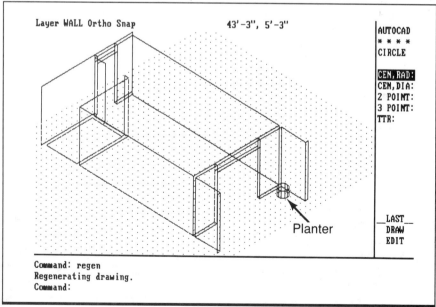

Figure 14.12:   The planter

Extruding forms is a very simple process, as you have seen. You just have to keep track of thicknesses and elevations. With these two properties, you can create nearly any three-dimensional form you need. Next you will discover how to control your view of your drawing.

VIEWING A 3D DRAWING

Your first 3D view of a drawing is a wire frame view. It appears as an open model made of wire; none of the sides appear solid. This section describes how to manipulate this wire frame view so you can see your drawing from any angle. We will also describe how, once you have selected your view, you can view your 3D drawing as a solid object with the hidden lines removed.

Getting a Wire Frame View

Pick the Vpoint command from the 3D menu again. The prompt

Enter view point<-0'-1",-0'-1",0'-1">:

appears. Here you specify the x, y, and z values for your position in relation to the origin of the *coordinate tripod*. The coordinate tripod graphically shows your orientation to the drawing. The coordinate values are not meaningful in themselves, only in relation to each other. The origin of the coordinate tripod, in this case, is your entire drawing and not the actual drawing origin (see Figure 14.13). The negative x value places your viewing position to the left of your drawing. The negative y places your position 270 degrees in relation to your drawing. The positive 1 value for the z axis lifts your view above the surface. As you go through the following exercise, you will see more clearly the relationship between your view and these coordinates.

Now press Return to accept the default or pick Axes from the 3D menu (the Axes option simply enters a Return). You get a screen that helps you visually select your 3D view (see Figure 14.14). The three lines converging at one point compose the coordinate tripod. As you move the cursor around, the tripod rotates to show your orientation. Each line is labeled to indicate which axis it represents. As the lines rotate about the origin, you begin to get a sense of what they are showing you.

Above and to the right of the tripod is a *target* with a small cursor. As you move your mouse, the cursor follows, staying near or

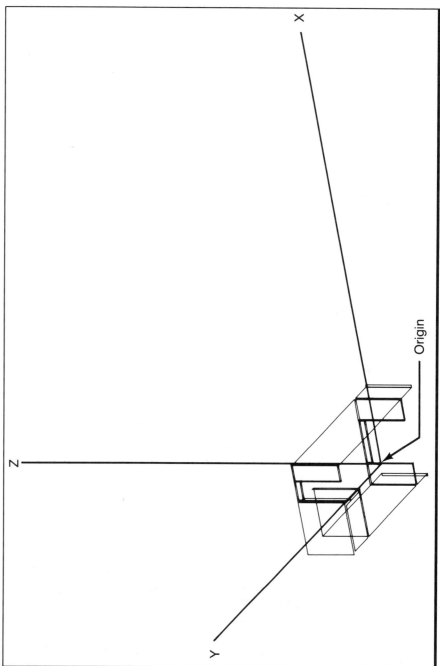

Figure 14.13: The coordinate tripod superimposed on the plan

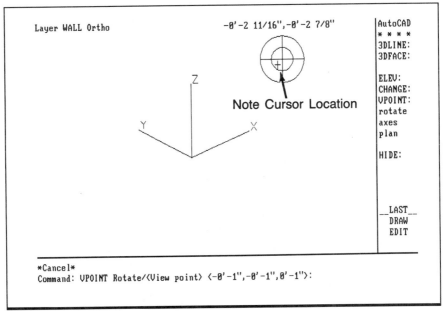

Figure 14.14: The coordinate tripod and target

within the target. The cursor's position in relation to the target's center is your viewpoint in relation to your drawing. For example, if you place the cursor just below and to the left of the center, your view will be from the lower-left corner of your object, like your view of the floor plan in the previous exercise. If you place the cursor above and to the right of the center, you will view your drawing from the upper-right corner. Moving the cursor around the center of the target is like circling your drawing. Try doing this and watch the tripod. Note how the tripod appears to rotate, indicating your changing view (see Figure 14.15).

Also note the coordinate readout. It tells you your x,y coordinates in relation to the target's center. As you move the cursor closer to the center, the coordinate readout approaches 0,0, and the z axis of the tripod begins to foreshorten until it is no longer visible (see Figure 14.16). This shows that you are almost directly above the drawing, as you would be in a 2D view. Position the cursor as shown in Figure 14.16 and pick this point.

Your drawing will look something like Figure 14.17. Now you can see that your view does indeed look like a plan view. The closer to the target's center you move the cursor, the higher in elevation your view will be.

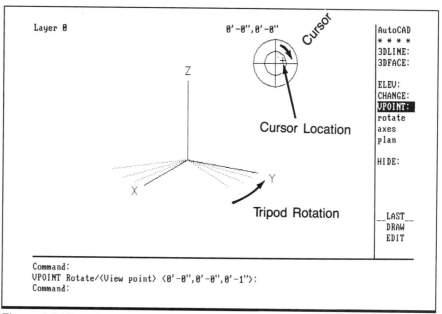

Figure 14.15: How the tripod rotates as you move the cursor around the target's center

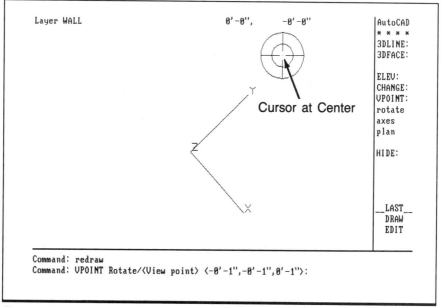

Figure 14.16: The z axis foreshortened

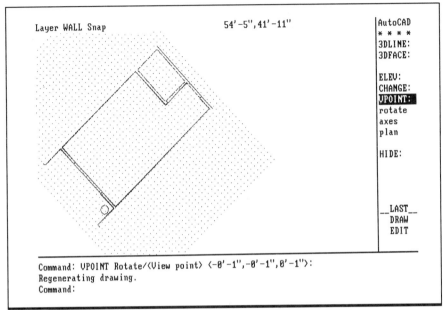

Figure 14.17: A 3D view that looks like a 2D view

Start the Vpoint command again and notice the default value at the prompt for a viewpoint. The x and y values are very low, while the z value is relatively high. This tells you that you are very close to the origin in the x and y axes but far from it in the z axis.

Press Return. Look at the target again. As you move closer to its inner ring, the x and y lines begin to flatten until, as you touch the circle, they are parallel (see Figure 14.18). This first ring represents a directly horizontal position on your drawing surface. Position the cursor as shown in Figure 14.18 and pick this position. Your drawing will look as if you are viewing the drawing surface edge on and the walls from the side (see Figure 14.19). (It is a little difficult to tell what is going on because you can see right through the walls.)

Start the Vpoint command again and note the default coordinates on the prompt. This time the x and y values are high, while the z value is 0 or close to it. This tells you that the previous view was from an elevation of 0. Go to the 3D graphic display again. As you move the cursor to the outermost ring of the target, the z axis line foreshortens again. This ring represents a view located underneath your drawing, as if you were looking at the back of the screen. Pick a point just inside this outer ring as shown in Figure 14.20.

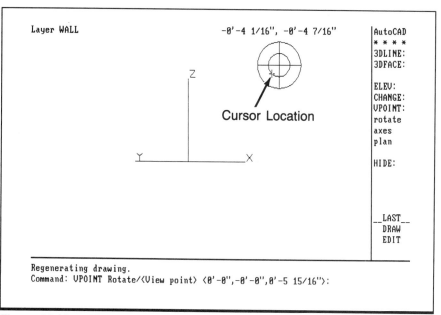

Figure 14.18: The parallel x and y axes

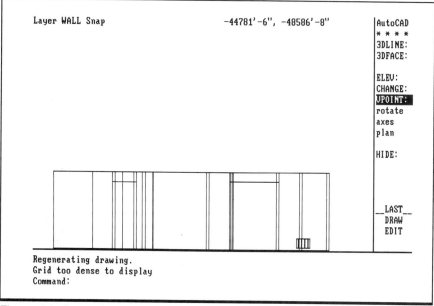

Figure 14.19: View of walls from side

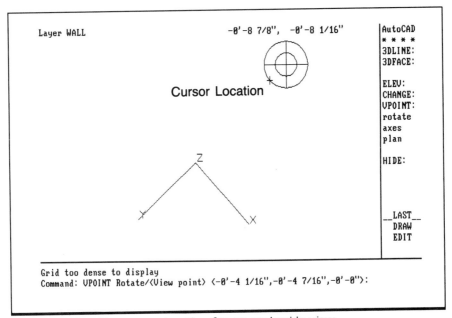

Figure 14.20: The cursor location for an underside view

You will get a view something like Figure 14.21. At first you might think that this is just another view from above the drawing. However, if you look carefully at the position of the bathroom in relation to the rest of the unit, you will notice that it appears to be mirrored, just like any drawing viewed from the back of the drawing sheet.

If you want to get back to a plan view of your drawing, use the Vpoint command and enter 0,0 or pick Plan from the 3D menu at the viewpoint prompt. When you do this, you will notice that your 2D view looks just the way it did before you extruded the walls. As we explained earlier, this is because you are viewing the wall lines edge on. Now return to the view you used to edit the Unit drawing, -1,-1,1.

You can save and recall a 3D view just like any other view. Just set it up, then start the View command. Then use the Save option on the View menu or enter S; you can give the 3D view any name you please. Save this view and give it the name 3D.

Turn on all the layers except Notes. Notice that when you extruded the walls, the interior bathroom walls did not change with the others. This is because those walls are part of a block. You can change the elevation of a block, but you cannot change its thickness. You must redefine the block to change the thickness of the

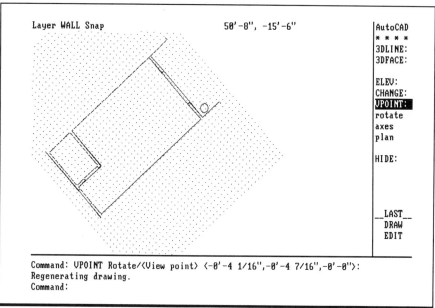

Figure 14.21: The plan from below the drawing surface

objects it contains. If you have forgotten how to redefine a block, refer to Chapter 7.

Using the Rotate Command

A more direct way of obtaining a view from a 3D drawing is by using the Rotate command. Pick Vpoint from the 3D menu, then pick Rotate from the same menu or enter R. The following prompt appears:

Enter angle in X-Y plane in X axis <225>:

The number in brackets tells you the rotational angle for the current view. If you imagine looking at a 2D view of the apartment, as in Figure 14.4, this value represents a position toward the lower left of the view. Enter 45 to get a view at the opposite side of the apartment. Another prompt appears:

Enter angle from X-Y plane <35>:

The number in brackets tells you the angle of the current view above the current floor elevation. If you imagine looking at the side of the apartment as in Figure 14.19, this value represents the direction of your point of view above the floor. Press Return to accept the default value. You get a new view of the apartment from the opposite side of your current view (see Figure 14.22). Figure 14.23 illustrates what these values represent.

If you like, you can visually choose the rotational angle of your view. To do this, first select the Id command from the Inquiry menu and pick a point at the center of the apartment. Next, start the Vpoint command and select the Rotate command as before. A rubber-banding line will appear with one end at the point you selected and the other end on the cursor (see Figure 14.24). At the prompt for an angle, pick a point indicating the position you wish to view the model from. The position of the cursor will determine your view position. With the Osnap modes you can even use part of your apartment model as a reference.

The next angle from the x,y plane prompt appears. You cannot use the rubber-banding line to select the view height; you must enter a value as before.

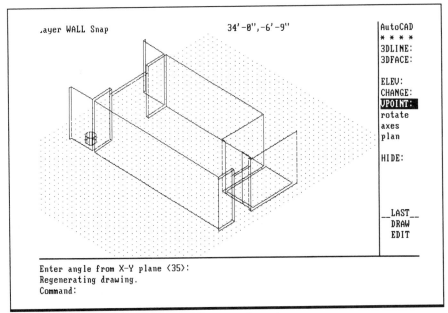

Figure 14.22: The new view of the apartment

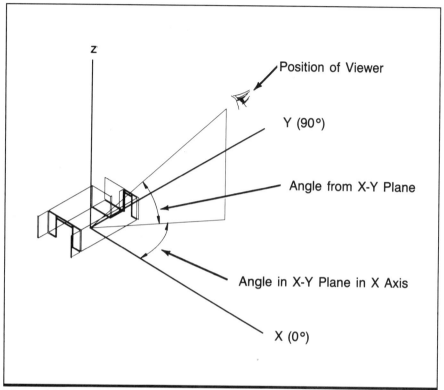

Figure 14.23:   *The view angles and what they represent*

Using a Dialog Box to Select 3D Views

A third way to select 3D views is by using the pull-down menus. Pick 3D View from the Display pull-down menu. An icon menu labeled Select 3D View appears, showing you several view-selection buttons (see Figure 14.25). If you select the button labeled Plan, you will get a plan or 2D view of the drawing much like Figure 14.4. Several buttons surrounding the plan box represent view orientations in relation to the plan view. This is similar to selecting the rotational angle of your view in the previous example.

Pick the button in the upper-left corner of the dialog box. The dialog box disappears and a new side menu appears labeled Enter the Eye Level (see Figure 14.26). This menu contains numbers ranging from − 5 to 5, arbitrary values representing the height of your

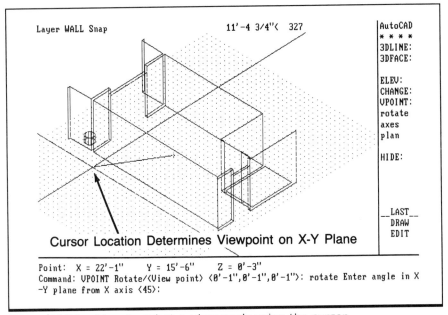

Figure 14.24: How to select a view angle using the cursor

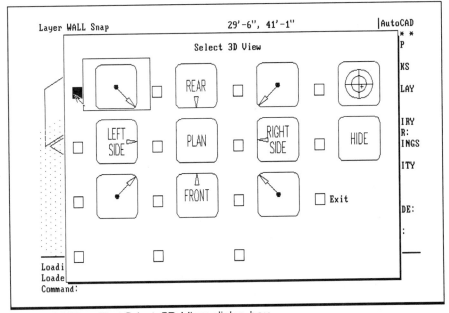

Figure 14.25: The Select 3D View dialog box

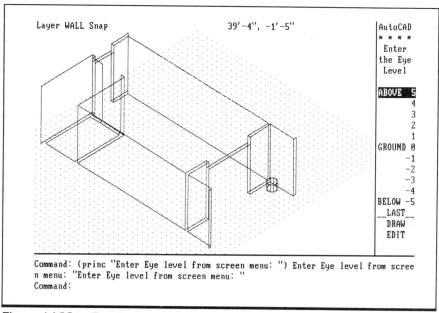

Command: (princ "Enter Eye level from screen menu: ") Enter Eye level from scree
n menu: "Enter Eye level from screen menu: "
Command:

Figure 14.26: *The Enter the Eye Level side menu*

view. Negative numbers indicate views looking from below your 3D model. Positive numbers indicate views looking from above. 0 indicates a view perpendicular to the walls of the model. Pick 5, and a new view, taken from the top left-hand side of your model, appears (see Figure 14.27).

Now return to the view you saved earlier by using the Restore command on the View menu and entering 3D for the name of the view to restore.

Removing Hidden Lines

Wire frame views will be adequate for most of your modeling needs. However, you will sometimes want to view your drawing as a solid form showing all the vertical planes as opaque surfaces. AutoCAD provides the Hide command for this purpose. Because this command requires intense computation, it often takes a long time. We suggest you use Hide only when you must have a view of your drawing for presentation purposes. If you want to remove hidden lines from a complicated object, try to simplify your model as much

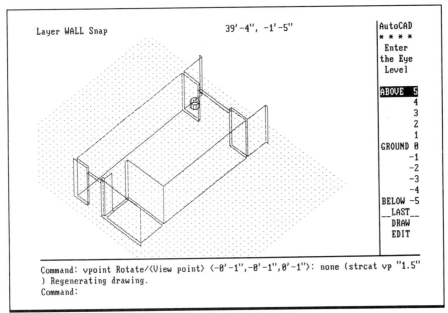

Figure 14.27: The new 3D view using the 3D dialog box

as possible. That way, AutoCAD has fewer objects to consider during its hidden line computation.

Pick Hide from the 3D menu, then pick Yes from the Hide menu (see Figure 14.28). Yes starts the Hide command just as when you enter it from the keyboard. The other option, No, returns you to the previous menu without entering a command.

You will get the prompt

Removing hidden lines:

followed by a number. The number continually changes, indicating that AutoCAD is in the process of removing hidden lines. Since the drawing area goes blank and doesn't change for a while during the Hide command, AutoCAD provides this prompt to tell you that the program hasn't locked up or otherwise bombed out. The time required to hide lines depends on how complicated your drawing is. The Unit drawing will take about two minutes on a PC/XT or compatible with a math coprocessor.

When Hide is done, your drawing will look like Figure 14.29. The hidden line view will remain until your drawing is regenerated. You may want to save this view as a slide.

Figure 14.28: The Hide menu

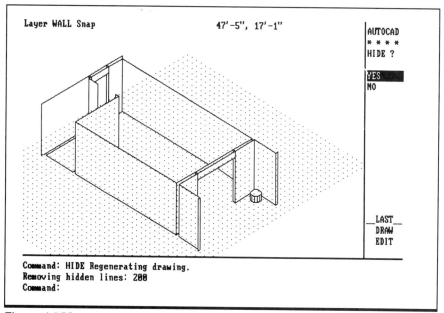

Figure 14.29: Hidden lines removed

To make a horizontal surface appear opaque, you must draw it with a wide polyline, a trace, or a solid. For example, if you were to draw a table, you could represent the table top with a rectangle and give it the appropriate thickness, but the top would appear to be transparent when the lines were hidden. Only the sides of the table top would become opaque. To make the table top opaque, you can use the Solid command (or a wide trace or polyline) to draw a filled rectangle and give it the appropriate thickness. When the lines are hidden, the table top appears to be opaque (see Figure 14.30). This technique works even with the Fill setting off.

If you use a circle as an extruded form, the top surface appears opaque when you use the Hide command. Where you want to show an opening at the top of a circular volume, as in a circular chimney, you can use two 180-degree arcs (see Figure 14.31).

If you prefer, you can have any hidden line appear in another color rather than disappear altogether. To do this, you must create a few new layers. The name of such a new layer must consist of the prefix "hidden," followed by the name of an existing layer. For example, if you want hidden lines on the Wall layer of your 3D view to appear as red lines, you would create a layer called Hiddenwall (Hidden + Wall) and give this layer the color red. Then when you perform a hidden line removal, you will see all the hidden lines associated with the Wall layer in red. You can then turn off Hiddenwall to view the drawing without hidden lines.

We should mention that the Hide command hides objects that are obscured by other objects on layers that are turned off. For example, if a couch in the corner of the studio unit is on a layer that is off when you use Hide, the lines behind the couch are hidden even though the couch does not appear in the view (see Figure 14.32). You can, however, freeze any layer containing objects that you do not want to affect the hidden-line removal process.

DRAWING 3D LINES AND 3D FACES

Extruded forms have their limitations. Using just extruded forms, you cannot draw diagonal lines in the z axis. AutoCAD provides two commands, 3Dline and 3Dface, that allow you to overcome the limitations of extruded objects. Unlike a regular line, which allows only x and y values for each endpoint, you can specify a different x, y, and z point for the beginning and end of a 3D line. A 3D line cannot be extruded, however. To create a 3D surface, you must use a 3D face, which is the

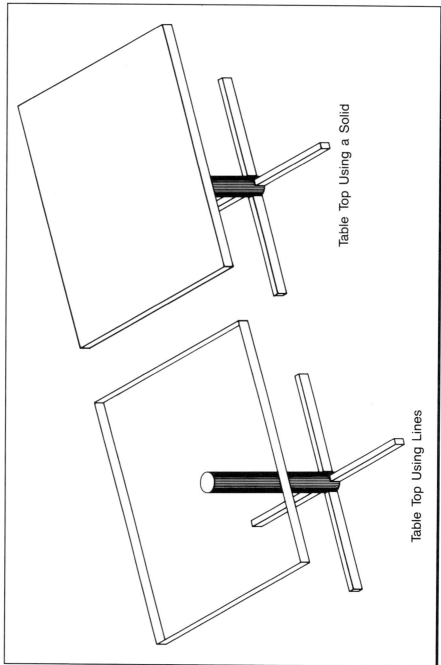

Table Top Using a Solid

Table Top Using Lines

Figure 14.30: One table using lines for the top and another using a solid

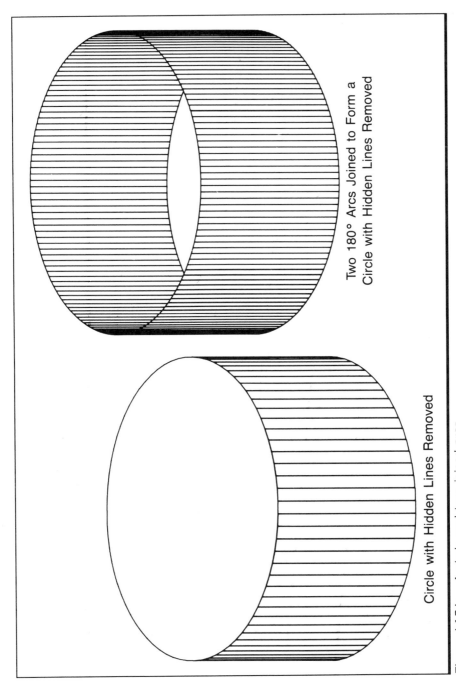

Figure 14.31:   A circle and two joined arcs

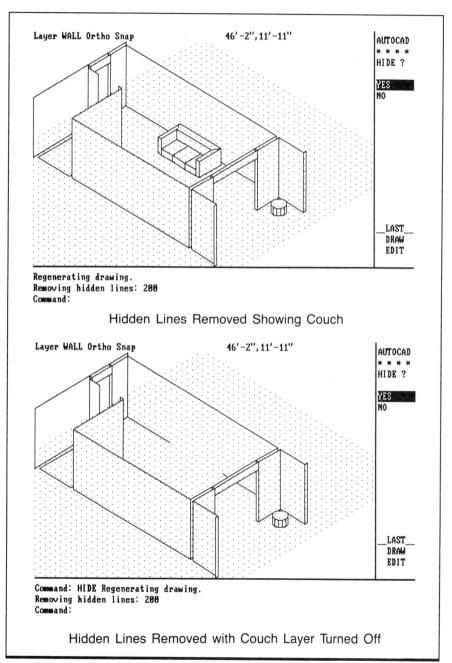

Figure 14.32:   A couch hiding a line whether the layer is on or off

equivalent of a solid. It produces a 3D surface where each corner can be given an x, y, and z value. By using these two commands in conjunction with extruded lines, you can create a 3D model of just about anything. When you view these 3D objects in a 2D plan view, you will see them as 2D objects showing only the x and y positions of their corners or endpoints.

Using 3D Lines and Filters

Before you start using 3D lines, you should have a good idea of what the z coordinate values are for your model. The simplest way to start using 3D lines is to use the plan view or top view of your drawing, then select the x and y coordinates as you normally would while drawing lines. You still have to enter a z coordinate, but by drawing in plan view you can control model creation more easily (at least at the beginning). AutoCAD offers a method for 3D point selection called *filtering* that makes the selection of z coordinates easier. Filtering allows you to enter an x, y, or z value by picking a point on the screen and telling AutoCAD to use only the x, y, or z value of that point or any combination of those values. If you don't specify a z coordinate, the current elevation setting is assumed.

In this exercise, you will add a stair rail to the studio apartment. In doing this, you will practice using 3D lines, 3D faces, and filters.

Use the View command to save the current 3D view with the name 3. End out of the Unit file and create a new file called Unitloft using the Unit file as a template. Next, start the Vpoint command. At the prompt for a viewpoint, enter 0,0. The plan view of the unit appears.

Set the current layer to Wall, then pick 3Dline from the 3D menu. The 3Dline menu appears (see Figure 14.33). Notice the .X, .Y, and .Z options on the menu. These are the 3D filters. By picking one of these options while you select points in a 3D command, you can filter an x, y, or z value, or any combination of values, from that selected point. You can also enter filters through the keyboard.

Also notice the Continue and Close options. Continue starts a regular line from the endpoint of the 3D line you are drawing. The Close option closes a 3D line, just as the Close option of the Line command closes a regular line. Undo deletes the last line segment you have drawn using the 3Dline command, just as it does for Line.

When you start the 3Dline command, you are prompted for a from point. Pick the .Xy option from the 3Dline menu, or enter .xy. By doing this you are telling AutoCAD that you are going to first

AUTOCAD
* * * *
3DLINE:

continue
close
undo
.x
.y
.z
.xy
.xz
.yz

__LAST__
DRAW
EDIT

Figure 14.33:   *The 3Dline menu*

specify the x and y coordinates for this beginning point, then indicate the z coordinate. Your prompt will change to

.xy of

The first line will be the bottom of the stair rail. Using your mouse, pick a point along the same axis as the bathroom wall 3'-6" from the right side wall of the unit near coordinate 25'-6",25'-5". The prompt changes to

.xy of (need Z):

telling you it needs a z coordinate. Enter 9'. The prompt for a to point appears. Pick .Xy again from the 3Dline menu. Then enter

@12'<270

You get the prompt for a z coordinate again. Enter O, then press Return to end the 3Dline command.

You just created a line that starts at an elevation of 9' and ends at an elevation of O'. As you can see, the 3Dline command works like the Line command with the exception of the filter options. Since you are looking at the 3D line from a plan view, it appears as a normal line. When you view it from a different viewpoint, you will see that it is actually a diagonal line. Use the View command to restore the 3D view you saved earlier. Now you can see that the 3D line really does rise in elevation from right to left (see Figure 14.34).

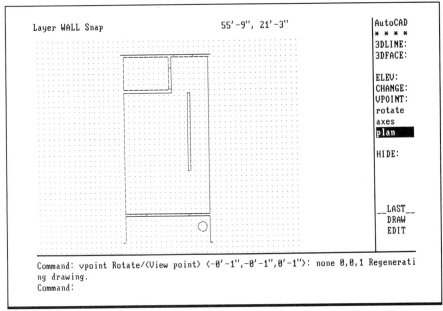

Figure 14.34: Plan view of the stair rail

Now copy the line vertically to draw the top of the stair rail. Start the Copy command and pick the 3D line you just drew. At the prompt for a base point enter an at sign. Then at the prompt for a second point, type .xy, Return, then another at sign and Return again. This tells AutoCAD that your copy will maintain the x,y coordinates of the original. At the prompt for a z coordinate, enter 3'6" to displace the copy 3'-6" on the z axis. A copy of the 3D line appears 3'-6" above the original. If you look at the plan view again, you see only one line because one lies directly on top of the other, as shown in Figure 14.34.

Using 3D Faces

Sometimes you will want to draw a solid surface so that when you perform a hidden line removal, objects will appear as surfaces rather than wire frames. The side of the stair rail will appear transparent if you continue to draw it using 3D lines, so the next step is to fill it in using 3D faces. It generally makes life easier to first draw a wire frame of your object using 3D lines, then use their endpoints to fill in the surfaces.

Zoom into the two lines you just created using the zoom window shown in Figure 14.35. Pick 3Dface from the 3D menu. The 3Dface

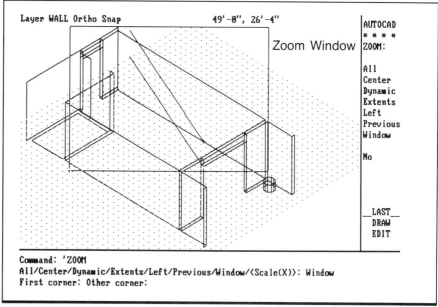

Figure 14.35: The zoom window

menu appears (see Figure 14.36). You also get the prompt

First point:

The 3Dface command acts like the Solid command except that with 3Dface, you pick four points in a circular fashion as shown in Figure 14.37. Use the Osnap overrides to pick the four endpoints of the 3D lines you drew. Be sure the ortho mode is off. As you pick the endpoints, you will get the following series of prompts:

Second point:
Third point:
Fourth point:

Once you have picked the fourth point, you again get the prompt

Third point:

indicating that you can draw more 3D faces if you like. The additional 3D face uses the last two points selected as the first two of its four corners, hence the prompt for a third point. This is similar to the way the Solid command allows you to continue to add solids to a drawing once you have already drawn one.

Figure 14.36:   The 3Dface menu

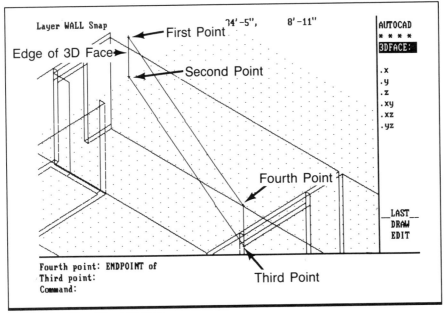

Figure 14.37:   The 3D face

Press Return to end the 3Dface command. A 3D face appears between the two 3D lines. It is difficult to tell if it is actually there until you use the Hide command, but you should see vertical lines connecting the endpoints of the 3D lines. These vertical lines are the edges of the 3D face (see Figure 14.37).

The filter options on the 3Dface menu enable you to enter points as you did for the 3Dline command. You can also use the Endpoint and Midpoint Osnap overrides to snap to the endpoints and midpoints of 3D lines and the edges of 3D faces. In addition, you can snap to the corners of 3D faces using the Intersect override.

Next, copy the 3D face five inches in the 0 angle direction. Then use the 3Dface command to put a surface on the top and front side of the rail as indicated in Figure 14.38. Use the Intersect Osnap override to snap to the corners of the 3D faces. Once you have done this, use the Hide command to get a view that looks like Figure 14.39.

End out of the Unitloft file. You won't be using it in any future exercise, but you can use it to experiment with 3D lines and 3D

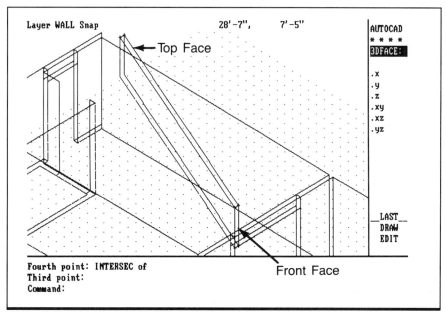

Figure 14.38: *The top and front face of the stair rail*

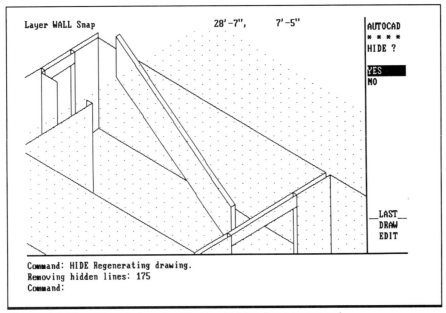

Figure 14.39: *The stair rail with the hidden lines removed*

faces. You may want to add some steps by using the Solid command, then copying them and using Change to alter their elevation.

Using AutoCAD's 3D Shapes

AutoCad provides several 3D shapes, among them cones, spheres,
and torus shapes. All are made up of 3D faces. To use them, pick 3D
Shapes from the Options pull-down menu. The Select 3D Object icon
menu shown in Figure 14.40 appears. If you pick an object, AutoCAD
will prompt you for its center point location and dimensions. Then
AutoCAD draws the object using an AutoLISP program written to
generate it. This provides quick access to shapes that would otherwise be time consuming to create.

Editing 3D Lines, 3D Faces, and 3D Shapes

You have seen how you can use the Copy command on 3D lines
and faces. You can also use the Move and Stretch commands on 3D
lines, faces, and shapes to modify their z coordinate values. The
Scale command can be used to change the size of an object, but
you should keep in mind that its z coordinate value is also scaled
(see Chapter 16 for information on the Scale command). For

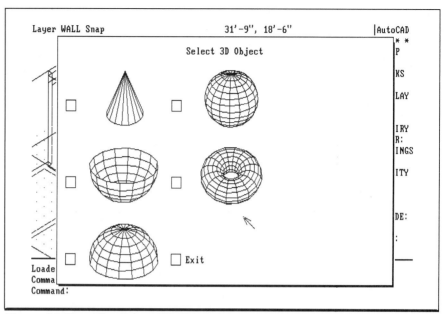

Figure 14.40: The Select 3D Object icon menu

example, suppose you have an object with an elevation of two units. If you use the Scale command to enlarge that object by a factor of four, the object will have a new elevation of two units times four, or eight units. If, on the other hand, that object has an elevation of zero, its elevation will not change because zero times four is still zero.

Array, Mirror, and Rotate can also be used on 3D lines, faces, and shapes but these commands won't affect their z coordinate values. Z coordinates can be specified for base and insertion points, so care should be taken when using these commands with 3D models.

Although using the filter options is the easiest way to specify z coordinates, you can use the transparent Setvar command to change the current elevation to a new one during the 3Dline and 3Dface commands. Remember that Setvar allows you to read or alter system variables. To use it you enter 'setvar at the AutoCAD command prompt. You get the prompt

Variable name or ?< >:

and you enter the word elevation. Then you get the prompt

New value for ELEVATION *<current elevation>***:**

Once you enter the desired elevation, you are returned to the previous command. If you use Setvar again, the default option is the elevation system variable, so you won't have to enter elevation each time you use Setvar.

PLOTTING A 3D VIEW

The plotting and printing options work the same for 3D drawings as for 2D, with two exceptions: plot rotation and hidden line removal. 3D plots cannot be rotated; they are always plotted in the same direction. To plot a drawing with hidden lines removed, you must answer Y at the plotting prompt to remove hidden lines. This option requires a good deal of computer time, so be prepared to tie up your computer for several minutes.

You can plot hidden lines as dashed or dotted instead of removing them. You do this by assigning a dashed or dotted line type to the color used for hidden layers. Then you assign a plotter pen to that color. Since this option uses the line type inherent in your plotter—and is not available on plotters without electronically built-in line types—the spacing of the dashes or dots doesn't vary with drawing scale and you can't control their appearance. Still, this option can be useful in drawings that require hidden lines to appear (see Figure 14.41).

CREATING A 2D DRAWING
FROM A 3D VIEW

At times you will want to convert a 3D view into a 2D drawing. For example, you may want to add notes to a 3D view of an object. If you are an architect, you will want to save and annotate elevation and isometric views of a building modeled using AutoCAD's 3D capabilities. If you are a mechanical engineer, you may want top, left, right, and isometric views of an object you have modeled.

To create a 2D drawing from a 3D view, first reconfigure your plotter setup for an ADI plotter. During configuration, you will be asked to select the output format. Select the AutoCAD DXB file option, which is item number 2 in the list of formats. Accept the default horizontal size, 11.0000. When you get to the prompt

Plotter steps per drawing unit <1000>:

enter 2900. This will give you the most accurate copy of your 3D view possible. Accept the default settings for all the other prompts

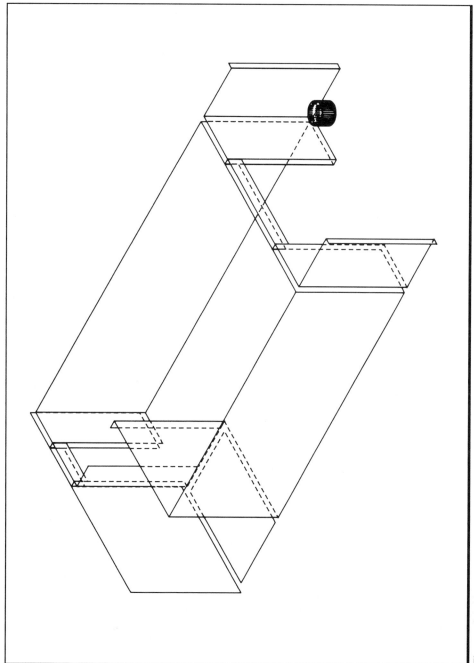

Figure 14.41:   A drawing with the hidden lines shown dashed

in the configuration. When you are done, exit the Configuration menu, answering yes to the keep configuration prompt.

With the plotter option configured in this way, AutoCAD will send the plot information to a file in the AutoCAD DXB file format, rather than to a plotter. This DXB file can then be read into a drawing file using the Dxbin command. DXB format, like the DXF file format described in Chapter 13, is an AutoCAD file standard, but in this case the file is in *binary* format rather than in ASCII. We won't go into the details of binary format files. Just understand that this is another type of file AutoCAD creates for the purpose of data exchange between software.

Open the Unit file and restore view 3, or pick any 3D view you want using the Vpoint command. Now use the Plot command to plot the drawing. You can set up the plot in the usual way, just as if you were going to get a hard copy. You will eventually get a prompt like

Enter file name for Plot<\acad\unit>:

This tells you that rather than sending the plot information to a plotter, AutoCAD will plot to a file on disk. You can enter a name for this file or accept the default. Press Return to accept the default file name, Unit. You will see the vector-processing prompt as you normally would during a plot. AutoCAD will send the plot information to a file called Unit.DXB. The DXB extension is automatically added to the file name you provide. When the process is complete, press Return to return to the drawing editor and quit the Unit file.

To view the 2D image you just created, open a new file called Unit2d. Pick Dxf/dxb from the Utility menu, then pick Dxbin from the Dxf/dxb menu. You will get the prompt

DXB file:

Enter Unit, the name of the file you just plotted to. AutoCAD will then look for the file Unit.DXB and bring it into the current file, Unit2d. The view you plotted appears in the drawing editor as a 2D image, not a 3D model.

You can edit this view like any other 2D image. Notes can now be added in the usual manner. If you like, when you first plot a drawing to a DXB file, you can use the hidden-line removal option to further enhance the final 2D image.

This conversion process is not perfect. You will have to use the Scale command to resize the drawing, and all the layer and color assignments are stripped away. Circles and arcs are broken into short line segments, and text is also broken into its component lines.

Some accuracy is also lost in the translation because AutoCAD must translate the drawing's floating-point database to an integer format (accuracy can be as much as 1/32000th of the overall plot file's drawing area). Still, the amount of accuracy lost is negligible, and this process can save you a great deal of time by eliminating the need to duplicate your work once a design has been modeled in 3D.

You could plot several views to DXB files, then combine them into one file. This technique could be used to create hard-copy presentations, or to generate exploded views of technical drawings. The possibilities are limited only by your imagination.

You may want to keep the ADI driver file and the driver for your particular plotter on your AutoCAD directory so you can reconfigure AutoCAD back and forth between the two plotter options. We also describe in Appendix B a method for maintaining several AutoCAD configurations, so you don't have to reconfigure AutoCAD every time you want to switch between plotter drivers.

DRAWING 3D VIEWS USING 2D

AutoCAD's 3D capability is quite useful as a design tool because it allows you to study an object from several angles. Unfortunately, creating a 3D model takes time, and when you want to use the Hide command to generate a view for a presentation, you can expect to wait while the computer processes the command. If you already know what your object is to look like, and you need a 3D view, you might consider drawing a 3D view in 2D just as you would by hand. This can be a faster route to a finished presentation drawing, and AutoCAD provides a few extra tools to aid you in creating isometric, axonometric, and perspective drawings.

Drawing Isometrics

AutoCAD's isometric grid option, in conjunction with a command called Isoplane, aids you in drawing isometric views. You will use these features to draw the partial universal joint shown in Figure 14.42. Isometric views are often used in mechanical drawings like this.

Open a file called Ujoint. Toggle the grid mode on. Pick Snap from the Settings menu, and at the snap prompt pick Style from the Snap menu. The prompt

Standard/Isometric<S>:

appears. Pick Iso from the Snap menu, then press Return to end the snap setting command. (If you had instead just pressed Return to accept the default setting, Standard, nothing would change in the drawing editor.) Pull-down menu users pick Isometric from the Drawing Aids dialog box. Your cursor and grid will change to look like Figure 14.43.

Using a standard line, draw the rectangle with the cross shown in Figure 14.44. This represents the left face of the universal joint. You will use the square to help draw the ellipses that form the joint. Now draw the top and left face of the view as shown in Figure 14.45.

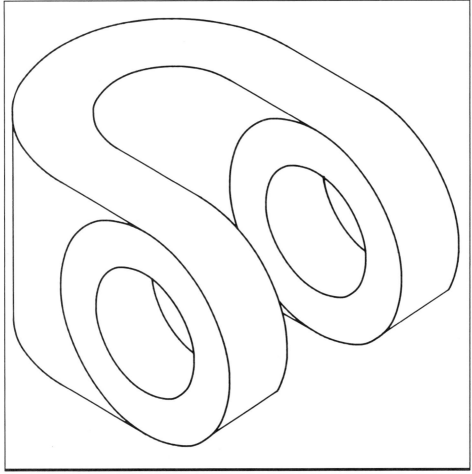

Figure 14.42:   *Part of a universal joint*

Next pick Ellipse from the Draw menu. At the prompt

\<Axis endpoint1\>/Center/Isocircle:

pick Iso from the Ellipse menu. You used this command in Chapter 3 to draw a regular ellipse. Here you are using it to draw an isometric ellipse, which has a specific shape and orientation. With the Isocircle subcommand, which is available only when the isometric snap mode is on, AutoCAD automatically sets the angle and axis dimensions to conform to the current Isoplane setting. All you need to do is tell AutoCAD the diameter or the radius of the circle. At the next prompt

Center of circle:

pick the intersection of the cross on the left face of the isometric view, as in Figure 14.46. You may have to toggle the snap mode off to pick the intersection. Now as you move the cursor, an ellipse appears in the proper orientation for the left plane of the view. At the prompt

\<Circle radius\>/Diameter:

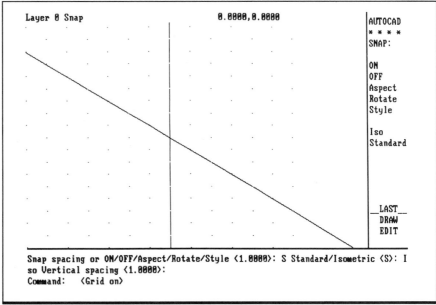

Figure 14.43: The isometric cursor

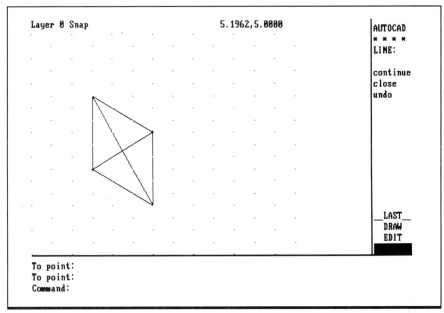

Figure 14.44: The left face of the isometric view

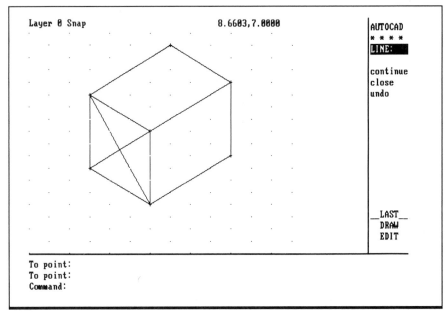

Figure 14.45: All sides of the view

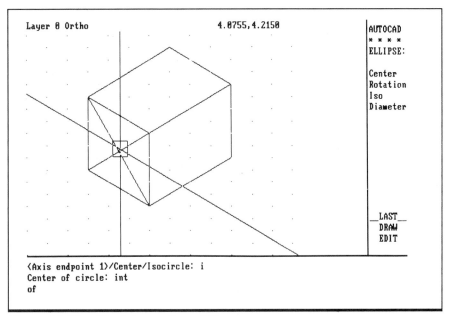

Figure 14.46: *The intersection of the cross*

set the ellipse by picking the midpoint of the top line of the left face (see Figure 14.47). You can also enter the radius value through the keyboard. (This prompt enables you to enter a diameter value instead by picking Diameter from the Ellipse menu, or entering D, then specifying the diameter value.) Your view will look like Figure 14.48.

Next you will draw an ellipse on the top of the isometric view to define the top arc of the joint. While using the isometric snap mode, you must tell AutoCAD which of the three isometric planes you wish to work on—left, top, or right. So far, you have drawn a cross and an ellipse on the left isometric plane. To change to another plane you use the Isoplane command. Enter isoplane through the keyboard. You get the prompt

Left/Top/Right/<Toggle>:

Press Return and your cursor will shift to align with the top face of the view as in Figure 14.49.

By pressing Return, you used the default option, Toggle, which shifts your current isoplane to the next plane in a clockwise direction. You can also enter the letter corresponding to the isoplane you wish to edit—L for left, T for top, and R for right. Now add an

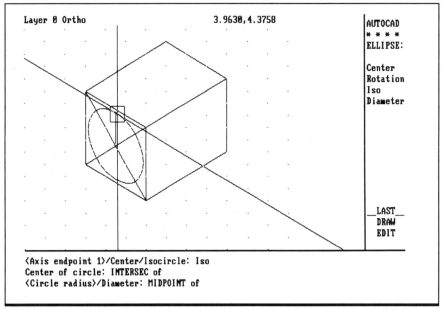

```
Layer 0 Ortho                      3.9630,4.3758          AUTOCAD
                                                          * * * *
                                                          ELLIPSE:

                                                          Center
                                                          Rotation
                                                          Iso
                                                          Diameter




                                                          __LAST__
                                                           DRAW
                                                           EDIT

<Axis endpoint 1>/Center/Isocircle: Iso
Center of circle: INTERSEC of
<Circle radius>/Diameter: MIDPOINT of
```

Figure 14.47:   *The ellipse's radius*

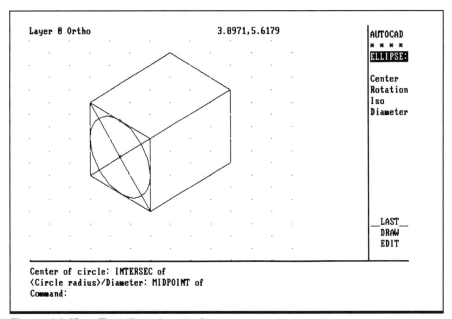

```
Layer 0 Ortho                      3.8971,5.6179          AUTOCAD
                                                          * * * *
                                                          ELLIPSE:

                                                          Center
                                                          Rotation
                                                          Iso
                                                          Diameter




                                                          __LAST__
                                                           DRAW
                                                           EDIT

Center of circle: INTERSEC of
<Circle radius>/Diameter: MIDPOINT of
Command:
```

Figure 14.48:   *The ellipse inserted*

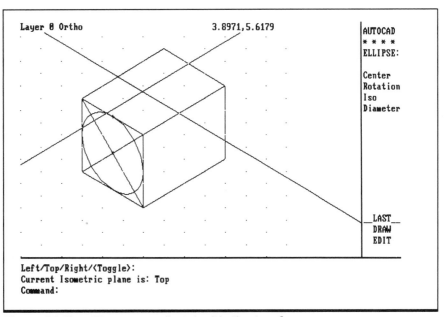

```
Layer 0 Ortho                        3.8971,5.6179         AUTOCAD
                                                           * * * *
                                                           ELLIPSE:

                                                           Center
                                                           Rotation
                                                           Iso
                                                           Diameter




                                                           _LAST_
                                                           DRAW
                                                           EDIT

Left/Top/Right/<Toggle>:
Current Isometric plane is: Top
Command:
```

Figure 14.49:   *The cursor aligned with the top face*

ellipse to the top of the view as shown in Figure 14.50. Use the midpoint of the top line as the center of the ellipse, then use the endpoint of that same line to define the radius.

Use Figure 14.51 to complete the joint. Step 2 in this figure shows the addition of ellipses concentric to the first two you created. These concentric ellipses form the inside surfaces of the part. Step 3 shows you where to break the top two ellipses into arcs, since only half of them are needed, and indicates the deletion of most of the guidelines. Step 4 indicates that you must copy three of the ellipses in the direction shown to help form other parts of the drawing. Step 5 shows where to break the ellipses to delete hidden parts. Finally, step 6 shows how to draw the other half of the joint by copying part of the existing drawing.

Once you are done, end out of the Ujoint file.

Drawing Axonometrics

If you want to draw an axonometric view of something, you don't even have to use the Isoplane command. You can just rotate a top or plan view of your object to the desired orientation, then copy

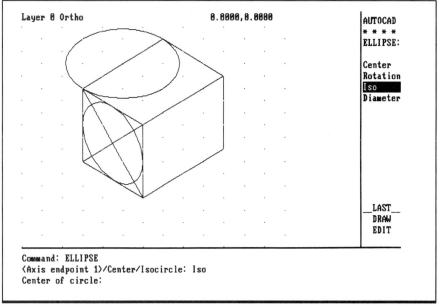

```
Layer 0 Ortho                          0.0000,0.0000          AUTOCAD
                                                              * * * *
                                                              ELLIPSE:

                                                              Center
                                                              Rotation
                                                              Iso
                                                              Diameter




                                                              _LAST__
                                                               DRAW
                                                               EDIT

Command: ELLIPSE
<Axis endpoint 1>/Center/Isocircle: Iso
Center of circle:
```

Figure 14.50:   *The ellipse at the top of the view*

objects at a 90-degree angle and project lines as you would by hand. Because you can rotate and copy objects easily, it is much easier to create an axonometric view with AutoCAD than by hand.

Figure 14.52 shows what might be done if you wanted to draw an axonometric view of a typical apartment unit. First you rotate the plan to a position that shows the view you want. Next you copy the plan in a 90-degree direction. Then you add lines connecting the two plans to indicate wall corners. Finally, you edit the drawing, erasing and breaking hidden objects.

Drawing Perspectives

AutoCAD does not currently support perspective 3D modeling. If you know how to lay out 3D perspectives by hand, however, you can create 3D drawings with AutoCAD as you would by hand and still save some time over hand drafting. For example, you can create various layers to keep your layout information. You can also save viewpoints so that when you need to draw a line from a vanishing point, you can specify the point by entering its coordinates. You can also store coordinates for vanishing points as variables and recall them later as needed; we will explain how to store coordinate locations in Chapter 18.

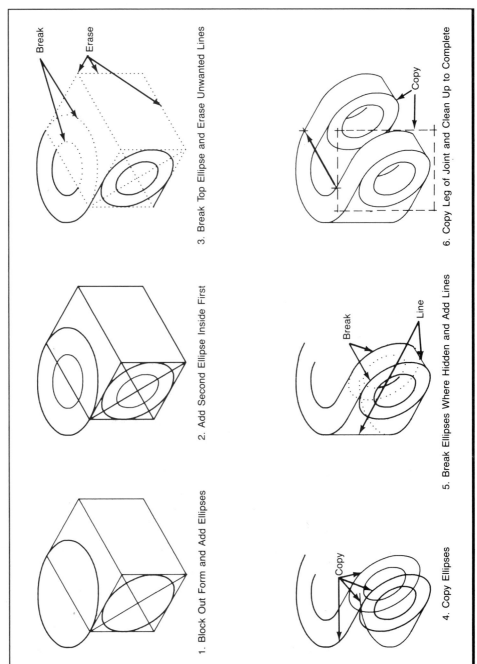

Figure 14.51: Finishing the universal joint

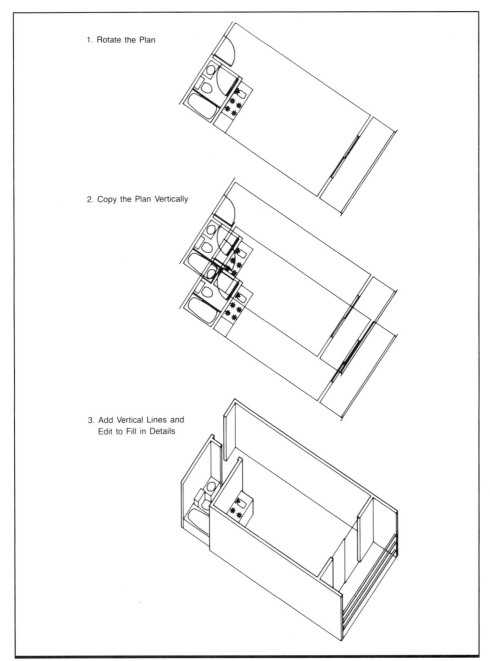

1. Rotate the Plan

2. Copy the Plan Vertically

3. Add Vertical Lines and
   Edit to Fill in Details

Figure 14.52: The construction of an axonometric view

CONCLUSION

Once you have used AutoCAD's 3D capabilities, you see how simple a process it really is. The 3D features have their limitations, but you can produce some credible results, especially if you want to create axonometric or isometric views. Most important, 3D can help you visualize an object without resorting to complex mathematics to input your image.

You may want to try turning the kitchenette into a 3D object. Make the cook top 30 inches high and add some cabinet doors. You may also want to try converting drawings you have done outside this tutorial into 3D images.

If you are not totally satisfied with the 3D views generated by AutoCAD alone, you may want to try using AutoShade to further enhance your 3D drawings. In the next chapter, you will use AutoShade to view your studio apartment unit in perspective and from different vantage points. You will also see how shading its surfaces can add solidity to your 3D model.

Chapter 15

Expanding AutoCAD's 3D Capabilities with AutoShade

THERE ARE TIMES WHEN YOU WILL WANT to view a design under different conditions and from different angles. An architect needs to study a building's design from various viewpoints to get a better idea of how it will appear from the street. An industrial designer needs to know how a product will look from different angles. If you create a 3D model of your design in AutoCAD, you can get a fairly good idea of its appearance by just using the Vpoint command. At times, however, this is not enough, and this is where you need AutoShade.

AutoShade is a rendering program produced by Autodesk, the makers of AutoCAD. It gives your 3D model a more realistic appearance by adding perspective and shading. It allows you to control not only your viewing angle, but also both the quality of lighting on the model and its surface reflectance. You can even choose among lens types that range from wide angle to telescopic.

AutoShade works in conjunction with AutoCAD as a postprocessor; that is, it works on AutoCAD drawings after they are created. Once you have a 3D model, you can use special AutoCAD commands to store views of it in special files. Later, AutoShade uses these files independently of AutoCAD to produce rendered images of your 3D model. In this chapter, you will explore the uses of AutoShade version 1.0 to produce a variety of views of your apartment unit.

MEETING AUTOSHADE'S HARDWARE REQUIREMENTS

AutoShade does not work on as many different types of hardware as AutoCAD. To use it you will need an IBM PC/XT, AT, or PS/2 compatible with at least 640K of memory and with a math coprocessor installed. Most AutoCAD users will already have this equipment.

You will also need an IBM EGA or PGC (Professional Graphics Controller) display adapter or compatible, or a Hercules display or compatible. The PGC gives the best results but is the most costly of the display options. An Orchid Turbo PGA is also an excellent display option. Both the PGC and the Orchid Turbo PGA offer 256 colors, which produce smooth, natural shading of your model. Some display systems using the AutoCAD Device Interface will also work, but since AutoShade is relatively new, only recently written ADI display devices will work with it. Check with your dealer for more information on your ADI display.

A mouse is highly recommended but you can use the cursor keys if you don't have one. A Microsoft mouse or compatible is supported, or any input device that uses the ADI. Other options are the Koala pad, which is like a small digitizing tablet, and the joystick.

Output devices are limited to some ADI-supported devices and PostScript printers, such as the Apple LaserWriter or QMS PS 800 series laser printers. You can also use a color PostScript printer when they become available. If you are interested in high-resolution shaded images, Linotronic 300 typesetters are capable of producing very high-resolution AutoShade prints. Because of its flexibility, the PostScript printer will be the device of choice for most AutoShade users. If you have an ADI input or output device, check with the manufacturer to determine whether it will work with AutoShade.

You cannot get AutoShade hard copy from plotters. Plotters are designed to output line drawings but are poor at producing shaded images, so AutoShade does not support them. You can, however, produce perspective wire frame images with AutoShade that can be sent back to AutoCAD and then plotted through AutoCAD's output options.

USING THE AUTOSHADE CAMERA

AutoShade uses the analogy of a camera to set up and view your 3D model. First, you set up the "shots" of your model while in AutoCAD by establishing your lighting, camera position, and view angle.

Then you take your "pictures." Once you have taken as many pictures as you need, you send your film to AutoShade for "processing." In this case, the pictures are called *scenes* and the film is a file on your disk that contains information about your model, plus information about the scenes you have created.

An exception to the camera analogy is that scenes can be manipulated *after* they have been taken. AutoShade can change camera locations. It can also adjust light intensities and the amount of light reflected by your model. You can even adjust the type of lens your camera uses. This means that if you want a wide-angle view of a scene, you can change a setting in AutoShade to allow a wider view.

Taking Pictures

Before you begin, install AutoShade by following the instructions in Appendix B. Next, set the DOS environment so that AutoCAD can use the AutoLISP programs required to create your views. At the DOS prompt, before you start AutoCAD, enter

```
set lispheap = 40000
set lispstack = 5000
```

Once you have done this, you can start AutoCAD and proceed with the tutorial. You will find a more detailed description of these settings and of the DOS SET command in Chapter 18, which discusses AutoLISP, and in Appendix C.

Start AutoCAD and open the Unit file. If you don't have a plan view of the unit in the drawing editor, change it to a plan view now so that it looks like Figure 15.1. Pick Ashade from the AutoCAD Root menu. Then pick Lights from the Ashade menu to bring up the Light menu (see Figure 15.2).

If you were instead to try to enter ashade from the AutoCAD command prompt, you would get an error message. When you pick Ashade from the menu, you are actually loading an AutoLISP program. The menu sends instructions to AutoCAD to load the program. To enter AutoShade through the keyboard, you would enter

```
(load "/acad/ashade")
```

at the AutoCAD command prompt.

Pull-down menu users should pick Ashade from the Options pull-down menu. The Select Ashade Command icon menu appears (see Figure 15.3). The icon menu contains several commands you will use in this tutorial: two light sources, a camera, a scene clapper, and a

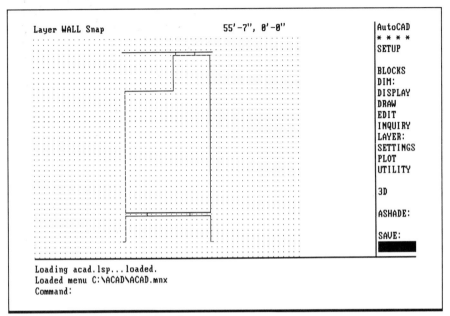

Figure 15.1: Plan view of unit

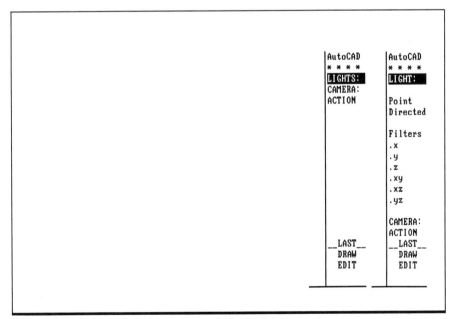

Figure 15.2: The Ashade menu and the Light menu

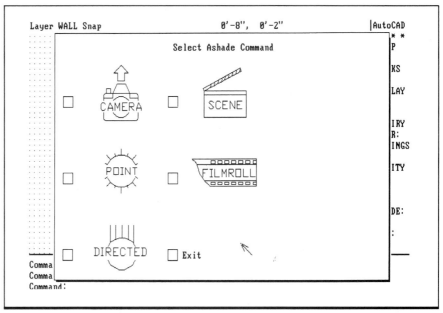

Figure 15.3:   *The Select Ashade Command icon menu*

filmroll. The Exit command allows you to close the icon menu without selecting a command.

Pick the Point command or icon. You will get the prompt

Enter light name:

Enter 1 for the light name. AutoShade allows you to use several light sources for a scene, and many scenes can use the same light source. You give each light source a name so you can distinguish among them. We arbitrarily name the light 1 for this exercise, but you can give it any name you like. The next prompt appears:

Point source or directed <P>:

A point source acts like a light bulb that shines light in all directions, while a directed light source is more like a spotlight that concentrates light on a small area. The point source works best for general lighting of objects, since it offers a softer lighting effect. The directed light source is good for more dramatic lighting, particularly on shiny materials such as glass or metal. As you practice using AutoShade, you will become more familiar with the subtleties of the two light source types. For now, you will be shown simply how to select and place them.

Press Return to accept the default, point source. If you used the icon menu to start this command, the point source option is automatically selected for you so you don't have to press Return. The following prompt appears:

Enter light location:

At this prompt, you can enter the location of your point light source in x, y, and z coordinates. You should consider how you want to light your model at this point. Think where you would place the light source if you were actually standing in the model. For the purposes of this exercise, we will choose a location for you.

Since the plan view of your unit is on the screen, you can pick the .Xy coordinate filter from the Light side menu or the icon menu, then pick the location of the light source at the center of the unit using your mouse (see Figure 15.4). If you have forgotten how to use the 3D filters, review the section entitled "Using 3D Lines and Filters" in Chapter 14.

Next, you will be prompted for a z coordinate representing the height of the light source. Enter a z value of 8'-0". A graphic appears on your screen representing point light source 1 (see Figure 15.5). The number 1 inside the graphic is the name you gave this

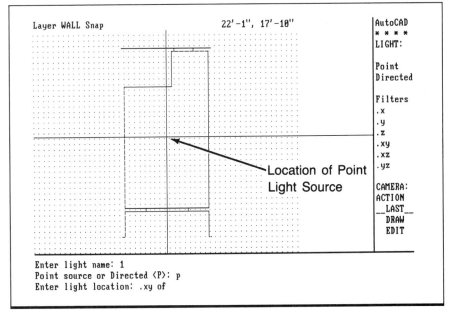

Figure 15.4: The location of the point light source

light source earlier in this command. This graphic is actually a block containing attributes needed to generate your shaded view. The attributes hold such information as the coordinates of the light source and its name. This information will be used by AutoShade to determine how to shade your model. The graphic is automatically inserted into a layer called Ashade. If this layer does not exist, Auto-CAD will create one before it inserts the graphic so you can isolate the graphic by either freezing or turning off the Ashade layer. You can save the lighting and any other information that appears on this layer without the graphic interfering with your drawing.

You can also add a directed light source. In fact you can add as many point or directed light sources as you want, depending on the kind of lighting you require for your shaded model. Of course, you can also use just one light source if that is all you need. In this exercise you will add a directed light source, since the procedure for placing it is slightly different from that for placing a point source.

Press Return to start the Light command again. If you are using the pull-down menus, the Ashade icon menu will reappear once you finish inserting the point source light. You can then pick the Directed command from the side or icon menu. The prompt for a light name appears again. Enter 1D for one directed. At the prompt for a point

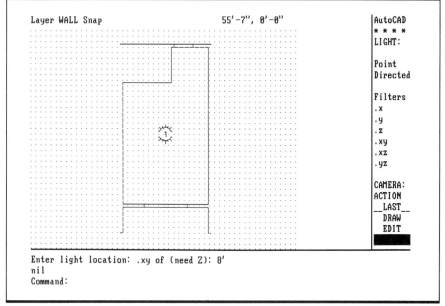

Figure 15.5: The point light source graphic

or directed light source, enter D. Pull-down menu users need not enter D at this point since AutoCAD automatically enters it for you. A new prompt appears:

Enter light aim point:

At this prompt you must select a location on the plan to which you want to point your directed light source. In general, when selecting the aim point, think of an area on your model that you want to highlight. The directed light source will concentrate light on that area. For this exercise, select a point in the middle of a wall in the unit.

You can specify a point in the x, y, and z axis just as you did when you placed the point light source. Pick the .Xy filter and select a point in the middle of the wall at the left of the unit (see Figure 15.6).

Next, enter 4'-0" for the height of the aim point. The next prompt appears:

Enter light location:

At this prompt you must pick the location of the directed light source. In general, think how you want the light to reflect off the light aim point. In the unit, the location of the directed light source is not too

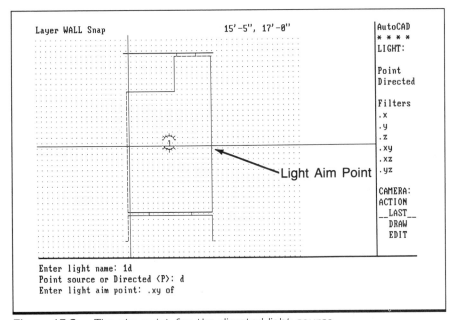

Figure 15.6: The aim point for the directed light source

critical, since the surfaces are not highly reflective. But for an object that reflects a lot of light, a polished metallic object for example, the location of the light source affects specular reflection from the object. In this exercise, the light source is chosen to cast light at a slight angle to the aim point.

Pick the .Xy filter and pick a point in the upper right of the drawing area (see Figure 15.7). Enter 20'-0" for the z value or height of the directed source. Another graphic appears. This time the graphic looks like a spotlight (see Figure 15.8). Notice the 1D inside the graphic. This graphic, like the point source graphic, is a block on the Ashade layer.

Now select a camera location by thinking of the viewpoint from which you would like to see your model. To some degree, the location you choose doesn't matter since you can change it later in AutoShade. Selecting the viewpoint you want now, however, will save time later.

Pick Camera from the Light side menu or from the Ashade icon menu. The Camera side menu will appear (see Figure 15.9) and you will get the prompt

Enter camera name:

Enter 1 for the camera name. Just as with the light sources, you

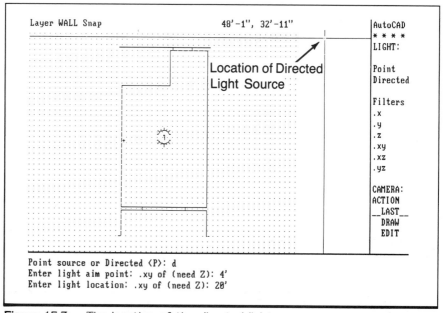

Figure 15.7: *The location of the directed light source*

can use any name and insert as many cameras as you like. For example, you may want to make several scenes in AutoCAD using different camera angles before you send them over to AutoShade. Doing this can save some time in AutoShade, since you won't have to adjust the camera location for every view you want.

The next prompt

Enter target point:

asks for the center of the view you wish to save. This will determine the direction the camera is pointed. Think where you would like to place the center of the view and pick that point at the prompt.

Pick a point at the center of the unit and five feet from the floor by using the .Xy filter (see Figure 15.10). The next prompt

Enter camera location:

asks you to position your camera. Place the camera to the lower right of the drawing area at a height of 30 feet (see Figure 15.11).

Now you are ready to take a picture of the scene. Pick Action from the Camera menu shown in Figure 15.11, then pick Scene from

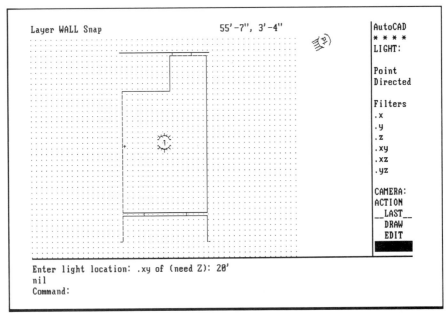

Figure 15.8:   *The directed light source graphic*

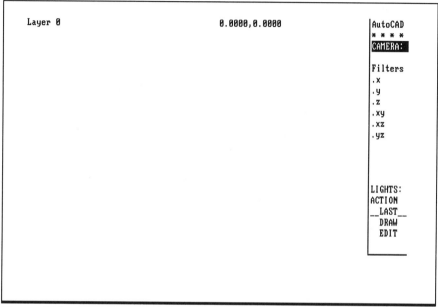

Figure 15.9: The Camera menu

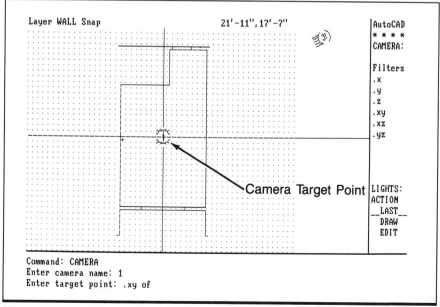

Figure 15.10: The center of the view you wish to save

the Action menu (see Figure 15.12), or pick the scene clapper from the icon menu.

At the prompt

Enter scene name:

enter scene1 for the scene name. The next prompt

Select the camera:

asks you to pick the camera you want to use for this scene. Pick the one in the lower-right corner. The next prompt

Select a light:

asks you to pick a light source for this scene. Pick the point source in the center of the unit. The light-selection prompt appears again. Pick the directed light source in the upper right of the drawing area. Again, the light-selection prompt appears. You can continue to select light sources but since you have only two, press Return. A new prompt appears:

Enter scene location:

Pick a point to the upper left of the unit. A graphic appears

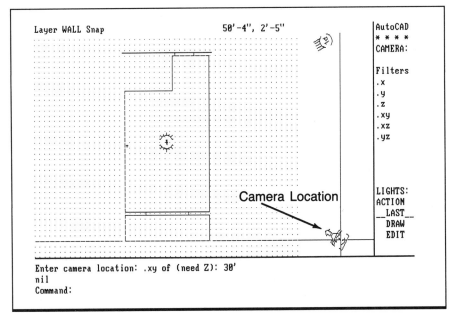

Figure 15.11:   The camera location

indicating the scene name, the camera used, and the light sources (see Figure 15.13). It doesn't matter where you place the scene graphic; it is just a reference device. Notice that it contains the names of the lights and camera used for the scene. You can create as many scenes as you like, but for our example you will use just one.

Now pick Filmroll from the Action menu or from the icon menu. You will get the prompt

Enter filmroll file name <UNIT>:

AutoCAD provides a default name for the filmroll file derived from the name of the 3D model file you are currently making scenes of. Press Return to accept the default name of Unit. The following prompt appears:

Creating the filmroll file
Processing faces: 17
Filmroll file created

A filmroll file is created on your disk drive with the extension .FLM. This file contains information about lighting and camera angles, and

Figure 15.12: The Action menu

about the model itself. The processing faces comment that appears on the prompt indicates the number of surfaces or "faces" that need to be shaded for this particular model. The value given is approximate. Now quit this drawing.

You have just "shot" a filmroll, although you used only one frame or scene. You could have added more light sources and made more scenes, but for this tutorial one is sufficient. You don't need to save the AutoShade information on this tutorial, so quit this file and exit AutoCAD. Next, you will use AutoShade to see what your film looks like.

VIEWING YOUR SCENE

Start AutoShade by entering shade at the DOS prompt. You will get a screen similar to Figure 15.14. At the top center of the screen is the program title. To the left of the title are the pull-down menu names. To the right are the timer, where the current time is displayed, and the memory-use area, where a number appears indicating the percentage of system memory used when a view is being processed. The bottom of the screen shows the drawing title.

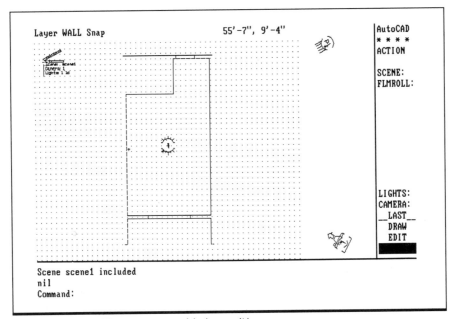

Figure 15.13:   The scene graphic in position

Other messages also appear in this area as shaded and wire frame views are processed. The rest of the screen is the view area.

Figure 15.15 shows you the commands available on the pull-down menus. To the right of some commands are codes that indicate keys you can press to invoke the command. If you prefer to use the keyboard for command input, you should pay special attention to these codes.

Codes beginning with F indicate function keys. For example, the Open command on the File pull-down menu shows F10. This means you can open an AutoShade filmroll file using the F10 key. Codes beginning with A tell you the Alt key must be used in conjunction with the function key number that precedes it. For example, the Replay command on the Display pull-down menu shows A1. This means that to start the Replay command through the keyboard, you must simultaneously hold down the Alt key while pressing the F1 key. As you go through the exercises, you may want to refer to Figure 15.15 from time to time to help you remember the keyboard equivalents to AutoShade commands.

Highlight and pick the File pull-down menu using your mouse. As you can see, the AutoShade pull-down menus operate in the same way as the AutoCAD pull-down menus. Highlight and pick the Open command (see Figure 15.16). A dialog box appears listing the names

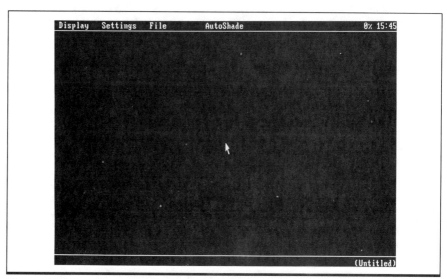

Figure 15.14: The AutoShade screen

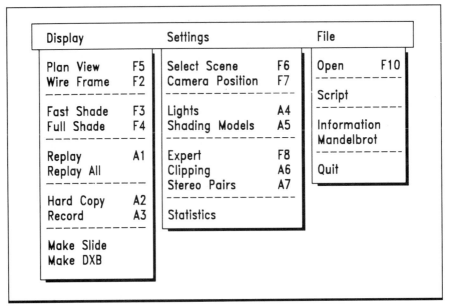

Figure 15.15: *The AutoShade pull-down menus*

of filmroll files available (see Figure 15.17). Several Autodesk sample files are listed: Openplan, Pushpin, Robot, etc.

Scroll down the list of files by picking the Page Down button. Pick Unit from the list. The unit name appears in the File input button. You can also highlight the File input button, then enter the name of the file you want. Pick the OK action button. Another dialog box appears listing the scenes contained in the chosen filmroll file (see Figure 15.18). Pick the Scene1 selection button, then pick the OK action button.

Getting a Wire Frame View

Now highlight and pick Display from the menu bar, then pick Wire Frame from the Display pull-down menu. As the command implies, you get a wire frame perspective view of your unit. The Wire Frame command gives you a quick look at your scene to make sure you have a view you want. Not all of the unit is visible; some of it is cut off by the limits of the display. As we mentioned earlier, AutoShade is analogous to a camera. The typical camera uses a 50mm lens which, placed in the position we chose when creating this scene, clips the image as you see it in Figure 15.19. To see the entire unit, you can change to a wide-angle lens.

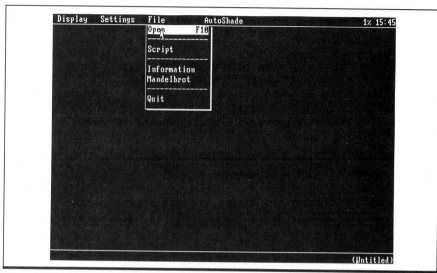

Figure 15.16: The Open command on the File pull-down menu

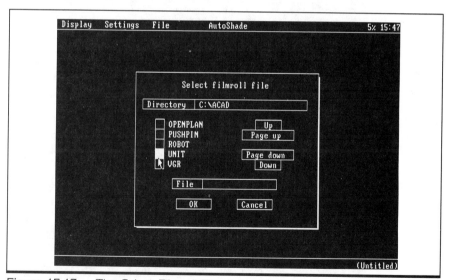

Figure 15.17: The Select Filmroll File dialog box

Adjusting the Lens Type

Highlight and pick Settings from the menu bar, then pick Camera Position from the Settings pull-down menu. The Camera Specifications dialog box appears (see Figure 15.20). This dialog box allows you to change both the lens and the camera location. We will cover the camera location settings later in this chapter.

For a view looking through a 20mm wide-angle lens, highlight the Lens in Mm input button and enter 20. AutoShade gives you a

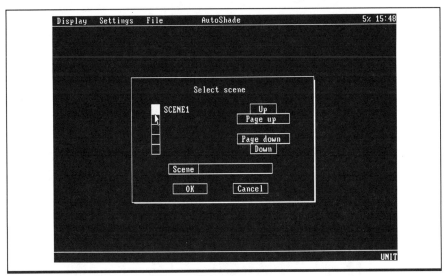

Figure 15.18: The Select Scene dialog box

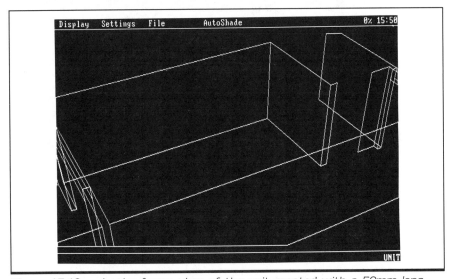

Figure 15.19: A wire frame view of the unit created with a 50mm lens

range of values from 5mm to 2000mm to choose from. As you type, two action buttons will appear to the right of the input button, just as in AutoCAD. Press Return after you type 20 and the action buttons disappear. Pick the OK action button at the bottom of the dialog box, then pick the Wire Frame command on the Display pull-down menu to redraw the scene. You will get the image shown in Figure 15.21, with most of the unit in view.

Getting a Shaded View

Now that you have selected your view, you can shade it. Shading creates the most realistic representation of your 3D model because it removes hidden lines and gives the appearance of solidity. Pick Fast Shade from the Display pull-down menu. AutoShade will begin calculating and soon you will see the shaded model appear on your screen (see Figure 15.22).

Fast Shade gives a quick preview of your shaded model so you can see how the current light settings affect the shaded view. In complex 3D models, Fast Shade lets you preview the effects of shading in much less time than Full Shade requires. Because it is less accurate, however, it distorts some surfaces. Full Shade gives an accurate shaded view, but in complex 3D models it takes much longer to generate. Since the apartment unit model is not too complex, there is hardly any difference in speed between Fast Shade and Full Shade.

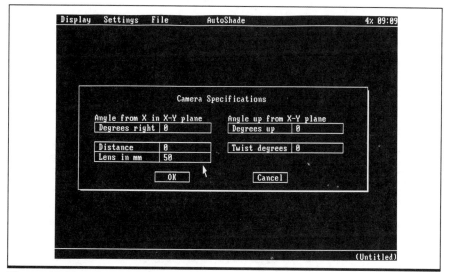

Figure 15.20: The Camera Specifications dialog box

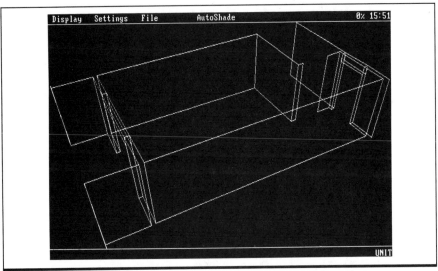

Figure 15.21:   *A wire frame view of the unit using a 20mm lens*

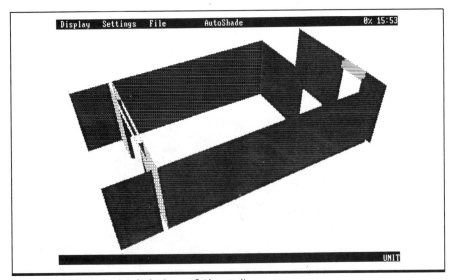

Figure 15.22:   *A shaded view of the unit*

Adjusting Lighting Conditions

As the shaded view appears, you can see that many of the surfaces seem to have the same light intensity, giving the view a flat
appearance. You can adjust aspects of the lighting that affect your

shaded model by using the Shading Models command on the Settings menu.

Pick Shading Models to bring up the dialog box shown in Figure 15.23. This dialog box allows you to adjust variables that affect the lighting of your model. It is beyond the scope of this book to discuss all of these options. The AutoShade manual gives detailed descriptions of each variable, and only experience and experimentation can give you a full understanding of what they do. You may, though, want to consider how a few of these variables can affect your shading model.

Highlight Ambient Factor and enter .2. This decreases the intensity of ambient light acting on your model. Ambient light is comparable to the light on an overcast day; it casts no shadows and has no direction. Next, change the Diffuse Factor to .5. This decreases the model's light reflectance from diffuse light sources, which is similar to toning down colors on the model's surface. Lowering both ambient light and surface reflectance gives the light reflected by your model a greater variety of intensity. This is comparable to the difference between a gray room lit with only a single light bulb and a spotlight, and a white room lit with a skylight providing lots of ambient light, a light bulb, and a spotlight. The walls of the white room will appear to have the same intensity, while the walls of the gray room will reflect a more varied range of light.

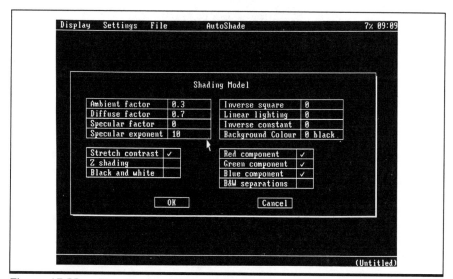

Figure 15.23:   *The Shading Model dialog box*

Two other buttons labeled Specular Factor and Specular Exponent control the shininess of a model's surfaces. The greater these two values, the shinier the object. By increasing the Specular Factor, you increase the shininess of surfaces, while increasing Specular Exponent has the effect of polishing the surfaces. We won't try to adjust these values in our tutorial, but you may want to experiment with them on your own (see Figure 15.24).

Now pick the OK action button and pick Fast Shade from the Display pull-down menu. The unit appears again with the walls more differentiated by shading than before. This is an example of how you can fine-tune the lighting of your model. Now pick Full Shade from

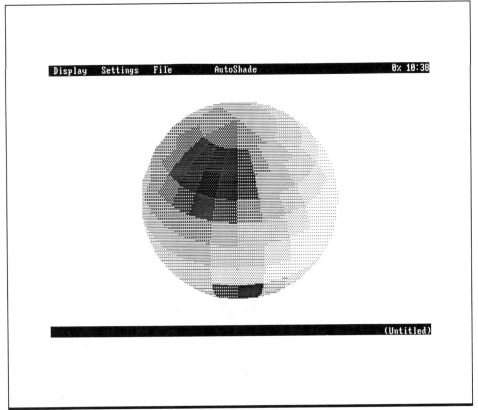

Figure 15.24: A view of a sphere with high values for Specular Factor and Specular Exponent

the Display pull-down menu. A complete shaded model will appear (see Figure 15.25).

The variety of shades is still not what you'd like. The walls at the entrance of the unit are the same shade, and you want more differentiation between them. You can adjust the difference of light-source intensity to give your model a more subtle shading effect. Pick Lights from the Settings pull-down menu. The Set Light Intensities dialog box appears (see Figure 15.26). Both the point source, 1, and the directed light source, 1D, are listed, and both have an intensity value of 1. This value is somewhat arbitrary in that one value is relative to the other, which means that if both values are 1, each light source is of equal intensity. Change the directed light source, 1D, to .5, then pick the OK action button at the bottom of the screen. By doing this, you reduce the intensity of the directed light source to half that of the point source. Redraw the image using the Full Shade command. Now your model shows more variety of shading than in previous views (see Figure 15.27).

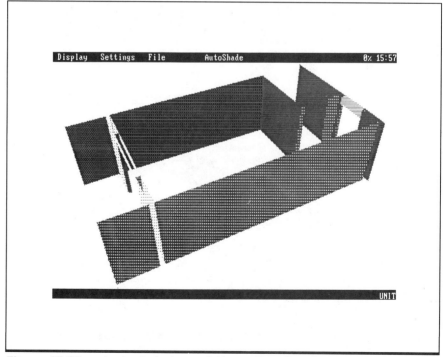

Figure 15.25:   *A shaded view of the unit using the new Ambient and Diffuse factors*

Changing the Camera's Position

You may find that the camera position you chose in AutoCAD is not exactly what you wanted. AutoShade allows you to relocate your camera by altering the x, y, and z values associated with its

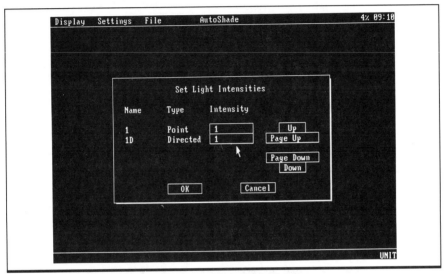

Figure 15.26: The Set Light Intensities dialog box

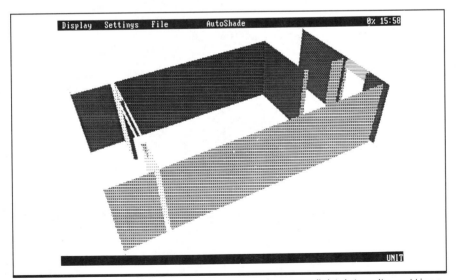

Figure 15.27: A shaded view of the unit using new light intensity settings

position. Pick Camera Position from the Settings pull-down menu. The Camera Specifications dialog box appears. Highlight the Degrees Right input button and enter 45. This moves the camera closer to the directed light source. Notice that you can also change the degrees up and the distance from the model using this dialog box. The Twist Degrees option allows you to "tilt" your camera so your view is not level with the x,y plane or floor (see Figure 15.20). Pick the OK action button to accept these new settings, then pick the Full Shade command from the Display menu. Your image will change to reflect the new camera location (see Figure 15.28).

Using Clipping to Control a View

At times, you may want a view that would normally be obscured by objects in the foreground. For example, if you try to view the interior of a room, the walls closest to the camera obscure your view. AutoShade's Clipping command facilitates greater control over what generates your views. In the following exercise, you will use Clipping on an interior view of the unit.

First change your camera position so that you will view the interior of the unit as if you were standing at floor level. Use the Camera Specifications dialog box and change the Degrees Right value to −85 to position your camera in front of the balcony. Remember,

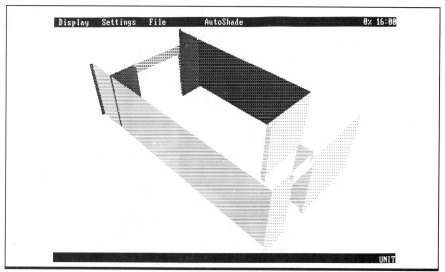

Figure 15.28:   *A shaded view of the unit using a new camera location*

this value is based on the angle in the x,y plane in the top or plan view of the original AutoCAD drawing. – 85 degrees places the camera slightly to the right of the balcony.

Next, change the camera's Degrees Up setting to 2. This positions the camera at nearly human-eye level from the floor instead of the bird's-eye level used previously. Pick the OK action button to accept the new settings.

To see your camera location from a top view, pick Plan View from the Display menu. You will get the view shown in Figure 15.29. This view not only shows you the camera position from the top of your model, but also the light source locations and view angle of the camera.

Use the Wire Frame command to get a quick preview of what you will see in this new view (see Figure 15.30). This will save you some time fine-tuning your views, since wire frame views appear in a fraction of the time shaded views require. If you look carefully, you will notice that the wall separating the balcony from the interior of the unit is in the way of your interior view. The Fast Shade command will give you a view of the balcony but you still won't be able to see the interior very well (see Figure 15.31).

Pick Clipping from the Settings menu. You will get the Clipping Specifications dialog box (see Figure 15.32). Change the check button

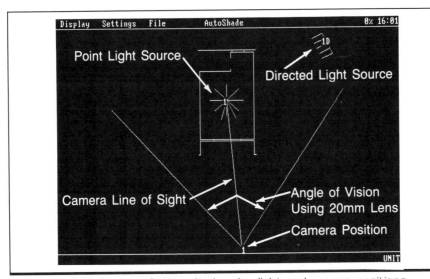

Figure 15.29: A view of the unit showing light and camera positions

next to Clip at Camera so no check mark appears there; then change the Front Clip Z input button to 120 for 120 inches or ten feet. Like AutoCAD, AutoShade uses inches as the base drawing unit. A check by the Clip at Camera check button will force

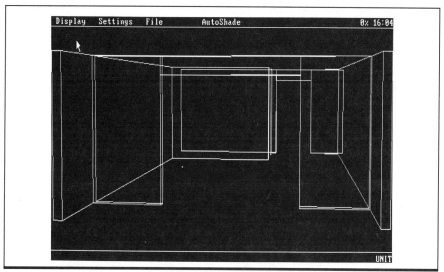

Figure 15.30: A wire frame view of the new camera position

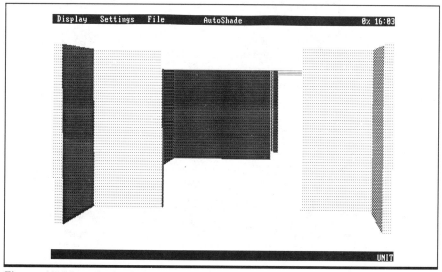

Figure 15.31: A shaded view of the unit from the new position

AutoShade to show all of your model right up to the camera location. By changing this setting, you can set your own view clip position. The new z clip value you entered is the distance from the camera target point toward the camera. Figure 15.33 illustrates these locations.

Other values in this dialog box, Left Clip, Right Clip, Top Clip, and Bottom Clip, determine the width and height of your view frame. The values set for these items may seem small compared to the Front Clip Z value. These values represent the distances from the center of an imagined frame of a 35mm film. Negative values represent distances to the left of center or below center. That is why the Left Clip and Bottom Clip values are negative. Changing these values will change the view frame (see Figure 15.34). Back Clip Z has a similar effect to Front Clip Z, but instead of clipping your view in front of the camera target position, it clips the view behind the camera target. This can be useful in 3D wire frame views that contain lines behind the area you want to view.

Now pick the OK action button, then do a wire frame view to check the results of the new clipping specifications (see Figure 15.35). You can see that the balcony wall is no longer in the view. Now do a full shade of your model. It will look like Figure 15.36.

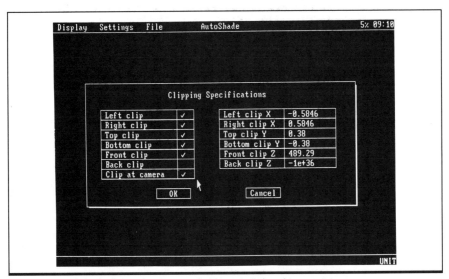

Figure 15.32: The Clipping Specifications dialog box

Saving Views for Quick Recall

You cannot save the settings you just made, but you can save the view for later replay. By saving a view, you can recall it without having to load the filmroll and readjust the settings. Saved views can also be displayed sequentially for presentations. AutoShade saves views on disk as rendering replay files, recognizable by their extension, .RND.

Pick Record from the Display menu, then pull down the Display menu again. Notice that Record now has a check mark by it, telling you that AutoShade is in *record mode*. Any view you display will be

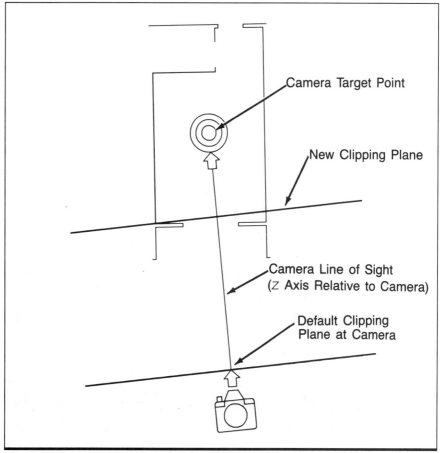

Figure 15.33:   *The clipping plane locations*

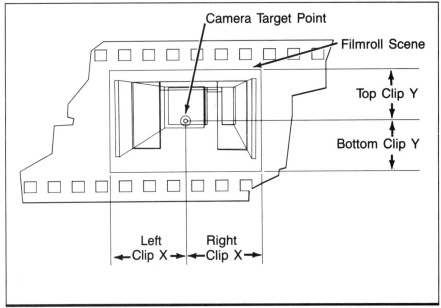

Figure 15.34:   Diagram showing other clipping values

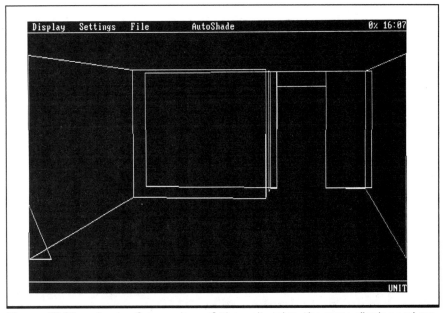

Figure 15.35:   A wire frame view of the unit using the new clipping values

recorded to disk. Now pick Full Shade. A new dialog box appears labeled Create Rendering Replay File (see Figure 15.37). It shows the default name of the replay file it will create, including the full directory path. You can either give the file a different name or accept

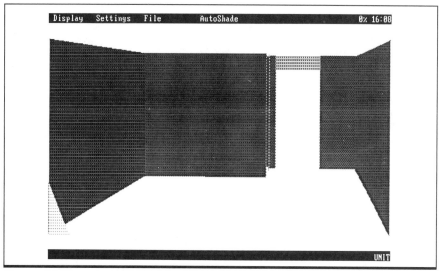

Figure 15.36: A shaded view of the unit using the new clipping values

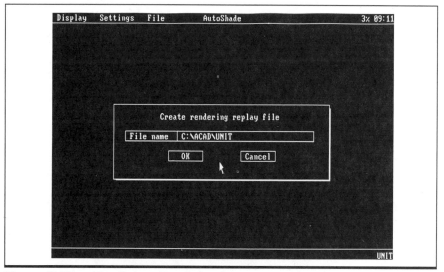

Figure 15.37: The Create Rendering Replay File dialog box

the default name by picking the OK input button. Accept the default name. The view will redraw and you will notice hard disk activity.

To see a recorded view, pick Replay from the Display pull-down menu. A dialog box appears listing the recorded views available (see Figure 15.38). Pick Unit and the OK action button, and the unit view will redisplay without going through the view calculations.

Viewing Several Views in Sequence

To look at a series of views, pick Replay All from the Display menu. A dialog box appears showing the name of the directory in which the replay files you wish to see are located (see Figure 15.39). You can either enter a different directory, or accept the directory displayed in the dialog box. AutoShade then displays all the saved views in the chosen directory sequentially. This dialog box also allows you to adjust the number of seconds a view remains on the screen before the next view is displayed.

PRINTING AUTOSHADE VIEWS

If you want hard copy of your AutoShade view, you have a limited range of alternatives. During the installation and configuration of AutoShade, you have a choice of four output device options: AutoCAD Device Interface, PostScript, rendering file (256-color map), and rendering file (continuous color). Only two of these options—the AutoCAD Device Interface and PostScript—really offer hard-copy output. Both also allow you to save output to a file that can later be read by an output device or other program. The rendering file options are similar to the AutoCAD DXF file format, in that they are a means of exchanging AutoShade files with other programs. They are intended for use by software developers who wish to import AutoShade files into programs they are using or marketing.

The ADI option allows you to print your view to a device that supplies an ADI interface (see Appendix A for more information on ADI hardware options). Unfortunately, not all hard-copy devices using the ADI format can output hard copy from AutoShade. Check with the manufacturer who supplies the ADI software interface to be certain that you can use their device for AutoShade output.

The PostScript option is the most flexible, because it enables you to get hard copy from any device that works with the PostScript programming language. An added feature is that with a little modification, you can import AutoShade PostScript files to desktop-publishing software that accepts files in the Encapsulated PostScript format. We will discuss this capability in detail later in this chapter.

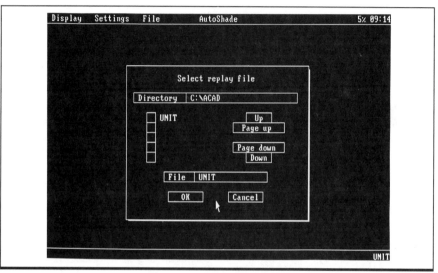

Figure 15.38: The Select Replay File dialog box

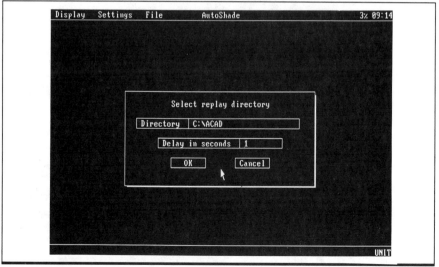

Figure 15.39: The Select Replay Directory dialog box

To get hard-copy output of a shaded view, first pick Hard Copy from the Display menu. Set up your view, then pull down the Display menu. Notice that the Hard Copy option now has a check mark by it telling you that whenever you use the Shade command, you will be sending your view to a printer or file for hard copy. Then pick Full Shade. If a printer is connected to your computer, the printing process will begin. Otherwise, you will get a dialog box displaying the name of the output file AutoShade will create (see Figure 15.40). You can enter a new name or accept the default. Pick the OK action button, and the shading process will begin. This time, however, the view will be saved to disk in a file rather than displayed on your screen. If you configured AutoShade for a PostScript output device, and printed to a file instead of the device, you can exit AutoShade and send the file directly to a remote PostScript printer by using the method described in Chapter 5.

EXPORTING AUTOSHADE VIEWS

Once you have an AutoShade view you like, you can use it in other programs. Wire frame views are easily exported to any program that accepts the AutoCAD DXB file format. Shaded views can

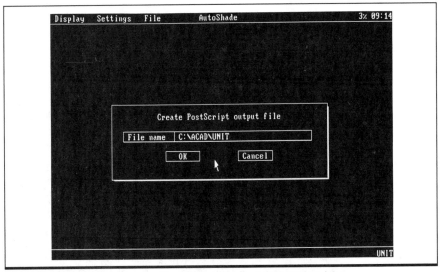

Figure 15.40:   *The Create PostScript Output File dialog box*

also be exported to programs that accept the Encapsulated Post-Script format. Most desktop-publishing programs use this format for importing both text and graphics. In this section, we will look at how to export wire frame and shaded views.

Exporting Wire Frame Views

To create a DXB file from AutoShade, first set up your AutoShade drawing as described above in the section on viewing your scenes. Then, pick Make Dxb from the Display pull-down menu. A dialog box prompting you for the DXB file name appears (see Figure 15.41). You can use a different name or accept the default. A file with the extension .DXB is created on disk. Once this is done, you can import the DXB file into AutoCAD and you will have an editable 2D drawing of a 3D view. This process is similar to the one described in Chapter 14, where you turn a 3D AutoCAD view into an editable 2D drawing. AutoShade enables you to do the same with perspective views.

You can use AutoShade to turn an AutoCAD 3D model into a 2D perspective line drawing. Just send your 3D model to AutoShade, set up the perspective view, then create a DXB file while still in Auto-Shade. Once this is done, you can start AutoCAD, open a new file, and

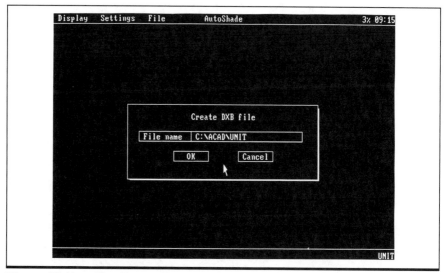

Figure 15.41:   *The Create Dxb File dialog box*

use the Dxbin command to import the DXB file created by AutoShade. This imported drawing will be a 2D representation of your AutoShade perspective view that you can edit like any other 2D drawing, or plot out for use as an underlay for hand-rendered illustrations.

Wire frame views can also be exported from AutoShade using the Make Slide command on the Display pull-down menu. This command operates in the same way as Make Dxb, but in this case the file created has the .SLD file extension. AutoShade slide files can be read by any program, including Ventura Publisher, that will accept slide files from AutoCAD versions 2.6 and earlier. Detailed information on how to create and view slides in AutoCAD can be found in Chapter 16. For more on using AutoCAD drawings with desktop-publishing software, see Chapter 13.

Exporting Shaded Views

Shaded views can only be exported to programs that accept the Encapsulated PostScript format. If you want to export shaded images, you must configure AutoShade to a PostScript printer. If you currently have AutoShade configured for a different printer and would like to change the configuration, delete the file Shade.CFG in the directory containing AutoShade, then start AutoShade. You will be asked the same series of questions as when you first installed AutoShade (see Appendix B). Another way to reconfigure AutoShade is to start the program by entering

shade -r

at the DOS prompt.

Once you have configured AutoShade for a PostScript printer, adjust the settings for your view and print the view to a file on disk as described earlier in the section on printing a view. Then convert this file into the Encapsulated PostScript format as outlined in Chapter 13.

Just as with AutoCAD PostScript files, AutoShade PostScript files are not in the Encapsulated PostScript format. Chapter 13 describes how you can easily convert AutoShade and AutoCAD PostScript files into Encapsulated PostScript files.

Once you have done all this, you can import the file into Ventura, PageMaker, or any other program that accepts Encapsulated PostScript. As we cautioned in Chapter 13, an Encapsulated PostScript file viewed in these programs does not display as the original drawing and it will only print on PostScript printers. However, if you have a Post-Script printer, and are using Ventura or PageMaker, you can get high-quality AutoShade images with this method (see Figure 15.42).

USING SCRIPT FILES TO BATCH YOUR WORK

The unit plan model is a fairly simple form for AutoShade to handle; shading the unit can be done quickly. If your 3D models become more complex, shading will take considerably longer. This can be a problem if you want to generate several shaded views of a complex model. You can, however, use AutoShade's script file capabilities to allow shading to proceed without your intervention.

Basically, AutoShade script files work the same way as AutoCAD script files (see Chapter 8 for detailed information on the use of script files in AutoCAD). You write a script file in DOS or ASCII format containing the AutoShade commands you wish to use. They should be in the sequence normally required to accomplish your task when you are using AutoShade interactively. But since AutoShade

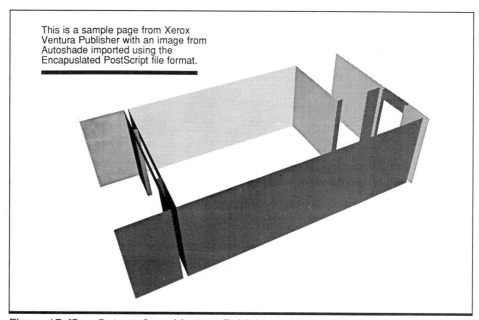

This is a sample page from Xerox Ventura Publisher with an image from Autoshade imported using the Encapuslated PostScript file format.

Figure 15.42: Output from Ventura Publisher using an AutoShade PostScript file

accepts keyboard input only through function buttons and Alt key input, you will have to translate the pull-down menu commands. Table 15.1 shows the AutoShade script commands. They perform the same functions as their counterparts in the pull-down menus and dialog boxes.

Your script file can have any name, but it must have the extension .SCR. You can run a script file from DOS by entering

shade -*script file name*

You don't have to add the .SCR extension.

Command	Description
Display commands	
Delay *seconds*	Pauses the script file for the number of seconds specified. This is similar to the Delay command in AutoCAD
DXB *file name*	Creates a DXB file
Fastshade *file name*	Performs a fast shade of the file given as *file name.* The file name is not required unless the record mode or hard-copy mode is on
Fullshade *file name*	Performs a full shade. The file name is not required unless the record mode or hard-copy mode is on
Record *on/off*	Toggles the record mode on or off
Replay *file name*	Replays the file with the name that follows the command
Rewind	Repeats the commands in the script file from the beginning
Settings commands	
Camera *x,y,z*	Moves the camera to a new location described by the *x, y,* and *z* values that follow the command
Target *x,y,z*	Changes the camera target position to one specified by the *x, y,* and *z* values that follow the command
Distance *distance*	Changes the distance of the camera from its target point
Twist *angle*	Sets the rotational angle of the camera along the line of sight
Intersection *on/off*	Toggles the intersection checking on or off
Lens *mm*	Sets the lens value to that which is specified after the command
Spercent *number*	Changes the screen percent value to one specified by the number that follows the command
File commands	
Open *file name*	Loads a filmroll with the file name given after the command
Scene *name*	Selects the scene in a filmroll specified by the name that follows the command

Table 15.1: AutoShade script file commands

CONCLUSION

In this brief tutorial, you were exposed to some of AutoShade's basic operations. It is a deceptively simple program that contains many more adjustment options than we can cover in one chapter. For more detailed information on AutoShade, consult the AutoShade manual. We hope that despite its brevity, this tutorial has given you a sense of AutoShade's potential as a rendering tool. Designers can use AutoCAD and AutoShade together to help develop and document their designs. With AutoCAD's and AutoShade's file export capabilities, product manuals can easily incorporate 2D and 3D design drawings using desktop-publishing systems. Illustrators can also take advantage of AutoShade's PostScript capabilities to add shaded images to desktop-publishing and other typesetting systems capable of importing Encapsulated PostScript files.

The 3D model of the unit is stark looking when viewed as a shaded model. You may want to make a copy of the unit drawing and add some details like furniture and lamps, then look at it again in AutoShade. You may want to create other 3D models more in line with the type of work you do. Experiment with some of the settings we mentioned but didn't use in the tutorial.

In the next chapter, you will draw on all that you have learned about AutoCAD thus far to complete a floor of your studio apartment building.

Chapter 16

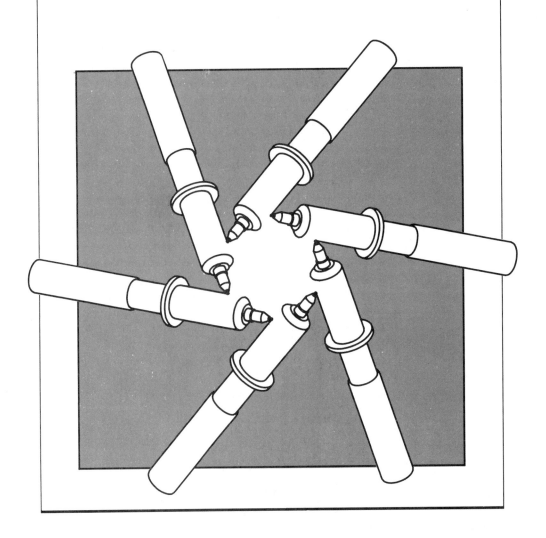

Managing the Drawing Process

BECAUSE YOU MAY NOT KNOW what all the requirements are at the beginning of a project, you usually base the first draft of a design on the early requirements. As the project proceeds, you make adjustments for new requirements as they arise. As more people enter the project, more design restrictions come into play and the design is further modified. This process continues throughout the project, from first draft to end product.

In this chapter you will review much of what you've already learned. In the process, you will look at some ways to handle continuous changes in a project and what you can do to minimize duplication of work. You will also see how to use your computer as a presentation device, a means to communicate your design ideas to others quickly.

EDITING MORE EFFICIENTLY

The apartment building plan is currently incomplete. For example, the utility room you created needs to be added. In the real world, this plan would also undergo innumerable changes. Wall and door locations would change, and more notes and dimensions would be added. In the space of this tutorial, we can't develop these drawings to full completion. However, we can give you a sample of what is in store while using AutoCAD on such a project.

In this section, you will add a closet to the Unit plan (you will update the Plan file later in this chapter). In the editing you've already done, you've probably found you use certain commands frequently: Move, Copy, Change, Break, Fillet, Trim, and the Osnap overrides. Now you will learn some ways to shorten your editing time by using them more efficiently.

Editing an Existing Drawing

Open the Unit plan and freeze the Notes and Flr-pat layers to keep your drawing clear of objects you won't be editing. To create the closet, first copy the right side wall two feet toward the center of the unit (see Figure 16.1). Next, you will use the Copy command to draw the other side of this new wall. You could enter a relative distance through the keyboard. Another approach would be to pick two reference points that represent the distance of the copy, similar to the way you used lines in previous chapters.

To use an existing wall as a reference for a wall thickness, first zoom into the entry area and start the Copy command. Pick the wall

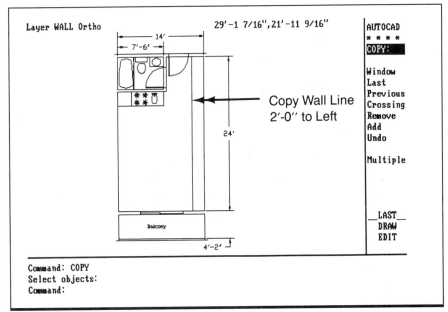

Figure 16.1: Where to copy the wall to start the closet

line you just copied at the object-selection prompt. Then, at the prompt for a base point, use the Nearest Osnap override and pick the outside wall of the bathroom near the door (see Figure 16.2). At the prompt for a second point, use the Perpend Osnap override and pick the other side of that wall (see Figure 16.2 again). The line copies over the same distance as the bathroom wall thickness.

Now zoom back so you can see the kitchenette in your screen view. Copy the wall at the top of your view to define the other side of the closet (see Figure 16.3). Use the upper-right corner of the bathroom and the lower-right corner of the kitchenette as reference points.

Break the wall lines at the wall intersections, as shown in Figure 16.4. Remember to use the F option with the Break command when you join wall lines. Use the Trim command to shorten the long wall lines to a point that will allow you to use the Fillet command to join the corner (see Figure 16.5). Now fillet the walls that don't meet at the corners to finish the closet walls (see Figure 16.6).

Add the closet door shown in Figure 16.7. This is similar to the sliding door to the balcony, so if you get stuck refer to Chapter 6. Your drawing should look like Figure 16.8.

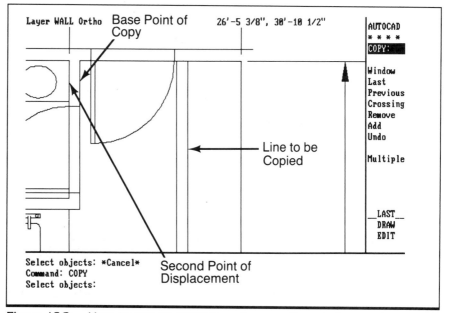

Figure 16.2: *How to use an existing wall as a reference for copying*

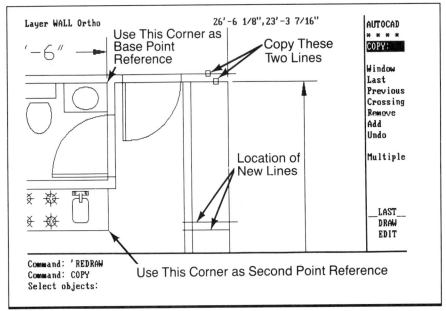

Figure 16.3: How to add the second closet wall

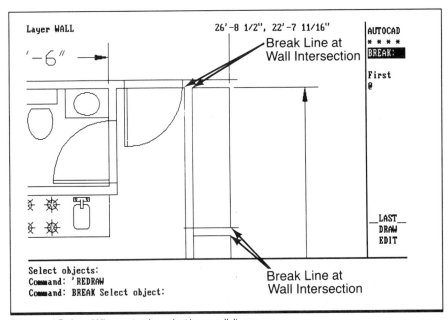

Figure 16.4: Where to break the wall lines

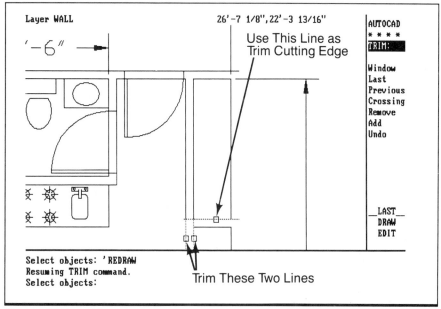

Figure 16.5:   *Where to trim the walls*

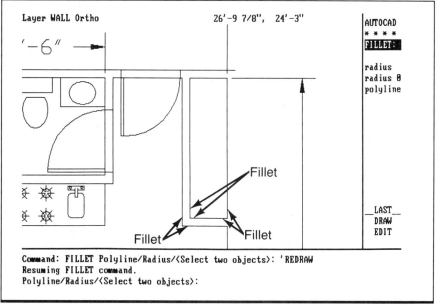

Figure 16.6:   *Where to fillet the corners*

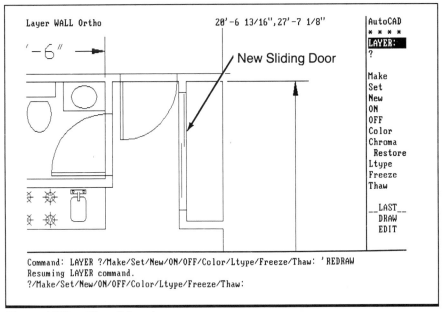

Figure 16.7: The sliding door

Now use the End command to close the Unit file.

Building on Previously Drawn Objects

Suppose your client decides your design needs a few one-bedroom units. In this exercise, you will use the drawing of the studio unit as a basis for the drawing of a one-bedroom unit. To do so, you will double the studio's size, add a bedroom, move the kitchenette, re-arrange and add closets, and move the entry doors. In the process of editing this new drawing, you will see how you can build on pre-viously drawn objects.

Open a new file called Unit2 and use the Unit file as a template. Since you will move the kitchenette, first erase its floor pattern. Do this by thawing the Flr-pat layer, exploding the hatch pattern, and erasing the tiles. Move the dimension string at the right of the unit 14'-5" further to the right, and copy the unit the same distance to the right (see Figure 16.9).

Now erase the bathroom, kitchenette, door, closet, and wall lines as shown in Figure 16.10. Use the Fillet or Change command to join and extend walls where they have been broken, as shown in Figure 16.11. You could have added line segments where wall lines were removed, but it is a good idea to keep lines continuous, rather than

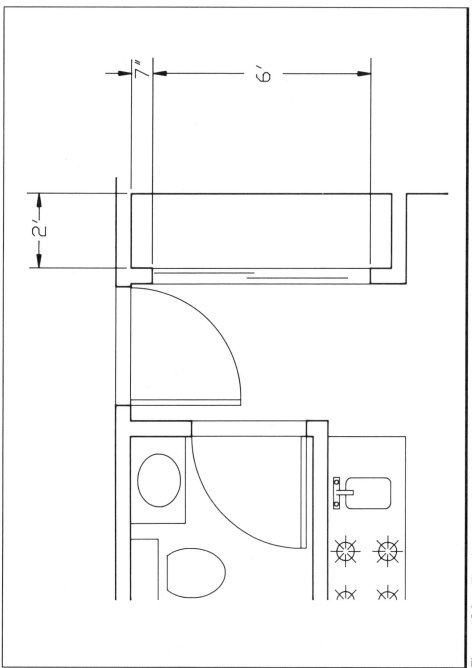

Figure 16.8: The finished closet

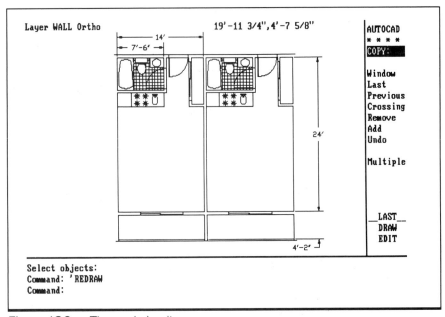

Figure 16.9: *The copied unit*

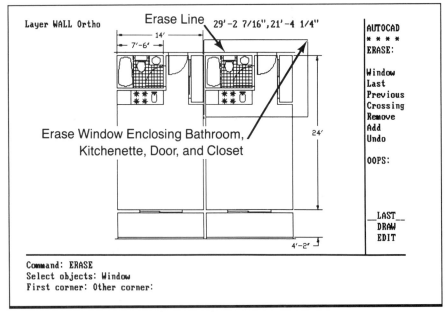

Figure 16.10: *Objects to be erased*

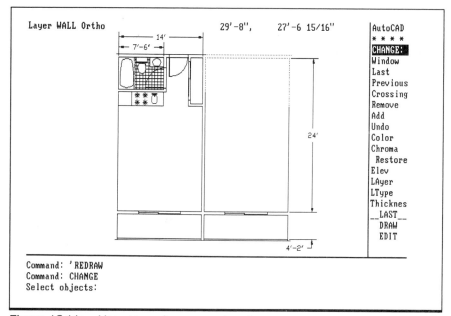

Figure 16.11: How to replace erased walls

fragmented. Adding line segments to a drawing increases the size of the drawing database and slows down editing operations. Fragmented lines also affect the final plot of your drawing, causing the plotter pen to jog or blob where two lines meet end to end, as shown in Figure 16.12.

Move the kitchenette to the opposite corner of the unit as shown in Figure 16.13. Move the remaining closet down 5'-5" as shown in Figure 16.14. You can use the corners of the bathroom as reference points.

Zoom into the area that includes the closet and the two doors. Copy the existing entry door down (see Figure 16.15). Clean up the walls by adding new lines and changing existing ones, as shown in Figure 16.16. Mirror the door you just copied so it swings in the opposite direction. Use the Stretch command to move the entry door from its current location to near the kitchenette, as shown in Figure 16.17. Once you've moved the door, mirror it as you mirrored the other door.

Now set the view of your drawing so it looks like Figure 16.18. Use the Extend command to extend the closet wall lines to the balcony wall. Extend is helpful when you want to lengthen a line or arc to touch a selected object. Pick Extend from the Edit menu to bring up the Extend menu (see Figure 16.19).

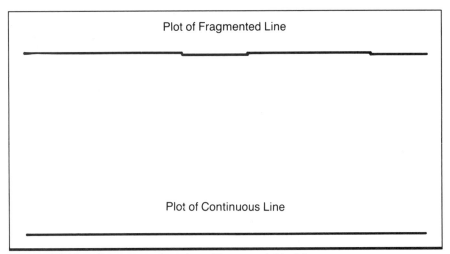

Plot of Fragmented Line

Plot of Continuous Line

Figure 16.12:   *Fragmented and continuous plotted lines*

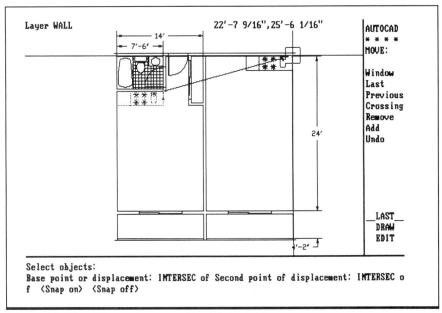

Layer WALL   22'-7 9/16", 25'-6 1/16"   AUTOCAD
                                                                     * * * *
                                                                     MOVE:

                                                                     Window
                                                                     Last
                                                                     Previous
                                                                     Crossing
                                                                     Remove
                                                                     Add
                                                                     Undo

                                                                     __LAST__
                                                                       DRAW
                                                                       EDIT

Select objects:
Base point or displacement: INTERSEC of Second point of displacement: INTERSEC o
f <Snap on> <Snap off>

Figure 16.13:   *Where to move the kitchenette*

The Extend menu offers the object-selection options, plus the
Zoom and Select commands. Select enables you to preselect objects
for processing. It works like the object-selection prompt, except that
no action is taken on the selected objects. They are just marked for

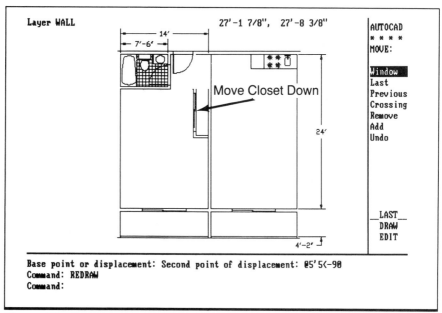

Figure 16.14:   The closet's new location

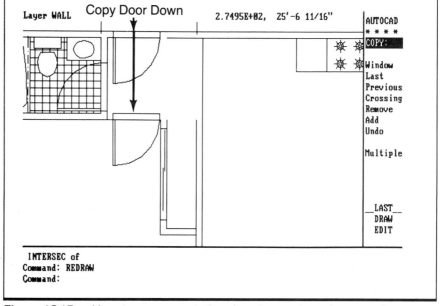

Figure 16.15:   How to use an existing door to create a door opening

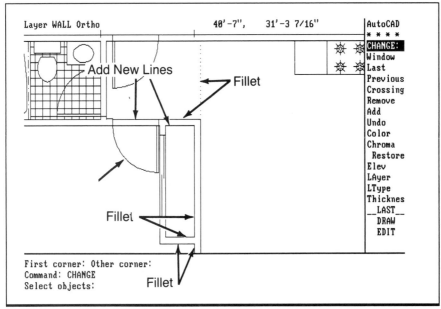

Figure 16.16: How to clean up the walls

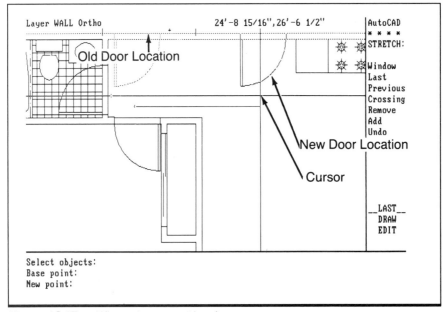

Figure 16.17: Where to move the door

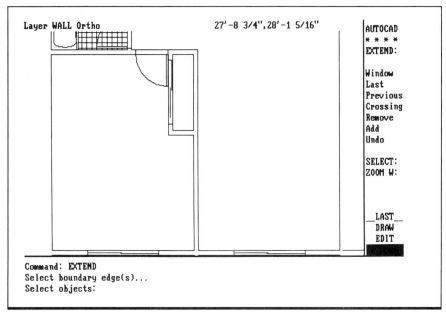

Figure 16.18: View of the new bedroom

Figure 16.19: The Extend menu

editing. You then choose the desired editing command and enter the Previous option when you are prompted to select objects. The objects you picked using the Select command will ghost.

Pick the Extend option. Next, you will get the prompt

Select boundary edge(s)...
Select object:

At this prompt, you must select the object to which you want your objects extended. Pick the wall at the bottom of the screen as shown in Figure 16.20. Press Return. At the next prompt

Select object to extend:

you select the objects you want to extend. Pick the two lines just below the closet door. As you pick the lines, they will extend to the wall you picked as the boundary. You may have to pick the lines several times if they don't extend on the first try. Then clean up the wall corners.

You could have used the Change command to extend these lines. We showed you the Extend command as an alternate because, unlike Change, it enables you to extend arcs and to pick several objects as boundaries.

Now suppose you want to change the location and orientation of the kitchenette. Set up your view to one similar to Figure 16.20. Go to the Edit menu and pick Next, then pick Rotate. You will get the

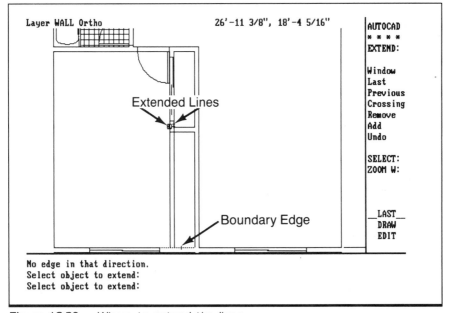

Figure 16.20: Where to extend the lines

object-selection prompt. Pick the kitchenette and press Return. At the base point prompt, pick the upper-left corner of the kitchenette as your rotation base (see Figure 16.21). You will get the prompt

<Rotation angle>/Reference:

and the kitchenette will appear to rotate with the cursor as in Figure 16.22. Toggle the ortho mode on and pick a point to orient the kitchenette as in Figure 16.23. Now move the kitchenette into the corner as in Figure 16.24.

Now suppose you want to widen the entrance door from 36 to 42 inches. First, widen the door opening by using the Stretch command to move the left door jamb six inches to the left, as in Figure 16.25. Notice that Stretch ignores the Door block.

Now you can enlarge the door using the Scale command. Scale allows you to change the size of an object or a group of objects. You can change the size visually, by entering a scale value, or by using an object for reference. In this exercise, you will use the current door width as a reference.

Pick Next from the Edit menu, then pick Scale to bring up the Scale menu (see Figure 16.26). At the object-selection prompt, pick the entry

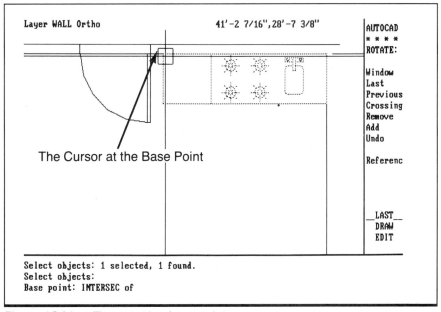

Figure 16.21: *The rotation base point*

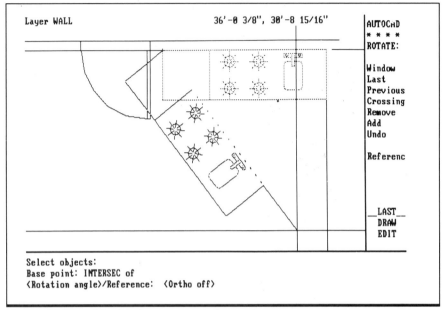

Figure 16.22: *The kitchenette rotating*

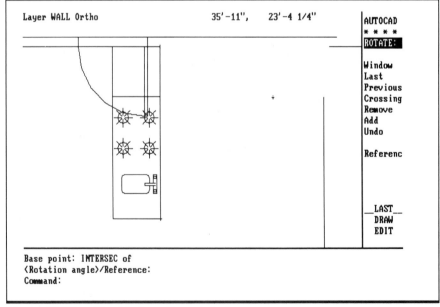

Figure 16.23: *The kitchenette rotated*

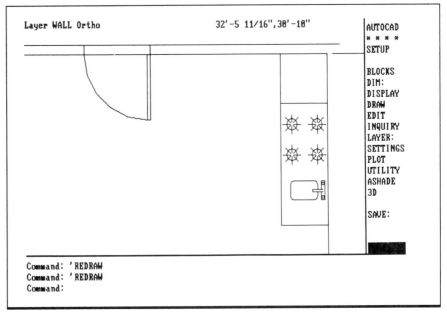

Figure 16.24: The revised kitchenette

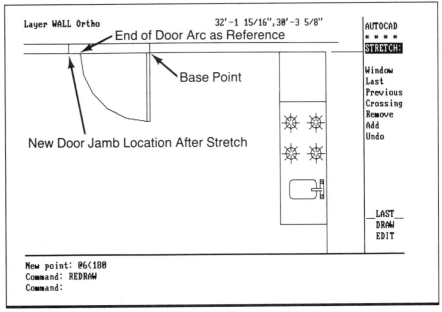

Figure 16.25: The widened door opening

Figure 16.26:   *The Scale menu*

door, then press Return. At the base point prompt, pick the corner
where the door meets the jamb. Now as you move the cursor, you will
see the door enlarge and contract depending on how close you move
the cursor to the base point. At the prompt

<Scale factor>/Reference:

you could enter a value for the new door size proportional to the
current size. Instead, you will use the Referenc option to visually
change the door size to fit the new opening.

Pick Referenc from the Scale menu. At the next prompt

Reference length <1>:

pick the point you used for the base point. At the next prompt

Second point:

pick the end of the door arc as in Figure 16.25. Now as you move
the cursor horizontally to the left of the base point, the door arc
follows, enlarging or reducing the size of the door. At the prompt

New length:

pick the left door jamb as shown in Figure 16.27.

You have finished drawing your one-bedroom unit, which should look
like Figure 16.28. Now end out of the Unit2 file. In the next section, you

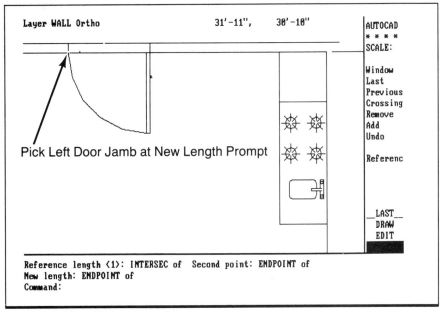

Figure 16.27: The enlarged door

will update the Plan file to include the revised studio apartment and the one-bedroom unit you just created. Changes like these will continue into the later stages of your design project. As you have seen, Auto-CAD's ability to make changes easily and quickly can ease your work and help you test your design ideas more accurately.

USING BLOCKS AND LAYERS

We mentioned in Chapter 6 that careful use of blocks and layers can help you improve your productivity. In this section you will see firsthand how to use them to help reduce design errors and speed up delivery of an accurate set of drawings. You do this by controlling layers in conjunction with blocks to create a common drawing database for several drawings.

Layering Your Drawing

You may recall that in Chapter 7 we discussed using the Freeze option to control layers. You can think of layers as being different z coordinate locations in your drawing. For example, you can create a

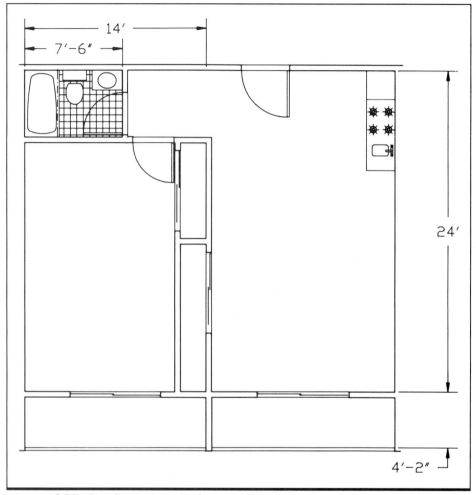

Figure 16.28: The finished one-bedroom unit

layer for each of the three floors of your apartment building, then insert the Unit blocks on the appropriate layers. You can create a fourth layer to contain the blocks common to all the floors, such as the lobby, stairs, utility room, and some of the units (see Figure 16.29). To display or plot a particular floor, you freeze all the layers except that floor and the layer containing the common information. The following exercise shows you how to do this.

Open the Plan file. Create a layer called Gridline and add the grid and dimension information shown in Figure 16.30. The grid line and

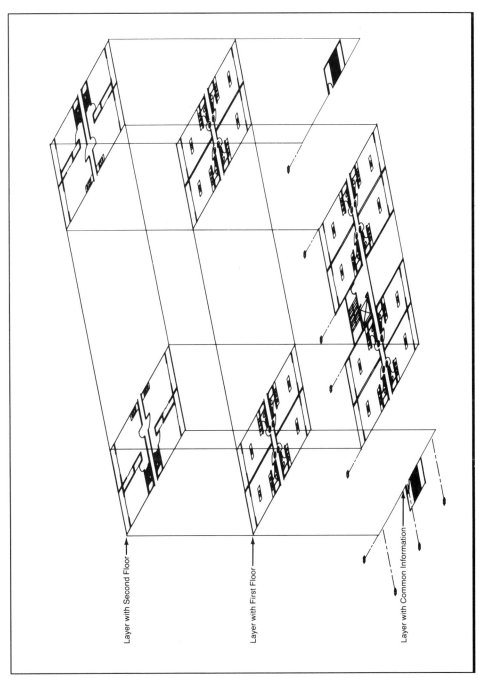

Layer with Second Floor →

Layer with First Floor →

Layer with Common Information →

Figure 16.29: 3D representation of how layers might be considered

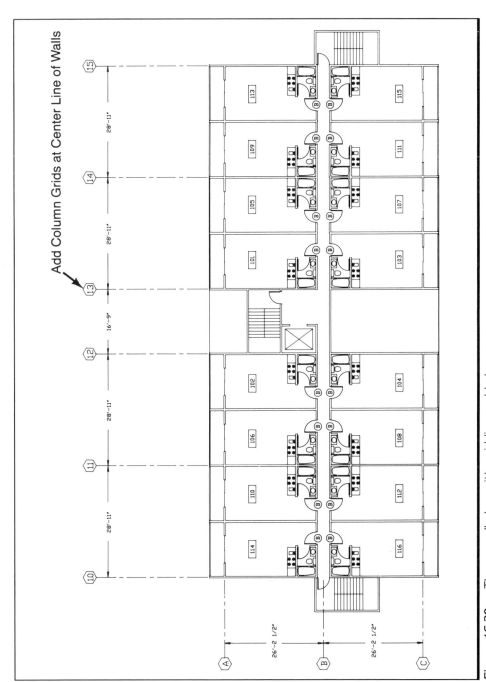

Add Column Grids at Center Line of Walls

Figure 16.30: The overall plan with grid lines added

related dimensions are used in architectural drawings as a system to establish references from which accurate dimensions can be taken. They are usually based on key structural elements, such as columns and foundation wall locations.

Use Change to make the grid lines a Center line type. This is a typical center line composed of a long line, then a short dash, then another long line. It is usually used to denote the center of an object; in this case, a wall. Be sure Ltscale is set to 96.

Make two more layers called Floor1 and Floor2 and change the eight units in the corners of your plan to the Floor1 layer. Change the door symbols for those units to the Floor1 layer also (see Figure 16.31). All the information specific to the first floor is now on the Floor1 layer and can be isolated with the Freeze command. Now freeze Floor1. The eight units you changed to that layer will disappear.

Now insert Unit2 into the corners where the other units had been. Use Figure 16.32 as a guide. Be sure the Unit2 drawings are on the Floor2 layer. The Floor2 layer now contains information specific to the second floor. Now you have the information for two floors combined in one drawing. By alternately freezing and thawing layers, you can view the different floors. To view the first floor,

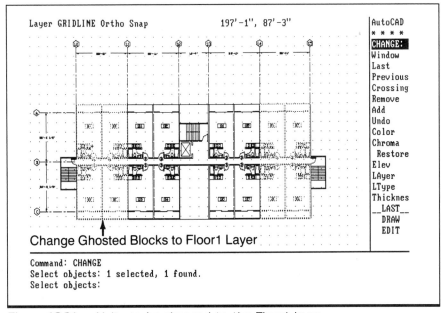

Figure 16.31:   *Units to be changed to the Floor1 layer*

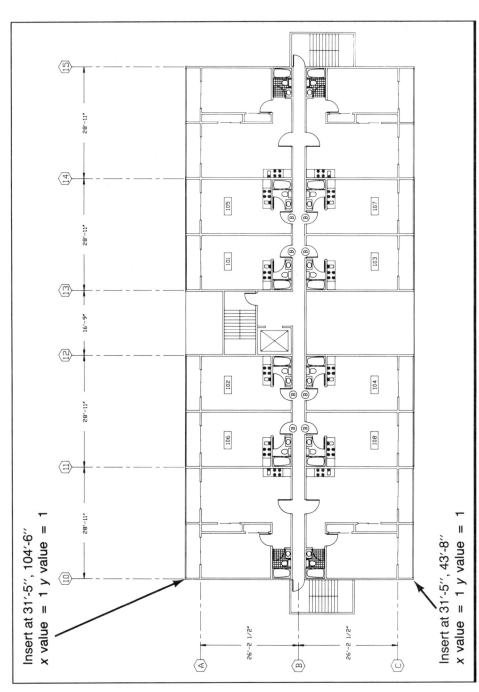

Insert at 31'-5'', 104'-6''
x value = 1 y value = 1

Insert at 31'-5'', 43'-8''
x value = 1 y value = 1

Figure 16.32:   Insertion information for Unit2

thaw the Floor1 layer and freeze Floor2. If you have Regenauto turned off, use Regen to view the change in layers.

Now create a Plan1 layer containing blocks common to all the floors. Because the second and third floors are the same, you don't have to create a separate Floor3 layer. Since you have all the information for the building in one file, whenever one element of the building changes, that change is reflected on all the floors. In other words, you have a common database for all your floor plans. For example, if for some reason the grid lines change, you can change them once in this file and they are changed for all the floors. This helps maintain accuracy and consistency between floors, since they all use the same points of reference, namely the grid lines.

If the studio unit plan changes, you can edit the Unit file and update it once in the Plan file. All the units in all the floor plans will be updated. If you had the floors in separate files, you would have to update each floor individually, doubling or tripling your work and making it easier for you to make errors by forgetting to update a file.

Now save the Plan file. You will continue to edit this file in the next section.

Assembling Blocks to Form a Drawing

The drawing setup described in the previous section may not be a workable solution for some types of drawings. A drawing can become difficult to manage, especially when more than three or four layers of information are involved. If the previous example contained six different floors, each associated with a different apartment unit type, the file would become too large to edit easily, and switching from floor to floor would be a time-consuming proposition.

Another approach is to have each final drawing be an assembly of smaller drawings. You already did this when you copied and mirrored the Unit plan to form the overall floor plan. You can take this method one step further by separating groups of components into drawings, then assembling the component drawings into the final drawing (see Figure 16.33).

For example, each of the blocks combined into the Floor1, Floor2, and Plan1 layers could be made into an individual file. Still another would contain the column grid. For the finished drawing, you would assemble these drawings into one. To edit such a drawing, you edit the components that need changing. Components common to several drawings can be edited in the individual files. This exercise shows you how this method works.

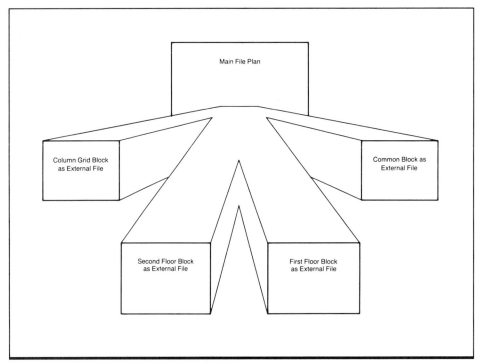

Figure 16.33:   *The components of a large, complex file*

Create a block of all the unit plans on the Plan1 layer. Name this block Common and give it an insertion point of 0,0. Turn all the door type symbols into a block called Symbol, and use 0,0 as the insertion point of this block as well. Do this for the column grids, units on the Floor1 layer, and units on the Floor2 layer. You can name the column grid block Col-gr and name the other blocks after the Floor1 and Floor2 layers.

Now insert all these blocks back into the drawing using 0,0 as the insertion point. Be sure you insert them into their proper layers (the Floor1 block should be on the Floor1 layer, the Common block on the Plan1 layer, etc.). Because the insertion points of all the blocks are the same, they will all fit together perfectly when they are inserted back into the drawing.

Now you can either freeze the layers that contain the floors you don't want to show, or erase the blocks of the floors. Since erasing a block does not remove it from the drawing's database even when you exit the drawing, you can reinsert the block at any time (unless you have purged it). You can Wblock the floors, edit them outside the Plan drawing, then reinsert them into the Plan drawing as we showed you in Chapter 7. This way you won't have to deal with such a large file.

You could also create new files from the blocks that have been turned into drawing files. For example, you may want to have one drawing containing the information for just the first floor. You can accomplish this by opening a new file and inserting the Common block, the Floor1 block, the Col-gr block, and the Symbols block. This technique can be used to split work among several people working on the same project. One person could edit the Common block while another works on Floor1, and so on.

If you operate in this manner, coordinating the various drawings is a major concern. You have to keep track of the various blocks and their associated drawing files. You must also take care in updating blocks. The next exercise will show you what to expect if you aren't careful about updating files.

Use the Wblock command and write the Common block out as a file. If you have problems remembering how to do this, refer to Chapter 4. End out of the Plan file. Now open the Common file and enter a Control-C to stop the drawing regeneration. Don't be alarmed if nothing appears on the screen. The drawing is still there.

Update the units by inserting the Unit plan you just edited. Remember to enter unit = when you are prompted for a block name. At the insertion point prompt, enter a Control-C. Regenerate the drawing. You will see the new Unit plan in place of the old one (see Figure 16.34). You will also see all the dimensions and notes for each unit. Freeze the Notes layer to keep the notes from interfering with the drawing. Your drawing should now look like Figure 16.35.

Replace the empty room across the hall from the lobby with the utility room you created in Chapter 11 (see Figure 16.36). End out of the Common file.

Open the Plan file again and update the Common block. If you have Regenauto off, regenerate the drawing. The utility room appears, but the typical units are still the old ones. While you may have updated the Common block, you haven't updated the Unit block in the Plan file, so no change appears. Update the units in the Plan file the same way you did for the Common file. Once you regenerate the drawing, you will see the new unit plans in their proper places. Again, freeze the Notes layer to keep the text from interfering with the rest of the drawing. Your drawing should look like Figure 16.37.

We should mention that you cannot update exploded blocks in the manner just described. Remember, once a block has been exploded, it breaks down into its drawing components. However, blocks nested within an exploded block remain as blocks.

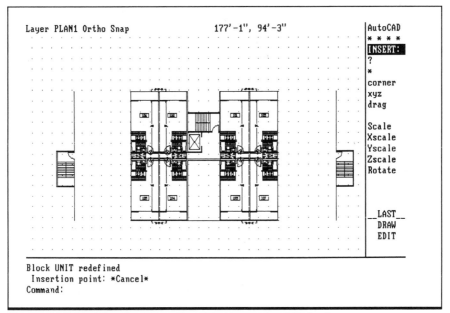

Figure 16.34:   The Common file with the revised Unit plan

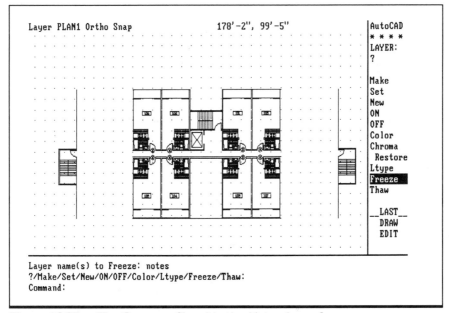

Figure 16.35:   The Common file with the Notes layer frozen

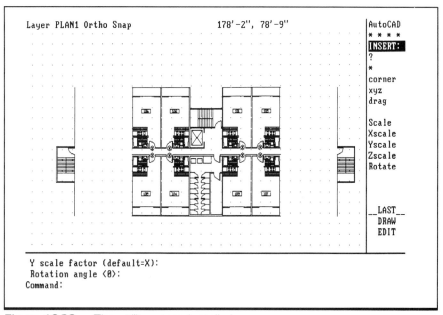

Figure 16.36:   *The utility room installed*

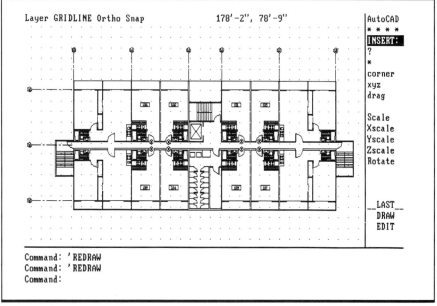

Figure 16.37:   *The Plan file with the units updated*

This exercise demonstrates the necessity for careful tracking of blocks and files, especially when nested blocks are used. It would be a good idea to keep a list of blocks and layers that is easily accessible to people working on your projects. Some sample lists are provided in Chapter 19.

Making One Drawing Serve as Many

Your set of drawings for this studio apartment building would probably have a larger-scale, more detailed drawing of the typical unit plan. You already have the beginnings of this drawing in the form of the Unit file. As you have seen, the notes and dimensions you entered into the Unit file can be frozen in the Plan file so they don't interfere with the graphics of the drawing. By selectively freezing layers, you can have one drawing fulfill two uses. The Unit file can be part of another drawing file that contains more detailed information on the typical unit plan at a larger scale. To this new drawing you can add other notes, symbols, and dimensions. Whenever the Unit file is altered, you simply update it in both the large-scale drawing of the typical unit and the Plan file (see Figure 16.38). By doing this, you can update the units quickly and assure good correspondence between all the drawings for your project.

CREATING AND USING SLIDES

At times you may want to display views of your drawings on the computer. You may want these views to appear quickly or in a predetermined sequence. AutoCAD enables you to save a *slide* of an entire drawing or a view as a file on disk. You can then display the slide at any time you are in the AutoCAD drawing editor. Slides can be used as a reference tool during editing sessions, instead of panning, zooming, or viewing, or for presentation. They can also be used for file management. A slide cannot be edited, however, nor will it be updated when you edit the drawing.

Creating Slides

In this exercise you will make a few slides of the Unit file. Open the Unit file and pick Slides from the Utility menu to bring up the Slides menu (see Figure 16.39). Next, the prompt

Slide file <unit>:

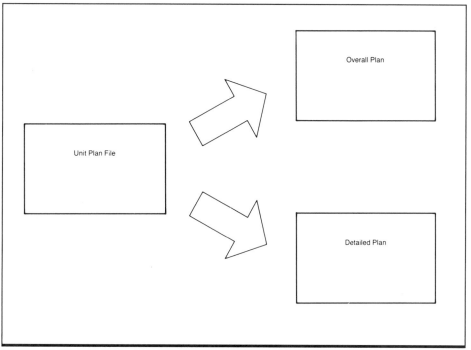

Figure 16.38:   *Relationship of drawing files*

Figure 16.39:   *The Slides menu*

appears. You can enter a name for the view to save as a slide or press Return to accept the default, which is the name of the current drawing. Press Return to accept the default name. AutoCAD will save the current view on disk as a slide with the file name Unit and the extension .SLD. The actual drawing file is not affected.

Zoom into the bathroom and use the Mslide command to save another view called Unitbath.

Viewing Slides

Zoom back to the previous view and pick Vslide from the Slides menu. Vslide enables you to view a slide created with the Mslide command. Enter Unitbath. The slide of the bathroom appears. Although you can move the cursor around the view and start commands in the normal way, you cannot edit or obtain information from this slide. To return to the drawing being edited, pick Redraw from the Osnap menu or enter redraw. Any command that performs a redraw will also return you to the current drawing. Now quit out of this file.

Open the Plan file and use the Vslide command to view the Unitbath slide again. You are able to call up the slide from any file, not just the file you were in when you created the slide. If you need to refer to another drawing from time to time, you can just save slides of the desired views. Another use for slides is in file management. You may reach the point where you can't remember which Auto-CAD drawing file goes with which drawing. Making a slide of every drawing you do gives you visual references for your drawing files. To hunt for a file, you just open a temporary drawing file, then look through your slide files to find the drawing. This is much faster than opening each drawing file until you find what you're looking for. Note that slide files created by version 9 are not compatible with those created by earlier versions of AutoCAD, but version 9 can read files from earlier versions.

Now create a slide of the Plan file and call it Plan1. Then quit out of this file.

Automating a Slide Presentation

As we mentioned in Chapter 8, Script can be used like the batch file in DOS to automatically run a sequence of commands. Now you will create a script file to automatically show your slides.

Open a new file called Show and use the Shell command to enter DOS. Use a word processor, the COPY CON command, or EDLIN to create a file called Show.SCR, and enter the following lines into this file. (If you have forgotten how to use COPY CON and Shell, see Chapters 8 and 10.) If you use COPY CON, remember to use the F6 key to add a Control-Z at the end of the file.

```
vslide
unit
delay 3000
vslide
unitbath
delay 3000
vslide
Plan1
```

These lines of text are a sequence of predetermined instructions to AutoCAD that can be played back later. Each line is entered at the AutoCAD command prompt, just as you would enter it through the keyboard. Note that the Vslide command appears before the name of each slide, then the line delay 3000. Delay 3000 tells Auto-CAD to pause roughly 3,000 milliseconds after each Vslide command is issued. You can substitute another value if you like. If no delay is specified, as soon as the slide is completed the next slide comes up.

Enter Script or pick Script from the Utility menu. You will get the prompt

Script file (show):

and the Script menu will appear (see Figure 16.40). Press Return to accept the default, show. The slides you saved will appear on the screen in the sequence you entered in the Show.SCR file.

Note the Delay, Resume, and Rscript commands on the Script menu. When you pick Delay, you get the prompt

Delay time in milliseconds:

You can enter a value at this prompt and AutoCAD will suspend operations for the amount of time you specify. During this time, no input is accepted. We are not sure why this is offered as a menu option since we cannot think of any time when we would want to suspend AutoCAD's operations for a fixed length of time while editing.

You can have the slides continually repeat themselves by adding the Rscript command after the plan1 line in the script file you just created. You may want to do this if your presentation is more like an exhibit where people can browse through your display area. To

Figure 16.40:   *The Script menu*

do this now, use COPY CON to create a file called Add containing
the line

Rscript

Then add it to the Show.SCR file by entering

copy show.scr + add

in the DOS shell. The Add file will be appended to the Show.SCR file.
Use the Script command again and start the Show script. The
sequence of slides will be repeated until you enter a backspace. If you
want to restart the script, you can enter resume or pick Resume
from the Script menu at any time. You can also restart any script
file from its beginning by picking Rscript from the Script menu.

Creating a Slide Library

With version 9, you can create *slide libraries*, files that organize
your slides by groups. For example, you could group slides by project
or drawing type. Slide libraries also save disk space as they often
use less space than the total used by the individual slide files.

Slide libraries are also used to create icon menus. AutoCAD provides a file called Acad.SLB for this purpose. This file contains all the
slides used for the font, hatch pattern, and 3D view icon menus. We
will discuss how to create icon menus in Chapter 18.

To create a slide library, you must first use a word processor and
make a list of the slides you want to include in the library. Make a

list of the slides you just created. It should look like the following:

    unit
    unitbath
    plan1

Save this list as a DOS text file or ASCII file. You can give this file any name you like. For this example, call it Sample.LST. Be sure it is saved in the same directory as your slide files.

Next, use the Slidelib.COM program on AutoCAD disk five to generate the slide library file. Be sure your Slidelib.COM file is in the same directory as your slide list file and slide files. At the DOS prompt enter

    slidelib *library name* < sample.lst

The library name can be any legal DOS file name. A file named *Library name*.SLB will be created. Do not include the file extension; the Slidelib utility program automatically adds the file extension .SLB. For example, if you enter Plans as the library name in the above example, a slide library file called Plans.SLB is created.

Now open a new temporary file called Temp to test your slide library. To view a slide from a slide library, you use the Vslide command. This time, however, you specify the file name differently. Instead of following the Vslide command with the slide name, you must give the library name followed by the individual slide name in parentheses. At the AutoCAD command prompt enter

    vslide *library name* (plan1)

The slide will appear in the drawing area. If you placed the slide library file in a directory different from the current one, be sure you enter the directory name before the slide library name.

You can also display slides in a slide library automatically by creating the appropriate slide library and slide name following the Vslide command script file, as in the following example:

    vslide
    libname(unit)
    delay 3000
    vlside
    libname(unitbath)
    delay 3000
    vslide
    libname(plan1)
    delay 3000
    rscript

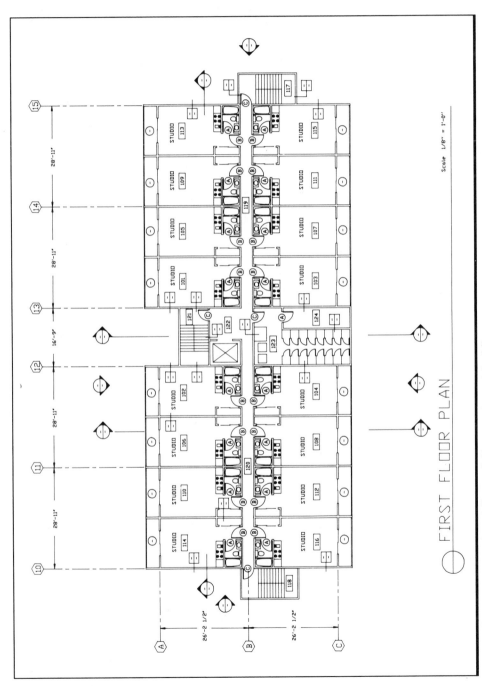

FIRST FLOOR PLAN

Scale 1/8" = 1'-0"

Figure 16.41:   A completed floor of the apartment building

CONCLUSION

This chapter concludes the apartment building tutorial. Although you haven't drawn the complete building, you've already learned all the commands and techniques you need to do so. Figure 16.41 shows you a completed plan of the first floor. You can add the symbols shown in this figure to the Plan file to complete your floor plans and practice using AutoCAD. Since buildings like this often have the same plans for different floors, the plan for the second floor can also represent the third floor. Combined with the first floor, this will give you a three-level apartment building. This project would also have a ground-level garage, which would be a separate file. The Gridline file you created earlier can be used in the garage file as a reference for dimensions. The other symbols can be blocks stored as files that can be retrieved in other files.

You may want to try the ideas we've presented in this chapter on a drawing more suited to your particular needs. A printed circuit board may use different layers and blocks to keep track of traces, or a mechanical drawing may use layers as a means of displaying alternate parts for a piece of machinery. It's up to you to think of ways these tools can be used.

In the next chapter, we will introduce you to ways of enhancing your editing speed. We will show you how to use DOS to create keyboard macros, as well as how to improve your computer's performance.

Chapter 17

Increasing Input and Processing Speed

As you become more comfortable with AutoCAD, you may begin to feel that getting to the command you want through the screen menus is a tedious process. If you are using a digitizing tablet, you may feel annoyed that you have to take your eyes off the screen to find a command. In this chapter you will explore some command input alternatives that may help you speed the drawing process. You will also find out what can be done to increase your PC's processing power.

USING MENUS

Menus are a way of aiding you in accessing commands. When you are new to a program, they can be of great help in learning the commands. AutoCAD provides the on-screen menus, and, for those who have digitizing tablets, an icon-based tablet menu. Both have their good points and bad points.

Using the On-Screen Menu

The on-screen menu system has the advantage of allowing you to keep your eyes on the screen while picking different commands. Its biggest disadvantage is its tree structure, which can get in the way of an experienced user. However, you can rearrange the menu system to reduce the numbers of menus you must go through to get to commands. You can also create your own menus containing your most frequently used commands, or commands you have created yourself. Customized on-screen menus are best suited to large macros that are used frequently and situations where you want to set up predetermined responses that can be selected from a menu. Because customized menus have many uses not directly related to increasing input speed, we give instructions for creating them in Chapter 18.

Using the Digitizing Tablet Menu

The tablet menu allows you to select commands directly instead of digging through the many levels of the on-screen menu's tree structure. Its *icons*, or graphic representations of commands, are designed to ease command selection. Its chief drawback is that it requires you to look away from the screen to pick a command. This may seem like a minor point, but when you are spending five to six hours a day editing drawings, such little annoyances can have a great effect on your productivity. The tablet menu has a space for customization at the top of the menu area (see Figure 17.1). A custom tablet menu is best used for symbol libraries or large macros that are not frequently used. We'll look at tablet menu customization in Chapter 18.

If you have a multibutton puck, you can program the buttons to start your most commonly used commands. This technique increases productivity in the same way as keyboard macros (see below). Programming puck buttons is discussed in Chapter 18.

USING THE KEYBOARD

Throughout the exercises in this book, you have been asked to pick items from the screen menu. We also describe how to enter most commands through the keyboard. Keyboard entry circumvents the menu search process, but it means learning the commands by heart. Still, the keyboard is the quickest way to enter commands. Once you are comfortable with AutoCAD you may find yourself using the keyboard without even thinking about it. We should remind you, however, that the options on the menu and the actual command names are not always the same. You may want to print a hard copy of the main help screen as a reference to the legal AutoCAD commands.

In the following section we suggest ways to speed up your keyboard input, which in turn will speed your access to commands.

Using Keyboard Macros

A keyboard macro is a single keystroke entry that automatically enters a command or a series of commands and responses. For example, you could have a keyboard macro that enters the AutoCAD Line command. You might assign the F5 key to this macro, so that whenever you want to draw a line you just press F5. You

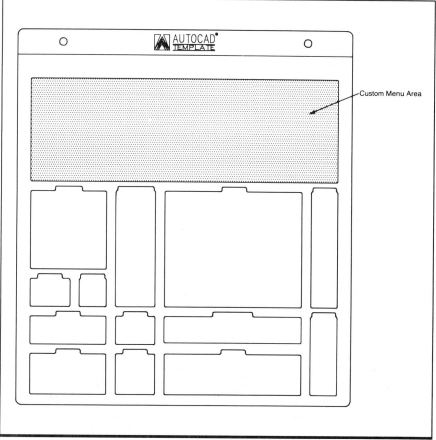

Figure 17.1: *The tablet's custom menu area*

could even assign a string of commands to F5, so that you could enter them at the press of a single key. Keyboard macros are perhaps the single most effective way of improving drawing input speed. Even if you are not a touch typist, once you become familiar with the locations of keys you have defined as macros, you can enter commands nearly as fast as you can think of them.

You can create AutoCAD keyboard macros with the DOS ANSI-.SYS device driver, with AutoLISP, or with a commercially available keyboard macro program. This chapter will give you experience in creating macros with ANSI.SYS and AutoLISP. You may later want to invest in a keyboard macro program that will give you more power and flexibility.

Such programs are priced from $50 to $200 retail. Many of them have features that give you flexibility in assigning macros to keys and allow as many macros as there are keys on your keyboard, or more. SmartKey is one commercially available keyboard macro program that works well with AutoCAD. It is capable of redefining each key on your keyboard with seven macro definitions. It also lets you move the locations of Control, Alt, Shift, and other keys.

Another advantage of SmartKey and programs like it is the ability to store several sets of macros that can be loaded and unloaded at any time within any program. They also allow you to create macros on the fly, which is helpful when you find yourself in a situation where you could use a macro but don't have an appropriate one set up. However, with any keyboard macro program, you must be careful to flip the screen to text mode before creating a macro on the fly.

Using ANSI.SYS to Define Your Keys

It is difficult to appreciate the usefulness of macros until you try working with them. You can create macros on your own with the help of a DOS file called ANSI.SYS. This can give you a feel for what keyboard macros can do for your productivity without your having to purchase a new program.

DOS provides the ANSI.SYS device driver to allow programs to control the display using a standardized system of codes. (ANSI stands for the American National Standards Institute, but few programs actually use this system.) It can be used to control color and highlights on the screen and, as we mentioned, to alter keyboard definitions.

As a keyboard macro program, however, ANSI.SYS is limited compared to the commercially available programs. You cannot easily change your keyboard definitions, and the number and size of the macros you can create is limited to roughly 25, depending on their complexity. This limit is due to the fixed amount of memory the ANSI driver is given when it is installed. The commercial programs allow a much greater number of macros, limited only by the amount of RAM you allocate to the program during its initial setup.

To create a keyboard macro with ANSI.SYS, first go to the DOS root directory and see if you have a file called Config.SYS. If your computer came with AutoCAD already installed, your dealer may have installed this file. If you don't have ANSI.SYS, enter

```
copy con config.SYS
device = ansi.SYS
buffers = 30
files = 24
 ^Z
```

at the DOS prompt.

DOS looks for this Config.SYS file when it starts up. If DOS finds Config.SYS, it reads the file to see if there are any special conditions it should know about before it sets up the computer. By entering the line

```
device = ansi.SYS
```

you tell DOS you want to use the ANSI.SYS device driver. The next two lines

```
buffers = 30
files = 24
```

tell DOS to create a buffer space in RAM for parts of files that are frequently read from disk, and to also make space in RAM to allow 24 files to be open at one time. (These files may be overlay files, drawing files, font files, or any number of program files Auto-CAD needs quick access to while working on a drawing.) These two options are not required, but they can improve hard disk access noticeably, thereby improving AutoCAD's performance.

Once you have done this, copy the ANSI.SYS file from your DOS disks to your DOS root directory. If you don't know how to copy files, look in Appendix C of this book or your DOS manual for instructions on using the COPY command.

If you already have a Config.SYS file, use your word processor or the DOS line editor, EDLIN, to open Config.SYS as an ASCII file or DOS text file. Then add the line

device = ansi.SYS

to the end of the file.

Next create a file called Macros.BAT with the contents

```
prompt $e[0;60;"inter";13p
prompt $e[0;61;"endp";13p
prompt $e[0;62;"mid";13p
prompt $e[0;63;"cen";13p
prompt $e[0;64;"per";13p
prompt $e[0;65;3;"line";13p
prompt $e[0;66;3;"arc";13p
prompt $e[0;67;3;"list";13p
prompt $e[0;68;3;"dist";13p
prompt $e[0;84;3;"fillet";13p
prompt $e[0;85;3;"change";13p
prompt $e[0;86;3;"move";13p
prompt $e[0;87;3;"copy";13p
prompt $e[0;88;3;"mirror";13p
prompt $e[0;89;3;"break";13p
prompt $e[0;90;"'redraw";13p
prompt $e[0;91;3;"erase";13p
prompt $e[0;92;"'pan";13p
prompt $e[0;93;"'zoom";13p
prompt $e[0;115;"<180";13p
prompt $e[0;116;"<0";13p
prompt $e[0;117;60p
prompt $e[0;118;"<270";13p
prompt $e[0;119;64p
prompt $e[0;132;"<90";13p
prompt $p$g
```

This file contains the codes that tell the ANSI device driver which keys to redefine and how to redefine them. Macros.BAT will be displayed on the monitor when its name is entered at the DOS prompt. The ANSI.SYS driver will read information displayed to the monitor. The text

prompt $e

tells the ANSI.SYS driver that the text that follows is code intended for the driver.

The left bracket along with the following number tells ANSI.SYS that it is to redefine a key. The number is a code representing a specific key to be redefined (see Table 17.1). The next group of letters tells ANSI.SYS the new definition for that key. If it is a string of text, it is enclosed by double quotes.

For example, the first line in the Macros.BAT file is

prompt $e[0;60;"inter";13p

This definition causes the Intersect Osnap override to be issued whenever the F2 key is pressed. The code 0;60 represents the F2 key. The semicolon that follows the 60 separates the old and new key codes. This is followed by

"inter"

This text tells ANSI.SYS that whenever the F2 key is depressed, the word inter is to be entered. The next semicolon tells ANSI.SYS that additional codes follow that are included in the definition. 13 represents the Return key; a Return is entered following the text "inter". Finally, the

p

tells ANSI.SYS that this is the end of this key definition.

To replace the letter or symbol a key represents with a different letter or symbol, you follow the code representing the key to redefine with the code representing the new letter or symbol. For example, the third from the last line in the Macros.BAT file is

prompt $e[0;119;64p

This definition causes the at sign to be entered whenever the Control-Home key combination is depressed. The 0;119 is the code for that key combination. The number 64 is the code for the at sign. Again, the p tells ANSI.SYS that this is the end of this key definition.

You may notice that some of the key definitions in the Macros.BAT file contain the number code 3, as in the sixth line from the top

prompt $e[0;65;3;"line";13p

This line redefines the F7 key to issue a Control-C, then start the Line command. The code 0;65 represents the F7 key, and the 3 represents the Control-C key combination. As you enter commands in AutoCAD, you may decide to issue a command while you are in the middle of another command. To do this normally, you have to cancel the current command by pressing Control-C. By including the Control-C character in your macro, you can start the command

Code Value	Key or Character
1	^ A
2	^ B (AutoCAD snap mode toggle)
3	^ C (AutoCAD Cancel command)
4	^ D (AutoCAD coordinate readout toggle)
5	^ E (AutoCAD isoplane toggle)
6	^ F
7	^ G (beep or AutoCAD grid mode toggle)
8	^ H (Backspace)
9	^ I (Tab)
10	^ J (Line Feed)
11	^ K (Home)
12	^ L (Form Feed)
13	^ M (Return)
14	^ N through ^ Z
15	^ O (AutoCAD ortho mode toggle)
16	^ P
17	^ Q (AutoCAD printer echo toggle)
18	^ R
19	^ S
20	^ T (AutoCAD tablet mode toggle)
21	^ U
22	^ V
23	^ W
24	^ X (AutoCAD Delete command line)

Table 17.1:   *The ANSI codes and their meanings*

Code Value	Key or Character
25	^ Y
26	^ Z
27	^ [(Escape)
28	^ \ (cursor right)
29	^] (cursor left)
30	^ ^ (cursor up)
31	^ _ (cursor down)
32	(space bar)
33	!
34	"
35	#
36	$
37	%
38	&
39	'
40	(
41	)
42	*
43	+
44	,
45	-
46	.
47	/
48 through 57	0 through 9

Table 17.1: *The ANSI codes and their meanings (cont.)*

Code Value	Key or Character
58	:
59	;
60	<
61	=
62	>
63	?
64	@
65 through 90	Uppercase A through uppercase Z
91	[
92	\
93	]
94	^
95	_
96	'
97 through 122	Lowercase a through lowercase z
123	{
124	¦
125	}
126	~

Extended Codes (codes that begin with 0;)

0;15	(Shift-Tab)
0;16 through 0;25	Alt-Q, W, E, R, T, Y, U, I, O, P
0;30 through 0;38	Alt-A, S, D, F, G, H, J, K, L

Table 17.1:   *The ANSI codes and their meanings (cont.)*

Extended Codes (codes that begin with 0;)

0;44	through 0;50	Alt-Z, X, C, V, B, N, M
0;59	through 0;68	Function keys F1 through F10
0;71		Home
0;72		(cursor up)
0;73		Page Up
0;75		(cursor left)
0;77		(cursor right)
0;79		End
0;80		(cursor down)
0;81		Page Down
0;82		Insert
0;83		Delete
0;84	through 0;93	Shift-F1 through Shift-F10
0;94	through 0;103	Ctrl-F1 through Ctrl-F10
0;104	through 0;113	Alt-F1 through Alt-F10
0;114		Control-Print Screen
0;115		(previous word)
0;116		(next word)
0;117		Control-End
0;118		Control-Page Down
0;119		Control-Home
0;120	through 0;131	Alt-1, 2, 3, 4, 5, 6, 7, 8, 9, -, =
0;132		Control-Page Up

Table 17.1:   The ANSI codes and their meanings (cont.)

associated with the macro while in another command without entering Control-C. If the command associated with the macro is a transparent command, you must include the apostrophe in the macro instead of the 3.

Now reboot your computer by pressing the Control, Alt, and Delete keys simultaneously. This is necessary because, as we mentioned earlier, DOS reads the Config.SYS file when the computer first starts up. Since you just created the Config.SYS file, DOS has not had a chance to read it and load the ANSI.SYS driver.

Once you see the DOS prompt, enter Macros. The list will display on the screen and once it is done, your function keys and some of your cursor keys will be redefined as shown in Figure 17.2.

Now try drawing Figure 17.3 using the function keys to start commands and the Alt-cursor keys to specify distances. It may take a little practice to get used to the key locations, but once you have memorized the key meanings, you will find that your input time is greatly reduced.

If you like, use Table 17.1 to create some definitions of your own by modifying the Macros.BAT file. Remember that there are three components to each definition: the prompt $e that gets the ANSI.SYS driver's attention, the code representing the key you wish to define, and the key definition ending with a p.

If you want to return your keys to their original definitions, create a file called Nokeys.BAT with the contents

```
prompt $e[0;60;0;60p
prompt $e[0;61;0;61p
prompt $e[0;62;0;62p
prompt $e[0;63;0;63p
prompt $e[0;64;0;64p
prompt $e[0;65;0;65p
prompt $e[0;66;0;66p
prompt $e[0;67;0;67p
prompt $e[0;68;0;68p
prompt $e[0;84;0;84p
prompt $e[0;85;0;85p
prompt $e[0;86;0;86p
prompt $e[0;87;0;87p
prompt $e[0;88;0;88p
prompt $e[0;89;0;89p
prompt $e[0;90;0;90p
prompt $e[0;91;0;91p
```

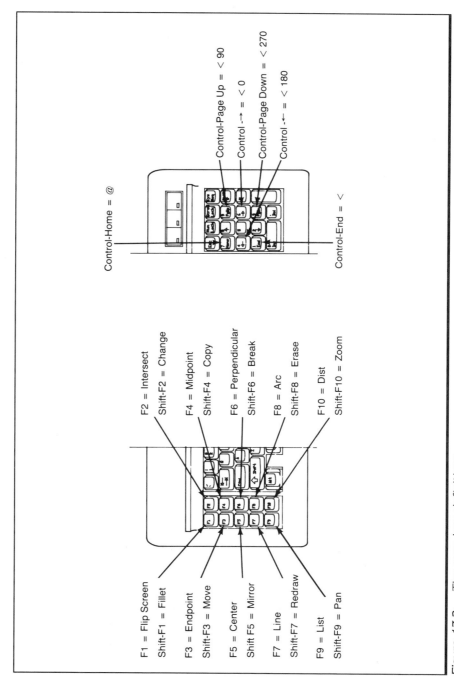

Figure 17.2: The new key definitions

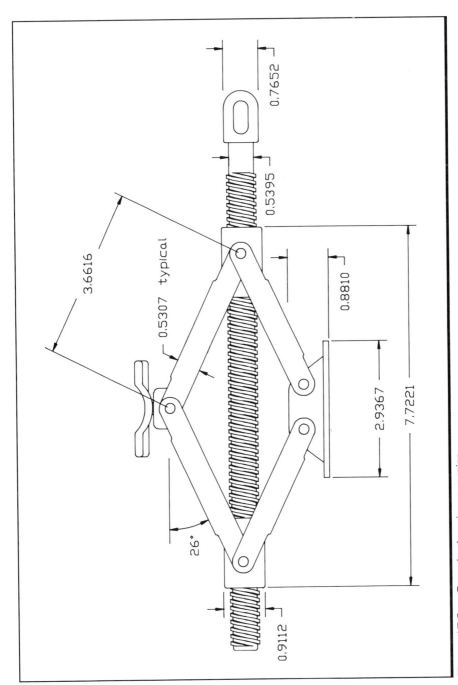

Figure 17.3: Sample drawing exercise

```
prompt $e[0;92;0;92p
prompt $e[0;93;0;93p
prompt $e[0;115;0;115p
prompt $e[0;116;0;116p
prompt $e[0;117;0;117p
prompt $e[0;118;0;118p
prompt $e[0;119;0;119p
prompt $e[0;132;0;132p
prompt $p$g
```

In this file, you are simply telling ANSI.SYS to give each key its original definition. Notice how the first code representing the key is followed by the same code. Once you have created this file, enter Nokeys. The keys will return to their previous definitions.

If you find you do not want the ANSI.SYS driver installed, delete the line

device = ansi.SYS

from the Config.SYS file.

Creating Keyboard Macros with AutoLISP

You can use the AutoLISP programming language to create macros. Unlike most keyboard macros, the macros you create using AutoLISP must be started by pressing Return after you press the key associated with the macro. This is a drawback because you cannot use macros as input to AutoCAD commands like the Osnap overrides. Also, the number of macros is limited by the amount of memory AutoCAD allocates to AutoLISP functions. AutoLISP macros can greatly reduce the amount of keyboard entry necessary to start commands, however.

An advantage of using AutoLISP to create macros is that you can create them any time you like while you are in AutoCAD. You could create macros while in AutoCAD using AutoCAD's Shell command to access ANSI.SYS, but this would be a cumbersome way to redefine your keys. You would have to memorize the complex codes ANSI.SYS requires, or at least keep a copy of Table 17.1 around.

The other advantage to using AutoLISP is that you can set up a sequence of keys to start a certain macro, rather than being limited to a single key. For example, you can create a macro that starts the Change command with the entry of the letters CH.

Appendix D contains a sample AutoLISP program called Macro.LSP that allows you to create macros while in AutoCAD. You can copy it into your computer as an ASCII file and load it into AutoCAD by placing the file in your AutoCAD directory and entering

(load "macro.lsp")

at the AutoCAD command prompt. After the program is loaded, enter

macro

and follow the prompts. See Appendix D for full details on this program.

Another AutoLISP program in Appendix D, Keycad.LSP, contains a number of AutoCAD commands abbreviated to simple two-keystroke macros. To use it, copy it into your computer as an ASCII file and load it into AutoCAD by placing the file in your AutoCAD directory and entering

(load "keycad")

at the AutoCAD command prompt. Once it is loaded, you can use the abbreviated versions of the commands as described in Appendix D.

Through the combined use of the ANSI.SYS driver and the Auto-LISP macro program, you can customize your system to your particular needs. But for flexibility and convenience, you may want to try one of the commercially available keyboard macro programs.

SWITCHING RAPIDLY BETWEEN PROGRAMS

At times you will want to switch frequently from one program to another. This can become bothersome, especially if the programs are large. You can speed up this process by using a special program that allows you to run more than one other program at a time. AutoCAD will work with two such commercially available programs, DesqView and Software Carousel.

DesqView is a multitasking program for DOS. This means that you can have two or more programs running simultaneously. Some speed degradation is noticeable, however, when two programs are running at the same time. This program also places limitations on the amount of memory available to AutoCAD. In some cases, you may not be able to use AutoLISP with DesqView.

Software Carousel, on the other hand, allows you to start several programs, then switch between them rapidly. With Carousel, only one program is actually running at a time; the others are suspended. Carousel works much like the popular terminate and stay resident programs. Unlike DesqView, no speed degradation occurs when more than one program is open.

If you find yourself having to jump in and out of large programs frequently, you may want to purchase DesqView or Software Carousel.

ENHANCING SPEED WITH HARDWARE

One area that can determine your productivity is the type of computer you have and how it is equipped. AutoCAD places large demands on the PC, and speed can become a real problem. In the following section, we examine some of the factors that affect Auto-CAD's processing speed and what can be done to improve it.

We will look at computer hardware additions that can enhance your computer's speed, such as *clock crystals*, which control the rate at which your computer works, and *accelerator cards*, which are like fast computers on a card. We will also look at the role the math coprocessor plays in enhancing AutoCAD's speed.

Increasing Processing Speed

PCs depend on precise timing to operate properly. A device known as a clock crystal regulates the timing of your PC's main processor and keeps it synchronized with other system components, such as the integrated circuits that make up the RAM and other optional equipment you have installed in your computer. The main processor is an integrated circuit that controls most of your PC's activities. You could think of it as the computer's brain. The speed of this brain is limited to about 4.7 million cycles per second, or 4.7 megahertz in the IBM PC or XT, though many compatibles have eight-megahertz processors. The AT runs at 6 or 8 megahertz depending on the model, though many AT compatible manufacturers offer up to 12-megahertz processors.

Understanding Processors

IBM PC/XTs use a processor called the Intel 8088. This is a 16-bit processor with an 8-bit data bus. What this means in simplified terms is that the processor can process 16 bits of information at once, but can move only 8 bits of information in and out of RAM at a time. This is like having a factory made up of two buildings, one building storing parts while the other assembles them into machines. The assembly building obtains parts from the storage building through a conveyer. The building can assemble 16 parts at a time, but the conveyer that connects the buildings can transport only 8 parts at a time. This factory's ability to produce machines is limited by its conveyer system. In the same way, the 8088 is limited by the amount of data that can be transmitted over an eight-bit data bus (see Figure 17.4).

Another processor, the 8086, is a 16-bit processor with a 16-bit data bus. These processors are found in the IBM model 30 PC and some IBM PC compatibles, such as the AT&T 6300. These computers are noticeably faster than computers equipped with the 8088 processor.

The IBM PC/AT uses an 80286 processor. This is still a 16-bit processor, but its design includes many features that make it faster than either the 8088 or the 8086. It is designed to make use of greater amounts of memory and to offer true multitasking. Computers having the 80286 processor, such as the IBM PC/AT, are the most common among AutoCAD users because of their speed. For example, a drawing that takes 32 seconds to regenerate on the XT equipped with a math coprocessor takes 17 seconds on an eight-megahertz AT also equipped with a math coprocessor. It is interesting to note, however, that this same drawing takes only a fraction of a second more on a computer equipped with the eight-megahertz 8086 processor with a math coprocessor installed. This is probably due to the differences in the way math coprocessors work. We will discuss these differences later in this chapter.

Most recently, computers using the new Intel 80386 processor are appearing. These are 32-bit processors capable of operating at 16 to 25 megahertz. Potentially, these processors can be four times faster than the 80286 running at eight megahertz, since they can process twice as much information at twice the speed. At these higher speeds, however, the memory access speed becomes a constraint.

The currently available PC-DOS does not use the 80286 and 80386 processors to their fullest potential. Like the 80286, the 80386 is capable of managing large amounts of memory and of multitasking, but PC-DOS does not support these features. Also, many of the fast AT compatibles have processing speeds close to those of the 80386-equipped computers. For example, the drawing that took 19 seconds to regenerate on the standard AT can take as little as half the time, or 7 seconds, on some 10- or 12-megahertz AT compatibles. This similarity in speed is partly due to the limited speed of RAM.

Understanding Memory Speed

The speed of your system's memory access can influence overall processing speed. Your computer's main processor constantly accesses RAM while it works, so if RAM cannot keep up with the processor, *wait states* must be employed. A wait state can be loosely described as a way of synchronizing a processor with RAM. When a processor can process data faster than RAM can manage it, wait states must be inserted.

The standard AT operates using one wait state. Some AT compatibles provide RAM fast enough to keep up with the processor, thereby eliminating the need for wait states. The integrated circuits

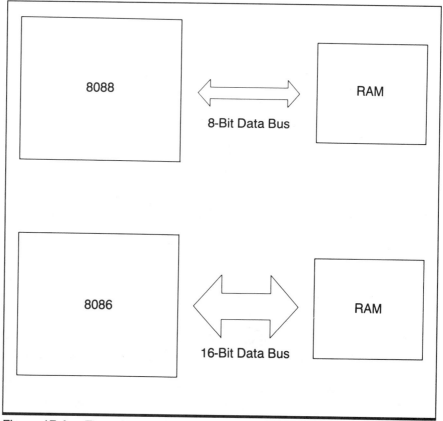

Figure 17.4: *The difference between the 8088 and the 8086*

that make up the RAM in these fast computers are rated at a higher speed than the most commonly used RAM-integrated circuits. This can result in faster processing, but it also means higher cost because these RAM *chips*, as they are frequently called, are more expensive. An AT compatible computer with zero wait states running at eight megahertz can regenerate the previously mentioned drawing in about 14 seconds. Wait states are not an issue with the PC/XT or 8086-based computers, as their processors are not fast enough to require wait states.

As processors operate at faster speeds, the speed of these RAM chips becomes more of a constraint. The 80386 processor is especially bound by memory access speed because it can access RAM twice as fast as the 80286 processor. The 80286 is already reaching the speed limit of the less expensive RAM chips.

Understanding the Math Coprocessor

We mentioned in Chapter 1 that the math coprocessor is essential if you are using version 9 of AutoCAD or want to do large, complex drawings in version 2.5 or 2.6. The math coprocessor shares information processing with the main processor by taking care of floating-point calculations. Math coprocessors made by Intel are designated as 8087, 80287, and 80387. The 8087 is used with the 8088- and 8086-based computers, such as the IBM PC/XT and compatibles, while the 80287 is used with the 80286-based computers, like the IBM PC/AT, the IBM model 50, and some 80386-based computers. An 80387 is used strictly with the 80386-based computers. This section describes the effect of these coprocessors on AutoCAD's speed.

A drawing that takes 150 seconds to regenerate on an 8088-based computer without an 8087 will take 32 seconds with one installed. A similar speed gain can be accomplished on an 8086-based computer. In the PC/XT and other 8088- or 8086-based computers, the main processor and the math coprocessor are controlled by the same timing crystal. If you have a PC/XT that runs at 4.7 megahertz, you need a coprocessor that is rated for 4.7 megahertz. You could install one that is rated for a higher clock speed, but your processing speed won't improve.

On an 80286-based computer, the speed increase is less dramatic. Generally, the speed improvement of math-intensive programs, such as AutoCAD, on the 80286 is at best one-third that of the 8088 or 8086. This is because of the differences in the way the 80286 and the 8088 operate. A thorough discussion of these differences is beyond the scope of this book. In very general terms, however, the

8088 and 8086 can access data from RAM independently from the 8087, while the 80286 controls some of the 80287's data access (see Figure 17.5). This difference in design contributes in part to the smaller 80287 performance increase. Also, the 80286 offers some degree of 80287 emulation already.

But unlike the 8087, the 80287 coprocessor speed can be controlled by a separate clock crystal. In the PC/AT you can potentially have a math coprocessor that operates at a faster or slower rate than the main processor. In fact, the normal 80287 operating speed is two-thirds that of the 80286. Because AutoCAD makes use of both types of processors, you can improve its regeneration speed by increasing the speed of either or both processors. Several manufacturers currently produce devices that allow you to do just that.

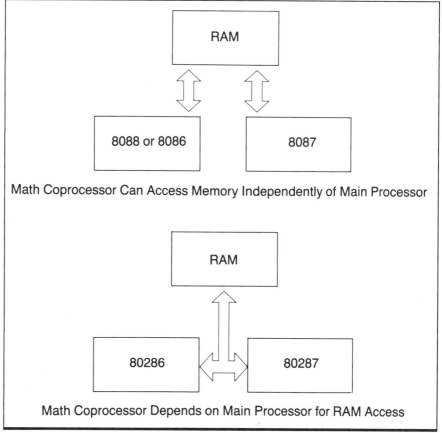

Figure 17.5:   The difference between the 8087 and the 80287

We will look at these devices later in this chapter.

So, as a rule, the most dramatic speed improvements using Auto-CAD on an IBM PC/XT or compatible can be gained by installing a math coprocessor. The PC/AT shows less, though still noticeable, speed improvement.

Using Accelerators

There are other devices besides the math coprocessor that will improve the performance of your PC. These devices are often referred to as *accelerators*, and they consist of a fast micropro-cessor, or a fast clock crystal, or some combination of the two. Accelerators come in many sizes, shapes, and prices. The majority of them are aimed at the PC/XT and compatibles, but they are also available for the AT.

Using Accelerators with the PC/XT

Accelerators offer a way for the PC/XT to approach or exceed the speed of the PC/AT and extend its life without the expense of buying a new computer. Accelerators can be loosely classified into three categories: the *computer-on-a-board* type of accelerator, the *caching* accelerator, and the *clock-crystal* accelerator. A fourth option is also available to XT users, and that is replacing your com-puter's motherboard with an 80286 or 80386 motherboard. This section describes each type of accelerator and how they compare when using AutoCAD.

Nearly all accelerators plug into an *expansion slot* in your computer. The expansion slot is a place where you can install optional equipment, such as a modem, additional printer and serial ports, and additional RAM. Your display adapter, for example, plugs into one of these slots. The slots are located inside your computer and you must remove the computer casing to access them (see Figure 17.6).

The largest and most expensive type of accelerator is like a com-puter on a board that fits into one of the expansion slots, or even two slots. These accelerator boards contain not only a faster pro-cessor, but 640K or more of RAM to go with it. They contain their own RAM because they can access it much faster than the mem-ory of the main system. Some of these accelerators require that you remove your current processor and replace it with a cable con-nected to the accelerator.

If you want the greatest possible speed improvement, this is the type of accelerator to choose. Some can make your PC/XT faster

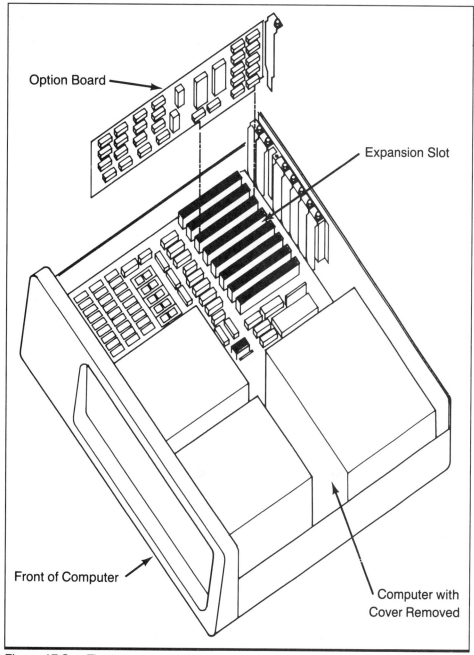

Figure 17.6: The expansion slots

than a standard PC/AT. However, they often won't work with all your software at their fastest speeds. For this reason, they usually offer different speed settings to allow you to run programs that are sensitive to the speed of your computer. They also do not work properly in some PC compatibles.

You can find everything from the 8086 to the 80386 processor on these full-board accelerators, and most of them will accept math coprocessors. Generally, the 8086 accelerators offer the best compatibility with most software in combination with a substantial improvement in AutoCAD's speed. You can expect performance equivalent to an 8-megahertz AT while using AutoCAD with a 10-megahertz 8086 accelerator, for example. A sample drawing that takes 32 seconds to regenerate on an XT with a math coprocessor takes 13 seconds on an XT equipped with an 8086 accelerator running at 10 megahertz. A six-megahertz AT with a standard math coprocessor regenerates the same drawing in 19 seconds.

You can pay anywhere from $500 for an 8086-based accelerator to as much as $2,500 for some of the 80386-based accelerators. Add another $200 for a math coprocessor to go with the 8086, or $500 for a coprocessor to go with the 80386.

Another type of accelerator is the caching accelerator. These boards have a faster processor, but they don't contain a large amount of RAM. Instead, they use a small amount of memory for what is called *caching*. Caching is a process where parts of a program's code are temporarily stored in a small amount of very fast memory to which the main processor has direct access. The frequency of access determines which code is placed in this cache. The theory is that 10 percent of a program's code is used 80 percent of the time. Therefore, the processor only needs quick access to that 10 percent. The rest can be kept in slower memory without severe speed degradation.

Caching accelerators are generally less expensive than those with their own RAM, but they will not match the speeds of the full-board accelerators. They also come in clock speeds varying from 8 to 12 megahertz. Nearly all these boards use the 80286 processor and come with a socket for the math coprocessor. Our sample drawing will regenerate in 14 to 20 seconds using a caching accelerator with a math coprocessor, depending on the clock speed of the accelerator.

Clock-crystal accelerators modify the PC's main board by replacing the components that control the timing of your system. These are by far the least expensive and can provide the most speed improvement per dollar spent, especially if you want to improve the speed of math-intensive programs such as AutoCAD. Their prices range from $100 to $250.

For the PC/XT, these devices usually use a faster version of the same processor that is currently in the PC/XT; special circuitry allows this processor to operate at its fastest rate. The main limitation of this type of accelerator is the speed of your PC's current memory. Since most clock-crystal accelerators can also speed up the math coprocessor, you can expect to increase AutoCAD's regeneration speeds by as much as 31 percent. Our sample drawing will regenerate in 22 seconds on an XT equipped with a math coprocessor and one of these accelerators. Bear in mind, however, that you will have to purchase a math coprocessor capable of these higher speeds. Also, a clock-crystal accelerator won't improve the speed of the so-called Turbo-XT compatibles, since these compatibles already operate at a faster speed.

Finally, there are replacement motherboards for the PC/XT and compatibles, which contain the 80286 processor running at 10 megahertz and using zero wait states. The motherboard is the main circuit board in your computer system. It contains the main processor, RAM, and all the support circuits. By replacing the motherboard, you are essentially replacing your computer (see Figure 17.7).

These replacement motherboards can cost as little as $400 and can regenerate our sample drawing in seven seconds. You must still add the cost of RAM chips and a math coprocessor, which will boost the price by another $500. 80386 motherboards are also available, but are more costly at around $1,600, not including the math coprocessor. If you are willing to take your current computer apart and install one of these boards, however, you can have a system that is two to three times as fast as a standard 80286-based computer.

Many factors that influence the effectiveness of these accelerators are too complex for discussion here, so we aren't too detailed in our descriptions. You should be aware that these accelerators vary in installation difficulty, and they can affect compatibility between your computer and other software and hardware. If you decide you want to use an accelerator, you can get fairly detailed reviews of them in the PC-oriented magazines such as *CADalyst*, *Byte*, *PC World*, and *PC Tech Journal*.

Using Accelerators with the PC/AT

There are also accelerators available for the PC/AT. These are usually just faster clock crystals that increase the rate at which the main processor operates. Some accelerators increase only the speed of the

MASTERING AUTOCAD

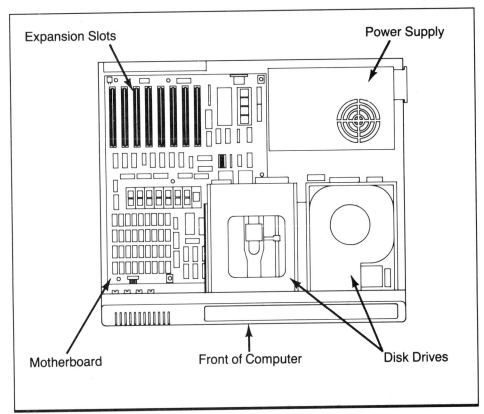

Figure 17.7: The insides of an XT-type computer

math coprocessor while maintaining the stock speed of the main processor. These types of accelerators can provide noticeable speed
improvements at a modest price and are worth consideration. You
will get the best improvements by increasing the clock speed of the
80286, while increasing the speed of the 80287 has less effect.

Board-type accelerators and replacement motherboards that contain
the 80386 processor running at 16 or 20 megahertz are also available
for the PC/AT. These are the most expensive accelerators available, so
you should carefully consider whether you really need one.

Ensuring OS/2 Compatibility

If you are thinking of using the new OS/2 operating system in the
future, be sure your accelerator board or replacement motherboard
will work with it. Only a few accelerator boards are rated to work
with OS/2. Boards using 8086 processors or accelerators that

increase the clock rate of 8088 processors are not compatible with OS/2. Most replacement motherboards that use the 80286 and 80386 processors are compatible, but be sure the manufacturer backs its compatibility claims.

Speeding Up RAM

When a drawing becomes too big to fit into RAM, AutoCAD makes room by storing infrequently used parts of it on the hard disk. This is called *memory paging*, and it allows AutoCAD to be free of any RAM limitations on drawing size. Unfortunately, this process slows AutoCAD down because the hard disk is considerably slower than RAM. You can improve paging speed by using expanded memory, extended memory, or a *RAM disk*.

Using Expanded and Extended Memory

Normally, DOS allows a maximum of 640K for RAM. Some programs, like AutoCAD, are capable of using up this memory rapidly. Expanded and extended memory allow AutoCAD to use up to eight megabytes of RAM for quick-access storage space, rather than paging to the hard disk (see Figure 17.8). This enables you to edit complex drawings more quickly. For example, on an XT, a drawing that normally takes 160 seconds to regenerate can take 120 seconds using expanded memory.

Expanded and extended memory differ in the ways they are accessed by the main processor. We won't try to explain the details. Just be aware that both these types of memory accomplish the same thing as far as AutoCAD is concerned: they offer page space that is faster than the hard disk. In the case of the AT and its compatibles, this RAM page space offers less improvement than for the XT. This is because the AT has a faster hard disk, which approaches the speed of RAM memory used as extended memory. The XT, on the other hand, has a slow hard disk, especially when compared to the speed of expanded memory.

To use expanded or extended memory, you must install a memory board, plus any software it requires. This memory board must conform to the *Lotus/Intel/Microsoft* memory specification. After that, you don't have to do anything special; AutoCAD automatically detects the board's presence and makes use of it.

MASTERING AUTOCAD

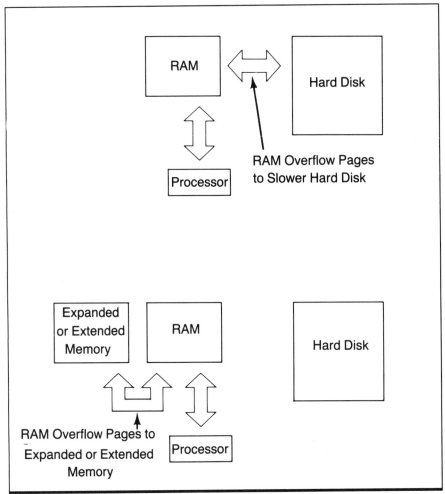

Figure 17.8: *How expanded or extended memory allows faster paging of large files*

Using a RAM Disk

You can accomplish a similar speed gain by using a RAM disk. A RAM disk is like a disk drive, except that it is in the form of RAM. Files can be stored on a RAM disk just like any other disk drive. A RAM disk offers very fast access compared to a hard disk.

Most RAM disks are installed through the use of special software and they often use some of the 640K system memory. This software usually comes with memory expansion boards that are designed to bring your system's RAM capacity up to 640K. However, there are memory boards that allow you to have RAM disks above the 640K limit. They can offer as much as eight megabytes of RAM disk space. These memory boards should not be confused with those that conform to the Lotus/Intel/Microsoft standard.

AutoCAD offers a way to use a RAM disk as page space, just as it uses expanded or extended memory. This option is offered for those users who have memory expansion boards that allow the creation of RAM disks but do not conform to the Lotus/Intel/Microsoft standard. The following is a description of how you can set up AutoCAD to use a RAM disk for page space.

Start AutoCAD in the normal way. When you get the Main menu, enter 5 to select the Configure AutoCAD option. You will get a screen showing your current hardware configuration. Press Return. Next you get the Configuration menu shown in Figure 17.9. Enter 8 to select the Configure Operating Parameters option. You will get the Operation Parameter menu shown in Figure 17.10. Enter 5 to select the Placement of Temporary Files option. You get the prompt

Enter directory name for temporary files, or DRAWING to
place them in the same directory as the drawing being edited.
<DRAWING>:

At this prompt enter the drive specification for your RAM drive (it will be given in the drive's installation instructions), followed by a colon. Be sure to add the colon or AutoCAD will not recognize the drive.

You will be returned to the Operation Parameter menu. Exit this menu and the Configuration menu by entering 0 twice. You will see the prompt

If you answer N to the following question, all configuration
changes you have just made will be discarded.
Keep configuration changes? <Y>

Press Return to accept the default, Y for yes. You will be returned to the Main menu. Now, whenever you work on a large file, you should notice less hard disk activity.

CHANGING A DISPLAY SYSTEM FOR PRODUCTIVITY

There are many ways a display system can influence your productivity. We briefly mentioned some of these in Chapter 1, such as the

```
                    A U T O C A D
        Copyright (C) 1982,83,84,85,86,87 Autodesk, Inc.
        Release 9.0 (9/17/87) IBM PC
        Advanced Drafting Extensions 3
        Serial Number:  10-113610

        Configuration menu

           0.   Exit to Main Menu
           1.   Show current configuration
           2.   Allow I/O port configuration

           3.   Configure video display
           4.   Configure digitizer
           5.   Configure plotter
           6.   Configure printer plotter
           7.   Configure system console
           8.   Configure operating parameters

        Enter selection <0>:
```

Figure 17.9:   *The Configuration menu*

```
                    A U T O C A D
        Copyright (C) 1982,83,84,85,86,87 Autodesk, Inc.
        Release 9.0 (9/17/87) IBM PC
        Advanced Drafting Extensions 3
        Serial Number:  10-113610

        Operating parameter menu

           0.   Exit to configuration menu
           1.   Alarm on error
           2.   Initial drawing setup
           3.   Default plot file name
           4.   Plot spooler directory
           5.   Placement of temporary files
           6.   Network node name
           7.   AutoLISP feature

        Enter selection <0>:
```

Figure 17.10:   *The Operation Parameter menu*

resolution of the display and its clarity and sharpness. In the following section we look at some of the special features available in display systems and how they affect your use of AutoCAD.

Deciding on Resolution

The resolution of your display can have the greatest influence on your ability to work quickly. The popular IBM Enhanced Graphics Adapter is capable of a 640 x 350-pixel resolution. As we mentioned in Chapter 1, this is barely adequate for most serious AutoCAD applications. Higher resolutions offer not only better detail, but less jagged lines. For example, the resolution of 640 x 480 offered by the IBM Professional Graphics Adapter and the IBM Personal System/2 computers is closer to the height-to-width ratio of most monitors, and therefore gives a smoother-looking line or circle. This is important because a better screen representation helps you create a more accurate drawing. Also, resolution is often only as good as the lowest of the two values given for vertical and horizontal pixels.

A higher resolution also reduces the number of times you have to perform pans and zooms, since more information can be displayed on the screen at one time. A display system with a resolution of 800 x 600 enables you to accurately see nearly double the area you can see with the EGA adapter. In fact, many EGA-compatible boards offer 800 x 600 resolution as an added feature. Even though these higher-resolution display systems cost more, in the long run they can save you money in time spent panning and zooming. Figure 17.11 gives you an idea of the different resolutions and how they compare.

Using Hardware to Pan and Zoom

Some display systems offer what is called *hardware panning and zooming*. This is a way of accomplishing instantaneous pans and zooms by storing a large part of the drawing display in memory separate from RAM used by the main processor. Because this memory is dedicated for use by the display, it is often called *display memory*. (This shouldn't be confused with AutoCAD's drawing database.) For example, the Graph Ax 20/20 made by ACS, Inc., and the BNW model 10 made by BNW, Inc., are capable of storing the equivalent of 2,000 x 2,000 pixels in display memory. By storing this large amount of display information, they can show all or part of your drawing in varying amounts of detail, instantaneously (see Figure 17.12). You can view all of the display memory at one time or

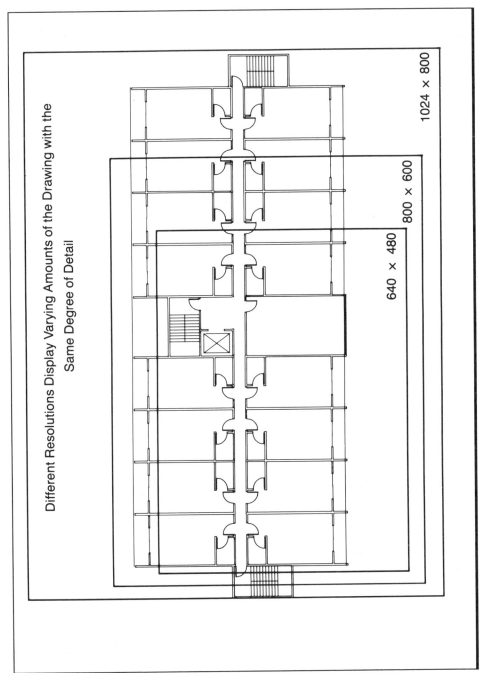

Different Resolutions Display Varying Amounts of the Drawing with the
Same Degree of Detail

1024 × 800

800 × 600

640 × 480

Figure 17.11: Areas represented by various display resolutions

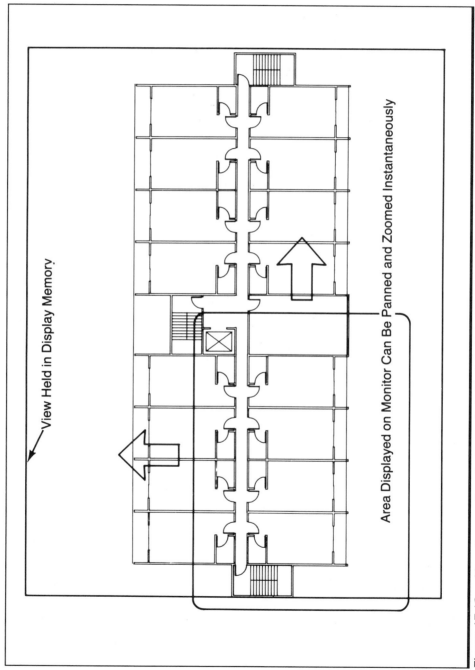

View Held in Display Memory.

Area Displayed on Monitor Can Be Panned and Zoomed Instantaneously

Figure 17.12:   How the monitor displays a "window" to the display memory using hardware panning and zooming

part of it without ever having to issue an AutoCAD Pan or Zoom command, which forces a redraw or regeneration.

Not all displays offering hardware panning and zooming are capable of storing 2,000 × 2,000 pixels. Most offer around 1,024 × 800. As a rule, the fewer pixels the display adapter can store, the less helpful magnification it is capable of when performing a hardware zoom. We say "helpful" because although nearly all high-resolution displays offering hardware zooming give you as many as 16 levels of magnification, after two or three magnifications the pixels begin to fatten noticeably rather than showing you more detail. This fattening of pixels is often called *pixel multiplication*. Pixel multiplication causes the lines of your drawing to appear thicker as you magnify your image. As you continue to magnify the image, the pixel elements also magnify.

Some display adapters store the drawing in what is called a *display list*. This is different from storing pixels because display memory actually stores a list of vectors that compose the displayed image. A display list is very much like the virtual screen (discussed in Chapter 7), where the drawing vectors are held in integer format. Hardware pans and zooms are like very fast redraws in a display using this technique. *Display list processors*, as they are called, have the added feature of allowing greater zoom magnifications without pixel multiplication.

The chief drawback of these adapters is they tend to be very slow when you issue a Regen or Redraw command through Auto-CAD. They can be twice as slow as a system without display list processing. This is a problem because you will inevitably have to perform regenerations in the course of your work. These adapters are also limited in the complexity of the drawings they can display. A very complex drawing may not be completely displayed, due to the adapter's memory limits. Some display systems that use display list processing use expanded or extended memory to resolve this memory limitation.

If your work involves large, complex drawings, you may want to consider a display with around 800 × 600 resolution, and you may even want the hardware panning and zooming feature. The cost of a monitor and display adapter combination with these features is approximately $1,700 to $6,000. Because of the complex nature of these hardware features, it is best to get a thorough demonstration before you make a purchase. You may want to test a sample AutoCAD file on the display you are considering. Also note the environment in which it is being demonstrated. A display system that looks good in a darkened room may look terrible in normal office lighting. Keep in mind that you will be looking at this monitor for hours at a time, so you will want to avoid a system that tends to give you eyestrain.

DRAWING IN COMFORT

Perhaps the most overlooked productivity factor is the computer operator's comfort. Too many times, the computer is placed in a makeshift workstation with no consideration at all for the user. But the computer system is only as good as the person operating it. This is especially true of complex programs like AutoCAD. If you, the operator, are not reasonably comfortable while using your computer, it won't matter how fast your computer is or how well you know the program. A poor workstation setup can cause eyestrain, headaches, backaches, and fatigue, which all lead to lack of concentration. It can mean frequent trips to the coffee machine or walks around the office just to relieve tension or discomfort.

Lighting should be arranged so that no glare occurs on the monitor while enough light is available to read drawings and notes. Good ventilation will help keep both the computer and operator happy and alert. A convenient place for hard copies of notes and drawings should be part of the workstation. You might consider using a monitor stand that lifts the monitor off the table surface, freeing space for documents. The keyboard, monitor, and mouse should be placed comfortably, and a comfortable chair is a must.

CONCLUSION

As you spend more time using AutoCAD, you will begin to develop personal preferences for commands and working methods. You may decide you need more speed or an easier way to access commands. We hope this chapter offers some information to aid you in finding the perfect interface with AutoCAD.

At times, you may wonder if there is a way to accomplish a task more easily than just using the standard AutoCAD commands. In the next chapter, we will discuss ways you can customize AutoCAD to your needs. Often a simple menu addition or an AutoLISP function can make a big difference in how easily you create and edit drawings. We can't anticipate your needs, but we can show you some of the possibilities for customizing AutoCAD.

Chapter 18

Customizing AutoCAD

THE MICROCOMPUTER'S ADAPTABILITY may be the biggest factor influencing its popularity. Some microcomputer programs, such as AutoCAD, offer a high degree of flexibility and customization, allowing you to tailor the software to your needs. In this chapter, we will look at ways you can customize AutoCAD to suit your production environment.

LOOKING AT THE MENU STRUCTURE

In Chapter 17, we introduced you to the keyboard macro as a way of aiding command selection. A screen menu is like a macro in that it allows you to create predefined strings of commands and responses. For example, you could create a screen menu item that automatically sets a new angle for the cursor. This might be useful if you find that you frequently need to work at an angle other than 0 and 90 degrees. Or you might create a macro that "remembers" specific coordinates for you. This could be used to store vanishing point locations while drawing 3D perspective views. You can also use the screen menu to provide predetermined responses to command prompts. For example, if you have a list of layer names you use all the time, you could turn that list into a screen menu from which you can pick names rather than entering them from the keyboard.

Modifying the AutoCAD menu or creating your own is the easiest way to customize the program. Before you try this, you should be familiar with the way AutoCAD commands work. To write custom menu files, you must also understand the menu structure. There really isn't much to it. In this section we will explore this structure and show you how to create your own menu. It will be helpful if you have a word processor that can read and write ASCII files, especially if you want to modify the (quite large) default AutoCAD menu. Otherwise you can use DOS's EDLIN program.

We will concentrate on creating on-screen menus, although the digitizing tablet menu and the puck and mouse button definitions can be created and modified by the method described here.

Knowing Which Menu File to Edit

When AutoCAD first opens a drawing file, it looks on the hard disk for a file called Acad.MNX. This file contains the menu you see displayed on the screen. It also contains the information AutoCAD needs to operate the digitizing tablet menu and the commands on the buttons of your puck or mouse.

This Acad.MNX file originates as an ASCII file that contains the menu options in a form that can be easily edited. This ASCII file has the name Acad.MNU; it comes on the disk you get when you send in your registration card. The Acad.MNX file is the *compiled* version of the Acad.MNU file, which means that it is in a form that AutoCAD can load and read quickly. You can make modifications to the Acad.MNU file but not the Acad.MNX file. If you want to customize your menu, you must work on Acad.MNU. If you modify Acad.MNU in any way, AutoCAD will detect this modification and automatically compile Acad.MNU into a new Acad.MNX file when you open a new drawing file. Once the file is compiled, AutoCAD uses only the compiled version.

You can also create other menu files with different names. A menu you create must always have the .MNU extension, however. You load an alternate menu using the Menu command on the Utilities menu. When you load a menu with a name other than Acad, it is compiled and the compiled version is given the file extension .MNX. The next time this new menu is loaded, AutoCAD uses the compiled version. Also, whenever you load an alternate menu while editing a file, AutoCAD remembers the name of the menu you loaded so that when that file is opened again, this alternate menu will be used instead of the Acad menu. AutoCAD will also use the alternate menu if you use the drawing file as a template, as long as you saved the drawing file after loading the menu.

Looking at the Acad.MNU File

The Acad.MNU file is a list of menu items containing the commands related to the items. There are six major menu groups: the *side* menu, the *pull-down* or *pop* menu, the *icons*, the *tablet*, the *buttons*, and the *auxiliary*. Figure 18.1 shows schematically how the file is structured. The side menu group controls the side screen menu, and the tablet menu group controls the tablet menu. The pop menu group controls pull-down menus, and the icon menu group controls the display of icon menus. The button menu group controls the buttons on your mouse or puck. The auxiliary menu group controls optional equipment, such as special keyboards, that we will not cover in this book.

All the menu items in each menu group enter commands individually, but some tablet, pull-down, and button menu items call up side menus to allow you to pick command options from the screen.

File organization is linear: each menu group follows the next, and starts with the group name preceded by three asterisks. Here is the beginning of the Acad.MNU file:

```
***BUTTONS
;
$p1 = *
^ c ^ c
^ B
^ O
^ G
^ D
^ E
^ T
***AUX1
;
$p1 = *
^ C ^ C
^ B
^ O
^ G
^ D
^ E
^ T
```

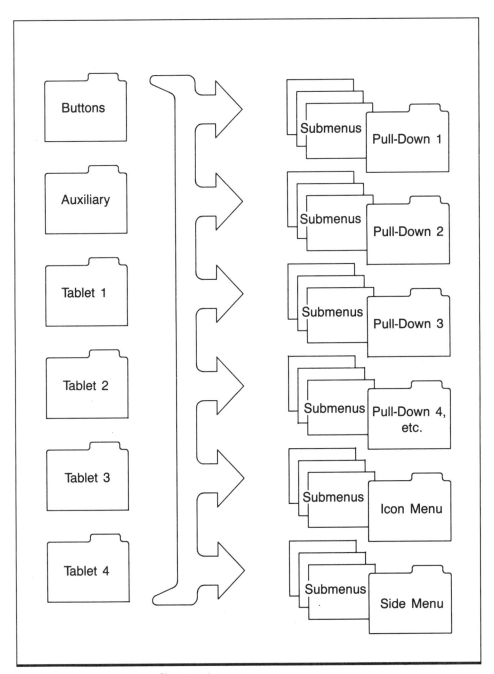

Figure 18.1: The menu file structure

```
***POP1
[Tools]
[OSNAP] ^C^C$p1=  $p1=* OSNAP \
[CENter]CENTER
[ENDpoint]ENDPOINT
[INSert]INSERT
etc.
```

You can see the three groups, Buttons, Aux1, and the beginning of Pop1, in the above sample. Pop1 is the first of seven pull-down menu groups—one group for each pull-down menu. The pull-down, icon, and side menu groups can have submenus, though the Acad.MNU file provided with your program does not make use of submenus in the pull-down group.

The menu groups are set up in similar ways. Side, icon, and pull-down menu options always start with the name of the menu option in brackets. This is done to distinguish the actual word that appears on the screen menu from the rest of the menu instructions. Icon menus start with the name of the slide library and slide in brackets to identify which slide to display for a particular icon menu option. We will discuss these points in detail next.

Understanding the Side Menu

This section shows you how a typical submenu from the screen menu group is put together. In the Acad.MNU file, the Draw submenu looks like

```
**DR 3
[ARC]$S=X $S=ARC
[ATTDEF:]$S=X $S=ATTDEF ^C^CATTDEF
[CIRCLE]$S=X $S=CIRCLE
[DONUT:]$S=X $S=DONUT ^C^CDONUT
[DTEXT:]$S=X $S=DTEXT ^C^CDTEXT
[ELLIPSE:]$S=X $S=ELLIPSE ^C^CELLIPSE
[HATCH:]$S=X $S=HATCH ^C^CHATCH
[INSERT:]$S=X $S=INSERT ^C^CINSERT
[LINE:]$S=X $S=LINE ^C^CLINE
[MINSERT:]$S=X $S=MINSERT ^C^CMINSERT
[OFFSET:]$S=X $S=OFFSET ^C^COFFSET
[PLINE:]$S=X $S=PLINE ^C^CPLINE

[next]$S=DR2
```

Each item on the list starts with a word enclosed in brackets. Each word is an option on the Draw menu. If you were to remove everything else, you would have the Draw menu as it appears on the screen with the exception of the Last, Draw, and Edit options at the bottom (see Figure 18.2).

The text that follows the item in brackets conveys instructions to AutoCAD in the form of a special code. The code

$S =

tells AutoCAD to display another submenu. The word that follows this code is the name of the submenu to be displayed. If you look at the line containing the Offset command, two menus are called for, one named X and another named Offset. The X submenu displays the Last, Draw, and Edit options. The Offset menu displays the rest of the Offset options:

**OFFSET 3
[OFFSET:] ^ C ^ COFFSET

Through
[last];

The submenu name is located at the top of the submenu and it begins with two asterisks. If you look at the top of the Offset submenu, you will see two asterisks followed by the word Offset. A 3

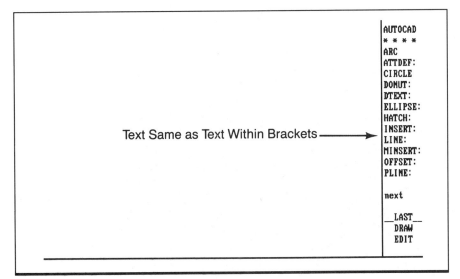

Figure 18.2: *The Draw menu*

follows the word Offset in the menu file. This number tells Auto-CAD to begin displaying the Offset menu on the third line of the menu area. This way, it won't overwrite the two top menu options that help you get around in the menu hierarchy (see Figure 18.2).

Finally, the Offset menu line ends with

^C^COFFSET

The two Control-Cs at the beginning of this text cancel any command that is currently operative. The Offset command follows. This last sequence is written just as it would be entered through the keyboard. Two cancels are issued in case you are in a command that has two levels, such as the Dim command. We should mention that the Control-C is typed into the Acad.MNU file as a carat symbol followed by a C, rather than an actual Control-C key sequence.

You may also notice that there is no space between the second Control-C and the word offset. A space on the menu line indicates a Return, which means that if there were a space between the two, a Return would be entered between the last Control-C and the Offset command.

Another way to indicate a Return is by using the semicolon as in the line

[continue] ^C^CLINE;;

This is how the Continue option appears in the Line menu file. The two semicolons following the word Line tell AutoCAD to start the Line command, then press Return twice to begin a line from the endpoint of the last line entered. AutoCAD automatically issues a Return at the end of a menu line. However, in this case, you want two Returns, so they must be represented as semicolons.

Also, a space must be used after a menu call as in

[DIM:]$S = X $S = DIM ^C^CDIM

where the calls to the X menu and the Dim menu are followed by a space. This is the only case where the space and the semicolon have different meanings; otherwise they are interchangeable.

Another symbol used in the menu file is the backslash. This is used when a pause is required for user input. For example, the Break F option on the tablet menu automatically starts the Break command's F subcommand after you pick an object to be broken. The line from the menu looks like

[BREAK:] ^C^CBREAK \F

The Break command is issued and the object-selection prompt appears. The backslash indicates a pause to allow you to select the object you wish to break. Once you have made your selection, the F is entered starting the First Point option under the Break command.

The length of each line in the menu file is limited to about 79 characters. You can break a line into two or more lines by adding a plus sign at the end of the line that continues, as in

[DR-SYMB] ^ C ^ CINSERT;S-DOOR;\96;;;A;1004;1-1//2;20-min; + wood;hc;CHANGE;LAST;;PROPERTIES;LAYER;NOTES;;

This example inserts the door type symbol you created in Chapter 9 into a drawing and automatically provides predetermined attribute values, then changes the symbol to the Notes layer. Everything is entered just as it would be through the keyboard, with the exception of the backslash used to pause the menu item for input, the plus for the continuation of the menu line to the next line, and the semicolon in place of the Return.

Understanding the Pull-Down Menu

Pull-down menus act in exactly the same way as side menus. Like the side menus, pull-down menus can also contain submenus. There are seven pull-down menu groups currently in the Acad.MNU file, but there may be as many as ten. If you look in your Acad.MNU file, the pull-down menu sections appear as follows:

```
***POP1
[Tools]
[OSNAP] ^ C ^ C$p1 = $p1 = * OSNAP \
[CENter]CENTER
[ENDpoint]ENDPOINT
[INSert]INSERT
[INTersec]INTERSEC
[MIDpoint]MIDPOINT
[NEArest]NEAREST
[NODe]NODE
[PERpend]PERPEND
[QUAdrant]QUADRANT
[QUICK,]QUICK, ^ Z
[TANgent]TANGEN
NONE
[˜ --]
```

```
[Cancel] ^ C ^ C
[U] ^ C ^ CU
[Redo] ^ C ^ CREDO
[Redraw]'REDRAW


***POP2
[Draw]
[Line]* ^ C ^ C$S = X $s = line line
[Arc]* ^ C ^ C$S = X $s = poparc arc
[Circle]* ^ C ^ C$S = X $s = popcircl circle
[Polyline]* ^ C ^ C$S = X $s = pline pline
etc.
```

Notice the three asterisks preceding the menu group names. As we mentioned earlier, the Acad.MNU file that comes with AutoCAD does not use submenus in the pull-down groups. Submenus can be easily added, however, following the same rules used in the side menu group, with the only difference being that you use the $P*n* = code instead of the $S = code to call submenus. The *n* in the $P*n* is the number of the pull-down menu group.

For example, if you want to add a submenu to the Pop1 menu group, you first add a submenu name right after the Pop1 group name. This turns the current single pull-down menu into a submenu of Pop1, which allows you to call it later from other submenus. The submenu name starts with two asterisks immediately followed by a keyword, P1a for example. The beginning of the submenu looks like

```
***POP1
**P1a
[Tools]
[OSNAP] ^ C ^ C$p1 = $p1 = * OSNAP \
[CENter]CENTER
[ENDpoint]ENDPOINT
[INSert]INSERT
etc.
```

At the end of the P1a submenu, you can append your new P1b submenu:

```
[QUICK,]QUICK, ^ Z
[TANgent]TANGEN
NONE
[~ --]
```

```
[Cancel] ^ C ^ C
[U] ^ C ^ CU
[Redo] ^ C ^ CREDO
[Redraw]'REDRAW
[Page 2]$P1 = P1b $P1 = *


**P1b
[Page 2]
[Regen] ^ c ^ cREGEN
[Regenauto] ^ c ^ cREGENAUTO
[Directory] ^ c ^ cdir
[Tools]$P1 = P1a $P1 = *
```

In the sample above, a second page is added to the Tools pull-down menu. Notice that an item called Page 2 is added to the end of sub-menu P1a. This allows you to access submenu P1b. The additional code $P1 = * forces AutoCAD to display the new pull-down menu once it is chosen. If this code is not added, the Page 2 menu will be switched with the Tools menu, but will not display.

At the beginning of the submenu you may also have noticed a word placed in brackets without a command following it. This first line in the submenu is the text that appears on the menu bar. Also note that we included a Tools menu option in submenu P1b to allow you to return to the original Tools menu (see Figure 18.3).

Two additional options not present in other menus are available in the pull-down menus. One is the *double hyphen symbol*, which is used to divide groups of items in a menu and will expand to fill the entire width of the pull-down menu. The other option is the *tilde symbol*. When the tilde precedes a bracketed option name, that option will be grayed out when displayed; when picked, it will have no effect. If you have used other programs that offer pull-down menus, you are probably familiar with this effect. When you see a grayed-out menu item, it usually means that the option is not valid under the current command.

Understanding the Icon Menus

Icon menus operate in a slightly different way from other menus. Each icon menu is actually a submenu of the icon menu group. Instead of starting with the name of the option as it might appear on the screen, icon menu options begin with the slide library file and

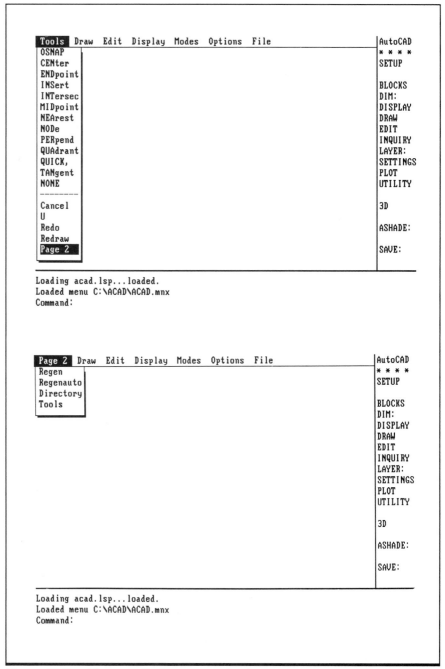

Figure 18.3: The new Tools menu and submenu

slide name in brackets. The following are two fonts icon submenus:

```
**fonts1
[Select Text Font]
[acad(romans)] ^ c ^ cstyle romans romans
[acad(romanc)] ^ c ^ cstyle romanc romanc
[acad(italicc)] ^ c ^ cstyle italicc italicc
[acad(romand)] ^ c ^ cstyle romand romand
[acad(romant)] ^ c ^ cstyle romant romant
[acad(italict)] ^ c ^ cstyle italict italict
[acad(monotxt)] ^ c ^ cstyle monotxt monotxt
[ Next]$i = fonts2 $i = *
[ Exit] ^ c ^ c

**fonts2
[Select Text Font]
[acad(gothice)] ^ c ^ cstyle gothice gothice
[acad(greeks)] ^ c ^ cstyle greeks greeks
[acad(scripts)] ^ c ^ cstyle scripts scripts
[acad(gothicg)] ^ c ^ cstyle gothicg gothicg
[acad(greekc)] ^ c ^ cstyle greekc greekc
[acad(scriptc)] ^ c ^ cstyle scriptc scriptc
[acad(gothici)] ^ c ^ cstyle gothici gothici
[ Next]$i = fonts3 $i = *
[ Exit] ^ c ^ c
```

Notice that the name of the slide associated with an icon is entered as it would be using the Vslide command: the slide library name is followed by the slide name in parentheses.

An icon menu can be called from any other menu by using the code $I = . This code serves the same purpose as $S = in the side menus and $P = in the pull-down menus. For example, the Select Text Font icon menu in the sample above is called from the Options pull-down menu using the following line:

```
[Fonts] ^ C ^ C$I = fonts1 $I = *
```

Notice that the Next option in the Fonts1 submenu calls the Fonts2 submenu. Options that do not call a slide file—such as Next and Exit—are displayed as they appear in the submenu. Also notice that the first item in the submenu is not followed by any instructions or commands. The first item is always the text that appears as the icon menu title.

You may want to create an icon menu of new line types or hatch patterns you design. To do this, you make slides of each individual line type or hatch pattern, create a slide library, then write an icon menu following the example above, but substituting your own slide library for the Acad font slide library.

Understanding the Tablet Menu

A tablet menu is written in exactly the same way as a side menu. The only real difference between the two is in the way the file is presented to you. The tablet menu is set up as rows and columns of boxes, with each box containing a menu item, while the on-screen menu is a long list. It is fairly easy to see how the list structure relates to the screen menu. To understand how the list is converted to the rows and columns of the tablet menu, think of the tablet menu as a list starting from the upper left and moving to the right. When the top row of the tablet menu is full, the next row continues the list, and so on until each item on the list has a box. A tablet menu containing 200 menu items might appear on the tablet as 25 columns and 8 rows. In fact, this is exactly how the customizable area of your tablet menu template is set up. Figure 18.4 is provided to help you find the corresponding position in the menu file.

You can have up to four tablet menu areas. Your Acad.MNU file uses three of them, reserving the first tablet area for your custom menu items. If you open your Acad.MNU file and go to the heading

* * *Tablet1

you will see the list:

* * *TABLET1
[T1-1]
[T1-2]
[T1-3]
[T1-4]
[T1-5]
[T1-6]
[T1-7]
[T1-8]
[T1-9]
[T1-10]
[T1-11]
[T1-12]

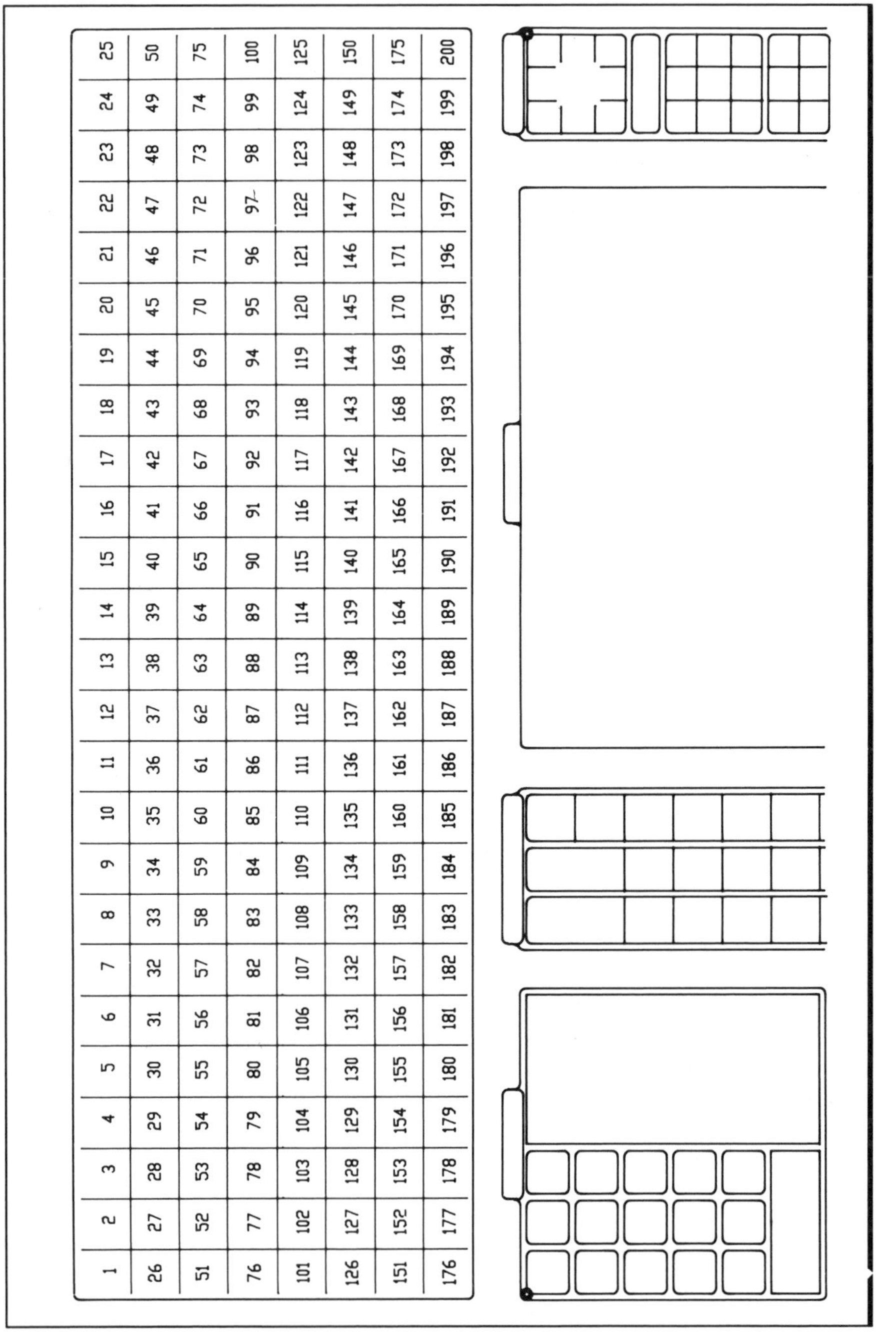

1	2	3	4	5	6	7	8	9	10	11	12	13	14	15	16	17	18	19	20	21	22	23	24	25
26	27	28	29	30	31	32	33	34	35	36	37	38	39	40	41	42	43	44	45	46	47	48	49	50
51	52	53	54	55	56	57	58	59	60	61	62	63	64	65	66	67	68	69	70	71	72	73	74	75
76	77	78	79	80	81	82	83	84	85	86	87	88	89	90	91	92	93	94	95	96	97	98	99	100
101	102	103	104	105	106	107	108	109	110	111	112	113	114	115	116	117	118	119	120	121	122	123	124	125
126	127	128	129	130	131	132	133	134	135	136	137	138	139	140	141	142	143	144	145	146	147	148	149	150
151	152	153	154	155	156	157	158	159	160	161	162	163	164	165	166	167	168	169	170	171	172	173	174	175
176	177	178	179	180	181	182	183	184	185	186	187	188	189	190	191	192	193	194	195	196	197	198	199	200

Figure 18.4:   The tablet menu template with numbers corresponding to those in Acad.MNU

[T1-13]
[T1-14]
[T1-15]
[T1-16]
[T1-17]
[T1-18]
[T1-19]
[T1-20]
[T1-21]
[T1-22]
[T1-23]

This list continues to T1-200. These 200 spaces are reserved for your custom menu items in the area at the top of your digitizing tablet.

Each number on the menu template corresponds to a number in the brackets, less the T1 prefix. If you want to add an item to the custom menu area, you find the square you want to assign it to, then add the appropriate text to the corresponding line in the tablet menu.

In summary, the codes to remember when writing a menu file are the dollar sign s equal to call other screen menus, the backslash to pause for data entry, the semicolon to signify a Return, and the plus sign for long menu items. Also remember that screen submenu names start with double asterisks, and the optional number that follows determines the line to begin the submenu on the screen. Menu group names start with three asterisks. Everything else works as standard command entry through the keyboard, including the space bar.

CREATING CUSTOM LINE TYPES AND HATCH PATTERNS

As your drawing needs expand, you may find that the standard line types and hatch patterns are not adequate for your application. Fortunately, you can create your own. In this section, we explain how you go about creating custom line types and patterns.

Creating Line Types

Although AutoCAD provides the line types most commonly used in drafting, the dashes and dots may not be spaced the way you would like, or you may want an entirely new line type (see Figure 18.5). In this section, we show you two methods for creating your own line types. One method allows you to create line types while in an AutoCAD drawing file, while the other uses a word processor outside AutoCAD.

AutoCAD stores the line types in a file called Acad.LIN, which is in the ASCII format. When you create a new line type, you are actually adding information to this file or creating a new file containing your own definitions. If you create a separate line type file, it will also have the extension .LIN. Both methods described below are ways of editing these files.

To create a custom line type while in an AutoCAD drawing file, you use the Linetyp command on the Settings menu. When you pick Linetyp, you get the prompt

?/Create/Load/Set:

and the Linetype menu appears (see Figure 18.6).

Four options are available. The question mark option allows you to view the currently available line types. If you enter a question mark or pick it off the Linetype menu, you will get the prompt

File to list <ACAD>:

The default is ACAD, the file we mentioned earlier that contains line type definitions. AutoCAD does not show the file extension .LIN.

If you press Return to accept the default, you get the following listing.

Linetypes defined in file C:\ACAD\ACAD.lin:

Name	Description
DASHED	__ __ __ __ __ __ __ __ __ __ __ __ __ __ __
HIDDEN	- - - - - - - - - - - - - - - - - - - -
CENTER	____ _ ____ _ ____ _ ____ _ ____ _ ____
PHANTOM	_____ _ _____ _ _____ _ _____ _ _____ _ _____
DOT	. . . .
DASHDOT	__ . __ . __ . __ . __ . __ . __ . __ . __
BORDER	__ __ . __ __ . __ __ . __ __ . __ __ . __ __
DIVIDE	__ . . __ . . __ . . __ . . __ . . __

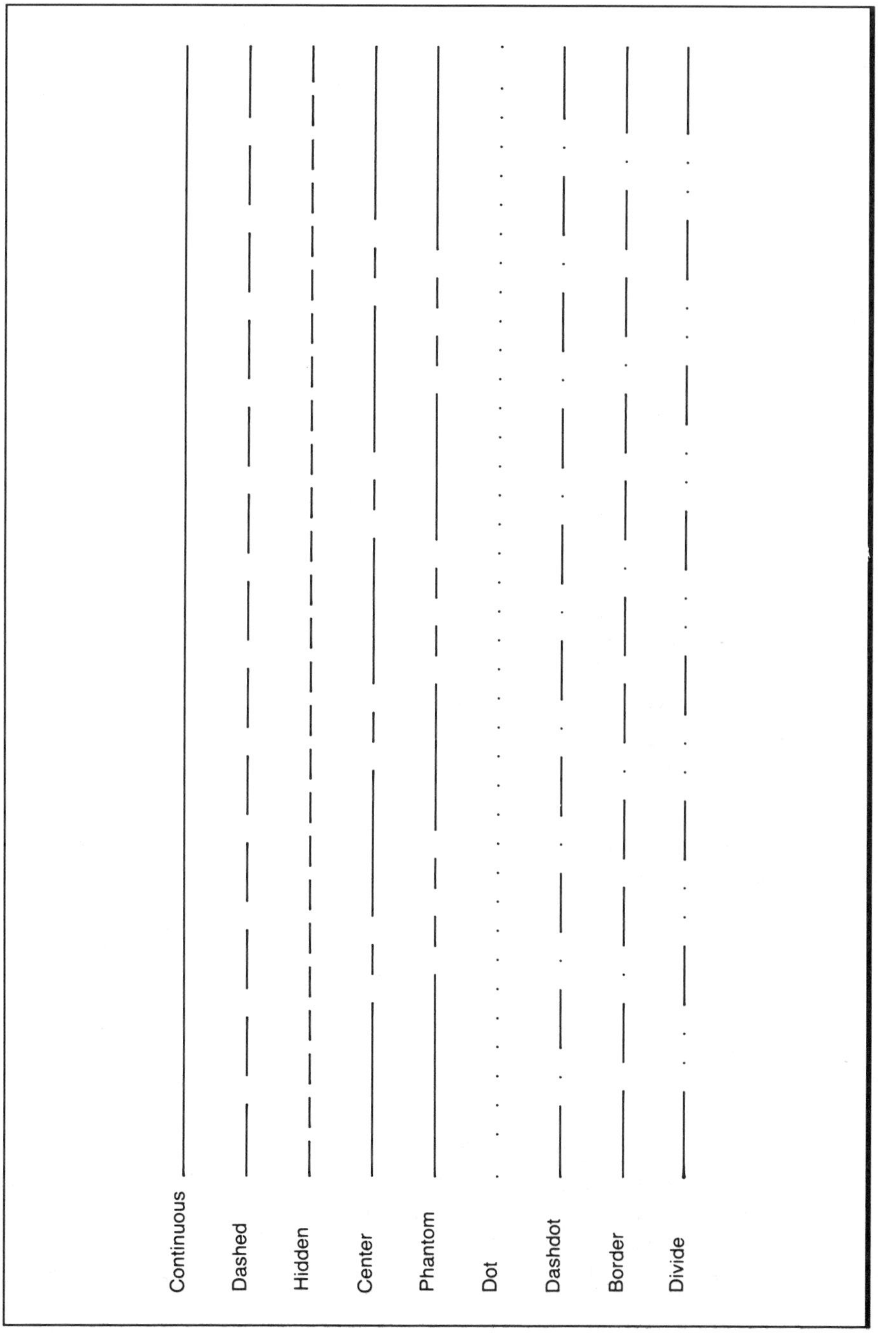

Figure 18.5: *The standard AutoCAD line types*

Figure 18.6: *The Linetype menu*

This is a list of the line types available in the Acad.LIN file, along with a simple graphic description of each line. The graphic description is generated using the underline key and the period and is only a rough representation of the actual line.

To create a new line type, you pick Create from the Linetype menu or enter C at the prompt listing the line types. You then get the prompt

Name of linetype to create:

Enter the name of your line type. For this exercise, call it Custom. Once you've entered the name, the next prompt appears.

File for storage of linetype <ACAD>:

At this prompt, you can either tell AutoCAD to store the line type you are about to define in the Acad.LIN file, or to create a new file to store your own line types. If you pick the default, Acad, your new line type will be added to the Acad.LIN file and whenever you list this file using the question mark option, your line type will also appear. If you choose to create a new line type file, AutoCAD will create a file containing only the line type you create, adding the extension .LIN to the file name you supply. You can add more line types to your new file just as you add them to the Acad.LIN file.

Let's assume you want to start a new line type file called Newline. Once you enter the name Newline the next prompt appears.

Creating new file
Descriptive text:

If you had accepted the default, ACAD, you would get the prompt

Wait, checking if linetype already defined...

This is done so you don't inadvertently overwrite an existing line type you may want to keep. After this step, you enter the name of your line plus any other description you desire. You can use any keyboard character as part of your description, but your actual line type can only be composed of a series of lines, points, and blank spaces. For this exercise, enter

custom _____ _ _____

Once you have entered this name and description of the new line type, you get the next prompt.

Enter pattern (on next line):
A,

A line type is composed of a series of line segments and points. The A, which is supplied by AutoCAD automatically, is a code that forces the line type to start and end on a line segment rather than a blank space in the series of lines. At times AutoCAD stretches the last line segment to force this condition, as in Figure 18.7.

At this prompt, you proceed to enter a series of numbers representing the length of each line segment:

A,1.0,-.125,.25,-.125

This example shows a series of numbers separated by commas. The commas separate the different lengths of the components that

Figure 18.7:   Stretched beginning and end of line

make up the line type. The 1.0 following the A is the length of the first part of the line. The values you enter for the line segment lengths are multiplied by the Ltscale factor, so you must enter values for the *plotted* lengths.

The -.125 is the blank or broken part of the line. The minus sign tells AutoCAD that the line is not to be drawn for the specified length, which is .125 units in this example. Next comes the positive value of .25. This tells AutoCAD to draw a line segment .25 units long after the blank part of the line. Finally, the last negative value, -.125, tells Auto-CAD to skip drawing the line for the distance of .125 units. This series of numbers represents one segment that is repeated to form the line (see Figure 18.8). You could create a very complex line type that looks like a random broken line, as in Figure 18.9.

Once you are finished entering these values you press Return and the next prompt appears.

New definition written to file.
?/Create/Load/Set:

Note that these options also appear on the Linetype menu. They enable you to create more line types, load a new line type, or set the current line type to a different predefined one. The standard

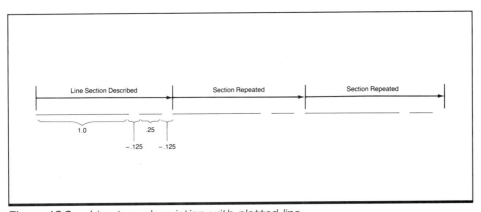

Figure 18.8:   *Line type description with plotted line*

Figure 18.9:   *"Random" broken line*

default is the Bylayer line type, which is discussed in Chapter 13, but you can set AutoCAD to draw using a different predefined line type. If you change this setting, no matter what layer you are on, you will get the line type to which you set AutoCAD. You can use the Load option to access line type definitions in line type files other than Acad.LIN.

As mentioned in the beginning of this section, you can also create line types outside AutoCAD by using a word processor or EDLIN and editing the Acad.LIN file. The standard Acad.LIN file looks like this.

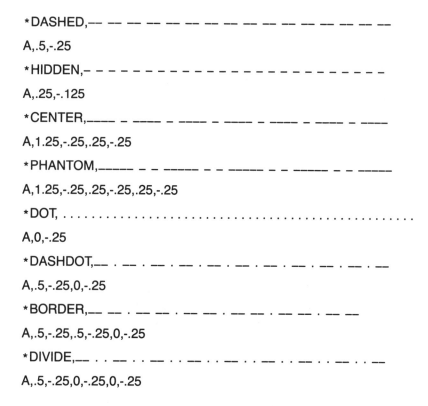

```
*DASHED,— — — — — — — — — — — — — — — —
A,.5,-.25
*HIDDEN,- - - - - - - - - - - - - - - - - - - - -
A,.25,-.125
*CENTER,____ _ ____ _ ____ _ ____ _ ____ _ ____ _ ____
A,1.25,-.25,.25,-.25
*PHANTOM,____ _ _ ____ _ _ ____ _ _ ____ _ _ ____
A,1.25,-.25,.25,-.25,.25,-.25
*DOT,. . . . . . . . . . . . . . . . . . . . . . . . . . . . . . . . . . . . . . . .
A,0,-.25
*DASHDOT,__ . __ . __ . __ . __ . __ . __ . __ . __ . __ . __
A,.5,-.25,0,-.25
*BORDER,__ __ . __ __ . __ __ . __ __ . __ __ . __ __
A,.5,-.25,.5,-.25,0,-.25
*DIVIDE,__ . . __ . . __ . . __ . . __ . . __ . . __ . . __ . . __
A,.5,-.25,0,-.25,0,-.25
```

This is the same file you saw earlier, with the addition of the code used by AutoCAD to determine the line segment lengths.

Normally, to use a line type you have created, you have to enter its name through the keyboard when you are prompted for a line type during the Change, Layer, or Linetype command. If you use one of your own line types frequently, you may want to add it to the Acad.MNU file so it will be available on the Linetype setting submenu. The name for this particular submenu is Chlt and it looks like

```
**CHLT 3
LTYPE

[bylayer]BYLAYER
[byblock]BYBLOCK

[contin.]CONTINUOUS
[dashed]DASHED
[hidden]HIDDEN
[center]CENTER
[phantom]PHANTOM
[dot]DOT
[dashdot]DASHDOT
[border]BORDER
```

Chlt stands for Change line type. You can get to it by opening the Acad.MNU file and paging through the file until you find it. If you have a word processor with a search capability, you can tell it to search for **CHLT. Otherwise you can find it on line number 1676.

You could add the line type created in the previous example by adding the line

```
[custom]CUSTOM
```

just below the last item on the submenu.

Creating Patterns

AutoCAD provides 41 predefined hatch patterns you can choose from (see Figure 18.10). If the hatch pattern you want is not available, you have the option to create your own. In this section we show you the basic elements of pattern definition.

Unlike the line types, hatch patterns cannot be created while you are in an AutoCAD file. The pattern definitions are contained in an external file named Acad.PAT. This file can be opened and edited with a word processor that can handle ASCII files or with EDLIN. Here is one hatch pattern definition from that file.

```
*square,Small aligned squares
0, 0,0, 0,.125, .125,-.125
90, 0,0, 0,.125, .125,-.125
```

You can see some similarities between the pattern description and the line description. They both start with a descriptive text line,

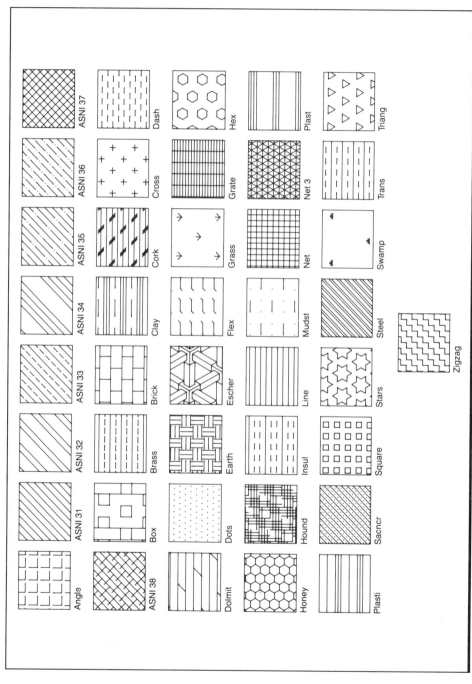

Figure 18.10: The standard hatch patterns

then give numeric values defining the pattern. The numbers have a different meaning, however. This example shows two lines of information. Each line represents a line in the pattern, much like a line in the line type definition. The first line determines the horizontal line component of the pattern, and the second line represents the vertical component. Figure 18.11 shows the hatch pattern defined in the example.

Figure 18.11:   *Square pattern*

A pattern is made up of *line groups*. A line group is like a line type that is arrayed a specified distance to fill the area to be hatched. A group is defined by a line of code, much as a line type is defined. In the square pattern, two lines are used, one horizontal and one vertical. Each of these lines is duplicated in a fashion that makes them appear as boxes when they are combined. Figure 18.12 illustrates this point.

Look at the first line in the definition.

0, 0,0, 0,.125, .125,-.125

As in a line type definition, this example shows a series of numbers separated by commas. This line of codes representing one line group actually contains four sets of information. The commas separate these different components. The first component is the 0 at the beginning. This value indicates the angle of the line group as determined by the line's orientation. In this case it is 0 for a horizontal line that runs from left to right. If you have forgotten what the numeric values for the different directions are, refer to Chapter 2.

The next component is the origin of the line group, 0,0. This does not mean that the line actually begins at the drawing origin (see Figure 18.13). It gives you a reference point to determine the location of other line groups involved in generating the pattern.

The next component is the 0,.125. This determines the distance the line is to be arrayed. Figure 18.14 shows what this means in terms of the pattern. This value is like a relative coordinate indicating x and y distances for a rectangular array. This coordinate is not based on the drawing coordinates, but on a coordinate system relative to the orientation of the line. If the line is oriented at a 0-degree angle, then the code 0,.125 indicates a precisely vertical direction. If

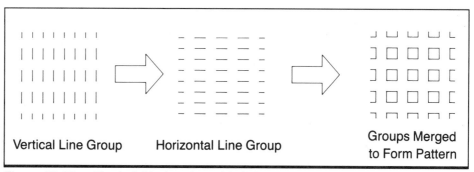

Vertical Line Group   **Horizontal Line Group**   **Groups Merged to Form Pattern**

Figure 18.12:   *The individual and combined line groups*

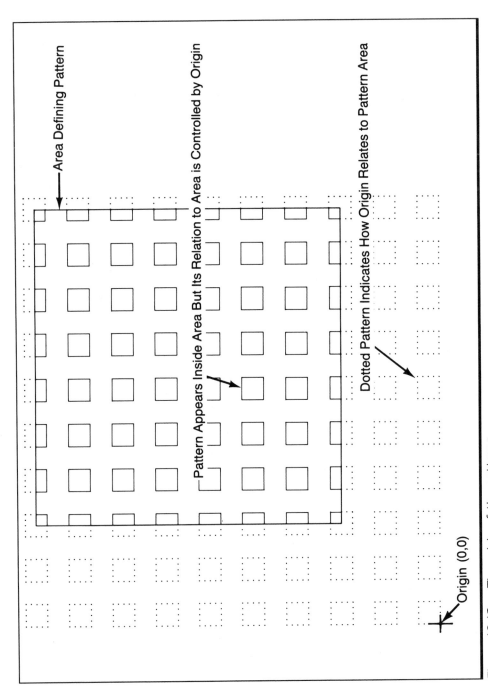

Figure 18.13: The origin of the patterns

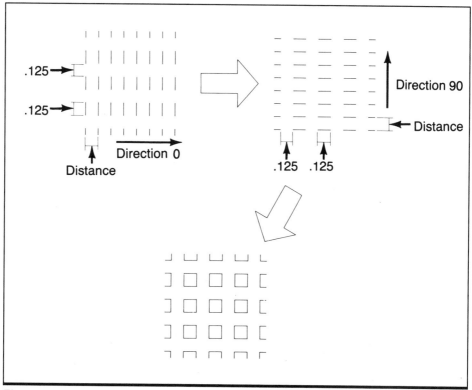

Figure 18.14: *The distance and direction of duplication*

the line were oriented at a 45-degree angle, then the code 0,.125 would represent a 135-degree direction. In this example, the duplication occurs 90 degrees in relation to the line group, since the x value is 0. Figure 18.15 illustrates this point.

Finally, the actual description of the line pattern is given. This value is equivalent to the value given when you create a line type. Positive values are line segments, and negative values are blank segments. This part of the line group definition works exactly like the line type definitions you looked at in the previous section.

This system may seem somewhat limiting, but you can actually do a lot with it. AutoCAD managed to come up with 41 patterns and that is really only scratching the surface. Still, if you want to create a random pattern such as concrete texture, you are better off creating a block and arraying it, rather than trying to create a hatch pattern.

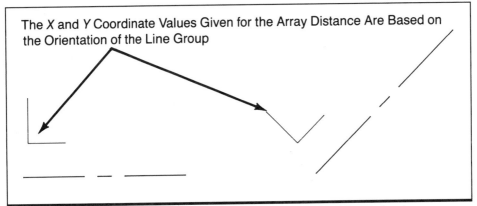

The X and Y Coordinate Values Given for the Array Distance Are Based on the Orientation of the Line Group

Figure 18.15:   *How the direction of the line group copy is determined*

USING AUTOLISP

To get the most from any CAD/CAM software, you will want to create some applications. No one software product can be all things to all people and it is likely that no matter what software you use, you will find it lacking in some feature or another. Perhaps this is why nearly every advanced CAD/CAM software package provides some programming capabilities.

The language you use to create AutoCAD applications is AutoLISP. AutoLISP is a form of Common LISP, the newest dialect of the oldest artificial-intelligence programming language, LISP. We are not attempting to teach you LISP programming in this book. There are a number of books available that will serve that purpose. We will show you how you can use AutoLISP and encourage you to give it a try. If you like, open an AutoCAD drawing file and follow the examples we give to see firsthand how AutoLISP works.

Understanding the Interpreter

AutoLISP is accessed through the AutoLISP *interpreter*. The interpreter is like a hand-held calculator. When you enter information at the command prompt, the interpreter *evaluates* it, then returns an answer. By evaluate, we mean perform the instructions described by the information provided. We will look at different ways Auto-LISP evaluates data as we go along.

The information you give the interpreter is like a formula—2 plus 2, for example. To enter this into the AutoLISP interpreter, you would enter

(+ 2 2)

at the command prompt. The answer, 4, appears on the prompt line. AutoLISP evaluates the formula (+ 2 2) and returns the answer, 4. By entering information this way, you can perform calculations, or even write short programs on the fly.

Another calculator-like capability of the interpreter is its ability to remember values. You probably have a calculator that has some memory. This capability allows you to store the value of an equation for future use. In a similar way, you can store values using *variables* with the AutoLISP interpreter. We will discuss variables in more detail in the next section.

You can also store your programs on disk for future use. Through special commands, AutoLISP will read these programs and run them through the interpreter. By storing programs to disk, you are able to create complex formulas and equations capable of manipulating your drawings.

In Appendix D, we have included several useful AutoLISP programs that you can copy into your computer and use with Auto-CAD. These programs will give you an idea of what can be done with AutoLISP. They provide such functions as continuous parallel lines, ASCII text importation, attribute template generation, and so on. If you copy them carefully as ASCII files into your computer, then load them as described in this chapter, you will be able to add these features to your system.

We say "copy carefully" because if you leave out double quotes and parentheses, a program will not work properly. However, Auto-LISP is not *case-sensitive:* it does not care whether you write code in uppercase letters or lowercase letters. The AutoLISP interpreter will convert all code written in lowercase to uppercase. Values given to variables, however, are case-sensitive. We will discuss this further when you learn about variables. (In this book we have lowercased all AutoLISP code in examples because you will probably find it most convenient to enter it that way, but capitalized function and variable names in text to distinguish them from English words.

Defining Variables

AutoLISP allows you to define variables. A variable is like a container that holds a value. That value can change in the course of a program's operation. A simple analogy to this is the title of a government position. The position of *president* could be thought of as a variable. This variable can be assigned a value, such as Ronald Reagan or Jimmy Carter.

When AutoLISP evaluates a variable, the value held by that variable is returned. Variables can take on four types of values: *integers*, *real numbers*, text, and coordinates. We refer to text as *string* values and coordinates as *lists*. Here is what these variables look like in AutoLISP.

integer	24
real number	0.618
string	"20 feet 6 inches"
coordinate list	(4.5021 6.3011)

Real numbers with values of less than one must begin with zero. Notice that strings are enclosed in double quotes and that coordinate lists are two numbers enclosed in parentheses. Actually, a list can be made up of any number of integers, real numbers, strings, and even other lists. We single out coordinates because they are used frequently in AutoLISP, though in fact anything enclosed by parentheses is considered a list.

These data types are important to remember as they can be a source of confusion if not carefully used. For example, you cannot mix data types in most operations. It is also important that quotes and parentheses are closed. We will discuss this requirement in more detail a little later.

There are actually two basic elements in AutoLISP: *atoms* and *lists*. We have already described lists. An atom is an element that cannot be taken apart. Atoms are further grouped into two categories, *numbers* and *symbols*. A number can be a real number or an integer. A symbol, on the other hand, is usually text, but it can also contain numbers like *point1* or *dx2*. A symbol must, however, start with a letter. You could think of a symbol as a name given to a variable or *function* as a means of describing it.

Using Functions

Variables are assigned values through the use of the Setq function. A function is an instruction telling the AutoLISP interpreter what to do. A very simple example of a function is the math function Add. The plus sign is a symbol representing the Add function. A function can also consist of complex instructions to perform more than one activity, like a small program within a program. You can create your own functions by using Defun. We will discuss Defun later in this section.

The Setq function tells AutoLISP to assign a value to a variable. For example, to assign the value 1.618 to the variable named Golden you would enter

(setq golden 1.618)

This line, when entered at the AutoCAD command prompt, will return the value 1.618, the new value of the variable Golden. The Setq function is like saying "Set equal to." Actually, Setq is an abbreviation for set quote. Quote is a function that prevents evaluation of an atom or list.

AutoLISP tries to evaluate everything it encounters after a function in a list. In some situations you will not want to have an atom or list evaluated, most commonly when you are assigning a value to a symbol representing a variable. If you entered

(set golden 1.618)

AutoLISP would try to evaluate the symbol Golden first, then assign the value 1.618 to whatever Golden evaluated to be. However, Golden cannot be evaluated because it is a symbol holding no value, so AutoLISP will return an error message. Even if Golden has a value assigned to it, the number 42 for example, this expression would still return an error message because Set will try to assign the value 1.618 to the number 42, an impossible feat. You cannot assign a number to another number, nor can you assign a string to another string.

However, if Golden has a symbol assigned to it, AutoLISP is able to evaluate Golden, and Set will assign the value to the symbol held by Golden. For example, you could assign the symbol X to the symbol Golden.

(setq golden (quote x))

The quote is used to prevent evaluation of X. You could then use Set to assign the value 1.618 to the symbol X indirectly through the symbol Golden.

> (set golden 1.618)

Whenever you call for the value held by the variable Golden, you will get the symbol X, and whenever you call for the value held by the symbol X, you will get the real value, 1.618.

As you can see, things can get very confusing. It is much easier to just remember that Set Quote and Setq are interchangeable and that when you want to assign a value to a variable, use Setq.

Setq will assign a value to a variable even if the variable already has a value assigned to it. For example, if you were to enter

> (setq golden 0.618)

after you entered the previous line, Golden would be reassigned the value 0.618 and the old value, 1.618, would be discarded. You can even reassign a value to a variable by using that variable as part of the new value as in

> (setq golden (+ golden 1))

In this example, Golden is assigned a new value by adding 1 to its current value.

Using Arguments and Expressions

Functions act on *arguments* to accomplish a task. An argument can be a symbol, a number, or a list. A simple example of a function acting on numbers is the addition of .618 and 1. In AutoLISP, this would be entered as

> (+ .618 1)

When this is entered at the AutoCAD command prompt, it will return the value 1.618. This (and the last example in the previous section) is called an *expression*. An expression returns the value evaluated within the parentheses. The proper syntax for an expression is the left parenthesis first, then the function symbol, then the arguments, and finally the closing right parenthesis. An expression is actually a list that contains a function and arguments for that function.

Arguments can also be expressions, which means you can nest expressions. For example you could combine the first example with the second to assign the value returned by 0.618 + 1 to the variable Golden by entering the following at the command prompt.

(setq golden (+ 0.618 1))

Whenever expressions are nested, the deepest nest is evaluated first, then the next deepest, and so on. In this example, the expression adding 0.618 to 1 is evaluated first.

Once this is done, you can retrieve the value of Golden by entering

!golden

at the AutoCAD command prompt. The exclamation point preceding the variable name tells AutoCAD to return the variable's value.

The variable Golden can now be used within an AutoCAD command to enter a value at a prompt, or within another function to obtain other results. For example, you might have used Setq to assign the value 25.4 to a variable called Mill. You could then find the result of dividing Mill by Golden:

(/ mill golden)

The slash sign is the symbol for the division function. This returns the value 15.698393. You can assign this value to yet another variable as in

(setq b (/ mill golden))

Now you have three variables, Golden, Mill, and B, which are all assigned values that you can later retrieve, either within an AutoCAD command by entering an exclamation point followed by the variable, or as an argument within an expression.

You must remember to close all parentheses when using nested expressions. Otherwise you will get the error message

n>

where *n* is the number of missing parentheses. If you see this prompt, you must enter the number of closing parentheses indicated by *n* to return to the command prompt. AutoCAD will not evaluate an Auto-LISP program that has the wrong number of parentheses. Double quotes enclosing strings must also be carefully closed.

Our examples have shown numbers being manipulated, but text can also be manipulated in a similar way. Variables can be assigned text strings that can later be used to enter values in commands that require text input. Strings can also be joined together or *concatenated* to form new strings. Strings and numeric values cannot be evaluated together, however. This may seem like a simple statement but if not carefully considered, it can lead to confusion. For example, it is possible to assign the number 1 to a variable as a text string by entering

> (setq foo "1")

Later, you may accidentally try to add this string variable to an integer or real number and AutoCAD will return an error message.

In our examples, we used Setq and the addition and division functions. These are three functions out of many available to you. All the usual math functions are available, plus many other functions used to test and manipulate variables. Table 18.1 shows some commonly used functions. Look at the *AutoLISP Programmer's Reference* for a full list of available functions and their use.

Since AutoLISP will perform mathematical calculations, you can use it as a calculator while you are drawing. For example, if you need to convert a distance of 132 feet 6 inches to inches, you could enter

> (setq in2 (+ (* 132 12) 6))

at the command prompt. The asterisk is the symbol for the multiplication function. The value 1590 will be assigned to the variable In2, which can later be used as input to prompts that accept numeric values. This is a very simple but useful application of AutoLISP. In the next section, you will explore some of its more complex uses.

Using Points

When you draw, you are actually specifying points on the drawing area in coordinates. Because a coordinate is a pair of values rather than a single value, it must be handled as a list in AutoLISP. You must use special AutoLISP functions to access single values in a list. For coordinate variables, these functions are Car and Cadr. The following example illustrates their use.

Say you have created a variable defining a point by entering

> (setq pt1 (list 12.004 14.002))

The List function in this expression combines the values following it to form a list. This list is assigned to the variable Pt1. Now suppose you want to get the x coordinate value from this example. You would enter

> (car pt1)

Function	Description
+	Add
−	Subtract
*	Multiply
/	Divide
sin	Sine
cos	Cosine
atan	Arctangent
sqrt	Square root
pi	3.1415926
=	Equal to (returns T or nil)
/=	Not equal to (returns T or nil)
>	Greater than (returns T or nil)
<	Less than (returns T or nil)
>=	Greater than or equal to (returns T or nil)
<=	Less than or equal to (returns T or nil)
abs	Absolute value

Table 18.1: A partial list of AutoLISP functions

You get the value 12.004000. If you wanted to get the y value, you would enter

   (cadr pt1)

which returns the value 14.002000. These values can in turn be assigned to variables, as in the line

   (setq x (car pt1))

By using the List function, you can construct a point variable using x and y components of other point variables. For example, you may want to combine the y value of the variable Pt1 with the x value of a point variable Pt2, which you define as

> (setq pt2 (list 16.002 15.005))

You combine the two by entering

> (list (car pt2) (cadr pt1))

You get the value (16.002000 14.002000).

These lists can be used to enter values during any AutoCAD command that prompts for points. By now you may be wondering how these AutoLISP variables can be assigned values easily. It would be hardly worth the time if you always had to enter values by hand.

Entering Values for Variables

In this section we show you how custom menus allow you to store functions and variables so you can use them freely. To do this, you need a way of prompting yourself so you can enter values and points to be processed. This is done through the use of special functions that pause and allow input of values from the keyboard or the mouse as in the line

> (setq pt1 (getpoint))

This expression will blank the command line and wait until you enter a point either through the keyboard or by picking a point on the drawing area. The coordinate of the point you enter will become the value assigned to the variable Pt1 in the form of a list.

Table 18.2 shows a list of these Get functions. They accept single values or, in the case of points, a list of two values. String values are case-sensitive. This means that if you enter a lowercase letter in response to Getstring, it will be saved as a lowercase letter. Uppercase letters will be saved as uppercase letters. You can enter numbers in response to the Getstring and Getkword functions, but they will be saved as strings and cannot be used in mathematical operations. Also, AutoLISP will automatically add quotes to string values, so you don't have to enter them.

All these Get functions allow you to create a prompt by following the function with the prompt enclosed by quotation marks as in the expression

> (getpoint "Pick the next point:")

This expression will cause the prompt

> **Pick the next point:**

Function	Description
Getint	Allows entry of integer values
Getreal	Allows entry of real values
Getstring	Allows entry of string values
Getkword	Allows filtering of string entries through a list of keywords. These keywords are defined by using a function called Initget
Getangle	Allows key or mouse entry of angles based on the standard AutoCAD compass orientation of angles. Returns values in radians
Getorient	Allows key or mouse entry of angles based on Units command setting for angles. Returns values in radians
Getdist	Allows key or mouse entry of distances. This always returns values as real numbers regardless of the unit format used
Getpoint	Allows key or mouse entry of point positions. This always returns values as lists of two values, the x and the y
Getcorner	Allows selection of a point by using a window. This function requires a base point value defining the first corner of the window. A window appears, allowing you to select the opposite corner

Table 18.2:   Functions that pause to allow input

to appear while AutoCAD waits for your input.

The functions Getangle, Getorient, Getdist, Getcorner, and Getpoint allow you to specify a point from which the angle, distance, or point is to be measured, as in the expression

(getangle pt1 "Pick the next point:")

where Pt1 is a previously defined point variable. A rubber-banding line will appear from the coordinate defined by Pt1. Once you pick a point, the angle defined by Pt1 and the point you pick are returned. You can also enter a relative coordinate through the keyboard in the unit system currently used in your drawing. Getangle and Getdist prompt you for two points if a point variable is not provided. Getcorner always requires a point variable and will generate a window instead of a rubber-banding line.

Getvar, which we have referred to in earlier chapters, is a function that allows you to retrieve system variables. The variable name must be enclosed by quotes, as in the expression

(setq pt1 (getvar "lastpoint"))

where Lastpoint is the system variable describing the last point selected. It is the same point accessed by the at sign while entering points in response to AutoCAD commands.

Using AutoLISP in a Menu

Once you understand the basic principles of AutoLISP, you can create functions and add them to a menu. The following is an example of a menu item using AutoLISP. Create an ASCII file called Box.MNU and copy this example exactly as it appears into the file. This example draws a box based on your input of height, width, and beginning corner.

```
[BOX] ^ C ^ C +
(setq dx (getreal "Enter horizontal dimension of box: "));\ +
(setq dy (getreal "Enter vertical dimension of box: "));\ +
(setq pt1 (getpoint "Starting corner: "));\ +
(setq pt2 (list (+ (car pt1) dx) (cadr pt1) )); +
(setq pt3 (list (car pt2) (+ (cadr pt1) dy) )); +
(setq pt4 (list (car pt1) (cadr pt3))); +
line;!pt1;!pt2;!pt3;!pt4;C;
```

In this example, the variable Dx is assigned a value for the horizontal dimension of the box, which you are prompted for. Next, the vertical dimension is assigned to the variable Dy in the same way. Then a point value is assigned to the variable Pt1 by prompting you to enter a point. The point can be entered as a coordinate through the keyboard, or by being picked from the screen. The point will be the lower-left corner of the box unless negative vertical and horizontal values are entered. The rest of the expressions create point values for the other corners of the box by using the Dx and Dy values and adding them to the x and y components of the point variable Pt1 (see Figure 18.16).

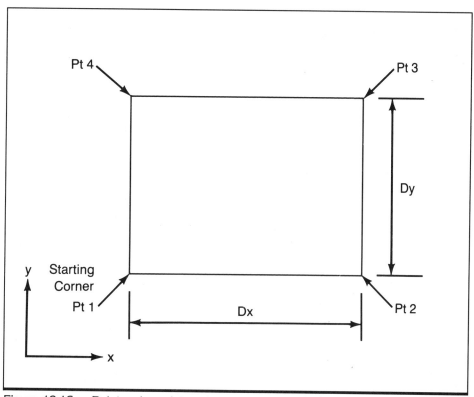

Figure 18.16: *Point values determined by the variables Dx and Dy*

Note that the backslash is used to pause for input, just as you would have a backslash in other commands that require mouse or keyboard input. Also note the use of the plus sign indicating the continuation of the menu item. Finally, note that the last line of the menu item uses the exclamation point to enter the values of the variables as responses to the Line command. The last C is the Close option of the Line command.

Open a file in AutoCAD called Test, then use the command Menu to load the Box menu you just created. The AutoCAD menu will disappear and will be replaced by the single word Box. Pick the Box option from the menu, and you will see the prompts you entered when you created the Box menu above. You can enter positive or negative values. The values must be in real numbers, however. Feet and inches are not allowed. Once you pick a point for the starting corner, a box will be drawn to your specifications. The starting corner will be the lower-left corner if you enter positive values for vertical and horizontal dimensions. To get the AutoCAD menu back, enter the command Menu and enter acad at the menu name prompt.

You could have added the Box program to the Acad.MNU file as a menu item under one of the submenus, such as the Draw submenu.

Creating an External AutoLISP File

The Box program can be made into an external AutoLISP file that can be loaded and used like any other AutoCAD command. In an ASCII file called Box.LSP, it would appear as

```
(defun c:box (/dx dy pt1 pt2 pt3 pt4)
        (setq dx (getreal "Enter horizontal dimension of box: "))
        (setq dy (getreal "Enter vertical dimension of box: "))
        (setq pt1 (getpoint "Starting corner: "))
        (setq pt2 (list (+ (car pt1) dx) (cadr pt1)))
        (setq pt3 (list (car pt2) (+ (cadr pt1) dy)))
        (setq pt4 (list (car pt1) (cadr pt3)))
        (command "line" pt1 pt2 pt3 pt4 "c" )
    )
```

You can have several functions within a single AutoLISP file. If you do this, all the functions contained in that file will be loaded at once.

The first line in this example

```
(defun c:box (/dx dy pt1 pt2 pt3 pt4)
```

defines the entire set of expressions that follow as a command called Box. Defun is a function that defines other functions. The c: tells Auto-LISP that this function is to act like an AutoCAD command. This means that if the function name is entered at the AutoCAD command prompt, the function will be executed as an AutoCAD command. The list that follows the name Box is an argument list. We'll explain argument lists in a moment.

Notice that a closing parenthesis is not included in this line. The closing parenthesis is at the very end of the set of expressions. AutoLISP will keep reading the program until it finds the closing parenthesis. This is why it is important to keep track of all parentheses.

The last line

```
(command "line" pt1 pt2 pt3 pt4 "c")
```

shows you how AutoCAD commands are used in an AutoLISP

expression. Command is an AutoLISP function that calls AutoCAD commands. The command to be called following the Command function is enclosed in quotation marks. Anything in quotation marks after the Command function is treated as keyboard input. Variables follow, but unlike the menu version, they do not have to be preceded by an exclamation point. The C enclosed in quotation marks at the end of the expression indicates a Close option for the Line command. Also notice that the semicolons and plus signs are omitted in the Box.LSP file.

The argument list mentioned earlier is a list of arguments that will be evaluated in that function. An argument list is used for two purposes. First it is used where the function is called from another function to evaluate a set of values. For example, you could define a function that adds the square of two variables.

```
(defun square (x y)
(+ (* x x) (* y y))
)
```

In this example, the c: is left out of the Defun line. By doing this, you create a function that can be used in other functions like a subprogram. We'll discuss this item in more detail later. Note that an X and Y are included in the parentheses after the name of the function, Square. This is the argument list. To use this function you would enter

```
(square a b)
```

within another function. The X and Y in the Square function take on the values held by A and B in the order they are listed. X takes on the value of A, and Y takes on the value of B. If A held the value 2 and B held the value 4, you would get 20. You could also enter the function at the AutoCAD command prompt as

```
(square 2 4)
```

and AutoCAD would return 20. The Square function must be loaded before it can be used, however.

The second use for the argument list is to determine *global* and *local* variables. Global variables are variables that remain in the system's memory even after a function has been executed. For example, where you assigned the value 1.618 to the variable Golden, Golden holds that value no matter where it is used. Any function can evaluate Golden to get its value, 1.618. This is an example of a global variable.

A local variable, on the other hand, exists only within the function it is found in. For example, the variable X in the Square function exists only while the Square function is evaluated. Once the function is used, X is discarded and no other function can use the value assigned to X.

Since an argument list is used for two purposes, the slash symbol is used to separate simple local arguments from function arguments that are assigned values from outside the functions. The assignable variables are listed first. Then a slash is entered, then the list of local variables as in the following example:

```
(defun square2 (x y / dx dy)
(setq dx (* x x))
(setq dy (* y y))
( + dx dy)
)
```

X and Y are variables that will be assigned values when the function is called initially, as in the Square function given earlier. Dx and Dy, on the other hand, are variables assigned values within the function, so they follow the slash sign. In either case, the variables are local. Arguments left out of the list become global. If, for example, Dy is left out of the argument list, it will remain in the AutoLISP system memory for as long as the current editing session lasts, and its value can be evaluated by any other function.

In both the Square and Square2 functions above we left out the c:. As we mentioned, this allows the function to be used by other functions like a subprogram. You can also use functions defined in this way in the middle of other commands by entering the name of the function enclosed by parentheses at the command prompt. For example, you could use the Square function above as a response to the scale factor prompt of the Insert command. Suppose you started the Insert command to insert the Door file into a drawing. When the prompt

X scale factor (1) / Corner / XYZ:

appears, you could enter

(square 2 4)

and AutoCAD will enter the value 20, returned from this function, as the x scale factor for the door currently being inserted. This can be quite useful where a value conversion or any other type of data conversion is wanted.

Loading an AutoLISP Program

To use the Box program, you must first load it by entering

(load "box")

at the AutoCAD command prompt. Be sure the Box.LSP file is in the default directory. You get the response

C:BOX

which tells you the Box program is loaded and available. You can then enter Box and the prompts appear in the following sequence:

Enter horizontal dimension of box:

At this prompt, you enter the desired width of the box in inches, leaving off the inches symbol. Remember, the data type called for is a real number, so only real numbers are accepted. The next prompt is

Enter vertical dimension of box:

Again you enter the desired value in inches. Finally the prompt

Starting corner:

appears. At this prompt you pick the point representing the lower-left corner of the box or enter its coordinate through the keyboard. Once you are done, a box appears with the dimensions you specified originating from the point you pick or enter.

Dx and Dy require real values to be entered. If you use this program and try to enter feet and inches, you will get an error message and the program will stop running. You will have to enter values in inches only and leave off the inches sign. You could create a function that converts the foot-and-inch format into real numbers to get around this limitation, but that could be a lengthy program.

Look at the Pbox.LSP example in Appendix D to see how the Box program can be made to accept any input format by using the Get-corner function. This function allows Pbox.LSP to be simplified over the Box.LSP example given here. Compare the two while referring to your AutoLISP manual to see how Pbox.LSP was simplified.

Loading AutoLISP Functions Automatically

Once you have created some new commands and functions, you may want them available every time you enter AutoCAD. This can be accomplished by combining your code into one file called Acad.LSP and including it in your Acad directory. AutoCAD will look for this file when it opens a drawing file and if it is present, AutoCAD will load its entire contents.

If you are planning to load many functions during your editing session, you should include the line

    (vmon)

at the beginning of your Acad.LSP file. This tells AutoCAD to page infrequently used functions to disk. AutoLISP functions can use up memory quickly and when this occurs, you are unable to load more functions. You must then close the file you are editing and reopen it to use the other functions. By using (vmon), you can avoid this problem.

Another way of dealing with the limited function storage is to place the following function at the end of your Acad.LSP file.

    (defun c:clear ( )
    (setq atomlist (member 'c:clear atomlist))
)

Whenever you run out of space for functions, enter clear and all the functions you load after Acad.LSP will be cleared from memory. You cannot use both methods to manage memory for your functions, however. You may want to try them both and see which suits your needs best. There is also a third method for managing memory for AutoLISP, which we explain in the following section.

ALLOCATING AUTOCAD WORK SPACE

AutoCAD can make use of the DOS environment to set up its own work space. Using the DOS SET command, you can adjust the total amount of RAM AutoCAD allocates for its work space and the amount of memory allocated to AutoLISP functions. The following sections discuss how to set these parameters.

Adjusting the Free RAM

In Chapter 13, we mentioned that you can control the amount of RAM available to AutoCAD for calculations. The RAM work space, or *free RAM* as it is referred to by AutoCAD, is normally about 14K. This is the default value when the SET command is not used to adjust it. Complex drawings, combined with the use of certain commands such as the 3D Hide command, will reach and exceed the free RAM work space. When this happens, you get the message

Out of RAM

and AutoCAD automatically closes the file. If this happens to you, use the DOS SET command to adjust AutoCAD's free RAM by entering

set acadfreeram = 15

at the DOS prompt. This will increase the amount of RAM work space to 15K. You must enter this value every time you start your computer, as it is lost whenever you turn your computer off or reset it.

If the out of RAM message persists, raise the value by 1 again. Keep raising the value until AutoCAD stops giving you the message. The maximum allowable value for Acadfreeram is 20. This fine tuning may take some time and experimentation, but it will save you from being dumped out of a file unexpectedly.

This is not likely to happen to you unless you create some very large files, so don't think it is a common occurrence. You can, in fact, lower the default to give AutoCAD more I/O page space for storing unused parts of files. This will help AutoCAD's speed by allowing it to store more of the drawing in RAM before it must start paging to your hard disk. Follow the same procedure as above but instead of raising the value by 1, lower it by 1 to 13. Open your most complex file and try editing it for a while. Try copying or moving large parts of your drawing or importing or exploding large blocks. If it is a 3D drawing, try a hidden line removal on it. If everything is OK, try lowering the value by 1 and test the file again. Keep doing this until you get the out of RAM message, then raise the value by 1. This will be the optimum Acadfreeram value for your work. The minimum value for Acadfreeram is 5.

Once you have established an Acadfreeram value you feel comfortable with, you can have it set automatically every time you start your computer by including it in a file called Autoexec.BAT on your DOS Root directory. This is an ASCII file that contains a series of commands to DOS. They are listed in the file just as they would be entered through the keyboard. This file is read by DOS when you first start your computer and any instructions it reads in this file will be executed, hence the name Autoexec. If you would like to know more about this file, look in Appendix C or in your DOS manual for information on batch files.

If you purchased your computer and software together from a dealer who installed the software for you, chances are the Autoexec.BAT file already exists on your hard disk. The Acad-freeram setting may even be present in this file. If this is the case, use your word processor to edit the Autoexec.BAT file to either modify the existing SET command or add the command to the file.

If you don't have this file, you can create it using your word processor, COPY CON, or EDLIN. Since we show you how to create an Autoexec.BAT file in Appendix C, we won't explain the method here.

Adjusting the Memory Available for LISP Functions

You can also use the SET command to set the amount of RAM AutoCAD allocates for your LISP functions. AutoCAD allocates two types of memory where AutoLISP is concerned, *heap* and *stack*. In very general terms, heap is memory used to store your functions and variables. This is also called *node space*. The stack holds arguments and partial results during the evaluation of expressions. The stack is critical when you have complex expressions. The default values for these types of memory are 5,000 bytes each. This is usually adequate, but if you get the message

insufficient node space

while attempting to run an AutoLISP program, you can increase these values. In most cases, the heap is the limiting space. If you get this message, exit AutoCAD and enter the following while in DOS:

set lispheap = 15000
set lispstack = 5000

In this example, you triple the heap space while keeping the stack space the same. If your expressions become very complex, you may want to increase the stack as well. The total amount of heap and stack space cannot exceed 45,000 bytes. This means that if you have 5,000 bytes set for the stack, the most you can have for the heap is 40,000 bytes.

You can include these lines in your Autoexec.BAT file if you find you do need to increase the amount of space allocated to these types of memory permanently. If you purchased your system with a software add-on like AutoCAD AEC, or a similar product, the Autoexec.BAT file probably exists on your system and these values are probably already set, so you needn't alter them in any way. If they aren't set, follow the instructions that came with your add-on.

CONCLUSION

In this chapter we have given you simplified descriptions of some very powerful tools. You have seen how you can customize menus, line types, and hatch patterns with a word processor. This ease of customization is one of AutoCAD's most significant features and we encourage you to take advantage of it. If you would like to explore this subject further, *Advanced Techniques in AutoCAD*, by Robert M. Thomas (SYBEX, 1988) is a good source book.

We also hope that you will be enticed into trying some programming on your own and learning more about AutoLISP. *Advanced Techniques in AutoCAD* discusses AutoLISP as well as AutoCAD customization. Although AutoLISP is somewhat different from other forms of LISP, you may want to consider studying LISP as background for using AutoLISP. Versions of LISP are available for the PC, and there are a few good introductory books on LISP as well. *LISP: A Gentle Introduction to Symbolic Computation*, by David S. Touretzky (Harper & Row, 1984) is a good beginning book for the nonprogrammer.

AutoCAD offers many tools to accomplish the task of designing and drafting, but the people using the program are ultimately responsible for its success or failure in a production environment. Though the program is quite flexible, many factors come into play that are beyond its reach. In the next chapter, we will look at some of the factors influencing AutoCAD's use and what can be done to make it as productive as possible.

Chapter 19

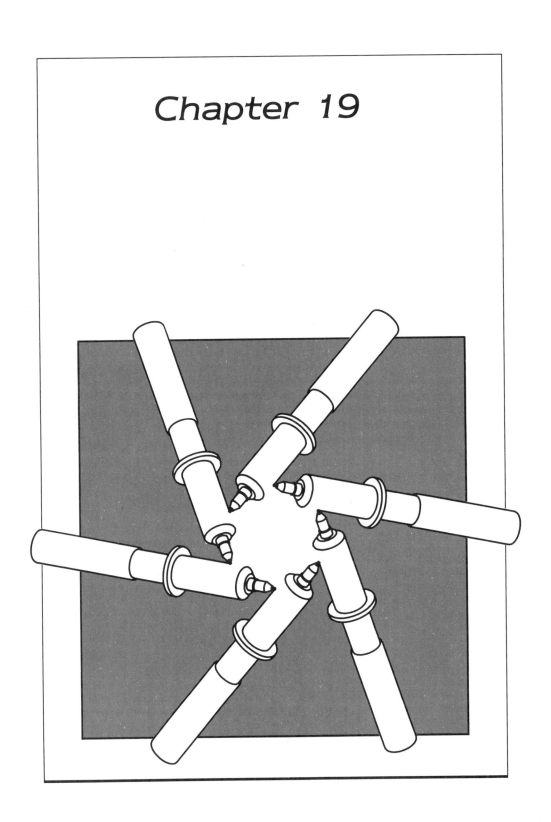

Incorporating AutoCAD
into Your Projects

SO FAR IN THIS BOOK you have related to AutoCAD as an individual learning a program. However, you are usually not alone when you use AutoCAD on a project. Your success in using it may depend as much on the people you work with as on your knowledge of the program. In this final chapter, we discuss some of the issues you may face as a member of an interactive group.

We will first look at general issues, such as selecting a system and obtaining support for it. Then we will discuss what happens once that system arrives in the office. Finally, we will look at some of the ways you can manage your system.

SELECTING A SYSTEM

Many factors other than cost influence the selection of a computer system. It is important to take a long-term view of your computer and how it integrates into your office both physically and socially. Although you probably have a system already, we will cover this subject briefly for those who do not or who are thinking of fine-tuning their hardware configurations for AutoCAD.

System requirements vary from profession to profession and office to office. A large architectural, engineering, or construction firm is likely to be involved in large projects and will have to coordinate with many consultants and client representatives. An AutoCAD system in such an office should be able to handle large drawings easily, and color is a must to help keep drawing information organized and easily controlled. A powerful microcomputer based on the 80386 microprocessor, with a high-resolution display system that allows dynamic hardware panning and zooming, is most desirable in this situation. Its high cost may well be offset by the time it saves. At least one large-format tablet for entering existing drawings is also a great time saver.

You should also consider integration with other software. AutoCAD might be used in conjunction with mini or mainframe CAD systems. Very large projects could be broken down into pieces easily managed by AutoCAD, while the larger assemblies of a design would be taken care of by the larger systems. Many translators are available that enable AutoCAD drawing files to be converted to files compatible with larger systems. Because PCs and the software that runs on them are so common, integration of spreadsheets, database managers, and AutoCAD is fairly easy. Integrating information processing can further improve productivity by enabling users to easily transfer information from one source to another.

Output might be produced with a large-format, high-quality plotter, plus one or two smaller plotters for small-scale drawings. You might want to consider doing all your plots on bond paper, then later having them photographically transferred to reproducible media. A service bureau may also be used for high-volume output of hard copy.

At the other end of the spectrum is the technical illustrator or technical writer who works only with line drawings that don't necessarily require the use of layers and colors. This person can use a less powerful computer and a high-resolution monochrome monitor. The choice of the display adapter and monitor may be influenced by the requirements of the desktop-publishing software the illustrator uses for combining text and graphics. Output might be produced with a PostScript device, such as an Apple LaserWriter. Systems are available that allow resolutions of up to 2,500 dots per inch.

Chances are you fall somewhere between these two extremes. A medium-sized firm may need less processing power than a large one. It may be more advantageous to have several medium- and low-cost workstations, rather than a few very expensive ones. In many cases, a mouse will work just as well as a digitizing tablet, so consideration should be given to where and when you need a tablet.

Whatever your situation, you should consider upgrade ability and system enhancement because technology changes daily. You may also want to integrate AutoCAD into a desktop-publishing system to produce proposals, reports, and other documentation.

If you don't already have a system, you may want to develop a checklist of system requirements (see the sample checklist in Table 19.1). Consider thoroughly all your foreseeable needs in the near and distant future. Also consider the nature of your clients' needs, and how your consultants' CAD systems fit in.

Hardware	Description
Computer	80286 or 80386 microprocessor. If budget is a problem, computer based on 8086 microprocessor can work well. Math coprocessor a must in any case
RAM	640K minimum with additional memory for memory page space preferred
Hard Disk	Fast-access hard disk with at least 40-millisecond access time. 20-megabyte capacity minimum
Floppy Disk	5¼-inch 1.2-megabyte capacity on AT-type computer, or 3½-inch 1.44-megabyte capacity on IBM System/2 computer. Additional 5¼-inch 360K capacity disk drive optional on AT-type computer
Tape Backup (optional)	Tape cartridge or cassette backup system matching hard disk capacity
Monitor for Drafting and Design	High-resolution color. 640 × 400 minimum. (EGA barely acceptable.) Higher resolution if budget allows. Sharp, flicker-free image. Hardware panning and zooming capability optional (see demo first or better yet, use for a while)

Table 19.1:   Checklist of system requirements

Monitor for Technical Illustration	High-resolution monochrome. 720 × 350 minimum. Sharp, flicker-free image. Compatible with desktop-publishing system
Input Device	Digitizing tablet with puck preferred, especially if tracing drawings is foreseen. Good quality is important. Large-format digitizer a must if you are tracing drawings larger than 11 × 11. Otherwise mouse is a reasonable alternative and inexpensive
Printer	Dot-matrix printer for quick draft plots. Limited to 11 × 17-inch if popular brand is chosen. Lesser-known brands can print larger drawings. Even if not used for printing drawings, the printer is very helpful for getting layer and block listings
Plotter	High-quality plotter for drawings larger than 11 × 17. Spare no expense in this category
Workstation Furniture	A comfortable chair and solid tables and monitor stands

Table 19.1:   Checklist of system requirements (cont.)

SUPPORTING YOUR SYSTEM

It helps to have knowledgeable people to turn to when questions arise. Most often, the vendor who sells the CAD system is also the source for technical support. Another source is the independent CAD consultant. You might even consider asking the advice of colleagues who have had some solid experience with AutoCAD. Most likely you will look to all three of these alternatives at one point or another as you start to implement an AutoCAD system in your work.

Getting Outside Support

It can be difficult to find a vendor who understands your special needs. This is because the vendor must have specialized knowledge of both computers and design or production. It is well worth searching for a knowledgeable vendor, however. He or she can save you several times the sales commission just in person-hours your office might spend trying to solve hardware and software problems. The vendor can help you set up a file organization and management system, something that can become a nightmare if left unattended. A good vendor should offer training and phone support, which are a must with a program that has as much depth as AutoCAD. Some vendors even offer user groups as a means of maintaining an active and open communication with their clients. Finally, you should consider a good service contract, especially if you are using some of the more exotic display systems and output devices.

Avoid the discount software sellers. Though you may get a deal on AutoCAD, you may be left in the cold when you need training or have questions. This situation eventually leads to higher costs for you than if you had purchased the system from a full-service dealer in the first place.

Another source for training and technical support is an independent consultant who is familiar with AutoCAD. Although it may be harder to find a CAD consultant than a vendor, his or her view of your needs is unbiased by the motivation to make a sale. The consultant's main goal is to help you gain productivity from your CAD system, so he or she will be more helpful than your average vendor.

Since this whole field is so new, consultants and vendors vary widely in their ability to give you real help. It is a good idea to get references before you use anyone's services. Your own colleagues may be the best source of information on vendors, consultants, and even hardware. You may be able to learn from their good fortune or mistakes.

Don't rely on magazine reviews and product demonstrations at shows. These can often be misleading or offer incomplete information. If you see something you like, test it before you buy it. This may be difficult for some products, but because of the complex nature of computer-aided design and drafting, it is important to know exactly what you are getting. You may even want to ask the prospective vendor to lend you a system and someone who knows AutoCAD for at least a week to run it through its paces on a real project.

Choosing In-House Experts

Perhaps even more important than a good vendor is an individual within your office who knows your system thoroughly. Ideally, everyone closely involved in your drafting and design projects is a proficient AutoCAD user, but it is impractical to expect everyone to give time to system management. So, usually one individual is chosen for this task. It can often be a thankless one, but when the going gets rough, an in-house expert is indispensible.

If you find that a task can be automated, a knowledgeable person can create custom macros and commands on the spot, saving your design or production staff hundreds of person-hours—especially if several people are performing that task. The in-house expert can also train new personnel and answer questions from less knowledgeable users.

In a smaller office, the in-house expert may be the design staff, production staff, and computer expert rolled into one. The point is: to really take advantage of AutoCAD or any CAD system, you should provide some in-house expertise. AutoCAD is a powerful tool, but that power is wasted if you don't take advantage of it.

You must be aware, however, that the role of the in-house expert requires a large amount of time away from other tasks he or she must perform. Not only are questions about using the program disruptive to the expert's own work, but writing custom applications can be at least a part-time job in itself. It is important to keep this under consideration when scheduling work or managing costs on a project.

The in-house expert should be a professional trained in whatever field your firm is involved in, rather than someone with a computer background. For example, an AutoCAD expert in an architectural firm should have an architectural background. It is vastly easier to train someone to use a computer than it is to train him or her to be an architect. However, the expert-to-be should be willing to develop some computer expertise.

Running a CAD system is not a simple clerical task. It takes clear thinking and good organizational skills, and good communication skills as well. The expert should have some interest in teaching and be patient when dealing with interruptions and "stupid" questions. He or she may well be a manager and should have access to the same information as any key player on your design team.

If you have several computers, you may also want to obtain some general technical support. If your company is new to computers, many questions will arise that are not directly related to AutoCAD.

The technical support person may be more familiar with computers than with your profession, but will be able to answer highly technical questions for which a computer background is required.

You could also contract an outside consultant to come in from time to time to augment the in-house expert. This way you can develop custom applications without waiting for your staff to develop the necessary skills. A consultant can also help train your staff and even fill in from time to time when production schedules become too tight.

ACCLIMATIZING THE STAFF

When an AutoCAD system is installed and operational, the next step is to acclimatize the staff to it. This can be the most difficult task of all. In nearly every office, there is at least one key person who resists the use of computers. This can be a tremendous problem, especially if that individual is at management level, though nearly anyone involved in a project can do damage. The human capacity to undermine the sincerest efforts is astounding, and when coupled with a complex computer system, results can be disastrous. Unfortunately, we don't have any easy solution to this problem aside from trying to foster a positive attitude toward the CAD system's capabilities and its implementation.

AutoCAD has a way of enhancing everything you do, both good and bad. Since it is capable of reproducing work rapidly, it is very easy to multiply errors until they are out of hand. This also holds true for project management. Poor management tends to be magnified when AutoCAD comes into the picture. Another dimension of information has to be dealt with in the form of blocks, symbols, and layers. If the users cannot manage and communicate this information, problems arise. Unlike traditional drafting methods, AutoCAD does not allow easy viewing of a drawing's current condition, so it is more difficult to know how your drawings stand at any given moment.

On the other hand, a smoothly running, well-organized project is reflected in the way AutoCAD enhances your productivity. In fact, good management is essential for realizing productivity gains with AutoCAD. A project on AutoCAD is only as good as the information you provide and the manner in which it is administered. Open communication and good record keeping are essential to the development and integrity of a design or a set of drawings. The better managed a project is, the fewer problems arise, thereby reducing the time required to get results.

Discussing CAD management procedures in your project kickoff meetings can help get people accustomed to the idea of using it. Exchanging information with your consultants regarding your CAD system standards is also an important step in keeping a job running smoothly from the start, especially if they are also using AutoCAD.

Learning the System

Learning AutoCAD can be time consuming. If you are the one who is to operate the AutoCAD system, at first you won't be as productive as you were when you were doing everything manually, nor can you perform miracles overnight. Once you have a good working knowledge of the program, you still have to integrate it into your day-to-day work. It will take you a month or two to get to a point where you are entering drawings with any proficiency, depending on how much time you spend regularly to learn AutoCAD. It also helps to have a real project you can work on while you are in training. You may want to select a job that doesn't have a tight schedule, so that if anything goes wrong you have enough time to make corrections.

It is important that you communicate to others what they can expect from you. Otherwise, you may find yourself in an awkward position because you haven't produced the results people thought you could produce.

Making AutoCAD Use Easier

Not everyone needs to be an AutoCAD expert, but almost everyone involved in design or production should be able to use AutoCAD in order for your firm to obtain maximum productivity from it. Designers especially should be involved, as AutoCAD can show significant time savings in the design phase of a project. You may want to consider an add-on software package to aid those in your office who need to use AutoCAD, but who are not likely to spend a lot of time learning it. These add-ons automate some of the more frequently used functions of a particular application. They can also provide ready-made office standards for symbols and layers. Autodesk's AEC is an enhancement intended for architects, engineers, and construction professionals. Other add-ons are available for circuit board designers, electrical engineers, civil engineers, and mechanical designers, to name a few.

Add-ons shouldn't be viewed as the only means of using AutoCAD within your office, but rather as an aid to casual users and a partner to your own custom applications. No two offices work alike and no two projects are exactly the same, so a system like AEC cannot be all things to all people. If you are serious about being as productive as possible with AutoCAD, you will want to develop custom applications.

Managing an AutoCAD Project

If you are managing a project that is to be put on AutoCAD, be sure you understand what it can and can't do. If your expectations are misled, and you don't communicate them to your design or production team, you can create friction and problems where they should never have occurred. Open and clear communication is of the utmost importance, especially when using AutoCAD or any CAD program.

If your office is just beginning to use AutoCAD, be sure you allow time for staff training. Generally, an individual can become independent on the program after 24 to 36 hours of training. By "independent," we mean able to produce drawings without having to constantly refer to a manual or call in the trainer. We hope this book will be enough to accomplish this and more. Once at that point, you might have to wait another month before the individual reaches a speed comparable to hand drafting. After that, the individual's productivity depends on his or her creativity and problem-solving ability. These are very rough estimates, but they should give you an idea of what to expect.

If you are using a software add-on product, the training period will be shorter, but the user won't have the same depth of knowledge as someone who isn't using the enhancements. As we mentioned earlier, this may be fine for casual users, but you will reach an artificial upper limit on productivity if you rely too heavily on add-ons.

You might consider a method of organization where designers are given AutoCAD workstations using the add-on software. They generate their preliminary designs, then pass them on to the CAD manager, along with any red-marked check plots (drawings with comments written on them, usually with a red pencil). The CAD manager then has the drawing set up to take advantage of Auto-CAD's features in the context of that particular job's requirements. Any further design changes are handled through red marks.

As you or your staff members are learning AutoCAD, you will also have to learn how to best utilize this new tool in the context of your office's operation methods. This may mean rethinking how you go about running a project. It may also mean training others you work with to operate differently. For example, one of the most common problems is scheduling work so that check plots can be produced on a timely basis. Normally project members are used to looking at drawings at convenient times as they progress, even when there are scheduled review dates. With AutoCAD, you won't have that luxury. You will have to keep plotting time in mind when scheduling drawing review dates. This means that the person doing the drawings must get accurate information in time to enter last-minute changes and to plot the drawings.

All this points to the fact that managers must be on top of scheduling. Communicating information to the people involved in a project on a timely basis should be a top priority.

ESTABLISHING OFFICE STANDARDS

Communication is especially important when you are one of many people working on the same project on separate computers. A well-developed set of standards and procedures helps to minimize problems that might be caused by miscommunication. In this section, we give some suggestions on how to set up these standards.

Establishing Layering Conventions

You have seen how layers can be a useful tool, but they can easily get out of hand when you have free reign over their creation and naming. This can be especially troublesome when more than one person is working on the same set of drawings. The following scenario illustrates this point.

One day the drawing you are working on has 20 layers. Then the next day you find that someone has added six more layers, each with some name that has no meaning to you whatsoever. You don't dare delete those layers or modify the objects on them for fear of retaliation from the individual who put them there. You ask around, but no one seems to know anything about these new layers. Finally, after spending an hour or two tracking down the culprit, you discover that the layers are not important at all.

With a naming convention, you can minimize this type of problem (though you may not eliminate it entirely). A too-rigid naming convention can cause as many problems as no convention at all, so it is best to give general guidelines rather than forcing everyone to stay within narrow limits. As we mentioned in Chapter 6, you can create layer names in a way that allows you to group them using wild cards. AutoCAD allows up to 31 characters in a layer name, so you can use descriptive names. Table 19.2 shows a list of layer names for an architectural project. They are organized by wall, ceiling, floor, and common elements and allow the use of the asterisk wild card to group layers.

Establishing Drawing Name Conventions

Just as you will want to keep track of layers, you will need a system to keep track of your drawing files and blocks. This is a little more difficult than keeping track of layers because DOS limits file names to eight characters. Although blocks can have 31-character names, because you will want to turn blocks into external files you should limit block names to 8 characters.

You can design a file-naming system that allows you to identify your drawing files by job number, drawing type, and revision number. The job number may be three digits, the drawing type may be an alphabetic code, and the revision may be an alphanumeric code. For example, a coded file name could be 704B061A.DWG.

In this example, the first three numbers could be an abbreviation of job number 8704. The next two characters could be a symbol for drawing type B on sheet number 6. Finally, the last two characters could mean revision number 1 and series designation A. You may even want to include a code number to designate symbols.

Layer Name	Description
Edge	Building features that appear on both floor and ceiling
Mechanical	Items that appear on both floor and ceiling, such as plumbing lines or ventilation ducts
Notes	Notes common to floor and ceiling
Wall	Wall information common to floor and ceiling

Table 19.2: Sample layer names

Layer Name	Description
F-casework	Floor-mounted casework
F-ceiling	Ceiling features reflected in floor plan
F-curb	Street curbs
F-door	Door symbols, since they appear on floor plans only
F-fixture	Plumbing fixtures that appear on floor plans only
F-jamb	Door jambs or window jambs
F-notes	Floor-plan-related notes
F-pattern	Floor patterns, such as tile or carpet
F-rail	Guardrail and handrails
F-stair	Stairs
F-wallpat	Wall pattern symbols designating wall material
C-casework	Casework outline on ceiling
C-edge	Edge of ceiling openings
C-fire	Ceiling-mounted fire system
C-fixture	Ceiling fixtures, such as fans and vents
C-header	Ceiling plan door and window headers
C-lights	Ceiling light fixtures
C-notes	Ceiling-related notes
C-pattern	Ceiling pattern, as for suspended ceiling

Table 19.2: *Sample layer names (cont.)*

Unfortunately, this type of code is difficult to learn. Most people prefer easily recognizable names, such as ELM02.DWG for Elm Street project sheet number 2. This recognizable type of name can't convey as much information as a coded name. Still, because most designers and drafters have enough to think about without remembering special codes, it is usually better to base your file-naming system on recognizable names. You may be able to devise a combination of the two systems that offers a word or phrase in conjunction with a code.

Organizing Directories

The more files you generate, the harder it is to find them on your hard disk. A good directory system can help you keep track of your files by breaking them into manageable groups. Using subdirectories to organize files is a must in any commercial setting. Figure 19.1 shows a sample directory structure that can help keep your drawings organized.

Line weights should be standardized in conjunction with layers. If you intend to use a service bureau for your plotting, you may want to check with them first because they may ask you to conform to their color and line weight standards.

You can have subdirectories under your AutoCAD directory for each job. Then, whenever you want to work on a set of drawings for a particular job, you set the directory associated with that job as your current directory in DOS, set a path to the AutoCAD directory, then start AutoCAD. This way, whenever you call up a file name, AutoCAD looks in the current directory for that file.

The following shows a batch file named Cad.BAT that automatically sets the path and default subdirectory for a given file name.

```
set acad = c:\ACAD
path \ACAD;\DOS;\BATCH
CD \ACAD\%1
acad
autoexec
```

The %1 at the end of the third line tells DOS to place the subdirectory name there.

Before using this batch file, you should create a directory called Dos that contains your external DOS command files, a directory called Batch containing all your batch files, and subdirectories under your AutoCAD directory containing files for your various jobs. To use the batch file, you enter CAD *subdirectory name* at the DOS prompt. It

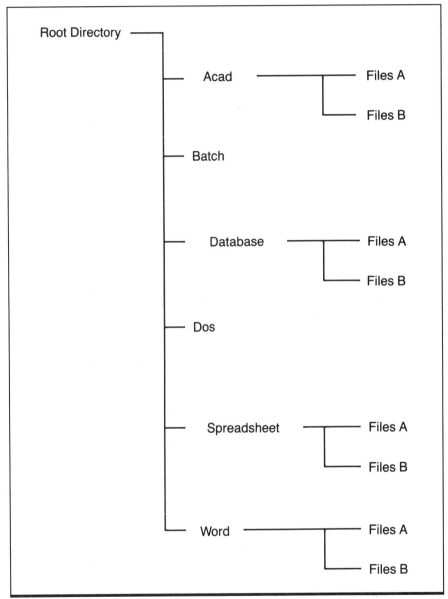

Figure 19.1:   *A sample DOS directory structure*

then sets a path to the most commonly used directories, Acad, Dos, and Batch, and changes the directory to \Acad*subdirectory name.* Finally, it starts AutoCAD. See Appendix C of this book or your DOS manual for more details on batch files.

MAINTAINING FILES

As you use your computer system you will generate files rapidly. Some files will be garbage, some will be necessary but infrequently used, and others will be current job files or system files that are constantly used. Also, AutoCAD automatically creates backup files (they have the extension .BAK), which you may or may not want to keep. An AutoCAD backup file is a copy of the most recent version of the file before the last Save or End is issued in AutoCAD. If you save the .BAK files, you will always have the next-to-the-most-recent version of a file. If something is wrong with the most recent version, you can restore the .BAK file to a drawing file by simply changing the .BAK extension to .DWG.

All these files take up valuable space, and you may end up with insufficient room for your working files. Because of this, you will want to clear the unused files off the hard disk by erasing unwanted files and archiving infrequently used ones on a daily basis. You will also want to erase current files from your hard disk once they have been backed up on floppy disks. Ideally, you should do this at every editing session so you don't forget which files are meaningful and which are garbage. You may want to erase all your .BAK files as well if you don't care to keep them.

Managing Active Files

You could think of the hard disk as a desktop where you lay out the files you want to use that day. When you start work in the morning, you take the files you want to work with out of a file drawer. When you are done, you put them back in the drawer. Old, unused files are archived in another file drawer, and unwanted documents are thrown away. On your computer, you might think of floppy disks as your file drawers. You store your files there when they are not in use. You copy the files you want to work with onto your hard disk where AutoCAD has quick access to them. When you are done, you copy them back onto the floppy disk and put the disk away. Then you erase those files from your hard disk, including any .BAK files AutoCAD has created. Inactive files should be stored for safekeeping on another set of floppy disks. All of these floppy disks should be clearly labeled in a manner others can easily understand (see Figure 19.2).

This process not only helps you save space on your hard disk, it helps you keep track of the latest files, especially when several people are working on the same ones. You may even want to have

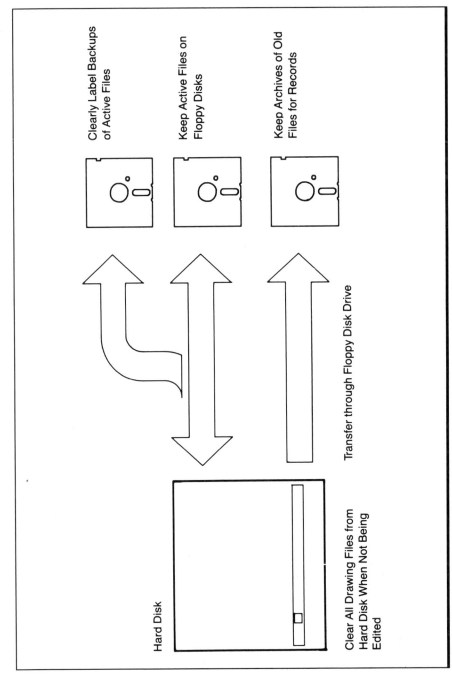

Figure 19.2: Typical procedure for storing and retrieving active files

a central place where the latest versions of files are kept on disks stored by job or by file type.

It is a good idea to keep separate copies of active files in a separate place, perhaps even a separate building, in case the originals are lost or corrupted in some way. These backup files should be clearly labeled as such; otherwise you could confuse them with original files and end up with some serious version control problems.

For example, if more than one person is working on the same project, one person may edit the original file and the other the backup, each thinking they have the original. When they realize what they have done, they must spend extra time merging their efforts into one file. If original files are clearly marked, this error will not occur so easily. While it is being edited, the original will be away from its storage area, so any individual wanting to work on it will have to wait until the other is done.

Backing Up Files

Besides keeping your hard disk clear of unused and inactive files, you may also want to back it up periodically, say once a week. This might be done by the in-house expert or the technical support staff. By backing up the hard disk, you save the configuration of all your programs and the directory structure. In the event of a hard disk failure, you won't have to reinstall and reconfigure all your software. You just restore the backups once the problem with the hard disk is remedied.

There are two methods for backing up a hard disk. One is through software using your existing floppy disk drive and removable disks as the backup media. DOS provides software for this purpose, but it is slow and difficult to use. You may want to look at some of the commercially available hard disk backup utility programs, such as Fastback. Many of them can back up a 20-megabyte hard disk in less than 10 minutes using standard floppy disks.

Prices of backup utilities vary from $50 to $150. You must also consider the cost of the disks used for backup storage. A full 20 megabytes usually requires 60 disks. At a dollar per disk, it costs $60 to back up one 20-megabyte hard disk. An AT-type computer can back up a 20-megabyte disk using about 20 1.2-megabyte floppy disks. These high-density disks generally cost three times as much as standard-density disks, so there is no cost saving.

Tape backup systems are an alternative way to back up a hard disk. These systems transfer the contents of your hard disk onto a cartridge or cassette tape similar to the type used for stereo recordings. A tape system also requires software to operate, but the software is usually provided as part of the system.

Tape backup systems cost considerably more than the software alternative, but they offer more flexibility and ease of use. For example, with backup software, you must constantly insert and remove disks from the computer as they are filled up. A tape backup system allows you to start the backup process, then walk away to do something else. Tape backup systems can take from 5 to 15 minutes to back up a 20-megabyte hard disk. These systems cost from $500 for a system that is installed inside your PC, to $2,000 for an external unit. The cartridges or cassettes used for storage cost around $30. While you initially spend more on a tape backup system, you can save time and pay less for storage media.

Both methods offer partial backup of your hard disk in addition to total backup, and in most cases, files can be restored selectively if you so desire.

Labeling Hard Copies

A problem you will run into once you start to generate lots of files is keeping track of which AutoCAD file goes with which hard-copy drawing. It is a good idea to place an identifying tag on the drawing in some inconspicuous place that will plot with the drawing. As well as the file name, you should include such information as the date and time the drawing was last edited, who edited it, and what submission the plot was done for. All these bits of information can prove helpful in the progress of a design or production project (see Figure 19.3).

KEEPING RECORDS

Computers are said to create the paperless office. As you work more and more with them, you may find that quite the opposite is true. Although you may store more information on magnetic media, you will spend a good deal of time reviewing that information on hard copy because it is very difficult to spot errors on a computer monitor. Another level of documentation must also occur when you use AutoCAD on large projects. You will have to have a way of keeping track of the many elements that go into the creation of drawings.

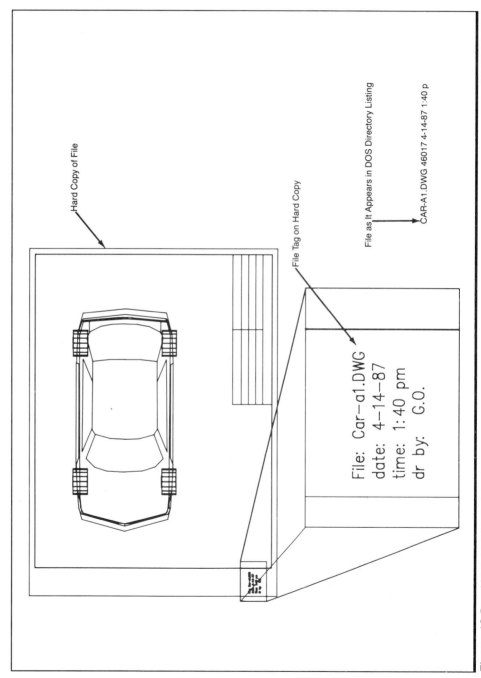

Hard Copy of File

File Tag on Hard Copy

File as It Appears in DOS Directory Listing

CAR-A1.DWG 46017 4-14-87 1:40 p

File: Car—a1.DWG
date: 4—14—87
time: 1:40 pm
dr by: G.O.

Figure 19.3:   How to tag a drawing

Because jobs vary in their requirements, you may want to provide a layer log to help keep track of layers and their intended uses for specific jobs. Figure 19.4 shows a sample layer log. Also, to keep track of blocks within files, you may want to keep a log of block names and their insertion values (see Figure 19.5). Finally, you may want to keep a log of symbols. You will probably have a library of symbols that everyone uses. This library will grow as your projects become more varied, so you may want to document these symbols to keep track of them (see Figure 19.6).

Plotting is an activity that you may also want to keep records for, especially if you bill your clients separately for computer time or for analyzing job costs. A plot log might contain such information as the time spent on plotting, the type of plot that was done, the purpose of the plot, and even plotting problems that arise with each drawing.

Although records may be the last thing on your mind when you are working to meet a deadline, in the long run they can save time and aggravation for you and the people you work with.

UNDERSTANDING WHAT AUTOCAD CAN DO FOR YOU

Many of us have only a vague idea of what AutoCAD can do for our work. We think it will make our drafting go faster but we're not sure exactly how, or we believe it will make us produce better-quality drawings. Some people believe it can make them better designers or allow them to produce professional-quality drawings without having much drawing talent. All these things are true to an extent, and Auto-CAD can help you in some ways that are less tangible than speed and quality.

Seeing the Hidden Advantages

We have discussed how AutoCAD can help you in both drafting and design work by allowing you to visualize your ideas more clearly and by reducing the time it takes to do repetitive tasks. AutoCAD also forces you to organize your drawing process more efficiently. It changes your perception of problems and, though it may introduce new ones, the additional accuracy and information it provides minimize errors.

Layer Log			Job # _____
Layer Name	Colors	Line Types	Remarks

Figure 19.4: *A sample layer log*

Block Log			Job # _____
Block Name	Insert Layer	Nested Blocks	Remarks

Figure 19.5: *A sample block log*

Symbol Log			Job # _____
Symbol Name	Insert Layer	Remarks	Symbol

Figure 19.6: *A sample symbol log*

AutoCAD also provides drawing consistency. A set of drawings done on AutoCAD is more legible and consistent, reducing the possibility of errors caused by illegible handwriting or poor drafting. In our litigious culture, this can be a significant feature.

Finally, since AutoCAD is becoming so pervasive, it is easier to find people who can use it proficiently. As this number of people grows, training will become less of a burden to your company.

Taking a Project Off AutoCAD

As helpful as AutoCAD can be, there are times when it is simply not worth keeping a project on AutoCAD. Last-minute changes that are minor but pervasive throughout a set of drawings are best made by hand on the most up-to-date hard copy. That way, you don't spend a long time plotting drawings or waste drawing media.

Only your experience can help you determine the best time to stop using AutoCAD and start making changes by hand. Many factors affect this decision, such as the size and complexity of the project, available people, and the nature of the revisions, to name a few. Once the project is done, however, you may still want to go back and enter the final changes in AutoCAD just to keep your files up-to-date.

CONCLUSION

Learning to manage an AutoCAD system can be as demanding as learning the program itself. It is also a task that is often forgotten until it is too late. When this happens, the blame for poor productivity or errors often falls on the program or even the computer user. No two offices operate exactly alike, so regard this last chapter as a reminder that there is more to using AutoCAD than just learning it.

Unlike words, drawings have few restrictions. The process of writing requires adherence to the structures of our language. The process of drawing, on the other hand, has no fixed structure. There are a million ways to draw a face or a building, for example. For this reason, AutoCAD is much less restricted in the way you use it. It has the potential for yet-to-be-discovered uses. We encourage you to experiment with AutoCAD and explore other possibilities for problem solving, as well as drawing.

Appendix A

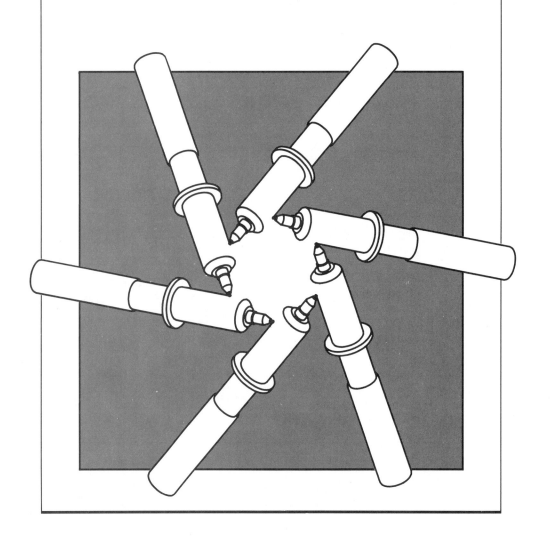

Hardware Options

THIS APPENDIX IS A LIST of hardware options supported by AutoCAD. Because the number of available options is constantly expanding, check with an AutoCAD dealer for the most up-to-date list. Some of the display adapters will not work on some IBM PC compatibles, so be sure you can use a device on your system before you purchase it. It is a good idea to get a guarantee from the vendor that if the board doesn't work in your computer, you can return it for a refund.

COMPUTERS

Each computer supported by AutoCAD requires a different version of the program, so be sure you specify which machine you have if you plan to purchase AutoCAD. Also, not all peripheral devices are supported for all the computers listed, other than the PC/XT and AT. Contact your AutoCAD dealer for a list of devices for each system.

Apollo Domain 3000 computers (32-bit)

AT&T 6300 and Olivetti M24

Compaq computers, all models

DEC MicroVAX 2000 (32-bit)

IBM /3270

IBM PC/AT and PC/XT and most compatibles

IBM PC/RT (32-bit)

IBM Personal System/2 computers (some models are 32-bit)

NEC APC III

Sun MicroSystems computers (32-bit)

Texas Instruments Professional Computer and Business Pro

Wang PCs

INPUT OPTIONS

Choose an input device that generates smooth cursor movement. Some of the lesser-quality input devices cause erratic movement. When looking for an input device other than a mouse, choose one that provides positive feedback, such as a button click or a beep, when you pick an object on the screen. Otherwise, it is easier to erroneously select objects and commands. Display adapters can affect tablet operation as well. Some display adapters will not work at all in conjunction with some tablets.

Mice

Product	Company
Hewlett-Packard Mouse. For use with Hewlett-Packard computers. Two-button.	Hewlett-Packard 1326 Kifer Rd. Sunnyvale, CA 94086
Logitech Logimouse R-5 and R-7. Microsoft Mouse and Mouse Systems Mouse compatible. Three-button.	Logitech, Inc. 805 Veterans Blvd. Redwood City, CA 94063
Microsoft Serial Mouse. Supports most popular software. Two-button.	Microsoft Corp. 16011 NE 36th Way Redmond, WA 98073

Product	Company
Mouse Systems Mouse. Supports most popular software. Also known as IBM mouse. Three-button.	Mouse Systems Corp. 2600 San Tomas Expressway Santa Clara, CA 95051
Summagraphics SummaMouse. Three-button mouse, requires serial port.	Summagraphics Corp. 777 State Street Ext. Fairfield, CT 06430
Torrington Mouse. Microsoft Mouse and Mouse Systems Mouse compatible. Three-button.	The Torrington Company P.O. Box 1008 Torrington, CT 06790

Digitizing Tablets

Product	Company
Calcomp 2000, 2100, 9000 Series, and 9100 Series. Tablets require serial port. Optional multibutton puck available on all models.	Calcomp Sub. of Lockheed Corp. 2411 W. La Palma Anaheim, CA 92801
Geographics Drafting Board. Tablet requires serial port. Uses foot switch as pick button. Connects to standard drafting table.	Geographics 1318 Alms Dr. Champaign, IL 61820
GTCO Digipad 5 Tablets and Micro DIGI-PAD (type 7). Tablets require serial port. Multibutton puck option available.	GTCO Corp. 7125 Riverwood Dr. Columbia, MD 21046
Hewlett-Packard HIL Devices. Tablets for the Hewlett-Packard computers. Multibutton puck option available.	Hewlett-Packard See section on mice for address
Hitachi HICOMSCAN HDG Series and Tiger Tablet. Tablets require serial port. Multibutton puck option available.	Hitachi America, Ltd. 2990 Gateway Dr., Suite 100 Norcross, GA 30071

Product	Company
Houston Instrument Series 7000 (COMPLOT) and HIPAD DT11AA. Tablets require serial port. Multibutton puck option available.	Div. of Ametek 8500 Cameron Rd. Austin, TX 78753
Kurta tablets. Tablets require serial port. Multibutton puck option available.	Kurta Corp. 4610 S. 35th St. Phoenix, AZ 85040
Numonics 2200 Series. Tablets require serial port. Multibutton puck option available.	Numonics Corp. 418 Pierce St. Sansdale, PA 19446
Pencept Penpad 320. Tablet with handwriting recognition capability. Stylus only.	Pencept, Inc. 39 Green St. Waltham, MA 02154
SAC GP-7 Grafbar and GP-8. Digitizers that use sound detection device rather than a tablet for locating points. The large-format digitizers are relatively inexpensive. Multibutton puck option available.	Science Accessories Corp. 970 Kings Hwy. West Southport, CT 06490
Scriptel SPD. Tablet requires serial port. Multibutton puck option available.	Scriptel Corp. 4145 Arlingate Plaza Columbus, OH 43228
Seiko DT-3103/4103. Tablets require serial port. Multibutton puck option available.	Seiko Instruments USA, Inc. 1130 Ringwood Ct. San Jose, CA 95131
Summagraphics Bit Pad One, MM Series Tablets, and MicroGrid. Tablets require serial port. Multibutton puck option available.	Summagraphics Corp. See section on mice for address

Trackballs

Product	Company
Honeywell LYNX Trackball. These devices can often emulate a mouse and offer multiple function buttons. See Chapter 1 for description of trackballs.	Honeywell Sub. of Disc Instruments 102 East Baker St. Costa Mesa, CA 92626

Joysticks

Kraft Joystick. Many joysticks are available for the PC that emulate the Kraft joystick. You must have a game port for these devices. See Chapter 1 for description of joysticks.	Kraft 18419 Park Grove Dallas, TX 95252

DISPLAY OPTIONS

We mentioned in Chapter 1 that because a display adapter often requires a matching monitor, the adapter and the monitor are often considered together as a system, especially in the higher resolutions. The list of display options we show is limited to the adapters. The manufacturer of each display adapter will give specific recommendations for monitors and often will sell the two together, so we have not discussed monitors in any detail. Many of the display systems will work with the popular *multiscan* or *multisync* monitors. These are most often used with the EGA display adapters, but are capable of working with a variety of adapters.

Many display systems offer *single-* or *dual-screen configurations*. A dual-screen configuration displays text on one monitor and graphics on the other. It requires a separate monochrome or color display system for the text screen because the graphic display is unable to display text. If you want a dual-screen system, be sure to take measures to reduce interference between monitors. Many color monitors can adversely affect the display of a monochrome monitor placed close by. Also, dual-screen systems take up more desk space and you can get tired looking back and forth between monitors. Their use is often a matter of preference.

Some display systems that operate with AutoCAD offer hardware panning and zooming. This feature allows instantaneous panning and zooming by storing the drawing display at a very high resolution in display memory. A discussion of this feature and its variations can be found in Chapter 17. If you are interested in hardware panning and zooming capability, we suggest you contact the display manufacturer for the name of a dealer who can give you a demonstration. Our list below indicates which display devices have this capability. Nearly all display devices listed under the ADI option at the end of this appendix also provide hardware panning and zooming.

We should also mention that the EGA, CGA, Hercules, and most compatible display adapters support the advanced user interface, which allows you to use pull-down menus and dialog boxes.

Finally, you should consider power requirements when looking for a display adapter. Some require great amounts of power, while others are more efficient. You risk ruining your computer if it does not have sufficient power to drive your adapter.

Display Adapter	Company
ADI Graphics Option. See list of manufacturers that have written ADI drivers at the end of this appendix.	
Bell and Howell CDI IV. 640 × 480, 16-color or 832 × 630, 16-color, dual-screen.	Bell and Howell 6800 McCormick Rd. Chicago, IL 60645
BNW Graphics Adapter. 1024 × 1024, 16-color, dual-screen.	BNW, Inc. 17419 Farley Rd. Los Gatos, CA 95030
Cambridge Big Picture. 1024 × 780, monochrome or color, dual-screen.	Cambridge Computer Graphics 6201 Ascot Dr. Oakland, CA 94611

Display adapter	Company
Conographic Model 40. 640 × 400, 16-color, single-screen. Early models may not work with ANSI.SYS.	Conographic Corp. 17841 Fitch St. Irvine, CA 92714
Control Systems Artist 1 and 2. 1 is 1024 × 1024, 16-color. 2 is 640 × 400, 16-color, dual-screen, hardware panning and zooming capability.	Control Systems 2675 Patton Rd. St. Paul, MN 55164
Control Systems Artist Transformer. 640 × 400, 16-color, single-screen, hardware panning and zooming capability, will not work with Ansi.SYS.	Control Systems See above for address
Cordata FastDraft 480. 640 × 480, 16-color, single- or dual-screen, will not work with Ansi.SYS.	Cordata, Inc. 275 E. Hillcrest Dr. Thousand Oaks, CA 91360
GraphAx 20/20. 2048 × 2048, 16-color, hardware panning and zooming capability, dual-screen.	ACS International, Inc. 2105 Luna Rd., Suite 330 Carrollton, TX 75006
Hercules Graphics Card. 720 × 348, monochrome, single-screen. This adapter and most of its compatibles support the advanced user interface.	Hercules Computer Technology 2550 Ninth St. Berkeley, CA 94701
Hewlett-Packard Multi Mode. For use with HP Vectra, 640 × 400, monochrome, single-screen.	Hewlett-Packard See section on mice for address
Hewlett-Packard 82960. For use with HP Vectra, similar to IBM PGA.	Hewlett-Packard See section on mice for address
IBM 8514/A for Personal System/2. 1024 × 768, 256 colors.	International Business Machines Corp. P.O. Box 1328-W Boca Raton, FL 33432

Display adapter	Company
IBM Color/Graphics Display (CGA). 640 × 200 monochrome or 320 × 200, four-color, single- or dual-screen. This adapter and most of its compatibles support the advanced user interface.	International Business Machines Corp. See above for address
IBM Enhanced Graphics Display (EGA). 640 × 350, up to 16-color depending on installed memory, single-screen. This adapter and most of its compatibles support the advanced user interface.	International Business Machines Corp. See above for address
IBM Professional Graphics Controller. 640 × 480, 256 colors, single- or dual-screen.	International Business Machines Corp. See above for address
Metheus 1004 and 1008 display. 1024 × 768, 16 colors on the 1004, 256 colors on the 1008, hardware panning and zooming, CGA emulation, single-screen.	Metheus Corp. P.O. Box 1049 Hillsboro, OR 97123
Number Nine NNIOS Graphics Display. 1024 × 768, 16-color, dual-screen.	Number Nine Computer 725 Concord Ave. Cambridge, MA 02138
Number Nine Revolution Board. 512 × 512, 256-color, dual-screen.	Number Nine Computer See above for address
Persyst BOB. 640 × 400, 16-color, single-screen.	Persyst 3545 Harbor Blvd. Costa Mesa, CA 92626
Quadram Quadscreen. 968 × 512, monochrome, single- or dual-screen.	Quadram One Quad Way Norcross, GA 30093
Quintar displays. 640 × 480, 16-color or 832 × 630, 16-color dual-screen.	Div. of Bell and Howell 411 Amapola Ave. Torrance, CA 90501

Display adapter	Company
Ramtek display. 1280 × 1024, 16-color, dual-screen.	Ramtek Corp. 2211 Lawson Ln. Santa Clara, CA 95050
Sigma Designs Color 400. 640 × 400, 16-color, single-screen.	Sigma Designs, Inc. 2023 O'Toole Ave. San Jose, CA 95131
STB Shauffeur. 640 × 352, monochrome, single-screen.	STB Systems, Inc. 601 N. Glenville, Suite 125 Richardson, TX 75081
STB Super Res 400. 320 × 400, 16-color and 649 × 400, four-color, dual-screen.	STB Systems See above for address
STB XVI. 320 × 200, 16-color, single- or dual-screen.	STB Systems See above for address
TAT Galaxy G-500 Graphics Card. 640 × 400, 16-color to 1024 × 768, 16-color, dual-screen.	GalaGraph, Inc. 1270 Lawrence Station Rd., Bldg. E Sunnyvale, CA 94089
Tecmar Graphics Master. 640 × 400, 16-color, single-screen.	Tecmar 6225 Cochran Rd. Solon, OH 44139
Vectrix PEPE. 1024 × 1024, 16-color, dual-screen.	Vectrix Corp. 2606 Branchwood Dr. Greensboro, NC 27408
Vectrix VX384 and Midas Card Set. 640 × 480, 256 colors, dual-screen.	Vectrix Corp. See above for address
Image Manager Series. 640 × 480, 256 colors to 1024 × 800, 256 colors. Uses display list for fast zooms and pans. Display list uses page memory.	Vermont Microsystems, Inc. P.O. Box 236 11 Tigan St. Winooski, VT 05404
Verticom H-Series. 1024 × 768, 16-color and store-view feature (similar in effect to hardware panning) single- or dual-screen.	Verticom, Inc. 545 Weddell Dr. Sunnyvale, CA 94089

Display adapter	Company
Verticom M-Series. 640 × 480, 16-color or 256-color with model M256, single- or dual-screen.	Verticom, Inc. See above for address
Wyse WY-700. 1280 × 800, monochrome, single- or dual-screen.	Wyse Technology 3571 North First St. San Jose, CA 95134

OUTPUT OPTIONS

Output options vary greatly in quality and price. Quality and format size are the major considerations in both printers and plotters. Nearly all printers give accurate drawings, but some produce better line quality than others. Some plotters give only acceptable results, while others are quite impressive in their speed and accuracy. Color is optional on both printers and plotters. Some printers produce color prints, while virtually all plotters allow color.

The following list will give you general information on printers and plotters. If at all possible, get a demonstration of these devices before you buy. It also helps if you can consult a colleague who has had experience with the device you are interested in.

Printers

Printer choice is mostly an issue of reliability and required drawing width, since most printers are used only for drafts. However, some of the laser printers can produce very high-quality prints and should be considered if you are doing small-format drawings. Also, printers and typesetting equipment that use the PostScript page description language are supported, so you can potentially get resolutions of up to 2500 dots per inch.

Product	Company
ADI Printer Plotter. See list of manufacturers that have written ADI drivers at the end of this appendix.	

Product	Company
Cordata LP300X Laser Printer. Laser printer capable of 300 × 300 dpi resolution on an 8 × 11-inch area. Requires serial port.	Cordata, Inc. 275 E. Hillcrest Dr. Thousand Oaks, CA 91360
Datacopy Model 90. This is not a hardware printer but a software package that converts AutoCAD drawings into a format that can be read by Datacopy's character-recognition software.	Datacopy Corp. 1215 Terra Bella Ave. Mountain View, CA 94040
Epson Fx-80, 100, or 286 dot-matrix printers. Depending on model, print sizes up to 11 × 13 are possible. Require either parallel or serial port.	Epson America, Inc. 2780 Lomita Blvd. Torrance, CA 90505
Hewlett-Packard LaserJet printers. Depending on the amount of memory installed in these printers, a 300 dpi resolution is possible over the entire page. Standard configurations, however, limit 300 dpi to a small area. Maximum print area is 8 × 11 inches. After the first copy is made, these printers can produce multiple copies at the rate of eight pages per minute. Require serial port.	Hewlett-Packard See section on mice for address
IBM Color JetPrinter 3852-2, Proprinter, and Proprinter XL. Color JetPrinter is limited to 8 × 11-inch prints, but is capable of printing in color. Proprinters can print up to 11 × 13-inch prints. Require parallel port.	International Business Machines Corp. See section on display options for address

Product	Company
JDL-750. Dot-matrix printer capable of up to 15 × 43-inch prints. Resolution is adjustable between 90 and 180 dpi. Can also print in color. Requires parallel port.	JDL, Inc. 2801 Townsgate Rd., #104 Westlake Village, CA 91361
Mitsubishi G500. Dot-matrix printer capable of 240 × 240 dpi. Can print in seven colors. Limited to 8 × 9-inch drawing area. Requires parallel port.	Mitsubishi International Corp. 520 Madison Ave. New York, NY 10022
Okidata 84, 93. Dot-matrix printers capable of up to 11 × 13-inch prints depending on model. Require parallel or serial port.	Okidata Corp. 532 Fellowship Rd. Mt. Laurel, NJ 08054
PostScript Writer for laser printers. Various resolutions can be specified up to 2540 dpi. Print area is limited to 8 × 11 inches. Connection requirement depends on device.	Adobe Systems, Inc. 1585 Charleston Rd. Mountainview, CA 94039
Printronix Model 4160. Dot-matrix printer capable of 11 × 13-inch prints. Requires parallel port.	Printronix, Inc. 17500 Cartwright Rd. Irvine, CA 92713
Texas Instruments Omni 800. Dot-matrix printer capable of 72 × 144-dpi resolution and a print area of up to 13 × 65 inches. Requires parallel or serial port.	Texas Instruments, Inc. P.O. Box 809063 Dallas, TX 75380
Toshiba 3-in-One Printer/Plotter. Dot-matrix printer capable of 180 × 180-dpi resolution and a print area of up to 11 × 13 inches. Requires parallel or serial port.	Toshiba America, Inc. 2441 Michelle Dr. Tustin, CA 92680

Plotters

Plotter quality can be determined by speed and accuracy. The better the quality, the faster and more accurate the plot and the more expensive the plotter. The best test for a plotter is a large, dense drawing. This will test both speed and *pen repeatability*. Pen repeatability is the capability of the pen to return to the same point on the drawing after moving across the drawing to another point. Poor repeatability can cause misalignment of line and arc endpoints. This is an important consideration for drawings that require accuracy.

Product	Company
ADI Plotter. See list of manufacturers that have written ADI drivers at the end of this appendix. This option can be used to create 2D drawings of 3D views. See Chapter 14 for details.	
Alpha Merics Alphaplot I and II. Up to 24 × 32-inch plots. Require serial port.	Alpha Merics Corp. 8031 Remmet Ave. Canoga Park, CA 91304
CalComp plotters. Plot sizes vary from model to model. Sizes up to 48 inches are available using multiple pens. Require serial port. Hardware line types are not supported by AutoCAD.	CalComp See section on digitizing tablets for address
Gould Colorwriter Models DS7, DS10, 6120, 6310, and 6320. Up to 11 × 17-inch plots using multiple pens. Require serial port.	Gould, Inc. 3631 Perkins Ave. Cleveland, OH 44114
Hewlett-Packard Plotters. Plot sizes vary from model to model. Sizes up to 36 × 48 are available using multiple pens. Require serial port.	Hewlett-Packard See section on mice for address

Product	Company
Houston Instrument DMP-xx Series (incl. DMP-56). Plot sizes vary from model to model. Sizes up to 32 × 48 inches are available. Scanner and multipen options are also available. Require serial port.	Houston Instrument See section on digitizing tablets for address
IBM Models XY/700 Series and Series 7300. Plot sizes vary from model to model. Sizes up to 36 × 48 inches are available. Hewlett-Packard manufactures some of these models. Require serial port.	International Business Machines Corp. See section on display options for address
Imagen Page Printers. Limited to 8 × 10-inch plots. Require parallel or serial port.	Imagen Corp. 2650 San Tomas Expressway Santa Clara, CA 95052
Ioline plotters. Capable of plots up to 36 × 81 inches. Require serial port.	Ioline Corp. 19417 36th Ave. West, D-1 Lynnwood, WA 98036
Nicolet plotters. Plot sizes vary from model to model. Sizes up to 32 × 44 inches available using multiple pens. Require serial port.	Bruning Computer Graphics 777 Arnold Dr. Martinez, CA 94553
Roland DG Plotters. Several models available offering up to 24 × 36-inch plots and multiple pens. Require serial port.	Roland DG 7200 Dominion Circle Los Angeles, CA 90040
Enter Computer plotters. Up to 24 × 36-inch plots, some with multiple pens. Require serial port.	Enter Computer 6867 Nancy Ridge Dr. San Diego, CA 92121
Western Graphtec plotters. Several models available offering sizes up to 32 × 44 inches using multiple pens. Require serial port.	Western Graphtec 12 Chrysler St. Irvine, CA 92718

ADI Drivers

ADI stands for Autodesk Device Interface. AutoCAD offers the ADI Toolkit for manufacturers who wish to write drivers for their own hardware. This frees Autodesk from having to write drivers for every device on the market.

The companies listed below currently have or are developing drivers for their products to interface with AutoCAD or other Autodesk products. If you don't see a hardware device you want on the lists above, check to see if its manufacturer is listed below. If so, contact the manufacturer directly.

Also, many products imitate devices on the above lists as a way of maintaining compatibility with AutoCAD, so even if they are not listed, they may still work. Check with the manufacturers and get a demonstration before you purchase such devices.

As a final note, ADI drivers tend to use up some of the computer system's memory, as they are usually terminate and stay resident-type software. The amount of memory used varies from driver to driver. You may find this to be an important consideration.

Product	Company
PTG1 Graphics Card. 800 × 600, 16-color, can be used with multisync monitors. Single-screen.	Aristocad 333 Cobalt Way #107 Sunnyvale, CA 94086 (408) 241-8020
Multi/4, Models 10, 12, 12e, 15, and 15e Graphics Cards. Multi/4 is MultiSync compatible, 800 × 600, 16-color. Other models are 1280 × 1024, 16-color. All models are single-screen and can handle software designed for the IBM EGA. All models offer hardware panning and zooming, with some offering a 2000 × 2000-pixel display memory option. BNW also offers high-resolution graphics cards for Wang computers.	BNW, Inc. 17419 Farley Rd. Los Gatos, CA 95030 (408) 395-7171

Product	Company
Artist 10 and 10-16. 1024 × 768, 16-color hardware panning and zooming. Some models offer 1600 × 1200-pixel display memory. Other models offer display list processors that use expanded or extended memory. Single- or dual-screen options.	Control Systems P.O. Box 64750 2675 Patton Rd. St. Paul, MN 55164 (612) 631-7800
Dolen MultiVID 16. 1024 × 1024, 16-color, hardware panning and zooming, dual- or single-screen options. Features fast redraws.	Dolen Computer Corporation P.O. Box 599 Norwalk, CT 06856 (203) 855-0895
Galaxy ADI Driver. Hardware panning and zooming, 6400 × 4800 virtual screen (similar to display list). Displays 1024 × 512, 16 colors.	GalaGraph, Inc. (formerly TAT) Galaxy EGX-2 1270 Lawrence Station Rd., Bldg. E Sunnyvale, CA 94089 (408) 734-2202
DGIS standard for drivers, which works with AutoCAD. Video 7 1280, Emulex Kaleidoscope, NDI Genesis, Quadram Quad HPG, are all display cards that support the DGIS standard. More display systems will be added to this list in the future. A feature of this standard is that it can support special graphics processors, such as the Intel 82786 and the TI TMS 34010. These processors offer very fast redraw speeds.	Graphic Software Systems P.O. Box 4900 9590 SW Gemini Dr. Beaverton, OR 97005 (503) 641-2200
Hercules InColor Card. A color version of their popular monochrome display card. Not to be confused with their CGA-compatible card.	Hercules Computer Technology 2550 Ninth St. Berkeley, CA 94710 (415) 540-6000

Product	Company
PG-640 and PB 1280. 1280 × 960, 16-color, 2048 × 1024-pixel display memory. Hardware panning and zooming.	Matrox Electronic Systems 1055 St. Regis Blvd. Dorval, Quebec, Canada H9P 2T4 (514) 685-2630
T4 Color Graphics Controller. 1024 × 800, 16-color, can emulate CGA, single- and dual-screen configurations available.	Microfield Graphics, Inc. 8285 SW Nimbus Ave., Suite 161 Beaverton, OR 97005 (503) 626-9393
GX-2102 PC Display. 1024 × 1024, 16-color.	Modgraph, Inc. 56 Winthrop St. Concord, MA 01742 (617) 371-2000
Viking 1 Graphics card. 1280 × 960, monochrome.	Moniterm Corporation 5740 Green Circle Dr. Minnetonka, MN 55343 (612) 935-4151
Nth Engine Display. Resolutions available from 640 × 480 to 1024 × 768, 16-color. 64000 × 64000 virtual display using display list. Feature fast pans and zooms.	Nth Graphics 1807 C. West Braken Ln. Austin, TX 78758 (512) 832-1944
AutoLISP debugger. Software product that aids the development of AutoLISP programs.	Pacific intelleData 5881 Balboa Dr. Oakland, CA 94611 (415) 769-7474
Photon Graphics Controllers. Resolutions from 800 × 600, 16-color, to 1024 × 1024, 16-color. Hardware panning and zooming. IBM EGA, CGA, and MDA available on Photon Mega.	Personal Computer Graphics Corp. 5819 Uplander Way Culver City, CA 90230 (213) 216-0055

Product	Company
Clipper Graphics Display. 1280 x 1024, 256 colors, hardware panning and zooming using display list. Uses expanded or extended memory for display list storage. Features fast redraw times.	Pixelworks 225A Lowell Rd. Hudson, NH 03051 (603) 880-1322
QDP offers several displays from 640 x 480, 16-color, to 1024 x 768, 16-color running a Sony Multiscan. Other models work with NEC MultiSync monitors. All models offer hardware panning and zooming, and some models offer a pop-up window for text screens and menus. Single-screen capable and 256-color option available on most systems. Very fast redraws.	QDP Computer Systems 23623 Mercantile Rd. Beachwood, OH 44122 (216) 464-6600
Laserview Display Adapter. 1664 x 1200 monochrome. Intended for use with desktop-publishing systems.	Sigma Designs 46501 Landing Pkwy. Fremont, CA 94538 (415) 770-0100
Shauffeur HT Display. 1056 x 352 monochrome.	STB Systems Incorporated P.O. Box 850957 1651 North Glenville Richardson, TX 75085 (214) 234-8750
Sun-Flex Touch Pen. This product is like a digitizer that allows you to draw directly on your monitor (not to be confused with a light pen). The ADI driver allows it to be used on a greater variety of monitors, including some color systems. An off-screen pad is available if you prefer to use the touch pen as a standard digitizer.	Sun-Flex Co., Inc. 20 Pimentel Ct. Novato, CA 94947 (415) 883-1221

Product	Company
EVA Graphics Card. 640 × 480, 16-color. EGA, CGA, MDA compatible. Hardware panning and zooming. Terminal emulation.	Tseng Laboratories, Inc. 10 Pheasant Run Newtown Commons Newtown, PA 18940 (215) 968-0502
Xerox 4045 Laser Printer. Requires 1.5-megabyte memory with vector graphics option. 300 dpi resolution. Diablo 630 emulation, Xerox 2700 emulation.	Xerox Corp. 701 S. Aviation Blvd. El Segundo, CA 90245 (213) 333-7527

Appendix B

Installing AutoCAD
and AutoShade

THIS APPENDIX CONTAINS instructions on installing AutoCAD and AutoShade. To follow them, you need to use some DOS commands. If you need more help with DOS than is provided here, refer to Appendix C or your DOS manual. For more information on the Auto-CAD package, refer to Chapter 1.

BACKING UP THE ORIGINAL DISKS

The program disks you got with your system are the most important part of your AutoCAD package. Without them, you have no AutoCAD program. It is therefore important that you make backup copies of them and use the copies to install your program. If you make any fatal errors during the installation, such as accidentally erasing files, you will still have the original disks to work with.

To back up your original disks, you can use the DOS DISKCOPY command. You should have eight blank disks ready for copying. Start your computer. Be sure you have the DOS file called Diskcopy-.COM in the current directory. If not, go to the directory that contains this file, then enter

DISKCOPY A: A:

at the DOS prompt. For a system with two floppy-disk drives, enter

DISKCOPY A: B:

This will copy the entire contents of one disk onto another. You will get the message

Insert source diskette in drive A:
Press Return when ready.

This tells you to place the original or source disk in drive A and press Return when it is ready to copy. This message will differ depending on which version of DOS you are using. Some versions tell you to strike any key when ready, rather than the Return key.

Insert disk 1 in drive A, then press Return. You will get the message

Copying 9 sectors per track, 2 side(s)

When the computer is done reading the original disk, you get the message

Insert target diskette in drive A:
Press Return when ready

Remove the original disk and place a blank disk in drive A. Be sure you place a new blank disk in the drive and not one of the program disks. Press Return. You will get the following message when the computer is done copying.

Copy complete
Copy another (Y/N)?

Press Y for yes and repeat the procedure for the rest of the disks.

Be sure to label your copies the same way the originals are labeled, including the serial number from disk 1, and place a write-protect tab on them once you are done. Put your originals in a safe place away from any magnetic sources. If you have a tablet, do not put disks on top of it because the tablet uses a small electrical field to operate. This field can destroy data on a disk.

PLACING AUTOCAD PROGRAM FILES ON YOUR HARD DISK

To install AutoCAD, you will use the MD command and the COPY command. MD creates a directory on your hard disk. COPY moves files from one disk to another.

Once your computer is on and you see the DOS prompt, check to be sure you are in the DOS root directory. Do this by entering CD. If you are in the root directory, you will get the message

C:

If you don't get this message, enter

CD

to change your current directory to the DOS root directory.
Next enter

MD ACAD

to create the AutoCAD directory. The light indicating hard disk activity will come on for a second. Place disk 1 in drive A and enter

COPY A:*.* C:\ACAD

This will place the entire contents of disk 1 in the Acad directory on the C drive. Do this for all the program disks except the ones containing the drivers and the sample files.

When this is done, place disk 6, the support files disk, back in drive A and enter the following at the DOS prompt.

COPY A:\SOURCE*.* C:\ACAD

Disk 6 contains a directory called Source that holds other files used by AutoCAD. By doing the above, you will copy those files onto the Acad directory where AutoCAD will have access to them.
While still in the root directory, enter

MD \DRV

This creates a directory where you will place the AutoCAD drivers. Next, place one of the driver disks in drive A. Enter

COPY A:*.* C:\DRV

When the computer is done, repeat the COPY command for the other driver disk. This process will place the AutoCAD drivers in a separate directory where they can be erased easily. AutoCAD uses these driver files to control the various hardware options when it configures your system. They are placed on your hard disk to allow quick access to them during configuration. The driver information you specify during configuration is saved in the Acad directory; the driver files are then erased to make room for other files. See Chapter 1 for more details on drivers.

When you are done copying the driver files, enter

COPY \DRV*.OVL \ACAD

Driver disk 1 contains an overlay that must be present on the Acad directory for AutoCAD to run. Since you copied both driver disks onto the Drv directory, the overlay is present in that directory. By doing the above, you ensure that all the overlay files are on the Acad directory. Once this is done, you can proceed with the Auto-CAD configuration.

CONFIGURING AUTOCAD

In this section, you will be shown how to configure AutoCAD. By configure, we mean to set up AutoCAD to work with the particular hardware you have connected to your computer. As we explained in Chapter 1, programs often rely on their own drivers to operate specialized equipment. By configuring AutoCAD, you tell it exactly what equipment it will be working with.

Doing the Basic Configuration

Change the current directory to Acad by entering

CD \ACAD

Next enter

ACAD

You will get the introductory message. Press Return and you will get the screen shown in Figure B.1. This tells you that AutoCAD needs to be configured. You will also get the prompt

Enter drive or directory containing the display device drivers:

This prompt is asking for the location of the drivers AutoCAD uses to operate the equipment it supports. Enter

\DRV

at this prompt.

You will get the screen shown in Figure B.2, numbers 1–20. The first item to configure is the display system. This is a partial list of the display systems AutoCAD supports directly. Below number 20 you will see the message to press Return for more. Before you do that, see if you can find your display system on the list. If you do, note its number.

```
              A U T O C A D
Copyright (C) 1982,83,84,85,86,87 Autodesk, Inc.
Release 9.0 (9/17/87) IBM PC
Advanced Drafting Extensions 3
Serial Number:  10-113610

AutoCAD is not yet configured.
You must specify the devices to which AutoCAD will interface.

In order to interface to a device, AutoCAD needs the
control program for that device, called a device driver.
The device drivers are files with a type of .DRV.

You must tell AutoCAD the disk drive or directory in
which the device drivers are located.  If you specify a
disk drive, you must include the colon, as in A:

Enter drive or directory containing the Display device drivers:
```

Figure B.1:   *Screen shown when AutoCAD is not configured*

Now press Return, and display options 20–40 will appear. Press Return again and the final two display options appear.

Enter the number of your display system at the prompt

Select device number or ? to repeat list <1>:

Next, you will be prompted by a series of questions similar to the ones shown in Figure B.3. These options vary somewhat among display devices, so we can't be too specific in our instructions. However, we will describe some of the more common prompts.

The first prompt usually asks if you have previously measured the height and width of a "square" on your screen. At this point, you haven't been able to even see what a square looks like in Auto-CAD; we suggest skipping over this prompt during the initial configuration. Press Return to accept the default, N for no. Later, if you notice that circles and squares appear stretched in one direction or another, you can compensate for that stretch by reconfiguring your display and answering yes to this prompt. You will be prompted for the current width and height of the "square," then AutoCAD will set up the display to make circles and squares appear correctly. However, this procedure is seldom required.

```
Serial Number:  10-113610

Available video displays:

     1.  ADI display v3.0
     2.  BNW Precision Graphics Adapter
     3.  Bell & Howell CDI IV
     4.  Cambridge Micro-1024
     5.  Compaq Portable III Plasma Display
     6.  Conographic Model-40 Color Display
     7.  Control Systems Artist I & II
     8.  Control Systems Transformer
     9.  Cordata 400 Line graphics
    10.  Cordata Fast Draft 480
    11.  Frontier CADgraph 2
    12.  GraphAx 20/20 display
    13.  HP Enhanced Graphics Adapter
    14.  Hercules Graphics Card
    15.  Hewlett-Packard 82960 Graphics Controller
    16.  Hewlett-Packard Multi Mode Video Adapter
    17.  IBM Color/Graphics
    18.  IBM Enhanced Graphics Adapter
    19.  IBM Personal System/2 8514/A Display
    20.  IBM Professional Graphics Controller
-- Press RETURN for more --
    21.  IBM Video Graphics Array
    22.  Matrox PG-640
    23.  Metheus Omega-PC Display, V2.2 Microcode
    24.  Micro-Display GENIUS
    25.  Number Nine NNIOS Graphics Display
    26.  Number Nine Revolution Board
    27.  Persyst BOB-16 Color/Graphics
    28.  Quadram Quadscreen
    29.  Quintar
    30.  Ramtek 4220 graphic displays
    31.  STB 16-Color
    32.  STB 4-Color
    33.  STB Chauffeur Monochrome
    34.  Sigma Designs Color 400
    35.  TAT Galaxy G-500
    36.  Tecmar Graphics Master
    37.  VMI Image Manager 1024
    38.  Vectrix Midas or VX384
    39.  Vectrix PEPE Graphics Controller
    40.  Verticom H-series Graphics Controller
-- Press RETURN for more --
    41.  Verticom M-series Graphics Controller
    42.  Wyse Technology WY700

Select device number or ? to repeat list <1>:
```

Figure B.2:   *List of display options*

```
If you have previously measured the height and width of
a "square" on your graphics screen, you may use these
measurements to correct the aspect ratio.

Would you like to do so? <N>

Do you want a status line? <Y>

Do you want a command prompt area? <Y>

Do you want a screen menu area? <Y>

Do you want dark vectors on a light background? <Y>

Do you have the Sun-Flex Touchpen? <N>
Press RETURN to continue:
```

Figure B.3:   *Typical display option questions*

You will also be asked if you want a status line, a prompt area, and a menu area. Normally you want these things, since they are part of AutoCAD's normal operation and you won't be able to use the tutorial part of this book without them. Press Return at each of these prompts to accept the default, Y for yes.

If you are using version 9, you will also be asked if you want to display dark vectors (lines) on a light background. Accept the default, Y, so that AutoCAD will display your drawings like plots or printouts, with black lines on a white medium. Earlier versions of AutoCAD offer white or colored lines on a black background as the default setup, and no other options are available unless you have a color display.

You may have options that are specific to your display device. For example, the prompts shown in Figure B.3 are for a Hercules display adapter. The last prompt asks if you have the Sun-Flex Touch Pen. This option is specific to the Hercules display, and you won't see it while configuring any other display device. This is where our discussion falls down since we cannot cover every option on every device AutoCAD supports. Check your AutoCAD installation guide for detailed instructions pertaining to your display device. As a rule, you can accept the defaults (shown in parentheses) provided by AutoCAD. You can always change them later if you like.

Once you are done configuring your display, you will get a list of input device options. Again, check the list for the number of your device and enter that number at the prompt at the bottom of the list. If you have no input device other than the keyboard, choose option 1, None. Answer any questions regarding your input device. Again, since different input devices offer different options, we cannot provide details on what to select. However, the prompts are usually quite clear, so you shouldn't have any problems. If you do have questions, refer to the AutoCAD installation guide for details.

If you have a digitizing tablet, you will also want to configure the tablet menu provided by Autodesk when you send in your registration card. Since this is done outside the system configuration menu, we will explain how to do it a little later.

Printer and plotter configuration works the same way as display and input device configuration. You are shown a numbered list, at the bottom of which is a prompt asking you to enter the number of the device you wish to connect to. You enter the number corresponding to your printer or plotter. You are also prompted for the printer and plotter default options that are displayed during Auto-CAD's Prplot and Plot commands. Chapter 5 describes the different options in detail.

Once you are done with the configuration, you will get a list of the devices you selected (see Figure B.4). Press Return and you will get the Configuration menu and a prompt asking you to enter a selection (see Figure B.5). Press Return to accept the default, 0, to exit to the Main menu. The following message will appear.

If you answer N to the following question, all configuration changes you have just made will be discarded.

Keep configuration changes? <Y>

If you wish to save your current configuration, press Return to accept the default, Y. You will return to the Main menu. Now you can begin drawing.

Changing Plotter Pen Selection Modes and Serial Port Assignments

If you have more than one serial port, you can configure Auto-CAD to assign different ports to your plotter and pointing device. Also, if you have a multipen plotter, you can control the pen selection sequence AutoCAD uses to draw your drawings. The default

```
                    A U T O C A D
         Copyright (C) 1982,83,84,85,86,87 Autodesk, Inc.
         Release 9.0 (9/17/87) IBM PC
         Advanced Drafting Extensions 3
         Serial Number:  10-113610

         Current AutoCAD configuration

            Video display:      Hercules Graphics Card

            Digitizer:          Mouse Systems Mouse [IBM]

            Plotter:            Hewlett-Packard 7475

            Printer plotter:    IBM Proprinter model


         Press RETURN to continue:
```

Figure B.4:   *Screen showing configured hardware options*

```
                    A U T O C A D
         Copyright (C) 1982,83,84,85,86,87 Autodesk, Inc.
         Release 9.0 (9/17/87) IBM PC
         Advanced Drafting Extensions 3
         Serial Number:  10-113610

         Configuration menu

            0.  Exit to Main Menu
            1.  Show current configuration
            2.  Allow I/O port configuration

            3.  Configure video display
            4.  Configure digitizer
            5.  Configure plotter
            6.  Configure printer plotter
            7.  Configure system console
            8.  Configure operating parameters

         Enter selection <0>:
```

Figure B.5:   *The Configuration menu*

setting causes the plotter to plot each color completely before selecting the next pen. This works fine if your plotter has a self-capping pen holder. If you have a plotter that does not have this feature, like the Nicolette plotters, you can set AutoCAD to alternate between pens more frequently so wet-ink pens are less likely to dry out.

After you have configured your system and are in the Main menu, select item number 5, Configure AutoCAD, by entering 5 at the option-selection prompt. If you are currently in DOS, start Auto-CAD to bring up the Main menu, then enter 5. You will get a list of your devices and a prompt to press Return to continue (see Figure B.4). Once you press Return, you will get the Configuration menu (see Figure B.5).

Pick item 2, Allow I/O Port Configuration, by entering 2 at the option-selection prompt. This option allows you to determine which serial ports your input and output devices are connected to. It also allows other options to be accessed. In this case, you are accessing plotter pen selection sequence options not normally shown during the plotter configuration.

You get the prompt

It is possible to configure the I/O ports to which some AutoCAD devices are connected, but doing so may require technical knowledge and is normally unnecessary.

Do you really wish to do I/O port configuration? <N>

Enter Y. You will get a display showing your devices, plus the *port address* the devices are connected to. The port address is the name assigned to the serial port. The addresses are normally COM1 and COM2. Other "names" for COM1 and COM2 are 3f8 and 2f8. Figure B.6 shows an example of this screen.

Press Return to continue. You will again get the Configuration menu. Enter 5, Configure Plotter, at the option-selection prompt. A prompt will appear asking if you wish to select a different plotter. Press Return to accept the default, N for no. Answer the prompts as you did when you first configured your plotter. Usually the defaults will reflect your current configuration, so you only need to press Return at each prompt.

```
Copyright (C) 1982,83,84,85,86,87 Autodesk, Inc.
Release 9.0 (9/17/87) IBM PC
Advanced Drafting Extensions 3
Serial Number:  10-113610

Current AutoCAD configuration


  Video display:       Hercules Graphics Card

  Digitizer:           Mouse Systems Mouse [IBM]
    Port: Asynchronous Communications Adapter COM1 at address 3F8 (hex)
    Interrupt: 4

  Plotter:             Hewlett-Packard 7475
    Port: Asynchronous Communications Adapter COM1 at address 3F8 (hex)

  Printer plotter:     IBM Proprinter model



  Port configuration questions will be asked during device configuration.

  Press RETURN to continue:
```

Figure B.6:   *An AutoCAD configuration with I/O port listed*

You will get the prompt

**Connects to Asynchronous Communications Adapter port.
Standard ports are:**

> **COM1**
> **COM2**

Enter port name, or address in hexadecimal <COM1>:

If you have two asynchronous communications ports, or serial ports as they are commonly called, you use this opportunity to tell Auto-CAD that you want to connect your plotter to a port other than COM1. This allows you to use two serial devices, such as a tablet and a plotter, without having to switch cables.

Enter 2F8 at this prompt to connect your plotter to COM2. As we mentioned earlier, 2F8 is the same as COM2. We ask you to enter 2F8 because sometimes entering COM2 does not work, while entering 2F8 always works. 2F8 is known as the *hexadecimal* address for COM2. Hexadecimal notation is a system of describing numeric values in a way more easily understood by computers. We won't go into an explanation of how it works. Just be aware that it is an alternate numbering system.

Be sure you plug your plotter into the proper serial port. If you don't know which port is COM2, you may have to experiment by switching ports and seeing which one works.

Next you will be asked if you wish to calibrate your plotter. Calibration allows you to adjust the plotter for accuracy in plotting to scale and is seldom required. Press Return to accept the default, N.

Next you will see the prompt

The pen motion optimization can be selected from the following list. Higher numbers represent more optimization.

0. None
1. Endpoint swap only.
2. Pen sorting + endpoint swap.
3. Pen sorting + endpoint swap + limited motion optimization.
4. Pen sorting + endpoint swap + full motion optimization.

Select degree of pen motion optimization, 0 to 4 <4>:

At this prompt you can select from four options that control pen selection and plotting optimization. The default setting is 4.

The first item in option 4, pen sorting, sorts pens so that all of one color is plotted at once. This is fine if your plotter has a self-capping pen holder, or if it is a single-pen plotter. You do not want this option active, however, if you have a multipen plotter that does not cap the pens. If this is the case, you should enter option 1. This will increase your plotting time somewhat, but the increase will be balanced by the time you save by not having to fix dry pens.

The second item in option 4, endpoint swap, means that if lines are parallel the plotter will draw one line, then start the next line from the nearest endpoint. Without this option, the plotter will plot lines in whatever direction they were entered.

Motion optimization causes the plotter to plot objects that are close together first before plotting objects in another area of the drawing. If this option is not used, as in option 2, the plotter will plot your drawing in the order the objects were added to it regardless of their proximity to other objects.

Once you have selected an option for this setting, you will be prompted for your plotter default settings as before. Refer to Chapter 5 for the meanings of these settings.

After you finish selecting the plotter settings, you are returned to the Configuration menu. Enter 0 at the option-selection prompt to return to the Main menu. You are asked if you want to save the current settings. Press Return to accept the default, Y for yes. You are returned to the Main menu. You can now start a new drawing, plot an existing drawing, or end out of AutoCAD. You may want to plot a drawing to test your current plotter configuration.

CLEARING YOUR HARD DISK OF UNUSED DRIVERS

Once you configure your system, enter DOS and go to the Drv directory by entering

CD \DRV

at the DOS prompt. Next enter

DEL C:\DRV*.*

Be sure you enter this exactly as shown here. You will see the prompt

Are you sure (Y/N)?

Enter Y. If you later change any device, you must reload the drivers onto the hard disk, then enter the Configuration menu and reconfigure your system to use the new device.

CONFIGURING YOUR DIGITIZING TABLET MENU

If you own a digitizing tablet, and you would like to use it with the AutoCAD tablet menu template, you must configure your tablet menu. The first step is to securely fasten your tablet menu template to the tablet using the plastic registration pins provided with the template. Be sure the area covered by the template is completely within the tablet's active drawing area.

Next, start AutoCAD by first changing directories to Acad, then entering acad. Because you must be in a drawing file to configure the tablet we ask you to open a file called Temp (actually, any drawing file will do). Select option 1 from the Main menu, then enter the word Temp at the prompt

Enter NAME of drawing:

Once the drawing editor is ready for your input, move your pointing device to the menu area to the right of the screen. Highlight the word Settings on the Root menu, then press your pick button. Next pick Tablet from the Settings menu. Then pick Config from the Tablet menu (if your tablet has already been configured once, pick Reconfig). You will get the prompt

Digitize upper left corner of menu area 1:

For the next series of prompts, you will be locating the four tablet menu areas, starting with menu area 1 (see Figure B.7). Locate the position indicated in Figure B.7 as the upper-left corner of menu area 1. Place your puck or stylus to pick that point. The prompt will change to

Digitize lower left corner of menu area 1:

Again, locate the position indicated in Figure B.7 as the lower-left corner of menu area 1. Continue this process until you have selected three corners for four menu areas.

Next you will get the prompt

Digitize lower left corner of screen pointing area:

Pick the position indicated in Figure B.7. Finally, you get the prompt

Digitize upper right corner of screen pointing area:

Pick the position indicated in Figure B.7. Now you are done.

AutoCAD will remember this configuration until you change it again. Quit out of this file by entering quit through the keyboard. Or quit it by picking Autocad from the top of the Tablet menu, then picking Utility from the Root menu, then Quit from the Utility menu, then Yes. You will exit the drawing editor. Enter 0 to exit AutoCAD.

SOLVING HARDWARE PROBLEMS

The most common problem when connecting devices to your computer's serial port is improper cabling and switch settings. Usually proper cabling is supplied with the device, but sometimes it is not. The wires connecting the various pins on your cable must be arranged a certain way. If your plotter or other serial device does not work, check the cabling on your plotter and be sure it conforms to the cabling diagram shown in your AutoCAD installation guide. Also be sure the switches are properly set on your plotter or other

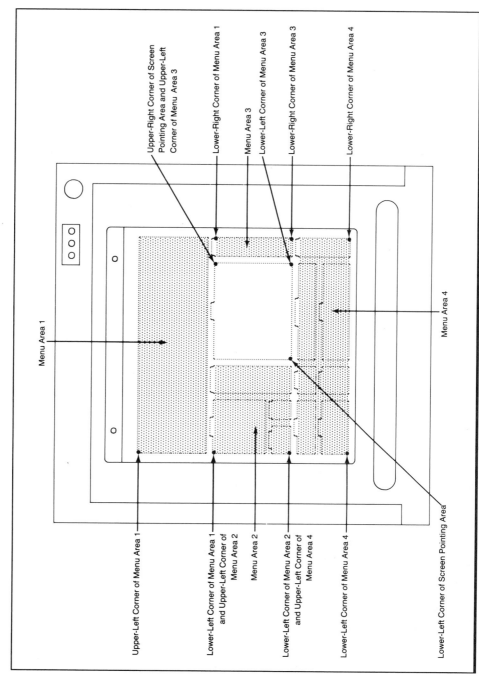

Figure B.7: How to locate the tablet menu areas

serial device to receive and send data to AutoCAD. Again, these settings can be found in the installation guide.

Some devices require special setting up even after AutoCAD has been configured. These usually come with setup instructions. Check the manual that came with the device to be sure you haven't missed its setup options. When all else fails, call your vendor or manufacturer.

KEEPING MULTIPLE CONFIGURATIONS

There may be times when you want to have AutoCAD configured in more than one way. For example, you may want to have one configuration where the drawing editor's status line, prompt area, and menu area are not shown so that a drawing fills the entire screen. (See Chapter 2 for the location and appearance of these areas on the display.) This configuration is desirable for presentations. At the same time, you will want to use the standard screen configuration when you create and edit drawings. Normally, you would have to reconfigure AutoCAD every time you want to switch between these two configurations. However, you can use DOS to maintain several configurations that you select by entering different words to start AutoCAD.

The DOS features that allow you to maintain several configurations are the batch files and the SET command. If you are unfamiliar with batch files and SET, take a moment to review the information on them in Appendix C.

As we mentioned earlier, when you configure AutoCAD, it stores the configuration information on files in the Acad directory. However, you can tell AutoCAD to store those configuration files in a specific place. This is done through the SET command.

First you establish locations for these configuration files. The simplest way to do this is to add subdirectories under the Acad directory, each one being the location for a different set of configuration files. For example, you could create two subdirectories, one called Acad\Standard for a standard configuration, and the other called Acad\Clrscrn for a clear-screen configuration. You would create these directories by entering

```
MD \ACAD\STANDARD
MD \ACAD\CLRSCRN
```

at the DOS prompt.

Once this is done, you need to create a batch file that will allow you to specify which directory AutoCAD should look in for the desired configuration. This batch file could be named Gocad.BAT and be written like

SET ACADCFG = C:\ACAD\%1
CD \ACAD
ACAD
**CD **

The first line in this batch file uses the SET command in conjunction with the ACADCFG name to tell AutoCAD to look in a specific directory for the configuration files. The %1 means that any word you enter after GOCAD will be placed where the %1 appears. For example, if you enter

GOCAD STANDARD

at the DOS prompt, DOS will place the word STANDARD in the first line in the batch and will read it as

SET ACADCFG = C:\ACAD\STANDARD

Then when AutoCAD starts, it will look in the Acad\Standard directory for the configuration files.

After you have set up the directories and created the batch file, you can start AutoCAD by entering

GOCAD STANDARD

You will be told that AutoCAD is not yet configured because there are actually no configuration files present in those directories. Configure AutoCAD as we described above, then exit it. Start AutoCAD again but this time enter

GOCAD CLRSCRN

Once again, you will be told that AutoCAD is not yet configured. Configure AutoCAD a different way by setting up the display to not show the menu, command prompt, and the status lines. Do this by entering N at the prompts

Do you want a status line? <Y>
Do you want a command prompt area? <Y>
Do you want a screen menu area? <Y>

during the display configuration. After you are done, you can enter either GOCAD STANDARD or GOCAD CLRSCRN to get the desired drawing editor screen.

INSTALLING AUTOSHADE

Before you install AutoShade, make backup copies of your original three disks by following the instructions given in the section "Backing Up the Original Disks" in the beginning of this appendix. Once you have done this, use your backup copies to perform the installation. You can install AutoShade before or after you install AutoCAD.

Copying AutoShade onto Your Hard Disk

First copy all the files on all three disks onto your AutoCAD directory. Begin by making your current directory the AutoCAD directory. For example, if your AutoCAD directory is called Acad, enter the following at the DOS prompt:

CD\ACAD

Next, place AutoShade disk number 1 in drive A and enter

COPY A:*.*

Repeat the COPY command for each of the three disks.

Configuring AutoShade

Before you actually configure AutoShade, you may have to install drivers for your input and display devices. AutoShade assumes you are using a Microsoft mouse, so if you have a mouse from another manufacturer you will have to install their Microsoft mouse driver. Other input devices like the joystick or Koala pad (similar to a digitizing tablet) are also supported. If you don't have a pointing device, you can use the keyboard cursor keys. Consult your user manual about these products before proceeding.

If you want to use an ADI display or input device, you will have to install that driver too (see Appendix A for a list of devices that use the ADI interface). Since ADI drivers are written by the suppliers of the associated devices, we can offer only a limited amount of information on the subject. Consult your dealer for more detailed information on your particular ADI device.

Once you have loaded the drivers you need, go to your AutoCAD directory and enter

SHADE

You will get the screen shown in Figure B.8. Enter the number corresponding to your pointing device. The next screen appears (see Figure B.9). Enter the number corresponding to your interactive display device. This display, which shows pull-down menus and other information, is the one you will use to communicate with AutoShade during your interaction with the program. Or you can select the None option, which enables you to run AutoShade through a script file. A script file is like a DOS batch file in that it contains a list of commands that are entered automatically by the computer. You may want to do this type of batch processing when you are generating a very complex shaded model. See Chapter 15 for more details on using script files with AutoShade.

The next screen asks you to select a rendering display device (see Figure B.10). This is the device that is used to show your shaded views. Usually, it will be the same as your interactive display device. If you have a display system that requires a separate display for rendering, such as a dual-screen ADI display, you will need two display systems, one for the interactive display and the other for renderings. If you select None, the output device you select later becomes the rendering device, and any shaded view you create will not be displayed on your display system, but will automatically be sent to your printer.

```
C:\ACAD>shade

Select pointing device:

     1.   Autodesk Device Interface Pointer
     2.   Microsoft Mouse
     3.   Joystick / Koala pad
     4.   Keyboard cursor keys

Pointer selection:
```

Figure B.8:   *The opening AutoShade configuration screen*

```
Select display device:

     1.   Autodesk Device Interface display driver
     2.   Hercules Graphics Card
     3.   IBM Color Graphics Adaptor (CGA - Monochrome mode)
     4.   IBM Enhanced graphics display (EGA)
     5.   IBM Alphanumeric display
     6.   None

Display selection:
```

Figure B.9:   *AutoShade's interactive display device selections*

```
Select rendering display device:

    1.   Autodesk Device Interface rendering driver
    2.   Hercules Graphics Card
    3.   IBM Color Graphics Adaptor (CGA)
    4.   IBM Enhanced Graphics Adaptor (EGA)
    5.   IBM Professional Graphics Controller (PGC)
    6.   Orchid TurboPGA
    7.   None

Rendering selection:
```

Figure B.10:   *AutoShade's rendering display device selections*

Next you will get the prompt

Do the display and rendering devices share a single screen (default = NO):

Enter Y if you are using one display system for both the interactive and rendering screens. If you are using an ADI display for your rendering device and you enter Y to the previous prompt, the following prompt appears:

Does FLIPSCREEN require a redraw (default = NO):

Some displays require you to press F1 to flip between interactive and rendering displays. If the device has sufficient memory to store both the interactive and rendering screens, flipping between them is instantaneous. Otherwise the rendering display must be redrawn, as in an AutoCAD redraw. If your device does have enough memory you can accept the default, No, to this prompt. Otherwise, enter Y.

Finally, the hard-copy selections appear (see Figure B.11). There are a limited number of hard-copy devices available. If you have an ADI output printer, you may be able to get hard copy by selecting item 1, the ADI rendering driver. Check with the manufacturer of your ADI output device to be certain that it will work with AutoShade (see Appendix A for a list of ADI output devices). The rendering file options are similar to AutoCAD's DXF file format in that they are a means of exchanging AutoShade files with other programs. They are intended for use by software developers who would like to import AutoShade files into programs they are using or marketing. If you select item 2, PostScript Device, you have the option to print your shaded view to a file that you can later send to a remote printer. You can also select None for the output, though it's unlikely you would want to because the PostScript option offers remote printing.

```
Select rendering hard copy device:

    1.   Autodesk Device Interface rendering driver
    2.   PostScript Device
    3.   Rendering file (256 colour map)
    4.   Rendering file (continuous colour)
    5.   None

Rendering hard copy selection:
```

Figure B.11:   *AutoShade's selection of hard-copy devices*

When you have finished configuring AutoShade, the opening AutoShade screen will appear. See Chapter 15 for the tutorial on using AutoShade.

Appendix C

Using Some Common DOS Commands

IN THIS APPENDIX, WE EXPLAIN some of the most common DOS commands. Consult your DOS manual for details and descriptions of others.

DOS commands can be broken into two categories: *internal* and *external*. Internal DOS commands reside in memory and can be called at any time. External commands exist as files outside memory that must be on your hard disk or floppy-disk drive. These external commands can be found on your DOS disk if they haven't already been installed on your hard disk. Later, we will discuss exactly how to access these external commands.

ENTERING COMMANDS AT THE DOS PROMPT

When you turn on your computer, you will see a prompt when it is ready to accept instruction. The prompt usually looks like this:

    C>

It tells you two things: which drive is currently active and that the computer is awaiting your instruction. Whenever you see this prompt, you can enter any DOS command or the name of a program you wish to start by typing the command or program name after the prompt, then pressing Return. The syntax is

> C:*program or command name [optional parameter]*

Some commands will accept optional *parameters*, which are like special instructions to the command. You will see how these parameters are used a little later.

SPECIFYING A DEFAULT DISK DRIVE

The default drive is usually C on a system with a hard disk. The A drive is usually the first floppy-disk drive. If you have two floppy-disk drives, the second is designated as B. If you have only one, A and B are both the same drive. To change from one drive to another, you enter the name of the drive you wish to activate followed by a colon, as in

> **A:**

This will change the default drive to A. The prompt will change to

> **A>**

to reflect the new default.

MANAGING DOS DIRECTORIES AND FILES

DOS allows you to arrange your disk into directories. These are like compartments that contain your files. The main directory is called the root directory. From it all other directories originate. Figure C.1 illustrates a typical directory system.

The directory system is called a *tree* because of its treelike structure. Directories spring from the root directory, which is like the roots of a tree. Still more subdirectories can originate from these directories. You could store all your files in the root directory instead of creating subdirectories, but once you had a hundred or so files on your disk, you would have a difficult time keeping track of them. Directories help you keep together files that have a common purpose, such as your program files, your database records, or your drawing files.

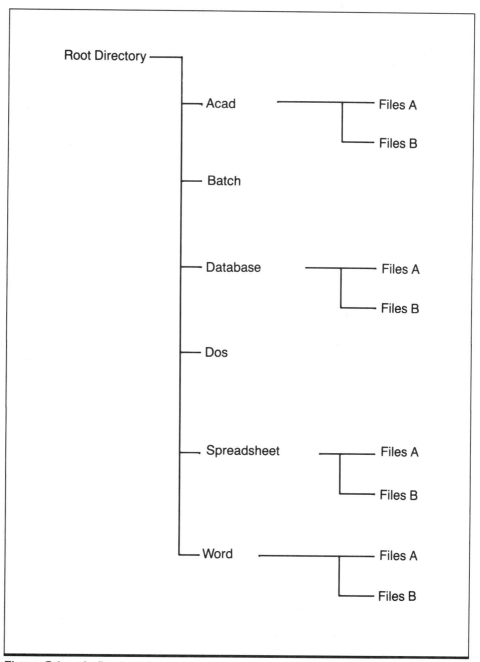

Figure C.1:   *A directory tree*

The internal command CD, or Change Directory, can be used to find out what directory you are in. If you enter

CD

at the DOS prompt while in the root directory, you will get the DOS prompt followed by a backslash. (Actually, DOS doesn't care whether you enter CD, Cd, or cd, but we capitalize DOS commands in this book for the sake of clarity.) If you are in a directory other than the root directory, you will get the DOS prompt followed by a backslash and the name of the directory you are in.

You can customize your DOS prompt to show the current directory automatically. See the section on the PROMPT command below.

Creating a Directory

To create a directory, you enter

MD *name*

MD stands for Make Directory. This is an internal DOS command. It creates a subdirectory under your current directory. For example, if you are currently in the root directory and you enter

MD LOTUS

DOS will create a directory called Lotus under the root directory. If you are already in a directory called Lotus and you enter

MD 123

DOS will create a subdirectory under Lotus called 123.

To create a subdirectory of a directory while you are in the root directory, you enter the name of that directory first as in

MD \LOTUS\123

The backslash indicates the name of a directory originating from the root directory. If you leave off the backslash, DOS will look for the directory under your current directory.

Changing a Directory

To change to a different directory, you enter CD followed by the name of the directory. For example, entering

CD\LOTUS

will place you in the Lotus directory, or

CD\

will place you in the root directory. If you are in a subdirectory and you want to get to its *parent* directory, you can enter

CD ..

As you use AutoCAD, you may find it useful to create directories under the directory you designate for AutoCAD to keep files separated by job or type.

Deleting a Directory

You may want to delete a directory that is not used or was created by accident. To do this you enter

RD *name*

where *name* is the directory name. RD stands for Remove Directory and it is an internal command. You must be sure that the entire contents of the directory are deleted, or the directory will not be removed.

Listing a Directory

To find out what is on a disk and directory, you can use the internal DIR command. You can get a listing of the current directory by just entering

DIR

This will give you a list similar to the one shown in Figure C.2.

This list shows the contents of a directory called Util. Because this directory is too long to fit on the screen, the first several items have scrolled off. You can tell DOS to pause the screen once it is full by entering

DIR /P

The screen will look like Figure C.3. You can now press any key to view the next screen of the directory.

Another parameter that can help you view the contents of a large directory is /W. If you enter

DIR /W

you will get a listing that looks like Figure C.4. The /W parameter

```
MORE        COM      282    3-07-85    1:43p
PRINT       COM     8291    3-07-85    1:43p
SORT        EXE     1664    3-07-85    1:43p
HGC         COM     1591    8-20-85
IMCAP       COM     9566    5-15-86    5:14p
MAKESFX     COM     1358    4-27-87
MAPMEM      COM    18511    7-20-86    1:42p
MARK        COM     1408    7-20-86    1:33p
RELEASE     COM    16647    7-20-86    1:32p
TEST        MRK     1030    9-07-86   12:55p
RAMFREE     COM      102    8-11-85   11:09a
NOKEY       COM     8738    6-08-87    5:05p
MSMOUSE     COM     4764    1-08-85   12:19p
MSMOUSE     SYS     4620    1-08-85   12:20p
MSMOUSE     LIB     5120    1-24-85    4:42p
COPYIIPC    EXE    44324    6-09-87    4:15p
RN          COM     4352   11-14-87   11:15a
NOGUARD     COM    10730    6-08-87    5:03p
EXPLORER    COM    46048   10-15-84    3:27p
DXFTOGEM    EXE    35840   10-12-86   11:02a
DR          COM     4096   12-02-87    1:25p
PRN2FILE    COM     1408   12-02-87    8:39a
        57 File(s)      804864 bytes free

C:\UTIL>
```

Figure C.2:   A directory listing using DIR

```
.                 <DIR>      11-17-87    1:02p
..                <DIR>      11-17-87    1:02p
JET         COM     7680    7-26-85    7:17a
XTREE       EXE    43076   12-12-85    1:46a
XTREEINS    EXE     8968   11-03-85    9:33a
XTREEINS    DAT    20608   11-03-85    9:33a
READ        ME     12928   11-03-85    9:33a
ED          EXE    35184    4-01-84    6:25p
BAC         COM     1392    4-24-86    5:32p
BROWSE      COM      958    1-02-86    3:54a
COLD        COM       16    4-23-86   12:27p
DD          COM      800   11-14-87   11:15a
DIREX       COM     1992   11-14-87   11:15a
DIRNOTES    COM     1792    9-01-87    8:12a
EATMEM      COM      256    8-07-85    3:40p
FINDFILE    BAT       20    4-25-86    8:40a
LOC         COM      517    4-24-86    5:30p
LOCATE      EXE    17024    8-14-84   12:00p
NO          COM      736    4-24-86    5:33p
FMARK       COM      640    7-20-86    1:33p
START       BAT      383    4-21-86   12:51p
WARM        COM       16    4-23-86   12:27p
WHERES      BAT       32    3-01-86    3:27p
Strike a key when ready . . .
```

Figure C3:   A directory listing using the /P parameter

condenses the directory listing by leaving out the file sizes and dates.

If you want to list a different directory from the one you are in, you can add its name to the DIR command as in

DIR \UTIL

If you enter this while in the root directory, for example, you get a list of the contents of the Util directory. You can also add a drive designation to the command as in

DIR A:\UTIL

This will display the contents of the directory Util on drive A. Directories can be listed for any type of drive.

Finally, you can use wild cards to filter file names. If you enter

DIR \UTIL*.EXE

you get a listing like the one in Figure C.5. We will discuss wild cards in the next section.

```
C:\UTIL>dir /w

 Volume in drive C has no label
 Directory of  C:\UTIL

.                    ..                   JET      COM    XTREE    EXE    XTREEINS EXE
XTREEINS DAT    READ     ME    ED       EXE    BAC      COM    BROWSE   COM
COLD     COM    DD       COM   DIREX    COM    DIRNOTES COM    EATMEM   COM
FINDFILE BAT    LOC      COM   LOCATE   EXE    NO       COM    FMARK    COM
START    BAT    WARM     COM   WHERES   BAT    ZERODISK COM    PAD      COM
PARK     COM    ASSIGN   COM   CHKDSK   COM    DEBUG    COM    DISKCOPY COM
FIND     EXE    FORMAT   COM   GRAPHICS COM    LABEL    COM    MODE     COM
MORE     COM    PRINT    COM   SORT     EXE    HGC      COM    IMCAP    COM
MAKESFX  COM    MAPMEM   COM   MARK     COM    RELEASE  COM    TEST     MRK
RAMFREE  COM    NOKEY    COM   MSMOUSE  COM    MSMOUSE  SYS    MSMOUSE  LIB
COPYIIPC EXE    RN       COM   NOGUARD  COM    EXPLORER COM    DXFTOGEM EXE
DR       COM    PRN2FILE COM   SCREEN00 CAP    SCREEN01 CAP
         59 File(s)     792576 bytes free

C:\UTIL>
```

Figure C.4:   *A directory listing using the /W parameter*

```
C:\>dir \util\*.exe

   Volume in drive C has no label
   Directory of  C:\UTIL

XTREE    EXE     43076  12-12-85    1:46a
XTREEINS EXE      8968  11-03-85    9:33a
ED       EXE     35184   4-01-84    6:25p
LOCATE   EXE     17024   8-14-84   12:00p
FIND     EXE      6403   3-07-85    1:43p
SORT     EXE      1664   3-07-85    1:43p
COPYIIPC EXE     44324   6-09-87    4:15p
DXFTOGEM EXE     35840  10-12-86   11:02a
          8 File(s)      780288 bytes free

C:\>
```

Figure C.5: *A directory listing using a wild-card filter*

MANAGING FILES

To work with DOS successfully, it helps to know a little about how files are named. All DOS file names have two parts, the actual name and the extension. The name is the first part and must consist of one to eight characters. The characters can be letters, numbers, or any combination of the two. The extension is added to the end of the name. The name and extension are always separated by a period, and the extension can be up to three characters long.

Certain extensions have special meanings to DOS. A file with the extension .COM is likely to be a command or program. A file with the extension .EXE is also likely to be a program, probably with a larger memory requirement than the file with the .COM extension. Finally, there are files with the .BAT extension. These files contain a series of instructions to DOS called a batch file. Whenever you enter a file name that has this extension, DOS reads its contents as if they were entered from the keyboard.

Using Wild Cards

When manipulating a file in DOS, you must give its full name, including the extension. You are also allowed to use what are called wild cards. Wild card characters are the asterisk and the question mark. They indicate an undefined character. For example, to delete a series of files all starting with the letter A, you could enter each file by name as in

```
DEL ALLAN.TXT
DEL ADRIAN.TXT
DEL APPLE.TXT
DEL AUTOCAD.TXT
DEL APRIL.TXT
DEL ANIMAL.TXT
DEL ACREATE.TXT
DEL A.....
```

The DEL preceding the file name tells DOS to delete that file from the current disk and directory. Deleting 40 or 50 such files could take some time. You could accomplish the same thing by entering

```
DEL A*.TXT
```

to tell DOS to delete all files that start with A and have the extension .TXT. The asterisk tells DOS to accept any character that appears between the A and the period. You could also enter

```
DEL A*.*
```

to tell DOS to delete all files that start with A no matter what the extension is.

Care must be taken when using the asterisk because every character that follows it is ignored. You cannot designate a file name like

```
DEL A*TE.TXT
```

because DOS will ignore the te at the end of the name.

The question mark works in the same way, except that it is used to replace individual letters rather than groups of letters. If you want to filter out file names that start and end with specific characters, use the question mark as in

```
DEL A?????TE.TXT
```

Here DOS will delete only files with names that start with A, are eight characters long, end with te, and have the extension .TXT.

Renaming Files

To rename files you use the REN internal command. REN is short for Rename. You enter REN, then the name of the file you wish to change followed by the new name. For example, to rename the file Chair.DWG to Rocker.DWG, you would enter

REN \ACAD\CHAIR.DWG \ACAD\ROCKER.DWG

You can change any part of the name you like, including the extension.

Copying Files

To copy a file, you use the internal command COPY. Enter the word COPY, then the name of the file you wish to copy followed by the copy's destination, as in

COPY A:ACAD.EXE C:\ACAD

Notice how the drive name is used before the name of the actual file, and how the directory name is used for the destination. This line will copy the file Acad.EXE from drive A to the Acad directory on drive C. If Acad.EXE were located in a directory called Prog on drive A, you would have to include that directory in the file name, as in

COPY A:\PROG\ACAD.EXE C:\ACAD

You can use wild cards to designate groups of files. Also, if the destination or source of the files to be copied is the current drive and directory, you can leave off the drive and directory name. For example, if your current directory is C:\Acad, you can enter

COPY A:\PROG\ACAD.EXE

to copy Acad.EXE to your current directory. Likewise, you can enter

COPY ACAD.EXE A:\PROG

to copy Acad.EXE from your current directory to the Prog directory on drive A.

Care must be taken when using this command because files with the same names will be overwritten. For example, if you have a file in drive A with the name 3rd-qtr.TXT and you copy a file from drive C with the same name to drive A, the 3rd-qtr.TXT file on drive A will be overwritten. This is fine if you want to update backup files, that is, files you put on disks for safe storage. But sometimes you may want to keep an older version of a file, as well as the new version. In this case, we suggest you rename the old version to avoid the possibility of overwriting it with the new one.

FORMATTING A DISK

The FORMAT external command will format a disk. It is usually used with a new, unformatted floppy disk, or to recycle a disk containing unwanted files. To use FORMAT, you must have the file Format.COM on your default directory or one you have set a path to. We will discuss setting paths a little later.

Care must be taken when using this command as it will remove all data on any disk being formatted, including your hard disk. When giving it, you specify the drive, then any optional parameters, as in

FORMAT A:/V

This command will format a disk in drive A. It is essential that you enter the drive letter. If you don't, you can accidentally format your hard disk and destroy all its files. The /V parameter causes the FORMAT command to prompt you for a volume label. (The volume label is simply a name you can assign to a disk.) It then adds that label to the disk. Later, when you display the contents of that disk using the DIR command, the volume label will also be displayed. See your DOS manual for other parameters and details on the FORMAT command.

SETTING UP DOS

DOS can be set up to perform repetitive tasks or to work with your programs in special ways. This section describes some options for setting up DOS.

Telling DOS Where to Look For Files

Normally, DOS looks only in the current directory for files. If you are in the root directory and you want to use a program in a different directory, you will have to go to that directory first before DOS can find it.

PATH is an internal command that allows you to direct DOS and other programs to look for files in specified directories, no matter what directory you are currently in. Enter the PATH command, then the directory name, including the drive name where the drive is other than the current one. When you specify more than one directory, separate directory names with a semicolon as in

PATH \;\DOS;\ACAD;A:\FILES

In this example, DOS is directed to the root directory, as well as directories called Dos, Acad, and a directory on drive A called Files.

(If you place all the DOS external files in the Dos directory, DOS will always be able to find them.) To display the current path setting, you can enter the PATH command by itself.

Customizing the DOS Prompt

The normal C prompt doesn't convey much information. You can use the PROMPT internal command to set up a custom prompt that displays more information, such as the directory you are in or the current date. If you have several computers, you can give each computer an identification name or number and have it display that name as part of the prompt. For example, you could enter

PROMPT CAD STATION 1; DRIVE PG

to create a prompt that looks like

CAD STATION 1; DRIVE C:\>

You enter the word PROMPT, followed by the text you want to appear as the prompt. Special codes can also be used. The code $P tells DOS to display the current drive and directory. The code $G tells DOS to display the greater-than sign. Other codes are shown in Table C.1.

PROMPT can also be used in conjunction with the Ansi.SYS driver provided with DOS to perform other tasks, such as creating keyboard macros. See your DOS manual for other parameters and more details on this command.

Setting Up Parameters for Application Programs

The internal command SET allows you to set up special parameters for application programs, which look for information in the DOS environment. The DOS environment contains the names and parameters established using the PATH, PROMPT, and SET commands. This information is stored in RAM and available to any program that can use it. AutoCAD locates drawing files by looking at the PATH parameters.

AutoCAD also examines this environment to find other parameters set by the user. These include the amount of available Auto-CAD work space (ACADFREERAM) and space for AutoLISP functions and nodes (LISPHEAP and LISPSTACK), and the location of AutoCAD's configuration file (ACADCFG) and program files (ACAD). If these items are not found in the environment, AutoCAD will use its

Prompt Code	Meaning
$T	Displays the time
$D	Displays the date
$G	Displays the greater-then sign
$V	Displays the DOS version number
$N	Displays the default drive
$L	Displays the less-than sign
$P	Displays the current directory
$B	Displays the ¦ character
$_	Causes the prompt to go to the next line
$Q	Displays the equals sign
$H	Causes the prompt to enter a backspace

Table C.1:   *Prompt codes*

own default settings. Chapter 18 describes how to use SET to set ACADFREERAM, LISPHEAP, and LISPSTACK. Appendix B describes setting the ACAD and ACADCFG parameters.

For example, to tell AutoCAD to look in the directory Acad\Config on drive C to find the configuration file it created, enter

SET ACADCFG = C:\ACAD\CONFIG

To see the contents of the current environment, enter SET without any parameters. A list of the current parameters will appear, for example

COMSPEC = C:\COMMAND.COM
PATH = \Util;\BAT
ACADCFG = C:\ACAD\CONFIG
PROMPT = (1) pg

The first line is always present in hard-disk systems. It tells DOS where to look for the *DOS command interpreter,* which is like a program that contains all the DOS internal commands. This example also shows a path set to two directories called Util and Bat. The ACADCFG line tells

AutoCAD that its configuration files should be placed in a directory called Acad\Config (a more detailed description of ACADCFG is in Appendix B). Finally, a special prompt is also shown.

Creating Batch Files

You may find yourself frequently entering several DOS commands in the same sequence. For example, you may enter CD \ACAD, then ACAD, every time you start your computer. You can combine several DOS commands into one file that will execute them together. Such a file is called a batch file. A batch file always has the extension .BAT. For the example above, you could use a word processor or COPY CON and create a small file with the lines

```
CD \ACAD
ACAD
CD\
```

As you can see, this file contains a simple list of the commands entered when you want to run AutoCAD. The CD\ at the end of this file causes DOS to change directories to the root directory when you are done using AutoCAD. The backslash represents the root directory. Through this example, you can see that batch files pick up where they leave off even when a program is started in the middle of one. Any legal DOS command will work.

Save this file as an ASCII file with the name Gocad.BAT and place it in your DOS root directory. You can also create a directory called Batch, set a path to it, and place all the batch files you have there. The next time you turn on your computer, you can just enter GOCAD, and AutoCAD will start.

DOS also recognizes a file named Autoexec.BAT as a special batch file that is executed automatically when you start your computer. If you find you use your computer solely for AutoCAD, you may want to rename the Gocad.BAT file Autoexec.BAT, so AutoCAD automatically starts whenever you turn on your computer. See your DOS manual for more information on batch files.

GETTING STATUS INFORMATION

DOS provides a few general commands to help you keep track of disk space, the current date, and the current time. These commands are CHKDSK, DATE, and TIME.

Checking Disk Space

CHKDSK is an external command that displays the current status of your disk, including the total space in bytes, the amount of disk space used, and the amount of available RAM. The name stands for Check Disk. To use CHKDSK, you must have the file Chkdsk.COM on your default directory or one you have set a path to. You enter the command CHKDSK, followed by the drive name and an optional parameter. For example, to check the C drive and display information on disk usage and available disk space, you would enter

CHKDSK C: /F

The /F option tells the CHKDSK command to write any *lost clusters* to files.

In general terms, files are stored on your hard disk not as a contiguous stream of information, but as bits of information called *clusters* scattered throughout the disk. Another part of your disk contains the file names and a kind of map called the *file allocation table*, or *FAT*, telling DOS the locations of the clusters associated with that file name. Sometimes clusters get lost when a program opens a file but fails to close it properly. This often occurs when you have a power outage while you are editing a file.

These lost clusters can be removed by using the DOS CHKDSK command with its /F option. You will get a list similar to the following if you have no lost clusters.

31236096	bytes total disk space
32768	bytes in 2 hidden files
417792	bytes in 50 directories
29515776	bytes in 1830 user files
1269760	bytes available on disk
655360	bytes total memory
551440	bytes free

If you do have lost clusters, you will get a list like

18 lost clusters found in 11 chains.
Convert lost chains to files (Y/N)?

The *chains* referred to in the first line are lists in the FAT that point to the cluster locations. You could think of chains as a way DOS links clusters to form a file. If you enter Y to the prompt, you get a list like

31236096	bytes total disk space
32768	bytes in 2 hidden files
417792	bytes in 50 directories
29360128	bytes in 1818 user files
147456	bytes in 11 recovered files
1277952	bytes available on disk
655360	bytes total memory
551440	bytes free

Note the line that says you have 147456 bytes in 11 recovered files. This tells you that DOS converted those lost clusters to files. These files can be found on the root directory, each with a name in the format

FILE0001.CHK

You can delete these files because they are probably of no use to you. By doing this you release the space taken up by the lost clusters. You may want to do this check from time to time to clear your disk of unused space and to see what space you have left.

In some older programs for the PC written before DOS 2.0, file creation is handled differently. The CHKDSK command with the /F option can corrupt files created by these programs. If you are using such a program, you may want to check these lost clusters to see if you haven't inadvertently modified a file created by your program. If you like, you can use the DOS TYPE command to display the contents of these recovered files. See below for information on TYPE. Programs written for DOS 2.0 and later should not have this problem.

Displaying the Date and Time

The DATE internal command displays the current date that has been set on the computer. It also allows you to reset an incorrect date by prompting you to enter a new one. If you have a PC/AT, the date is constantly maintained with an independent battery. You can have a battery-operated clock installed in other PCs and compatibles. If you do not have a battery-operated clock, you must enter the correct date each time you start your computer.

To use the DATE command, simply enter it at the DOS prompt.

You will get a message like

Current date is Thu 3-26-1987
Enter new date:

If you want to reset the date, enter the current date at this prompt. Otherwise, press Return.

TIME is an internal command that operates exactly like DATE, except that it displays the current time. Again, you enter TIME at the DOS prompt and get a message like

Current time is 9:51:29.06
Enter new time:

You can enter a new time or press Return to leave the time alone.

VIEWING ASCII FILES

ASCII files are used by AutoCAD in a number of different ways. Line types, hatch patterns, fonts, menus, and AutoLISP programs all use this file format. At times, you may want to view these files on the fly while you are in DOS. The following commands can aid you in doing this.

The TYPE internal command allows you to view an ASCII file while in DOS. You enter TYPE, followed by the full file name including the drive and directory, for example

TYPE C:\WORD\SAMPLE.TXT

This command will display the contents of an ASCII file called Sample.TXT in the Word directory on drive C.

The command works fine for small files containing 24 or fewer lines of text. For larger files, you should use the MORE external command. MORE allows you to view the contents of an ASCII file that is larger than the screen will display. To use MORE you must have the file More.COM on your default directory or one you have set a path to. You specify the file name in the same way as for TYPE.

For example, if you enter

MORE <C:\WORD\SAMPLE.TXT

the file Sample.TXT appears on the screen. When the screen is full, the display will pause, and the word "– More –" will appear at the bottom. To continue to view the file, you can press any key.

You may want to clear the screen before you display files so you can see files you have typed more clearly. To do this, enter the CLS command at the DOS prompt. CLS stands for Clear Screen.

Appendix D

AutoLISP Programs

THIS APPENDIX CONTAINS a few AutoLISP programs that can be
entered into your computer as ASCII files and later used with Auto-
CAD to give you some new features. They are intended to show
you some of AutoLISP's capabilities. Be sure to read Chapter 18
before you try to use them. The AutoLISP manual provided with
AutoCAD will help you to analyze these programs.

You can create these files individually, or combine several of them
into one file so they can be loaded all at once. You may have to
adjust the DOS environment to enable AutoCAD to accept these
programs. This technique is explained in Chapter 18.

EDITING UTILITIES

This first group of programs contains utilities that will help you
edit your drawings. The first aids you in the placement of objects
during any command that prompts you for points. The next two
allow you to match properties of other objects.

Di.LSP

```
(defun di (/ b )
(setq b (getpoint "\nPick reference point: "))
```

```
(getpoint b "\nEnter distance from reference point: ")
)
```

The Di function can be used with version 2.5 or later. It allows you to specify an exact location in a drawing in reference to an existing object. For example, you may want to move box A to a location that would place its upper-left corner exactly 4.5 inches away from the upper-right corner of box B. You start the Move command, select box A, then pick the corner of box A as a starting point as you normally would for the Move command. Then, at the prompt for a second point, you enter

```
(di)
```

The following prompts appear:

Pick reference point:
Enter distance from reference point:

At the first prompt, you pick the corner of box B to be used as a reference point for box A. At the second prompt, you enter the distance you wish box A to be from that reference point. You can enter the distance through the keyboard using relative or polar coordinates. Box A then moves to the exact distance and direction from box B that you specified. This function can be used with any command that prompts you for a point (see Figure D.1)

Match.LSP

```
(defun match (/ x p v )
(setq x (entsel "\nSelect object whose property is to be matched: "))
(initget 1 "Layer Elev Thickness")
(setq p (getkword "\nLayer/Elev/Thickness of object: "))
    (cond ((= p "Layer") (setq v 8))
          ((= p "Elev") (setq v 38))
          ((= p "Thickness") (setq v 39))
    )
(command "p" p)
(command (cdr (assoc v (entget (car x)))) "")
)
```

This function, available for versions 2.6 and later, allows you to change an object or objects to match the layer, elevation, or thickness of another object that appears on the screen. You use it in

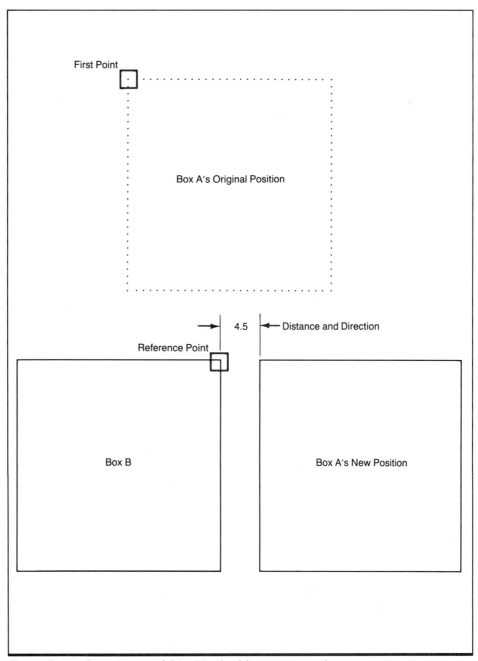

First Point

Box A's Original Position

4.5 ← Distance and Direction

Reference Point

Box B

Box A's New Position

Figure D.1: *Sample use of Di with the Move command*

conjunction with the Change command. First you enter Change, then select the object or objects you wish to change. After you press Return to confirm your selection, you enter

(match)

You will be prompted to select an object whose property you want to match, then for the specific property to be matched. After you do this, the selected objects change to match the properties of the first object you selected.

The Entsel function in the second line of this program allows the processing of a chosen set of objects. AutoLISP considers these sets as one object.

Matchl.LSP

```
(defun c:matchl (/ x )
    (setq x (entsel "\nSelect object whose layer is to be matched: "))
    (command "layer" "S" (cdr (assoc 8 (entget (car x)))) "" )
    )
```

This is a variation of the Match function (for version 2.6 and later) shown earlier. This program allows you to change the current layer setting by selecting an object whose layer you want to be on.

Fence.LSP

```
(defun mem (d 1 / h)
(setq h (list 1 d))
    (while (/ = 1 nil)
        (setq h (cons (setq 1 (getpoint 1 "\nNext point: ")) h))
    )
)
(defun c:fence (/ x y u a d b v1 v2 pt1 pt2 int)
(setvar "cmdecho" 0)
(setq x (getpoint "\nPick first point of fence: "))
(setq y (getpoint x "\nNext point: "))
(setq u (mem x y))
(setq u (cdr u))
    (while (/ = u nil)
        (setq a (car u))
        (setq u (cdr u))
        (setq b (car u))
```

```
(setq v1 (ssget "c" a b))
(setq v2 0)
  (if (/= v1 nil)
    (while (< v2 (sslength v1))
      (setq pt1 (cdr (assoc 10 (entget (ssname v1 v2)))))
      (setq pt2 (cdr (assoc 11 (entget (ssname v1 v2)))))
      (setq int (inters a b pt1 pt2))
      (command "break" int "@")
      (setq v2 (+ v2 1))
    )
  )
)
)
```

This program (for versions 2.5 and later) will cut out a section of a drawing, much like the Scissors command in many of the available paint programs. It prompts you to enter a series of points that determine the area to be cut. Once you are done, you can use another command, such as Erase, Move, or Copy, to edit the area that has been cut. For example, you could use Fence to cut a square area out of an exploded hatch pattern, then use Erase and window the cut-out area to delete it.

Fence has some limitations, however. It does not cut blocks, arcs, or circles. It also does not reliably cut lines that are close together. Still, this program can be quite useful.

KEYBOARD MACROS

The next three programs, also for version 2.5 or later, are used together to create and keep track of keyboard macros. The first two programs actually create macros that can be initialized by single or multiple keystrokes. The second program allows you to list and load any macros you save to disk. The third is a utility to help you manage memory use in conjunction with AutoLISP programs in general.

Keycad.LSP

```
(defun c:zw () (command "zoom" "w"))
(defun c:zp () (command "zoom" "p"))
(defun c:mo () (command "move"))
(defun c:co () (command "copy"))
```

```
(defun c:st () (command "stretch" "C"))
(defun c:fl () (command "fillet"))
(defun c:br () (command "break"))
(defun c:ch () (command "change"))
(defun c:ro () (command "rotate"))
(defun c:ex () (command "extend"))
(defun c:tr () (command "trim"))
(defun c:mi () (command "mirror"))
(defun c:li () (command "line"))
(defun c:ci () (command "circle"))
(defun c:ar () (command "arc"))
(defun c:of () (command "offset"))
```

This set of keyboard macros (for versions 2.5 and later) substitutes two-keystroke commands for command names. If you study the macros, you will see that it is quite simple to create one. You can add to the list on your own, specifying your own choices of command names and keystroke sequences. The commands translate as follows:

```
zw zoom window
zp zoom previous
mo move
co copy
st stretch
fl fillet
br break
ch change
ro rotate
ex extend
tr trim
mi mirror
li line
ci circle
ar arc
of offset
```

Macro.LSP

```
(defun c:macro (/ kys mac next sv dt )
   (setq kys (strcat "c:"(getstring "Enter keys to define:")))
   (setq mac (list(getstring "Enter macro <enter / when done>:")))
```

```
(setq next "")
(while (/= next "/")
(setq next(getstring "<enter / when done>: "))
  (if (= next "/") (progn
                    (setq prt (cons 'command (reverse mac)))
                    (setq prt (list 'defun (read kys) 'nil prt))
                    (eval prt)
                    )
     (setq mac (cons next mac))
  )
)
(initget 1 "No Yes")
(setq sv (getkword "Save this macro to disk <N>? "))
  (if (= sv "Yes") (progn
                    (setq dt (open (strcat kys ".LSP") "w"))
                    (print prt dt)
                    (close dt)
                    )
  )
)
```

This program allows you to create keyboard macros for your most frequently used commands. You can, for example, create a macro to start the Change command by entering ch instead of the entire word change. You can even have it enter other keyboard entries after the command. However, you cannot have it pause for point or other keyboard input.

Loadmac.LSP

```
(defun c:loadmac (/ name )
(setvar "cmdecho" 0)
(setq name (getstring "\n? or name of Macro to load: "))
  (if (= name "?") (progn
                    (command "CATALOG" "*.LSP")
                    (setq name (getstring"\n? or name of Macro to
                            load: "))
                    )
  )
(load name)
)
```

This is a simple program to help you load any AutoLISP macros you have created with the Macro program listed above. It also provides a question mark option to list your AutoLISP macros and any AutoLISP programs, in case you have forgotten the name of the one you want to load.

Clear.LSP

```
(defun c:clear ( )
(setq atomlist (member 'clear atomlist))
)
```

This short program is intended to help you manage memory usage while using AutoLISP programs. Load it before any other AutoLISP program. If and when you get the prompt

insufficient node space

you can enter

(Clear)

to recover some memory to run other programs.

Clear cannot be used in conjunction with the (VMON) option described in Chapter 18. If you use (VMON) you probably won't need this function, but you still have to use the Set command to set the LISPHEAP and LISPSTACK values for AutoCAD (also described in Chapter 18).

TEXT-ORIENTED PROGRAMS

These programs allow you to more easily handle some of Auto-CAD's text-related functions. One program simplifies the creation of attribute template files, while another simplifies the process of importing ASCII files.

Attmplt.LSP

```
(defun plc1 (p / d x zr)
(setq x 3)
(setq d (strlen p))
```

```
(setq zr "")
  (while (> x 0)
        (if (< d x) (setq zr (strcat "0" zr)))
        (setq x (- x 1))
  )
(setq p (strcat zr p))
)


(Defun c:attmplt (/ tag cn dgt pt dt tx lng1 p tt)
(setq tt (getstring "\nName of attribute template file: "))
(setq dt (open (strcat tt ".txt") "w"))
(setq tag (getstring "\nEnter name of attribute tag: "))
  (while (/ = tag "")
    (initget 1 "C N")
    (setq cn (getkword "\nIs the attribute a Number or Character
        <C/N>? "))
    (setq dgt (getstring "\nEnter number of digits or
                    characters: "))
      (if (= cn "C")
        (setq pt "0")
        (setq pt (getstring "\nEnter number of decimal places
            wanted: "))
      )
    (setq dgt (plc1 dgt))
    (setq pt (plc1 pt))
    (setq tx (strcat tag " " cn dgt pt))
    (Write-line tx dt)
    (setq tag (getstring "\nEnter name of attribute tag: "))
  )
(close dt)
)
```

This program (for versions 2.5 and later) automates the creation of attribute template files. It prompts you to enter the variables required in the template file, then constructs a template file based on the information you provide.

Once this program is loaded, you enter

(Attmplt)

at the command prompt. You will be asked a series of questions regarding the attributes. Once you are done answering the prompts for one attribute the questions repeat, allowing you to add more attributes to the template file. To end out of this program, press Return without entering anything at the prompt

Enter name of attribute tag:

The template file will then be created on your hard disk in the current default directory.

Imprtext.LSP

```
(Defun c:imprtext (/ txt sp th lns ht wd stl ls dt)
    (setvar "cmdecho" 0)
    (setq txt (open (getstring "\nName of text file: ") "r"))
    (setq sp (getpoint "\nText starting point: "))
    (setq lns (getstring "\nEnter line spacing in drawing units: "))
    (setq ht (getstring "\nEnter text height in drawing units: "))
    (setq wd (getstring "\nEnter text width factor: "))
    (initget 1 "Txt Simplex Complex Italic Monotxt")
    (prompt "Use the Monotxt font for aligned columns of text")
    (setq stl (getkword "\nEnter font
        /Txt/Simplex/Complex/Italic/Monotxt: "))
    (setq ls (strcat "@" lns "<-90"))
    (setq dt (read-line txt))
    (command "style" "import" stl ht wd "" "" "" "")
    (command "text" sp "" dt)
        (while (/= dt nil)
            (setq dt (read-line txt))
            (command "text" ls "" dt)
        )
    (command "redraw")
    (close txt)
)
```

This program (for version 2.6 and later) automatically imports ASCII text files into a drawing. It prompts you for the insertion point, font, line spacing, text height, and text width.

Seqns.LSP

```
(defun c:seqns (/ a c v dtx delta sc z z1 z2 z3 d )
  (setvar "cmdecho" 0)
  (setq a (Getpoint "\nPick beginning location of sequence: "))
  (setq c (Getpoint a "\nPick direction of sequence: "))
  (setq v (Getint "\nEnter beginning value: "))
  (setq dtx (Getint "\nEnter number of values in sequence: "))
  (setq delta (getstring "\nEnter distance between values in
sequence: "))
  (setq sc (Getint "\n Enter scale factor for drawing: "))
  (setq z (* (angle a c) 57.2958))
  (setq z3 (fix z))
  (setq z2 (itoa z3))
  (setq z1 (strcat "@" delta "<" z2))
  (command "insert" "number" a sc "" z v)
  (setq d 1)
    (while (< d dtx)
          (setq v (+ 1 v))
          (setq d (+ 1 d))
          (command "insert" "" z1 sc "" z v)
    )
  (command "redraw")
  )
```

This program (for versions 2.5 and later) will insert a sequence of numbers of increasing value. Each number in the sequence is increased by one. This can be helpful if you are numbering a sequence of objects. For example, you could use this macro to number a series of 24 lockers in a floor plan. You are prompted for the starting point, beginning value, distance between values, number of values, and the drawing scale.

Before you try to use this program, you must have a drawing on the default directory that contains a single attribute. The drawing must have the name Number.DWG. This can also be a block within the drawing you wish to use the program in. The attribute should be the size you want the text to appear when it is plotted.

This program works by inserting a block with an attribute several times. Each time the block is inserted, a numeric value is entered automatically by the program. This value is increased by one each time the block is inserted. The number of times the block is inserted is determined by a variable you supply.

DRAWING AIDS

These are two programs that will help you draw simple objects. One draws parallel lines, while the other draws boxes. Though they both draw simple objects, the amount of code required to do each is quite different.

Paraline.LSP

```
(defun c:paraline (/ w cud a b dx dy a1 a2 a3 a4 b1 b2 b3 b4 ca1
                ca2 b4 bgn ab1 ab2 ai1 ai2 ai3 ai4 )
  (setvar "cmdecho" 0)
  (setq w (getreal "\nEnter width: "))
  (initget 1 "Center Up Down")
  (setq cud (getkword "\nCenter/Up/Down of line: "))
  (setq a (getpoint "\nPick beginning of parallel lines: "))
  (setq b (getpoint a "\nPick next point: "))
    (cond ((= cud "Center") (setq dx (/ w 2) dy (/ w 2)))
      ((= cud "Up") (setq dx 0 dy w))
      ((= cud "Down") (setq dx w dy 0))
    )
  (setq a1 (polar a (- (angle a b) 1.57079) dx))
  (setq b1 (polar b (- (angle a b) 1.57079) dx))
  (setq a2 (polar a (+ (angle a b) 1.57079) dy))
  (setq b2 (polar b (+ (angle a b) 1.57079) dy))
  (command "line" a1 b1 "")
  (command "line" a2 b2 "")
  (setq ca1 a1 ca2 a2 )
  (setq a b b3 b1 a3 a1 b4 b2 a4 a2)
  (setq b (getpoint a "\nPick next point: "))
  (setq bgn 0)
    (while (/= b nil)
      (setq bgn (+ bgn 1))
  (setq a1 (polar a (- (angle a b) 1.57079) dx))
  (setq b1 (polar b (- (angle a b) 1.57079) dx))
  (setq a2 (polar a (+ (angle a b) 1.57079) dy))
  (setq b2 (polar b (+ (angle a b) 1.57079) dy))
  (setq ab1 (inters a1 b1 a3 b3 nil))
  (setq ab2 (inters a2 b2 a4 b4 nil))
  (command "erase" "1" "")
  (command "erase" "1" "")
```

```
      (command "line" a4 ab2 "")
      (command "line" a3 ab1 "")
      (command "line" ab2 b2 "")
      (command "line" ab1 b1 "")
      (if (= bgn 1) (setq ai4 a4 ai2 ab2 ai3 a3 ai1 ab1))
      (setq a b a4 ab2 a3 ab1 b4 b2 b3 b1)
      (setq b (getpoint a "\nPick next point: "))
    )
  (initget 1 "Yes No")
    (setq b (getkword "clean up last corner? <Y/N>: "))
      (if (= b "Yes")(progn
              (command "erase" "1" ""
                       "erase" "1" ""
                       "erase" ai4 ""
                       "erase" ai3 ""
              )
            (setq ab1 (inters a1 b1 ai1 ai3 nil))
            (setq ab2 (inters a2 b2 ai2 ai4 nil))
              (command "line" ai2 ab2 ""
                       "line" ai1 ab1 ""
                       "line" ab2 a4 ""
                       "line" ab1 a3 ""
              )
          )
      )
    )
  )
```

This program (for versions 2.6 and later) draws parallel lines. It prompts you for the width of each line and whether it is to be centered on, below, or above selected points. You are then prompted to select points to locate the line. You can pick points on the screen or enter distances through the keyboard just as with the Line command. When you are done, press Return. You will be asked if you would like to have the last corner closed. If you enter Y, the last set of parallel lines will join with the first set you drew.

This does not work like the AutoCAD Line or Pline command, where entering a C during the command causes the first and last lines to close. Instead, you must draw the entire closed area first. By entering Y at the end of the Paraline program, you are saved from having to clean up the last corner of a rectangle or other polygon drawn using Paraline.

You may notice that in some places, the Setq function is used to set several variables as in the line

```
(setq a b a4 ab2 a3 ab1 b4 b2 b3 b1)
```

Here, a is set to b, ab2 is set to a3, and so forth. This is perfectly legal in AutoLISP.

Pbox.LSP

```
(defun c:pbox (pt dpt)
    (setq pt(getpoint "\nStarting corner: "))
    (setq dpt(getcorner pt "\nDiagonal corner: "))
    (command "pline" pt ".x" dpt ".y" pt dpt ".x" pt ".y" dpt "C")
)
```

This program (for versions 2.5 and later) draws a polyline rectangle based on two opposite corners entered by either cursor input or numeric input from the keyboard. It is a streamlined version of the one given as an example in Chapter 18.

Appendix E

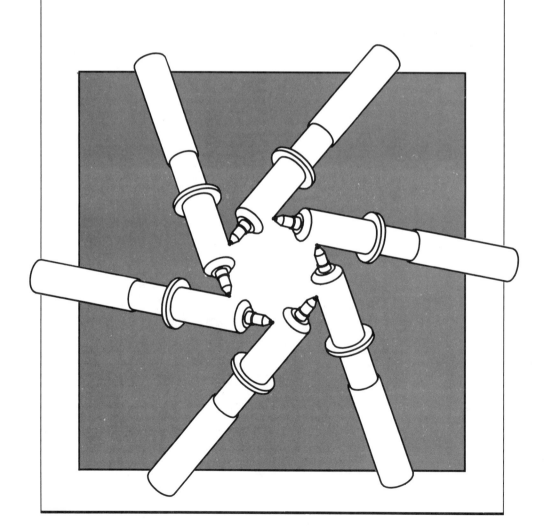

Setvar Options

THIS APPENDIX CONTAINS A LIST of system variables accessible through the Setvar command, plus a brief description of each variable. These system variables are also accessible through the AutoLISP interpreter. We have divided the variables into sections listing adjustable variables, read-only variables, and variables accessible only through Setvar. Most of these variables are accessible through the commands they are associated with, but at times you will want to use Setvar to read or change them while you are in another command.

ADJUSTABLE VARIABLES

These are variables that can be adjusted either through the Setvar command or through the commands associated with the variable. For example, the first three variables can be adjusted using the Units command, as well as Setvar.

Aflags
Controls the attribute mode settings: 1 = invisible, 2 = constant, 3 = verify.

Angbase
Controls the direction of the 0 angle.

Angdir
Controls the positive direction of angles: 0 = counterclockwise, 1 = clockwise.

Aperture	Controls the Osnap cursor target height in pixels.
Attdia	Controls the appearance of attribute dialog box: 0 = no dialog box, 1 = dialog box.
Attmode	Controls the attribute display mode: 0 = off, 1 = normal, 2 = on.
Attreq	Controls the prompt for attributes. 0 = no prompt or dialog box for attributes. Attributes use default values. 1 = normal prompt or dialog box upon attribute insertion.
Aunits	Controls angular units: 0 = decimal degrees, 1 = degrees-minutes-sec., 2 = grads, 3 = radians, 4 = surveyors' units.
Auprec	Controls the precision of angular units determined by decimal place.
Axismode	Controls the axis mode: 0 = off, 1 = on.
Axisunit	Controls the axis spacing.
Blipmode	Controls the appearance of blips: 0 = off, 1 = on.
Chamfera	Controls first chamfer distance.
Chamferb	Controls second chamfer distance.
Coords	Controls coordinate readout: 0 = coordinates are displayed only when points are picked. 1 = absolute coordinates are dynamically displayed as cursor moves. 2 = distance and angle are displayed during commands that accept relative distance input.
Dragmode	Controls dragging: 0 = no dragging, 1 = on if requested, 2 = automatic drag.
Elevation	Controls current 3D elevation.
Filletrad	Controls fillet radius.
Fillmode	Controls fill status: 0 = off, 1 = on.
Gridmode	Controls grid: 0 = off, 1 = on.
Gridunit	Controls grid spacing.
Insbase	Controls insertion base point of current drawing.

Limcheck	Controls limit checking: 0 = no checking, 1 = checking.
Limmax	Controls the coordinate of drawing's upper-right limit.
Limmin	Controls the coordinate of drawing's lower-left limit.
Ltscale	Controls the line type scale factor.
Lunits	Controls unit styles.
Luprec	Controls unit accuracy by decimal place or size of denominator.
Orthomode	Controls ortho: 0 = off, 1 = on.
Osmode	Sets the current default Osnap mode: 0 = none, 1 = endpoint, 2 = midpoint, 4 = center, 8 = node, 16 = quadrant, 32 = intersection, 64 = insert, 128 = perpendicular, 256 = nearest, 512 = quick. If more than one mode is required, enter the sum of those modes.
Qtextmode	Controls the quick text mode: 0 = off, 1 = on.
Regenmode	Controls the regenauto mode: 0 = off, 1 = on.
Sketchinc	Controls the sketch record increment.
Snapang	Controls snap and grid angle.
Snapbase	Controls snap, grid, and hatch pattern origin.
Snapisopair	Controls isometric plane: 0 = left, 1 = top, 2 = right.
Snapmode	Controls snap toggle: 0 = off, 1 = on.
Snapstyl	Controls snap style: 0 = standard, 1 = isometric.
Snapunit	Controls snap spacing given in x and y values.
Splframe	Controls the display of spline vertices. 0 = no display, 1 = display.
Splinesegs	Controls the number of line segments used for each spline patch.
Textsize	Controls default text height.

Thickness   Controls 3D thickness of objects being drawn.

Tracewid   Controls trace width.

READ-ONLY VARIABLES

These are variables that can be read either through their associated commands or through Setvar. They are not changeable, so in a sense they are not really variables.

Acadver   Displays the AutoCAD version number.

Area   Displays the current area being computed.

Cdate   Displays calendar date/time read from DOS.

Cecolor   Displays current object color.

Celtype   Displays current object line type.

Clayer   Displays current layer.

Date   Displays Julian date/time.

Distance   Displays last distance read using Dist, List, or Dblist.

Dwgname   Displays drawing name.

Lastangle   Displays the end angle of last arc or line.

Lastpoint   Displays coordinates of last point entered. Same point referenced by at sign.

Menuname   Displays the current menu file name.

Perimeter   Displays the perimeter value currently being read by the Area, List, or Dblist commands.

Popups   Displays the availability of the advanced user interface. 0 = not available, 1 = available.

Tdcreate   Displays time and date of drawing creation.

Tdindwg   Displays total editing time.

Tdupdate   Displays time and date of last update of file.

Tdusrtimer   Displays user-elapsed time.

Vpointx	Displays the x value of the current 3D viewpoint.
Vpointy	Displays the y value of the current 3D viewpoint.
Vpointz	Displays the z value of the current 3D viewpoint.

VARIABLES ACCESSIBLE ONLY THROUGH SETVAR

The following variables are accessible only through the Setvar command. Take a close look at them. Some may serve little purpose, while others may be quite useful.

Adjustable Variables

These variables can be altered, but only through the Setvar command.

Cmdecho	Used with AutoLISP to control what is displayed on the prompt line. See the AutoLISP manual for details.
Dragp1	Controls regen-drag input sampling rate.
Dragp2	Controls fast-drag input sampling rate.
Expert	Controls prompts, depending on level of user's expertise. 0 = issues normal prompts. 1 = suppresses "are you sure" prompts.
Highlight	Controls object-selection ghosting: 0 = no ghosting, 1 = ghosting.
Menuecho	Controls menu prompts displayed to prompt line. Also used with AutoLISP to select and display screen menus.
Mirrtext	Controls mirroring of text: 0 = no mirroring of text, 1 = mirroring of text.
Pdmode	Controls the type of symbol used as a point during the Point command. Several point styles are available. See the *AutoCAD Reference Manual* for a complete description of these styles.
Pdsize	Controls the size of the symbol set by Pdmode.

Pickbox   Controls the size of the object-selection box. Integer values can be entered to control the box height in pixels.

Skpoly   Controls whether the Sketch command uses regular lines or polylines. 0 = line, 1 = polyline.

Read-Only Variables

These read-only variables can be read only through the Setvar command, unlike the variables in the first two sections in this appendix.

Dwgprefix   Displays drive and directory prefix for drawing file.

Extmax   Displays upper-right corner coordinate of extents view.

Extmin   Displays lower-left corner coordinate of extents view.

Screensize   Reads the size of the graphics screen in pixels.

Viewctr   Displays the center coordinate of the current view.

Viewsize   Displays the height of the current view in drawing units.

Index

Mastering AutoCAD on Disk

If you would like to use the AutoLISP programs shown in this book but do not want to enter them into your computer yourself, you can obtain a copy of them on disk. The disk also contains a full-featured AutoCAD AEC overlay that includes functions like automatic door insertion, parallel line creation for walls, and a library of architectural symbols combined with an on-screen icon menu for easy symbol selection. This icon menu system works on versions 2.5 and later. We also include a utility for converting AutoCAD and AutoShade PostScript plot files into Encapsulated PostScript files, enabling you to import high-quality images from AutoCAD to your favorite desktop-publishing software.

Just complete this order form and return along with a check or money order for $30.00. California residents add the proper sales tax for your city and county.

Omura Illustration
829 Pomona Avenue
Albany, CA 94706
(415) 526-1113

Name _____

Address _____

City/State/Zip _____

Phone Number _____

Enclosed is my check or money order: _____
(Make check payable to Omura Illustration)

Check version of AutoCAD you are using:
2.5xx   2.6xx   9.0

Earlier versions are not supported